DELIVERING BUSINESS INTELLIGENCE

with **Microsoft® SQL Server® 2016**

About the Author

Brian Larson served as a member of the original Reporting Services development team as a consultant to Microsoft. In that role, he contributed to the original code base of Reporting Services. Brian is currently the Chief Creative Officer for Superior Consulting Services in Minneapolis, Minnesota.

Brian has presented at national conferences and events, including the SQL Server Magazine Connections Conference, the PASS Community Summit, and the Microsoft Business Intelligence Conference, and has provided training and mentoring on Reporting Services across the country. He has been a contributor to and columnist for *SQL Server Magazine*. In addition to this book, Brian is the author of *Microsoft SQL Server 2016 Reporting Services* and co-author of *Visualizing Data with Microsoft Power View*, both from McGraw-Hill Professional.

Brian is a Phi Beta Kappa graduate of Luther College in Decorah, Iowa, with degrees in physics and computer science. He has 31 years of experience in the computer industry, and 27 years of experience as a consultant creating custom database applications. Brian is a Microsoft Certified Solutions Expert (MCSE) in Business Intelligence and a Microsoft Certified Database Administrator (MCDBA).

Brian and his wife Pam have been married for 31 years. Pam will tell you that their first date took place at the campus computer center. If that doesn't qualify someone to write a computer book, then I don't know what does. Brian and Pam have two children, Jessica and Corey.

Brian can be contacted at blarson@teamscs.com. Follow Brian on Twitter at @Brian_Larson or connect on LinkedIn at www.linkedin.com/in/brianlarsonscs.

About the Technical Editor

Jared Zagelbaum is a highly experienced IT professional, specializing in the Microsoft Data Platform suite of technologies since 2007. He expertly leads projects and teams through enterprise solution design and implementation for data management, analytics, and information delivery. Jared regularly speaks at user groups and events across the Midwest, as well as blogging and providing technical review for SQL Server publications. He is a Microsoft Certified Solutions Expert (MCSE) in Business Intelligence, and a graduate of the University of Florida with a BS in Finance, Accounting, and Economics.

DELIVERING BUSINESS INTELLIGENCE

with **Microsoft® SQL Server® 2016**

Fourth Edition

Brian Larson

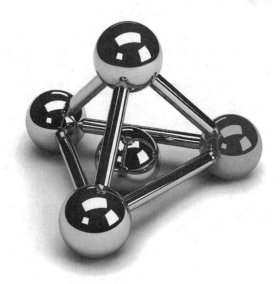

McGraw Hill Education

New York   Chicago   San Francisco
Athens   London   Madrid
Mexico City   Milan   New Delhi
Singapore   Sydney   Toronto

Library of Congress Cataloging-in-Publication Data

Names: Larson, Brian, author.
Title: Delivering business intelligence with Microsoft SQL server 2016 /
  Brian Larson.
Description: Fourth edition. | San Francisco : McGraw-Hill Education, 2016.
Identifiers: LCCN 2016041674 (print) | LCCN 2016043727 (ebook) | ISBN
  9781259641480 (paperback) | ISBN 9781259641497
Subjects: LCSH: Business intelligence. | SQL server. | Client/server
  computing. | BISAC: COMPUTERS / Database Management / General.
Classification: LCC HD38.7 .L37 2016 (print) | LCC HD38.7 (ebook) | DDC
  658.4/038—dc23
LC record available at https://lccn.loc.gov/2016041674

McGraw-Hill Education books are available at special quantity discounts to use as premiums and sales promotions, or for use in corporate training programs. To contact a representative, please visit the Contact Us pages at www.mhprofessional.com.

Delivering Business Intelligence with Microsoft® SQL Server® 2016, Fourth Edition

23456789   LCR   21 20 19 18

ISBN   978-1-25-964148-0
MHID   1-25-964148-1

Sponsoring Editor Hilary Flood	**Technical Editor** Jared Zagelbaum	**Production Supervisor** James Kussow
Editorial Supervisor Janet Walden	**Copy Editor** Nancy Rapoport	**Composition** Cenveo® Publisher Services
Project Editor Patty Mon	**Proofreader** Paul Tyler	**Illustration** Cenveo Publisher Services
Acquisitions Coordinator Claire Yee	**Indexer** Karin Arrigoni	**Art Director, Cover** Jeff Weeks

This book is dedicated to my parents. To my father, Robert, who even after 50-plus years as a junior high mathematics teacher and computer instructor has a love of teaching. He has shown me what a real commitment to sharing knowledge with others looks like. To my mother, Beverly, who was my first editor, coaching me through elementary school papers on this state or that president. She taught me the value of sticking with a job and seeing it through to the end. I owe them both a debt of love, caring, and support that can never be adequately repaid.

Contents at a Glance

Contents

Part III Working with a Tabular BI Semantic Model

Acknowledgments

No project of this size is the work of a single person. I need to thank a number of people for their assistance, professionalism, dedication, and support. So, a *ginormous* thank you…

To Wendy Rinaldi, my original contact person at McGraw-Hill Professional who allowed me to lean on her as part editor, part coach, part literary agent, and part psychoanalyst. Her professionalism, humor, understanding, and faith truly made the many editions of this book possible.

To the McGraw-Hill Professional staff, who shepherded this book through to the end.

To John Miller, who founded Superior Consulting Services as a place where people can grow and learn, produce solid technology solutions, serve customers, and have a good time to boot.

To Jessica and Corey, my children, who allowed me time to pursue this passion.

To my wife, Pam, who continues to be gracious in her understanding of my affliction with the writing bug. She has given generously of her time to proof and review this book and its Learn By Doing exercises. Her incredible attention to detail has made this a better product.

Last, but certainly not least, to you, the reader, who plunked down your hard-earned cash for this purchase. I hope you view this as a helpful and informative guide to all of the truly exciting business intelligence features in SQL Server 2016.

All the best,
Brian Larson
blarson@teamscs.com

The Maximum Miniatures Databases and Other Supporting Materials

All of the samples in this book are based on business scenarios for a fictional company called Maximum Miniatures, Inc. You can download the data, image files, and other supporting materials from the book's web page on the McGraw-Hill Professional website. This download also includes the complete source code for all of the Learn By Doing activities and the applications demonstrated in the book.

You can download the Zip files from the McGraw-Hill Professional website at www .mhprofessional.com. Simply enter the book's title or ISBN in the search box and then click the Downloads & Resources tab on the book's home page. Follow the instructions in the Zip file to install or prepare each item as needed.

Part I

Business Intelligence

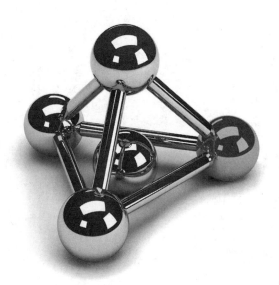

Chapter 1

Equipping the Organization for Effective Decision Making

In This Chapter

► **Effective Decision Making**
► **Keys to Effective Decision Making**
► **Business Intelligence**

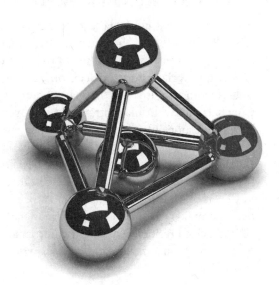

"Would you tell me please, which way I ought to go from here?" asked Alice. "That depends a good deal on where you want to get to," said the Cat. "I don't much care where," said Alice. "Then, it doesn't matter which way you go," said the Cat.

Alice's Adventures in Wonderland
—Lewis Carroll

L ife is filled with decisions. Should I have the burger and fries or the salad for lunch? Should I get my significant other that new watch they've had their eye on, or should I buy them a new vacuum cleaner? Do I invest my holiday bonus or head for the casino? Should I buy this book or go browse the comics section? (Here is your first bit of business intelligence: buy this book!)

The choices we make can have life-changing consequences. Even seemingly trivial decisions can have big consequences down the road. It's like your parents always told you: the key to success in life is to make good choices!

Effective Decision Making

Good decision making is as important in the working world as it is in the rest of our lives. Every day a number of decisions must be made that determine the direction and efficiency of the organizations we work for. Decisions are made concerning production, marketing, and personnel. Decisions are made affecting costs, sales, and margins. Just as in our personal lives, the key to organizational success is to make good choices. The organization must have effective decision making.

Who Is a Decision Maker?

Just who is it that must make good choices within an organization? At first blush, it may seem that only the person at the top, the chief executive officer (CEO), the president, or the chairperson needs to be an effective decision maker. If that person makes appropriate strategic decisions, the organization will succeed!

Unfortunately, it is not that easy. There are countless examples throughout history where absolutely brilliant strategic plans went awry because of poor decisions made by those responsible for their implementation. As emperor and leader of "La Grande Armée," Napoleon Bonaparte had a fairly decent strategic plan for his campaign in Belgium. However, due to some poor decision making by his marshals, Napoleon suffered a major defeat at a little place called Waterloo.

Given this, perhaps it is important for the next level of management to be effective decision makers as well. The chief financial officers (CFOs), chief information officers (CIOs), vice presidents, assistant chairpersons, and department heads (and marshals of the army) must make good choices when creating the policies and setting the priorities to implement the strategic plan. With all of upper management making effective decisions, the organization is guaranteed to go places!

In fact, success is not even assured when this is true. Effective plans and policies created at the top of the organization can be undone by poor decisions made further down as those plans and policies are put into action. The opposite is also true. Good decisions made by those working where the rubber meets the road can be quickly overwhelmed by poor decisions made further up the line.

The answer, then, is to have effective decision makers throughout an organization. Those lower down the organizational chart will have much better morale and will invest more energy in an activity if they have some assurance that their efforts will not be undone by someone higher up. In addition, the success of the person in the corner office is, in large part, simply a reflection of the effective decisions and successes of the people who report to them. Effective decision making at every level leads to success.

What Is an Effective Decision?

The organization that has the desired products or services, provided in the proper place, at the correct time, produced at the appropriate cost, and backed by the necessary customer support will be successful. This, of course, is fairly obvious. Any business plan or mission statement worth its salt professes to do just this.

What is not so obvious is how an organization goes about making sure it provides what is desired, proper, correct, appropriate, and necessary. The answer, as we learned in the previous section, is to have people making effective decisions at all levels of the organization. But what exactly is an effective decision?

DEFINITION

Effective decisions *are choices that move an organization closer to an agreed-on set of goals in a timely manner.*

An effective decision moves an organization toward its goals in a timely manner. This definition is extremely broad. In fact, this makes a good slogan, but is too broad to be of much use in day-to-day operations. Using this definition, however, we can define three key ingredients necessary for making effective decisions:

► A set of goals to work toward.

► A way to measure whether a chosen course is moving toward or away from those goals.

► Information based on those measures provided to the decision maker in a timely manner.

This information serves both as the foundation for the initial decision making and as feedback showing the results of the decision. Defining effective decision making is the easy part. Taking this rather nebulous definition and turning it into concrete business practices requires a bit more work.

DEFINITION

Foundation information *serves as the basis for making a particular decision as that decision is being made.*

DEFINITION

Feedback information *is used to evaluate the effectiveness of a particular decision after that decision is made.*

Keys to Effective Decision Making

In the previous section, we learned that three keys are necessary for effective decision making: specific goals, concrete measures, and timely foundation and feedback information, as shown in Figure 1-1. In this section, we take a detailed look at each of these three keys to learn how to encourage effective decision making.

Are We Going Hither or Yon?

In Mel Brooks's film *The Producers,* Max and Leopold set out to stage an absolutely horrible Broadway musical, certain to fail, so they can abscond with the investors' money. Aside from this entertaining exception, organizations do not set out to fail.

Figure 1-1   *Three keys to effective decision making*

On the contrary, they come together, raise capital, create organizational charts, draw up business plans, prepare massive presentations, and have endless meetings, all to succeed. The first, largest, and ultimately fatal problem for many of these organizations is they do not define exactly what that success looks like. They don't know what the destination is.

An organization may have some nebulous goals in its mission statement. Phrases such as "superior customer satisfaction," "increased profit margin," or "better meeting our community's needs" grace the reception area, the annual report, and the entryway to the shareholders' meeting. These are great slogans for building a marketing campaign or generating esprit de corps among the employees. They do not, however, make good milestones for measuring business performance.

"Superior customer satisfaction" is a wonderful goal. (The world would be a much happier place if even half the companies that profess to strive toward superior customer satisfaction would actually make some progress in that direction.) The issue is how to measure "customer satisfaction." How do we know when we have reached this goal or if we are even making progress in that direction? What is required is something a bit more concrete and a lot more measurable.

Rather than the ill-defined "superior customer satisfaction," a better goal might be "to maintain superior customer satisfaction as measured by repeat customer orders with a goal of 80 percent repeat orders." This goal may need a few more details filled in, but it is the beginning of a goal that is specific and measurable. We can measure whether our decisions are taking us in the right direction based on the increase or decrease in repeat orders.

"Increased profit margin" makes the shareholders happy. Still, the organization must decide what operating costs impact profit margin and how they are divvied up among a number of concurrent projects. We may also want to state how large the increase to profit margin must be in order to satisfy the investors. Does a 1 percent increase put a smile on the shareholders' faces, or does our target need to be more in the 5 percent range? Once these details are added, we have a specific target to work toward.

"Better meeting our community's needs" is a noble goal, but what are those needs and how can we tell when they are met? Instead, we need to select a specific community need, such as increasing the number of quality, affordable housing units. We can then define what is meant by quality, affordable housing and just what size increase we are looking to achieve.

To function as part of effective decision making, a goal must

▶   Contain a specific target

▶   Provide a means to measure whether we are progressing toward that target

As with the dartboard in Figure 1-2, we need both a bull's-eye to aim for and a method for scoring how close we came to that target.

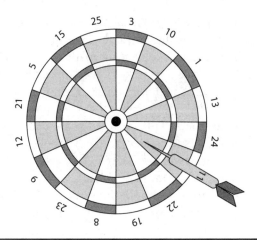

Figure 1-2   *Required elements of a goal to be used in effective decision making*

Is Your Map Upside-Down?

Goals are important. In fact, they are essential to effective decision making, as discussed in the previous section. However, goals are useless without some sort of movement toward reaching them. The finish line can only be reached if the ladies and gentlemen start their engines and begin the race.

This is where decision making comes into play. Each decision moves the company in a particular direction. Some decisions produce a giant leap. These are the policy and priority decisions usually made in the upper levels of management. These decisions determine the general course the organization is going to take over a lengthy period, a fiscal year, a school calendar period, or perhaps even the entire lifetime of the organization. It is essential that these decisions point the organization toward its goals if those goals are ever going to be reached.

Some decisions cause the organization to make smaller movements one way or another. These decisions range from workgroup policies to daily operating decisions. It could even come down to the way a particular employee decides to handle a specific customer complaint or which phone number a sales representative decides to dial next. These small variations in the organization's direction, these small steps forward or backward, when added together become a large determinant of whether the organization ultimately reaches its goals. For this reason, effective decision making is needed at all levels of the organization.

But how do we know when a decision moves the organization, either by a leap or a baby step, toward the goal? We need a method of navigation. As shown in Figure 1-3,

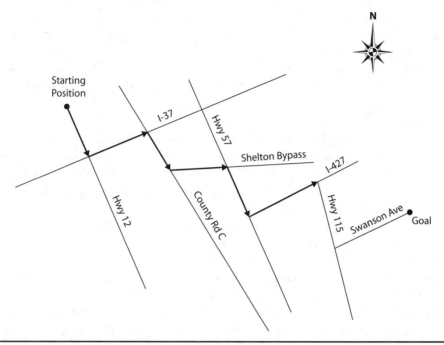

Figure 1-3   *Measuring progress toward the goal*

we need a map or, these days, perhaps a global positioning system (GPS), to tell us where we are relative to our goal and to show us if we are moving in the right direction.

This is the reason why goals must include a means of measuring progress. By repeatedly checking these measures, we can determine whether the organization is making effective decisions. When the measures show we are heading away from the goals, the decision making can be adjusted accordingly. As long as our measures are correctly defined to match our goals, we have a good chance of moving ever closer to those goals.

Panicked Gossip, the Crow's Nest, or the Wireless

The sinking of the *Titanic* provides a catastrophic illustration of poor decision making. The ship was traveling at high speed in ice-laden waters—an unfortunate decision. This tragedy also provides us with an illustration of how important it is to receive feedback information in a timely manner.

News that there were "icebergs about" reached different people aboard the ship at different times. Most passengers found out about the fatal iceberg through panicked gossip as they were boarding the lifeboats. Of course, the passengers were not in a position to take direct action to correct the situation and, by the time they found out, it was far too late.

The ship's captain got news of the iceberg from the lookout in the crow's nest of the *Titanic*. This warning was received before the collision, and the captain attempted to correct the situation. However, the *Titanic* could neither stop nor turn on a dime so, ultimately, this warning turned out to be too late.

Another warning had been received earlier on board the *Titanic*. The wireless operator received an ice warning from another ship, the *America*, and even passed that warning on to a land-based wireless station. This message was received hours ahead of the collision—plenty of time to take precautions and avoid the tragedy. Because of the large workload on the wireless operator, however, this warning was never relayed to anyone on the *Titanic* with the authority to take those precautions. The feedback information aboard the *Titanic* is shown in Figure 1-4.

In the previous section, we learned about the need to use defined measures to get information to our decision makers. As the story of the *Titanic* illustrates, the timing of this feedback information is as important as its content. Feedback information that does not reach the proper decision makers in a timely manner is useful only to those investigating the tragedy after it has occurred. The goal of effective decision making is to avoid the tragedy in the first place!

As with the passengers on the *Titanic*, information in our organizations may come in the form of panicked gossip among lower-level personnel. Unlike those passengers, these people might even pick up some important information in advance of a calamity.

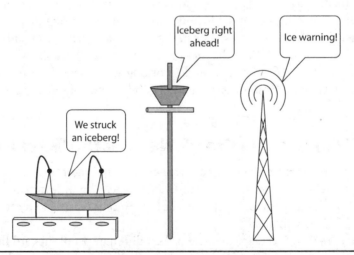

Figure 1-4   *Aboard the* Titanic, *feedback information was not given to the decision makers in a timely manner.*

Even if this is the case, these people are not in a position to correct the problem. Furthermore, we need to base our decision making on solid information from well-designed measures, not gossip and rumors.

Like the captain of the *Titanic*, the decision makers in our organizations often get feedback information when it is too late to act. The information may be extremely accurate, but if it does not get to the decision makers in time to make corrections, it is not helpful. The numbers in the year-end report are not helpful for making decisions during that year.

Similar to the wireless operator, our organizations often have a person who has the appropriate information at the appropriate time. The situation breaks down when this person does not pass the information along to the appropriate decision maker. This may occur, as in the case of the *Titanic*'s wireless operator, because that person is overworked and has too much information to get out to too many people. It may also occur because organizational policies or structures prevent the flow of information. Finally, this may occur because the infrastructure is not in place to facilitate this communication.

Business Intelligence

The first step in effective decision making is to set specific, measurable goals. As these goals are being set, the objective is to get accurate, useful information to the appropriate decision makers to serve as a foundation for the decision and as feedback on the effectiveness of that decision. Having the foundation and feedback information available at the appropriate time is extremely important. The question becomes: How does an organization go about obtaining and distributing this information? As the title of this book suggests, the answer is through the use of business intelligence. In fact, this objective serves as our definition of business intelligence.

DEFINITION

Business intelligence *is the delivery of accurate, useful information to the appropriate decision makers within the necessary timeframe to support effective decision making.*

Business intelligence is not simply facts and figures on a printed report or a computer screen. Rows upon rows of numbers showing detailed sales figures or production numbers may be extremely accurate, but they are not business intelligence until they are put in a format that can be easily understood by a decision maker who needs to use them. Concise summaries of customer satisfaction or assembly-line efficiency may be easily understood, but they are not business intelligence until they can be delivered in time to meaningfully affect daily decision making.

We also discovered earlier in this chapter that effective decision making is important at all organizational levels. Timely foundation and feedback information is needed as part of that effective decision making. Therefore, we need to make business intelligence available throughout our organizations.

Business Intelligence and Microsoft SQL Server 2016

Fortunately, Microsoft SQL Server 2016 provides tools to support all aspects of business intelligence. Integration Services enables us to create automated processes to cleanse data and move it into a business intelligence warehouse, when necessary, to ensure we have accurate information available in a timely manner. Numerous online analytical processing (OLAP) features, such as key performance indicators (KPIs), multidimensional expression (MDX) queries and scripts as well as data analysis expressions (DAX), and the BI Semantic Model (BISM), enable us to slice, dice, and summarize information so it can be presented in a meaningful manner. Finally, Reporting Services (along with other Microsoft end-user tools) facilitates the delivery of this information to decision makers throughout the entire organization.

In Chapter 2 of this book, we learn more about the concepts used when creating and delivering business intelligence. We see the types of questions business intelligence can help us answer. We also examine the kinds of information and the timeliness of that information required at various levels within an organization.

Finally, we become acquainted with Maximum Miniatures, Incorporated, the sample company we use throughout the remainder of the book. To make the business intelligence features of SQL Server 2016 easier to understand, we perform several hands-on exercises to create business intelligence solutions. Rather than looking at code snippets without any business context, we use the business needs of Maximum Miniatures. The goal of this book is not to enable you to use this or that feature of SQL Server 2016, but to help you understand how to use these features to meet business needs.

Chapter 2

Making the Most of What You've Got: Using Business Intelligence

In This Chapter

Out of clutter find simplicity. From discord find harmony.

—Albert Einstein's First Two Rules of Work

In the previous chapter, we discussed the importance of effective decision making to the success of any organization. We also learned that effective decision making depends on specific goals, concrete measures to evaluate our progress toward those goals, and foundation and feedback information based on those measures. The latter two items, concrete measures and foundation/feedback information, we referred to as business intelligence.

In this chapter, we take a look at the types of questions this business intelligence can help us answer. We also discuss the types of business intelligence that are needed at various levels of an organization. The chapter ends by talking about Maximum Miniatures, Incorporated, the company we are going to use for our examples throughout the book.

What Business Intelligence Can Do for You

In Chapter 1, we saw how business intelligence is used to support effective decision making. It provides foundational information on which to base a decision. Business intelligence also provides us with feedback information that can be used to evaluate a decision. It can provide that foundational and feedback information in a number of different ways.

Types of Data Exploration

There are two types of data exploration we can use as we look to our data for answers. We may know exactly what we are looking for and where to find it. Alternatively, we may want the data itself to lead us to new questions or areas of concern. Each of these two types of data exploration requires a different approach to the data.

Layout-Led Discovery

When we know the question we want answered and have a good idea where that answer is going to be found, we can use reports to deliver our business intelligence. This is the most common form of business intelligence and one we are all familiar with. For many situations, this format works well.

For example, if we want to know the dollar amount of the sales or services provided in each region, we know where to find this information. We can design a report to retrieve the information, and the report will consistently deliver what we need. The report serves as an effective business intelligence tool.

This is an example of *layout-led discovery*. With layout-led discovery, we can only learn information that the report designer thought to put in the report layout when it was first designed. If the information wasn't included at design time, we have no way to access it at the time the report is run.

Suppose our report shows the dollar amount for a given region to be unusually low. If the report designer did not include the supporting detail for that region, we have no way to drill into the region and determine the cause of the anomaly. Perhaps a top salesperson moved to another region. Maybe we have lost a key client. The report won't give us that information. We quickly come to a dead end.

Data-Led Discovery

In some cases, we know the question, but we don't know exactly where to look for our answer. This often occurs when the information we initially receive changes the question slightly. As in the example from the previous section, an anomaly in the information may cause us to want to look at the data in a slightly different way. The unusually low dollar amount for sales or services provided in a specific region led us to want detailed numbers within that region.

In other cases, we know where to look, but it is not practical to search through all of the detailed information. Instead, we want to start at an upper level, find a number that looks interesting, and then drill to more detail. We want to follow the data that catches our attention to see where it leads.

This is *data-led discovery*: The information we find determines where we want to go next. The developer of this type of solution cannot know everywhere the report user may want to go. Instead, the developer must provide an interactive environment that enables the user to navigate at will.

To implement data-led discovery, we need some type of drilldown mechanism. When we see something that looks interesting, we need to be able to click that item and access the next level of detail. This is, of course, not going to happen on a sheet of paper. Data-led discovery must be done online.

Business Intelligence at Many Levels

In Chapter 1, we discussed the fact that business intelligence should be utilized at all levels of an organization to promote effective decision making. While it is true that business intelligence is useful throughout the organization, the same type of information is not needed at each level. Different levels within the organization require different types of business intelligence for effective decision making.

As we look at what is required at each level, keep in mind the Effective Decisions Triangle from Figure 1-1. We will transform that triangle into a pyramid as we examine

Figure 2-1 *Specific goals at each level of the organization*

the specific goals, concrete measures, and the timing of the foundation and feedback information required at each level. (See Figures 2-1, 2-2, and 2-3.)

The Top of the Pyramid

Decision makers at the upper levels of our organizations must look at the big picture. They are charged with setting long-term goals for the organization. Decision makers need to have a broad overview of their area of responsibility and not get caught up in the minutiae.

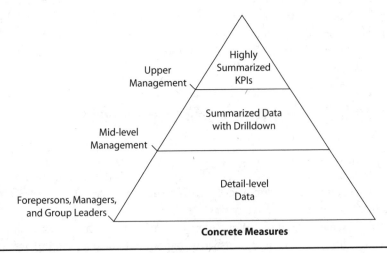

Figure 2-2 *Concrete measures at each level of the organization*

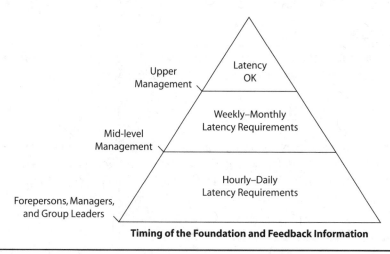

Figure 2-3   *Timing of the foundation and feedback information at each level of the organization*

Highly Summarized Measures

The business intelligence utilized at this level needs to match these characteristics. The measures delivered to these decision makers must be highly summarized. In many cases, each measure is represented, not by a number, but by a status indicator showing whether the measure is in an acceptable range, is starting to lag, or is in an unacceptable range. These highly summarized measures are known as key performance indicators.

> ### DEFINITION
>
> Key performance indicators *(KPIs)* are highly summarized measures designed to quickly relay the status of that measure. They usually reflect the most vital aspects of the organization.

KPIs are used to provide these high-level decision makers with a quick way to determine the health of the essential aspects of the organization. KPIs are often presented as a graphical icon, such as a traffic light or a gauge, designed to convey the indicator's status at a glance. We discuss KPIs in greater detail in Chapters 10 and 12 of this book.

Higher Latency

Because these upper-level decision makers are dealing in long-term policies and direction, they do not need up-to-the-minute business intelligence. Another way to state this is to say they can have more *latency* in their business intelligence. These decision makers need to see downward trends in time to make corrections. They do not need to see the daily blips in the organization's operation.

DEFINITION

The latency *of business intelligence is the amount of time between the occurrence of a transaction and the loading of that transaction's information into the business intelligence system.*

Mid-Level

Mid-level decision makers are managing the operation of departments and other working units within the organization. They are setting short-term goals and doing the planning for the functioning of these areas. Mid-level decision makers are still at a level where they should not be involved in the details of day-to-day processes.

Summarized Measures with Drilldown

These mid-level decision makers need business intelligence that is still summarized. However, they often need to drill down into this information to get at more detail. Therefore, these decision makers can utilize reports along with interactive systems, allowing data-led discovery.

Some Latency Acceptable

Because these decision makers are closer to the everyday functions, they may require business intelligence with less latency. In some cases, they may need to see measures that are updated daily. In other cases, these decision makers are looking for trends discernible from weekly or monthly loads.

The Broad Base

At the broad base of our business intelligence pyramid are the forepersons, managers, and group leaders taking care of daily operations. These people are setting daily operational goals and making decisions on resource allocation for the next week, the next day, or perhaps the next shift. They are planning the next sales campaign or maybe just the next sales call. These decision makers usually need business intelligence systems with high availability and high responsiveness.

Measures at the Detail Level

These decision makers are dealing with the details of the organization's operations. They need to be able to access information at the detail level. In some cases, the work groups these decision makers are responsible for are small enough that they can see the detail for the work group directly without being overwhelmed. In other cases, measures need to be summarized, but drilldown to the detail level will probably be required.

Low Latency

Because these low-level decision makers are managing day-to-day operations, they need to react quickly to changes in feedback information. For this reason, they can tolerate little latency. In some cases, these decision makers require data that is no more than one day old, one hour old, or even less.

Maximum Miniatures, Inc.

Throughout the remainder of this book, Maximum Miniatures, Incorporated serves as the basis for all of our examples. Maximum Miniatures, or Max Min, Inc., as it is referred to by most employees, manufactures and sells small, hand-painted figurines. It has several product lines, including the Woodland Creatures collection of North American animals; the Mythic World collection, which includes dragons, trolls, and elves; the Warriors of Yore collection, containing various soldiers from Roman times up through World War II; and the Guiding Lights collection, featuring replica lighthouses from the United States. The miniatures are made from clay, pewter, or aluminum.

Max Min markets these miniatures through three different channels. It operates five of its own "Maximum Miniature World" stores dedicated to selling the Max Min product line. Max Min also operates MaxMin.com to sell its products online. In addition, Max Min sells wholesale to other retailers.

Business Needs

Max Min, Inc., has experienced rapid growth in the past three years, with orders increasing by over 300 percent. This growth has put a strain on Max Min's only current source of business intelligence, the printed report. Reports that worked well to support decision making just a few years ago now take an hour or more to print and even longer to digest. These reports work at the detail level with little summarization. Max Min's current systems provide few, if any, alternatives to the printed reports for viewing business intelligence.

In addition, Max Min, Inc., is facing tough competition in a number of its product areas. This competition requires Max Min to practice effective decision making to keep its competitive edge. Unfortunately, Max Min's current business intelligence infrastructure, or lack thereof, is making this extremely difficult.

Because of these issues, Max Min has launched a new project to create a true business intelligence environment to support its decision making. This project includes the design of a data warehouse structure, the population of that data warehouse from its current systems, and the creation of analytical applications to serve decision makers at all levels of the organization.

The new business intelligence platform is based on SQL Server 2016. After an extensive evaluation, it was decided that the SQL Server 2016 platform would provide the highest level of business intelligence capability for the money spent. SQL Server 2016 was also chosen because it features the tools necessary to implement the data warehouse in a relatively short time.

We will examine each step of Max Min's implementation project as we learn about the various business intelligence tools available in SQL Server 2016. Before we begin, let's take a quick look at Max Min's current systems.

Current Systems

Max Min has three data processing systems that are expected to serve as sources of business intelligence (see Figure 2-4).

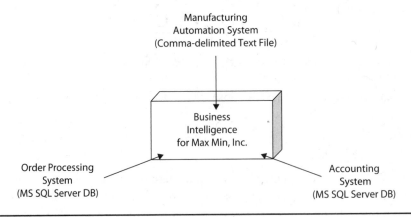

Figure 2-4   *Sources of business intelligence at Max Min, Inc.*

Manufacturing Automation

The manufacturing automation system tracks the materials used to make each product. It also stores which products are manufactured on which production lines. Finally, this system tracks the number of items manufactured during each shift.

The manufacturing automation system uses a proprietary data-storage format. Data can be exported from the manufacturing automation system to a comma-delimited text file. This text file serves as the source for loading the manufacturing data into the business intelligence systems.

Order Processing

The order processing system manages the inventory amounts for all products. It tracks wholesale orders placed by non–Max Min retailers. The system also records product amounts sold through the Max Min retail stores and the Max Min online store to maintain inventory amounts.

The order processing system tracks order fulfillment, including product shipping. It also generates invoices and handles the payment of those invoices. In addition, this system records any products returned from the retailer.

The order processing system uses a Microsoft SQL Server database as its backend.

Accounting

The accounting system tracks all the financial transactions for Max Min, Inc. This includes the purchase of raw materials for manufacturing. The accounting system uses a SQL Server database for its backend.

Building the Foundation

In Chapter 3, you will learn more about the foundations of our business intelligence systems. We explore possible sources for our business intelligence data. We also look at what the structure of those data sources might look like.

Chapter 3

Seeking the Source: The Source of Business Intelligence

In This Chapter

- ▶ Seeking the Source
- ▶ The Data Mart
- ▶ Why Analysis Services?

Planning ahead is a good idea. It wasn't raining when Noah built the ark.

—Anonymous

In the previous chapter, we discussed the various ways business intelligence can aid in making effective business decisions. We also looked at the characteristics of the business intelligence used at different levels within our organizations. Finally, we were introduced to Maximum Miniatures, Incorporated, the source for all sample data in this book.

In this chapter, we begin planning the database structures to serve as the source of our business intelligence. In some cases, we can extract our business intelligence information directly from the same database used to store the data from our daily business operations. In many cases, however, we need to move that data into another location before we can use it as business intelligence. This "other location" is known as a data mart.

Seeking the Source

We have seen that business intelligence is important for effective decision making in our organizations. This, however, leads to a big question. Just where is this business intelligence going to come from? Is business intelligence a form of corporate espionage? Do we need to send up spy satellites to watch our competitors and tap the phone lines of our clients? Should we be hiring secret agents to infiltrate our rivals' facilities? Of course not!

Does business intelligence require us to take the pulse of the people? Do we need to commission large studies of our potential customers? Do we need to conduct a survey to determine what people are thinking about our products or services? While some business intelligence may come from customer satisfaction surveys or market research, the customer's buying behavior is a better gauge of their tendencies and satisfaction. At any rate, this is not what we are going to focus on in this book.

The bulk of business intelligence for most organizations comes from something they already have: their transactional data.

Transactional Data

Most organizations need to keep track of the things they do to conduct their business. Orders taken, products produced, services rendered, payments received from clients, and payments made to vendors are all interactions that usually result in one or more entries in some type of data store. Each of these interactions is a business transaction, so we refer to this as transactional data.

DEFINITION

Transactional data *is the information stored to track the interactions, or business transactions, carried out by an organization.*

The business transactions of an organization need to be tracked for that organization to operate. Payments must be collected for products and services. Payments must be made for goods and services received. Orders and service requests need to be fulfilled. In general, the organization needs to keep track of what it has done and what it needs to do. When these transactions are stored on and managed by computers, we refer to this as online transaction processing, or OLTP.

DEFINITION

Online transaction processing (OLTP) *systems record business interactions as they happen. They support the day-to-day operation of an organization.*

The totality of these transactions stored in OLTP systems is the history of an organization. This transactional data contains the raw numbers necessary to calculate the measures we discussed in the previous chapters. Here, then, is the data we need to create our business intelligence.

Difficulties Using Transactional Data for Business Intelligence

OLTP systems are the treasure chests holding the raw data we need to calculate measures and create business intelligence. Problems arise, however, when we try to extract these nuggets of raw data from our OLTP systems. Let's take a look at some of the difficulties.

The Nature of the Beast   Well-designed OLTP systems are optimized for efficiently processing and storing transactions. This means breaking data up into small chunks using the rules of database normalization. This allows OLTP systems to process a number of transactions at the same time without one transaction getting in another's way. Information of this type is best stored in a relational database.

The measures we are using for business intelligence, on the other hand, are not designed to reflect the events of one transaction, but to reflect the net result of a number of transactions over a selected period. Business intelligence measures are often aggregates of hundreds, thousands, or even millions of individual transactions. Designing a system to provide these aggregates efficiently requires an entirely different set of optimizations.

DEFINITION

An aggregate *is a number that is calculated from amounts in many detail records. An aggregate is often the sum of many numbers, although it can also be derived using other arithmetic operations or even from a count of the number of items in a group. For example, the total amount invoiced to a client in a given year is the aggregate sum of all the invoice amounts for that client in the selected year.*

OLTP systems, because of the way they are designed, are usually not good at delivering large aggregates. This is not what they were intended to do. We need to look to a different type of data storage optimization to make these aggregates work efficiently.

Interfering with Business Operations   OLTP systems are used by our organizations to support their daily operations. In many cases, the organizations' operation depends on the performance of these systems. If the order processing system or the client management system becomes too bogged down, our organizations can grind to a halt.

We've already discussed the fact that OLTP systems are not good at delivering the aggregates needed for business intelligence. When OLTP systems are called on to produce such aggregates, they typically use a large amount of processing power and take a long time to produce a result. It is also possible that a large number of records will be locked while the aggregate is being produced, rendering those records unavailable to participate in transactional processing. Either of these two events can have a serious impact on transactional processing efficiency.

In other words, requiring an OLTP system to create business intelligence aggregates can tax the system. This can have a detrimental effect on our organizations' daily operations.

Archiving   Because OLTP systems are concerned with the day-to-day operations, they aren't too worried about data from the distant past. These systems may only save data for a relatively short time (and/or the data may only represent the current state, such as current quantity in stock). The data may be saved for a year, and then a year-end process may remove it from the database. It may be archived in another format, a text file, or a database backup file, or it might simply be deleted. Whether deleted or archived, the data is no longer easily accessible.

OLTP systems use this archive process to ensure that the system continues to operate efficiently. If a transaction table contains too many records, the OLTP system can become bogged down and begin to operate slowly. Archiving allows an OLTP system to stay lean and mean.

This archiving causes problems for business intelligence. When we are looking for trends in our measures, we want to compare last year's numbers to this year's numbers.

We may even want to compare numbers over several years of operation. This is hard to do when the data from past years has been archived or deleted.

Divided They Stand   Our organizations probably use a number of different OLTP systems to manage different aspects of their operations. One system is used for order processing, a different system for accounting, another for manufacturing, and still another for personnel. As we saw in the previous chapter, Maximum Miniatures, Incorporated has three different systems that will provide data for their current business intelligence project. Even with the move toward integrated Enterprise Resource Planning (ERP) systems, it is unlikely that all of an organization's transactional data will be in one location.

The measures used to provide business intelligence, on the other hand, do not respect these lines of separation. Instead, they treat the organization as a whole. For example, a reasonable measure to require is the profit margin for a particular product. To calculate this measure, we need the list of raw materials from the manufacturing system, the cost of those materials from the accounting system, the cost of labor required to produce the product from the time entry system, and the amount paid for the product from the order processing system. To calculate this type of measure, then, we need to combine data across systems to get what we need.

Aside from the necessity for communication between systems, this need to pull data from multiple systems leads to another problem. Each of these systems maintains its own set of product numbering schemes, codes, and calendars. The same product may be known as "12593" in the manufacturing system and "SD125RDS" in the order processing system. The payroll system may work on two-week pay periods, while the accounting system works on fiscal months. When data from these disparate systems is brought together, we need to find some common ground.

The Data Mart

A number of problems can result when we try to use our organizations' OLTP systems as the source for our business intelligence. What we need to do is take the information stored in these OLTP systems and move it into a different data store. This intermediate data store can then serve as the source for our measure calculations. We need to store the data so it is available for our business intelligence needs somewhere outside of our OLTP systems. When data is stored in this manner, it is referred to as a *data mart*.

DEFINITION

A data mart *is a body of historical data in an electronic repository that does not participate in the daily operations of the organization. Instead, this data is used to create business intelligence. The data in the data mart usually applies to a specific area of the organization.*

NOTE

In this book, we discuss the creation of data marts rather than the perhaps more familiar term, data warehouse. Data warehouses tend to be large, one-stop-shopping repositories where all the historical data for the organization would be stored. Nothing is wrong with this as a concept; however, attempting to create a data warehouse often led to huge, multiyear technology projects that were never quite finished or were outdated when they finally did get done. In this book, we concern ourselves with creating data marts—smaller undertakings that focus on a particular aspect of an organization.

Features of a Data Mart

Because the data mart is meant to serve as a source for business intelligence rather than managing the organization's day-to-day transactions, it is not designed the same as an OLTP database. Instead of being built around the rules of normalization, data marts are built for speed of access. A data mart is still a relational database, but it is designed to require fewer table joins when data is output for analysis and reporting. In a data mart, it is acceptable to have data repeated (denormalized) for the sake of speed.

When designing a data mart, the rules of normalization are replaced by different methods of design organized around "facts." One of these new design approaches uses structures called stars and snowflakes. We discuss stars and snowflakes in the sections "The Star Schema" and "The Snowflake Schema." Stars and snowflakes may seem like the stuff of children's fantasies, but, in reality, they provide quite grownup and down-to-earth approaches to creating information that is quick and easy to access. The other design approach we will discuss is a denormalized relational structure. This is covered in the section "Denormalized Relational Schema."

Not Real-Time Data

OLTP systems store data from business transactions as they occur throughout the day. Data marts, on the other hand, are updated at set intervals. Data is copied from the OLTP systems periodically and written to the data mart. This is known as a *data load*.

Because the data mart exists separately from the OLTP systems, accessing the data mart for business intelligence information does not put any stress on the transactional systems vital to the business's operation. The only exception to this is during the data load. During the data load, the OLTP systems may have to work hard to prepare the data for copying to the data mart. The good news here is the data load is an automated process that can be scheduled to run during off-peak hours.

As we discussed in Chapter 2, information in a data mart has some latency. In most cases, some time elapses between the moment a transaction is completed and the moment when the transaction is copied to the data mart. If a data mart load is scheduled to run each month right after the month-end processing, then the data mart has a latency of one month. If the data load runs nightly, the data mart can have a latency of up to one day.

The latency of the data mart must be set properly to fulfill the business intelligence requirements of that data mart. The information provided by the data mart must be up-to-date enough to facilitate effective decision making. However, the data loads should not occur so often that they cause unneeded stress on the OLTP systems.

Consolidation and Cleansing

Data from a number of different OLTP systems may be combined into a single data mart. This enables us to calculate some complex measures for our business intelligence. As we discussed earlier, this may also cause problems. Multiple OLTP systems can have different ways of representing data. Inconsistent data types used for the same data, dissimilar unique identifiers used for the same entity, and different time periods and calendar systems can all cause a great deal of difficulty when trying to combine data from heterogeneous systems.

In fact, problems can even arise when using data from a single system. The business rules necessary for a meaningful measure calculation may be stricter than those enforced within the OLTP system itself. If this is the case, some of the data coming from the OLTP system may not meet the stricter rules. Inconsistencies with data types and unique identifiers could also exist within the same system if the database has been poorly designed or poorly maintained.

These problems must be resolved before the data can be stored in the data mart. We must scrub out all the problem data. To do this, the data is put through a data cleansing process.

DEFINITION

Data cleansing *removes inconsistencies and errors from transactional data so it has the consistency necessary for use in a data mart.*

Data cleansing transforms data into a format that does not cause problems in the data mart environment. It converts inconsistent data types into a single type. Data cleansing translates dissimilar identifiers to a standard set of codes for the data mart. In addition, it repairs or removes any data that does not meet the business rules required by the measures calculated from this data mart.

Data cleansing is usually done as part of a larger process. This process extracts the data from the OLTP systems and loads it into the data mart. Thus, the entire procedure is known as extract, transform, and load—or ETL.

DEFINITION

The extract, transform, and load (ETL) *process extracts data from one or more OLTP systems, performs any required data cleansing to transform the data into a consistent format, and loads the cleansed data by inserting it into the data mart.*

Data Mart Structure

The data we use for business intelligence can be divided into four categories: measures, dimensions, attributes, and hierarchies. These four types of data help us to define the structure of the data mart. Let's look at each of these types of data and see how they are stored in the data mart.

Measures

The measure forms the basis of everything we do with business intelligence. In fact, without measures, there would be no business intelligence. As we learned in Chapter 1, the measures are the whole reason for pursuing business intelligence. They are the basic building blocks for effective decision making.

DEFINITION

A measure *is a numeric quantity expressing some aspect of the organization's performance. The information represented by this quantity is used to support or evaluate the decision making and performance of the organization. A measure can also be called a fact.*

Measures are the facts we use for our foundational and feedback information. Therefore, the tables that hold measure information are known as *fact tables*. Don't let the name fool you, though, Sergeant Friday—fact tables hold more than just the facts.

Dimensions

Total sales is an example of a measure that is often required for effective decision making. However, it is not often that decision makers want to see one single aggregate representing the total sales for all products for all salespersons for the entire lifetime of the organization. Instead, they are more likely to want to slice and dice this total into smaller parts. Dimensions are used to facilitate this slicing and dicing.

DEFINITION

A dimension *is a categorization used to spread out an aggregate measure to reveal its constituent parts.*

A dimension enables us to apply a categorization to an aggregate measure. The categorization lets us see the constituent numbers that create the aggregate measure. For example, we can think of the measure of total sales as a single point of information. In geometry, a point has no dimensions.

Total Sales

$145,346,834

We can apply a categorization or a dimension to that single point of data to spread it out. In this case, let's spread the total sales out into the total sales for each year.

Total Sales

$33,708,421

2011   2012   2013   2014   2015   2016

Years

We now have a line made up of measures of total sales at various points along that line, one point for each year in the dimension. In geometry, a line is a one-dimensional object. Thus, we have added a dimension to our measure: 2011, 2012, 2013, 2014, 2015, and 2016 are each said to be *members* of the year dimension.

We can again spread out the total sales, this time for each product type.

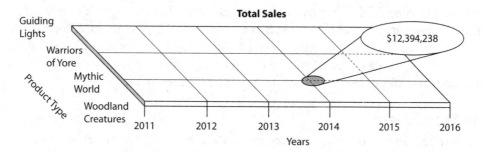

Total Sales

$12,394,238

Guiding Lights
Warriors of Yore
Mythic World
Woodland Creatures

Product Type

2011   2012   2013   2014   2015   2016

Years

The measures of total sales are now arranged in a square. Because a square is a two-dimensional object, we have added another dimension to our measure. Woodland

Creatures, Mythic World, Warriors of Yore, and Guiding Lights are each members of the Product Type dimension.

Let's spread out the total sales once more—this time by sales region. The measure of total sales has become a cube, which is a three-dimensional object. You can see that each time we add a new criteria to spread out the measure, we increase the dimensionality of our measure, thus, the name dimension.

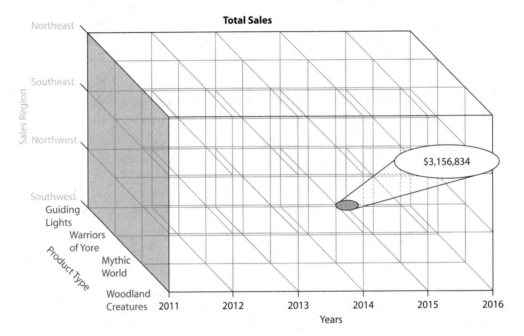

We can continue to spread out the measure using additional dimensions, such as a marketing campaign dimension and a buyer's age bracket dimension, to get a four-dimensional object, and then a five-dimensional object. Even though this becomes difficult to represent in an illustration, it is a perfectly valid thing to do. Also, because we are more familiar with three-dimensional objects than four- or five-dimensional ones, if there is such a thing, we continue to refer to these structures with four, five, or even more dimensions as cubes. We talk more about cubes in Chapter 4.

The Star Schema

Measures and dimensions can be stored in the data mart in a number of different layouts, or schemas. We will look at three schemas, the first of which is the star schema. The name of this schema comes from the shape formed by the relational database diagram for the data mart, as we will see in a moment. The star schema uses two types of tables: fact tables and dimension tables.

DEFINITION

A star schema is a relational database schema used to hold measures and dimensions in a data mart. The measures are stored in a fact table, and dimensions are stored in dimension tables.

The center of the star is formed by the fact table. The fact table has a column for the measure and a column for each dimension containing the foreign key for a member of that dimension. The primary key for this table is created by concatenating all of the foreign key fields. This is known as a *composite key*. Fact tables are named for the set of measures they contain, with the word "Fact" added to the beginning. The fact table for the example in the previous section is shown in Figure 3-1.

The dimensions are stored in dimension tables. The dimension table has a column for the unique identifier of a member of the dimension. The dimension table has another column for a description of the member. One dimension is stored in each dimension table, with one row for each member of the dimension. Dimension tables are named for the dimension they contain, with the letters "Dim" added to the beginning. The rows of the DimProductType dimension table would be:

ProductTypeID	ProductTypeDescription
1	Woodland Creatures
2	Mythic World
3	Warriors of Yore
4	Guiding Lights

When we add the dimension tables to the schema, we get the characteristic star design, as shown in Figure 3-2.

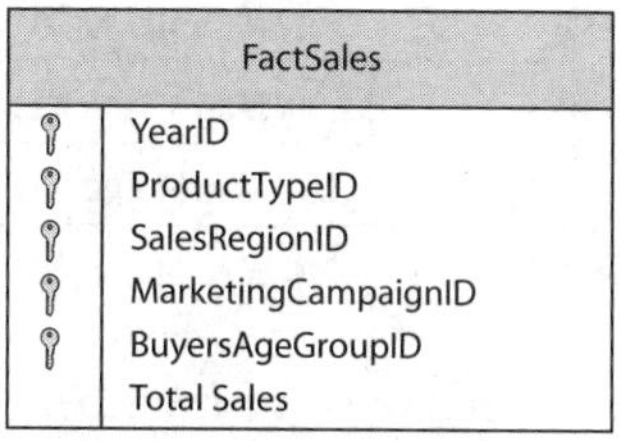

FactSales
YearID
ProductTypeID
SalesRegionID
MarketingCampaignID
BuyersAgeGroupID
Total Sales

Figure 3-1   *The FactSales table*

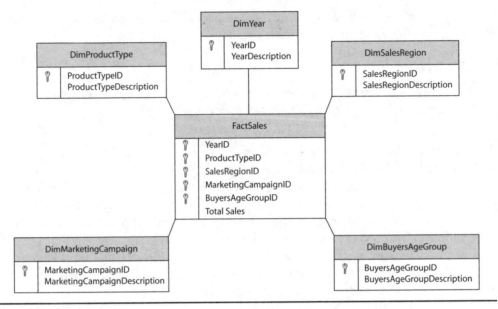

Figure 3-2 *The star schema*

Potentially, one row will be in the fact table for every unique combination of dimension members. The word "potentially" is used here because there may be some combinations of dimension members that do not have a value. In some cases, a particular combination of dimension members may not even make sense.

In our example, if History Magazine Spring Ad is a member of the marketing campaign dimension, some of the rows in the FactSales table would be:

Year	Product Type	Sales Region	Marketing Campaign	Buyer's Age	Total Sales
2011	Mythic World	Northeast	History Mag Spring Ad	0–25	56,342
2011	Mythic World	Northeast	History Mag Spring Ad	25–35	104,547
2011	Mythic World	Northeast	History Mag Spring Ad	35–45	234,385
2011	Mythic World	Northeast	History Mag Spring Ad	45–55	534,532
2011	Mythic World	Northeast	History Mag Spring Ad	55–65	829,282
2011	Mythic World	Northeast	History Mag Spring Ad	65+	284,540

If, in our example, we assume there are eight members of the marketing campaign dimension to go along with six members of the year dimension, four members of the product type dimension, four members of the sales region dimension, and six members of the buyer's age dimension, we have a potential for

$$8 \times 6 \times 4 \times 4 \times 6$$

or 4608 rows in the FactSales table. This is not a huge number, but you can see when you have dimensions with tens or hundreds of members, the size of the fact table can grow rather large.

In reality, the fact table should contain the identifiers for the dimension members rather than their descriptions. This cuts down on the size required to store each fact row, which becomes important in fact tables with a potential for millions or even hundreds of millions of rows.

In addition, a single fact table may contain multiple measures. This can occur when two or more measures use exactly the same dimensions. Putting a number of measures with the same dimensions in the same fact table is also a way to save on storage space required for the data mart.

Attributes

In some cases, we may want to store additional information about dimension members in our data mart. This helps us further define the members of the dimension. These bits of additional information are known as *attributes* of the dimension.

DEFINITION

An attribute *is an additional piece of information pertaining to a dimension member that is not the unique identifier or the description of the member.*

Attributes can be used to more fully describe dimension members. They may contain information about a dimension member that the users are likely to want as part of their business intelligence output. Attributes are also used to store information that may be used to limit or filter the records selected from the data mart during data analysis. They are stored as additional columns in the dimension tables, as shown in Figure 3-3.

Hierarchies

In many cases, a dimension may contain one or more multilevel structures. These structures are known as *hierarchies*. In our sample, the year, product type, and sales region dimensions each contain hierarchies.

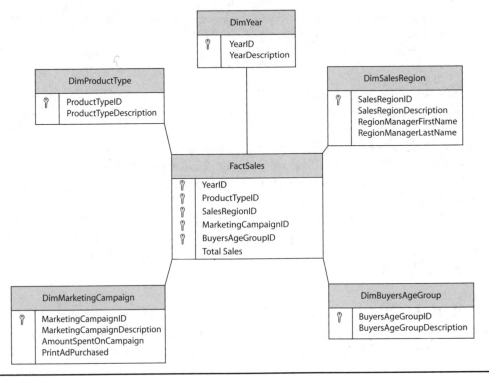

Figure 3-3   *Attribute columns in the dimension tables*

DEFINITION

A hierarchy is a structure made up of two or more levels within a dimension.

Hierarchies enable the users to navigate to different levels of granularity within the measures of the data mart. Users can look at the measures at one level of the hierarchy and then drill into a selected member to see the next lower level. For example, a user can look at the product subtypes within the Mythic World product type. He or she can look at the sales territories within the Northeast sales region. A user can also look at the months within Q1, 2011. In fact, all of these can be combined at once so the user can view the sales totals by the product subtypes of the Mythic World product type, by sales territories of the Northeast sales region, and by months in Q1, 2011. By moving up and down the hierarchy, users can find exactly the right measure to aid in making the decision at hand.

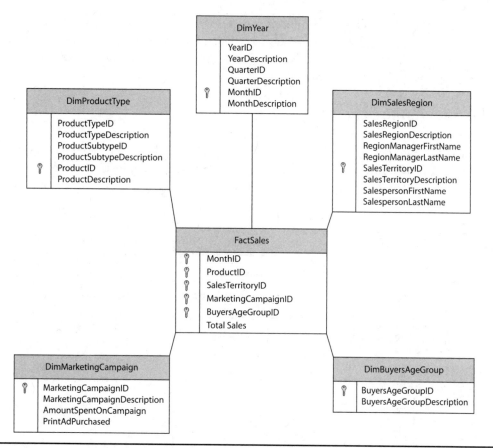

Figure 3-4   *A star schema with hierarchies*

In a star schema, the information about the hierarchies is stored right in the dimension tables, as shown in Figure 3-4. The primary key in each of the dimension tables is at the lowest level of the hierarchy. At the same time, we adjust the name of some of the dimension tables to better represent the data they contain. In addition, the fact table must be changed so its foreign keys point to the lowest levels in the hierarchies as well. This means, then, the fact table will have one row (and one set of measures) for each unique combination of members at the lowest level of all the hierarchies.

Measures for hierarchy levels above the lowest level are not stored in the data mart. Instead, these measures have to be calculated by taking an aggregate of the measures stored at the lowest level. For example, if the user wants to see the total sales for the Northeast sales region, that measure has to be calculated by aggregating the total sales for all of the territories within the Northeast sales region. In this case, the aggregation is the sum of the total sales of the territories.

The Snowflake Schema

An alternative to the star schema is the snowflake schema. The *snowflake schema* represents hierarchies in a manner that is more familiar to those of us who have been working with relational databases. In a snowflake schema, each level of a hierarchy is stored in a separate dimension table. This is shown in Figure 3-5. These chains

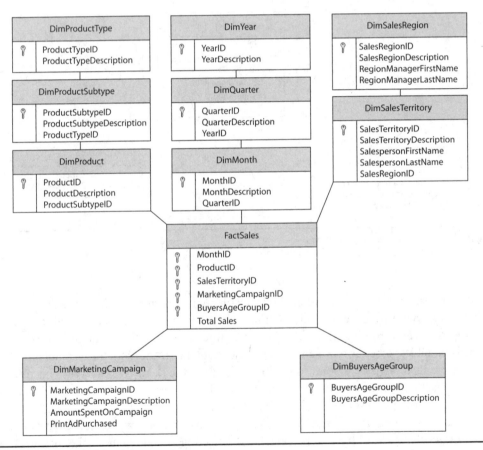

Figure 3-5   *The snowflake schema*

of dimension tables are supposed to resemble the intricate patterns of a snowflake. Although the resemblance may not be too strong in Figure 3-5, this is how the snowflake schema got its name.

As with the star schema, the foreign keys in the fact table at the center of the snowflake schema point to the lowest level of each hierarchy. Therefore, the fact table in the snowflake schema also contains one row for each unique combination of members at the lowest level of each hierarchy. Measures for hierarchy levels above the lowest level have to be calculated by taking an aggregate, just as they were with the star schema.

The snowflake schema has all the advantages of good relational design. It does not result in duplicate data and is, therefore, easier to maintain. It also looks more proper to those of us who have been working with relational databases. The disadvantage of the snowflake design is that it requires a number of table joins when aggregating measures at the upper levels of the hierarchy. In larger data marts or in data marts that experience heavy utilization, this can lead to performance problems.

Denormalized Relational Schema

The third data mart layout we will look at is the denormalized relational schema. When constructing a denormalized relational schema, we look at each dimension related to a given set of measures. If that dimension is only related to this set of measures and no others, we put the dimension information and all of its attributes right in the same table with that set of measures. We do not include the dimensional unique identifier in this table unless it has meaning to the business users.

Dimensional information that is related to more than one set of measures remains in its own table. In these cases, the unique identifier is placed in both the measure table and the dimension table to create a relationship, as we did in the star and snowflake schemas. Because the table holding the measures is likely to contain both measure and dimension information, we do not use the "Fact" and "Dim" prefixes in the table names.

In Figure 3-6, we have added a set of measures related to manufacturing. Both the manufacturing measures and the sales measures are related to the date information and the product information, so we leave these in their own tables. The sales territory, marketing campaign, and buyer's age group information is only related to the sales measure, so we put all of this information into the Sales table.

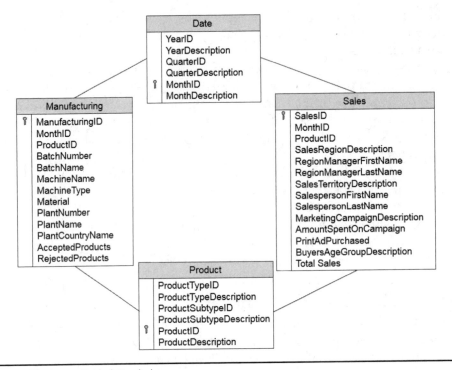

Figure 3-6 *The denormalized relational schema*

Why Analysis Services?

In all three of our schemas, we have to calculate aggregates on-the-fly when the user wants to see data at any level above the lowest level in each dimension. In a schema with a number of dimensions or with dimensions that have a large number of members, this can take a significant amount of time. The whole idea of business intelligence is to make information readily available to our decision makers.

We could calculate all the measures at every level of our hierarchy and store them in the data mart. However, this would make the data mart much too complex and, therefore, much harder to maintain. How do we get good performance from our data mart at every level of the hierarchy without driving the data mart administrator crazy? The answer is Microsoft SQL Server 2016 Analysis Services, as we see in Chapter 4.

Two, Two, Two Models in One: The BI Semantic Model

In This Chapter

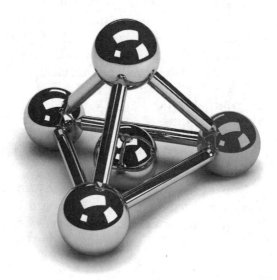

Snowflakes are one of nature's most fragile things, but just look at what they can do when they stick together.

—Vesta M. Kelly

In Chapters 1 and 2, we learned how business intelligence can be used to support effective decision making. In Chapter 3, we began the search for the data that serves as the source for this business intelligence. In most cases, the data we need can be found in our online transaction processing (OLTP) systems.

On close examination, we discovered that an OLTP system is not a good candidate for the direct source of business intelligence. OLTP systems are designed for processing business transactions and storing the detail from each of these transactions. They are not optimized for delivering the aggregated information typically required for business intelligence.

The shortcomings of OLTP systems as a source for business intelligence led us to the data mart. The *data mart* is a relational database structure specifically designed for storing large amounts of historical data. Data must be copied from the OLTP systems into the data mart.

At the end of Chapter 3, we were left with a concern about the data mart. Namely, how do we improve performance when the user wants to view aggregate information derived from a large number of detail records? For the answer to this, we look to online analytical processing.

Online Analytical Processing

In 1993, E. F. Codd, one of the fathers of relational database and OLTP theory, proposed a different type of system that would be tuned to the needs of data analysts. He called this an online analytical processing, or OLAP, system. The criteria Codd originally laid out for an OLAP system were not widely accepted. However, the OLAP name continues to be used for systems designed to quickly provide users with business intelligence.

DEFINITION

Online analytical processing (OLAP) systems enable users to quickly and easily retrieve information from data, usually in a data mart, for analysis. OLAP systems present data using measures, dimensions, hierarchies, and cubes.

As the first word—online—in the name implies, OLAP is designed to let the user interact with the data during analysis. It is geared toward having the user online with the data, slicing and dicing the data to view it in different ways, drilling down into the data to see more detail. This is a different approach from the static reports produced by most OLTP systems.

The BI Semantic Model

Microsoft provides two tools for implementing OLAP systems. The first of these is Microsoft SQL Server Analysis Services (SSAS). SSAS hosts one or more data repositories that are optimized for online analytical processing. The second of these is Microsoft Power BI.

To facilitate interactive data exploration, SSAS and Power BI create a model of the underlying data. This model presents the data to the user in a manner that more closely matches the way business decision makers think about their business. It provides the business users a more natural way to view the data. This model is referred to as the BI Semantic Model (BISM).

The BI Semantic Model, as implemented in SQL Server Analysis Services 2016, provides two alternative ways of working with the data. The data can be stored and presented to the user in the form of measures, dimensions, attributes, and hierarchies. This is implemented using the Multidimensional model within SSAS. Data can also be presented in the more traditional form of tables, fields, and relationships. This second format is implemented through the Tabular model within SSAS. Power BI only supports the second of these two modeling approaches—the Tabular model.

This book looks at both of the architectures available within the BI Semantic Model. Exercises are provided for creating implementations using the Multidimensional model in SSAS and Tabular model in SSAS and in Power BI.

Building OLAP Out of Cubes: The Multidimensional Model

An OLAP system is designed to provide its users with quick and easy access to business data. That data is usually stored in a data mart. The OLAP system simply provides a mechanism for viewing and analyzing the data mart information quickly. When using the Multidimensional model, the business data takes the form of measures, dimensions, hierarchies, and cubes.

In fact, the Multidimensional model's focus is on cubes. We briefly discussed cubes in Chapter 3. Before we get into the specifics of the Multidimensional model, let's take a more detailed look at cubes. We again create a cube using the total sales measure. This time, we use month, product, and salesperson as our dimensions. The resulting cube is shown in Figure 4-1.

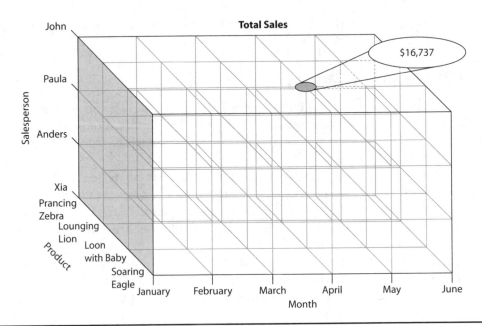

Figure 4-1   *Total Sales cube*

DEFINITION

A cube is a structure that contains a value for one or more measures for each unique combination of the members of all its dimensions. These are detail, or leaf-level, values. The cube also contains aggregated values formed by the dimension hierarchies or when one or more of the dimensions is left out of the hierarchy.

Within the cube is a measure value for each intersection of members of the three dimensions. Figure 4-1 illustrates the total sales for the Loon with Baby figurine by John in April. Loon with Baby is a member of the product dimension. John is a member of the salesperson dimension. April is a member of the month dimension. The total sales at this intersection are $16,737.

A measure value that exists at an intersection of all of the dimensions is called a *detail*, or *leaf-level, value*. In Figure 4-1, total sales for the Loon with Baby figurine by John in April is an example of a leaf-level value. This is a leaf-level value because members (John, April, and Loon with Baby) are specified for each dimension (salesperson, month, and product).

To determine the total sales by John in April, we need to add together John's total sales of each individual product in April. In other words, John's total sales for April are

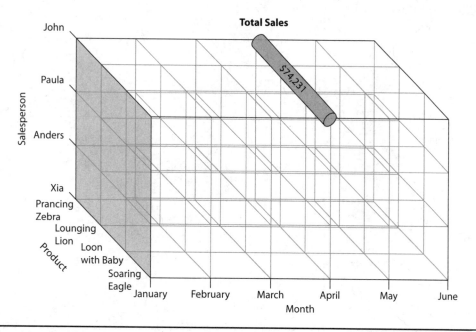

Figure 4-2   *Total Sales cube with an aggregation for John's total sales for April*

equal to John's total sales of Soaring Eagle in April, plus his total sales of Loon with Baby in April, plus his total sales of Lounging Lion in April, plus his total sales of Prancing Zebra in April. In OLAP terminology, we aggregate all the leaf-level values from the product dimension using the sum aggregation. This is shown in Figure 4-2.

DEFINITION

*An **aggregate** is a value formed by combining values from a given dimension or set of dimensions to create a single value. This is often done by adding the values together using the sum aggregate, but other aggregation calculations can also be used.*

To determine the total sales for April for all salespersons, we need to do another aggregation. This time, we need to aggregate all the total sales for all the salespersons across all the products they sold in April (see Figure 4-3).

We also use aggregate values within the cube when we traverse the hierarchy of one or more dimensions. Recall that salespersons can be grouped, or rolled up, into sales regions; products can be rolled up into product subtypes and product types; and months can be rolled up into quarters and years. Each time one level of a hierarchy is rolled up

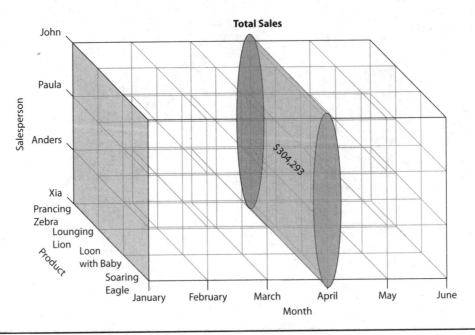

Figure 4-3   *Total Sales cube with an aggregation for total sales for all salespersons for April*

into a higher level, aggregations are used to combine values from the lower level into the groupings at the upper level. For example, the total sales for the Loon with Baby figurine by John in Quarter 1 would be the total sales for the Loon with Baby figurine by John in January, plus the total sales for the Loon with Baby figurine by John in February, plus the total sales for the Loon with Baby figurine by John in March.

You can see that cubes with a number of dimensions and a number of hierarchies require quite a few aggregate calculations as the user navigates through the cube. This can slow down analysis significantly. To combat this, some or all of the possible data aggregates in the cubes are calculated ahead of time and stored within the cube itself. These stored values are known as *preprocessed aggregates*.

Features of a Multidimensional Model Implementation

A Multidimensional model implementation offers many advantages for us as we seek to produce business intelligence. It provides an architecture that is focused on the presentation of information for analysis. This focus makes the Multidimensional model implementation a natural environment for users looking to use information for effective decision making.

Multidimensional Database

The Multidimensional model implementation is built around data that is structured as measures, dimensions, hierarchies, and cubes. This multidimensional approach makes it easy for users to slice and dice information as needed. Users can use dimensions to view the data in different ways. They can use hierarchies to drill into the data and find more detail when needed.

DEFINITION

A multidimensional database is structured around measures, dimensions, hierarchies, and cubes rather than tables, rows, columns, and relations.

A multidimensional database is a natural way to store information used for business intelligence, where measures are analyzed by dimensions. Aside from this innate fit, the multidimensional database offers another big advantage. It provides the structure for storing preprocessed aggregates.

Preprocessed Aggregates

In a data mart, when a decision maker wants to see the value of a measure for a certain set of dimension members, that value must be calculated on the fly. The decision maker must wait while the aggregate value is calculated from all the detail information that rolls up into that aggregate. This can cause a significant delay that distracts from productive research and leads to frustration.

If the goal of an OLAP system is to get the decision maker to interact with the data, then aggregates must be returned quickly. For this reason, Multidimensional model systems preprocess a portion of the aggregates that are found throughout the cube. This preprocessing is done as part of the task that loads or updates the data in the multidimensional database. This is usually done in a manner that does not impact the end users. As the aggregates are preprocessed, they are stored within the cube in the multidimensional database.

Now, when a decision maker wants to see the value of a measure for a certain set of dimensional members, that value can be read from the database rather than being calculated on the fly. This greatly improves the responsiveness of the system, which, in turn, encourages online interaction and provides the decision maker with a higher probability of finding the correct piece or pieces of information necessary to make an effective decision.

Easily Understood

In OLTP systems, the data is normalized and dependencies are represented by complex foreign key relationships; the goal is to reduce redundant data. Any decision maker querying this data must reconstruct the dependencies with the appropriate INNER

JOINs and OUTER JOINs. Business rules that define the way a measure is to be calculated are kept in programmatic structures that are used for transaction processing, not reporting. When including a measure, the decision maker must re-create these calculations each time they are used in a report.

Fields and tables in an OLTP system are given names that make sense to the developer, but not necessarily the end user. The database system may impose a limit on the length of a name, or the database administrator may not like typing long names in his or her maintenance scripts. In either case, the result is cryptic abbreviations in field and table names. The decision maker must decipher the code to be sure the correct data is being queried from the tables.

In a Multidimensional model implementation, just the opposite is true. The structure of the data is represented by dimensions and hierarchies. If the Multidimensional model implementation is designed properly, these dimensions and hierarchies should match the structure of the organization. Thus, the data structure is familiar to the decision maker using the system.

The business rules that pertain to each measure in the Multidimensional model implementation are contained within the calculation defined for that measure. The user does not need to re-create this calculation each time that particular measure is used. For example, suppose your organization defines net profit as:

```
Selling Price - (Cost of Materials + Cost of Labor + Sales Commissions)
```

In a relational environment, net profit might be incorrectly reported as

```
Selling Price - (Cost of Materials + Cost of Labor)
```

in one place and as

```
Selling Price - (Cost of Materials + Sales Commissions)
```

in another. This inconsistency can lead to confusion and, worse yet, poor decisions. In the Multidimensional model implementation, the measure for net profit is defined in one place so it is always calculated properly whether the decision maker is looking at net profit by product, net profit by month, or net profit by sales region.

Finally, because the Multidimensional model implementation exists solely for producing business intelligence, all of the measures, dimensions, and hierarchies are given names that can be easily understood by the decision maker. The Multidimensional model implementation allows additional metadata, such as a long description, to be stored along with the name of the object. This provides the decision maker with enough information to ensure they know exactly what business information they are looking at.

Architecture of a Multidimensional Model Implementation

The key part of the Multidimensional model implementation is the cube and the preprocessed aggregates it contains. The Multidimensional model uses one of three different architectures for storing cube data. Each architecture has certain advantages and disadvantages. The basics of each are shown in Figure 4-4.

Relational OLAP

Relational OLAP (ROLAP) stores the cube structure in a multidimensional database. The leaf-level measures are left in the relational data mart that serves as the source of the cube. The preprocessed aggregates are also stored in a relational database table.

When a decision maker requests the value of a measure for a certain set of dimension members, the ROLAP system first checks to determine whether the dimension members specify an aggregate or a leaf-level value. If an aggregate is specified, the value is selected from the relational table. If a leaf-level value is specified, the value is selected from the data mart.

A ROLAP architecture, because of its reliance on relational tables, can store larger amounts of data than other Multidimensional model architectures. Also, because the ROLAP architecture retrieves leaf-level values directly from the data mart, the leaf-level

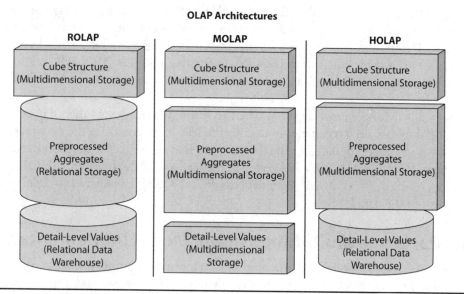

Figure 4-4   *OLAP architectures*

values returned by the ROLAP system are always as up-to-date as the data mart itself. In other words, the ROLAP system does not add latency to leaf-level data. The disadvantage of a ROLAP system is that the retrieval of the aggregate and leaf-level values is slower than the other Multidimensional model architectures.

Multidimensional OLAP

Multidimensional OLAP (MOLAP) also stores the cube structure in a multidimensional database. However, *both* the preprocessed aggregate values and a copy of the leaf-level values are placed in the multidimensional database as well. Because of this, all data requests are answered from the multidimensional database, making MOLAP systems extremely responsive.

Additional time is required when loading a MOLAP system because all the leaf-level data is copied into the multidimensional database. Because of this, at times the leaf-level data returned by the MOLAP system is not in sync with the leaf-level data in the data mart itself. A MOLAP system, therefore, does add latency to the leaf-level data. The MOLAP architecture also requires more disk space to store the copy of the leaf-level values in the multidimensional database. However, because MOLAP is extremely efficient at storing values, the additional space required is usually not significant.

Hybrid OLAP

Hybrid OLAP (HOLAP) combines ROLAP and MOLAP storage. This is why we end up with the word "hybrid" in the name. HOLAP tries to take advantage of the strengths of each of the other two architectures while minimizing their weaknesses.

HOLAP stores the cube structure and the preprocessed aggregates in a multidimensional database. This provides the fast retrieval of aggregates present in MOLAP structures. HOLAP leaves the leaf-level data in the relational data mart that serves as the source of the cube.

This leads to longer retrieval times when accessing the leaf-level values. However, HOLAP does not need to take time to copy the leaf-level data from the data mart. As soon as the data is updated in the data mart, it is available to the decision maker. Therefore, HOLAP does not add latency to the leaf-level data. In essence, HOLAP sacrifices retrieval speed on leaf-level data to prevent adding latency to leaf-level data and to speed the data load.

The Parts of a Multidimensional Model Implementation

A Multidimensional model implementation is made up of a number of parts. We look at creating each of these parts in subsequent chapters. For now, we take a quick look at each part and how they fit together.

Data Sources

A Multidimensional model begins with one or more data sources. A data source stores the information necessary to connect to a database that provides data to the Multidimensional model. The data source includes the server name, database name, and the database logon credentials, among other things. A number of data providers are available for accessing different databases, including Oracle and Microsoft Directory Services.

The database being pointed to by the data source could be a data mart. It could point directly to a table in an OLTP system. When a data source points directly at an OLTP system, the data source view is used to transform the data into more of a star or snowflake structure.

Data Source Views

Data source views are used to determine which tables and fields in a particular data source are utilized within the Multidimensional model. The data source view can combine tables and fields from a number of different data sources. For instance, tables from the order processing system can be combined with tables from the sales management system so a measure of actual sales versus sales quota can be created.

Once the tables and fields have been added to the data source view, the data source view can then be used to filter out unnecessary items in the database. Only those tables and fields being used to create business intelligence are included in the view. The underlying table structures in the data sources are not changed. The data source view merely controls what is available as building blocks for the next step in the definition process.

This is especially helpful when a data source is a large, highly normalized OLTP system. The data source view makes available only those tables that contain the data for the measures, dimensions, and hierarchies we need to define. The same is true within a table. Only those fields that contain required data are visible. All the extraneous tables and fields are filtered out by the data source view.

To make the data source view even easier to understand, user-friendly names and descriptions can be assigned to tables and fields. This metadata is used throughout the Multidimensional model. Any measures, dimensions, and hierarchies created from these fields will utilize the user-friendly names.

In addition, we can use the data source view to make virtual additions to the table and field structures. These additions are not made in the database itself, but in the virtual view that exists only in the Multidimensional model. Therefore, we can make these virtual additions without any fear of breaking the OLTP systems that use the relational tables.

One example of these virtual additions is the creation of a relationship between two tables that is not defined in the database itself. Another example is the addition of a calculated field in a database table. For instance, a calculation involving a number of different fields from different tables can be created for use as a measure. Or, a number of strings can be concatenated for use as a dimension attribute. These calculated fields are given names and descriptions so they appear just like any other field included in the Multidimensional model.

Once the data source view is completed, its content is used to create measures, dimensions, hierarchies, and cubes.

Proactive Caching

To obtain maximum performance, a Multidimensional model uses preprocessed aggregates. To facilitate high availability, these preprocessed aggregates are stored in the *proactive cache.*

This structure is referred to as cache because it is created when needed and is changed when the underlying data or the underlying structure changes. It works much the same way as Internet Information Services (IIS) caches web pages, as shown in Figure 4-5. The results of a processed web page are stored in the IIS page cache so subsequent accesses to that page are faster, as shown in Figure 4-6. When changes are made to the underlying page, that page is deleted and eventually re-created in the page cache, as in Figure 4-7.

The major difference between Multidimensional model caching and other caching mechanisms, such as the IIS example, is summed up in the word "proactive." With IIS, a page is put into cache only after it has been accessed the first time. The first user to request a particular page must wait until the page is read from the disk and processed before the user receives the contents of the page, as you see in Figure 4-5.

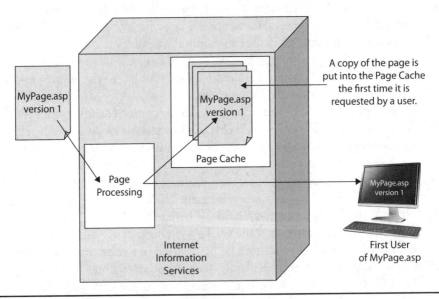

Figure 4-5 *Creating a cached web page in Internet Information Services*

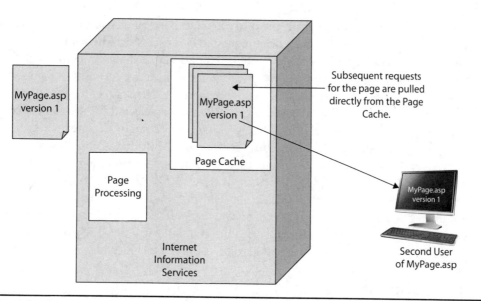

Figure 4-6   *Retrieving a web page from the Internet Information Services page cache*

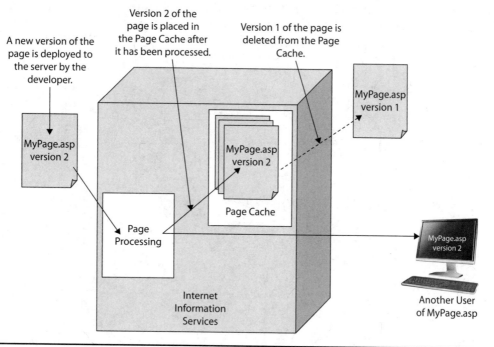

Figure 4-7   *Updating the Internet Information Services page cache when a web page is modified*

The Multidimensional model, on the other hand, can use proactive caching. Items are created in the cache before they have been requested by a user. With the Multidimensional model, the preprocessed aggregates are created automatically, as shown in Figure 4-8. Even the first users receive their requested aggregates from the proactive cache, as in Figure 4-9.

The Multidimensional model monitors the data in the data source. As this data is modified, the Multidimensional model checks the options selected for the associated proactive cache. We look at just what these caching options are in Chapter 12. At the appropriate time, as defined by the caching options, the Multidimensional model deletes the current cache and rebuilds it with up-to-date values, as shown in Figure 4-10.

The proactive cache can be built using MOLAP, ROLAP, or HOLAP. The Multidimensional model provides an easy mechanism to assist you in making a decision among these three architectures. It points out the tradeoffs these three architectures make between latency and responsiveness. This enables you to determine which architecture to use based on the business needs without getting lost in the technical details.

XML Definitions

The definitions of all the objects in the Multidimensional model are stored as XML text files. Each of the data source, data source view, dimension, and cube definitions is stored in its own text file. These XML text files do not contain any of the data for the object—the dimension text file does not contain any of the members of the dimension; the cube text file does not contain any of the preprocessed aggregates. The XML text

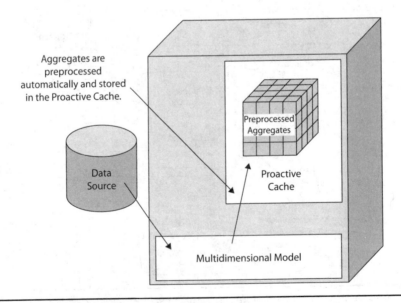

Figure 4-8   *Proactive caching with a Multidimensional model*

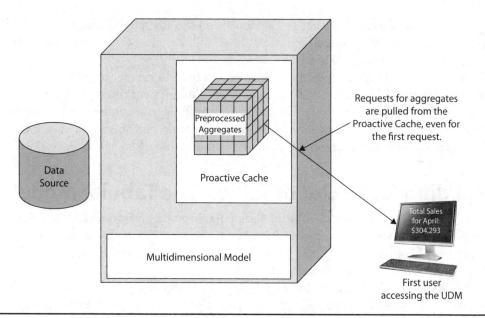

Figure 4-9   *Even the first user receives the requested aggregate from the proactive cache.*

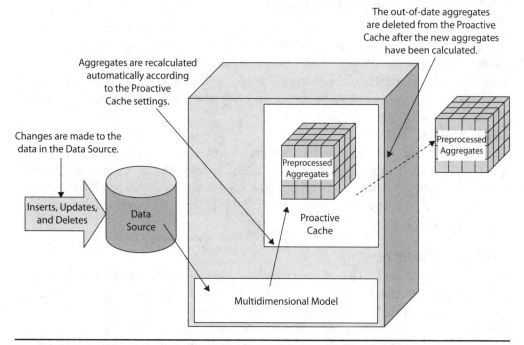

Figure 4-10   *The proactive cache is deleted and re-created in response to changes in the data source.*

files simply contain the definitions—the dimension text file tells which table and field hold the members of the dimension; the cube text file contains the information on how the preprocessed aggregates will be managed.

Because the definition for each of the objects in the Multidimensional model is stored in its own XML text file, the objects in the Multidimensional model can be managed by a source code utility. The source code utility can track these objects as you develop your Multidimensional model. It can also provide version control in case you need to undo a change to an object's definition and roll it back to an earlier version.

Building OLAP Out of Tables: The Tabular Model

The Multidimensional model implementation has been highly optimized to efficiently deal with aggregation and exploration of large amounts of data. Its maturity offers a number of compelling features. We will examine those features throughout the Multidimensional model sections of this book.

Advances in computing, including advances in processing power and the wide availability of low-cost memory, have made possible another approach for analyzing a sizeable amount of data in a reasonable manner. This is the Tabular model.

Features of a Tabular Model

The Tabular model is less complex than the Multidimensional model implementation. Currently, it does not have the breadth of features of a Multidimensional model implementation and, in some cases, cannot work with as large a set of data as a Multidimensional model implementation. That said, a Tabular model provides surprising capabilities with a fraction of the complexity of a Multidimensional model implementation.

Tabular Structure

The Tabular model does not use the measure, dimension, attribute, and hierarchy structure. Instead, it approaches the data as related tables with fields, just as is done in a relational database. With more and more business decision makers using the data table feature of Excel or having done some basic reporting from a relational database, this tabular approach is more familiar.

Quick to Implement

Because we do not need to transform the data into measures and dimensions, it may be possible to pull data directly from OLTP systems into a Tabular model. This is one of the ways a Tabular model may enable us to streamline the process of creating a BI system. Of course, considerations such as stress put on the OLTP system by data analysis and the need for data cleansing may still make it desirable to create a data mart as the source for our business intelligence.

As we see when we begin building our Tabular model example, the Tabular model creation process is more interactive and immediate than the creation of a Multidimensional model. Data is available to be viewed in the Tabular model immediately after it is added. This makes it easier to get started and easier to get things right as the implementation progresses.

Architecture of a Tabular Model

When we looked at Multidimensional models, we saw there were three different architectures that could be utilized: MOLAP, ROLAP, and HOLAP. In the Tabular world, there are two different architectures or modes of operation from which to choose. They are cached mode and direct query mode.

Cached Mode

When Tabular models were first demonstrated, their capabilities almost seemed like magic—even to us jaded BI professionals. The Tabular model (and the Vertipaq engine that powers it) is not magic, of course. What makes it possible is the in-memory processing of cached mode operation.

When operating in *cached mode*, a Tabular model loads all data into memory. Therefore, having large amounts of memory available and having the 64-bit Windows operating system available to address all that memory make it possible for a Tabular model to do some great things. However, the size of addressable memory does not necessarily define the limit on the amount of data that can be processed.

The Tabular model, operating in cached mode, also applies some extremely effective data compression techniques to the data as it is stored in memory. So, even more data can be crammed into the memory space available. With the data compression techniques in place, the Tabular model squeezes every bit of capability out of the memory provided.

The whole reason for working hard to put massive amounts of data into memory is speed. The processor can read through and analyze data in memory in a fraction of the time necessary to access data stored on a hard drive. Given this inherent speed advantage, the Tabular model can complete the analytical processing by sheer brute force. It doesn't need preaggregates and highly efficient data retrieval methods. It can simply read through the data in memory, looking to match criteria and produce aggregates.

This, then, is the magic.

Direct Query Mode

A Tabular model has a second mode of operation called direct query mode. When operating in *direct query mode*, the Tabular model does not load any data into memory. Instead, a Tabular model in direct query mode always queries the underlying data sources to get its results. This means, when running in direct query mode, we need to be mindful of the load any queries made through the model are putting on those data sources.

If in-memory processing provides all of the seeming magic for a Tabular model, why then would you ever run in direct query mode? Obviously, performance is going to suffer. Why not query the data directly without the model?

The answer to those questions is twofold. First, when operating in direct query mode, there is no latency to the data. As soon as data is changed in the underlying data source, that change is reflected in queries done through the model. This, then, has the same advantage as querying the data source directly.

Second, the model provides a metadata layer over the top of the underlying data source. This metadata layer, when done properly, exposes the data in a manner closer to the perception of the business user. A business user can query this data through the model without having to write complex SELECT statements. So, a direct query Tabular model still has the advantage of making data accessible to a business user.

Choosing an Implementation Method

With the Tabular model showing big advantages in simplicity and speed of implementation, why would you want to choose to do a Multidimensional model implementation (and why would I devote so many chapters of this book to telling you about it)? There may be a day when a Tabular model is the right answer for any and all BI needs. That day, however, has not yet arrived.

The Multidimensional model is a mature architecture. Its capabilities have been added to and refined over many years. Quite frankly, there are things that can be done in a Multidimensional model implementation that cannot yet be done in a Tabular model. Those differences are highlighted throughout the remainder of this book.

It is also the case that even with the data compression available within a Tabular model, there are still limits to what can be effectively processed in memory. What that limit is will vary depending on the memory available and on the content of your data and how well it lends itself to compression.

For these reasons, it is still important to learn how to create both Multidimensional and Tabular models.

Tools of the Trade

We utilize three environments for creating and managing business intelligence content throughout the rest of this book. They are SQL Server Data Tools, SQL Server Management Studio, and Power BI Desktop. In Chapter 5, you will be introduced to the first two. We then use those tools in Chapters 6 through 14. In Chapters 15 and 16, we work with Power BI Desktop. The final two chapters will explore ways to deliver business intelligence to our users through BI client tools and integrating BI into our applications.

Chapter 5

First Steps: Beginning the Development of Business Intelligence

In This Chapter

► **SQL Server Data Tools**
► **SQL Server Management Studio**
► **Don Your Hardhat**

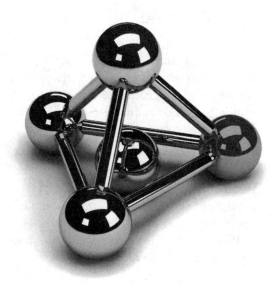

There is a great satisfaction in building good tools for other people to use.

—Freeman Dyson

Now that we have discussed the basics of business intelligence and the BI Semantic Model, it is time to become acquainted with some of the tools that we are going to be using. Microsoft has created a special tool for creating and managing business intelligence: SQL Server Data Tools.

We begin this chapter with a tour of this tool. SQL Server Data Tools looks familiar to those of you who have used Microsoft Visual Studio as part of front-end or middleware development projects. In fact, SQL Server Data Tools (SSDT) is Visual Studio with some special functionality.

With home improvement, having the right tool for the job makes things faster and easier. The same is true with BI development. Let's see how SQL Server Data Tools can make our job faster and easier.

SQL Server Data Tools

SQL Server Data Tools is our primary work environment for much of this book. All of our work building an ETL process to populate our data marts, all of our work creating BI Semantic Models for SQL Server Analysis Services, and all of our work developing reports in SQL Server Reporting Services will be done in SQL Server Data Tools. Because of this, it is important to become comfortable with the interface and capabilities of this product.

Visual Studio

SQL Server Data Tools is, in fact, Visual Studio, the same integrated development environment (IDE) used by Visual Basic and C# developers. Visual Studio is also used to author reports for use with SQL Server Reporting Services. Visual Studio provides the business intelligence developer with a robust environment that has been tested and proven by millions of developer hours of use.

Project Organization

Visual Studio organizes each development effort into projects. Each project produces its own type of output: a Windows application, a web service, or a set of Reporting Services reports. SQL Server provides additional project types: an Integration Services project and an Analysis Services project.

Projects are grouped together in solutions. Each solution represents an answer to a particular business problem. A solution could be an e-commerce website with a

Visual Basic web application project to produce the ASP.NET user interface pages and a Reporting Services project to provide reporting on sales. Another solution might contain a complete business intelligence application, with a C# Windows application project to produce the front-end application, an Analysis Services project to create the BI Semantic Model, and a Reporting Services project that produces reports for presenting the analysis to the user. This grouping of projects into solutions makes it easier to manage software systems built from several different parts.

Editing and Debugging Tools

Visual Studio also provides a rich set of editing and debugging tools. Some of you may say that color-coded editors and single-step debugging are only for wimps. After all, many of us grew up writing stored procedures in a text editor and debugging them with embedded PRINT statements, and we did just fine. Believe me, once you have these tools available, you will never want to go back!

Source Code Management Integration

Another benefit of using the Visual Studio environment for BI projects is its ability to integrate with source control. *Source control* copies the source code for your item definitions and report layouts to a central database. Source control then manages access to those definitions and layouts to provide version control and prevent two developers from trying to change the same item at the same time.

Each version of these items is saved. This makes it possible for us to roll back changes if we discover we have gone down the wrong path. It also makes it possible to determine what changed between two versions of an item. This can be helpful when troubleshooting or when copying changes from one server to another.

Source code also enables multiple developers or administrators to work on the same project at the same time without the danger of one person overwriting another's changes. You must check out an item from source control before you can edit it. Only one person can have a given item checked out at a given time. Once changes are made, the item is checked back in for the next person to use.

Visual Studio makes this check-out and check-in process straightforward. In fact, it is simply part of the editing process itself. No additional applications to open. No extra steps writing things out to temporary files.

Installing SQL Server Data Tools

In earlier versions of SQL Server, SQL Server Data Tools was installed as part of the SQL Server installation. Frankly, this didn't make a whole lot of sense. In most cases, SQL Server Data Tools was installed on a developer's workstation, not on a server where an instance of SQL Server must be installed. It was inconvenient to have to fire up the complete SQL Server install process just to install SQL Server Data Tools.

For this reason, Microsoft has now separated the SQL Server Data Tools install from the SQL Server installation. The SQL Server Data Tools installation is a free download from Microsoft. You will need to download and execute the SQL Server Data Tools install in order to complete the exercises in this book.

If you have not done so already, this might be a good time to download and install SQL Server Data Tools. It will be helpful to open the development environment and walk through the interface along with the description in this chapter. So, go ahead and complete the SQL Server Data Tools install. We will be here waiting when you are done.

Navigating SQL Server Data Tools

SQL Server Data Tools is found on the Start menu or on the Start window in the grouping for Microsoft SQL Server 2016. After the splash screen, you see the empty SQL Server Data Tools. No solution has been opened.

In this section, we create a solution and an Analysis Services project within that solution. Then, we explore the menus, toolbar, and windows within SQL Server Data Tools. In the next section, we look at some of the ways to customize this development environment.

Creating a Solution and an Analysis Services Project

The empty SQL Server Data Tools is not too exciting. Therefore, we begin by creating a solution and an Analysis Services project within that solution. We can then explore all of the windows, menu choices, and toolbar buttons available to us when working in this type of project.

In SQL Server Data Tools, we do not choose to create a solution. Instead, we create a new project. At the same time that project is created, we can create the solution that will contain it.

We can create a new project in SQL Server Data Tools in four ways:

► Select File | New | Project from the menu.
► Press CTRL-SHIFT-N.
► Click the New Project button on the toolbar, as shown in Figure 5-1.
► Click the New Project link on the Start Page tab.

No matter how you get there, once you request a new project, you see the New Project dialog box, shown in Figure 5-2. The left side of the dialog box contains a list

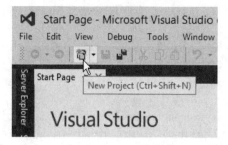

Figure 5-1   *The New Project toolbar button*

of the Visual Studio project templates installed on your development machine. In this book, we are interested in Business Intelligence Projects. Expand this group of project templates, if it is not already expanded.

The right side of the dialog box displays the various BI projects available to us within each template type. These can be displayed as small icons or as the medium icons shown

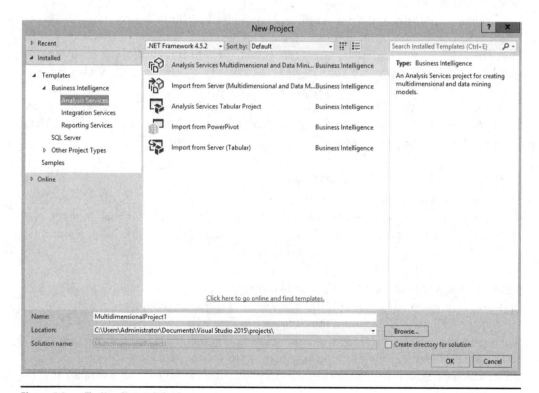

Figure 5-2   *The New Project dialog box*

in Figure 5-2. You can toggle between the two sizes using the buttons in the toolbar for the dialog box.

The lower portion of the dialog box displays the path and filename for the project we are about to create. Name refers to the name of the new project. Location is the file path where the new solution and project are to be stored. Solution Name is the name of the new solution.

By default, solutions and projects are stored in the Visual Studio 2015 Projects folder under Documents. You can use the Browse button to navigate to a different folder, if desired. When the Create directory for solution check box is not selected, only one folder is created. Both the new solution files and the new project files are placed in this folder.

When the Create directory for solution check box is selected, two folders are created. One folder is created to hold the solution files, and a second folder is created within this solution folder to contain the project files. By default, the solution folder and the project folder have the same name. You can override this default behavior by entering a unique name for both the Name and the Solution Name. If the solution is going to contain more than one project, it is usually a good idea to keep the solution files and the project files in separate folders.

If source control integration is set up and configured within Visual Studio, we also have the option of placing the project under source control. An Add to source control check box will appear under the Create directory for solution check box. If you are going to use source control for your BI projects, it is a good idea to use this check box to place them under source control right from the start.

To create our empty Analysis Services project, select Business Intelligence | Analysis Services in the Templates area, and select Analysis Services Multidimensional and Data Mining Project in the center area of the dialog box. Click OK.

SQL Server Data Tools Windows

Now that we have a solution and a project open, SQL Server Data Tools appears as shown in Figure 5-3. We now have some content in the two windows that are open on the right side of the main window. We begin by looking at these two windows and then at several other windows that are not visible by default.

Solution Explorer Window   The Solution Explorer window is visible in the upper-right portion of Figure 5-3. Just as Windows Explorer provides a hierarchical view of the Windows file system, the *Solution Explorer* window in SQL Server Data Tools provides a hierarchical view of your solution and the projects it contains. Both Windows Explorer and the Solution Explorer window use a tree view to let us navigate the hierarchical structure. We can browse through our solution to find and open any item it contains.

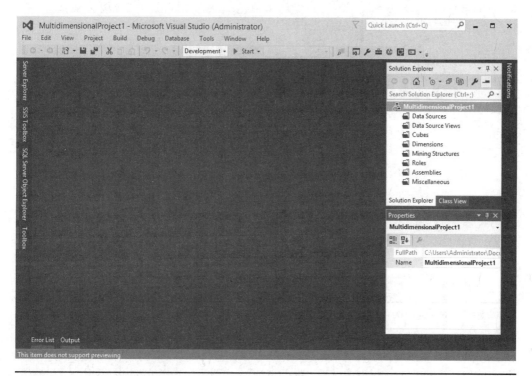

Figure 5-3   *SQL Server Data Tools with an empty Analysis Services project*

Each project node displays the name of the project. Within the project nodes are folders for each type of item the project can create. The number of folders and their labels vary, depending on the project type. In Figure 5-3, you can see that a Multidimensional project contains eight folders, one for each of the eight different types of items it can create.

In addition to the toolbar at the top of SQL Server Data Tools (where we found the New Project button), each window has its own toolbar. The content of this toolbar varies depending on which item or folder is selected. The toolbar button in the Solution Explorer window with the wrench icon is the Properties button. If this toolbar button is clicked when a project node is highlighted, the Project Property Pages dialog box is displayed.

Most other items in the solution do not have their own custom property pages dialog boxes. Instead, these items display their properties in the Properties window, which we discuss next. Clicking the Properties button in the Solution Explorer toolbar when any of these other items is highlighted causes the Properties window to gain focus.

The toolbar button to the left of the Properties button in the Solution Explorer toolbar is the Show All Files toggle. This toggle causes all the supporting files to be

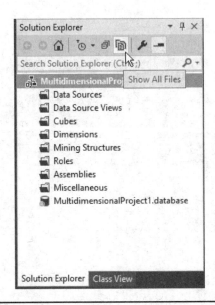

Figure 5-4   *The Solution Explorer window with the Show All Files toolbar button*

displayed for a project, as shown in Figure 5-4. In most cases, this is not necessary and toggling it on clutters up the Solution Explorer. However, at times, it is helpful to know exactly which files are being used by a project.

Properties Window   Below the Solution Explorer window in Figure 5-3 is the Properties window. This window displays the property settings of the item highlighted in the Solution Explorer window or elsewhere in SQL Server Data Tools. The drop-down list at the top of the Properties window shows the name of the item whose properties are currently displayed.

The main portion of the Properties window is composed of a list with two columns. The left column shows the name of each property. The right column shows the current value of that property. If the text in the right column is black, the value of that property can be changed in the Properties window. If the text in the right column is gray, the value is read-only.

The lower portion of the screen provides a little more information about the selected property. The name of the selected property is displayed in bold, along with a description of this property. This description can often help users understand a property without having to consult the online help.

There are three buttons on the Properties window toolbar. The left button causes the properties to be displayed by category. The category headings are shown as light-gray bands within the properties list. Figure 5-5 shows the properties of the Data Mart data source. These properties are divided into two categories: Location and Object Model.

Figure 5-5   *The Properties window with categorized properties*

The middle button on the Properties window toolbar causes the properties to be displayed in one continuous, alphabetical list without any grouping. Personally, I never remember which grouping contains the property I want to see, so I use the alphabetical list setting. However, you may find it more helpful to have properties grouped. Use whichever setting works best for you.

The right button on the Properties window toolbar displays the Property Pages dialog box for the selected item. However, only some items have a Property Pages dialog box associated with them. Therefore, this toolbar button does not function for all items.

Toolbox Window   On the left side of Figure 5-3 are several tabs, one of which is a tab labeled Toolbox. This tab provides access to the *Toolbox* window, which is set to Auto Hide. The *Auto Hide* setting causes the window to remain out of the way until it is needed. A window that is set to Auto Hide can be displayed by clicking the window's tab, as shown in Figure 5-6.

The Auto Hide feature is controlled by the pushpin icon at the top of the window. When Auto Hide is on, the pushpin is sideways, as shown in Figure 5-6. When Auto Hide is off, the pushpin is vertical. You can see this at the top of the Solution Explorer and Properties windows in Figure 5-4 and Figure 5-5. To toggle the Auto Hide setting for a window, click its pushpin icon.

The Toolbox window contains components used to build items in our projects. The contents of the Toolbox window change to match the type of item being built. For example, it contains data transformation tasks when we are creating Data Integration Services packages. The Toolbox window contains report items when we are building Reporting Services reports. The toolbox for report designing is shown in Figure 5-6.

Figure 5-6 *Displaying the Toolbox window when it is set to Auto Hide*

Opening Windows Not Visible in SQL Server Data Tools Any window in SQL Server Data Tools, including the three already discussed, can be closed using the Close icon in the upper-right corner of the window. Because this is the case, we obviously need a way to open a window that is not visible on the screen. This is done using the View menu. The Solution Explorer, Properties, and Toolbox windows are available right from the View menu, as shown in Figure 5-7. You may see other windows in the View menu. Additional windows are in the Other Windows submenu.

In addition to the View menu, windows can be opened directly using buttons on the toolbar. These toolbar buttons are illustrated in Figure 5-8.

Error List Window The Error List window can be opened from the View menu. In addition, this window automatically opens when we try to build a project or solution and there are problems. The *Error List* window contains an entry for each error,

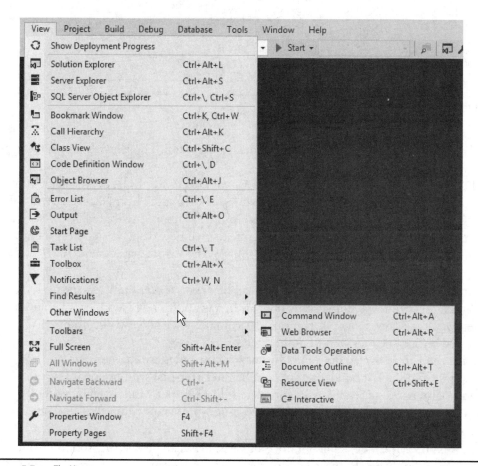

Figure 5-7   *The View menu*

Figure 5-8   *Toolbar buttons for opening SQL Server Data Tools windows*

Error List								
Entire Solution ▾	⊗ 1 Error	⚠ 0 Warnings	ⓘ 0 Messages	Build + IntelliSense ▾		Search Error List		🔎 ▾
	Description				Project	File	Line	
⊗	Could not load file or assembly 'Microsoft.AnalysisServices.AppLocal.Core, Version=13.0.0.0, Culture=neutral, PublicKeyToken=89845dcd8080cc91' or one of its dependencies. The system cannot find						0	

Figure 5-9   *The Error List window*

warning, and message that was produced during the build. The Error List window is shown in Figure 5-9.

Double-clicking an entry in the Error List window causes SQL Server Data Tools to open the item that caused the error, warning, or message. This makes it easy to fix a number of build errors that have occurred in various items distributed across several projects. Right-clicking an entry in the Error List window displays a context menu for navigating and controlling the display columns of the Error List entries.

Output Window   The Output window can be opened from the View menu. In addition, this window automatically opens when we try to build a project or solution. The *Output* window, shown in Figure 5-10, contains a narrative of the events that occurred during the most recent build attempt.

Like the Error List window, the Output window notes errors, warnings, and messages from the last build attempt. Unlike the Error List window, the Output window also notes successful tasks completed. The Output window includes toolbar buttons for clearing its contents and for toggling word wrap within the window.

Find Results Windows   The Find Results windows can be opened from the View menu. In addition, one of these windows automatically opens whenever we perform a Find in Files or a Replace in Files operation. The Find Results 1 window is shown in Figure 5-11.

When we execute a find or replace operation, we can choose to display the results in either the Find Results 1 window or the Find Results 2 window. In this way, we can move between the results of two different find operations. The *Find Results* window contains a list of all of the places where the desired text was found. We can move to any of these locations by double-clicking that line in the Find Results window.

Figure 5-10   *The Output window*

Find Results 1

```
Find all "MaxMin", Subfolders, Find Results 1, Current Project: MultidimensionalProject1.dwproj, ""
  C:\Users\Administrator\Documents\Visual Studio 2015\projects\MultidimensionalProject1\Max Min Accounting.ds(6):  <ConnectionS
  Matching lines: 1    Matching files: 1    Total files searched: 3
```

Figure 5-11   *The Find Results 1 window*

Designer Window   All of the windows we have discussed so far are usually found along the left, right, top, or bottom edge of SQL Server Data Tools (although they don't have to be, as we discuss in the next section). That leaves us with the large area in the center. This area is occupied by the Designer window.

The Designer window appears any time we view the code or the design of an item. In fact, the *Designer* window is where most of the work of creating business intelligence gets done. Figure 5-12 shows the Designer window with several designers and source

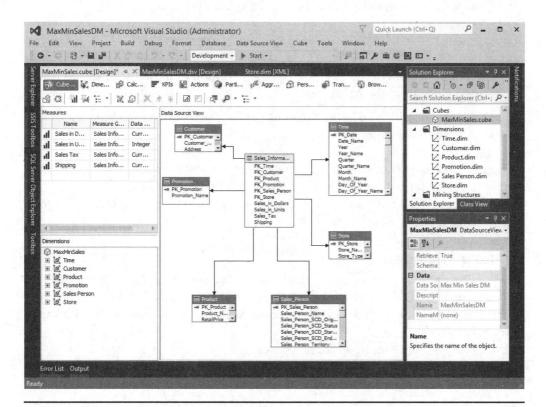

Figure 5-12   *The Designer window with the Dimension, Cube, and Data Source View designers open*

code editors open (note the three tabs across the top). The Cube designer is open for the Min Max Sales cube. The Data Source View designer is open for the Min Max Sales DM data source view. The Dimension source code editor is open for the store dimension. (We can tell this is a source code editor rather than a designer because of the "[XML]" in the tab. We talk more about code editors and designers throughout the rest of this book.)

A tab is created each time an item is opened in a code editor or a designer. The tabs enable us to move quickly from one item's designer or source code editor to another item's designer or source code editor with a single click. We can open an item's designer by doing one of the following:

► Selecting the item in the Solution Explorer window and then selecting View | Designer from the Main menu

► Right-clicking the item in the Solution Explorer window and selecting View Designer from the context menu

► Double-clicking the item in the Solution Explorer window

We can open an item's code editor by doing one of the following:

► Selecting the item in the Solution Explorer window and then selecting View | Code from the Main menu

► Right-clicking the item in the Solution Explorer window and selecting View Code from the context menu

We can close an item's designer or code editor by selecting the appropriate tab and then clicking the Close button (the *X*) on the right of the selected tab.

We discuss each designer and code editor as we use them to create and modify the various items in SQL Server Data Tools.

Window Management

The windows of SQL Server Data Tools can be rearranged any way that we like. This is done by setting various windows to be docked along the sides or bottom, to float, or to Auto Hide. In this way, each person can arrange the windows to suit their development style.

Each window can be set to one of five states:

► Float
► Dock

- ▶ Dock as Tabbed Document
- ▶ Auto Hide
- ▶ Hide

We can set a window's state by selecting that window, and then selecting Float, Dock, Dock as Tabbed Document, Auto Hide, or Hide from the Window menu. Alternately, we can right-click the title bar of a window and set its state using the context menu. This is shown in Figure 5-13.

Floating Windows   When a window's state is set to float, it exists as a separate *floating* window on top of the rest of SQL Server Data Tools windows. A floating window can be moved anywhere around the screen on top of any other part of the user interface. This is shown in Figure 5-14.

Dockable Windows   When a window's state is set to *dock,* it is able to dock with the left, right, top, or bottom edge of SQL Server Data Tools. After a floating window's state is set to dock, the window either automatically docks itself or it may be dragged to a docking position. To drag a dockable window (including one that is already docked), click the window's title bar and hold down the left mouse button while you move the window into the appropriate place.

As soon as you begin dragging the window, several docking guides appear on the screen. These docking guides make it easy to dock the window in the desired location. The docking guides are linked to each of the possible docking locations on the screen.

By moving the mouse pointer over one of the docking guides while dragging a dockable window, we can see exactly where that window is going to dock if the mouse

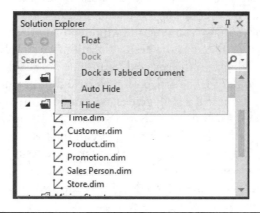

Figure 5-13   *Changing a window's state*

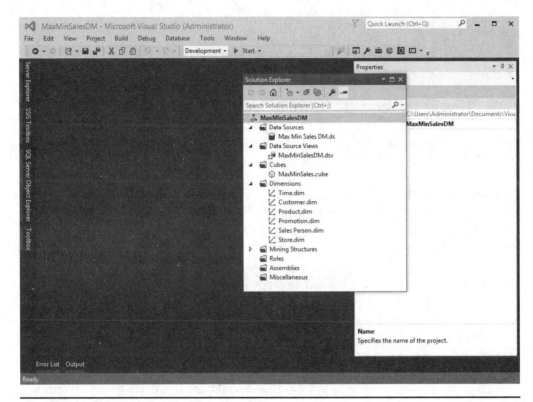

Figure 5-14   *The Solution Explorer as a floating window*

button is released at that point. The possible docking location linked to the docking guide under your mouse pointer displays as a blue shadow on the screen. If this is not the desired docking location, we can drag the window to another docking guide. When we find the docking guide linked to the desired location, we simply release the mouse button and the window docks in the selected location.

There are docking guides for the top, bottom, left, and right sides of SQL Server Data Tools. Using one of these docking guides, we can dock the window along the entire length of that side. Any other windows that might butt up against that side are moved out of the way. Also, a set of docking guides in the form of a diamond is in the center of the current window. Using one of the docking guides at the points of this diamond docks the window at the side of this current window. As we drag from one window to another, this diamond-shaped docking guide switches so that it is always in the center of the window we are dragging over.

In the center of the diamond is a tabbed-icon docking guide. Using this tabbed-icon docking guide causes the window being docked to fill the current window. The two windows now form a tabbed grouping. Figure 5-15 shows the Properties window and the Solution Explorer window combined to create a tabbed grouping. Note the tabs at the bottom of the window for switching between the Solution Explorer and the Properties window. To remove a window from a tabbed grouping, simply click that window's tab, hold down the left mouse button, and drag the window away.

Tabbed Document   You can even create a tabbed grouping with the Designer window. In Figure 5-16, the Solution Explorer is part of the tabbed grouping in the Designer window. When this is done, the window's state changes from dock to dock as tabbed document. Remember, this is only true when a window is in a tabbed group in the Designer window. A window in a tabbed group outside of the Designer window continues to have a dock window state.

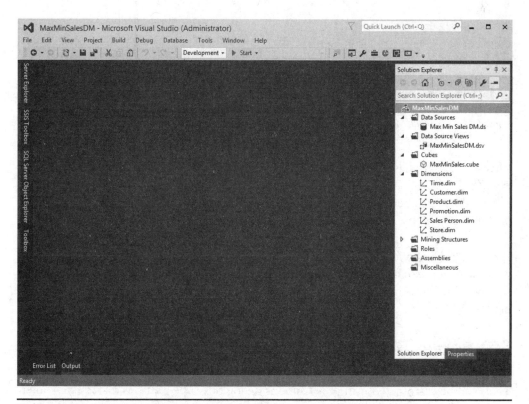

Figure 5-15   *The Properties window and the Solution Explorer window combined in a tabbed window*

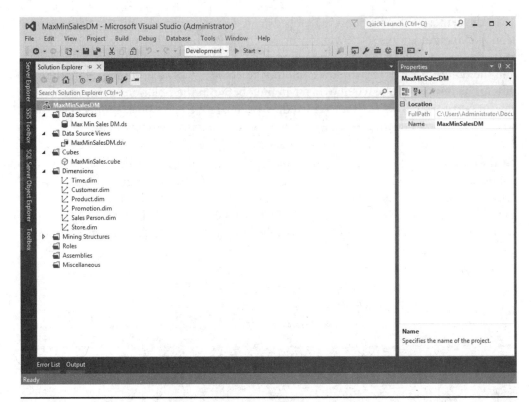

Figure 5-16 *The Solution Explorer window in a tabbed grouping on the Designer window*

Auto Hide We have already seen the behavior of an Auto Hide window when we examined the Toolbox window. Note that a window's state cannot be changed to Auto Hide unless it is already docked. A window must have Auto Hide turned off, using the pushpin icon, before it can be changed to another state.

Hide The final window state is the simplest one of all. This is the hide state. When a window is in the *hide state*, it is closed and no longer appears on the screen. If we want to view a hidden window, we need to use the Window menu or the toolbar, as discussed previously.

SQL Server Data Tools Options

In addition to the capability to rearrange the windows to our liking, SQL Server Data Tools can be customized using the Options dialog box. The Options dialog box, shown in Figure 5-17, is accessed by selecting Tools | Options from the Main menu.

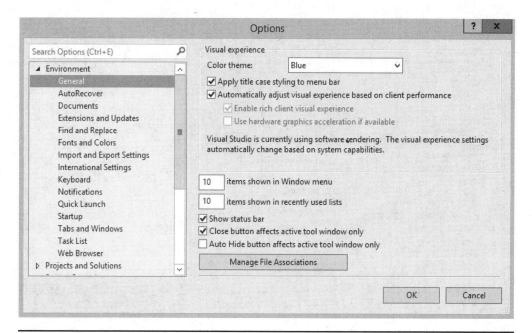

Figure 5-17   *The Options dialog box*

The Options dialog box provides the capability to modify a great number of settings for SQL Server Data Tools. We only discuss a few of those settings here. Feel free to explore this dialog box further on your own to learn about more of the customization options.

Fonts and Colors

Further down under the Environment options is the Fonts and Colors entry. This area lets us customize the font and color used for any category of text within SQL Server Data Tools. This is shown in Figure 5-18. The fonts and colors options can be used to change font size or typeface to make certain items more readable. They can also be used to change the color of a particular set of text to make it stand out.

To make a change, first make a selection from the Show settings for drop-down list. Next, select the text we want to change from the Display items list. Finally, we make the desired font and color changes, and then click OK to apply the changes.

Default File Locations

Another area that often needs customizing is the default location for creating solution and project files. This can be changed in the Projects and Solutions area, as shown in Figure 5-19. The path in the Projects location text box is the default location for

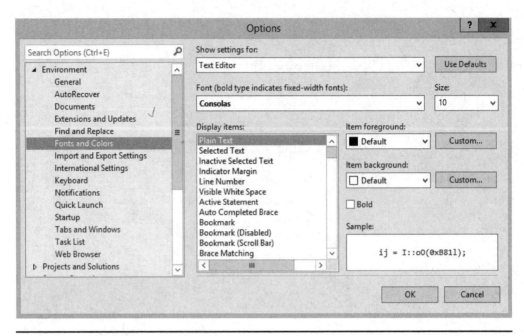

Figure 5-18 *Fonts and Colors options*

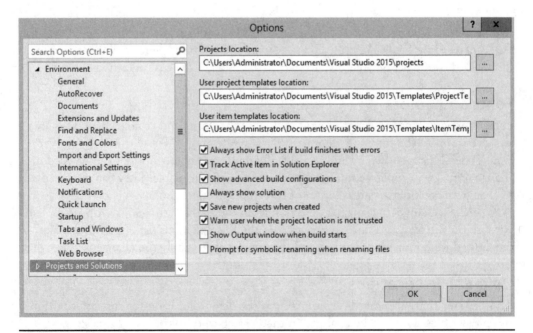

Figure 5-19 *Options in the Projects and Solutions area*

creating new solutions and projects. To change this, we simply browse to or type in a new path and click OK to apply the changes. Now, whenever the New Project dialog box is displayed, Location shows our updated path. (Refer to Figure 5-2 for another look at the New Project dialog box.)

SQL Server Management Studio

As we have seen in the previous section, we use SQL Server Data Tools to develop BI Semantic Models. We use another tool to manage our relational and Analysis Services databases during day-to-day operations. This is SQL Server Management Studio (SSMS).

Installing SQL Server Management Studio

As with SQL Server Data Tools, SQL Server Management Studio was installed as part of the SQL Server in earlier versions. SQL Server Management Studio now has its own separate installation. The SQL Server Management Studio installation is a free download from Microsoft. You will need to download and execute the SQL Server Management Studio install in order to complete the exercises in this book.

If you have not done so already, this might be a good time to download and install SQL Server Management Studio. It will be helpful to open the management environment and walk through the interface along with the description in this chapter.

The SQL Server Management Studio User Interface

SQL Server Management Studio has a user interface similar to SQL Server Data Tools. It has the same type of window states (floating, dockable, and so forth), and it features a tabbed work area. Let's take a quick look at SQL Server Management Studio so we have some familiarity with it when it is time to use this tool for managing databases.

When SQL Server Management Studio starts up, it attempts to connect to the last server we were working with. The Connect to Server dialog box is displayed, as shown in Figure 5-20. To connect to the server, we need to provide logon credentials, if necessary, and then click Connect. We can also enter SQL Server Management Studio without connecting to a server by clicking Cancel.

The SQL Server Management Studio Windows

By default, SQL Server Management Studio has one window open, as shown in Figure 5-21. The Object Explorer window is on the left. As with SQL Server Data Tools, additional windows can be displayed when needed using the View menu.

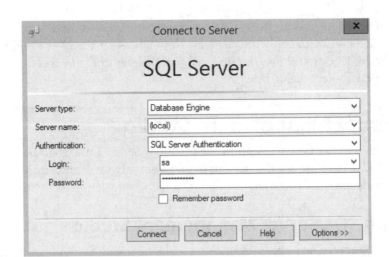

Figure 5-20 *Connecting to a server on startup*

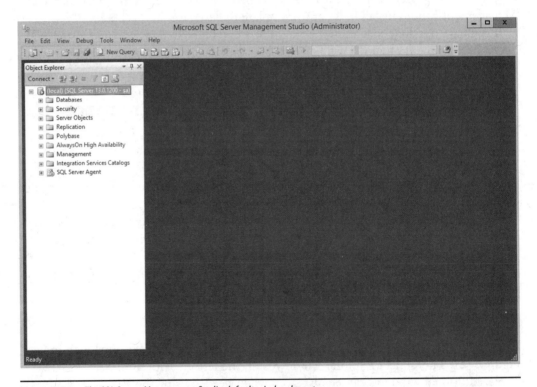

Figure 5-21 *The SQL Server Management Studio default window layout*

The Object Explorer window functions similarly to the dockable windows in SQL Server Data Tools. We can make them float over other windows or set them to Auto Hide. We can have them form tabbed groupings with other dockable windows or set them to be tabbed documents in the Designer window. The SQL Server Management Studio windows use the same menus, the same docking guides, and the same drag-and-drop functionality.

Object Explorer Window   The *Object Explorer* window lets us view and manage the objects on a particular server. These objects are displayed in a tree view, as shown in Figure 5-22. In most cases, objects are managed by right-clicking an object to display its context menu and then selecting the appropriate action from the context menu.

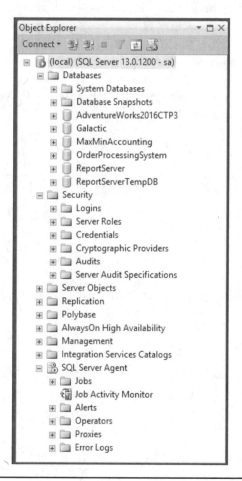

Figure 5-22   *The Object Explorer window*

We discuss the various objects in the Object Explorer window as we work with them in future chapters.

When SQL Server Management Studio first opens, the Object Explorer window displays objects for the server you connected to using the Connect to Server dialog box. We can add other servers to the Object Explorer window by clicking Connect in the Object Explorer window toolbar. The servers appear one below the next in the Object Explorer window's tree view.

Object Explorer Details Window   The *Object Explorer Details* window provides a brief overview of the entry currently selected in the Object Explorer window. If the selected entry is a folder, the Details window shows the contents of that folder. If the selected entry is an object, the Details window shows the current status of that object.

Query Windows   One of the functions of SQL Server Management Studio is the creation and execution of queries. These queries may be Transact-SQL for relational databases, MDX or XMLA for Analysis Services databases, or DMX for data mining. Each type of query has its own specific type of query window. We discuss how to use these query windows throughout the rest of this book.

DEFINITION

Multidimensional Expression *(MDX) language provides the programming language for BISM Multidimensional navigation.*

DEFINITION

Data Mining Expression *(DMX) language provides the commands to easily set up and analyze data mining structures.*

DEFINITION

XML for Analysis Services (XMLA) is an open, XML-based standard protocol for interacting with Microsoft SQL Server 2016 Analysis Services data over a Hypertext Transfer Protocol (HTTP) connection, such as an intranet or the Internet. XMLA uses the Simple Object Access Protocol (SOAP). (Because it is an open standard, XMLA is used by other vendors' OLAP tools as well.)

To create and execute queries, we need to open a query window of the appropriate type. This is done using the query buttons on the toolbar (see Figure 5-23). The New Query button opens the default type of query window for the database selected in the Object Explorer window. We can also select the specific type of query window we want to open by selecting the appropriate toolbar button. We can also open a query window by selecting the appropriate option under File | New on the Main menu or by using the context menu for objects in the Object Explorer window. Figure 5-24 shows SQL Server Management Studio with a SQL Server Query window open in the designer area.

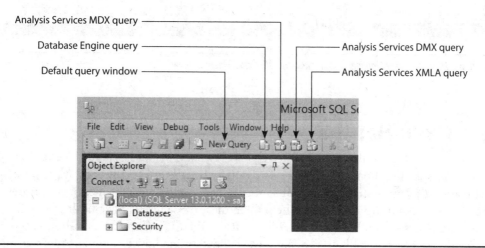

Figure 5-23   *The New Query toolbar buttons*

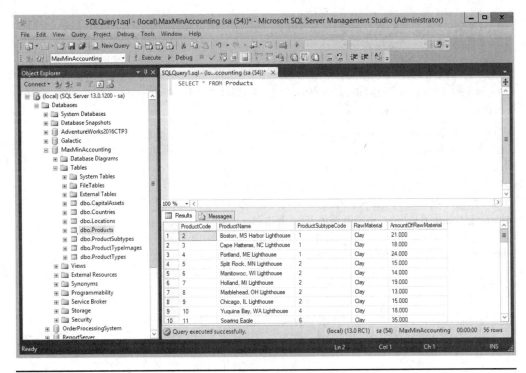

Figure 5-24   *SQL Server Management Studio with a SQL Server Query window*

Don Your Hardhat

Now that you are familiar with these SQL Server 2016 business intelligence tools, it is time to start building. In Chapter 6, we return to our sample company, Maximum Miniatures, Incorporated. We look at some of their specific business intelligence needs and begin to build the structures to help them meet those needs. Specifically, we build two data marts—one from scratch and one using the SQL Server Data Tools Cube Wizard. After these data marts are built, we will determine how to populate them using Integration Services.

Strap on your tool belt and let's go!

Part II

Defining Business Intelligence Structures

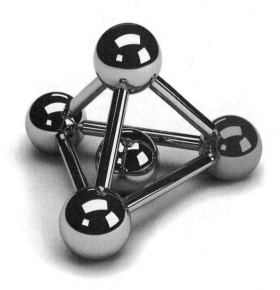

Chapter 6

Building Foundations: Creating Data Marts

In This Chapter

▶ Data Mart
▶ Designing a Data Mart
▶ Table Compression
▶ The Benefits of Integration

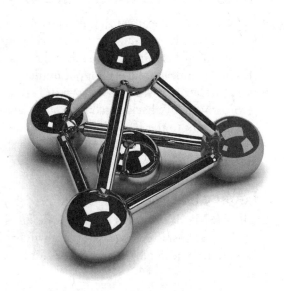

He who has not first laid his foundations may be able with great ability to lay them afterwards, but they will be laid with trouble to the architect and danger to the building.

The Prince
—Niccolò Machiavelli

Now that you have been introduced to the business intelligence and database management tools in SQL Server 2016, it is time to get to work. The first thing we need to do is lay some foundation. We need to examine our data sources and determine if we need to create one or more data marts.

This chapter examines the criteria to use when determining whether a data mart is needed. Next, we walk through the steps necessary for designing a data mart. Finally, we look at two different methods for creating data marts: using the SQL Server Management Studio and using SQL Server Data Tools.

Data Mart

Chapter 3 introduced the concept of the data mart. We learned that a data mart is a repository for data to be used as a source for business intelligence. The data mart is not used as part of day-to-day operations. Instead, the data mart periodically receives data from the online transactional processing (OLTP) systems. The data in the data mart is then made available to Analysis Services for creating BI Semantic Models (BISM). This is shown in Figure 6-1.

Who Needs a Data Mart Anyway?

In Chapter 4, we learned that it is possible for an Analysis Services BISM to utilize OLTP data without an intervening data mart. Either the Multidimensional or the Tabular model can incorporate data directly from OLTP systems. It is possible to do this in a manner that does not put undue stress on these systems, thus eliminating the need for data marts. This is shown in Figure 6-2.

So, why are we back to talking about data marts? Why don't we skip over all of this and get right to the BISM? The answer is this: Many situations still exist where a data mart may be the best choice as a source for business intelligence data. These situations are shown in Figure 6-3.

Legacy Databases

The BISM's data sources need appropriate data providers to make a connection to OLTP systems. In many cases, these will be .NET, OLE DB, or ODBC connections. However, some database systems do not have an appropriate data provider to make this

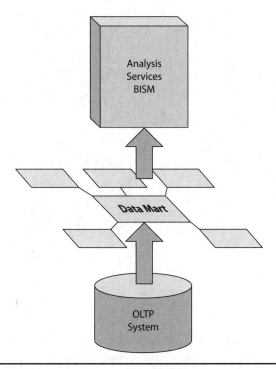

Figure 6-1   *An Analysis Services BI Semantic Model receiving data from a data mart*

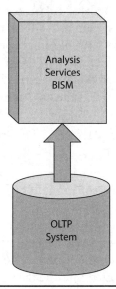

Figure 6-2   *The BISM eliminates the need for a data mart.*

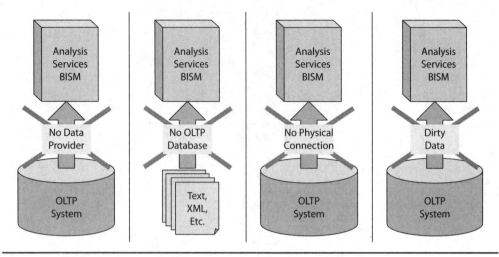

Figure 6-3 *Situations where a data mart is advised*

connection. Either the data provider available does not provide enough speed, flexibility, or reliability, or a data provider does not exist at all. In fact, some systems, especially legacy systems, do not have any way to allow this type of external access.

In these situations, the data must be exported from the legacy system and copied into a database that can be utilized by the BISM. This database is the data mart. The data must be exported from the legacy system into a format that can then be imported into the data mart. Usually, this is in the form of some type of text file: delimited columns, fixed-width columns, or, perhaps, Extensible Markup Language (XML).

Each time the export is run, a text file is created. This text file is then imported into the data mart. The import is accomplished using Integration Services.

Data from Nondatabase Sources

In some cases, the data needed for business intelligence is not even stored in a database. Production information from the automated manufacturing system could be written to a text file. Customer service call records might be logged to an XML file. Perhaps customer orders exist only on paper forms.

Again, in these situations, we need to import the data into a data mart before it can be utilized by a BISM. The text and XML files can be imported directly by Integration Services. The paper order forms must be scanned in or entered by hand into an electronic format that can be imported into the data mart.

No Physical Connection

In other cases, the data may exist in an OLTP database that has a data provider but does not have a full-time connection to the location where the business intelligence must be utilized. The BISM requires some type of physical connection that will support the data provider. If there is none, we again need to set up a data mart to serve as a repository for this data at the location where the business intelligence is utilized.

Of course, we also need some way to transport an export file from the OLTP database to the data mart so it can be imported. This might mean performing a File Transfer Protocol (FTP) transfer over a dial-up connection. It could mean putting the export file on a backup tape or burning it on a DVD-R and carrying it or shipping it between the two sites. However the data is transported, it is once again imported into the data mart using Integration Services.

Dirty Data

Dirty data can also trigger the need for a data mart. If the data in our OLTP systems contains a number of errors, inconsistencies, or duplicate information, we may need to clean the data before we can use it as a source of accurate business intelligence. Because of limitations in the OLTP systems, it may not be possible to properly cleanse the data in the OLTP database. Instead, the data must be exported from the OLTP system and then cleaned up as it is imported into a data mart by Integration Services.

Designing a Data Mart

Once you establish the need for a data mart, it is time to create a design. As we learned in Chapter 3, a data mart can utilize one of three different formats. The first two of these formats, the star schema and the snowflake schema, are made up of measures, dimensions organized in hierarchies, and attributes. The third format utilizes a denormalized relational schema made up of tables and fields.

We begin our design by identifying the information that our decision makers need for effective decision making. We then need to reconcile this with the data we have available from our OLTP systems and organize this data into the data mart components: measures, dimensions, hierarchies, and attributes; or tables and fields. When this is complete, we can build the database structure for the data mart using either a star, snowflake, or denormalized relational schema.

We discuss each step of the data mart design process in the following sections. This is followed by a section called "Learn By Doing." The Learn By Doing section helps make the concepts more concrete by applying what you just learned to a business scenario from Maximum Miniatures, Incorporated. I encourage you to work through these Learn By Doing exercises to make what can be complex and overwhelming concepts more tangible and straightforward. As Aristotle said, "One must learn by doing the thing, for though you think you know it, you have no certainty until you try."

Decision Makers' Needs

Business intelligence design should never be done in a vacuum. As we discussed in Chapter 1, the goal of business intelligence is to provide the tools for effective decision making. Therefore, any business intelligence design must start with the decision makers themselves. What foundation and feedback information do they need? How do they need that information sliced and diced for proper analysis? To create truly effective business intelligence, these questions need to be answered by the decision makers themselves.

There are two important reasons to have the decision makers involved in this design process. First, the decision makers are the ones in the trenches. They know the choices that are made each day in the organization's operation. They also have a pretty good idea of what information can aid them in making those choices.

Second, the decision makers are the ones who ultimately determine the success or failure of a project. They do this through their willingness or unwillingness to use the resulting business intelligence tools. Your tool may produce dynamite information, but, ultimately, it is a failure if no one uses that information to produce more effective decisions.

Involving decision makers in the design of the data mart structures distributes the perceived ownership of the project. Most people who get their brainstorming ideas on the whiteboard during a design meeting, or who are allowed to submit a design suggestion via e-mail, feel some sense of having contributed to the project. They feel a small piece of ownership in the project. Just as the owner of a single share in a billion-dollar corporation cares whether the company's stock goes up or down, the person who feels ownership in a project, no matter how small their actual contribution might be, cares about the success or failure of that project. A decision maker who has taken a small piece of ownership in our business intelligence project is far more likely to use the resulting tool and, if appropriate, to push for others to make use of it as well.

So, with the goal of both gaining important insight into the decision makers' needs and creating a sense of ownership among the future users of our business intelligence tool, we need to have decision makers answer the following questions:

▶ What facts, figures, statistics, and so forth do you need for effective decision making? (foundation and feedback measures)

▶ How should this information be sliced and diced for analysis? (dimensions)

▶ What additional information can aid in finding exactly what is needed? (attributes)

The answers to these questions form half of the required design information. The other half comes from the OLTP data itself.

Available Data

The input and the ownership buy-in of the decision makers are important to our data mart design. Next comes the reality check. The fact is we cannot place any measures, dimensions, hierarchies, attributes, tables, or fields in the data mart if they are not represented in the OLTP data source.

We need to analyze the data to be received from the data source to make sure that all of the information requested by the decision makers can be obtained from there. Measures and attributes can come directly from fields in the OLTP data or from calculations based on those fields. Dimensions and hierarchies must be represented in the data and relationships contained in the OLTP data.

If a piece of requested information is not present in the OLTP data source, we need to determine if it is present in another data source. If so, data from these two data sources can be joined during the population of the data mart to provide the decision makers with the desired result. If the requested information is unavailable, we have to work with the decision makers to either determine a method to gather the missing information in the future or identify an alternative bit of information already present in the OLTP data source.

Data Mart Structures

We are now ready to specify the structures that will be in our data mart. These are the measures, dimensions, hierarchies, and attributes or tables and fields. These structures lead us to the star schema, snowflake schema, or denormalized relational schema that is going to define our data mart. For our discussion here, we use the measure, dimension, hierarchy, and attribute nomenclature.

Measures

We start our data mart design by specifying the measures. The *measures* are the foundation and feedback information our decision makers require. We reconcile these requirements with what is available in the OLTP data to come up with a list of measures, as shown in Figure 6-4.

In Chapter 4, we learned measures are numeric quantities. The following are some examples of numeric data that can be used as measures:

Monetary Amounts

- ▶ The cost of raw materials
- ▶ The value of a sale
- ▶ Operational expenses
- ▶ Labor expenses

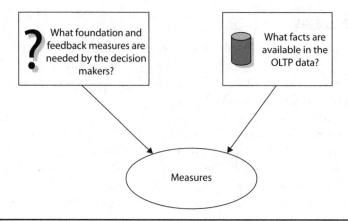

Figure 6-4 *Designing the measures in a data mart*

Counts

- ▶ The number of items produced
- ▶ The number of items ordered
- ▶ The number of items shipped
- ▶ The number of items returned
- ▶ The number of calls to customer service

Time Periods

- ▶ The number of minutes or hours required to produce a product
- ▶ The number of days required to fill an order
- ▶ Mean time between failure of a product

In the design, we need to note the following for each measure:

- ▶ Name of the measure
- ▶ What OLTP field or fields should be used to supply the data
- ▶ Data type (money, integer, decimal)
- ▶ Formula used to calculate the measure (if there is one)

As previously discussed, the data cannot appear out of thin air. It must be copied from or calculated from somewhere else. Therefore, identifying the OLTP fields that supply the data is important.

Refer to the "Learn By Doing: Designing the Maximum Miniatures Manufacturing Data Mart" section for an example of measure design.

Dimensions and Hierarchies

As we learned in Chapter 3, *dimensions* are used to spread a measure into its constituent parts. *Hierarchies* are used to organize dimensions into various levels. Dimensions and hierarchies are used to drill down into a measure to move from more general information to more specific information. While measures define *what* the decision makers want to see, the dimensions and hierarchies define *how* they want to see it.

When the decision makers tell us they want to see "total sales by salesperson by year," they are describing a measure, total sales, and two dimensions: salesperson and date. In discussions with decision makers, dimensions often are preceded with the words "by," "for each," or "for every." When the decision makers tell us they want to be able to "roll up salespersons into sales regions" or "drill down from year into quarter," they are describing hierarchies. The sales region dimension is above the salesperson dimension and the year dimension is above the quarter dimension in the hierarchy they are describing. These are all indications of how the decision makers want to view the measure.

We again reconcile the requested dimensions and hierarchies with what is available from the OLTP data to come up with the list of dimensions and their hierarchies for our design. This is shown in Figure 6-5. In the design, we need to have the following listed for each dimension:

▶   Name of the dimension

▶   What OLTP field or fields are to be used to supply the data

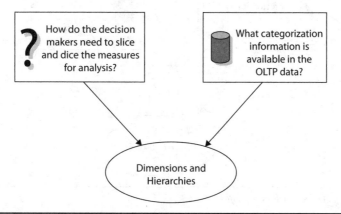

Figure 6-5   *Designing the dimensions and hierarchies in a data mart*

► Data type of the dimension's key (the code that uniquely identifies each member of the dimension)

► Name of the parent dimension (if there is one)

Refer to the "Learn By Doing: Designing the Maximum Miniatures Manufacturing Data Mart" section for an example of dimension and hierarchy design.

Attributes

Attributes provide additional information about a dimension. They may result from information decision makers want to have readily available during analysis. Attributes may also result from information decision makers want to filter on during the analysis process.

As before, we need to reconcile the requested attributes with the data available from the OLTP database to come up with the list of attributes in our design. This is shown in Figure 6-6. In the design, we need to include the following for each attribute:

► Name of the attribute

► What OLTP field or fields are to be used to supply the data

► Data type

► Name of the dimension to which it applies

Refer to the "Learn By Doing: Designing the Maximum Miniatures Manufacturing Data Mart" section for an example of attribute design.

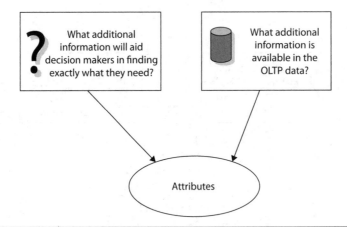

Figure 6-6   *Designing the attributes in a data mart*

Stars and Snowflakes

Data marts defined around measures and dimensions are architected using either a star schema or a snowflake schema. Refer to Chapter 3 if you need a refresher on these two layouts. Our last step is to turn our lists into either a star or a snowflake schema. Figure 6-7 shows a star schema, while Figure 6-8 shows a snowflake schema.

Recall that all the measures are placed in a single table called the fact table. The dimensions at the lowest level of the hierarchies are each placed in their own dimension table. In the *star schema,* all the information for a hierarchy is stored in the same table. The information for the parent (or grandparent or great-grandparent, and so forth) dimension is added to the table containing the dimension at the lowest level of the hierarchy.

The snowflake schema works a bit differently. In the *snowflake schema,* each level in the dimensional hierarchy has its own table. The dimension tables are linked together with foreign key relationships to form the hierarchy. Refer to Chapter 3 for a discussion of the advantages and disadvantages of star and snowflake schemas.

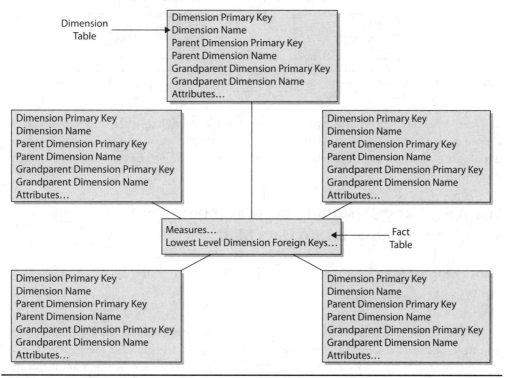

Figure 6-7   *A star schema*

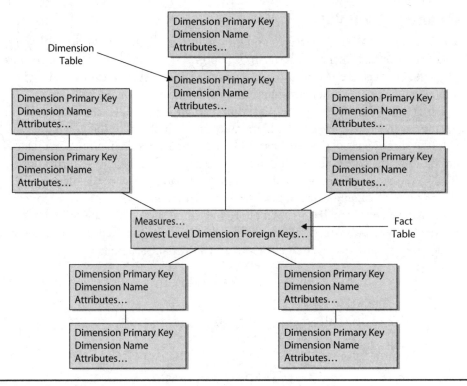

Figure 6-8   *A snowflake schema*

Once we create our schema, we are ready to implement that schema in a database. Before we look at implementing the schema, however, let's walk through an example of data mart design. Again, we are looking specifically at a design based on measures and dimensions here.

Learn By Doing: Designing the Maximum Miniatures Manufacturing Data Mart

Feature Highlighted

▶ Designing a data mart

In this section, we apply the knowledge gained in the previous sections to complete a sample task for Maximum Miniatures, Incorporated. In this case, we design the Manufacturing data mart to hold information that is initially logged by the manufacturing automation system in comma-delimited text files.

Business Need   The vice president (VP) of production for Max Min, Inc., wants to analyze the statistics available from the manufacturing automation system. He would like an interactive analysis tool, rather than printed reports, for this analysis. In keeping with Max Min's new business intelligence strategy, Microsoft SQL Server 2016 Analysis Services is the platform for this analysis tool. Because the manufacturing automation system does not use a database, logging everything to comma-delimited text files instead, a data mart must be designed and built as a repository for this information.

The manufacturing automation system controls all the machines used by Max Min to create its figurines. Each machine handles all the steps in the manufacturing process of a figurine. This includes the following:

▶ Filling a mold with the raw material (clay, pewter, or aluminum)

▶ Aiding the hardening of this material

▶ Removal from the mold when hardening is complete

▶ Computerized painting of the figurine, if necessary (pewter figurines are not painted)

▶ Curing the paint, if necessary

Multiple painting and curing cycles may be necessary, depending on the intricacy of the paint job required by a product. A quality assurance check is done by the machine operator as the figurine is completed.

Operators log onto a machine. As part of this logon process, the operator tells the manufacturing automation system what product is being produced, along with the batch number of the raw material being used by that machine. The operator also makes an entry in the system when a figurine is rejected.

An interview with the VP of production yielded the following data requirements for effective decision making:

▶ Number of accepted products by batch, by product, by machine, by day

▶ Number of rejected products by batch, by product, by machine, by day

▶ Elapsed time for molding and hardening by product, by machine, by day

▶ Elapsed time for painting and curing by paint type, by product, by machine, by day

▶ Product rolls up into product subtype, which rolls up into product type

▶ Machine rolls up into machine type, which rolls up into material (clay, pewter, or aluminum)

▶ Machine also rolls up into plant, which rolls up into country

▶ Day rolls up into month, which rolls up into quarter, which rolls up into year

▶ The information should be able to be filtered by machine manufacturer and purchase date of the machine

The export file from the manufacturing automation system contains one row for each product produced. Each row includes the following information:

▶ Product

▶ Batch number of the raw material

▶ Machine number

▶ Operator employee number

▶ Start of manufacture date and time (when the batch run begins)

▶ End of manufacture date and time (when the batch run is complete)

▶ Reject flag

Steps   In this particular Learn By Doing exercise, you don't have that much to do except follow along and make sure you understand each step. You can use these steps as an example when you have to create your own data mart design. Subsequent "Learn By Doing" sections require you to use the SQL Server 2016 tools to create part of a working business intelligence solution.

1. Prepare a list of the measures requested by the VP of production. This is shown in the Measure column of Figure 6-9.

2. Determine which fields in the OLTP data source supply the data for these measures. This is shown in the OLTP Fields column of Figure 6-9. The Reject Flag field tells us whether a product has been accepted or rejected. This can be used to determine the number of accepted and number of rejected products. The manufacturing system does not track the time spent in each individual production step. It only tracks the date and time at the start of manufacture and the date and time at the end of manufacture. Therefore, we need to put NOT AVAILABLE for these two items.

Measure	OLTP Fields
Number of Accepted Products	Reject Flag
Number of Rejected Products	Reject Flag
Elapsed Minutes for Molding and Hardening	NOT AVAILABLE
Elapsed Minutes for Painting and Curing	NOT AVAILABLE

Figure 6-9   *Requested measures for the Manufacturing data mart*

Measure	OLTP Fields	Data Type	Formula
Number of Accepted Products	Reject flag	Int	Count when reject flag is false
Number of Rejected Products	Reject flag	Int	Count when reject flag is true
Elapsed Minutes for Manufacturing	Start of manufacture date and time, End of manufacture date and time	Decimal(6,2)	DATEDIFF(mi, [Start of manufacture date and time], [End of manufacture date and time])

Figure 6-10   *Finalized measures for the Manufacturing data mart*

3. Resolve any problems with information that is unavailable. In this case, a follow-up interview with the VP reveals he will be satisfied with knowing the elapsed minutes for the entire manufacturing process. When our list is updated with this information, it appears as shown in the Measure and OLTP Fields columns of Figure 6-10.

4. Add the data types and calculations to the list. This is shown in the Data Type and Formula columns of Figure 6-10.

5. Prepare a list of the dimensions requested by the VP of production. This is shown in the Dimension column of Figure 6-11.

6. Determine which fields in the OLTP data source are going to supply the data for these dimensions. This is shown in the OLTP Fields column of Figure 6-11.

Dimension	OLTP Fields
Product	Product
Product Subtype	NOT AVAILABLE
Product Type	NOT AVAILABLE
Batch	Batch
Machine	Machine
Machine Type	NOT AVAILABLE
Material	NOT AVAILABLE
Plant	NOT AVAILABLE
Country	NOT AVAILABLE
Day	Start of Manufacture Date and Time
Month	Start of Manufacture Date and Time
Quarter	Start of Manufacture Date and Time
Year	Start of Manufacture Date and Time
Paint Type	NOT AVAILABLE

Figure 6-11   *Requested dimensions and hierarchies for the Manufacturing data mart*

7. Resolve any problems with information that is not available. The manufacturing automation system does not include information on the hierarchies within Max Min. To include these hierarchies in the data mart, we need to pull data from another system. It turns out that the accounting system has the data we need. We remove the Paint Type dimension because this data is not available electronically. When our list is updated with this information, it appears as shown in the Dimension and OLTP Fields columns of Figure 6-12.

8. Add the data type of the dimension's key, along with the name of the parent dimension. This is shown in the Data Type and Parent Dimension columns of Figure 6-12.

9. Prepare a list of the attributes requested by the VP of production. This is shown in the Attribute column of Figure 6-13.

10. Determine which fields in the OLTP data source will supply the data for these attributes. Remember, some of this data needs to come from the accounting system. This is shown in the OLTP Fields column of Figure 6-13.

11. Resolve any problems with information that is unavailable. In this case, we do not have any problem attributes so no changes need to be made to the list.

Dimension	OLTP Fields	Data Type	Parent Dimension
Product	Product	Int	Product Subtype
Product Subtype	Accounting System.ProductSubtype	Int	Product Type
Product Type	Accounting System.ProductType	Int	None
Batch	Batch	Int	None
Machine	Machine	Int	Machine Type, Plant
Machine Type	Accounting System.MachineType	Nvarchar(30)	Material
Material	Accounting System.Material	Nvarchar(30)	None
Plant	Accounting System.Plant	Int	Country
Country	Accounting System.Country	Nchar(2)	None
Day	Start of Manufacture Date and Time	Int	Month
Month	Start of Manufacture Date and Time	Int	Quarter
Quarter	Start of Manufacture Date and Time	Int	Year
Year	Start of Manufacture Date and Time	Int	None

Figure 6-12   *Finalized dimensions and hierarchies for the Manufacturing data mart*

Attribute	OLTP Fields	Data Type	Dimension
Machine Manufacturer	Accounting.Equipment	Nvarchar(50)	Machine
Date of Purchase	Accounting.Equipment	Datetime	Machine

Figure 6-13 *Finalized attributes for the Manufacturing data mart*

12. Add the data type of the attribute, along with the name of the dimension it is associated with. This is shown in the Data Type and Dimension columns of Figure 6-13.

13. Turn the lists in Figure 6-10, Figure 6-12, and Figure 6-13 into your choice of a star schema or a snowflake schema. In this case, we use a snowflake schema. Place the measures and their data types in the FactManufacturing table, as shown in Figure 6-14.

14. Place each dimension into its own dimension table, as shown in Figure 6-15. Include a table name beginning with "Dim" and a primary key designation in each table.

NOTE

The time-related dimensions of day, month, quarter, and year do not need dimension tables. Instead, a single datetime field is placed in the FactManufacturing table (DateOfManufacture). The entire time-related hierarchy will be extrapolated from this field when we create a cube based on this data mart in a later chapter. This is done using a feature of SQL Server Analysis Services.

FactManufacturing	
Field Name	**Data Type**
AcceptedProducts	Int
RejectedProducts	Int
ElapsedTimeForManufacture	Decimal(6,2)

Figure 6-14 *The Manufacturing data mart schema with measures in a fact table*

FactManufacturing

Field Name	Data Type
AcceptedProducts	Int
RejectedProducts	Int
ElapsedTimeForManufacture	Decimal(6,2)
DateOfManufacture	DateTime

DimMachine

Field Name	Data Type
MachineNumber (PK)	Int
MachineName	Nvarchar(50)

DimProduct

Field Name	Data Type
ProductCode (PK)	Int
ProductName	Nvarchar(50)

DimMachineType

Field Name	Data Type
MachineType (PK)	Nvarchar(30)

DimProductSubtype

Field Name	Data Type
ProductSubtypeCode (PK)	Int
ProductSubtypeName	Nvarchar(50)

DimMaterial

Field Name	Data Type
Material (PK)	Nvarchar(30)

DimProductType

Field Name	Data Type
ProductTypeCode (PK)	Int
ProductTypeName	Nvarchar(50)

DimPlant

Field Name	Data Type
PlantNumber (PK)	Int
PlantName	Nvarchar(30)

DimBatch

Field Name	Data Type
BatchNumber (PK)	Int
BatchName	Nvarchar(50)

DimCountry

Field Name	Data Type
CountryCode (PK)	Nchar(2)
CountryName	Nvarchar(30)

Figure 6-15   *The Manufacturing data mart schema with dimension tables added*

15. For any dimension that does not have an integer key, add your own integer key field. This is known as a *surrogate key*. We do this because integer keys are more efficient within the data models. The value of the surrogate key will be assigned when the data is loaded into the data mart. In our example, the country, machine type, and material dimensions will need surrogate keys. This is shown in Figure 6-16.

16. Create the dimensional hierarchies by adding foreign keys to the dimension tables. This is shown in Figure 6-16.

FactManufacturing

Field Name	Data Type
AcceptedProducts	Int
RejectedProducts	Int
ElapsedTimeForManufacture	Decimal(6,2)
DateOfManufacture	Date

DimBatch

Field Name	Data Type
BatchNumber (PK)	Int
BatchName	Nvarchar(50)

DimMachine

Field Name	Data Type
MachineNumber (PK)	Int
MachineName	Nvarchar(50)
MachineTypeKey (FK)	int
PlantNumber (FK)	Int

DimProduct

Field Name	Data Type
ProductCode (PK)	Int
ProductName	Varchar(50)
ProductSubtypeCode (FK)	Int

DimProductSubtype

Field Name	Data Type
ProductSubtypeCode (PK)	Int
ProductSubtypeName	Nvarchar(50)
ProductTypeCode (FK)	Int

DimMachineType

Field Name	Data Type
MachineTypeKey (PK)	int
MachineType	Nvarchar(30)
MaterialKey (FK)	int

DimPlant

Field Name	Data Type
PlantNumber (PK)	Int
PlantName	Nvarchar(30)
CountryKey (FK)	Int

DimProductType

Field Name	Data Type
ProductTypeCode (PK)	Int
ProductTypeName	Nvarchar(50)

DimMaterial

Field Name	Data Type
MaterialKey (PK)	int
Material	Nvarchar(30)

DimCountry

Field Name	Data Type
CountryKey (PK)	Int
CountryCode	NChar(2)
CountryName	Nvarchar(30)

Figure 6-16   *The Manufacturing data mart schema with hierarchies added*

17. Link the lowest-level dimensions to the fact table by adding foreign keys to the fact table. Also, add the attributes to the dimension tables. The final Manufacturing data mart schema is shown in Figure 6-17. This may be a pretty funny-looking snowflake, but it is, indeed, a snowflake schema.

The design of the Manufacturing data mart is complete. Next, we learn how to turn that design into a reality.

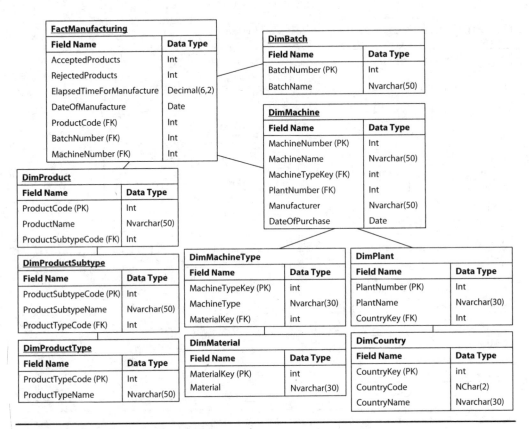

Figure 6-17   *The completed Manufacturing data mart schema*

Creating a Data Mart Using the SQL Server Management Studio

Now that we have a design for our data mart based on the decision maker's requests and the data available from the OLTP systems, it is time to turn that design into database tables. We are going to build the relational data mart as shown in Figure 6-18. We use the schema in Figure 6-17 to create a database with a fact table and several dimension tables.

Even though we identified several foreign key relationships among our tables, we are not going to create foreign key constraints in our data mart. Foreign key constraints put a strain on the database engine during a large data load. Large data loads are quite common in the data mart environment. Instead of using foreign key constraints, we will depend on our data extract, transform, and load (ETL) process in SQL Server

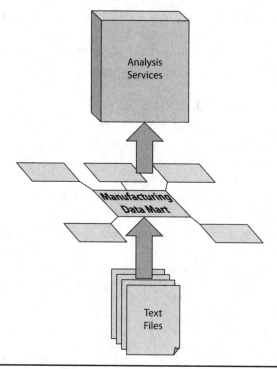

Figure 6-18   *Building the relational data mart*

Integration Services to enforce data integrity. We use the ETL because it can handle data integrity errors in a more robust fashion. We will see this in action in Chapter 8.

Follow the steps in the "Learn By Doing: Creating the Maximum Miniatures Manufacturing Data Mart Using the SQL Server Management Studio" section to create the Manufacturing data mart.

Learn By Doing: Creating the Maximum Miniatures Manufacturing Data Mart Using the SQL Server Management Studio

Features Highlighted

- ▶ Creating a data mart database
- ▶ Creating dimension tables
- ▶ Creating a fact table

Business Need   The business need was stated in the previous Learn By Doing section, where we created the schema for the Manufacturing data mart. In this section, we implement the Maximum Miniatures Manufacturing data mart schema using SQL Server Management Studio.

Steps to Create a Data Mart Using SSMS

1. Open SQL Server Management Studio, as we discussed in Chapter 5.
2. Connect to a development or test instance of the SQL Server database engine. (Do *not* perform this or any other Learn By Doing activity on a server instance used for production database operations!)
3. Right-click the Databases folder in the Object Explorer window. The context menu appears, as shown in Figure 6-19.
4. Select New Database from the context menu. The New Database dialog box appears, as shown in Figure 6-20.
5. Enter **MaxMinManufacturingDM** for the Database name. Select the Options page, and select Simple from the Recovery model drop-down list. Click OK to create the database.

NOTE

Because this is not a transactional database, there is no need to recover the content of this database to a point in time using the transaction log. The simple recovery model truncates the transaction log on checkpoint, keeping the size of the transaction log small. The Full and Bulk-logged recovery models require a backup of the transaction log before it is truncated.

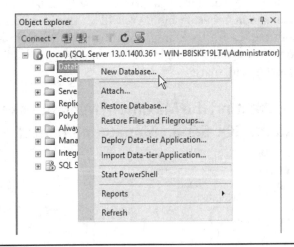

Figure 6-19   *The Database folder context menu*

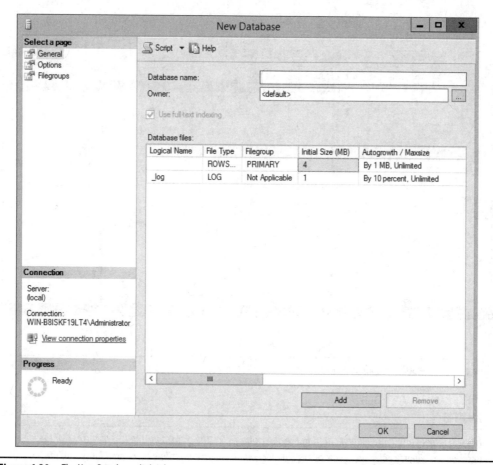

Figure 6-20   *The New Database dialog box*

6. Expand the Databases folder, and expand the MaxMinManufacturingDM
   database entry. Right-click the Tables folder, and select New | Table from the
   context menu. A Table Designer tab appears, as shown in Figure 6-21.

7. We use both the Properties window and the Column Properties window as we
   create our tables. If the Properties window is not visible, as in Figure 6-21, select
   Properties Window from the View menu. Be sure to note whether the entries in
   the following steps are being made in the Properties window or in the Column
   Properties window.

8. Begin by creating the DimProduct table from the schema (see Figure 6-17).
   In the Properties window, enter **DimProduct** for (Name) and **Product
   Dimension populated from the Manufacturing Automation System export
   file.** for Description.

Table Designer tab

Properties window

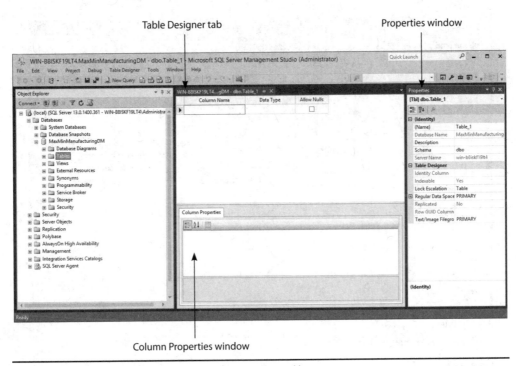

Column Properties window

Figure 6-21   *The SQL Server Management Studio ready to create a table*

NOTE

To use a larger editing area when entering the description, click the ellipses button (...) at the end of the Description property entry area. This opens a dialog window with a multiline entry area for typing the description.

9. In the first row of the Table Designer tab, enter **ProductCode** under Column Name, select int under Data Type, and uncheck Allow Nulls. Right-click this row and select Set Primary Key from the context menu to make this the primary key for this table.

10. In the second row of the Table Designer tab, enter **ProductName** under Column Name, select nvarchar(50) under Data Type, and uncheck Allow Nulls. (Leave Length in the Column Properties window set to the default value of 50.)

11. In the third row of the Table Designer tab, enter **ProductSubtypeCode** under Column Name, select int under Data Type, and uncheck Allow Nulls.

12. Click the Save toolbar button to save this table design. This creates the table in the database. Click the Close button (the *X* on the right side of the Table Designer tab).

13. Create the DimProductSubtype table from the schema. Right-click the Tables folder and select New | Table from the context menu. In the Properties window,

enter **DimProductSubtype** for (Name) and **ProductSubtype Dimension populated from the Accounting System.ProductSubtype table.** for Description.

14. In the first row of the Table Designer tab, enter **ProductSubtypeCode** under Column Name, select int under Data Type, and uncheck Allow Nulls. Right-click this row and select Set Primary Key from the context menu to make this the primary key for this table.

15. In the second row of the Table Designer tab, enter **ProductSubtypeName** under Column Name, select nvarchar(50) under Data Type, and uncheck Allow Nulls. (Leave Length in the Column Properties window set to the default value of 50.)

16. In the third row of the Table Designer tab, enter **ProductTypeCode** under Column Name, select int under Data Type, and uncheck Allow Nulls.

17. Click the Save toolbar button to create the table, and then click the Close button on the right side of the Table Designer tab.

18. Create the DimCountry table from the schema. Right-click the Tables folder and select New | Table from the context menu. In the Properties window, enter **DimCountry** for (Name) and **Country Dimension populated from the Accounting System.** for Description.

19. In the first row of the Table Designer tab, enter **CountryKey** under Column Name, select int under Data Type, and uncheck Allow Nulls. Right-click this row and select Set Primary Key from the context menu to make this the primary key for this table.

20. This is a surrogate key column, meaning the source tables are not going to be supplying a value for this column. We must supply our own value as this table is loaded. To do this, we set this column as an identity column. Scroll down in the Column Properties tab until you see an entry for Identity Specification.

21. Click the triangle to the left of Identity Specification to expand this section.

22. Select Yes from the (Is Identity) drop-down list. Leave the Identity Increment and the Identity Seed each set to 1.

23. In the second row of the Table Designer tab, enter **CountryCode** under Column Name, type **nchar(2)** under Data Type, and uncheck Allow Nulls.

24. In the third row of the Table Designer tab, enter **CountryName** under Column Name, type **nvarchar(30)** under Data Type, and uncheck Allow Nulls.

25. Click the Save toolbar button to create the table, and then click the Close button on the right side of the Table Designer tab.

26. Use the same process to create the DimProductType, DimBatch, DimMachine, DimMachineType, DimMaterial, and DimPlant dimension tables based on the schema in Figure 6-17. Be sure to uncheck Allow Nulls for all fields and to enter the appropriate data type and appropriate length. Also, create a primary key for each field that is followed by a (PK) in Figure 6-17. Finally, be sure to turn on Identity for the MachineTypeKey column in the DimMachineType table and for the MaterialKey column in the DimMaterial table.

27. Right-click the MaxMinManufacturingDM database entry in the Object Explorer window, and select Refresh from the context menu. When you expand the node for columns under each table, the entries should appear just as in Figure 6-22 and Figure 6-23.

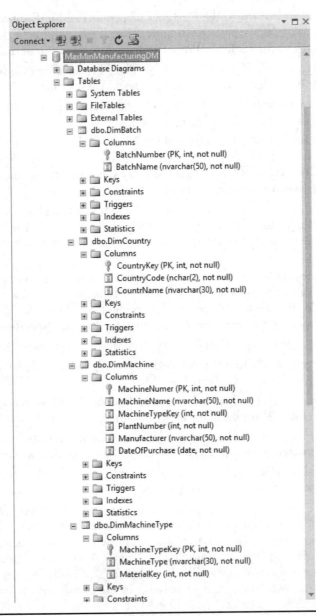

Figure 6-22 *The tables in the MaxMinManufacturingDM with columns (Part 1)*

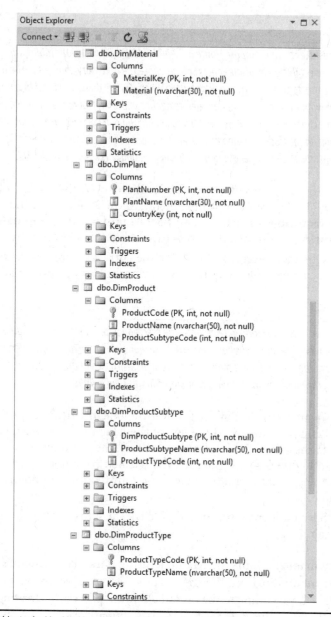

Figure 6-23   *The tables in the MaxMinManufacturingDM with columns (Part 2)*

NOTE

If you notice any mistakes as you compare Figure 6-22 and Figure 6-23 with your tables, right-click the table that is in error and select Design from the context menu. Make the necessary changes to the table structure to correct the error. Be sure to click the Save toolbar button when you are done. You need to refresh the contents of the Object Explorer window after your changes before again comparing Figure 6-22 and Figure 6-23. You may need to enable table changes in the SQL Server Management Studio. If you receive an error, select Tools | Options from the main menu. In the Options dialog box, select the Designers | Table and Database Designers page. Uncheck the Prevent saving changes that require table re-creation check box, and click OK.

28. Now, create the FactManufacturing table. Right-click the Tables folder, and select New | Table from the context menu. In the Properties window, enter **FactManufacturing** for (Name) and **Fact Manufacturing populated from the Manufacturing Automation System export file.** for Description.

29. Using the schema in Figure 6-17, create the entries for the seven columns in the FactManufacturing table. (Continue to uncheck Allow Nulls for all fields.)

NOTE

The decimal data type is used to store real numbers. The precision determines the total number of digits contained in the number. The scale tells how many of those digits are to the right of the decimal. The ElapsedTimeForManufacture field has a maximum of six digits, with two of those digits to the right of the decimal. Therefore, the largest number that can be stored in this field is 9999.99.

30. Click the square to the left of the DateOfManufacture field definition. Hold down SHIFT and click the square to the left of the MachineNumber field definition. This selects these two field definitions and all the field definitions in between, as shown in Figure 6-24. Right-click the selected columns and select Set Primary Key from the context menu to make these four fields a compound primary key for this table.

31. Click the Save toolbar button, and then click the Close button in the Table Designer tab.

We have now manually built the Manufacturing data mart structure using SQL Server Management Studio. Even though this process took 31 steps, we are only halfway done. In Chapter 11, we complete the other half of the process by creating an Analysis Services BISM that uses this data mart as its data source.

Creating a Data Mart Using SQL Server Data Tools

In the previous section, we completed the first half of a two-step process for creating a relational data mart and an Analysis Services BISM built on that data mart. This is a long and, as you will see, somewhat redundant process. SQL Server Data Tools comes

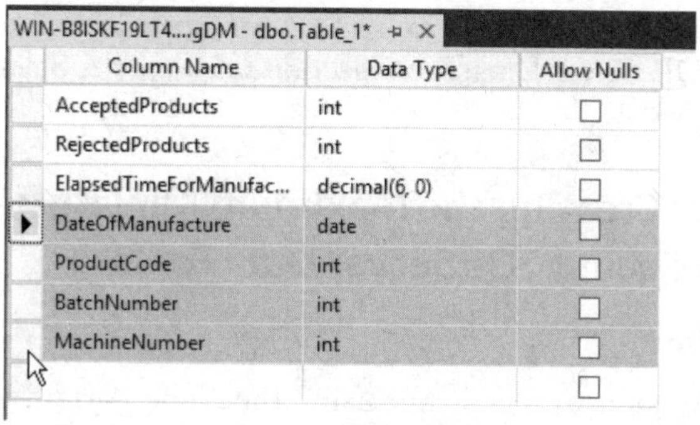

WIN-B8ISKF19LT4....gDM - dbo.Table_1*
Column Name
Data Type
Allow Nulls
AcceptedProducts
int
RejectedProducts
int
ElapsedTimeForManufac...
decimal(6, 0)
DateOfManufacture
date
ProductCode
int
BatchNumber
int
MachineNumber
int

Figure 6-24 *Selecting multiple fields to create a compound primary key*

to our rescue here. We will now use this tool to create the Analysis Services BISM and its underlying relational data mart for the Maximum Miniatures sales data at the same time. This is shown in Figure 6-25. The Cube Wizard creates an Analysis Services cube, and then creates the matching dimension and fact tables in the Sales data mart based on the cube definition.

Sales
Analysis
Services
BISM
Sales
Data Mart
Order Processing
OLTP
System

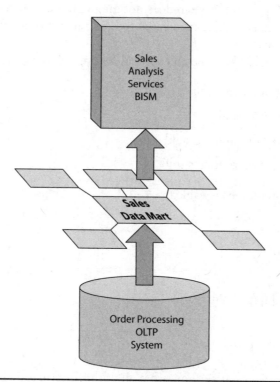

Figure 6-25 *Building the Sales relational data mart and the Sales Analysis Services cube*

Follow the steps in the "Learn By Doing: Creating the Maximum Miniatures Sales Data Mart Using SQL Server Data Tools" section to create the Sales data mart through the Cube Wizard.

Learn By Doing: Creating the Maximum Miniatures Sales Data Mart Using SQL Server Data Tools

Features Highlighted

▶ Creating an Analysis Services cube using the Cube Wizard in SQL Server Data Tools

▶ Creating a relational data mart from a cube definition in SQL Server Data Tools

Business Need   The VP of sales for Max Min, Inc., would like to analyze sales information. This information is collected by the Order Processing OLTP System (refer to Figure 2-4). The Order Processing System uses Microsoft SQL Server as its back-end database.

Microsoft SQL Server 2016 Analysis Services is the platform for this analysis tool. Because the Order Processing System does not maintain the history of sales staff assignments, a relational data mart is created to hold the information that is to serve as the data source for the cube.

The VP of sales would like to be able to analyze the following numbers:

▶ Dollar value of products sold

▶ Number of products sold

▶ Sales tax charged on products sold

▶ Shipping charged on products sold

These numbers should be viewable by:

▶ Store

▶ Sales Promotion

▶ Product

▶ Day, Month, Quarter, and Year

▶ Customer

▶ Salesperson

An analysis of the data source shows that all of this information is available.

In the previous Learn By Doing exercise, we first created our data mart structure on paper, and then implemented it in SQL Server. This time around, we will let the Cube Wizard guide us through the creation of the data mart structures.

NOTE

We need to use the SQL Server Management Studio to create a database for our Max Min Sales data mart. SQL Server Data Tools creates the dimension and fact tables in this database later in the process.

Steps to Create a Data Mart Using SSDT

1. Open the SQL Server Management Studio and connect to a development or test instance of the SQL Server database engine. Create a new database called **MaxMinSalesDM**, which uses the Simple recovery model. If you have any questions about creating this database, refer to Steps 3–5 in the "Learn By Doing: Creating the Maximum Miniatures Manufacturing Data Mart Using the SQL Server Management Studio" section of this chapter.

2. Close the SQL Server Management Studio.

3. Open the SQL Server Data Tools, as we discussed in Chapter 5.

4. Click the New Project button in the toolbar.

5. Select Business Intelligence | Analysis Services in the Installed Templates area, and then select Analysis Services Multidimensional and Data Mining Project from the center area.

6. Enter **MaxMinSalesDM** for Name and set the Location to the appropriate folder. Check Create directory for solution.

NOTE

You should create a folder to hold all of the Learn By Doing activities in this book. Make sure this folder is clearly named so it does not become confused with production source code.

7. Click OK to create the project.

8. Once the project is open, right-click the Cubes folder in the Solution Explorer, and select New Cube from the context menu. The Cube Wizard dialog box appears.

9. On the Welcome page, click Next.

10. On the Select Creation Method page, select the Generate tables in the data source radio button. Leave (None) selected in the Template drop-down list. Click Next.

11. On the Define New Measures page, click the highlighted cell in the Add new measures grid. Enter **Sales in Dollars** in the Measure Name column.

12. Enter **Sales Information** in the Measure Group column.

13. Select Currency in the Data Type column. Sum should be selected by default in the Aggregation column.

14. Click the cell containing "Add new measure" in the Add new measures grid.

15. Enter **Sales in Units** in the Measure Name column.

16. Make sure "Sales Information" is selected in the Measure Group column.

17. Select Integer in the Data Type column. Sum should be selected by default in the Aggregation column.

18. Click the cell containing "Add new measure" in the Add new measures grid.

19. Enter **Sales Tax** in the Measure Name column.

20. Make sure "Sales Information" is selected in the Measure Group column.

21. Select Currency in the Data Type column. Sum should be selected by default in the Aggregation column.

22. Click the cell containing "Add new measure" in the Add new measures grid.

23. Enter **Shipping** in the Measure Name column.

24. Make sure "Sales Information" is selected in the Measure Group column.

25. Select Currency in the Data Type column. Sum should be selected by default in the Aggregation column. The Define New Measures page should appear as shown in Figure 6-26.

26. Click Next.

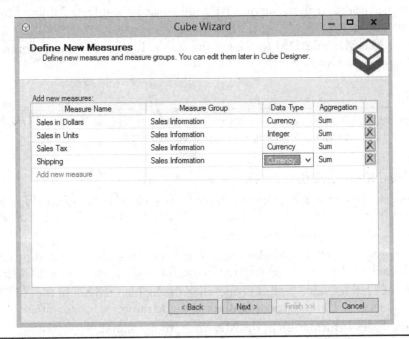

Figure 6-26   *After defining the measures in the Cube Wizard*

27. The Select dimensions from template grid at the top of the Define New Dimensions page will create the Time dimension for us from a time dimension template. Make sure the Time dimension line remains checked. In the Name column, replace "Time" with **Date**.

28. Click the cell containing "Add new dimension" in the Add new dimensions grid.

29. Enter **Customer** in the Name column, and press TAB.

30. Click the cell containing "Add new dimension" and enter **Product** in the Name column. Press TAB.

31. Click the cell containing "Add new dimension" and enter **Promotion** in the Name column. Press TAB.

32. Click the cell containing "Add new dimension" and enter **Sales Person** in the Name column. Press TAB.

33. Check the box under SCD in the Sales Person row.

DEFINITION

A Slowly Changing Dimension (SCD) varies over time. Of course, the data in many dimensions can change over time. What differentiates an SCD is the fact that the history of that change is important and must be tracked in the business intelligence information. For example, the salesperson dimension changes as salespeople are transferred from one sales territory to another. We need to track which territory a salesperson was in last year versus which territory they are in this year so sales can be rolled up into the correct territory for year-to-year comparisons.

34. Click the cell containing "Add new dimension" and enter **Store** in the Name column. Press TAB. The Define New Dimensions page should appear as shown in Figure 6-27.

35. Click Next.

36. The Define Time Periods page enables us to specify range, format, and hierarchy for the time dimension. Select Tuesday, January 1, 2013 from the First calendar day date picker. Check Month, Quarter, and Year in Time periods. (Leave Date checked as well.) The Define Time Periods page appears similar to Figure 6-28.

NOTE

If we use week in a time hierarchy, we can specify the first day of the week to use with this dimension. We can also specify the language to use for the members of the time dimension.

37. Click Next.

38. The Specify Additional Calendars page lets us add calendars other than the standard 12-month calendar to the date dimension. The Specify Additional Calendars page is shown in Figure 6-29. This might include a calendar for a fiscal year that starts on a day other than January 1 or the ISO 8601 standard calendar. Max Min tracks sales based on the standard 12-month calendar, so simply click Next.

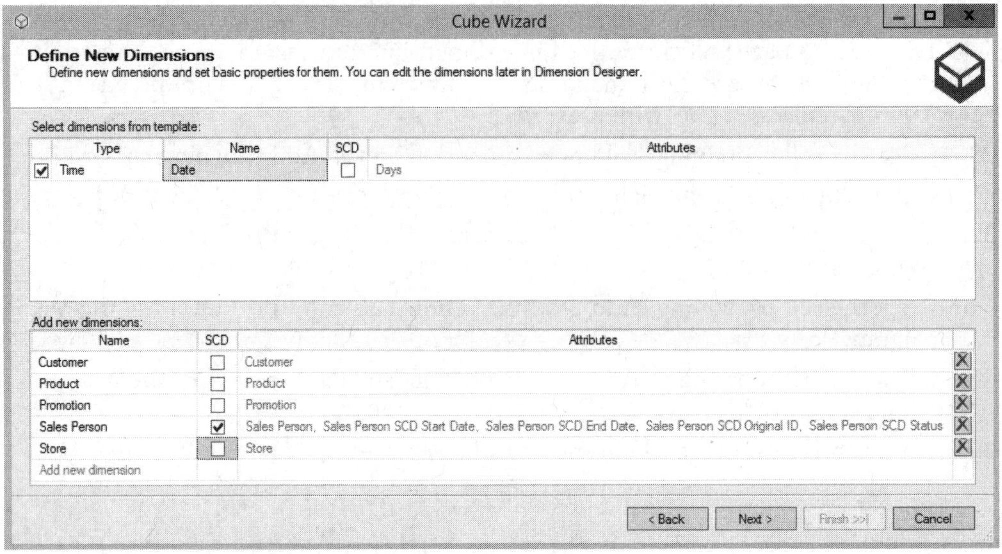

Figure 6-27 *After defining dimensions in the Cube Wizard*

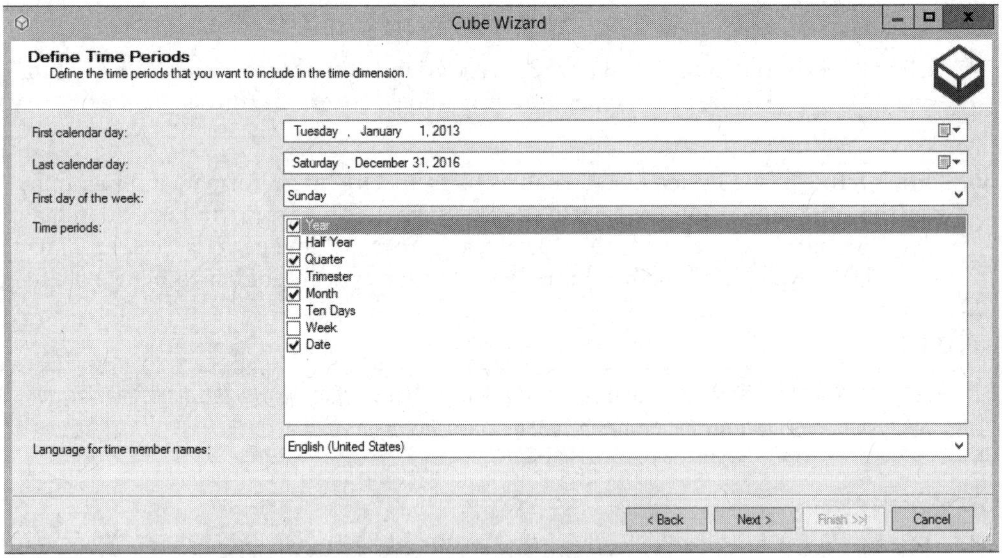

Figure 6-28 *After defining the time periods for the time dimension in the Cube Wizard*

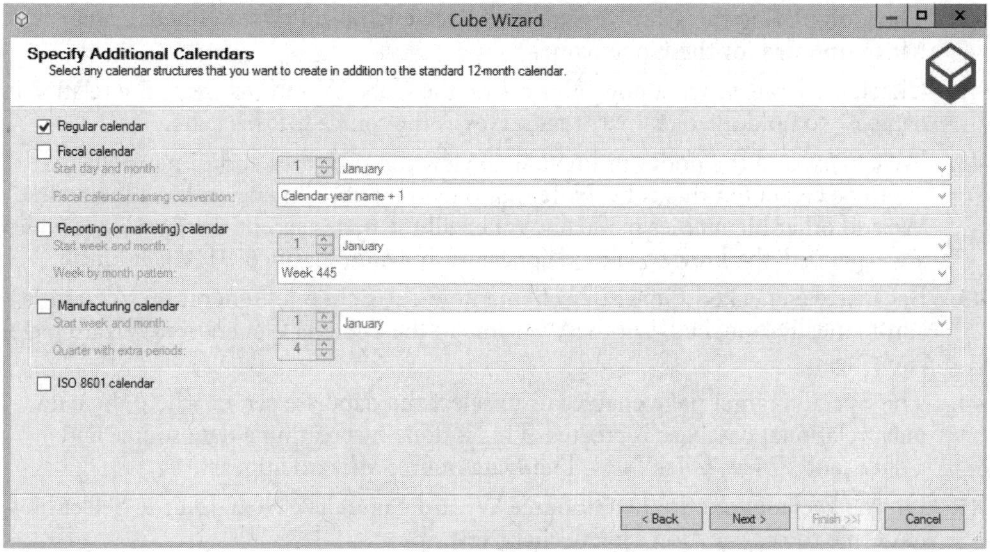

Figure 6-29 *Specifying additional calendars in the Cube Wizard*

39. The Define Dimension Usage page enables us to specify which dimensions are related to each group of measures. The Max Min Sales data mart is only using one group of measures, called Sales Information, so we want all the dimensions to apply to this group. Check the box in the Sales Information column for all of the dimensions, as shown in Figure 6-30. Click Next.

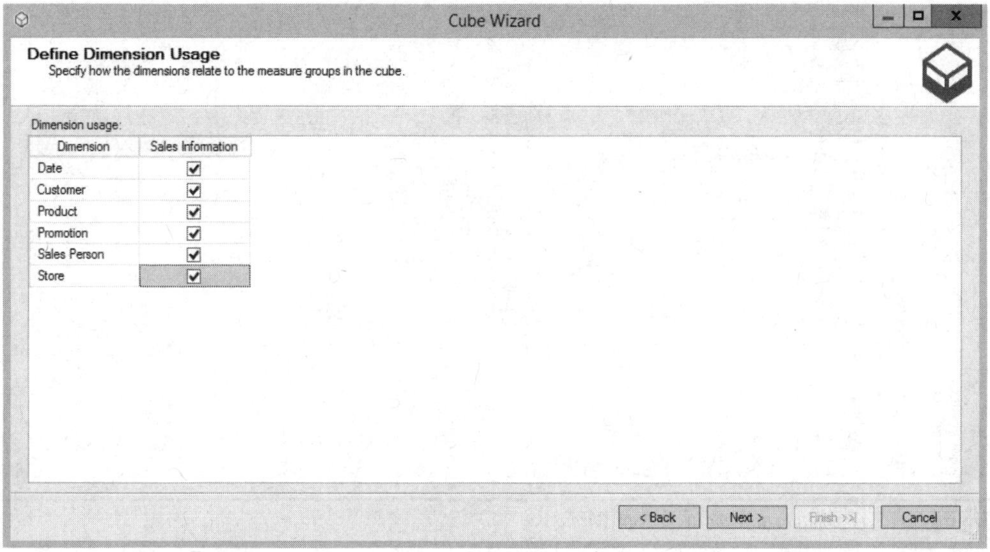

Figure 6-30 *Setting the dimension usage in the Cube Wizard*

40. The Completing the Wizard page lets us review the cube we defined. Enter **MaxMinSales** for the Cube name.

41. Check Generate schema now. This causes the Cube Wizard to create the relational database to hold the data mart that serves as the source for this cube.

42. We can expand the nodes in Preview to view the measures and dimensions that are to be created in this cube. Note that only the Date dimension has a hierarchy. We add other hierarchies manually. When all the nodes except the Attributes nodes are expanded, the Preview should appear as shown in Figure 6-31. Click Finish.

43. Because we checked Generate schema now, the Schema Generation Wizard is automatically launched. On the Welcome to the Schema Generation Wizard page, click Next.

44. The Specify Target page enables us to select the database server where the data mart relational database is created. This is done by creating a data source and a data source view. Click New. The Data Source Wizard appears.

45. On the Welcome to the Data Source Wizard page, click Next. On the Select how to define the connection screen, click New.

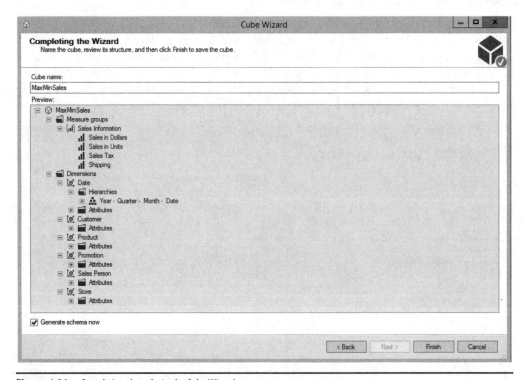

Figure 6-31   *Completing the cube in the Cube Wizard*

46. The Connection Manager dialog box lets us define a connection string used to access a database. Provider enables you to select between .NET and OLE DB data providers. In this case, we leave Provider set to Native OLE DB\SQL Server Native Client 11.0. For Server name, enter the name of the database server where you created the MaxMinSalesDM database in Step 1 of this section.

47. Select Use Windows Authentication under Log on to the server. The Schema Generation process requires Windows Authentication. Make sure that your current Windows credentials have rights to create tables in the MaxMinSalesDM database.

48. Select MaxMinSalesDM from the Select or enter a database name drop-down list. (A valid set of credentials must be specified before the drop-down list is populated.) The Connection Manager will appear as shown in Figure 6-32.

49. Click OK to exit the Connection Manager dialog box.

50. In the Select how to define the connection dialog box, click Next.

Figure 6-32 *The Connection Manager dialog box*

51. On the Impersonation Information page, select "Use a specific Windows user name and password" and enter a valid Windows user name and password for database access. Click Next. The Completing the Wizard page will appear.

NOTE

Analysis Services needs to access the data mart relational database in order to populate and update the information in the Multidimensional BISM. This is done using the information in the data connection selected in Step 46. The Analysis Services updates may run as a background process. This can be an issue if the data connection specifies Windows Authentication or if the connection is to a file-based database such as Access. In these situations, Analysis Services needs to know what Windows credentials to use when accessing the data source. In other words, it needs to impersonate a Windows identity while accessing the data.

52. The Completing the Wizard page shows the finished connection string. Click Finish to exit the Data Source Wizard.

53. We are now back to the Specify Target page of the Schema Generation Wizard. Click Next.

54. The Subject Area Database Schema Options page lets us select the operations we want the Schema Generation Wizard to perform. Uncheck the Enforce referential integrity check box. As stated earlier, we will let our ETL process enforce referential integrity. Populate should be selected from the Populate time table(s) drop-down list. Click Next.

NOTE

There are three options for handling the population of the table for the time dimension. The Populate option creates records in the time dimension table for the timeframe specified on the Define Time Periods page in Step 36.

55. The Specify Naming Conventions page enables us to determine how the tables and fields in the data mart are named. We use all the default settings. Click Next.

56. The Completing the Wizard page provides a summary of the schema generation we defined. Click Finish.

57. The Schema Generation Progress dialog box appears. This dialog box shows each step as the data mart (called the subject area database) is created. When the process has completed, the dialog box should appear similar to Figure 6-33. Click Close.

58. Click the Save All toolbar button.

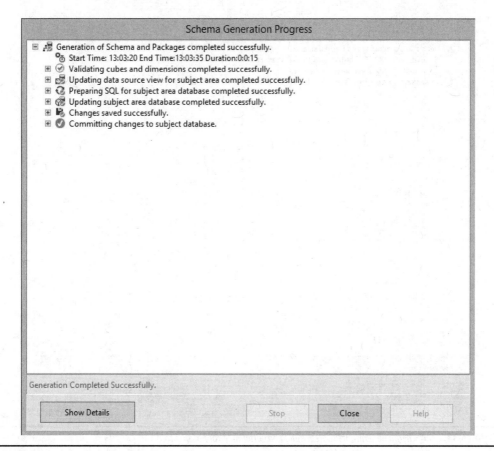

Figure 6-33   *The Schema Generation Progress dialog box with a successful process completion*

NOTE

If an error occurs during the process, a red circle with a white X appears next to the last step, as shown in Figure 6-34. The text next to the red circle with a white X describes the error. If an error occurs, use the description to determine the cause of the error, click Stop to terminate the process, click Close, and then repeat the process with the problem corrected. The cube and the dimensions may have been created in the Analysis Services project before the error occurred. To restart the entire process, the cube and dimensions need to be deleted from the project. The most common cause of an error is not using Windows Authentication in the data source or being logged onto Windows with credentials that do not have rights to create tables in the MaxMinSalesDM database.

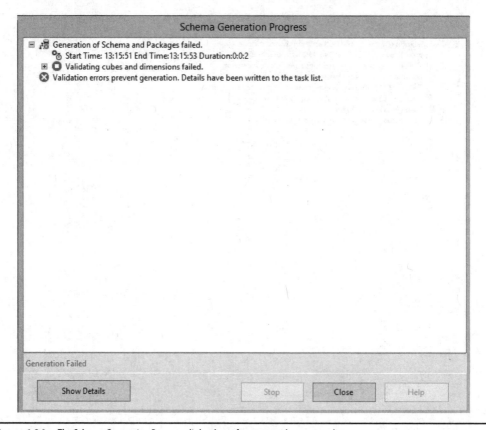

Figure 6-34 *The Schema Generation Progress dialog box after an error has occurred*

59. Beyond the basic fields created for us in the Sales data mart, we need to add some fields to hold additional information coming from our data source. We add these fields using the SQL Server Management Studio. Close SQL Server Data Tools.

60. Open the SQL Server Management Studio, and connect to the instance of the SQL Server database engine hosting the MaxMinSalesDM database.

61. Expand the Databases folder, and then expand the MaxMinSalesDM database. Finally, expand the Tables folder.

62. Right-click the dbo.Customer table entry, and select Design from the context menu.

63. Add the following columns to the Customer table:

Column Name	Data Type	Allow Nulls
Address	nvarchar(50)	Checked
City	nvarchar(50)	Checked
State	nchar(2)	Checked
ZipCode	nvarchar(10)	Checked
Homeowner	nchar(1)	Checked
MaritalStatus	nchar(1)	Checked
NumCarsOwned	smallint	Checked
NumChildrenAtHome	smallint	Checked

64. Close the table design tab. Click Yes when asked if you want to save changes.

NOTE

If you receive an error when trying to save changes to the table definition, select Tools | Options from the main menu. In the Options dialog box, select the Designers | Table and Database Designers page. Uncheck the Prevent saving changes that require table re-creation check box, and click OK.

65. Right-click the dbo.Product table entry, and select Design from the context menu.

66. Add the following columns to the Product table:

Column Name	Data Type	Allow Nulls
RetailPrice	money	Checked
Weight	real	Checked

67. Close the table design tab. Click Yes when asked if you want to save changes.

68. Right-click the dbo.Sales_Person table entry, and select Design from the context menu.

69. Add the following column to the Sales_Person table:

Column Name	Data Type	Allow Nulls
Sales_Person_Territory	int	Checked

70. Close the table design tab. Click Yes when asked if you want to save changes.

71. Right-click the dbo.Store table entry, and select Design from the context menu.

72. Add the following column to the Store table:

Column Name	Data Type	Allow Nulls
Store_Type	nvarchar(50)	Checked

73. Close the table design tab. Click Yes when asked if you want to save changes.

The Sales Data Mart

We now have a Sales data mart along with an Analysis Services cube built on that data mart. The star schema that defines both the data mart and the cube is shown in Figure 6-35. (Note, the data source view shown in Figure 6-35 does not include the fields we manually added to the tables.) We can tell this is a star schema rather than a snowflake schema because all the levels in the time hierarchy are contained in a single Date table, rather than multiple linked tables. We will add fields to these tables and hierarchies to this cube later.

Also, note the fields in the Sales_Person table. Several fields contain SCD in the field name. These fields are included to help maintain the history of a member of this dimension. We see this in action in future examples.

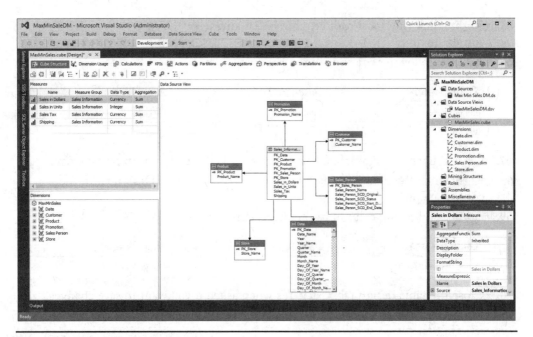

Figure 6-35   *The MaxMinSales star schema*

Table Compression

Our relational data warehouses may be called upon to store a copious amount of data. This can cause our fact tables and perhaps even some of our dimension tables to grow very large. Fortunately, SQL Server 2016 provides some relief in the form of table compression.

NOTE

The table compression features described in this section require the Developer or Enterprise Edition of SQL Server.

Table compression modifies the way data is physically stored on the disk drive in order to save space. It does not change the structure of a table, nor does it change the syntax used to SELECT, INSERT, UPDATE, or DELETE data in a table. Table compression is completely transparent to applications making use of the data. It simply makes more efficient use of disk space.

Types of Table Compression

SQL Server offers two flavors of table compression for us to take advantage of. The first is *row compression*. Row compression works within each row of data.

The second type of table compression is *page compression*. Page compression works within the page structure that SQL Server uses to store data. Let's take a closer look at each of the compression types.

Row Compression

Row compression reduces the space required to store a row of data. It does this by only using the bytes required to store a given value. For example, without row compression, a column of type int normally occupies 4 bytes. This is true if we are storing the number 1 or the number 1 million. SQL Server allocates enough space to store the maximum value possible for the data type.

When row compression is turned on, SQL Server makes smarter space allocations. It looks at the actual value being stored for a given column in a given row, and then determines the storage required to represent that value. This is done to the nearest whole byte.

Of course, this added complexity adds some overhead as data is inserted or updated in the table. It also adds a smaller amount of overhead when data is retrieved from that table. In most cases, the time taken for this additional processing is negligible. In fact, in some cases, the saving in disk read and disk write time can even be greater than the calculation time required for data compression.

Page Compression

Page compression takes things a bit further than row compression. In fact, page compression starts by utilizing row compression. It then adds two other compression techniques: *prefix compression* and *dictionary compression.*

Prefix compression looks for values of a given column that have a common beginning within a page of data. If the rows are sorted by account number, then the account number fields that fall within a given page will probably start with the same digits. The same is true if the rows are sorted by last name. The last name fields that fall within a given page are all likely to start with the same characters.

Prefix compression is designed to take advantage of these situations. It determines these common prefixes, and then stores a representative of this common beginning, or prefix, in a reference row in the page header. Rather than storing this repeating prefix data in every row, a pointer to the reference row is used. The pointer to the reference row can even show where a given value diverges from the reference row.

Dictionary compression is applied after prefix compression. This compression scheme looks for repeating values within the page. A representative of the repeated value is placed in the page header. A pointer to the header entry is then used in place of each occurrence of the repeated value.

It is not necessary to understand the technical details of table compression. What is important is to know that we have ways to reduce the storage space required by large tables and, in general, make these tables more manageable. Fortunately, using table compression is much easier than understanding what is happening under the hood.

Learn By Doing: Enabling Table Compression

Features Highlighted

▶ Turning on table compression

▶ Using the sp_estimate_data_compression_savings stored procedure

Business Need   We want to decrease the disk space required by our fact tables. These tables will grow quite large as we gather a number of years' worth of manufacturing and inventory data for reporting.

NOTE

The Developer or Enterprise Edition of SQL Server is required to complete this Learn By Doing exercise.

Steps to Enable Table Compression

1. Open the SQL Server Management Studio, if it is not already open, and connect to the SQL server hosting the MaxMinManufacturingDM database.

2. Expand the Database folder, and then expand the MaxMinManufacturingDM database entry. Finally, expand the Tables folder.

3. Right-click the FactManufacturing table entry and select Storage | Manage Compression. The Welcome page of the Data Compression Wizard appears.

4. Click Next. The Select Compression Type page of the Data Compression Wizard appears.

5. From the Compression type drop-down list, select Page. The Select Compression Type page will appear as shown in Figure 6-36.

6. Clicking the Calculate button will calculate an estimate of the amount of space that will be saved by turning on compression. To do this, the wizard looks at the actual data in the table. Of course, we don't have any data in this fact table currently, so the Calculate button doesn't do anything exciting for us at the moment. Click Next.

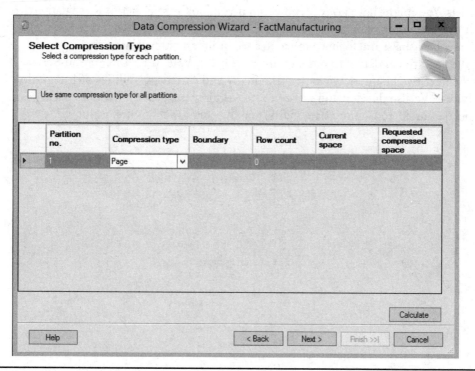

Figure 6-36 *The Select Compression Type page of the Data Compression Wizard*

7. On the Select an Output Option page of the Data Compression Wizard, select the Run immediately radio button.

8. Click Next. The Wizard Summary page appears. Click Finish. Compression is turned on for the FactManufacturing table in the MaxMinManufacturingDM database.

9. Click Close to exit the Data Compression Wizard.

10. Right-click the FactManufacturing table and select Properties. The Table Properties dialog box appears.

11. Select the Storage page of the dialog box. You will see at the top of the page that Compression type is set to Page for this table.

12. Select OK to exit the Table Properties dialog box.

13. Repeat this process to turn on Page compression for the Sales_Information table in the MaxMinSalesDM database.

The Benefits of Integration

We now have designed two data mart structures to serve as the source for BISM data models. You might have noticed, however, if you look into either of these data marts, that they are completely empty (except for the MaxMinSalesDM.Time table). There is not much business intelligence to be gleaned from an empty data mart!

We need to get data into our data marts. This is done using Integration Services. In the next two chapters, we look at the many and varied capabilities of Integration Services. We also develop and utilize some working Integration Services packages to populate our all-too-empty data marts, making them much more useful.

Chapter 7

Transformers: Integration Services Structure and Components

In This Chapter

► **Integration Services**
► **Package Items**
► **Getting Under the Sink**

There are painters who transform the sun to a yellow spot, but there are others who with the help of their art and their intelligence, transform a yellow spot into the sun.

—Pablo Picasso

I n the previous chapter, we created two data marts on our relational database server. As we pointed out at the end of Chapter 6, these data marts are not much use to us or our decision makers until they contain useful data. Fortunately, SQL Server 2016 has a tool designed for just such a purpose. This tool is SQL Server Integration Services.

Integration Services

Integration Services was introduced with SQL Server 2005. It facilitates changing the location of data by copying it from our online transaction processing (OLTP) databases and other locations into the data mart. As it is being copied, we can also transform the data from the format required by the OLTP systems to the format required by the online analytical processing (OLAP) systems we are creating. Finally, we can verify foreign key values as we load the data. This enables us to implement our data mart database without foreign key constraints.

Package Structure

We use SQL Server Data Tools to create an Integration Services project. A project defines one or more Integration Services packages. Each package defines a data extract, transform, and load (ETL) process.

The ETL process consists of two levels of operation. The top level defines the operations that need to be done to move the data from point A to point B. Perhaps log entries need to be created to track the ETL process. Perhaps files need to be moved from one location to another. These are the steps that control what the ETL process does.

The second level defines the individual data transfers that move the data itself. These data transfers also define how the data is cleansed and modified as it is transferred. Perhaps data types have to be changed. Perhaps product codes need to be validated.

The structure of an Integration Services package mirrors this two-level structure. The package's overall operation is defined by the control flow. The *control flow* is the sequence of tasks that will be performed by the package. One of those task types is the *data flow task*. Each data flow task has its own structure to define the plumbing for moving data from one or more sources to one or more destinations. The data flow task also defines how the data is manipulated along the way.

When we are creating an Integration Services project in SQL Server Data Tools, the Designer window contains five tabs, as shown in Figure 7-1. Three of these tabs—the Control Flow Designer tab, the Data Flow Designer tab, and the Event Handlers Designer tab—let us define various types of functionality for the package. The Parameters tab allows us to manage any parameters used to pass information to the package. The Package Explorer tab provides an alternative view of the contents of the package. In addition to the tabs, there is a special area at the bottom of the Designer window for defining Connection Managers, which is called the *Connections tray.*

As stated earlier, each Integration Services package contains a control flow to define the overall operation of the package. This is shown in Figure 7-2. The control flow is defined by dragging items from the SSIS Toolbox onto the Control Flow Designer tab. When the Control Flow Designer tab is selected, only those tasks that can be used on this tab are displayed in the SSIS Toolbox, as shown in Figure 7-1.

An Integration Services package may contain several data flows. Each data flow is represented by a data flow task placed on the Control Flow Designer tab, as shown in Figure 7-2. A data flow task is created by dragging a data flow item from the SSIS

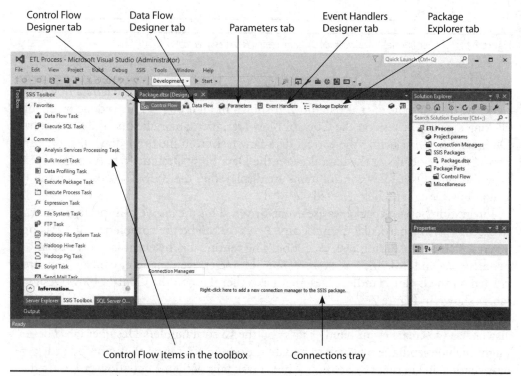

Figure 7-1   *The Integration Services package design layout in SQL Server Data Tools*

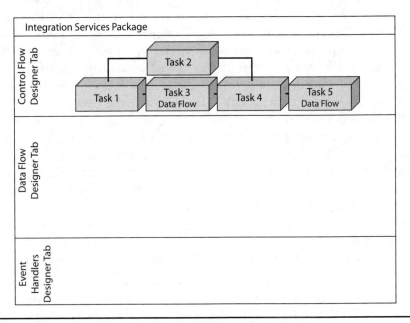

Figure 7-2   *The Integration Services package structure Control Flow Designer tab*

Toolbox and placing it in the control flow. We need to drill down into a data flow task to define the contents of that data flow, as shown in Figure 7-3. This is done by double-clicking a data flow task on the Control Flow Designer tab or clicking the Data Flow Designer tab and selecting the correct data flow task from the drop-down list. We can now define the details of the data flow on the Data Flow Designer tab. As might be expected, only Data Flow control items are displayed in the SSIS Toolbox when the Data Flow Designer tab is selected.

Integration Services packages are event-driven. This means we can specify routines to execute when a particular event occurs. An *event* can be the completion of a task or an error that occurs during task execution. The routine for the event is known as an *event handler* and is defined as a *control flow*. However, event handler control flows are created on the Event Handlers Designer tab rather than on the Control Flow Designer tab, as shown in Figure 7-4.

The same Control Flow items that can be used on the Control Flow Designer tab can also be used to create event handler tasks on the Event Handlers Designer tab. These might include sending an e-mail to update the administrator on the status of a package or executing an alternative data flow when a task fails. When a data flow task is used in an event handler, the details of the data flow are defined on the Data Flow Designer tab, as shown in Figure 7-5.

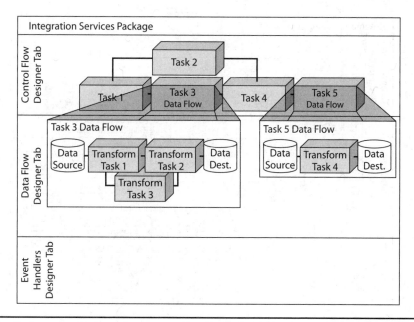

Figure 7-3   *The Integration Services package structure Data Flow Designer tab*

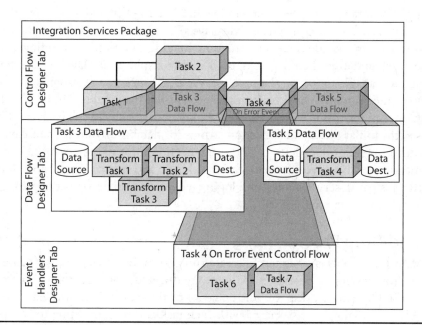

Figure 7-4   *The Integration Services package structure Event Handlers Designer tab*

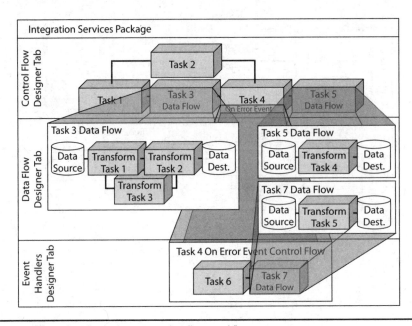

Figure 7-5 *Defining a data flow task in an event handler control flow*

The rightmost tab of the Designer window in Figure 7-1 provides access to the Package Explorer. The *Package Explorer* displays all the contents of the Integration Services package in a single tree-view structure. In addition to the control flow tasks, data flow tasks, and event handler tasks, the Package Explorer displays all the parameters and variables available for use in the package. We discuss the use of parameters and variables in Integration Services packages (as well as the Parameters tab) in Chapter 8.

The Connections tray is used to manage all the connections in the package. This includes paths to flat files and connection strings for databases. Rather than having this spread throughout the package, all this connection information is stored in the Connections tray. This makes it much easier to locate and manage the connection information as paths, server names, and login credentials change, or as the package is used in different server environments.

Drag-and-Drop Programming

SQL Server Data Tools is designed to create Integration Services packages using a drag-and-drop development style. Task items are dragged from the SSIS Toolbox and placed on the Designer workspace. The behavior of these tasks is controlled by setting properties in the dialog box associated with each task and by connecting the output from one task to the input of another. Some expressions may be required, but these tend to be straightforward, single-line comparison statements, rather than more complicated, multiline programming constructs.

Data manipulations can be done through Integration Services tasks without writing the data to disk. These tasks work with the data in buffers kept in physical memory. Pointers to these memory buffers are passed from one task to another throughout the processing. The only time data is written to disk during a data pipeline process is when it exceeds the size of the physical memory available. All of this makes it easy to develop complex packages while ensuring fast, efficient operation.

Control Flow Tasks

As we create our Integration Services packages, we use a top-down approach. First, we use the Control Flow Designer tab to define the tasks that the package will perform. Next, we use precedence arrows to define the tasks' order of execution and any dependencies between them. Then, we drill down into each of the data flow tasks to define their operation. Finally, we add any event handlers or other programming needed to get the package functioning in the manner required.

We begin, then, on the Control Flow Designer tab, by specifying the tasks that must be accomplished by the package. We create tasks by dragging Control Flow items from the SSIS Toolbox and placing them on the Control Flow Designer tab. Each item taken from the SSIS Toolbox becomes a control flow task. This is shown in Figure 7-6.

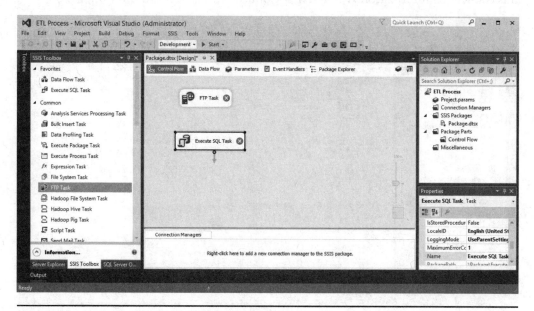

Figure 7-6   *Creating control flow tasks from the SSIS Toolbox*

The red circle with the white *X* on the control flow task indicates that the task is in an error state because some of the required properties for the task have not been set or have been set improperly. Hovering the mouse over a task with this symbol displays a message explaining the error. In other situations, a yellow triangle with a black exclamation point appears on a task. This indicates a warning message is associated with this task. Again, hovering the mouse over the task displays the warning message. A task with a warning executes, but a task with an error does not.

We can set the properties of a task by double-clicking the task to display its Editor dialog box. This is shown in Figure 7-7. We can also select the task and modify its properties using the Properties window. We look at the properties of each task in detail in the next section of this chapter.

When creating an Integration Services package, it is important to change the default name for each task that is placed in the package. The names should be changed to a phrase that accurately describes the functionality performed by that task. It is also a good idea to enter a short explanation of each task in the Description property of the task. The description is displayed when we hover over the task on the Control Flow Designer tab. Entering meaningful information for each task makes the package self-documenting and, consequently, much easier to test, debug, and maintain.

Connection Managers

Any time a control flow task must make a connection to a database or to the file system, this connection information is stored in a Connection Manager in the Connections

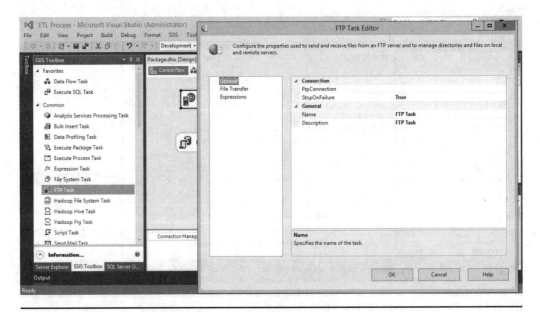

Figure 7-7   *Setting the properties of a task using the task's Editor dialog box*

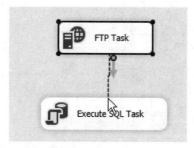

Figure 7-8   *Making a precedence connection between two tasks*

tray. This makes it easier to move packages from one server to another or from a development environment to a production environment. When database connection information or file system paths need to be modified to work on a different server, we do not need to look for them throughout the package. Instead, they are conveniently located in one place: the Connections tray.

We take a look at creating some of the most commonly used connections in the "Learn By Doing" sections in Chapter 8.

Precedence Arrows

We control the order in which tasks are executed by connecting the precedence arrow from one task to the task that is to run after it. To do this, we select a task and then click the green arrow that appears below that task. We drag this arrow until the mouse pointer is over the task that should follow during execution. This is shown in Figure 7-8. When we release the mouse button, the green arrow connects the two tasks, as shown in Figure 7-9. This is known as a *precedence constraint* because it constrains one task to run after another.

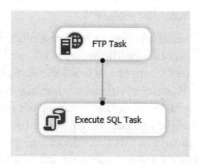

Figure 7-9   *The precedence arrow*

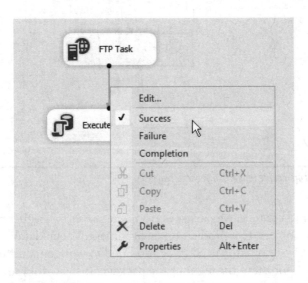

Figure 7-10 *The precedence arrow context menu*

By default, the precedence arrow is green, meaning the second task will execute only after the successful completion of the first task. This is the "Success" precedence. When we right-click the arrow, a context menu appears, as shown in Figure 7-10. Three options on the context menu—Success, Failure, and Completion—allow us to select the type of precedence the arrow represents.

NOTE

For those with red-green color blindness, you can use Tools | Options on the main menu to display the Options dialog box. In the Options dialog box, go to the Business Intelligence Designers | Integration Services Designers | General page, and select Show precedence constraint labels under Accessibility. This will display a label on each precedence constraint arrow, in addition to the color coding.

When we select Failure from the context menu, the precedence arrow changes from green to red. With "Failure" precedence, the second task executes only after the failure of the first task. When we select Completion from the context menu, the precedence arrow changes to blue. With "Completion" precedence, the second task executes after the first task has completed without regard to whether the first task succeeded or failed.

A single task can have multiple precedence arrows connecting it to other tasks. When we select a task that already has its precedence arrow connected to another task, a second precedence arrow automatically appears. This is shown in Figure 7-11. This second arrow can be connected to another task. When a task has two precedence

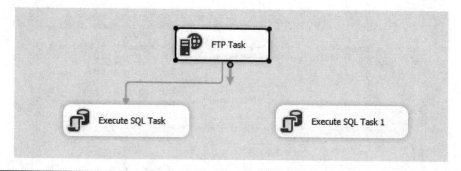

Figure 7-11 *A control flow task with a second precedence arrow*

arrows connected to subsequent tasks, a third arrow appears. And so on. Each of these precedence arrows can be set to Success, Failure, or Completion as appropriate. The result can be a complex sequence of tasks, such as the one shown in Figure 7-12.

We can double-click a precedence arrow or right-click the arrow and select Edit from the context menu to access the Precedence Constraint Editor dialog box, shown in Figure 7-13. The Value drop-down list on this dialog box provides another way to select among Success, Failure, and Completion. If these three options do not provide enough flexibility, we can also attach expressions to a precedence arrow.

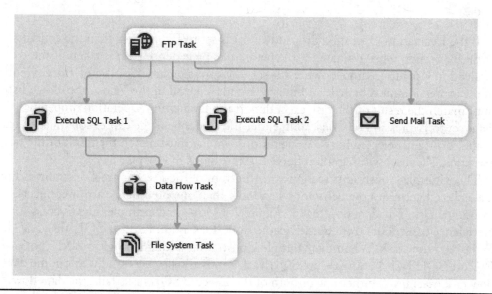

Figure 7-12 *Using precedence arrows to make a complex sequence of tasks*

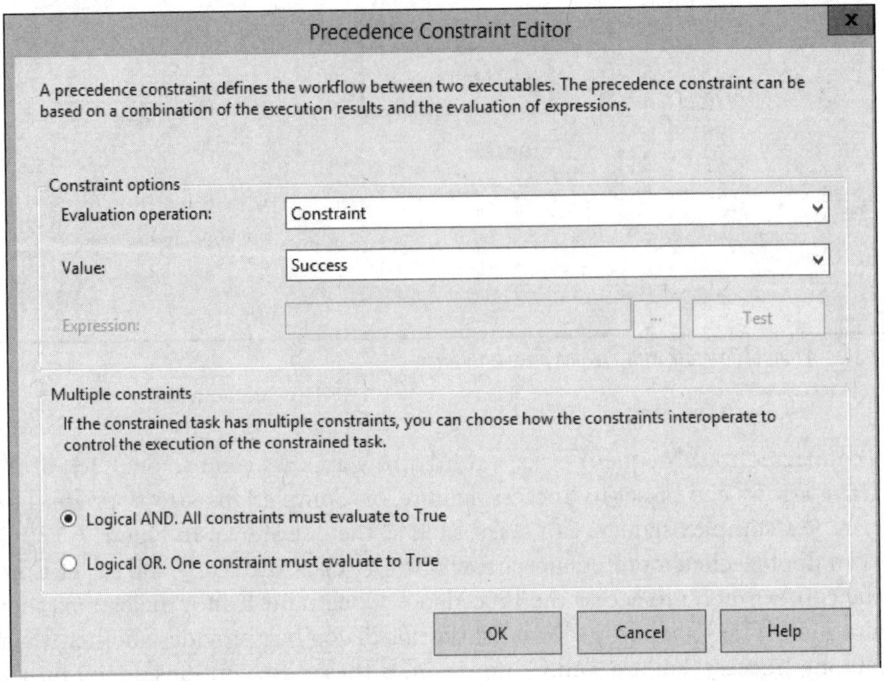

Figure 7-13   *The Precedence Constraint Editor dialog box*

If the Evaluation Operation drop-down list is set to Expression, then the contents of the expression must evaluate to true before this precedence path is taken. If the Evaluation Operation drop-down list is set to Expression and Constraint, the contents of the expression must be true and the constraint selected in the Value drop-down list must match the result of the task execution. If the Evaluation Operation drop-down list is set to Expression or Constraint, either the contents of the expression must be true or the constraint selected in the Value drop-down list must match the result of the task execution. We discuss Integration Services expressions in Chapter 8.

The Multiple Constraints section at the bottom of the Precedence Constraint Editor dialog box determines the behavior when more than one precedence arrow connects to a single task. The data flow task in Figure 7-12 is a good example. The Success precedence constraints from both Execute SQL Task 1 and Execute SQL Task 2 lead to the data flow task. When the Multiple Constraints setting is Logical AND, both Execute SQL Task 1 and Execute SQL Task 2 must finish successfully before the data flow task executes. If either one or both of the Execute SQL tasks fails, the data flow task cannot execute. When the Multiple Constraints setting is Logical OR, the data flow task executes if either one or the other of the Execute SQL tasks is successful. Changing the Multiple Constraints setting on any one of the precedence arrows leading into a task changes the Multiple Constraints setting for all of the precedence arrows leading into that task.

It is possible to have one or more control flow tasks in a package that are not connected by precedence arrows to any other task. These tasks are not constrained to execute in any particular order, and they are not constrained by the success or failure of any other task. These disconnected tasks execute every time the package is run, no matter what happens with the other tasks in the package.

Data Flow

Once we set the precedence constraints for the control flow tasks in the package, we can define each of the data flows. This is done on the Data Flow Designer tab. Each data flow task that was added to the control flow has its own layout on the Data Flow Designer tab. We can switch between different data flows using the Data Flow Task drop-down list located at the top of the Data Flow tab.

The Data Flow SSIS Toolbox contains three types of items: data flow sources, data flow transformations, and data flow destinations. Data flow sources enable us to read data from almost any vendor's relational database, flat file, or Extensible Markup Language (XML) source. Data flow destinations let us write data to these same locations, as well as to certain Analysis Services structures. Data flow transformations operate on the data as it moves through the data flow. In most cases, the transformations change the data to increase its appropriateness for the destination.

Data flow tasks are connected by flow path arrows. These are connected in the same way that control flow tasks are connected by precedence arrows. Green flow path arrows indicate the route that valid data will take through the task. This is the output flow of the task. Red flow path arrows indicate the route that invalid data follow. This is the error flow of the task.

The flow path from a data source to a data destination is called a *data flow segment*. The simplest data flow segment has only a single source and a single destination, connected by a flow path. This type of segment simply copies data from one place to another. Transformation tasks are added to the segment to modify the data as it moves from the source to the destination. In fact, as we see in the sections on data flow, we can do some sophisticated data manipulation using the transformation tasks in Integration Services.

Data flow segments may contain multiple data sources, with the data flow from each source being combined with a merge or union task. Likewise, a segment may have multiple data destinations, with the data flow being divided by an error path, a conditional split task, or a multicast task. We gain even more flexibility with the ability to have multiple, distinct data segments in the same data flow.

When a data flow has multiple segments, the order in which the segments are executed is determined by the execution plan created at run time. This means that we cannot depend on the order in which multiple segments are executed within a single data flow. If the multiple segments are performing independent tasks, such as loading data into different dimensions of a data mart, this is not a problem. However, if these multiple segments are performing dependent tasks, such that one segment must be completed before another segment can begin, the segments should be split up into different data flow tasks. The order of execution can then be enforced by a precedence arrow from one data flow task to the other on the Control Flow Designer tab.

Package Items

In this section, we take a look at the Control Flow and Data Flow items that can be used in an Integration Services package. We discuss how each item can be used in a package, and we look at the task dialog box provided for configuring each task. Because of the tremendous amount of capability and flexibility available from Integration Services tasks, it would take the remainder of this book, and then some, to provide a complete description. Instead, this section is intended to give you some familiarity with the purpose and capabilities of each task.

Control Flow

The Control Flow SSIS Toolbox contains three types of objects: Containers, Control Flow tasks, and Maintenance Plan tasks. Each object has a dialog box that lets us configure that component in a straightforward manner. The dialog box is launched by double-clicking the component in the design area or right-clicking the item and selecting Edit from the context menu.

Control Flow SSIS Toolbox Organization

The Control Flow SSIS Toolbox is divided into several sections: Favorites, Common, Containers, and Other Tasks. These divisions are designed to help you more easily find objects within the SSIS Toolbox. The Favorites section is for the objects you use most often. The Common section is for objects that are used often, but not as frequently as the favorites. Containers are set aside in their own section because they function differently than the other objects. Everything else ends up in the Other Tasks section.

You can move objects between sections to customize the arrangement to suit your tastes. Right-click an object in the SSIS Toolbox to bring up the context menu. Then select the section where you would like the object to be moved. You can expand or hide any of these sections by clicking the triangle to the left of the section name.

Containers

We begin by looking at the containers. *Containers* are a special type of item that can hold other Control Flow items and Maintenance Plan tasks. They help us repeat a set of tasks or organize groups of tasks within the package.

For Loop Container   The *For Loop container* enables us to repeat a segment of a control flow. In this way, it functions much the same as a FOR... NEXT loop in Visual Basic or a *for* loop in C#. The For Loop container in Figure 7-14 executes the Execute SQL task and the Data Flow task multiple times.

The number of times the content of the container is executed is controlled by three properties of the For Loop container: InitExpression, EvalExpression, and AssignExpression. These properties are shown in the For Loop Editor dialog box in Figure 7-15. The InitExpression is executed once at the beginning of the loop to initialize the variable (or other item) that is controlling the loop. The EvalExpression is then evaluated. If the EvalExpression evaluates to true, the loop's content is executed. If the EvalExpression is false, the loop is exited. After each execution of the loop's contents, the AssignExpression is evaluated, followed by another evaluation of the EvalExpression.

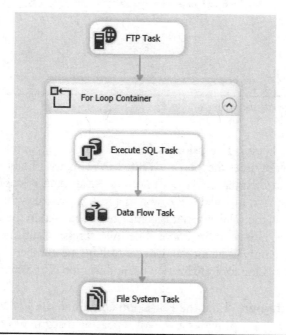

Figure 7-14   *A For Loop container in a control flow*

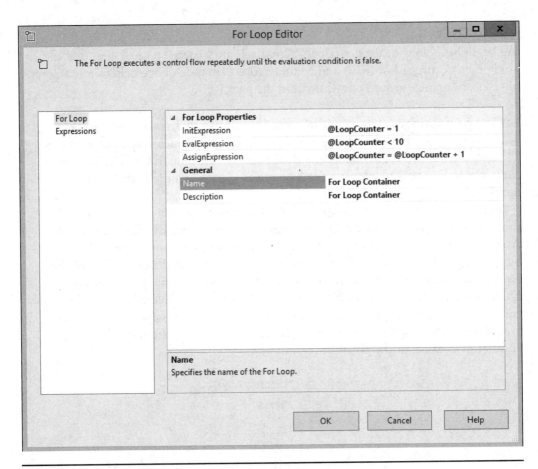

Figure 7-15 *The For Loop Editor dialog box*

The For Loop in Figure 7-15 is using a variable called @LoopCounter in the expressions to control the number of times the loop is executed. (We discuss variables and Integration Services expressions in Chapter 8.) We don't need to use an explicit loop counter variable to control the loop. In fact, any valid expression that results in a true value while the loop should continue and a false value when it is complete can be used in the EvalExpression property to control the number of iterations. The InitExpression and AssignExpression properties can be left empty if the mechanism controlling the number of iterations does not require a separate expression for initialization or modification of the counter.

Foreach Loop Container   Like the For Loop container, the Foreach Loop container also provides a way of repeating a segment of a control flow. However, rather than have an expression to control when the loop is exited, the *Foreach Loop container* iterates one time for each item in a collection. The following collections can be used:

▶ Each file in a given folder matching a given file specification

▶ Each row of the first table in an ADO recordset or an ADO.NET dataset

▶ Each row of all tables in an ADO.NET dataset

▶ Each table in an ADO.NET dataset

▶ Each item from a variable that holds a collection

▶ Each node in an XML nodelist

▶ Each object in an SMO collection

▶ Each file in an Hadoop Distributed File System (HDFS) directory matching a given file specification

Each time the Foreach Loop iterates, it selects a different object from the collection. The name of this object can then be mapped to one or more properties of the control flow tasks inside the container. In this way, the tasks inside the container can operate on each object in the collection.

For example, Figure 7-16 shows the Nightly Transfer package. This package uses FTP to transfer data files from a cloud-based line-of-business system to the C:\FTP_Rcv directory on the server. Several .dat files may be received by a given transfer. After the FTP transfer is complete, the Foreach Loop processes each of the files that is received. The Collection page of the Foreach Loop Editor dialog box in Figure 7-17 shows the configuration of the Foreach Loop necessary to accomplish this task.

The Data Flow task and the File System task within the Foreach Loop use the Received.DAT Files connection, shown at the bottom of Figure 7-16, to operate on a given data file received from the cloud. For the Data Flow task and the File System task to operate on each file received, we need a way to change the connection string of the Received.DAT connection for each iteration of the loop. To do this, we first assign the fully qualified filename to a variable. This is done on the Variable Mappings page of the Foreach Loop container as follows:

Variable	Index
User::FileName	0

User::FileName is a user variable in the package. The entry in the Index column is an index to the Foreach Loop collection. When used with a collection of files, index 0 contains the file specification and is the only valid index. Next we create an expression

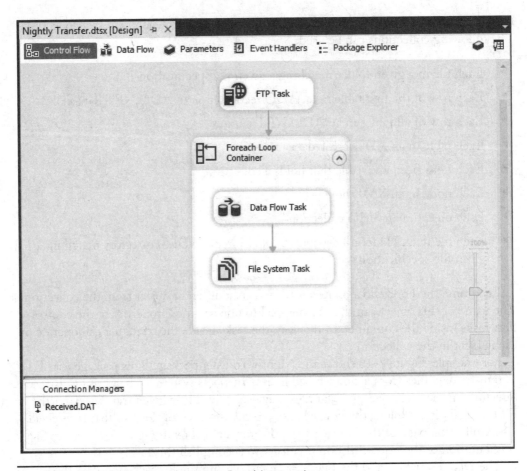

Figure 7-16 *The Nightly Transfer package using a Foreach Loop container*

in the Received.DAT Connection Manager to assign the value of the User::FileName to its ConnectionString.

Sequence Container Unlike the For Loop and Foreach Loop containers, the Sequence container does not change the control flow. Instead, the purpose of the *Sequence container* is to help organize tasks in a package. The Sequence container can be used to do the following:

▶ Organize a large package into logical sections for easier development and debugging

▶ Manage properties for a group of tasks by setting the properties on the container, rather than on the individual tasks

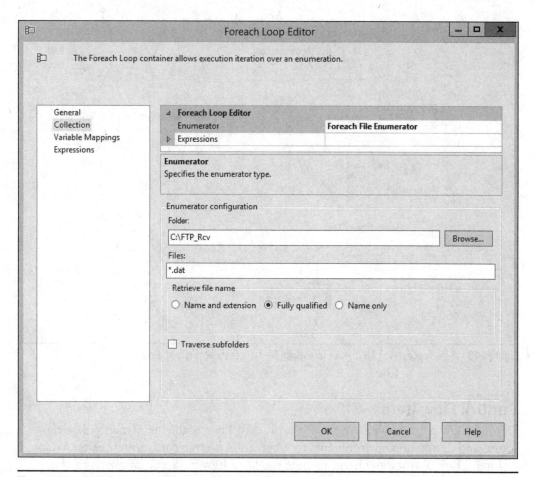

Figure 7-17   *The Collection page of the Foreach Loop container in the Nightly Transfer package*

▶ Allow a group of tasks to be easily enabled or disabled to aid package development and debugging

▶ Provide a variable scope that includes multiple tasks, but does not include the entire package

All of the container objects—For Loop, Foreach Loop, and Sequence—have the capability to hide their content. Figure 7-18 shows two Sequence containers. Sequence Container 2 is hiding its content. The content of a container is hidden or shown by clicking the down arrow.

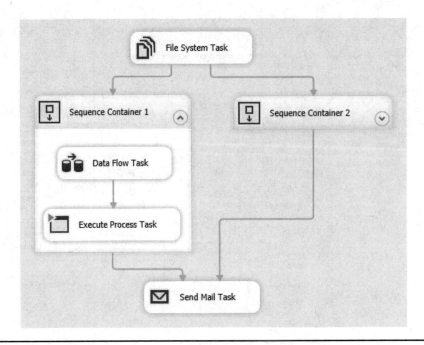

Figure 7-18 *Sequence Container 1 is showing its content. Sequence Container 2 is hiding its content.*

Control Flow Items

Control Flow items implement the ETL process. They enable us to manipulate the source and destination environments to prepare for, execute, and clean up after a data transfer. The Control Flow items include the Data Flow task that implements the actual transfer of data from source to destination.

Analysis Services Execute DDL Task   The *Analysis Services Execute DDL task* enables us to run a statement on an Analysis Services server. The statement must be a valid Data Definition Language (DDL) query, which lets us create, modify, delete, and process Analysis Services objects, such as tables or cubes and dimensions. The Analysis Services Execute DDL Task Editor dialog box is shown in Figure 7-19.

Analysis Services Processing Task   The *Analysis Services Processing task* enables us to process objects in Analysis Services. This can include tables, cubes, dimensions, and data mining models. This is important

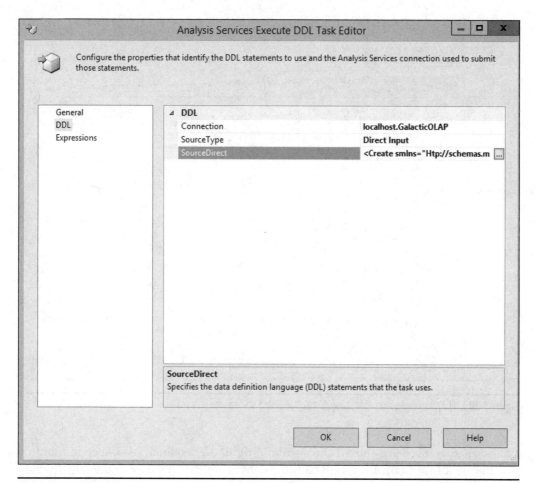

Figure 7-19 *The Analysis Services Execute DDL Task Editor dialog box*

after we have made major data changes that affect any of these objects. The Analysis Services Processing Task Editor dialog box is shown in Figure 7-20.

Bulk Insert Task The *Bulk Insert task* lets us rapidly copy data from a text file into a SQL Server table or view. This is equivalent to using the bcp utility program to do a bulk data load. In fact, we can use a bcp format file with the Bulk Insert task. The Bulk Insert Task Editor dialog box is shown in Figure 7-21.

The Bulk Insert task is the fastest way to move large amounts of data into a SQL table. Remember, however, that this data must come from a text file directly, it cannot be

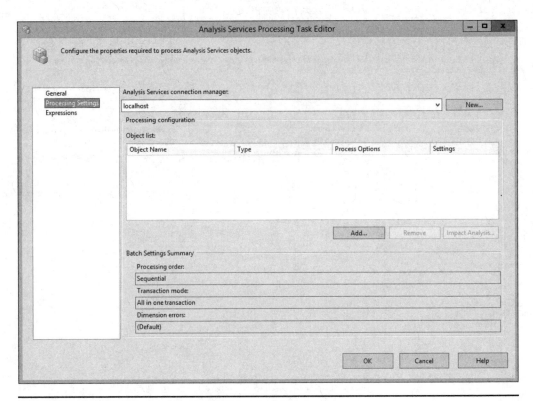

Figure 7-20   *The Analysis Services Processing Task Editor dialog box*

transformed as it is being moved and sysadmin rights are required. Also, keep in mind that the Bulk Insert task always appends the data to any existing data in the target table.

CDC Control Task   The *CDC Control task* is used to implement change data capture for a table within Integration Services. It plays four different roles in the change data capture process. This is determined by the CDC control operation property.

The change data capture process requires two Integration Services packages. The first package is run once to do the initial load of data from the source table to the destination table. This is the Initial Load package. The second package is run periodically to take the incremental changes made to the source table and apply them to the destination table. This is the Incremental Load package.

The CDC Control task is used in the Initial Load package to record the Log Sequence Number at the beginning of the data load and at the end of the data load. To accomplish this, a CDC Control task is placed at the beginning of the control

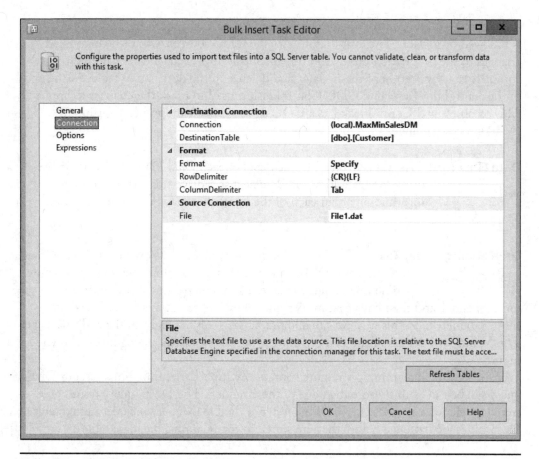

Figure 7-21   *The Bulk Insert Task Editor dialog box*

flow with the CDC control operation property set to "Mark initial load start." This is
followed in the control flow by the Data Flow task that copies the records from the
source to the destination. Finally, a second CDC Control task is placed in the control
flow after the Data Flow task. This second CDC Control task is configured the
same as the first CDC Control task with the exception of its CDC control operation
property, which is set to "Mark initial load end."

The CDC Control task is used in the Incremental Load package in conjunction
with the CDC source in the data flow. The CDC Control task determines which
changes to the source table have not yet been applied to the destination table. The
CDC source uses that information to ensure it only sends the unapplied data changes
through the data flow. (More on the CDC source in the "Data Flow Sources" section
of this chapter.) The CDC Control task is placed at the beginning of the control

flow with the CDC control operation property set to "Get processing range." This is followed by a Data Flow task that utilizes the CDC source to send the unapplied changes to the destination table. Additional control flow tasks may be required to complete the application of the updates and deletes on the destination table. At the end of the control flow, a second CDC Control task is used to mark the changes as applied. This second CDC Control task has a CDC control operation property setting of "Mark processed range."

Data Flow Task   As was stated earlier, the detail of each *Data Flow task* is configured using the Data Flow tab. The next section of this chapter contains information about each of the items that may be used on the Data Flow tab.

Data Mining Query Task   The *Data Mining Query task* lets us execute a Data Mining Expression (DMX) query against an existing data mining structure. The DMX query enables us to feed parameter values to a data mining model, and then have that mining model make predictions for us based on those parameters. In this way, we can add predictive analytics right in the SSIS package. The Mining Model tab of the Data Mining Query Task Editor dialog box is shown in Figure 7-22.

If the selected data mining structure contains multiple data mining models, our DMX query can be run against more than one of these models. The DMX query results are stored in relational database tables. If the result of the DMX query includes nested tables, those tables are flattened before they are stored in the relational database tables.

Data Profiling Task   The *Data Profiling task* gathers information about a set of data. This can be used to determine information about a particular set of data we intend to process through an Integration Services package. We can use this information to make intelligent decisions as we design the package that will process this data and the data mart tables that will contain it.

The following profiling operations can be done using this task:

- ▶ **Candidate Key Profile Request**   Determines whether a column or a set of columns is a unique identifier for the rows in a table. Valid for integer, character, and date/time data types.

- ▶ **Column Length Distribution Profile Request**   Provides a list of the distinct string lengths present in a column. Valid for character data types.

- ▶ **Column Null Ratio Profile Request**   Reports the number of NULLS in a column as a percentage of the total number of rows. Valid for all data types.

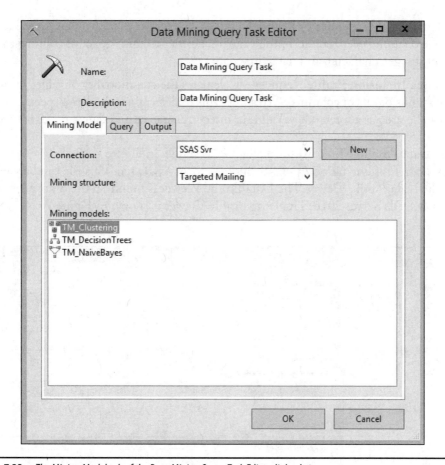

Figure 7-22   *The Mining Model tab of the Data Mining Query Task Editor dialog box*

- ► **Column Pattern Profile Request**   Determines a set of regular expressions that are valid for a specified percentage of the values in a column. Valid for character data types.

- ► **Column Statistics Profile Request**   Finds the maximum, minimum, average, and standard deviation of the data in a numeric column. Finds the maximum and minimum of the data in a date/time column. Valid for numeric and date/time data types.

- ► **Column Value Distribution Profile Request**   Reports the distinct set of values in a column and the number of occurrences of that value as a percentage of the total number of rows. Valid for integer, character, and date/time data types.

▶ **Functional Dependency Profile Request**   Determines how much the value in one column is dependent on the value in another column or set of columns. Valid for integer, character, and date/time data types.

▶ **Value Inclusion Profile Request**   Calculates the commonality of values in two columns or sets of columns. We can use this to determine whether a specific column can be used as a foreign key. Valid for integer, character, and date/time data types.

The Data Profiling Task Editor dialog box is shown in Figure 7-23.

The Data Profiling task outputs its findings to an XML file. This file can be viewed using the Data Profile Viewer. The Data Profile Viewer is found on the Start page under Microsoft SQL Server 2016. The Data Profile Viewer is shown in Figure 7-24.

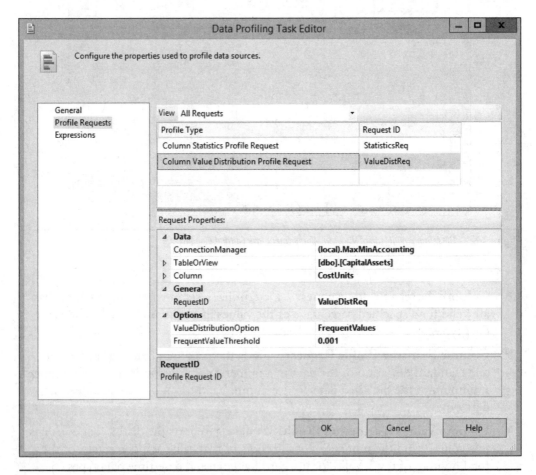

Figure 7-23   *The Data Profiling Task Editor dialog box*

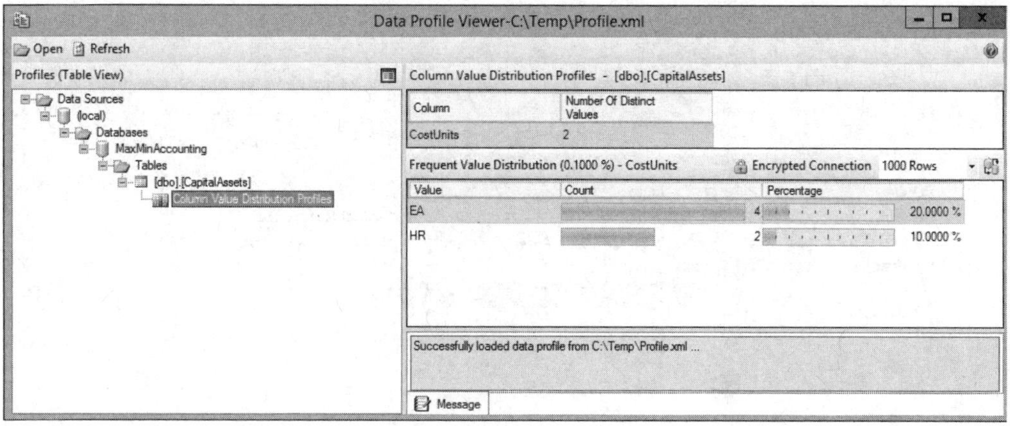

Figure 7-24   *The Data Profile Viewer*

Execute Package Task   The *Execute Package task* lets us execute a different Integration Services package. The package containing the Execute Package task is the parent package, and the package being executed by that task is the child package. The child package can be stored in SQL Server or in a structured storage file.

The child package can execute as a separate process by setting the ExecuteOutOfProcess property to true. Otherwise, it executes in the same process as the parent package. Executing a child package as a separate process means an error in the child process cannot crash the parent process. Creating separate processes for each child package does, however, add some overhead each time a child package is launched.

The Execute Package Task Editor dialog box is shown in Figure 7-25.

Execute Process Task   The *Execute Process task* enables us to execute a program or a batch file as part of an Integration Services package. This task can be used to do such things as unzipping compressed files. The Execute Process Task Editor dialog box lets us specify the command-line arguments and working directory, as shown in Figure 7-26. We can also specify variables for the standard input, standard output, and standard error of the process.

Execute SQL Task   The *Execute SQL task* enables us to execute SQL statements or stored procedures. The contents of variables can be used for input, output, or input/output parameters and the return value. We can also save the result set from the SQL statements or stored procedure in a package variable.

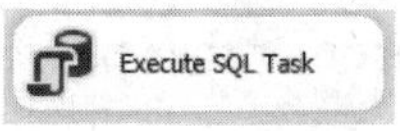

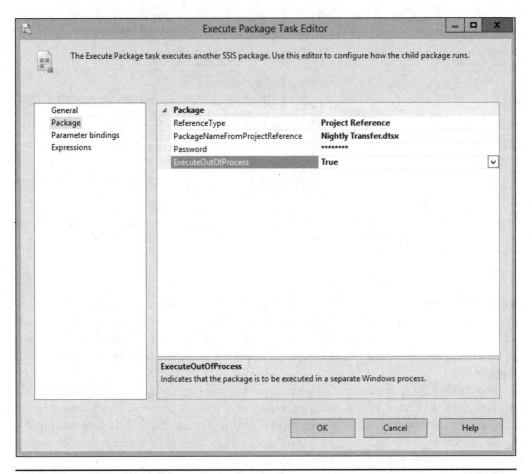

Figure 7-25   *The Execute Package Task Editor dialog box*

This result set could be a single value, a multirow/multicolumn result set, or an XML document. The Execute SQL Task Editor dialog box is shown in Figure 7-27.

Expression Task   The *Expression task* enables us to assign a value to a variable. Using the Expression Builder dialog box, shown in Figure 7-28, we can build a valid assignment statement in the Expression area. The Evaluate Expression button ensures the assignment statement is valid and shows the resulting value. During package execution, the value that results from the expression at that time will be assigned to the variable specified in the assignment statement.

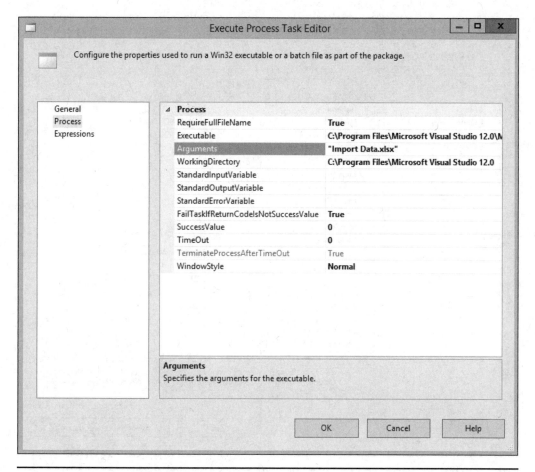

Figure 7-26   *The Execute Process Task Editor dialog box*

File System Task   The *File System task* lets us perform one of the following file system functions:

- ► Copy a directory
- ► Copy a file
- ► Create a directory
- ► Delete a directory

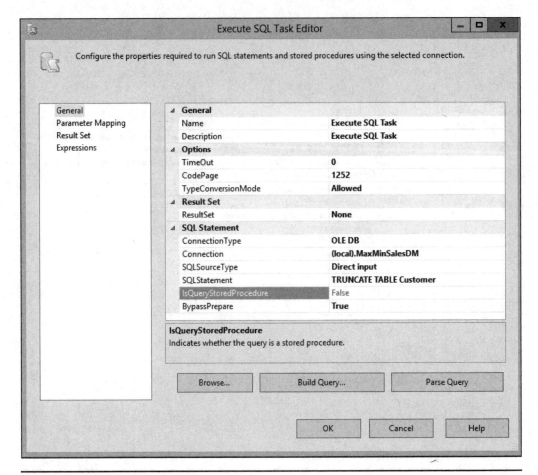

Figure 7-27 *The Execute SQL Task Editor dialog box*

- ▶ Delete the contents of a directory
- ▶ Delete a file
- ▶ Move a directory
- ▶ Move a file
- ▶ Rename a file
- ▶ Set the attributes of a directory or file

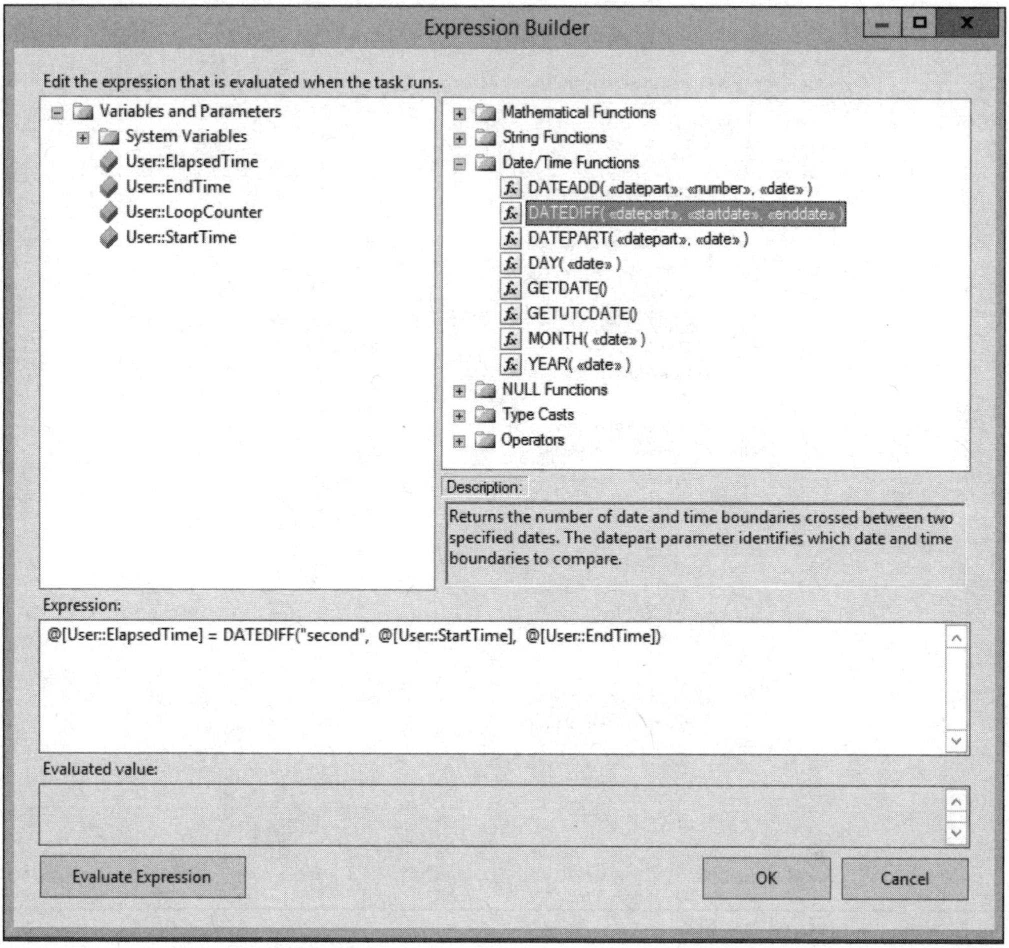

Figure 7-28   *The Expression Builder dialog box*

We must create a File Connection Manager in the Connections tray to specify the source and, if necessary, the destination for the file operation. The File System Task Editor dialog box is shown in Figure 7-29.

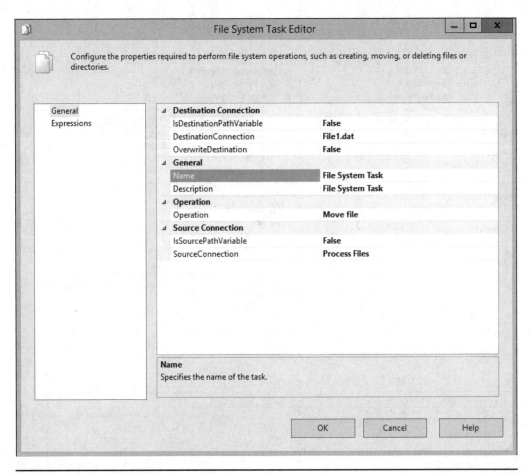

Figure 7-29   *The File System Task Editor dialog box*

FTP Task   The *FTP task* enables us to perform the following functions on an FTP site:

- ► Send files
- ► Receive files
- ► Create a local directory
- ► Create a remote directory

- ▶ Remove a local directory
- ▶ Remove a remote directory
- ▶ Delete local files
- ▶ Delete remote files

We must create an FTP Connection Manager in the Connections tray to specify the address and login credentials for the FTP server. In addition, a File Connection Manager or the content of a package variable is used to specify the local path for the transfer. The FTP Task Editor dialog box is shown in Figure 7-30.

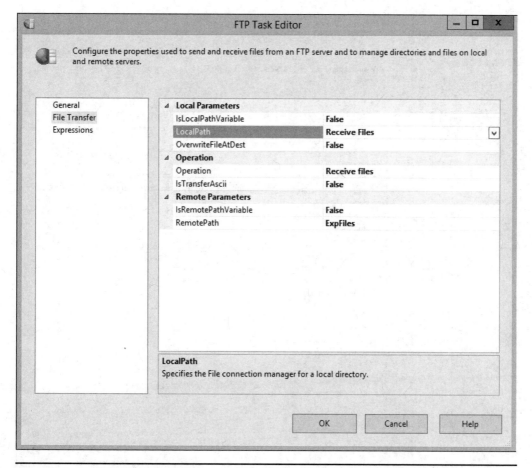

Figure 7-30   *The FTP Task Editor dialog box*

Hadoop File System Task   The *Hadoop File System task* enables us to copy files or directories as follows:

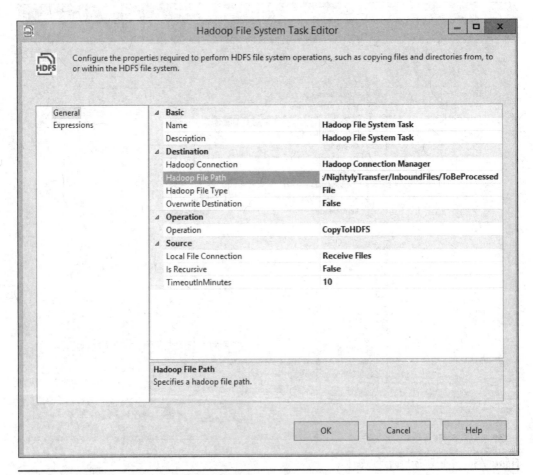

- ▶ From a Windows file system (NTFS) to a Hadoop Distributed File System (HDFS)
- ▶ From a Hadoop Distributed File System to a Windows file system
- ▶ From one location in a Hadoop Distributed File System to another

We must create a Hadoop Connection Manager in the Connections tray to specify the location of the Hadoop cluster. The Hadoop File System Task Editor dialog box is shown in Figure 7-31.

Figure 7-31   *The Hadoop File System Task Editor dialog box*

Hadoop Hive Task   The *Hadoop Hive task* enables us to execute a Hive script on a
Hadoop cluster. We must create a Hadoop Connection Manager in
the Connections tray to specify the location of the Hadoop cluster.
The Hadoop Hive Task Editor dialog box is shown in Figure 7-32.

Hadoop Pig Task   The *Hadoop Pig task* enables us to run Pig script on a Hadoop
cluster. We must create a Hadoop Connection Manager in the
Connections tray to specify the location of the Hadoop cluster.
The Hadoop Pig Task Editor dialog box is shown in Figure 7-33.

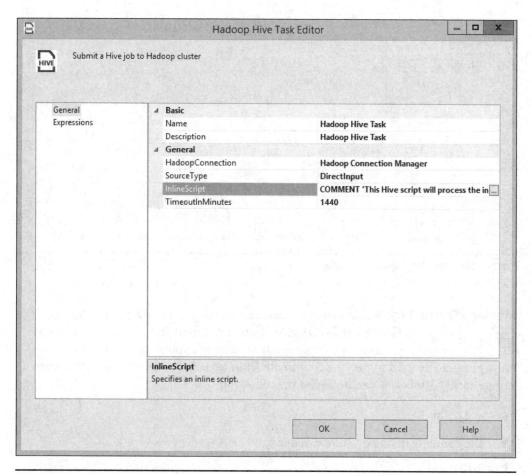

Figure 7-32   *The Hadoop Hive Task Editor dialog box*

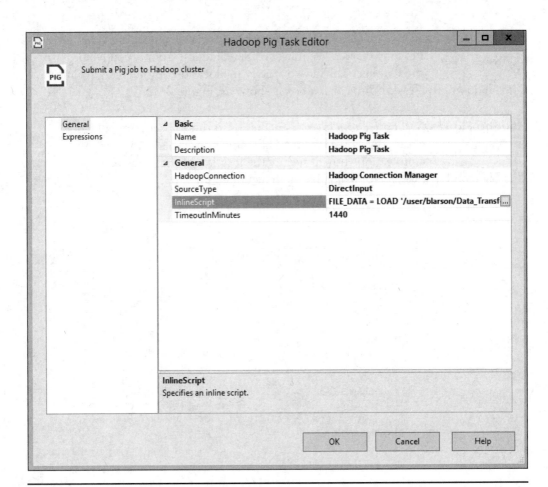

Figure 7-33 *The Hadoop Pig Task Editor dialog box*

Message Queue Task The *Message Queue task* lets us send a Microsoft Message Queue (MSMQ) message to a different Integration Services package or to the message queue of another application. This messaging can be used to provide coordinated, but asynchronous, processing between various tasks. A message can be any of the following:

► A data file

► The contents of one or more variables

► A string

We must create an MSMQ Connection Manager in the Connections tray to specify the MSMQ queue to use with this task. The Message Queue Task Editor dialog box is shown in Figure 7-34.

Script Task   The *Script task* enables us to create .NET code for execution as part of our Integration Services package. The Script task can be used to execute transformations, perform complex calculations, or implement business logic that cannot be created using the other Integration Services tasks. The code resulting from a Script task can be precompiled for superior performance and scalability.

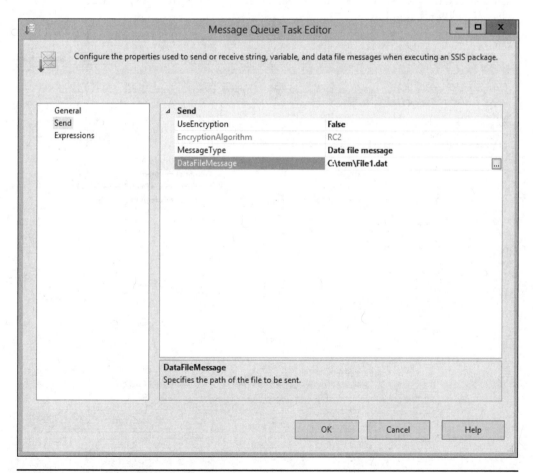

Figure 7-34   *The Message Queue Task Editor dialog box*

The Script Task Editor dialog box is shown in Figure 7-35. This dialog box is used to specify the .NET language used to create the script, as well as whether the script is precompiled. When a script is precompiled, the code is compiled as soon as the script is saved in the package. The compiled code is then saved in the package as well. This allows for much faster execution when the package is run. The only disadvantage to this approach: the size of the package becomes larger because it contains both the source code and the compiled version of that source code.

The EntryPoint property specifies which method is to be executed first when the Script task is run. The ReadOnlyVariables and ReadWriteVariables properties contain comma-separated lists of variables that are to be made available, either as read-only variables or as read-write variables, within the script. You can type in these variable names or use the ellipses (...) button to select the variables from a scrolling list in the Select Variables dialog box.

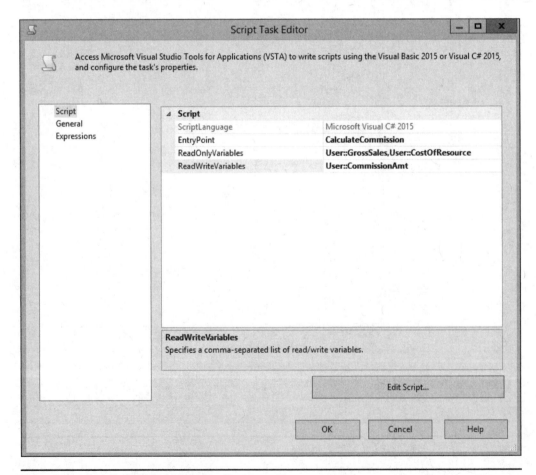

Figure 7-35   *The Script Task Editor dialog box*

Variables are accessed in our script using C# code similar to the following:

```
double GrossSales;

GrossSales = (double)Dts.Variables["GrossSalesAmt"].Value;

Dts.Variables["CurrentAmt"].Value = GrossSales;
```

where "GrossSalesAmt" and "CurrentAmt" are package variables. The equivalent Visual Basic code looks like this:

```
Dim GrossSales As Double

GrossSales = CDbl(Dts.Variables("GrossSalesAmt").Value)

Dts.Variables("CurrentAmt").Value = GrossSales
```

The value of a variable is always returned as a type object and must be cast to the appropriate type. Clicking Edit Script displays the Script Editing window, as shown in Figure 7-36.

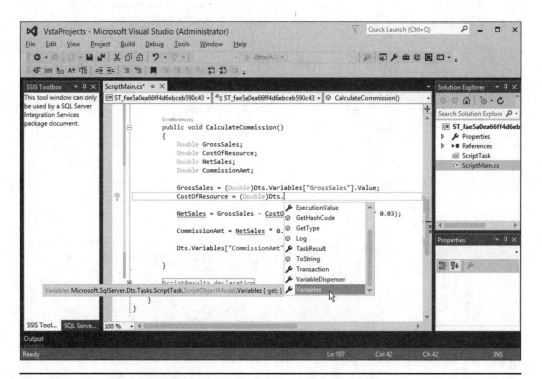

Figure 7-36   *The Script Task Script Editing window*

Send Mail Task   The *Send Mail task* lets us send an e-mail message as part of our
Integration Services package. This can be useful for alerting an
administrator to an error condition or notifying a key user that
a critical process has completed. The Send Mail task uses a Simple Mail Transfer
Protocol (SMTP) server to deliver the e-mail. We must create an SMTP Connection
Manager in the Connections tray to specify the SMTP server to use with this task.
The Send Mail Task Editor dialog box is shown in Figure 7-37.

The content of the e-mail message can come from a file or a package variable, or
it can be directly input as a string. If a file is used, we must create a File Connection
Manager in the Connections tray pointing to that file. One or more files can be
attached by specifying the path to each file in the Attachments property. If multiple
files are attached, the paths are separated by semicolons.

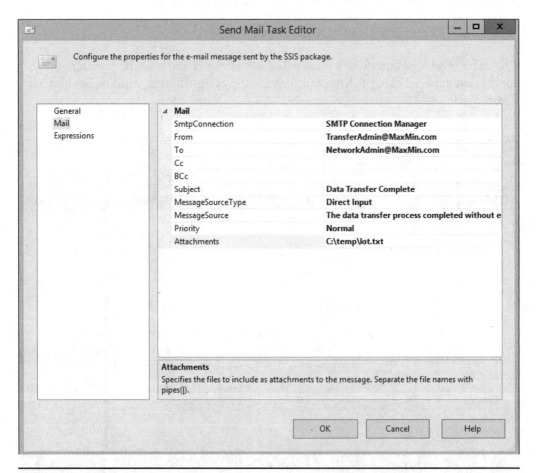

Figure 7-37   *The Send Mail Task Editor dialog box*

Transfer Database Task, Transfer Error Messages Task, Transfer Jobs Task, Transfer Logins Task, Transfer Master Stored Procedures Task, Transfer SQL Server Objects Task   There are a number of Control Flow items for transferring SQL Server objects from one server to another. The *Transfer Database task* is used to either transfer or move an entire database. Using the *Transfer Error Messages task*, we can copy user-defined error messages. The *Transfer Jobs task* is used to copy SQL Agent Jobs. The *Transfer Logins task* copies one or more SQL logins. Using the *Transfer Master Stored Procedures task*, we can copy user-defined stored procedures between master databases.

The *Transfer SQL Server Objects task* is used to copy any of the following items:

Object	SQL Server Version
Tables	2000 or later
Views	2000 or later
Stored Procedures	2000 or later
User-Defined Functions	2000 or later
Defaults	2000 or later
User-Defined Data Types	2000 or later
Partition Functions	2005 or later
Partition Schemes	2005 or later
Schemas	2005 or later
Assemblies	2005 or later
User-Defined Aggregates	2005 or later
User-Defined Types	2005 or later
XML Schema Collection	2005 or later

Web Service Task   The *Web Service task* lets us execute a web service method as part of our Integration Services package. We must create an HTTP Connection Manager in the Connections tray to specify the connection to the web service. Once a connection has been specified, a Web Services

Description Language file must be located to define the web methods that are available. We can then select the web method we want to execute, along with the parameters to be passed to that web method. This is shown in the Web Service Task Editor dialog box in Figure 7-38. The result returned by the web method call can be stored in a package variable or a file specified by a File Connection Manager in the Connections tray.

WMI Data Reader Task   The *WMI Data Reader task* enables us to execute a Windows Management Instrumentation (WMI) query to retrieve data about a computer. This could include data from an event log, a list of installed applications and their current versions, or the state of computer hardware. We must create a WMI Connection Manager in the Connections tray to specify the

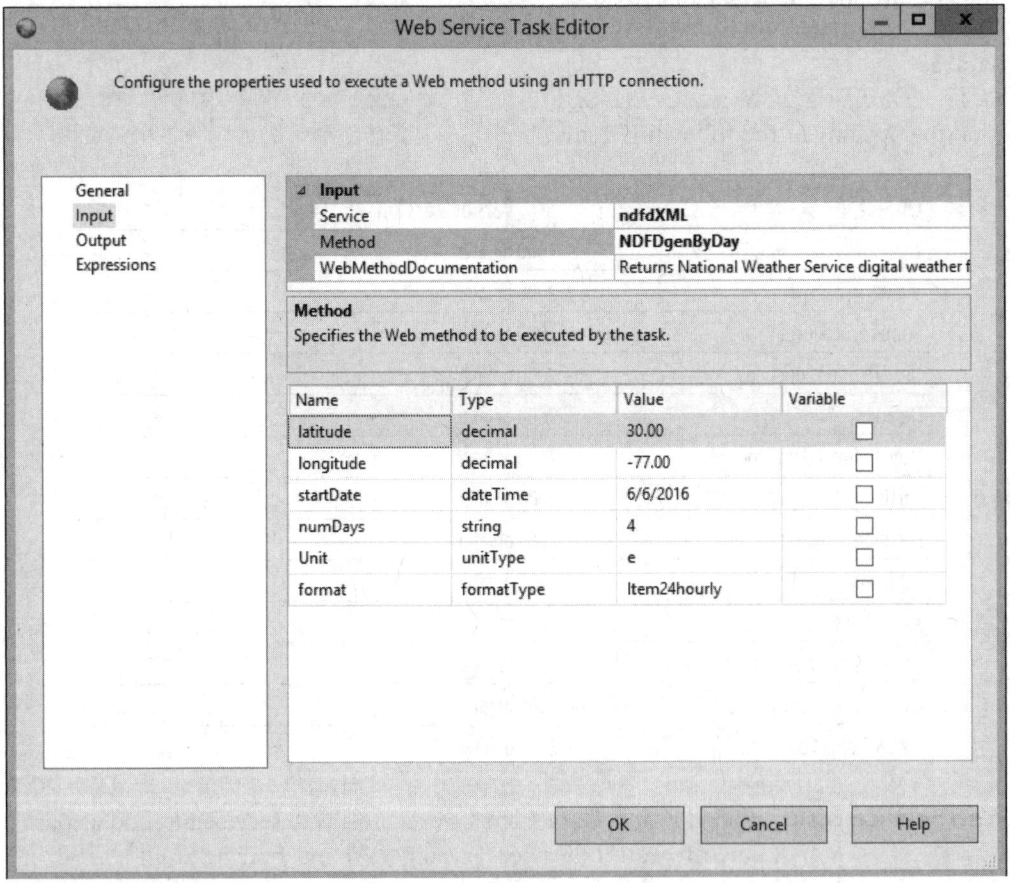

Figure 7-38   *The Web Service Task Editor dialog box*

computer that we want to query. The WMI Data Reader Task Editor dialog box is shown in Figure 7-39.

A *WMI query* is used to select the desired information. The output of the WMI query can be returned as a table, a set of property values, or a set of property name/value pairs. The output can be stored in a file, specified by a File Connection Manager, or in a package variable.

WMI Event Watcher Task   The *WMI Event Watcher task* lets us wait for a specific computer system event or state before continuing the execution of the Integration Services package. This enables us to do things,

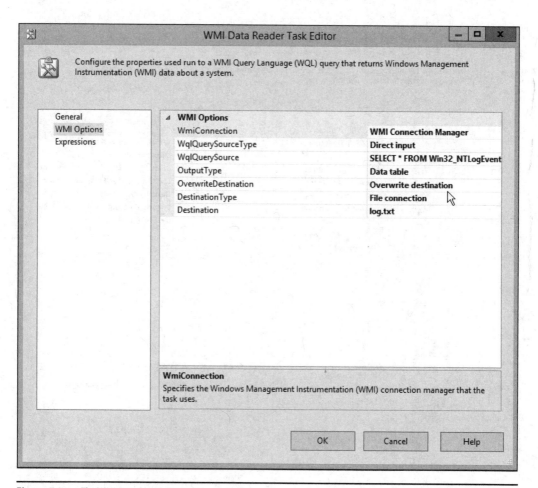

Figure 7-39   *The WMI Data Reader Task Editor dialog box*

such as wait for the server load to drop below a certain level or wait for a file to be copied to a specified folder. We must create a WMI Connection Manager in the Connections tray to specify the computer that we want to watch for the event. The WMI Event Watcher Task Editor dialog box is shown in Figure 7-40.

A WMI query is used to specify the event we want to watch for. We can then specify the desired behavior when the event occurs. The ActionAtEvent property determines if the event is simply logged or if it is logged and, at the same time, fires the Integration Services WMIEventWatcherEventOccurred event. If this Integration Services event is being fired, we can then provide an event handler. (This is covered in Chapter 8.) The AfterEvent property determines if this task exits with a success status after the event occurs, exits with a failure status after the event occurs, or waits for another event. If we

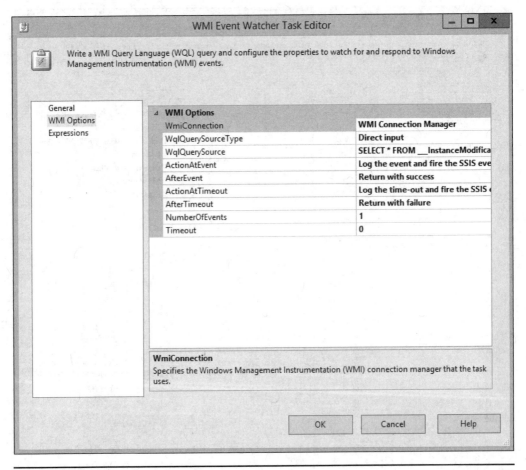

Figure 7-40   *The WMI Event Watcher Task Editor dialog box*

are waiting for multiple occurrences of the event, the NumberOfEvents property specifies how many occurrences to wait for before exiting the task. The Timeout property lets us specify how many seconds to wait for the event to occur. The ActionAtTimeout and AfterTimeout properties function similarly to their event counterparts.

XML Task   The *XML task* enables us to manipulate XML documents. Using the XML task, we can perform the following operations:

> ▶ Validate an XML document using an XML Schema Document (XSD) or a Document Type Definition (DTD)
>
> ▶ Apply an XSL Transformation (XSLT)
>
> ▶ Apply an XPath query
>
> ▶ Merge two XML documents
>
> ▶ Find the difference between two XML documents (Diff operation)
>
> ▶ Apply the output of a Diff operation

The XML source document can be supplied from a File Connection Manager in the Connections tray, a package variable, or directly input as a string. The XML document that results from the operation can be saved in a text file specified by a File Connection Manager, saved in a package variable, or discarded. The XML Task Editor dialog box is shown in Figure 7-41.

Maintenance Plan Tasks

In addition to containers and Control Flow items, the Control Flow SSIS Toolbox contains Maintenance Plan tasks. The Maintenance Plan tasks, as we might guess from the name, mirror tasks that can be accomplished as part of a database maintenance plan. In fact, when you create a database maintenance plan through SQL Server Management Studio, you are actually creating a SQL Server Integration Services package that utilizes these tasks. The Maintenance Plan tasks can also be used to perform database maintenance as we are loading data. This can be done to ensure that the database is ready for efficient operation at the conclusion of the data load.

Each Maintenance Plan task has a View T-SQL button on its dialog box. This button shows the T-SQL statements that would perform the equivalent operation in a query window. Looking at these T-SQL statements may be helpful to determine exactly how a Maintenance Plan task is operating.

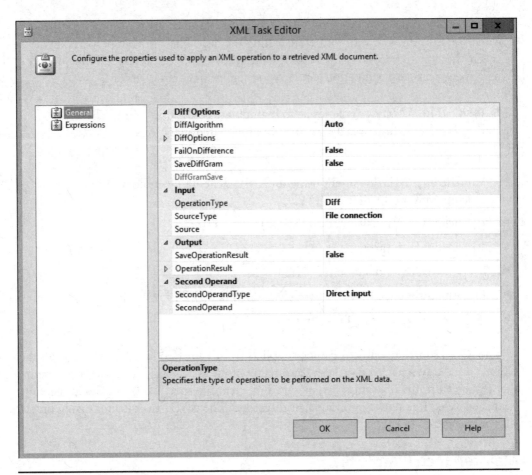

Figure 7-41 *The XML Task Editor dialog box*

Back Up Database Task   The *Back Up Database task* lets us run a database backup as part of an Integration Services package. This is a wise thing to do just before making major changes to the contents of a database. Often, some type of data load or other operation in an Integration Services package is responsible for these major changes. By using the Back Up Database task in a package, we can create the backup within the same process that makes the changes. We may also find this task useful to create a snapshot of the database contents immediately after a large data load.

Figure 7-42 shows the Back Up Database Task dialog box used to configure the Back Up Database task. The dialog box enables us to back up any combination of databases on a single server. A Full, Differential, or Transaction Log backup can be created. The backup can be stored in a single file or in multiple files, with one file for each database.

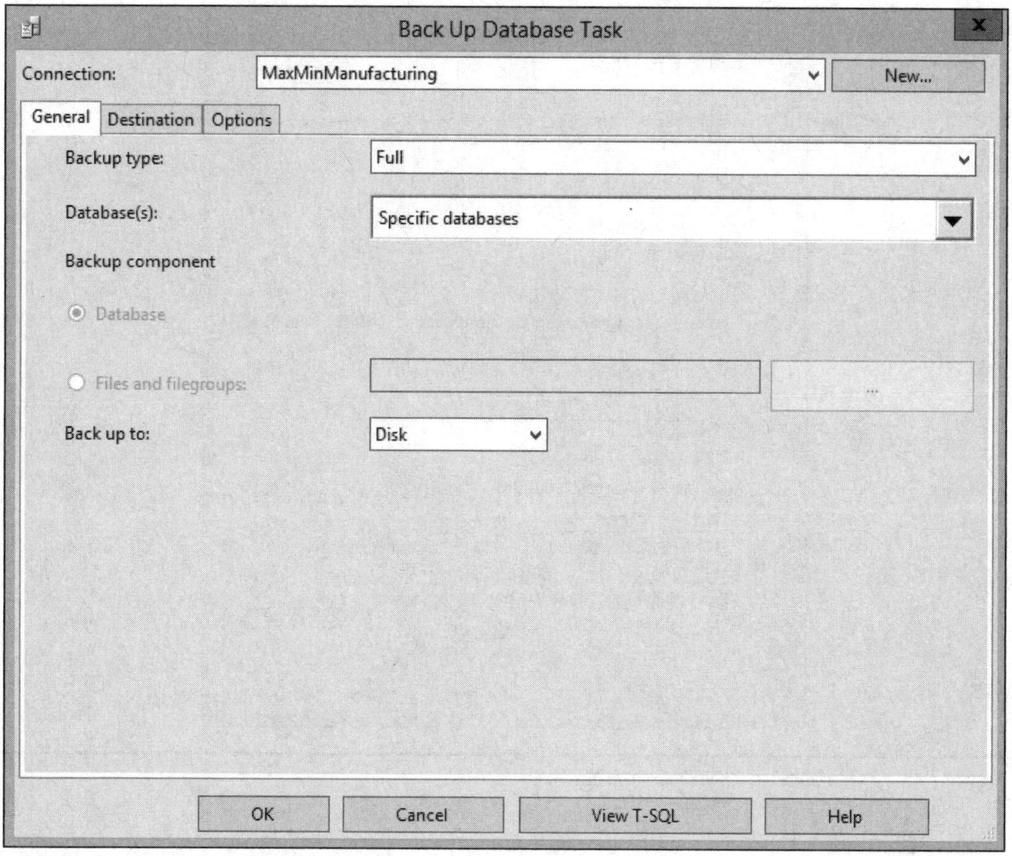

Figure 7-42   *The Back Up Database Task dialog box*

A special type of drop-down box is used to select the databases to be backed up. This is shown in Figure 7-43. This drop-down box contains predefined choices that let us select all of the databases on the server, all system databases on the server (master, msdb, and model), or all user databases on the server. In addition to the predefined choices, we can use the database list at the bottom of the drop-down box to create our own selection of databases using the check boxes.

Check Database Integrity Task   The *Check Database Integrity task* lets us check for corruption in one or more databases on a single server. This task executes a

DBCC CHECKDB WITH NO_INFOMSGS

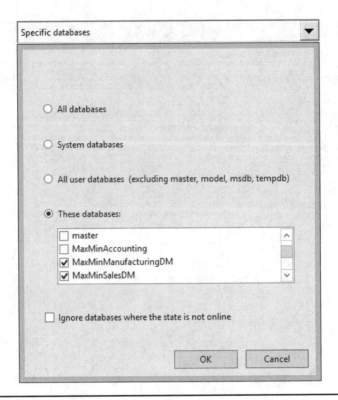

Figure 7-43 *The database selection drop-down box*

command against each database specified. This can be a good idea, either right before or right after major changes to the database.

The Check Database Integrity Task dialog box is shown in Figure 7-44. It uses the same database selection drop-down box as the one shown in Figure 7-43 for the selection of the databases to check. We can also specify whether we want indexes included in the integrity check.

If the integrity check is successful, the package execution continues with any tasks linked to the Check Database Integrity task, with either a success or a completion precedence constraint. If the integrity check finds database corruption, the package execution continues with any tasks linked to the Check Database Integrity task, with either a failure or a completion precedence constraint.

Figure 7-44 *The Check Database Integrity Task dialog box*

Execute SQL Server Agent Job Task   The *Execute SQL Server Agent Job task* lets us 
execute a single SQL Server Agent Job as part of a package.
A single job can be selected for execution. The Execute SQL
Server Agent Job Task dialog box is shown in Figure 7-45.

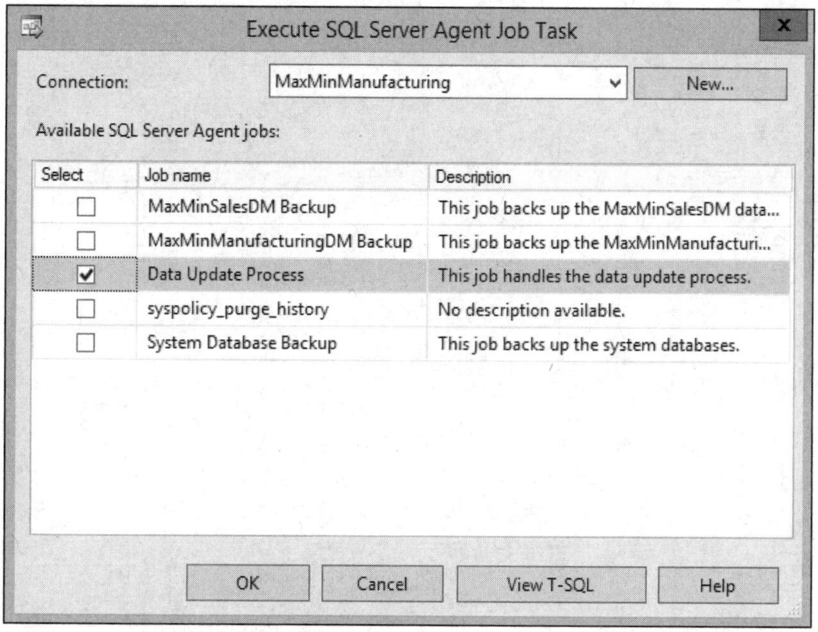

Figure 7-45 *The Execute SQL Server Agent Job Task dialog box*

Execute T-SQL Statement Task   The *Execute T-SQL Statement task* enables us to

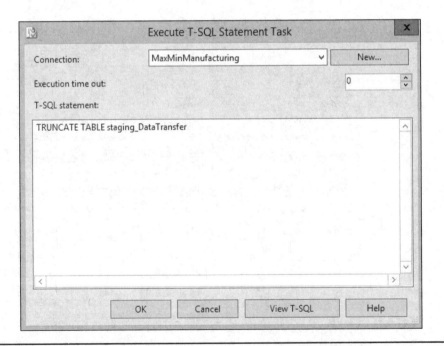

run one or more Transact SQL statements on a SQL server. Anything that can be executed from a query window in the SQL Server Management Studio can be executed here. The Execute T-SQL Statement Task dialog box is shown in Figure 7-46.

Notice that there is a task referred to as the Execute SQL task in the Control Flow items section of the SSIS Toolbox. The Execute T-SQL Statement task that we are looking at here is simple. It lets us type in T-SQL statements and execute them. The Execute SQL task in the Control Flow items has additional features for creating parameterized statements and dealing with result sets.

History Cleanup Task   The *History Cleanup task* enables us to remove historical entries from a database. This includes backup history, SQL Agent Job execution history, and database maintenance plan execution history. We can specify the timeframe for the historical entries we want to keep and, therefore, the timeframe for the historical entries we want to remove. The History Cleanup Task dialog box is shown in Figure 7-47.

Figure 7-46   *The Execute T-SQL Statement Task dialog box*

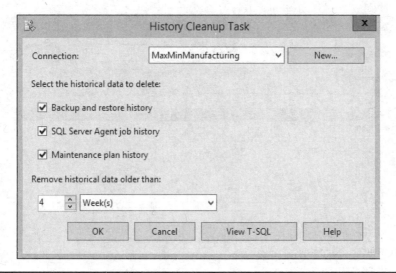

Figure 7-47 *The History Cleanup Task dialog box*

Maintenance Cleanup Task   The *Maintenance Cleanup task* allows us to remove files created by database maintenance plans and database backups. Specifically, we can remove maintenance plan text reports and database backups. We can remove a single file based on the filename or a number of files with the same file extension from a folder. We can specify the age of the files we want to remove.

Notify Operator Task   The *Notify Operator task* lets us send a message to one or more SQL Server operators. Operators must be set up in SQL Server before they can be notified using this task. The Notify Operator Task dialog box is shown in Figure 7-48.

Rebuild Index Task   The *Rebuild Index task* enables the rebuilding of indexes in one or more databases. Rebuilding indexes causes SQL Server to drop the existing indexes and rebuild them. The Rebuild Index task uses the same database selection drop-down box as the one shown in Figure 7-43 for the selection of the databases whose indexes are to be rebuilt. We can specify the free space that should be placed into the rebuilt indexes, along with several other advanced indexing options. The Rebuild Index Task dialog box is shown in Figure 7-49.

Reorganize Index Task   The *Reorganize Index task* lets us reorganize the indexes in one or more databases. It uses the same database selection drop-down box as the one shown in Figure 7-43 for the selection of the

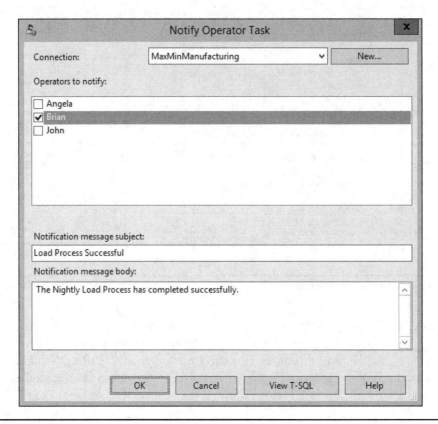

Figure 7-48   *The Notify Operator Task dialog box*

databases whose indexes are to be reorganized. The Reorganize Index Task dialog box is shown in Figure 7-50.

Reorganizing indexes defragments the leaf-level nodes of both clustered and nonclustered indexes. It does this by reordering the nodes to match the logical order of the leaf nodes. Reorganizing also compacts the indexes. The reorganization process does not, however, drop and re-create the indexes as the rebuild process does.

Shrink Database Task   The *Shrink Database task* enables the recovery of unused pages from tables in one or more databases. It uses the same database selection drop-down box as the one shown in Figure 7-43 for the selection of the databases that are to be shrunk. We can determine whether these recovered pages are to be returned to the operating system or remain allocated to the database. We can also specify how much free space is to be left in the pages allocated to the database to accommodate future growth. The Shrink Database Task dialog box is shown in Figure 7-51.

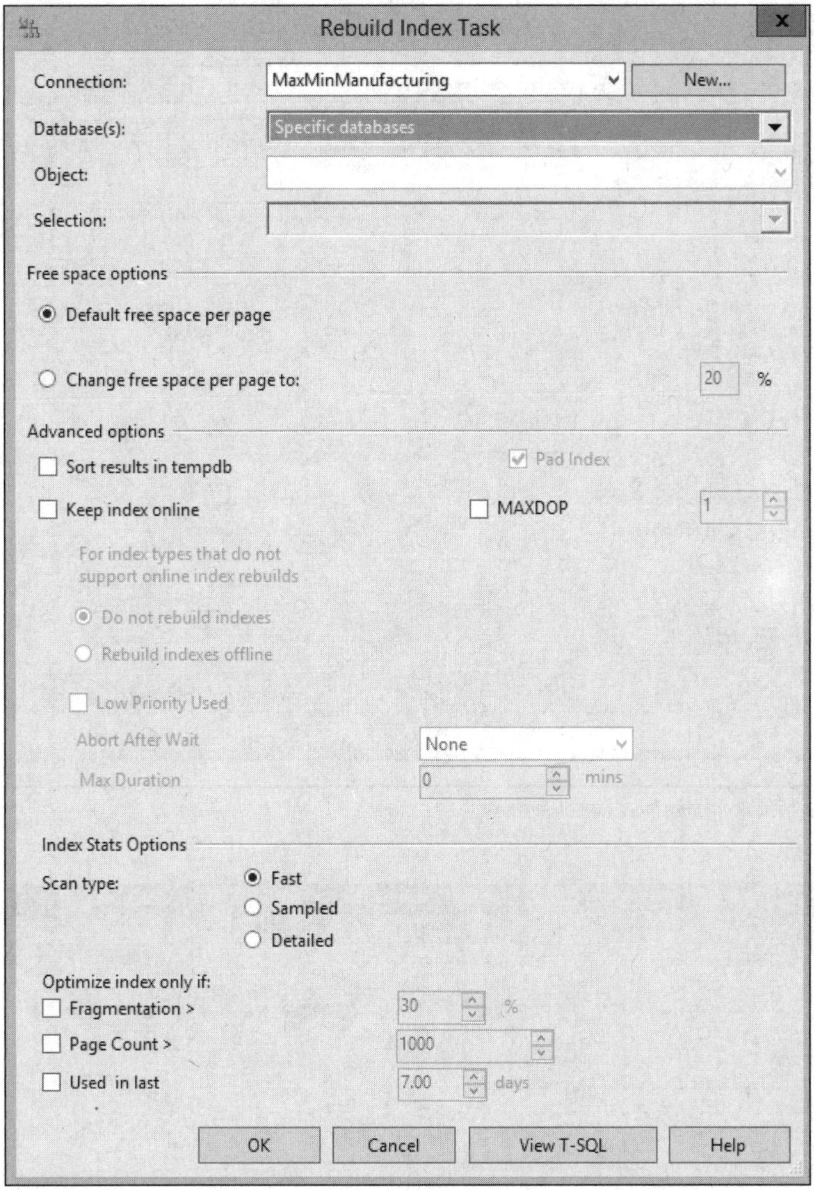

Figure 7-49 *The Rebuild Index Task dialog box*

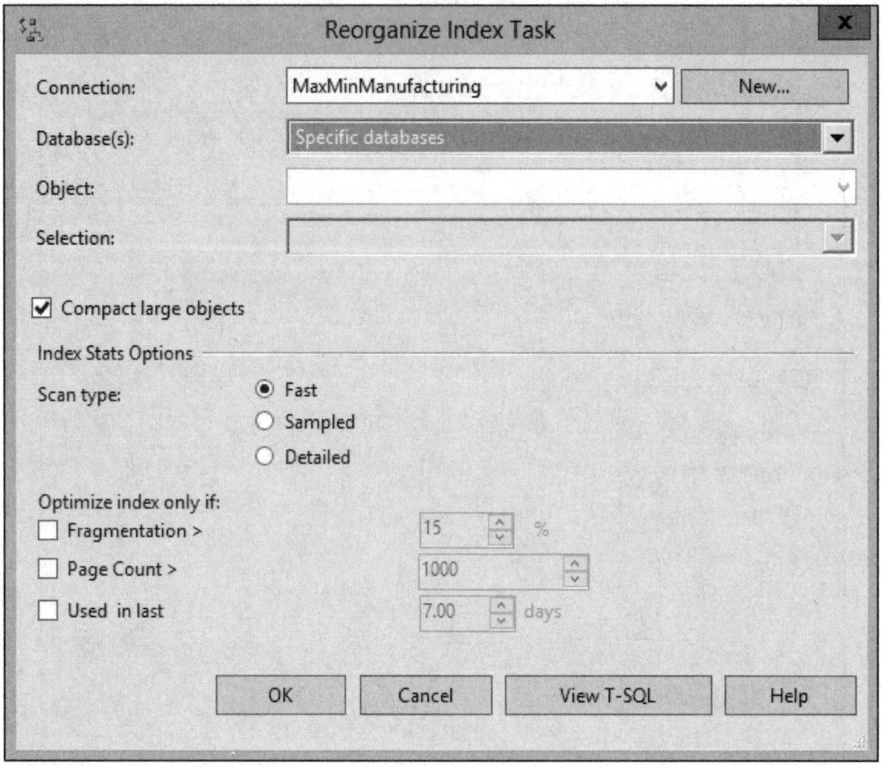

Figure 7-50   *The Reorganize Index Task dialog box*

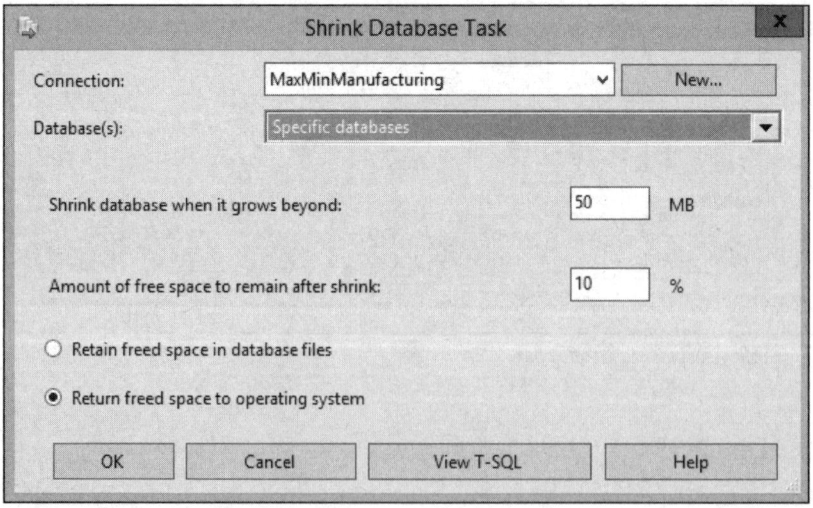

Figure 7-51   *The Shrink Database Task dialog box*

Update Statistics Task   The *Update Statistics task* lets us update the statistics in
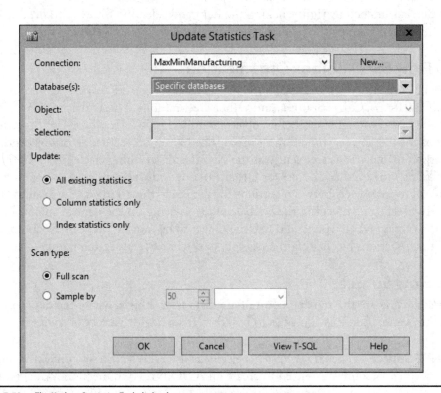 one or more databases. It uses the same database selection drop-
down box as the one shown in Figure 7-43 for the selection of the
databases whose statistics are to be updated. Because the database statistics are used by
SQL Server to calculate query execution plans, it is important for these statistics to be
up-to-date. A large data load can cause the statistics to be inaccurate. Therefore, it is a
good idea to use this task to update the database statistics after a major data operation.
The Update Statistics Task dialog box is shown in Figure 7-52.

Custom Tasks   If none of the control flow tasks included with Integration Services
fits your needs, it is possible to write your own. You can create a .NET assembly that
can integrate seamlessly with both Integration Services and SQL Server Data Tools.
Creating a custom task requires a solid knowledge of object-oriented programming in the
.NET Framework. Consult the SQL Server Books Online "Developing Custom Objects
for Integration Services" topic for more information on developing a custom task.

Figure 7-52   *The Update Statistics Task dialog box*

Data Flow

The Data Flow SSIS Toolbox contains three types of objects: data flow sources, data flow transformations, and data flow destinations. It also contains two assistants that aid in the process of creating a data flow source or a data flow destination. Each data flow item—source, transformation, destination, and assistant—has an editor dialog box that lets us configure that component or work with the assistant in a straightforward manner.

The editor dialog box for a data flow source, data flow transformation, or data flow destination is launched by double-clicking the item in the design area or right-clicking the item and selecting Edit from the context menu. The editor dialog box for the source assistant or the destination assistant is launched by double-clicking the assistant item in the SSIS Toolbox or dragging one of the assistant items onto the data flow design area.

Each of the data flow source, data flow transformation, and data flow destination items also has an advanced editor dialog box. Where the editor dialog box enables us to configure the item for use and make most of the necessary property settings for the item, the advanced editor dialog box contains all of the properties of an item. The advanced editor dialog box lets us set any property for the item. The advanced editor dialog box is launched by right-clicking the item and selecting Show Advanced Editor from the context menu.

Data Flow SSIS Toolbox Organization

The Data Flow SSIS Toolbox is divided into several sections: Favorites, Common, Other Transforms, Other Sources, and Other Destinations. These divisions are designed to help you more easily find objects within the SSIS Toolbox. The Favorites section is for the objects you use most often. The Common section is for objects that are used often, but not as frequently as the favorites. Everything else ends up in the Other Transforms, Other Sources, or Other Destinations sections.

You can move objects between sections to customize the arrangement to suit your tastes. Right-click an object in the SSIS Toolbox to bring up the context menu. Then select the section where you would like the object to be moved. You can expand or hide any of these sections by clicking the triangle to the left of the section name.

Data Flow Sources

Data flow sources are the starting point of any data flow. This is where the data comes from. Integration Services allows us to pull data from a wide variety of sources.

ADO.NET Source   The *ADO.NET source* lets us use ADO.NET to connect to a data source. We need to create an ADO.NET Connection Manager in the Connections tray for use with this data source. Once the ADO.NET

Connection Manager has been created, it can be selected on the Connection Manager page of the ADO.NET Source Editor dialog box. This is shown in Figure 7-53.

The Connection Manager page is also used to specify whether we are getting our data directly from a table or view, or from a SQL query. If the data is coming from a table or a view, the name of the Table or the View property is used to select a table or view in the database. Alternately, the table or view name can come from a package variable at run time.

If the data is coming from a SQL query, we have several ways to specify the content of the query. The simplest method is to type the query into the SQL command text property. This works only if we are comfortable with SQL query syntax and have the database structure memorized or an up-to-date copy of the database schema documentation handy. If this is not the case, we can create the query in the SQL Server Management Studio or some other query-authoring environment and save the completed query to a file. We can then load the query from the file by clicking Browse.

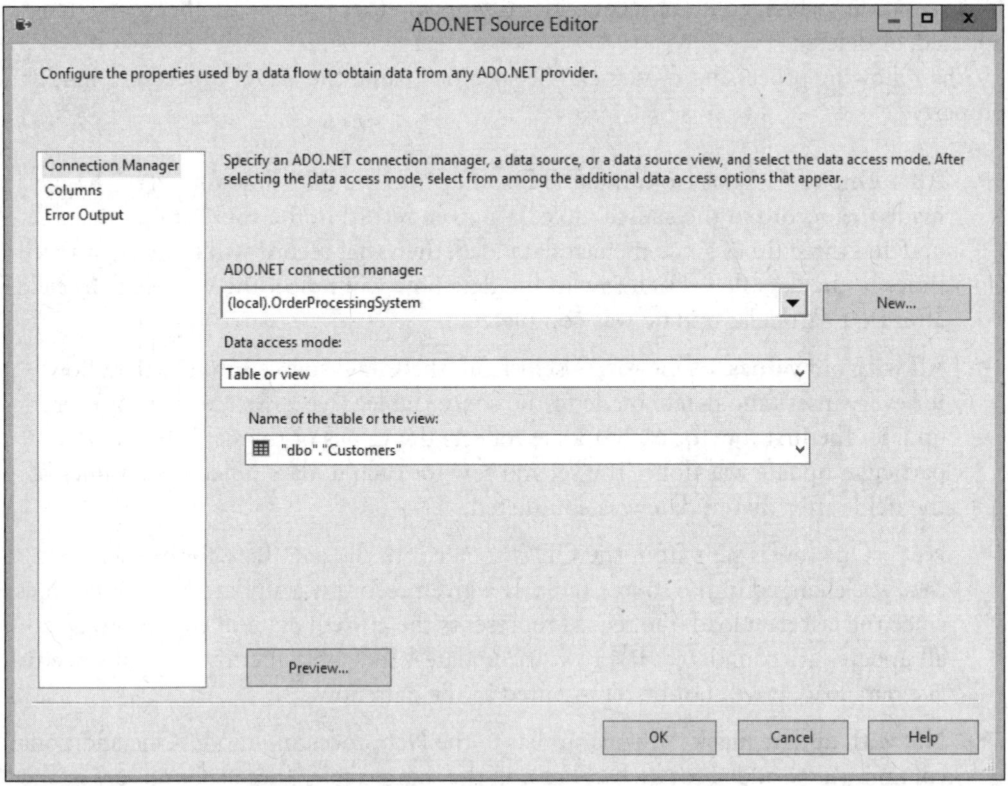

Figure 7-53   *The ADO.NET Source Editor dialog box*

Alternatively, we can click Build Query to create the query using the Query Builder. The Query Builder is discussed later in the "OLE DB Source" section. The Columns and the Error Output pages of the ADO.NET Source Editor dialog box are discussed in the "Flat File Source" section.

CDC Source   The *CDC source* is used to implement a change data capture

processing. The CDC source works in conjunction with the CDC Control task. The CDC Control task and the CDC source communicate with one another through the variable specified as the "Variable containing the CDC state."

The ADO.NET Connection Manager utilized by the CDC source must point to a database that has change data capture enabled. Once this is in place, you can select a CDC–enabled table from that database. Working with the CDC Control task, the CDC source provides only that data from the source table that has been modified since the last data load. Each row from the CDC source has an additional column called "__$operation", which contains a code identifying whether the row has been inserted, updated, or deleted.

The following processing modes can be specified using the CDC processing mode property:

▶ **All**   One row is sent from the CDC source into the data flow for every change made to a record in the source table. If a given record in the source table was updated three times since the last data load, then that record will be present three times in the data flow. Each row in the data flow will reflect the values of the fields after that particular update was completed.

▶ **All with old values**   One row is sent from the CDC source into the data flow for every insert and delete made to the source table. Two rows are sent for every update. The first row for each update reflects the values of the fields before that particular update was done. The second row for each update reflects the values of the fields after that update was completed.

▶ **Net**   One row is sent from the CDC source into the data flow for every record that was changed in the source table. If a given record was updated multiple times since the last data load, the record represents the current state of the record after all updates are completed. If a row was updated and subsequently deleted since the last data load, it will not be represented in the data flow.

▶ **Net with update mask**   This is similar to the Net processing mode. One additional column will be added for each column in the source table. These columns are in the format "__${*ColumnName*}__Changed" and indicate whether or not the associated column was changed since the last data load.

▶ **Net with merge**   This is similar to the Net processing mode; however, the updates and inserts are assigned the same code in the __$operation column. This optimizes the data for use with the MERGE T-SQL command.

Excel Source   The *Excel source* enables us to utilize data from an Excel spreadsheet. The Excel Source Editor dialog box is shown in Figure 7-54. We need 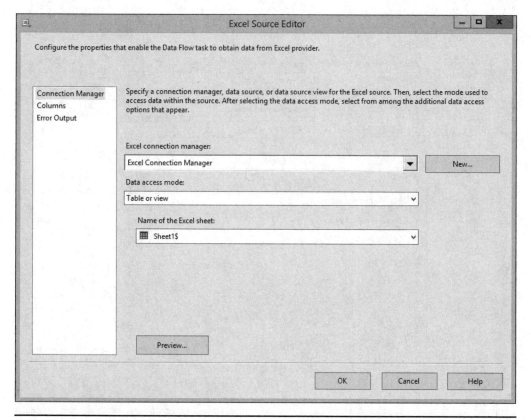 to create an Excel Connection Manager in the Connections tray for use with this data source. Once the Excel Connection Manager has been created, this Connection Manager can be selected on the Connection Managers page of the Excel Source Editor dialog box. A spreadsheet is then selected from the Excel file pointed to by this Connection Manager. The columns included in the result set are selected on the Columns page of the Excel Source Editor dialog box.

Figure 7-54   *The Excel Source Editor dialog box*

Flat File Source   The *Flat File source* lets us utilize data from text files. We need to create a Flat File Connection Manager in the Connections tray for use with this data source. The Flat File Connection Manager requires a bit more configuration than the OLE DB Connection Manager and most of the other Connection Managers. The other Connection Managers deal with specific data formats, so not a lot of configuration is required beyond the connection information. A flat file, on the other hand, can represent, format, and delimit the data in a number of different ways.

The first page of the Flat File Connection Manager, the General page shown in Figure 7-55, enables us to specify the file location in the File name text box. In addition,

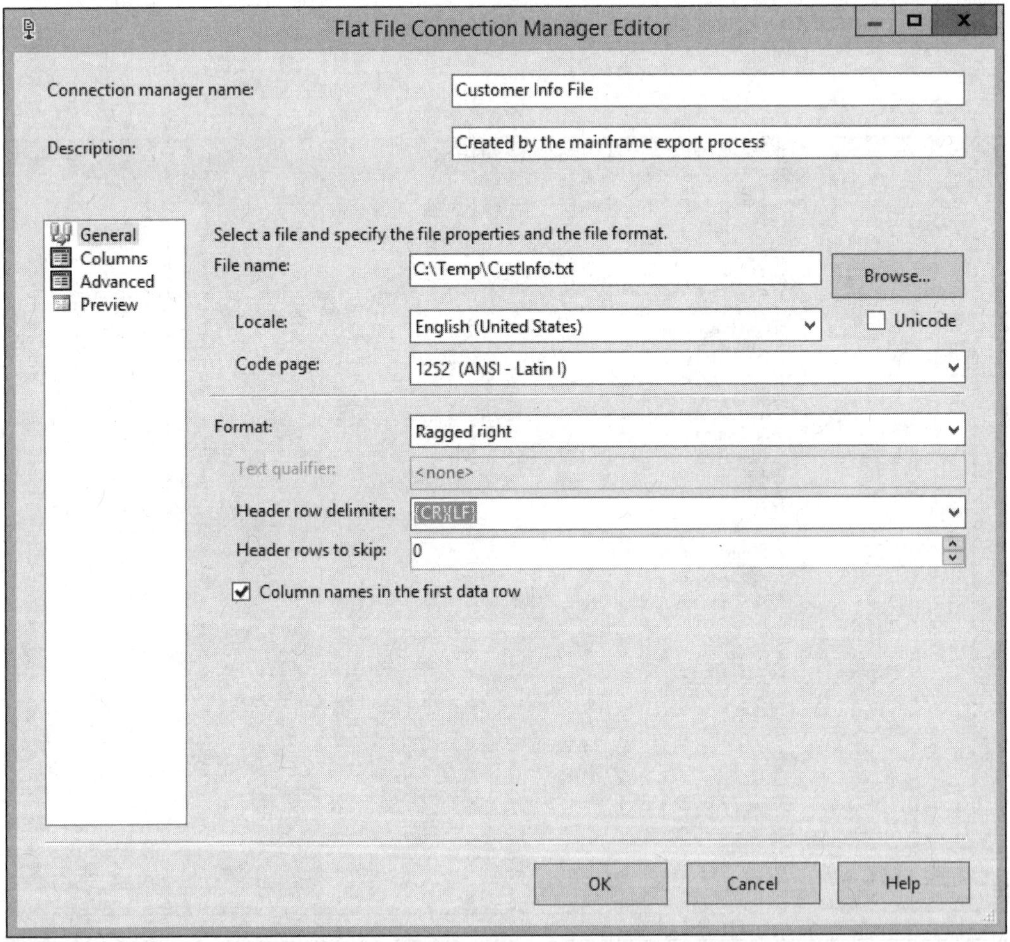

Figure 7-55   *The General page of the Flat File Connection Manager Editor dialog box*

we need to tell the Connection Manager how the data is represented with the Locale and Code page drop-down lists, along with the Unicode check box. Finally, we need to specify how the data is formatted: whether the data is a fixed-width layout or delimited by a comma, tab, or some other separator (Format); if the text is enclosed in some form of quotation character (Text qualifier); how the header row is delimited (Header row delimiter); if there are header rows to skip (Header Rows to Skip); and if the column names are in the first row (Column names in the first data row).

In this example, we are using the ragged-right format. The *ragged-right format* expects fixed-width columns in the text file. This means, for example, that the first 11 characters of each line are always the first column, the next 50 characters are always the second column, and so on. The ragged-right format expects some type of end-of-line indicator, such as a set of carriage return and line-feed characters. The *fixed-width format* also expects fixed-width columns, but it specifies the exact number of characters in each line, rather than using an end-of-line indicator. The length of the lines in the ragged-right format can vary because the end-of-line indicator tells the parser where to end one line and begin another. The length of the lines in the fixed-width format must be exactly the same for all lines.

As soon as we select the Columns page of the Flat File Connection Manager, shown in Figure 7-56, the Flat File Connection Manager uses the information from the General page to access the file. When the delimited format is selected on the General page, the Flat File Connection Manager attempts to figure out what the delimiter is and parse the file accordingly. If the wrong delimiter is chosen, you can edit the delimiter information. When the fixed-width format or, as in our example, the ragged-right format is used, we are given the opportunity to graphically specify the width of each column.

We specify column widths by creating column markers in the Source data columns area. The column marker is indicated by the mouse pointer in Figure 7-56. *Column markers* are created by clicking along the bottom of the ruler or below the ruler in the sample text area. We can drag the column markers to their appropriate positions, if necessary. We can remove an unneeded column marker by double-clicking it or by right-clicking it and selecting Delete from the context menu.

The Advanced page of the Flat File Connection Manager, shown in Figure 7-57, lets us specify additional information about each column that was defined on the Columns page. We can create, add, and delete column definitions here, as well as on the Columns page. The drop-down list alongside the New button, indicated by the mouse pointer in Figure 7-57, enables us to insert a column definition either before or after the column definition highlighted in the list. We can specify the Name property for each column definition. (If column names are supplied as the first row of the text file, these names appear in the Name property for each column definition.) The *Suggest Types button*

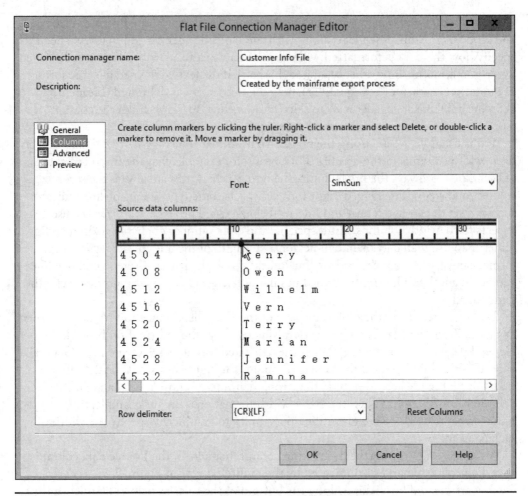

Figure 7-56 *The Columns page of the Flat File Connection Manager Editor dialog box*

instructs the Flat File Connection Manager to suggest a data type for each column definition based on the data in the text file. The final page in the Flat File Connection Manager Editor dialog box lets us preview the data from the text file when it is parsed according to our file layout and column definitions.

Once the Flat File Connection Manager has been created, this Connection Manager can be selected on the Connection Manager page of the Flat File Source Editor dialog box. We can then use the Columns page to specify which columns should be used in the data flow. The Error Output page enables us to specify the behavior of the Flat File

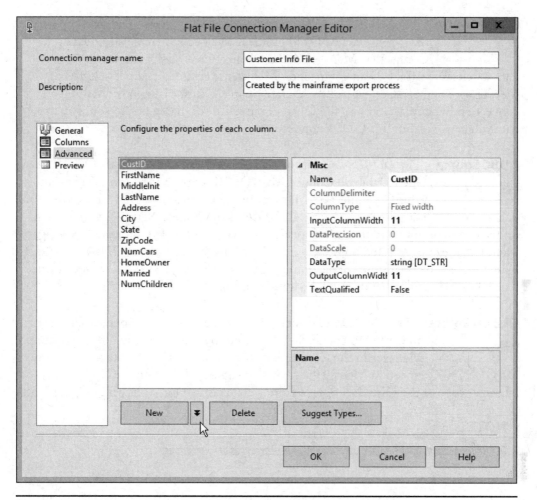

Figure 7-57 *The Advanced page of the Flat File Connection Manager Editor dialog box*

source when an error or truncation occurs in any given column. We can ignore the failure, direct the row containing the failure to the error output, or cause the process to fail.

HDFS File Source   The *HDFS File source* lets us utilize data from a file stored in the Hadoop Distributed File System (HDFS). We need to create an HDFS Connection Manager in the Connections tray for use with this data source. Once the HDFS Connection Manager is created, it can be selected in the HDFS Source Editor dialog box. With the connection in place, we can use the HDFS Source Editor dialog box to specify the file to use and the columns to be read from that file.

OData Source   The *OData source* lets us utilize data from any source that supports the Open Data (OData) protocol. We need to create an OData Connection Manager in the Connections tray for use with this data source. Once the OData Connection Manager is created, it can be selected on the Connection Manager page of the OData Source Editor dialog box. With the connection in place, we can use the OData Source Editor dialog box to specify what data will be read from this OData connection.

ODBC Source   The *ODBC source* lets us utilize data from any source that has an Open Database Connectivity (ODBC) driver. We need to create an ODBC Connection Manager in the Connections tray for use with this data source. We may also wish to have an ODBC Data Source Name (DSN) defined on the computer for use with this connection. Once the ODBC Connection Manager is created, it can be selected on the Connection Manager page of the ODBC Source Editor dialog box. With the connection in place, we can use the ODBC Source Editor dialog box to specify what data will be read from this ODBC connection.

OLE DB Source   The *OLE DB source* lets us utilize data from any source that supports an OLE DB connection. We need to create an OLE DB Connection Manager in the Connections tray for use with this data source. Once the OLE DB Connection Manager is created, it can be selected on the Connection Manager page of the OLE DB Source Editor dialog box. This is shown in Figure 7-58.

NOTE

OLE DB connections are being phased out in favor of other types of connections.

The Connection Manager page is also used to specify whether we are getting our data directly from a table or view, or from a SQL query. If the data is coming from a table or a view, the name of the Table or the View property is used to select a table or view in the database. Alternately, the table or view name can come from a package variable at run time.

If the data is coming from a SQL query, we have several ways to specify the content of the query. The simplest method is to type the query into the SQL Command Text property. This works only if we are comfortable with SQL query syntax and have the database structure memorized or an up-to-date copy of the database schema documentation handy. If this is not the case, we can create the query in the SQL Server Management Studio or some other query-authoring environment and save the completed query to a file. We can then load the query from the file by clicking Browse.

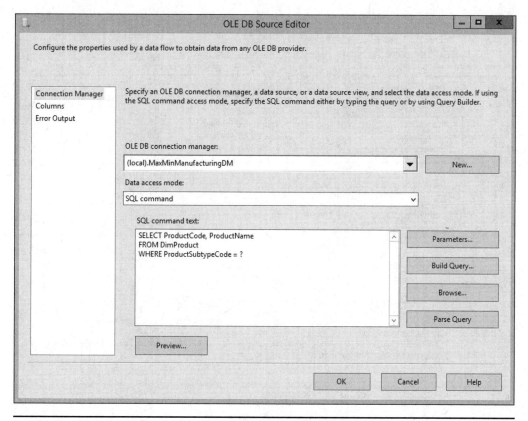

Figure 7-58   *The Connection Manager page of the OLE DB Source Editor dialog box*

Alternatively, we can click Build Query to create the query using the Query Builder. The Query Builder is shown in Figure 7-59. The top quarter of the Query Builder is the Diagram pane. The *Diagram pane* area is used for selecting tables from the database, creating join conditions between tables, and selecting fields to be used in the query, either in the field list or in the filter conditions. The next quarter of the Query Builder, moving downward, is the Grid pane. The *Grid pane* is used to select the fields to be included in the field list (the Output column), as well as for setting the sort order and filter conditions. The next quarter, again moving downward, is the SQL pane. The *SQL pane* shows the SQL SELECT statement that is equivalent to the contents of the Diagram and Grid panes. Changes made directly in the SQL pane are reflected in the Diagram pane and the Grid pane as soon as focus leaves the SQL pane. The bottom quarter of the Query Builder is the *Result pane,* which shows the results of executing the query.

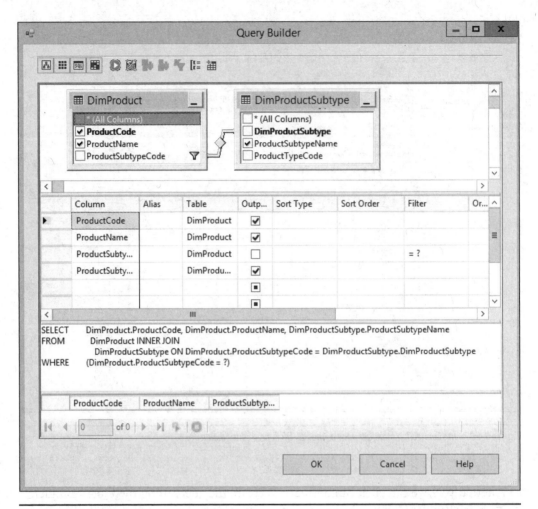

Figure 7-59 *The Query Builder*

The Columns and the Error Output pages of the OLE DB Source Editor function similarly to their counterparts in the Flat File source.

Raw File Source   The *Raw File source* lets us utilize data that was previously written to a raw data file by a Raw File destination. The *raw file format* is the native format for Integration Services. Because of this, raw files can be written to disk and read from disk rapidly. One of the goals of Integration Services is to improve processing efficiency by moving data from the original source to the ultimate destination without making any stops in between. However, on some occasions, the data must be staged to disk as part of an extract, transform, and load process. When this is necessary, the raw file format provides the most efficient means of accomplishing this task. The Raw File Source Editor dialog box is shown in Figure 7-60.

XML Source   The *XML source* enables us to utilize the content of an XML document in the data flow. The XML document can come from a file or from the contents of a package variable. If the XML document is coming from a file, we can specify the file path at design time or obtain the file path from a package variable at run time. We can also specify the location of an XSD that describes the structure of the XML document. If an XSD is unavailable, click Generate XSD to autogenerate an XSD from the XML document structure. The XML Source Editor dialog box is shown in Figure 7-61.

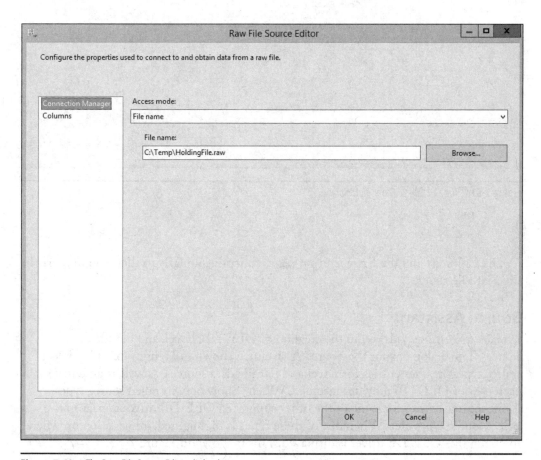

Figure 7-60   *The Raw File Source Editor dialog box*

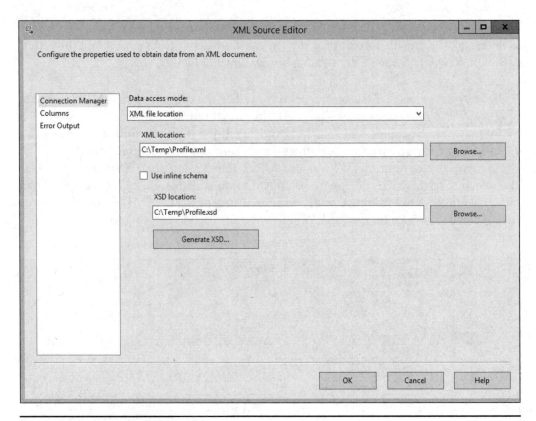

Figure 7-61   *The XML Source Editor dialog box*

The Columns and the Error Output pages function similarly to their counterparts in the Flat File source.

Source Assistant

The *Source Assistant* aids you in the creation of OLE DB, Excel, and flat file data sources. The dialog box for the Source Assistant is shown in Figure 7-62. The Select source types area has entries for Excel and flat file data sources, as well as an entry for each type of OLE DB provider installed. When "Show only installed source types" is unchecked, entries for some of the other supported OLE DB drives appear in the Select source types area. When one of these types is highlighted, information on where to obtain this OLE DB driver is displayed. This is shown in Figure 7-63.

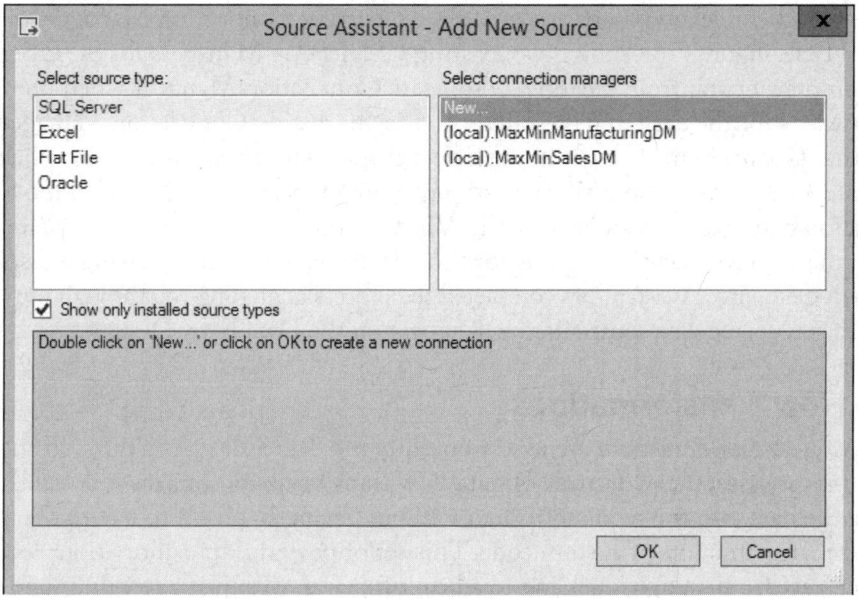

Figure 7-62   *The Source Assistant dialog box showing Excel, flat file, and installed OLE DB providers*

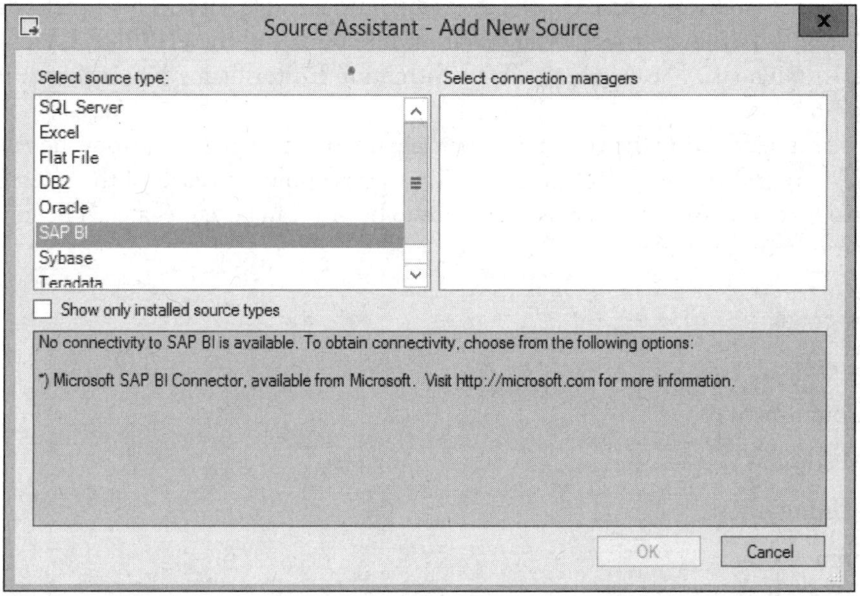

Figure 7-63   *The Source Assistant dialog box showing information on additional OLE DB providers*

The Select connection managers area shows existing Connection Managers of the selected type. Figure 7-62 shows two existing Connection Managers for SQL Server. This can prevent you from creating a duplicate Connection Manager when one already exists for the desired data source. To use an existing Connection Manager, select that Connection Manager in the Select connection managers area and click OK. To create a new Connection Manager of the desired type, select "<New>" in the Select connection managers area and click OK. When creating a new Connection Manager, the Connection Manager dialog box for the selected connection type will be displayed.

When the Source Assistant has completed the process of guiding you through the creation of a data source, the data source item will appear on the Data Flow Designer tab.

Data Flow Transformations

The *data flow transformations* are used to modify the data as it moves through the data flow. In most cases, the wide array of data flow transformations makes it possible to change the data into the required format without having to save it to a temporary table or utilize large amounts of custom code. This set of powerful transformations lets us take our data from an ugly duckling to a beautiful swan with just a few drag-and-drop operations.

Aggregate   The *Aggregate* transformation enables us to combine information from multiple records in the data flow into a single value. This functions in the same way as aggregation functions and the GROUP BY clause in a SQL statement. The Aggregate Transformation Editor dialog box is shown in Figure 7-64.

We begin by selecting the columns to participate in the aggregation from the Available Input Columns. We then select the operation that is applied to each of the selected columns. A column can either be used as a group by or it can be aggregated. The following aggregations are available:

► Average
► Count
► Count distinct
► Maximum
► Minimum
► Sum

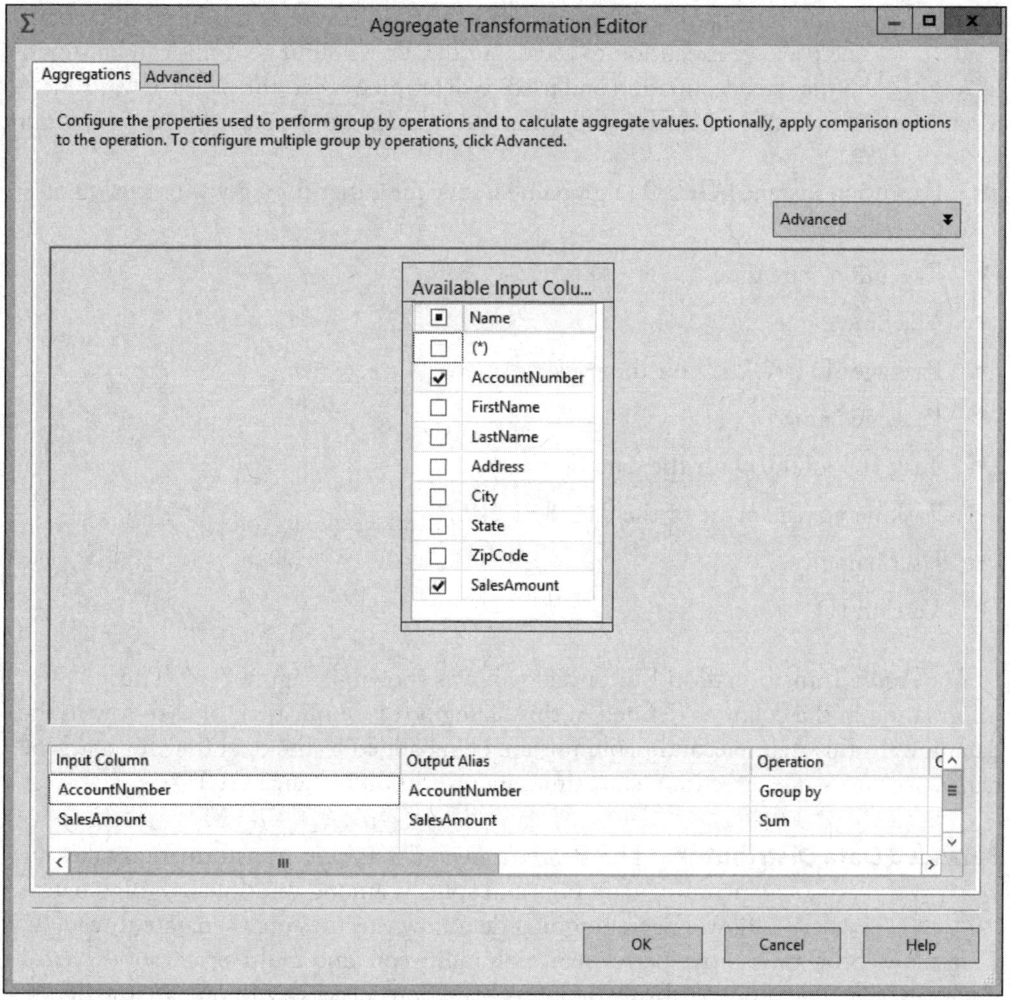

Figure 7-64   *The Aggregate Transformation Editor dialog box*

The example in Figure 7-64 calculates the sum of the SalesAmount column for each customer represented by the content of the AccountNumber column.

Audit The *Audit* transformation lets us add columns that contain information about the package execution to the data flow. These audit columns can be stored in the data destination and used to determine when the package was run, where it was run, and so forth. The following information can be placed in audit columns:

▶ Execution instance GUID (a globally unique identifier for a given execution of the package)

▶ Execution start time

▶ Machine name

▶ Package ID (a GUID for the package)

▶ Package name

▶ Task ID (a GUID for the data flow task)

▶ Task name (the name of the data flow task)

▶ User name

▶ Version ID

The Audit Transformation Editor dialog box is shown in Figure 7-65. The information in the columns defined in this dialog box is duplicated for each row in the data flow. In this example, audit columns are being added to the data flow for machine name, package name, execution start time, and execution instance GUID.

Balanced Data Distributor The *Balanced Data Distributor* transformation takes an incoming data flow and splits it among multiple outgoing data flows. Each outgoing data flow executes on a separate thread. This allows SSIS to improve performance on multi-core and multi-processor servers. Each outgoing data flow performs the transformations necessary to prepare the data. Each data flow ends with a data destination and all of these destinations point to the same destination table.

The Balanced Data Distributor can improve performance when the following are all true:

▶ The data coming through the incoming data flow is so large that multiple buffers are required to hold it.

▶ The data coming through the incoming data flow is arriving faster than the remainder of the data flow can process it.

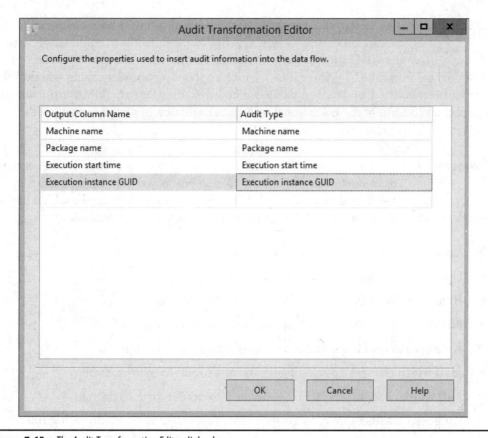

Figure 7-65   *The Audit Transformation Editor dialog box*

▶ The data does not need to be sorted at any point after it has passed through the Balanced Data Distributor.

▶ The data flow destination supports parallel operation.

Cache Transform   The *Cache Transform* transformation enables us to populate a cache that will be subsequently used by a Lookup transformation. Thus, the Cache Transform transformation enables us to apply any of the Integration Services data flow transformations to a set of data before using it as the lookup data set. The Cache Transform transformation can be configured to write the cached data to a cache file using a Cache Connection Manager. This persisted cache can then be used by several lookup transformations in a single package. Only one Cache Transform transformation in a package can write data to a given Cache Connection Manager.

CDC Splitter The *CDC Splitter* transformation is used to implement change data capture processing. The CDC Splitter task works in conjunction with the CDC source. Each row of data from the CDC source has an additional column called "__$operation", which contains a code identifying whether the row has been inserted, updated, or deleted. The CDC Splitter data flow transformation is a specialized form of the conditional split transformation designed to work with the codes in the __$operation column.

Character Map The *Character Map* transformation enables us to modify the contents of character-based columns. The modified column can be placed in the data flow in place of the original column, or it can be added to the data flow as a new column. The following character mappings are available:

▶ **Lowercase** changes all characters to lowercase.

▶ **Uppercase** changes all characters to uppercase.

▶ **Byte reversal** reverses the byte order of each character.

▶ **Hiragana** maps Katakana characters to Hiragana characters.

▶ **Katakana** maps Hiragana characters to Katakana characters.

▶ **Half width** changes double-byte characters to single-byte characters.

▶ **Full width** changes single-byte characters to double-byte characters.

▶ **Linguistic casing** applies linguistic casing rules instead of system casing rules.

▶ **Simplified Chinese** maps traditional Chinese to simplified Chinese.

▶ **Traditional Chinese** maps simplified Chinese to traditional Chinese.

Multiple character mappings can be applied to a single column at the same time. However, a number of mappings are mutually exclusive. For example, it does not make sense to use both the lowercase and uppercase mappings on the same column. The Character Map Transformation Editor dialog box is shown in Figure 7-66.

The Configure Error Output button displays the Configure Error Output dialog box, shown in Figure 7-67. The Configure Error Output dialog box lets us determine the error behavior of this transformation. For the Character Map transformation, the only error condition we need to worry about is a character truncation caused by one of the mappings. For each character mapping, we can choose to ignore truncation, send the row containing the truncation to the error output, or cause the entire transformation to fail.

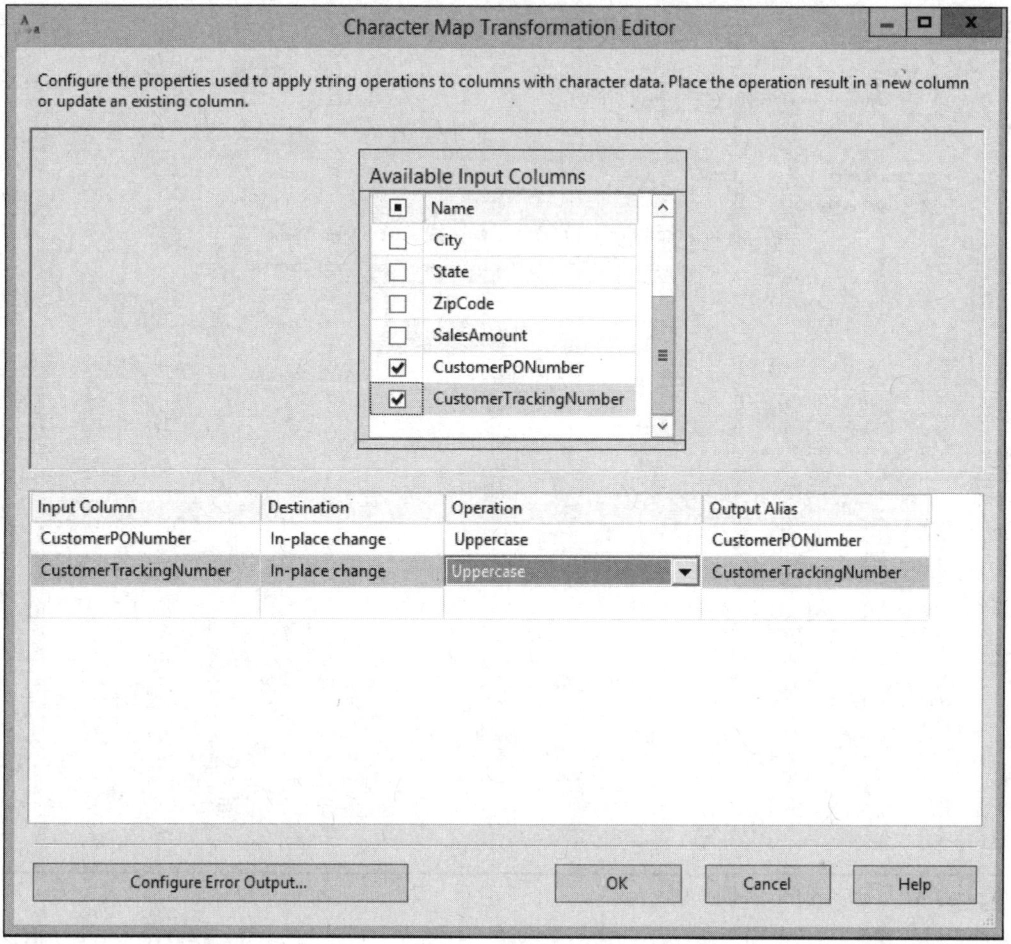

Figure 7-66 *The Character Map Transformation Editor dialog box*

Conditional Split   The *Conditional Split* transformation enables us to split the data

[Conditional Split icon] flow into multiple outputs. In the Conditional Split Transformation
Editor dialog box, shown in Figure 7-68, we define conditions for
each branch of the split. When the package executes, each row in the data flow is
compared against the conditions in order. When the row meets a set of conditions, the
row is sent to that branch of the split.

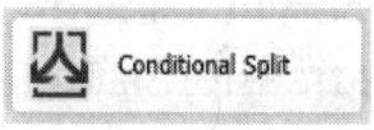

In Figure 7-68, the conditional split has been defined with three branches. If the content
of the SalesAmount column for a given row is less than $10, that row is sent to the

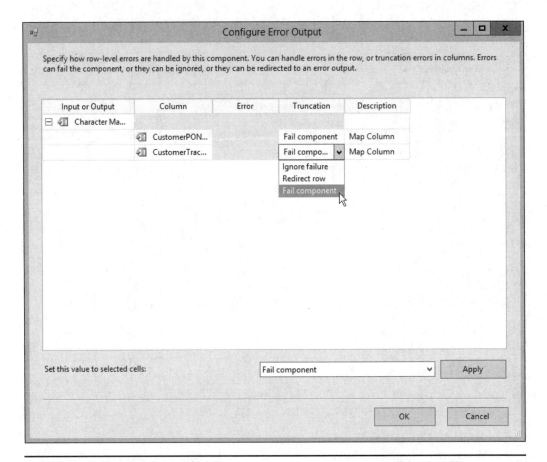

Figure 7-67 *Configure Error Output dialog box*

SmallSales output. If the content of the SalesAmount column is between $10 and $50 inclusive, the row is sent to the MediumSales output. If the content of the SalesAmount column does not fit either of these conditions, the row is sent to the default output, named LargeSales. Figure 7-69 shows the three outputs from the Conditional Split transformation being routed to three different paths through the data flow.

The Configure Error Output button displays the Configure Error Output dialog box, where we determine the error behavior of this transformation. In addition to truncation, we need to configure the behavior when the condition statement fails during evaluation. For each output column defined, we can choose to ignore an error, send the row containing the error to the error output, or fail the entire transformation.

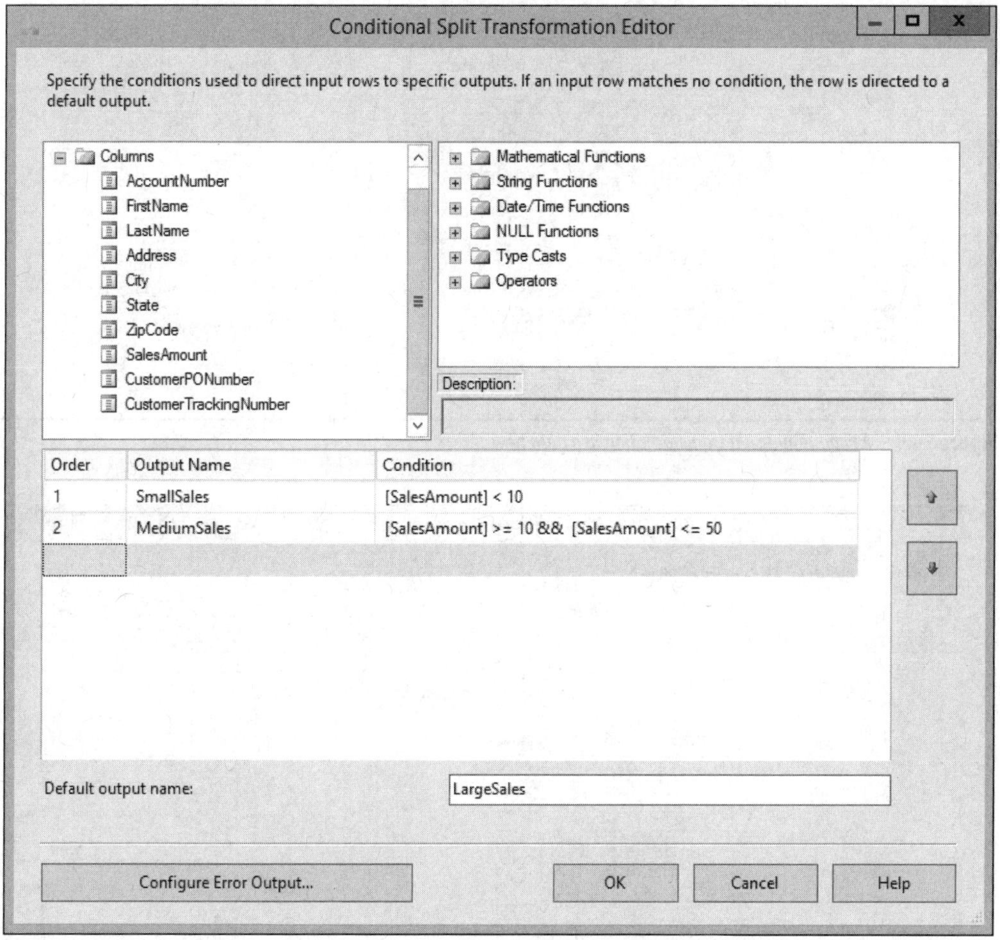

Figure 7-68 *The Conditional Split Transformation Editor dialog box*

Copy Column   The *Copy Column* transformation lets us create new columns in the
data flow that are copies of existing columns. The new columns can
then be used later in the data flow for calculations, transformations,
or mapping to columns in the data destination. Figure 7-70 shows the Copy Column
Transformation Editor dialog box with the SalesAmount column being copied to a new
column called SalesAmountForTaxCalculation.

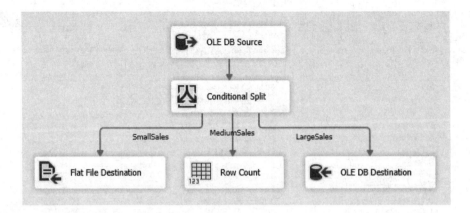

Figure 7-69 *A Conditional Split transformation in a data flow*

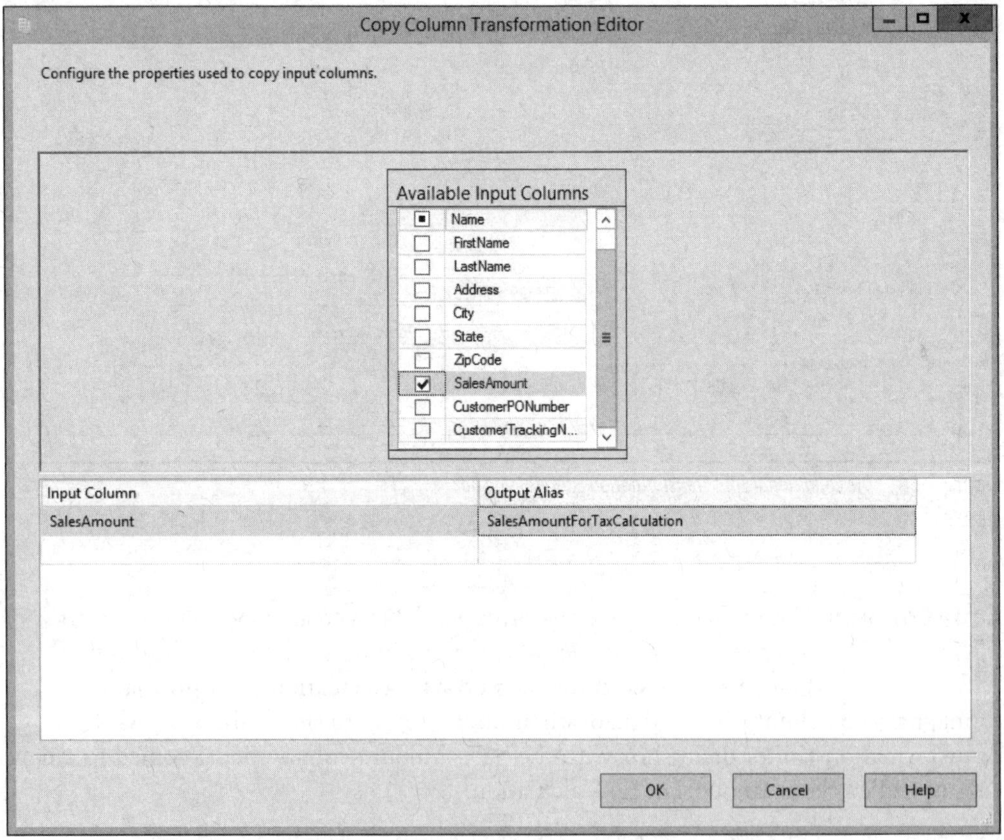

Figure 7-70 *The Copy Column Transformation Editor dialog box*

Data Conversion   The *Data Conversion* transformation enables us to convert columns
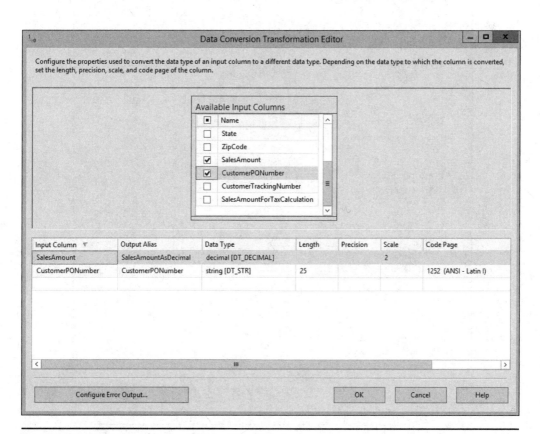from one data type to another. The converted data can either replace
the existing column or be added as a new column. The Configure Error
Output dialog box functions the same as it does for the Conditional Split transformation.

Figure 7-71 shows the Data Conversion Transformation Editor dialog box with two
columns set up for conversion. The currency type contents of the SalesAmount column
are converted to a decimal, with two places to the right of the decimal point. The decimal
value is placed in a new column called SalesAmountAsDecimal. The Unicode contents
of the CustomerPONumber column are replaced by its single-byte equivalent.

Data Mining Query   The *Data Mining Query* transformation lets us execute a DMX
query on the data flow. Using the DMX query along with a data
mining model, we can make predictions based on the data in each

Figure 7-71   *The Data Conversion Transformation Editor dialog box*

row of the data flow. These predictions can indicate other items that are likely to be associated with the column (that is, other products a customer is likely to purchase based on the current purchase) or the likelihood of a column to fit a certain condition (that is, the likelihood of a prospective client to be interested in a certain service).

The columns that result from the DMX query are added as new columns in the data flow. The new columns can be sent along with the rest of the data to the data destination, or they can be used along with the Conditional Split transformation to send rows to different data destinations based on the prediction. Figure 7-72 shows the Mining Model tab of the Data Mining Query Transformation Editor dialog box.

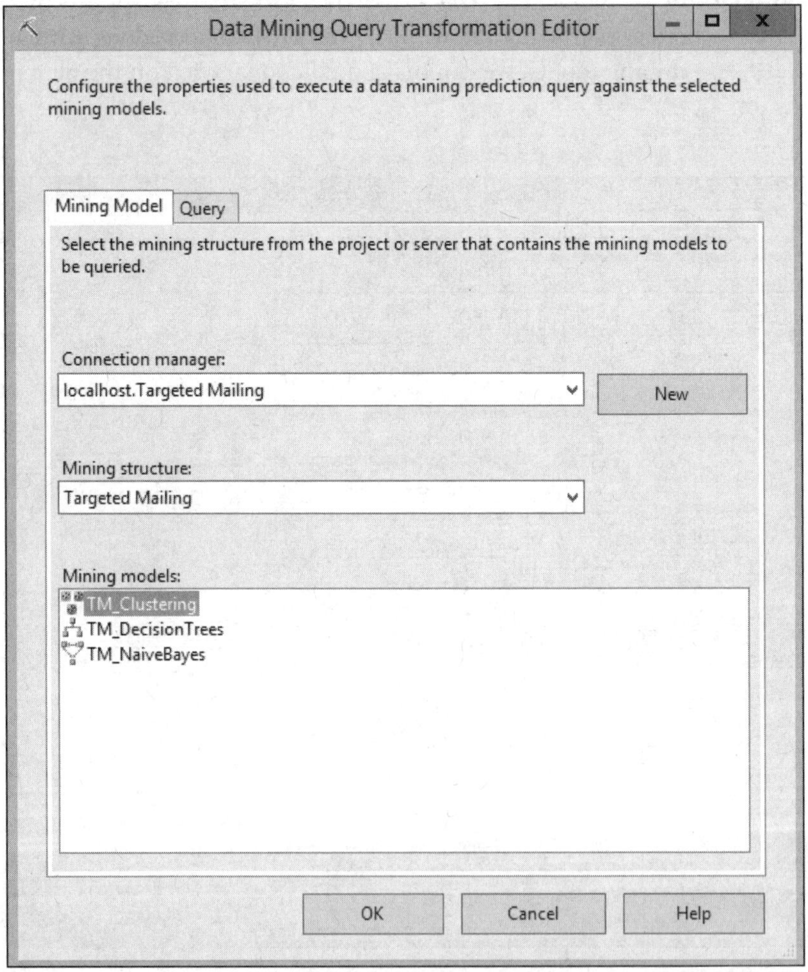

Figure 7-72   *The Mining Model tab of the Data Mining Query Transformation Editor dialog box*

Derived Column   The *Derived Column* transformation enables us to create a value

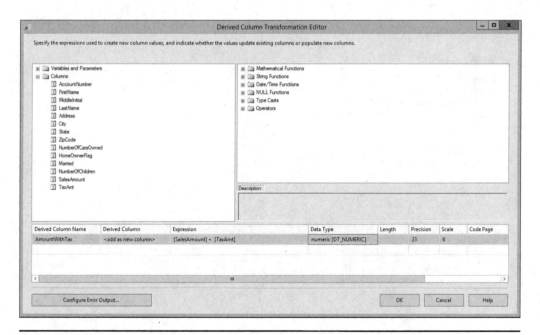 derived from an expression. The expression can use values from variables and the content of columns in the data flow. The value can replace the content of an existing column or be added to the data flow as a new column. Figure 7-73 shows the Derived Column Transformation Editor dialog box defining a new column, AmountWithTax, which contains the sum of the SalesAmount and TaxAmt columns. The Derived Column transformation uses the same Configure Error Output dialog box as the Conditional Split transformation.

DQS Cleansing   The *DQS Cleansing* transformation allows us to use a data quality knowledge base managed by SQL Server Data Quality Services (DQS) to evaluate and cleanse our data. A DQS knowledge base contains information about what does or does not make something a valid bit of data. This might be things like

▶ What are the valid country names

▶ What makes up a valid e-mail address

▶ What are the possible job titles in your organization

Figure 7-73   *The Derived Column Transformation Editor dialog box*

Each of these areas within the knowledge base (country names, e-mail addresses, job titles) is known as a domain.

Once we have captured the information about one or more domains in a knowledge base, we can use the DQS Cleansing transformation to apply that captured knowledge to our data. The Connection Manager tab of the DQS Cleansing Transformation Editor dialog box is shown in Figure 7-74. Here we can create or select a Connection Manager to an instance of SQL Server running Data Quality Services. When a connection has been chosen, we can select one of the knowledge bases on that server. Once the knowledge base is selected, we can see all of the domains within that knowledge base.

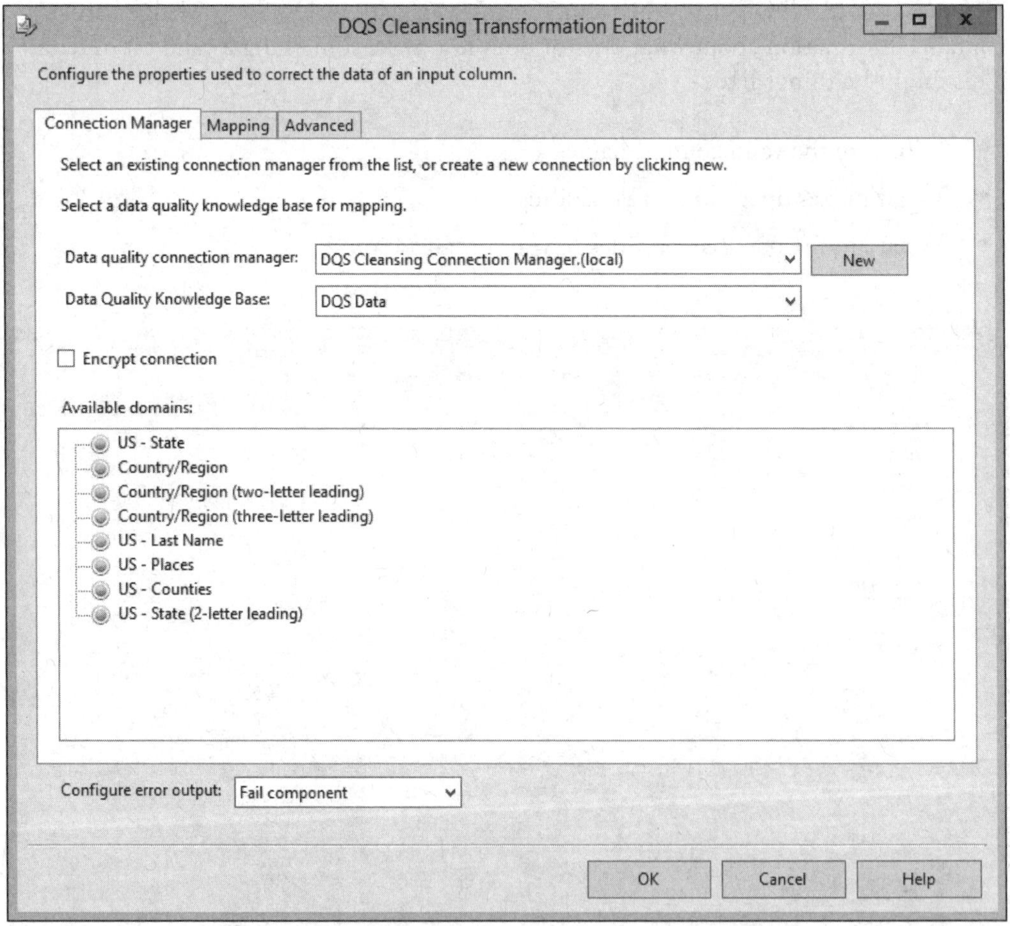

Figure 7-74   *The Connection Manager tab of the DQS Cleansing Transformation Editor dialog box*

On the Mapping tab of the DQS Cleansing Transformation Editor dialog box, shown in Figure 7-75, we select the columns in the data flow to which we apply the knowledge base. For each column selected, we pick a domain from the knowledge base to be used with that column. We also specify the output aliases for the source data, the corrected data, and the status for each column. These are all added as columns to the data flow. In addition to these, a Record Status column is added to the data flow.

The Record Status column, and possibly the statuses for the individual columns, can be used along with a Conditional Split transformation to determine how to handle each record in our data flow. Figure 7-76 shows one possible way to separate out data coming

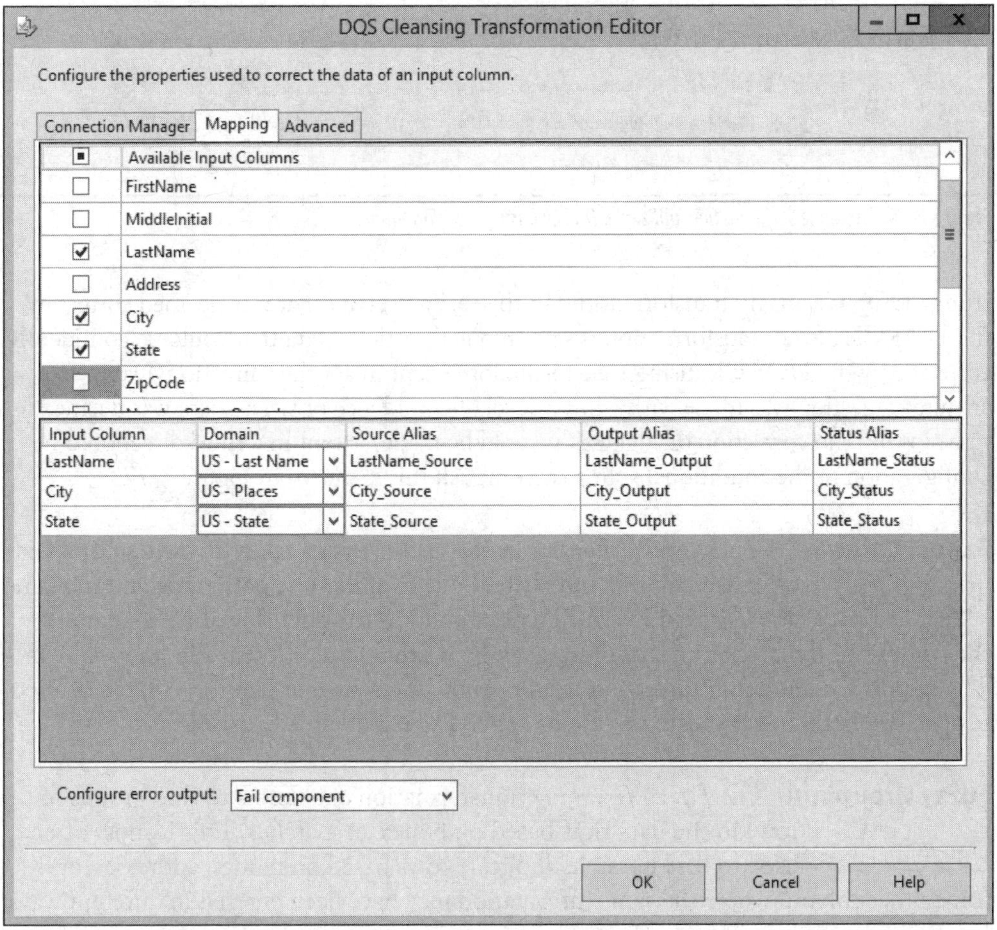

Figure 7-75   *The Mapping tab of the DQS Cleansing Transformation Editor dialog box*

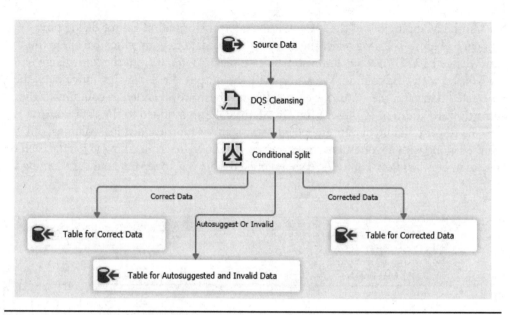

Figure 7-76   *A simple SSIS data flow utilizing a DQS Cleansing Transformation*

from a DQS Cleansing transformation. In this example, data that was deemed correct by the DQS Cleansing transformation is sent in one direction. Data that could be confidently corrected by the DQS Cleansing transformation is sent in another direction. Data where an autosuggestion was made with a lower level of confidence or where data was deemed to be invalid (no correction or suggestion could be made) is sent in a third direction. The configuration of the conditional split to accomplish this is shown in Figure 7-77.

Export Column   The *Export Column* transformation lets us take the content of a text or image column and write it out to a file. The pathname and filename are specified in a different column in the data flow. In this manner, the content of the text or image column can be written to a different file for each row. The Export Column Transformation Editor dialog box, shown in Figure 7-78, can be used to specify whether to truncate the file or append to it if it already exists.

Fuzzy Grouping   The *Fuzzy Grouping* transformation enables us to find groups of rows in the data flow based on nonexact matches. This is most often used to find possible duplicate rows based on names, addresses, or some other column where the same information may have been entered in different ways. For example, a row for Ms. Kathy Jones, a second row for Ms. Kathryn Jones, and a third row for Ms. Cathy Jones may be three entries for the same person.

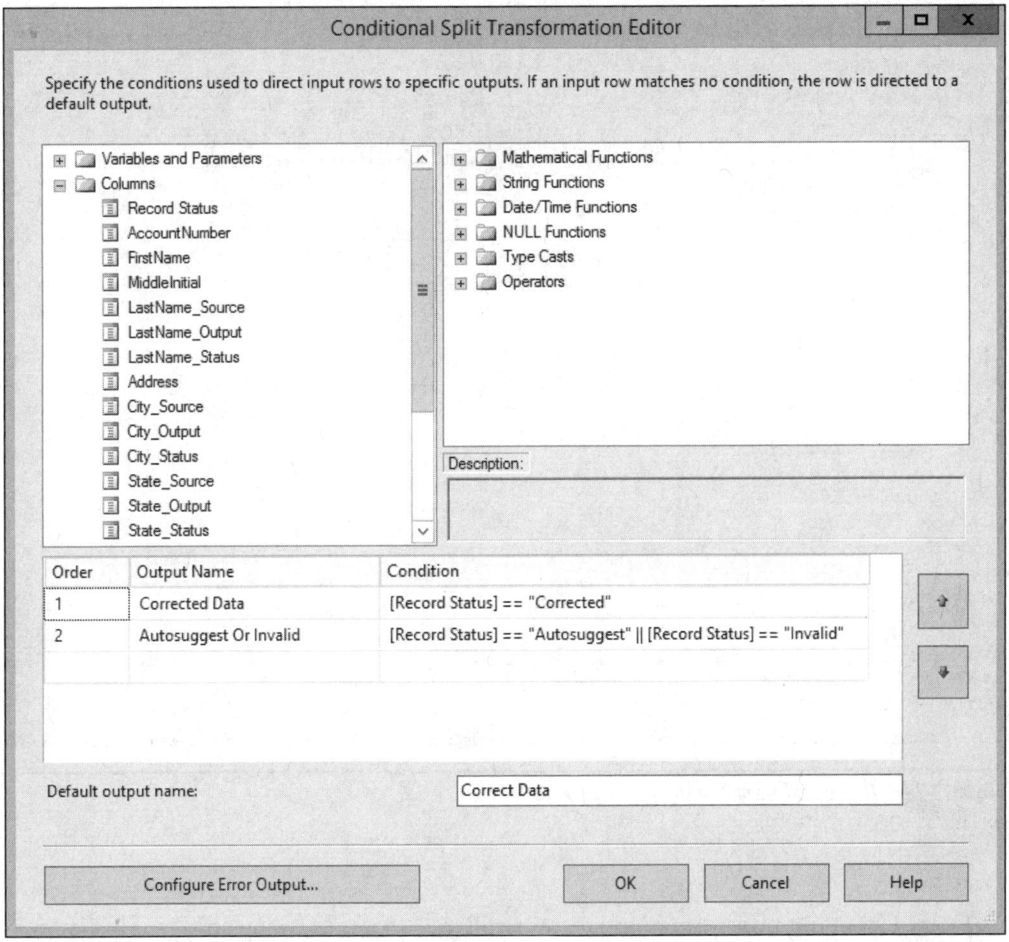

Figure 7-77   *A conditional split based on DQS Cleansing Transformation Record Status output*

The Fuzzy Grouping transformation selects one of the rows in the group as the best candidate for the other rows to be combined into, and this is the *model row*. Once the groups and their model rows have been identified, we can use another transformation to combine any unique information from the nonmodel rows into the model row and delete the nonmodel rows. This removes the duplication from the data. The Fuzzy Grouping transformation identifies row groups and model rows; it does not combine any data or delete any nonmodel rows. This must be done as a separate step in the package or as a manual operation.

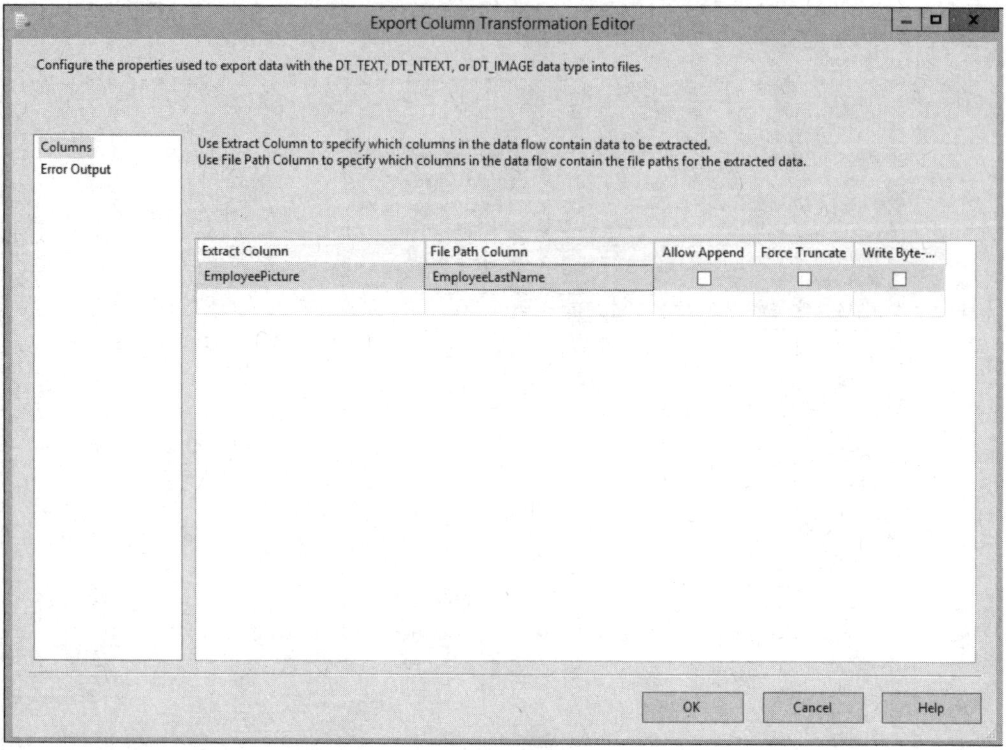

Figure 7-78 *The Export Column Transformation Editor dialog box*

Fuzzy Grouping transformation creates similarity scores between strings. This is done by considering the edit distance between two strings. In other words, how many character inserts, deletions, and replacements must be made in one string to produce the other string? Kathy and Kathryn have an edit distance of 2, because we need to insert an *r* and an *n* into the first word to get the second. Kathy and Cathy have an edit distance of 1, because we simply need to replace *K* with *C* in the first word to get the second.

In addition to edit distance, Fuzzy Grouping uses information, such as frequency of character occurrence and the positions of the characters, among other things, to increase its accuracy when creating similarity scores. Fuzzy Grouping is great at detecting character transpositions and other common spelling errors. All of the algorithms that create the similarity scores are language-independent, so Fuzzy Grouping can work with any language we care to throw at it.

NOTE

Fuzzy Grouping assumes a string that is all uppercase is an acronym. Because even acronyms that have a close edit distance, say, FTC and FCC, are not likely to be the same thing, it is unlikely that groups will be identified for strings in all uppercase. If your data was entered in all uppercase (this can be especially true for legacy data), it is important to use the Character Map transformation to change the string to lowercase before trying a Fuzzy Grouping transformation.

On the Columns tab of the Fuzzy Grouping Transformation Editor dialog box, shown in Figure 7-79, we select the columns to use when looking for groupings. These columns can be set for fuzzy matching that uses similarity scoring or for exact matching. In the example in Figure 7-77, the content of the Title column—Mr. or Ms.—must match exactly before we want to even think about trying a fuzzy match on the FirstName and LastName columns. In addition to the exact or fuzzy match setting, we can specify whether leading or trailing numerals (0–9) are significant or should be ignored. (Selecting Leading from the Numerals drop-down list indicates that leading numerals are significant, and so forth.)

The columns we select for grouping on the Columns page are automatically passed through to the output of the Fuzzy Grouping transformation. For each of the columns used in the grouping, the Fuzzy Grouping transformation adds a "clean" column to the output. These clean columns contain the values from the row that the Fuzzy Grouping transformation has selected as the model row for that group. In our previous example,

Fuzzy Grouping Transformation Editor

Configure the properties used to group input rows that are likely duplicates, and choose a canonical row for each group.

Connection Manager | Columns | Advanced

Specify which columns to join and the use of reference columns.

Available Input Columns

	Name	Pass Throu...
	AccountNumber	✔
✔	FirstName	▪
	MiddleInitial	✔
✔	LastName	▪
✔	Title	▪
	Address	✔

Input Column	Output Alias	Group Output Alias	Match Type	Minimum Similarity	Similarity Output Alias	Numerals	Comparison Flags
FirstName	FirstName	FirstName_clean	Fuzzy	0	_Similarity_FirstName	Neither	Ignore case, Ignore kana type, Ignore nonspacing characters, Ignore character width
LastName	LastName	LastName_clean	Fuzzy	0	_Similarity_LastName	Neither	Ignore case, Ignore kana type, Ignore nonspacing characters, Ignore character width
Title	Title	Title_clean	Exact	1		Leading and Trailing	Ignore case, Ignore kana type, Ignore nonspacing characters, Ignore character width

OK | Cancel | Help

Figure 7-79   *The Columns tab of the Fuzzy Grouping Transformation Editor dialog box*

if the row containing Ms. Kathy Jones is chosen as the model row for the group, the FirstName_clean column would contain Kathy for the Ms. Kathy Jones row, the Ms. Kathryn Jones row, and the Ms. Cathy Jones row.

We can also select columns to be passed through from the input to the output without participating in the transformation by placing a check mark in the Pass Through column. The Fuzzy Grouping transformation can add three more columns to the output. The default names for these columns are _key_in, _key_out, and _score. We can change the names of these columns on the Advanced tab of the Fuzzy Grouping Transformation Editor dialog box, shown in Figure 7-80.

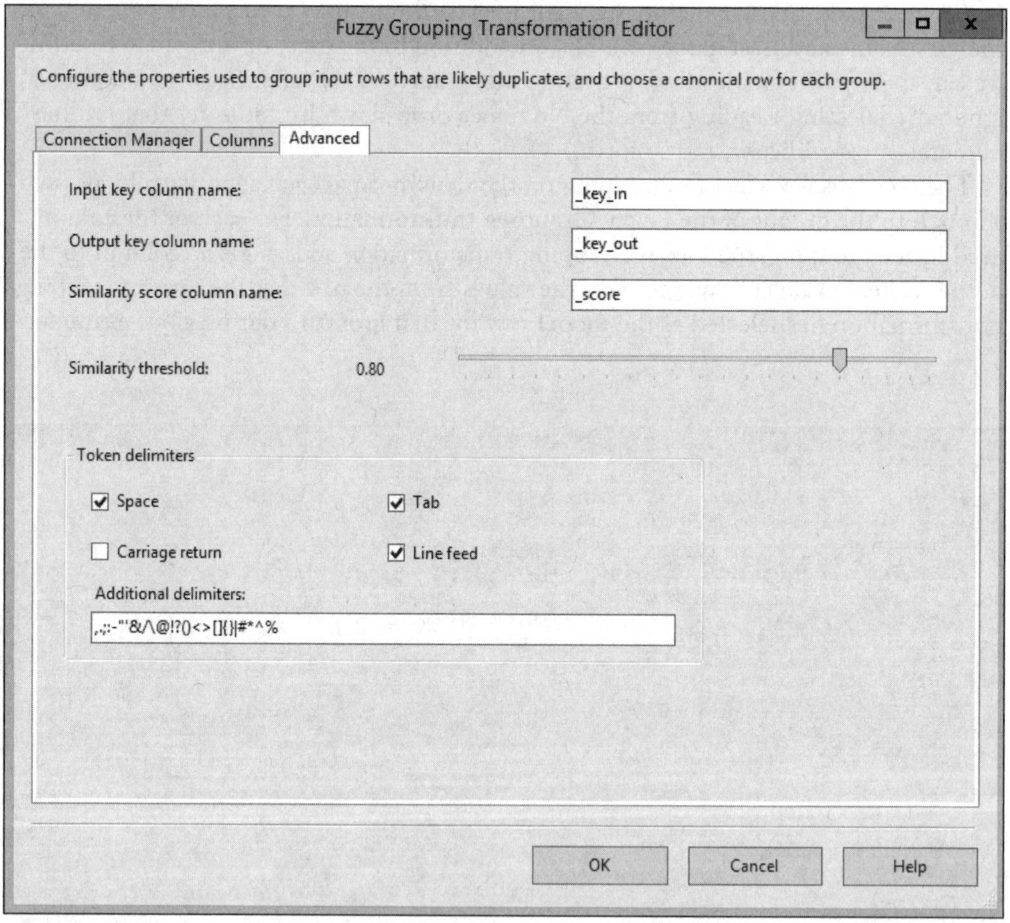

Figure 7-80   *The Advanced tab of the Fuzzy Grouping Transformation Editor dialog box*

The _key_in column contains a unique identifier for each field. This unique identifier is generated by the Fuzzy Grouping transformation. If a row is not grouped with any other rows, or if it is the model row for a group of rows, then it has the same identifier in its _key_out column as it has in its _key_in field. If a row is in a group and it is not the model row for that group, then it has the identifier of the model row in its _key_out column.

The _score column contains the similarity score assigned to the row. The higher the similarity score, the more confidence the Fuzzy Grouping transformation has in the match. A row that is not grouped or that is a model row for a group always has a similarity score of 1. A row that is in a group and is not a model row has a similarity score between 0 and 1, inclusive.

On the Advanced tab of the Fuzzy Grouping Transformation Editor dialog box, we can set the threshold for the similarity score. Similarity scores that fall below the threshold are not used to create groups. A lower threshold allows the Fuzzy Grouping transformation to find more groups of duplicate rows, but also increases the risk of false positives. A higher threshold makes fewer mistakes, but increases the risk that some actual duplicates will not be found. Some experimenting should be done with your data to determine the best threshold for each Fuzzy Grouping transformation.

The Fuzzy Grouping transformation creates a lookup list of items and does fuzzy matching on that lookup list to create the groupings. If we are dealing with the processing of a data flow with a large number of rows, the Fuzzy Grouping transformation may need to write the lookup list to disk. The OLE DB Connection Manager selected on the Connection Manager tab provides access to a tempdb database where this temporary lookup list can be written. Because of this necessity to create a lookup list, the Fuzzy Grouping task can be rather slow.

Fuzzy Lookup   The *Fuzzy Lookup* transformation lets us look up values using fuzzy matching logic. The Fuzzy Lookup transformation is closely related to the Fuzzy Grouping transformation. In fact, as was noted, the Fuzzy Grouping transformation creates its own lookup list and then does a fuzzy lookup.

The Fuzzy Lookup transformation is extremely useful when the data is moving from a database where a column was entered as freeform text to another database where that same column uses a lookup table and a foreign key constraint. Without the Fuzzy Lookup transformation, any typos in the freeform data leave us with a situation where we cannot determine the appropriate foreign key value to put in the destination table. However, with the Fuzzy Lookup transformation, we can determine a foreign key value even when typos are present.

The Fuzzy Lookup transformation uses an existing table or view as the source for its lookup operation. The transformation creates a copy of the source lookup table to use during the transformation processing. It then creates a second table that holds the information necessary for calculating the similarity score. This second table is called the *match index*. Don't let the name fool you—this is really a table created in the same database that holds the source lookup table.

The copy of the source lookup table and the match index table can be created as temporary tables each time the package is run. This is a good idea if the package performs a one-time data load operation. However, if the package is going to be run frequently, it is more efficient to create these tables as regular tables in the database. This is done using the Store new index check box on the Reference Table tab of the Fuzzy Lookup Transformation Editor dialog box, as shown in Figure 7-81. For the most

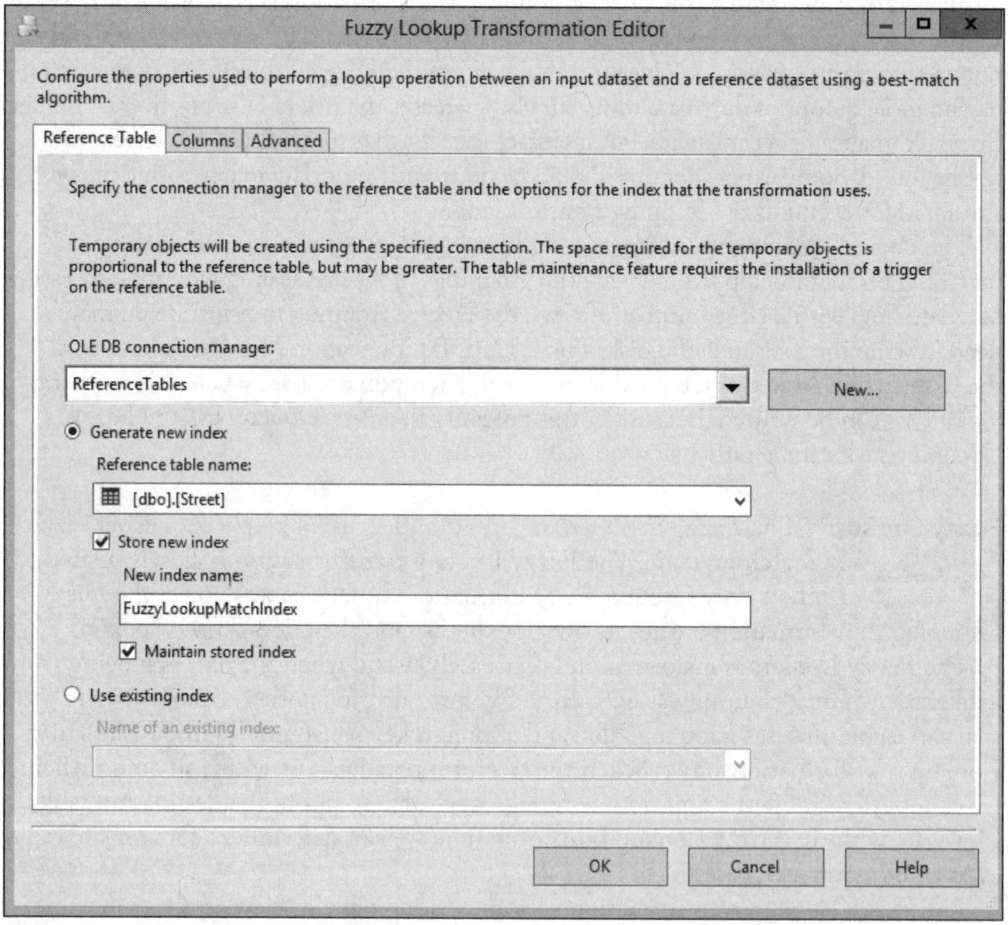

Figure 7-81   *The Reference Table tab of the Fuzzy Lookup Transformation Editor dialog box*

efficient operation of the package, we can have the database maintain the match index, so any changes to the source lookup table cause an update to the match index. If a match index already exists in the database, we can use it directly by selecting Use existing index and selecting the name of the index table.

Once the match index is configured, we can use the Columns tab to map one or more columns from the data flow to columns in the source lookup table. This is done by dragging a column from the Available Input Columns and dropping it on the corresponding column in the Available Lookup Columns. We can then set the behavior of the transformation using the Advanced tab. The Advanced tab enables us to specify the maximum number of source table records we want the transformation to find for each input row. This is usually one. We can also specify the similarity score threshold for this transformation. This works on the same scale as the Fuzzy Grouping transformation.

The Fuzzy Lookup transformation adds one column to the output for each column from the source lookup table that is used in the lookup. In addition to this, the _Similarity and _Confidence columns are added. The _Similarity column shows the similarity score for the lookup done for that row. The _Confidence column shows how much confidence to place on the lookup that was just completed. Like the similarity score, the confidence figure is a number between 0 and 1, inclusive. A confidence level of 1 represents a near certainty that a value is correct. A confidence level of 0 indicates no confidence in the match at all.

Import Column   The *Import Column* transformation lets us take the content of a set of files and insert it into a text or image column in the data flow. The pathname and filename are specified in a different column in the data flow. In this manner, the content of a different text or image file can be written to each row in the data flow. The Input Columns tab of the Advanced Editor for Import Column dialog box is shown in Figure 7-82.

Lookup   The *Lookup* transformation works similarly to the Fuzzy Lookup transformation. The difference is the Lookup transformation requires exact matches, rather than using similarity scores. The selection of the source lookup table and the column mapping is done in much the same way as for the Fuzzy Lookup transformation.

One difference between the Lookup transformation and the Fuzzy Lookup transformation is found on the Advanced page of the Lookup Transformation Editor dialog box, as shown in Figure 7-83. When the Lookup transformation executes, by default, it loads the entire source lookup table into cache for faster processing. If the source lookup table is too large to be completely loaded into cache, we can set a restriction on the amount

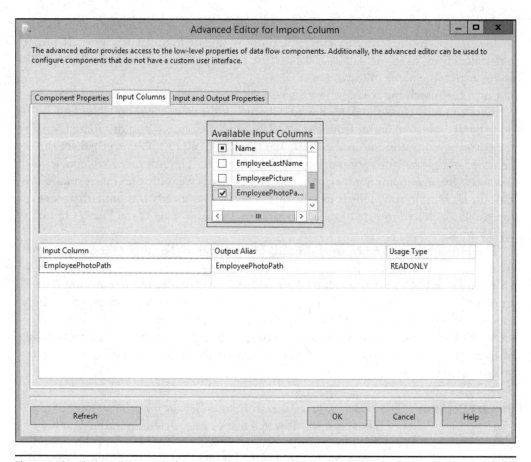

Figure 7-82   *The Input Columns tab of the Advanced Editor for Import Column dialog box*

of memory used. In Figure 7-83, the cache memory usage has been restricted to 5MB for both the 32-bit and 64-bit caching.

In addition, if only a portion of the records in the source lookup table is needed to resolve the lookups for a given Lookup transformation, we can load only the required portion of the source lookup table into memory. This is done by modifying the caching SQL statement and adding a WHERE clause. In Figure 7-83 a WHERE clause has been added so only the urban streets in the Street lookup table are loaded into memory. The additional WHERE clause is the highlighted portion of the Caching SQL statement.

The Error Output page of the dialog box lets us determine whether an unresolved lookup is ignored, sent to the error output, or causes the transformation to fail.

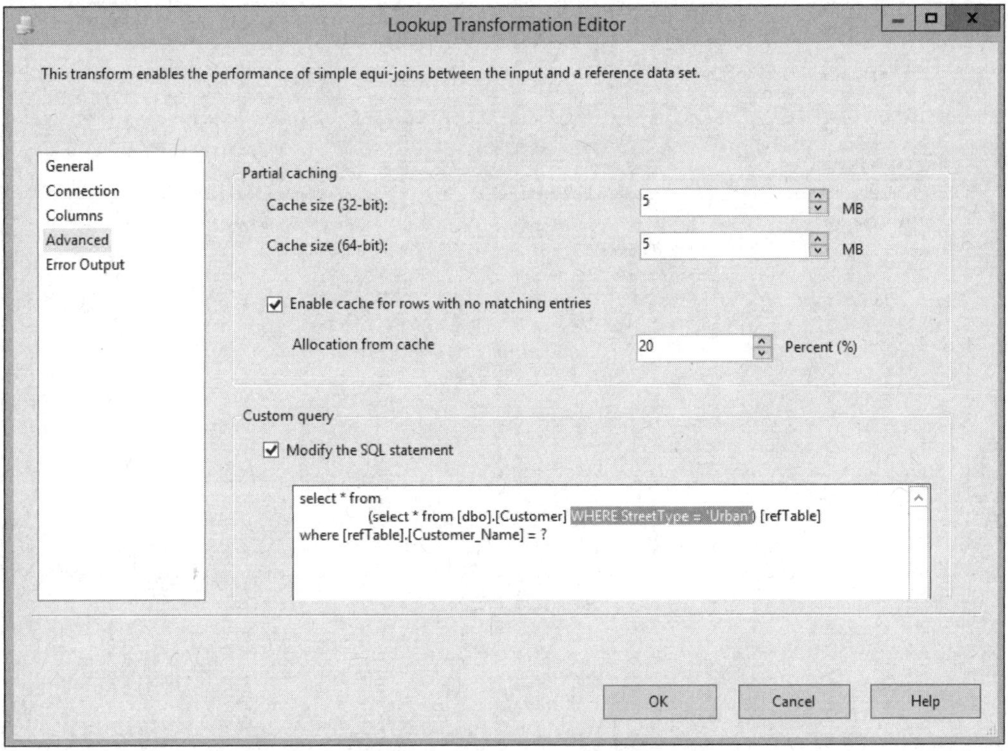

Figure 7-83 *The Advanced page of the Lookup Transformation Editor dialog box*

Merge The *Merge* transformation merges two data flows together. For the Merge transformation to work properly, both input data flows must be sorted using the same sort order. This can be done by using the Sort transformation in each data flow prior to the Merge transformation. Alternately, if the rows coming from the data source are already sorted by the data provider, you can set the IsSorted property to true for the output of that data provider. The IsSorted property is only available in the Advanced Editor dialog box for the data source. The two data flows are merged together, so the output is sorted in the same manner as the inputs.

Figure 7-84 shows the Merge Transformation Editor dialog box with two lists of street addresses that are being merged together. Each input is sorted first by the street name, and then by the street number. When the records from the two inputs are merged together, the resulting output will also be in street name, street number order.

All of the rows in both of the input data flows are present in the merged output. For example, say 450 rows are in the first input data flow and 375 rows are in the second input data flow. There will be 825 rows in the output data flow.

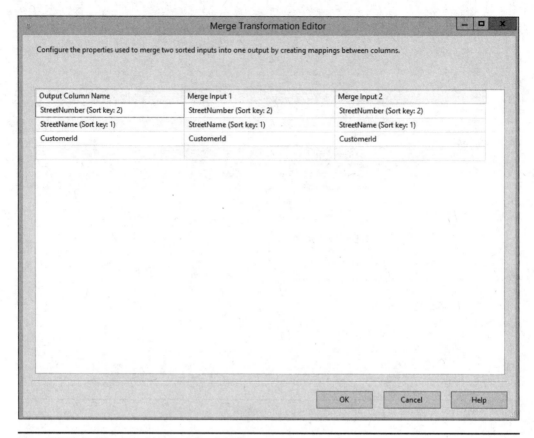

Figure 7-84 *The Merge Transformation Editor dialog box*

Merge Join The *Merge Join* transformation enables us to merge two data flows together by executing an inner join, a left outer join, or a full outer join. As with the Merge transformation, both of the input data flows must be sorted. With the Merge Join transformation, both of the data flows must be sorted by the columns to be used as the join condition.

Figure 7-85 shows the Merge Join Transformation Editor dialog box. In this example, an inner join is being used to join the Address Table data flow with the Street Lookup List data flow. The *join key* requires the StreetName column from the Address Table to match the CompleteName column from the Street Lookup List. Because an inner join is being used, only those rows that contain a match are included in the output.

If a left outer join were used in the example in Figure 7-85, all of the columns from the Address Table data flow would be included in the output, even if a matching column

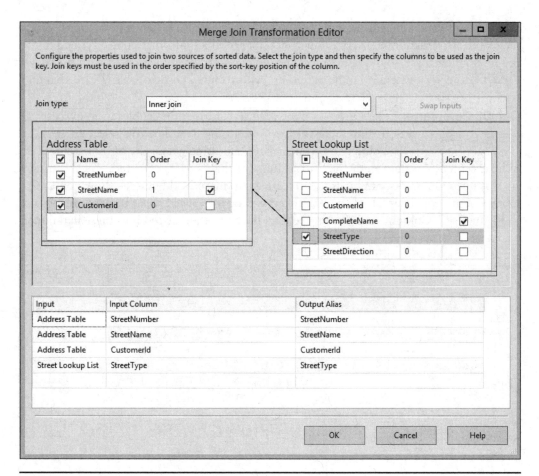

Figure 7-85   *The Merge Join Transformation Editor dialog box*

in the Street Lookup List data flow was not found. (The Address Table data flow was identified as the left input flow when it was connected to the Merge Join transformation.) If a full join were used in the example in Figure 7-85, all of the columns from both the Address Table data flow and the Street Lookup List data flow would be included in the output. The output of the Merge Join transformation is always sorted on the join key column or columns.

Multicast   The *Multicast* transformation lets us take a single data flow and use it as the input to several data flow transformations or data flow destination items. The Multicast transformation simply copies the data flow and sends it in multiple directions. Figure 7-86 shows the Multicast Transformation Editor dialog box. In this example, a data flow containing product information needs to go to the online store database, to the sales processing system, to the commissions system, and to the FTP directory, where it can be picked up by distributed point-of-sale (POS) systems.

OLE DB Command   The *OLE DB Command* transformation enables us to execute a SQL statement for each row in the data flow. We select an OLE DB Connection Manager to determine where the SQL statement is to be executed. We then enter the SQL statement that is to be executed. Placeholders, such as question marks, can be used to create a parameterized query, as shown on the Component Properties tab of the Advanced Editor for OLE DB Command dialog box in Figure 7-87. Column values from the data flow can then be fed into these parameters

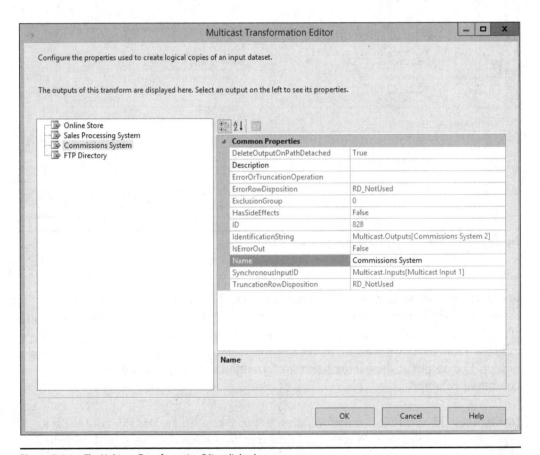

Figure 7-86   *The Multicast Transformation Editor dialog box*

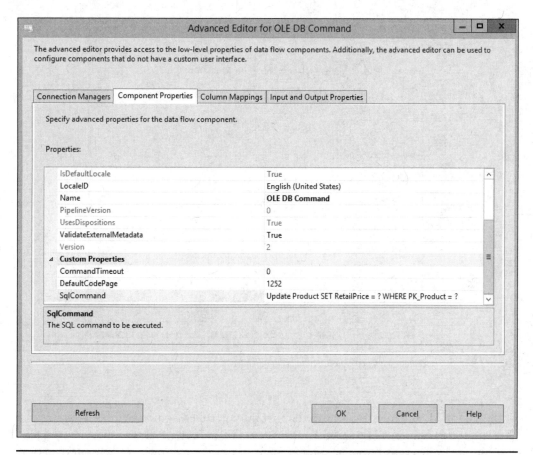

Figure 7-87   *The Component Properties tab of the Advanced Editor for OLE DB Command dialog box*

as the SQL statement is executed for each data flow. In the example in Figure 7-87, the retail price of existing product records is updated based on information in the data flow.

Percentage Sampling   The *Percentage Sampling* transformation lets us split the data flow into two separate data flows based on a percentage. This can be useful when we want to create a small sample of a larger set of data for testing or for training a data mining model. Figure 7-88 shows the Percentage Sampling Transformation Editor dialog box.

Two outputs are created from the Percentage Sampling transformation item. The first output contains the rows that were selected to be part of the sample. In the example in Figure 7-88, 10 percent of the total rows in the input data flow are selected to be part

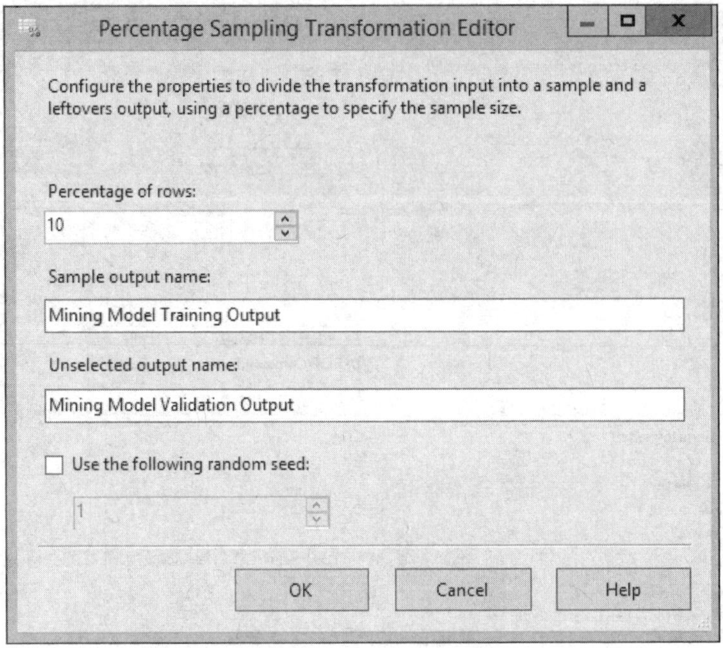

Figure 7-88   *The Percentage Sampling Transformation Editor dialog box*

of the sample. These rows are sent to the first output, called Mining Model Training Output in this example. The second output contains the rows that were not selected for the sample. In this case, the remaining 90 percent of the total rows in the input data flow are to be sent to the second output, called Mining Model Validation Output.

The Percentage Sampling transformation selects rows at random from the input data flow. This random sampling provides a more representative sample of the entire data flow than simply selecting the top *N* rows. Because of the workings of the random sampling algorithm, the number of rows included in the sample is going to be close to the percentage specified, but it may not hit it exactly.

Pivot   The *Pivot* transformation enables us to take normalized data and change it into a less normalized structure. This is done by taking the content of one or more columns in the input data flow and using it as column names in the output data flow. The data in these newly created columns is calculated by taking an aggregate of the contents of another column from the input data flow. An aggregate must be used because a number of rows from the input data flow may define a single row in the output data flow. Figure 7-89 shows the Pivot dialog box.

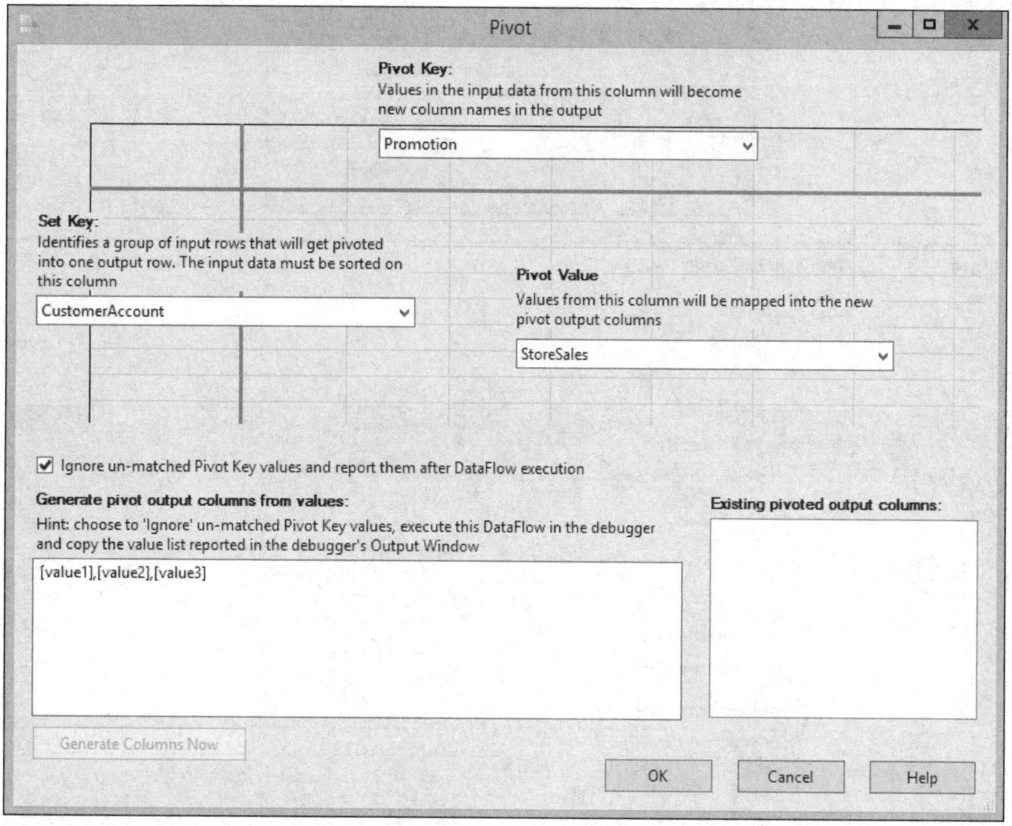

Figure 7-89   *The Pivot dialog box*

Row Count   The *Row Count* transformation lets us determine the number of rows in the data flow. This count is stored in a package variable. The package variable can then be used in expressions to modify the control flow or the data flow in the package. All of the columns in the Row Count transformation's input flow are simply passed on to the output flow. The Row Count dialog box is shown in Figure 7-90.

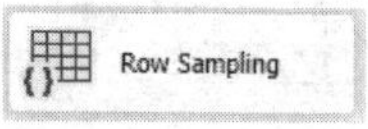

Row Sampling   The *Row Sampling* transformation enables us to split the data flow into two separate data flows based on the number of rows desired. The Row Sampling transformation works in the same manner as the Percentage Sampling transformation. The only difference is the Row Sampling transformation determines the number of rows in the sample based on a requested row count, rather than a requested percentage. The Row Sampling Transformation Editor dialog box is shown in Figure 7-91.

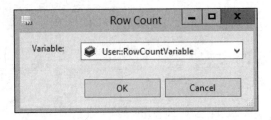

Figure 7-90 *The Row Count dialog box*

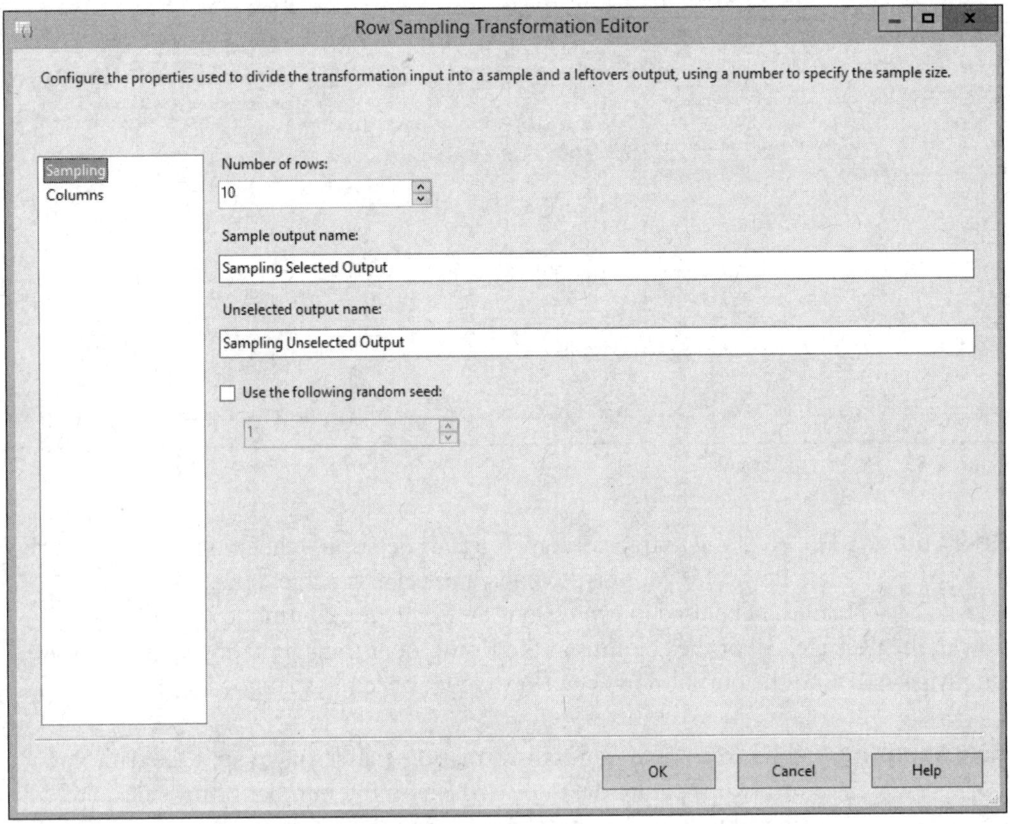

Figure 7-91 *The Row Sampling Transformation Editor dialog box*

Script Component   The *Script Component* transformation lets us create .NET 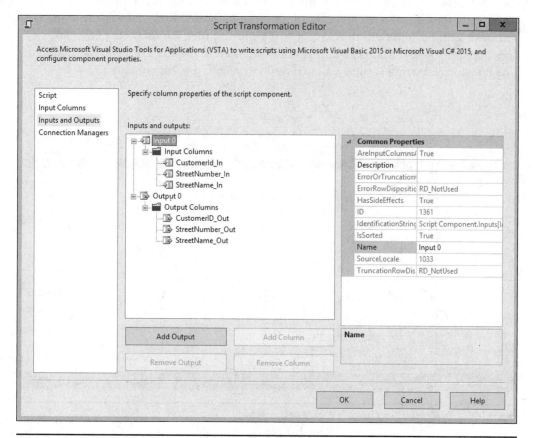 code for execution as part of our data flow. The Script Component transformation can be used as a data source, a data destination, or a data transformation. Our script code could read data from a file format that is not supported by any of the Connection Managers, and then expose those rows as its output data flow. In this case, the Script Component item functions as a data source. Our script code could take rows from its input data flow and write data to a file format that is not supported by any of the Connection Managers. In this scenario, the Script Component item functions as a data destination. Finally, the script code could take rows from its input data flow, modify the data in a way not supported by the other data transformations, and then expose those rows as its output data flow. Here, the Script Component item functions as a data transformation.

The data inputs and outputs that are going to be used in the script, even if they are just going to be passed through, must be defined on the Inputs and Outputs page of the Script Transformation Editor dialog box. This is shown in Figure 7-92. Make sure to

Figure 7-92   *The Inputs and Outputs page of the Script Transformation Editor dialog box*

use different names for the input and output columns. If we use the same name for both an input and an output, only the output column will be visible to the script code.

In the example shown in Figure 7-92, we have street names from a legacy system that were entered in uppercase. We want to change these to title case (sometimes known as proper case; the first character of each word in uppercase, with the remaining characters in lowercase) as part of our Integration Services package. The Copy Column transformation provides translations to lowercase and uppercase, but not to title case. We need to create a custom script to accomplish this task.

Clicking Edit Script on the Script page of the Script Transformation Editor dialog box displays the Microsoft Visual Studio dialog box, where we can edit the script. This is shown in Figure 7-93. The Input0_ProcessInputRow method is executed once for each row in the input data flow. The Row object parameter, which is passed to this method, contains the properties that provide access to both the input and output columns defined on the Inputs and Outputs page.

The sample code simply copies the CustomerIdIn and StreetNumberIn values from the input data flow to the CustomerIdOut and StreetNumberOut columns in the output data flow. The StreetNameIn column is transformed first to lowercase using the ToLower method, and then to title case using the ToTitleCase method. (ToTitleCase does not work on text that is all uppercase, so we need to use the ToLower method first.) The transformed string is then assigned to the StreetNameOut column.

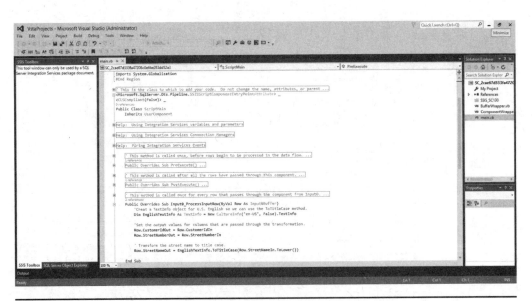

Figure 7-93 *The Microsoft Visual Studio for Applications dialog box*

Slowly Changing Dimension   The *Slowly Changing Dimension* transformation

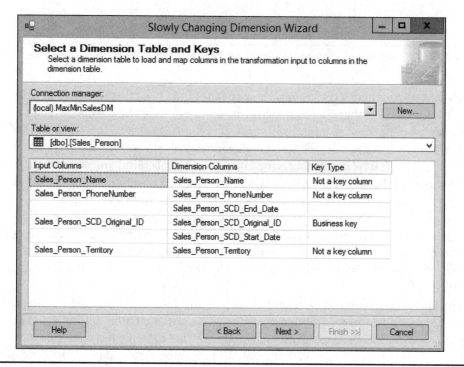

enables us to use a data flow to update the information in a slowly changing dimension of a data mart. This transformation is configured using the Slowly Changing Dimension Wizard. The wizard walks us through the steps necessary to use the input data flow columns to properly update the slowly changing dimension.

The first page of the wizard after the welcome page, the Select a Dimension Table and Keys page, is shown in Figure 7-94. This wizard page requires us to select the Connection Manager that lets us connect to the data mart and to select the table containing the slowly changing dimension. This wizard page also requires us to map the input data flow columns to the fields in the dimension table and to specify which column is the business key column (the unique identifier for the dimension information).

The next page of the wizard, the Slowly Changing Dimension Columns page, is shown in Figure 7-95. This wizard page enables us to specify how each of the nonkey columns in the dimension table should be treated when it changes. A column such as the Sales_Person_Name column is fixed relative to the salesperson ID. A situation

Figure 7-94   *The Select a Dimension Table and Keys page of the Slowly Changing Dimension Wizard*

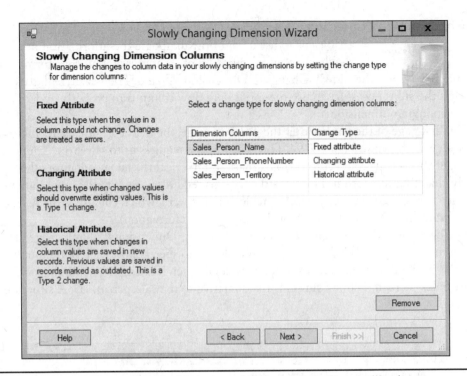

Figure 7-95 *The Slowly Changing Dimension Columns page of the Slowly Changing Dimension Wizard*

should not occur where a different person assumes the use of this salesperson ID. (Yes, names could change due to marriage or other events, but we will conveniently ignore that fact for this example.) This type of column is marked as a fixed attribute.

A column such as the Sales_Person_PhoneNumber column is changeable. We do not need to track previous phone numbers used by the salespeople. This type of column is marked as a changing attribute. A column such as the Sales_Person_Territory column is one whose changes we want to track. This type of column is marked as a historical attribute.

The next page of the wizard, the Fixed and Changing Attribute Options page, enables us to specify the transformation behavior when a fixed or a changing attribute is modified. We can choose to fail the transformation when a fixed attribute is modified. We can also choose to change all historic occurrences of a changing attribute when that attribute is modified.

The Historical Attribute Options page lets us specify the method used to determine which are the historical records and which are the current records. This page is shown in Figure 7-96. The salesperson dimension used in this example has a start date and an end date that determines the current records. We use the system date at the time the new record was created to populate the date fields.

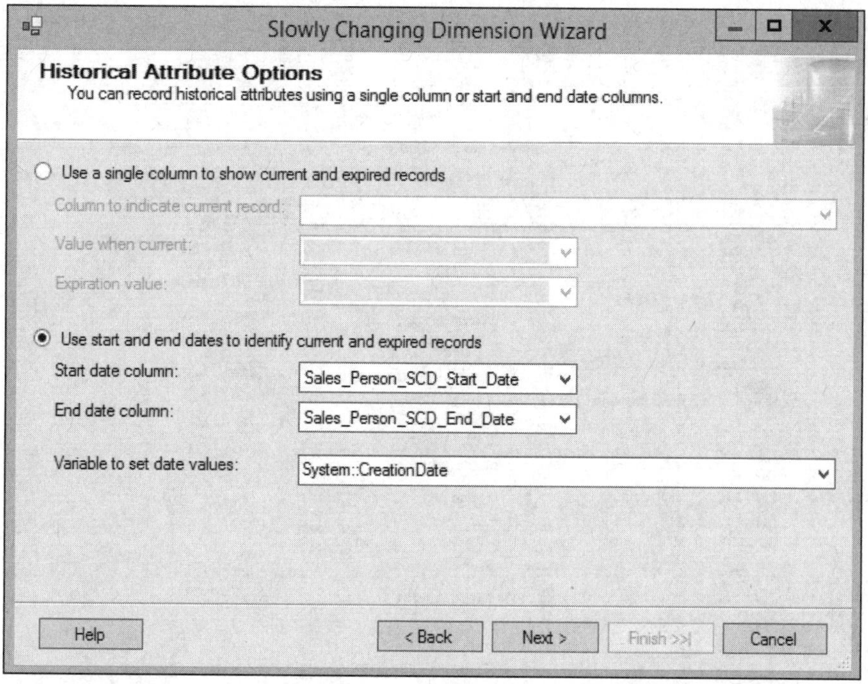

Figure 7-96   *The Historical Attribute Options page of the Slowly Changing Dimension Wizard*

The Inferred Dimension Members page lets us specify whether we can infer information for dimension members that do not yet exist. When the wizard completes, it adds a number of transformations to the package, as shown in Figure 7-97. These additional transformations provide the functionality to make the slowly changing dimension update work properly.

Sort   The *Sort* transformation enables us to sort the rows in a data flow. The Sort Transformation Editor dialog box is shown in Figure 7-98. In the example in this figure, the data flow is being sorted first by the StreetName column, and then by the StreetNumber column. The CustomerId column is not used as a sort column, but is passed through from the input data flow to the output data flow. The Sort transformation can remove rows with duplicate sort keys if "Remove rows with duplicate sort values" is checked.

Term Extraction   The *Term Extraction* transformation lets us extract a list of words and phrases from a column containing freeform text. The Term Extraction transformation identifies recurring nouns and/or noun

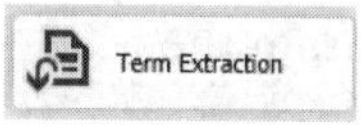

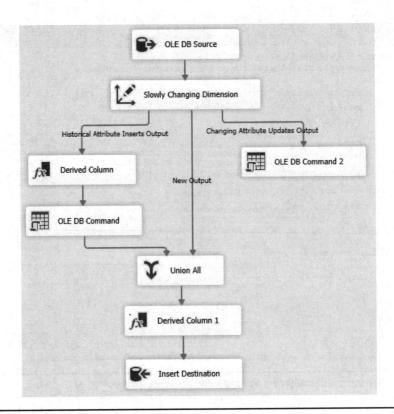

Figure 7-97   *The results of the Slowly Changing Dimension Wizard*

phrases in the freeform text, along with a score showing the frequency of occurrence for each word or phrase. This information can then be used to help discover the content of unstructured, textual data.

The Term Extraction transformation has two limitations. First, it only works with Unicode data (the DT_WSTR or DT_NTEXT Integration Services data types). This limitation is easily overcome by using the Data Conversion transformation to convert single-byte strings to Unicode. The second limitation is that the Term Extraction transformation only works with English-language text. The term extraction algorithms require knowledge of the structure and syntax of the language they are parsing. Currently, this intelligence is only available for English.

On the Term Extraction tab of the Term Extraction Transformation Editor dialog box, we simply select the column that contains the freeform text, and then specify the name of the term and score output columns. The Exclusion tab enables us to specify a database table or view that contains a list of words or phrases to exclude from the term

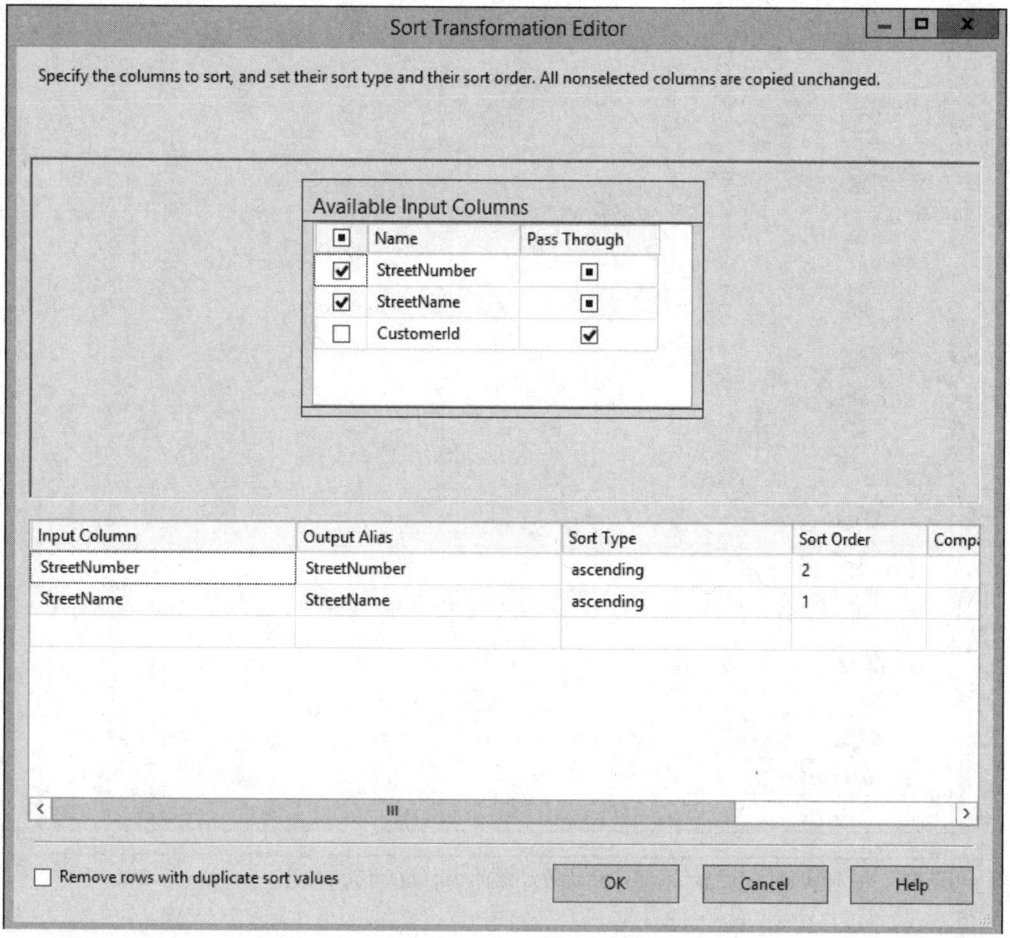

Figure 7-98   *The Sort Transformation Editor dialog box*

list. The Advanced tab, shown in Figure 7-99, lets us configure the operation of the term extraction, including whether nouns, noun phrases, or both are included in the extraction and the number of occurrences that must be found before a word or phrase is added to the list.

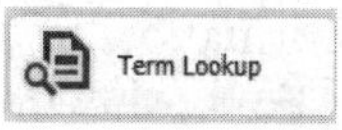

Term Lookup   The *Term Lookup* transformation enables us to look for occurrences of a set of words or phrases in a data flow column containing freeform text. The Term Lookup transformation functions almost identically

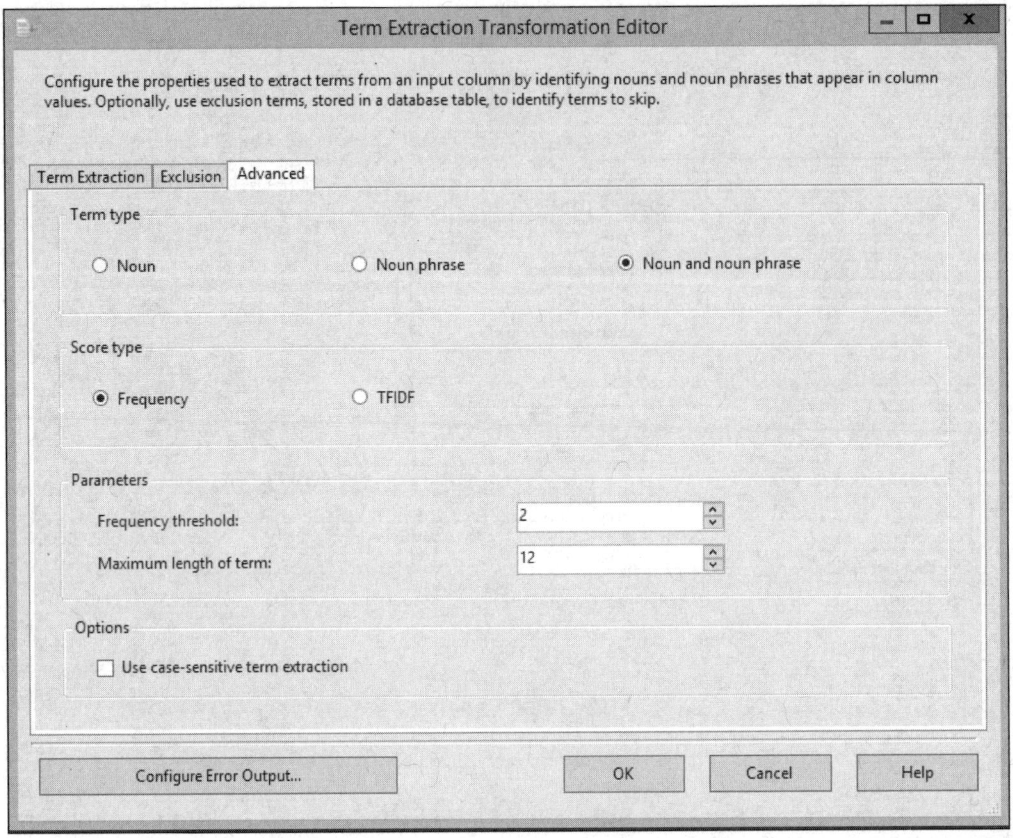

Figure 7-99 *The Advanced tab of the Term Extraction Transformation Editor dialog box*

to the Term Extraction transformation. The big difference is this: the Term Lookup transformation starts with a table of terms to look for in the freeform text, whereas the Term Extraction transformation creates its own list on-the-fly.

The Term Lookup transformation creates one row in the output data flow for each term found in the table of terms and in the text column. If the text column contains more than one term, more than one output row is created. For example, if a text column contains three of the terms from the lookup table, three rows are created in the output data flow. The same restrictions of Unicode text only and English only that applied to the Term Extraction transformation also apply to the Term Lookup transformation. The Term Lookup tab of the Term Lookup Transformation Editor dialog box is shown in Figure 7-100.

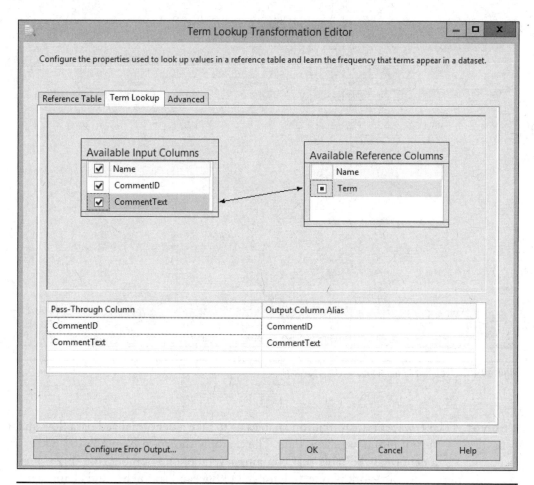

Figure 7-100 *The Term Lookup Transformation Editor dialog box*

Union All   The *Union All* transformation lets us merge several data flows into a single data flow. Any number of data flows can be unioned together. The only limitation is they all must be able to contribute fields to all of the columns defined in the output. The data flows used as inputs to the Union All transformation do not need to be sorted, as with the Merge and Merge Join transformations. Consequently, the output data flow is not sorted. The Union All Transformation Editor dialog box is shown in Figure 7-101.

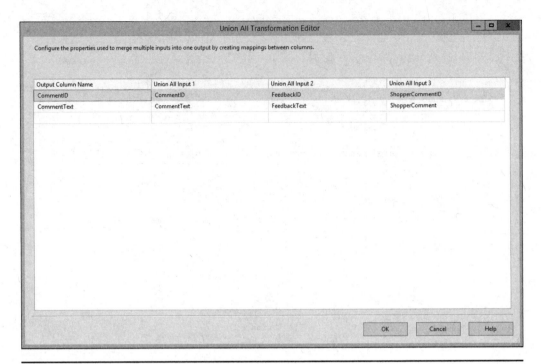

Figure 7-101 *The Union All Transformation Editor dialog box*

Unpivot The *Unpivot* transformation enables us to take a denormalized data flow and turn it into normalized data. The example shown in Figure 7-102 takes a denormalized table that contains several phone number columns—one for home phone, one for work phone, one for cell phone, and so forth—and changes it into a normalized table, with one record for each phone number. If the input data flow for our example contains the following rows:

CustomerID	HomePhone	WorkPhone	CellPhone	Fax
3843	891-555-2443	891-555-9384		891-555-2923
4738	891-555-9384		891-555-3045	

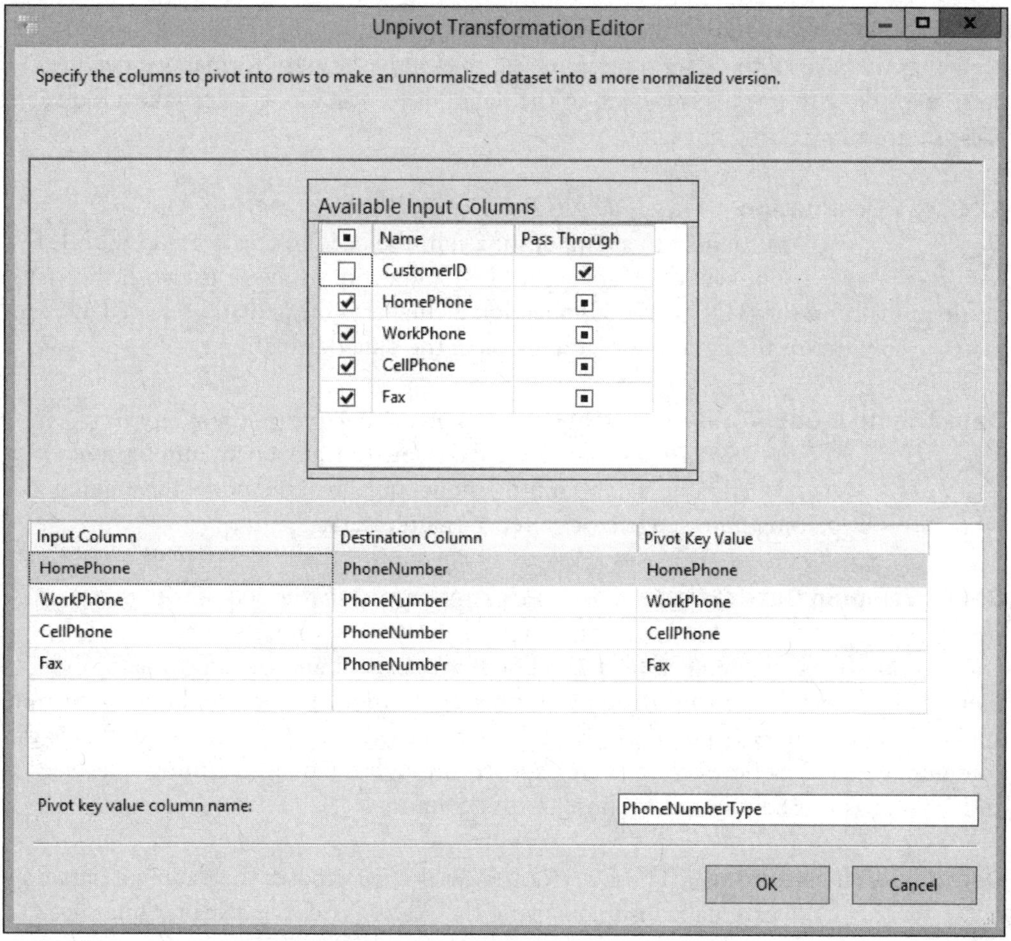

Figure 7-102 *The Unpivot Transformation Editor dialog box*

the output data flow would contain the following rows:

CustomerID	PhoneNumberType	PhoneNumber
3843	HomePhone	891-555-2443
3843	WorkPhone	891-555-9384
3843	Fax	891-555-2923
4738	HomePhone	891-555-9384
4738	CellPhone	891-555-3045

Data Flow Destinations

Now that we have all this data transformed into exactly the right format, we need to do something with it. This is the job of the data flow destinations. Let's take a look at these options for storing our data.

ADO.NET Destination　The *ADO.NET destination* enables us to use ADO.NET to connect to a data destination. We need to create an ADO.NET Connection Manager in the Connections tray for use with this data destination. Once the ADO.NET Connection Manager is created and selected, we can map the columns of the data flow to the fields in the data destination.

Data Mining Model Training Destination　The *Data Mining Model Training destination* lets us use a data flow to train a data mining model. Training a data mining model prepares the model for making predictions by gaining knowledge from a set of sample data.

Data Streaming Destination　The *Data Streaming destination* exposes the data in a data flow to external consumers using the SSISOLEDB connection. This allows us to extract and transform data, and then send that data to be consumed by another application. This can either be a custom application or it can be exposed as a SQL view and used in a SQL Server query. We can configure which data flow columns are exposed through the data streaming interface and what alias is used for each of those output columns.

DataReader Destination　The *DataReader destination* exposes the data in a data flow to external consumers using the ADO.NET DataReader interface. This allows, for example, a SQL Server Reporting Services report to use an Integration Services package data flow as a data source. We can configure which data flow columns are exposed through the DataReader interface and what alias is used for each of those output columns.

Dimension Processing Destination　The *Dimension Processing destination* lets us send a data flow to process a dimension. By using this destination, we can provide new values for a dimension in an Analysis Services cube. Columns from the data flow are mapped to the dimension and its attributes.

Excel Destination　The *Excel destination* enables us to send a data flow to an Excel spreadsheet file. We need to create an Excel Connection Manager in the Connections tray for use with this data destination. Once the

Excel Connection Manager is created and selected, we can map the columns of the data flow to the fields in the data destination.

Flat File Destination   The *Flat File destination* lets us send a data flow to a text file. We need to create a Flat File Connection Manager in the Connections tray and define the columns that are in the text file. Once the Flat File Connection Manager is created and selected, we can map the columns of the data flow to the fields in the data destination.

HDFS File Destination   The *HDFS File destination* lets us send a data flow to a file in a Hadoop Distributed File System (HDFS). We need to create a Hadoop Connection Manager in the Connections tray. Once the Hadoop Connection Manager is created and selected, we can specify the path and format of the file and map the columns of the data flow to the fields in the data destination.

ODBC Destination   The *ODBC destination* enables us to send a data flow to an ODBC data source. We need to create an ODBC Connection Manager in the Connections tray for use with this data destination. Once the ODBC Connection Manager is created and selected, we can map the columns of the data flow to the fields in the data destination.

OLE DB Destination   The *OLE DB destination* enables us to send a data flow to an OLE DB–compliant database. We need to create an OLE DB Connection Manager in the Connections tray for use with this data destination. Once the OLE DB Connection Manager is created and selected, we can map the columns of the data flow to the fields in the data destination.

Partition Processing Destination   The *Partition Processing destination* lets us send a data flow to process a partition. By using this destination, we can provide new values for a partition in an Analysis Services cube. Columns from the data flow are mapped to the items in the partition. We discuss Analysis Services partitions in Chapter 12.

Raw File Destination   The *Raw File destination* enables us to write a data flow to a raw data file. The Raw File format is the native format for Integration Services. Because of this, raw files can be written to disk and read from disk rapidly. One of the goals of Integration Services is to improve processing efficiency by moving data from the original source to the ultimate destination without making any stops in between. However, on some occasions, the data must be staged to disk as part of an extract, transform, and load process. When this is necessary, the Raw File format provides the most efficient means of accomplishing this task.

Recordset Destination   The *Recordset destination* lets us send a data flow to a record set. The record set is then stored in a package variable, which is visible outside of the current data flow. This allows the record set to be used by other items within the package.

SQL Server Compact Destination   The *SQL Server Compact destination* enables us to send a data flow to a SQL Server Compact database. We need to create a SQL Server Compact Connection Manager in the Connections tray for use with this data destination. Once the SQL Server Compact Connection Manager is created and selected, we can map the columns of the data flow to the fields in the data destination.

SQL Server Destination   The *SQL Server destination* lets us quickly insert records from a data flow into a SQL Server table or view. The SQL Server destination is the equivalent of using the Bulk Insert task with a data flow, rather than a text file, as the source of the data. Because of this, it results in a shorter load time than is required for the same load into SQL Server using the OLE DB destination.

The Bulk Insert task is extremely fast, but it can only use text files for the data source and it does not allow any transformations to the data. The SQL Server destination enables us to pull data from any of the supported data sources, apply transformations, and then do a fast insert into a SQL Server table or view. We need to create an OLE DB Connection Manager in the Connections tray for use with this data destination. Once the OLE DB Connection Manager is created and selected, we can map the columns of the data flow to the fields in the data destination.

The SQL Server destination achieves its speed by using special hooks into the SQL Server database engine itself. For this reason, the SQL Server destination can only be used in SSIS packages that are run on the same server where the destination SQL Server instance is executing.

Destination Assistant

As with the Source Assistant, the *Destination Assistant* aids you in the creation of OLE DB and Excel data destinations. The dialog box for the Destination Assistant

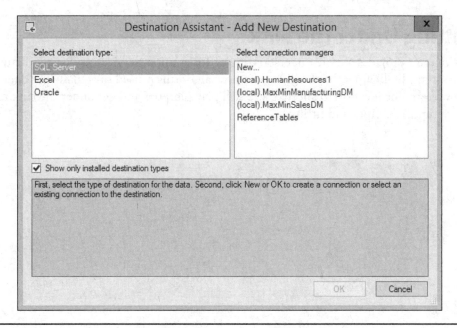

Figure 7-103 *The Destination Assistant dialog box showing Excel and installed OLE DB providers*

is shown in Figure 7-103. The Select destination type area has entries for Excel and each type of OLE DB provider installed. When "Show only installed destination types" is unchecked, entries for some of the other supported OLE DB drives appear in the Select destination type area. When one of these types is highlighted, information on where to obtain this OLE DB driver is displayed, just as with the Source Assistant.

The Select connection managers area shows existing Connection Managers of the selected type. Figure 7-103 shows four existing Connection Managers for SQL Server. This can prevent you from creating a duplicate Connection Manager when one already exists for the desired data destination. To use an existing Connection Manager, select that Connection Manager in the Select connection managers area and click OK. To create a new Connection Manager of the desired type, select "<New>" in the Select connection managers area and click OK. When creating a new Connection Manager, the Connection Manager dialog box for the selected connection type will be displayed.

When the Destination Assistant has completed the process of guiding you through the creation of a data destination, the data destination item will appear on the Data Flow Designer tab.

Getting Under the Sink

This chapter provides a basic understanding of Integration Services package structure and content. In Chapter 8, we will look at how all of this is used to actually get data to flow from one location to another. We will play plumber and get under the sink to connect up these pipes and fittings.

Chapter 8

Fill 'er Up: Using Integration Services for Populating Data Marts

In This Chapter

- ▶ Package Development Features
- ▶ Change Data Capture
- ▶ Loading a Fact Table

- ▶ Putting Integration Services Packages into Production
- ▶ Meanwhile, Back at the BI Semantic Model

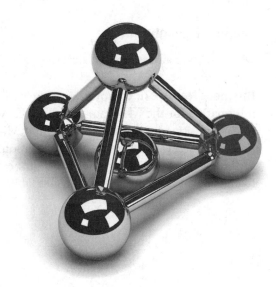

To change and to improve are two different things.

—Anonymous

We have become familiar with the structure and components of Integration Services. Now it is time to begin putting the tool to use. We will take a more in-depth look at Integration Services packages and how they are produced. We will also utilize several Learn By Doing activities to gain experience in Integration Services package development.

Package Development Features

Now you have seen all the wonderful tasks and transformations provided by Integration Services. However, just as with all those gadget commercials on TV, you need to wait because there's more. Integration Services also provides a number of features to aid in the package development process. In this section, we explore a number of features that make Integration Services packages easy to program and easy to debug.

Give It a Try

Before we begin to discover additional features of Integration Services, let's actually give it a try. We begin with a Learn By Doing exercise.

Learn By Doing: Using Integration Services to Populate the Maximum Miniatures Manufacturing Data Mart Dimensions

Feature Highlighted

▶ Creating an Integration Services package for loading data into a data mart

Business Need In Chapter 6, we created a relational database to hold the information for the Maximum Miniatures Manufacturing data mart. Now it is time to copy information from the Maximum Miniatures online transaction processing (OLTP) systems and load it into the relational database tables. We need to create two processes: one to initially populate all of the dimensional tables and one to add new manufacturing information to the fact table.

NOTE

To complete this Learn By Doing activity, you need the Maximum Miniatures Accounting database. If you have not done so already, go to www.mhprofessional.com and search for the book's web page using the ISBN, which is 9781259641480. Use the "Downloads & Resources" tab to download the zip file containing the book's material. Follow the instructions within the zipped folders in the zip file to install the Maximum Miniatures Accounting database.

Steps to Create the Integration Services Project

1. Open SQL Server Data Tools.
2. Click the New Project button on the toolbar.
3. Make sure Business Intelligence is selected from the Installed Templates, and then select Integration Services Project in the center of the screen.
4. Enter **MaxMinManufacturingDMLoad** for Name, and set the Location to the appropriate folder. The Create directory for solution check box should be unchecked.
5. Click OK to create the project.
6. Once the project is open, right-click the Package.dtsx entry in the Solution Explorer window and select Rename from the context menu. Enter **DimensionLoad.dtsx** for the package name and press ENTER.

Steps to Create the Data Source for the Load ProductType Data Flow

1. Drag the data flow task item from the SSIS Toolbox and drop it on the Control Flow tab design surface.
2. Right-click the Data Flow Task item you just created and select Rename from the context menu. Enter **Load ProductType** and press ENTER. (You can also single-click the Data Flow Task item to edit the name of the item.)
3. Double-click the Load ProductType item. This takes you to the Data Flow tab.
4. Right-click in the Connections tray and select New ADO.NET Connection from the context menu. Click New in the Configure ADO.NET Connection Manager dialog box to create a new data connection.
5. Enter the name of the server where the MaxMinAccounting database was created in Server name. Select the appropriate method for accessing this server in the Log on to the server section. Enter credentials if necessary. Select MaxMinAccounting from the Select or enter a database name drop-down list. Click OK to return to

the Configure ADO.NET Connection Manager dialog box. Click OK again to exit this dialog box.

6. Drag an ADO.NET Source item from the SSIS Toolbox and drop it on the Data Flow tab.

7. Double-click the ADO.NET Source item you just created. The ADO.NET Source Editor dialog box appears.

8. Select the MaxMinAccounting data connection that you just created in the ADO.NET connection manager drop-down list, if it is not already selected. (The server name will be in front of the database name.) Leave the Data access mode drop-down list set to Table or view. Select "dbo"."ProductTypes" from the Name of the table or the view drop-down list. Click OK.

Steps to Create the Data Destination for the Load ProductType Data Flow

1. Right-click in the Connections tray and select New OLE DB Connection from the context menu. Click New in the Configure OLE DB Connection Manager dialog box to create a new data connection.

2. Enter the name of the server where the MaxMinManufacturingDM database was created in Server name. Select the appropriate method for accessing this server in the Log on to the server section. Enter credentials if necessary. Select MaxMinManufacturingDM from the Select or enter a database name drop-down list. Click OK to return to the Configure OLE DB Connection Manager dialog box. Click OK again to exit this dialog box.

3. Drag a SQL Server Destination item from the Other Destinations section of the SSIS Toolbox, and drop it on the Data Flow tab.

4. Click the ADO.NET Source item. Click the blue data flow arrow, drag it on top of the SQL Server Destination item, and drop it on this item. This connects the source to the destination.

5. Double-click the SQL Server Destination item. The SQL Destination Editor dialog box appears.

6. Select the MaxMinManufacturingDM data connection that you just created in the Connection manager drop-down list, if it is not already selected. Select [dbo].[DimProductType] from the Use a table or view drop-down list.

7. Click Mappings to view the Mappings page. The columns from the data source (which are Available Input Columns to this data destination item) should be automatically mapped to the columns in the destination (the Available Destination Columns). You see an arrow going from each column name under Available Input Columns to the corresponding column name under Available Destination Columns. The automatic mapping occurs because the column names match. (The ProductTypeShortName column in the AccountingSystem.ProductTypes table is not mapped to a column in the MaxMinManufacturing.DimProductTypeTable.) Click OK to exit the SQL Destination Editor dialog box.

Steps to Create the Load ProductSubtype Data Flow

1. Click the Control Flow tab. Drag a second Data Flow Task item on to the Control Flow tab design surface. Rename this new Data Flow Task item **Load ProductSubtype**.

2. Click the Load ProductType item. Drag the precedence arrow onto the Load ProductSubtype item and drop it there. These two items are now linked by a precedence constraint. The Load ProductType item must complete successfully before the Load ProductSubtype item can execute. This is required because ProductType is a foreign key for ProductSubtype.

3. Double-click the Load ProductSubtype item. This takes you to the Data Flow tab, with Load ProductSubtype selected in the Data Flow Task drop-down list.

4. Drag an ADO.NET Source item from the SSIS Toolbox onto the Data Flow tab. Double-click this item. The ADO.NET Source Editor dialog box appears.

5. The MaxMinAccounting data connection will be selected in the ADO.NET connection manager drop-down list. Leave the Data access mode drop-down list set to Table or view. Select "dbo"."ProductSubtypes" from the Name of the table or the view drop-down list. Click OK.

6. Drag a SQL Server Destination item from the SSIS Toolbox, and drop it on the Data Flow tab.

7. Click the ADO.NET Source item. Click the blue data flow arrow, drag it on top of the SQL Server Destination item, and drop it on this item. This connects the source to the destination.

8. Double-click the SQL Server Destination item. The SQL Destination Editor dialog box appears.

9. The MaxMinManufacturingDM data connection will be selected in the Connection manager drop-down list. Select DimProductSubtype from the Use a table or view drop-down list.

10. Click Mappings to view the Mappings page. The input columns should be automatically mapped to the columns in the destination. Click OK to exit the SQL Destination Editor dialog box.

Steps to Create Additional Data Flow

1. Repeat the steps of the "Create the Load ProductSubtype Data Flow" section to take data from the AccountingSystem.Products table and copy it to the MaxMinManufacturingDM.DimProduct table. Create the precedence arrow to connect the Load ProductSubtype and Load Product data flow tasks. (The RawMaterial and AmountOfRawMaterial columns in the AccountingSystem.Products table are not mapped to columns in the MaxMinManufacturingDM.DimProduct table.)

2. Repeat the steps of the "Create the Load ProductSubtype Data Flow" section again to take data from the AccountingSystem.Countries table and copy it to the MaxMinManufacturingDM.DimCountry table. Create the precedence arrow to connect the Load Product and Load Country data flow tasks. (The CountryKey column is an auto-increment field, so it does not need to have an input column feeding it data.)

Steps to Create the Load Plant Data Flow   The Plant dimension references the Country dimension. However, the Country dimension uses a surrogate key rather than the CountryCode business key. Therefore, we need to use the business key to look up the surrogate key in this data flow.

1. Select the Control Flow tab. Drag another data flow task item onto the Control Flow tab. Rename this new data flow task item **Load Plant**.

2. Click the Load Country item. Drag the precedence arrow onto the Load Plant item, and drop it there.

3. Double-click the Load Plant item. This takes you to the Data Flow tab, with Load Plant selected in the Data Flow Task drop-down list.

4. Drag an ADO.NET Source item from the SSIS Toolbox onto the Data Flow tab. Double-click this item. The ADO.NET Source Editor dialog box appears.

5. We only want plant site records from the Locations table. We will use a query with a WHERE clause to filter out the records we don't want. The MaxMinAccounting data connection will be selected in the ADO.NET connection manager drop-down list. Select SQL command from the Data access mode drop-down list. Enter the following for SQL command text:

```
SELECT LocationCode AS PlantNumber,
       LocationName AS PlantName,
       CountryCode
FROM Locations
WHERE LocationType = 'Plant Site'
```

6. Click OK to exit the ADO.NET Source Editor dialog box.

7. Drag a Lookup item from the SSIS Toolbox, and drop it on the Data Flow tab.

8. Click the ADO.NET Source item. Click the blue data flow arrow, drag it on top of the Lookup item, and drop it on this item.

9. Double-click the Lookup item. The Lookup Transformation Editor dialog box appears.

10. Click Connection to view the Connection page.

11. The MaxMinManufacturingDM data connection will be selected in the Connection manager drop-down list. Select [dbo].[DimCountry] from the Use a table or a view drop-down list.

12. Click Columns to view the Columns page.

13. Drag CountryCode in the Available Input Columns list and drop it on CountryCode in the Available Lookup Columns list. This will cause the Lookup Transformation to find the record in the DimCountry table with a CountryCode field that matches the value in the CountryCode field in the data flow.

14. Check the check box next to CountryKey in the Available Lookup Columns list. This will add the content of the CountryKey column in the matching DimCountry record to the data flow.

15. Click OK to exit the Lookup Transformation Editor.

16. Drag a SQL Server Destination item from the SSIS Toolbox, and drop it on the Data Flow tab.

17. Click the Lookup item. Click the blue data flow arrow, drag it on top of the SQL Server Destination item, and drop it on this item. The Input Output Selection dialog box appears.

18. The Lookup transformation has two data flow outputs, one for matched records and one for unmatched records. Select Lookup Match Output from the Output drop-down.

19. Click OK to exit the Input Output Selection dialog box.

20. Double-click the SQL Server Destination item. The SQL Destination Editor dialog box appears.

21. The MaxMinManufacturingDM data connection will be selected in the Connection manager drop-down list. Select [dbo].[DimPlant] from the Use a table or view drop-down list.

22. Click Mappings to view the Mappings page. The PlantNumber and PlantName columns from the data source and the CountryKey lookup columns should be automatically mapped to the columns in the destination. Click OK to exit the SQL Destination Editor dialog box.

Steps to Create the Load Material Data Flow

1. Click the Control Flow tab. Drag another data flow task item onto the Control Flow tab. Rename this new data flow task item **Load Material**.

2. Click the Load Plant item. Drag the precedence arrow onto the Load Material item and drop it there.

3. Double-click the Load Material item.

4. Drag an ADO.NET Source item from the SSIS Toolbox onto the Data Flow tab. Double-click this item. The ADO.NET Source Editor dialog box appears.

5. The MaxMinAccounting data connection will be selected in the ADO.NET connection manager drop-down list. Leave the Data Access Mode drop-down list set to Table or view. Select "dbo". "CapitalAssets" from the Name of the table or the view drop-down list.

6. Click OK to exit the ADO.NET Source Editor.

7. Drag a Conditional Split item from the Common section of the SSIS Toolbox, and drop it on the Data Flow tab. Rename this new data flow transformation item **Filter For Molding Machines**.

8. Click the ADO.NET Source item. Click the blue data flow arrow, drag it on top of the Filter For Molding Machines item, and drop it on this item.

9. Double-click the Filter For Molding Machines item. The Conditional Split Transformation Editor dialog box appears.

10. We only want records for molding machines from the CapitalAssets table. We will use the Conditional Split transformation to filter out the records we don't want. Click the cell in the Output Name column, and enter **Molding Machine Records**.

11. Expand the Columns folder in the upper-left corner of the dialog box.

12. Click the AssetType column and drag it to the uppermost cell in the Condition column. This will create an "[AssetType]" placeholder for this column.

13. Complete the expression in the Condition cell so it appears as follows:

```
[AssetType] == "Molding Machine"
```

14. Click OK to exit the Conditional Split Transformation Editor dialog box.

15. Drag a Multicast item from the SSIS Toolbox and drop it on the Data Flow tab.

16. Click the Filter For Molding Machines item. Click the blue data flow arrow, drag it on top of the Multicast item, and drop it on this item. The Input Output Selection dialog box appears. This dialog box appears because the Conditional Split Transformation item has two outputs: one that we created called "Molding Machine Records," containing only those records that satisfy our condition expression, and the "Conditional Split Default Output," containing all other records in the data flow.

17. Select Molding Machine Records from the Output drop-down list. Click OK.

18. Drag an Aggregate item from the SSIS Toolbox and drop it on the Data Flow tab. Rename this new aggregate item **Aggregate by Material**.

19. Click the Multicast item. Click the blue data flow arrow, drag it on top of the Aggregate by Material item, and drop it on this item.

20. Double-click the Aggregate by Material item. This opens the Aggregate Transformation Editor dialog box. Check RawMaterial under Available Input Columns. This groups the data by the RawMaterial column to give you a unique list of materials. You can use this unique list to populate the DimMaterial table. Only the RawMaterial column is included in the output of the Aggregate by Material item.

21. In the Output Alias column, change RawMaterial to **Material**.

22. Click OK to exit the Aggregate Transformation Editor dialog box.

23. Drag a SQL Server Destination item from the SSIS Toolbox and drop it on the Data Flow tab.

24. Click the Aggregate by Material item. Click the blue data flow arrow, drag it on top of the SQL Server Destination item, and drop it onto this item.

25. Double-click the SQL Server Destination item. The SQL Destination Editor dialog box appears.

26. The MaxMinManufacturingDM data connection will be selected in the Connection manager drop-down list. Select DimMaterial from the Use a table or view drop-down list.

27. Click Mappings to view the Mappings page. The Material column should be automatically mapped to the Material column in the destination. The MaterialKey is automatically populated as an identity column, so we don't need to map anything to this column. Click OK to exit the SQL Destination Editor dialog box.

Steps to Create the Load Machine Type Flow

1. Click the Control Flow tab.

2. Click the Load Material item to select it.

3. Press CTRL-C to copy this item.

4. Press CTRL-V to paste a copy of this item onto the Control Flow design surface. A new data flow item called "Load Material 1" will appear on the design surface.

5. Rename this new data flow task item **Load Machine Type**.

6. Drag the Load MachineType item below the Load Material item.

7. Click the Load Material item. Drag the precedence arrow onto the Load MachineType item and drop it there.

8. Double-click the Load MachineType item.

9. Rename the Aggregate by Material item to **Aggregate by Machine Type**.

10. Double-click the Aggregate by Machine Type item. This opens the Aggregate Transformation Editor dialog box. Check AssetClass in addition to RawMaterial in the Available Input Columns. This groups the data by the AssetClass and RawMaterial columns to give you a unique list of machine types and their materials. You can use this unique list to populate the DimMachineType table.

11. In the Output Alias column, change AssetClass to **MachineType**.

12. Click OK to exit the Aggregate Transformation Editor dialog box.

13. Select the SQL Server Destination item and press DELETE. The SQL Server Destination is removed from the data flow.

14. Drag a Lookup item from the SSIS Toolbox and drop it on the Data Flow tab.

15. Click the Aggregate by Machine Type item. Click the blue data flow arrow, drag it on top of the Lookup item, and drop it on this item.

16. Double-click the Lookup item. The Lookup Transformation Editor dialog box appears.

17. Click Connection to view the Connection page.

18. The MaxMinManufacturingDM data connection will be selected in the Connection manager drop-down list. Select [dbo].[DimMaterial] from the Use a table or a view drop-down list.

19. Click Columns to view the Columns page.

20. Drag Material in the Available Input Columns list and drop it on Material in the Available Lookup Columns list. This will cause the Lookup Transformation to find the record in the DimMaterial table with a Material field that matches the value in the Material field in the data flow.

21. Check the check box next to MaterialKey in the Available Lookup Columns list. This will add the content of the MaterialKey column in the matching DimMaterial record to the data flow.

22. Click OK to exit the Lookup Transformation Editor.

23. Drag a SQL Server Destination item from the SSIS Toolbox and drop it on the Data Flow tab.

24. Click the Lookup item. Click the blue data flow arrow, drag it on top of the SQL Server Destination item, and drop it on this item. The Input Output Selection dialog box appears.

25. Select Lookup Match Output from the Output drop-down.

26. Click OK to exit the Input Output Selection dialog box.

27. Double-click the SQL Server Destination item. The SQL Destination Editor dialog box appears.

28. The MaxMinManufacturingDM data connection will be selected in the Connection manager drop-down list. Select [dbo].[DimMachineType] from the Use a table or view drop-down list.

29. Click Mappings to view the Mappings page. The MachineType column from the data source and the MaterialKey lookup columns should be automatically mapped to the columns in the destination. The MachineTypeKey is automatically populated as an identity column so we don't need to map anything to this column. Click OK to exit the SQL Destination Editor dialog box.

Steps to Create the Load Machine Flow

1. Click the Control Flow tab.

2. Click the Load MachineType Item to select it.

3. Press CTRL-C to copy this item.

4. Press CTRL-V to paste a copy of this item onto the Control Flow design surface. A new data flow item called "Load MachineType 1" will appear on the design surface.

5. Rename this new data flow task item **Load Machine**.

6. Drag the Load Machine item below the Load MachineType item.

7. Click the Load MachineType item. Drag the precedence arrow onto the Load Machine item and drop it there.

8. Double-click the Load Machine item.

9. Rename the Aggregate by Machine Type item to **Aggregate by Machine**.

10. Double-click the Aggregate by Machine item. This opens the Aggregate Transformation Editor dialog box. Check AssetCode, AssetName, LocationCode, Manufacturer, and DateOfPurchase in addition to AssetClass and RawMaterial in the Available Input Columns. This groups the data by these columns to give you a unique list of machine and their machine types. You can use this unique list to populate the DimMachine table.

11. Select Group by from the drop-down list in the Operation column for AssetCode and LocationCode.

12. Click OK to exit the Aggregate Transformation Editor dialog box.

13. Double-click the Lookup item.

14. Click Connection to view the Connection page.

15. Select [dbo].[DimMachineType] from the Use a table or a view drop-down list.

16. Click Columns to view the Columns page.

17. Drag the MachineType column from Available Input Columns and drop it on MachineType in Available Lookup Columns.

18. Uncheck MaterialKey in Available Lookup Columns.

19. Check MachineTypeKey in Available Lookup Columns.

20. Click OK to exit the Lookup Transformation Editor.

21. Select the SQL Server Destination item and press DELETE. The SQL Server Destination is removed from the data flow.

22. Drag a Data Conversion item from the SSIS Toolbox and drop it on the Data Flow.

23. Click the Lookup item. Click the blue data flow arrow, drag it on top of the Data Conversion item, and drop it on this item. The Input Output Selection dialog box appears.

24. Select Lookup Match Output from the Output drop-down.

25. Click OK to exit the Input Output Selection dialog box.

26. Double-click the Data Conversion item. The Data Conversion Transformation Editor dialog box appears.

27. Check DateOfPurchase in Available Input Columns. This will create a row in the grid.

28. In the new grid row, click in the Data Type column to activate the drop-down list.

29. Select database date [DT_DBDATE] from the drop-down list.

30. In the Output Alias column, replace Copy of DateOfPurchase with **Converted DateOfPurchase**.

31. Click OK to exit the Data Conversion Transformation Editor dialog box.

32. Drag a SQL Server Destination item from the SSIS Toolbox and drop it on the Data Flow tab.

33. Click the Data Conversion item. Click the blue data flow arrow, drag it on top of the SQL Server Destination item, and drop it on this item.

34. Double-click the SQL Server Destination item. The SQL Destination Editor dialog box appears.

35. The MaxMinManufacturingDM data connection will be selected in the Connection manager drop-down list. Select [dbo].[DimMachine] from the Use a table or view drop-down list.

36. Click Mappings to view the Mappings page. The Manufacturer and DateOfPurchase columns from the data source and the MachineTypeKey lookup columns should be automatically mapped to the columns in the destination. Drag the AssetCode column from Available Input Columns and drop it on MachineNumber in Available Destination Columns.

37. Drag the AssetName column from Available Input Columns and drop it on MachineName in Available Destination Columns.

38. Drag the LocationCode column from Available Input Columns and drop it on PlantNumber in Available Destination Columns.

39. Drag the Converted DateOfPurchase column from Available Input Columns and drop it on DateOfPurchase. This will replace the default mapping.

40. Click OK to exit the SQL Destination Editor dialog box.

Steps to Save and Execute the Integration Services Package

1. Click the Save All button on the toolbar to save the completed package.

2. Click the Control Flow tab.

3. Click the Start button (the green triangle) on the toolbar to execute the completed package. When the execution is complete, click Stop Debugging or click the Package execution completed link to return to design mode.

Executing the DimensionLoad package copies data from the AccountingSystem database tables into the dimension tables of our MaxMinManufacturingDM database.

NOTE

When package execution is complete, all items should have a green circle with a check mark. If any item has an "X" in a red circle, there has been an error during execution. Look at the Excecution Results tab to determine the error that occurred, and then recheck the steps in this exercise associated with that item to determine the cause of the error and re-execute the package. If you see a message stating you need to run the package as an administrator, click Save All, close SQL Server Data Tools, and then right-click SSDT and select Run as Administrator from the context menu.

Programming in Integration Services Packages

Integration Services uses a program development paradigm. We can create variables with strong types and scopes. We can use those variables in expressions throughout our Integration Services packages while still maintaining speed and scalability. In addition, we can define event handlers to react to certain occurrences within a package.

Variables

Variables are used within Integration Services packages to pass information between the various parts of the package. This could be from one data transformation to another, from a control task to a Connection Manager, and so forth. In prior discussions of tasks, data sources, data transformations, and data destinations, we have already seen several examples of variables in use.

Variables are managed using the Variables window, shown in Figure 8-1. (The Variables window can be opened by selecting View | Other Windows | Variables from the Main menu, by right-clicking the designer area and selecting Variables from the context menu, or by clicking the Variables button in the upper-right corner of the designer area.) Variables are added using the Add Variable button in the Variables window toolbar. The variable's name and data type must be specified when the variable is created. In addition, an initial value can be provided, if desired. As opposed to other scripting environments, variables in Integration Services are strongly typed.

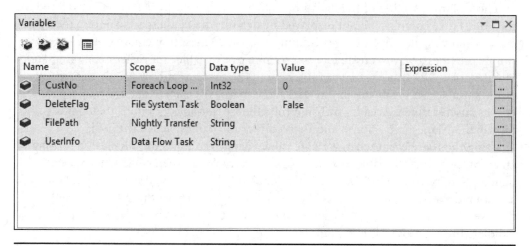

Figure 8-1   *The Variables window*

This allows for memory allocation planning to be done in advance rather than at run time, leading to more efficient operation. A variable's name, data type, and initial value can be edited right in the grid of the Variables window. Variables are deleted using the Delete Variable button in the Variables window toolbar.

Each variable has its own scope, which is displayed in the Scope column in Figure 8-1. The variable's *scope* is the set of locations where the variable can be accessed and utilized. A variable is initially created with its scope set to the entire package. The scope can be changed using the Move Variable button in the Variables window toolbar. A variable can be used in expressions and other code that resides in the item specified in the variable's Scope column. The variable can also be used within any items that are contained inside this item. For example, if a variable called LoopCounter is scoped to a For Loop container, that LoopCounter variable can be used in any task that is placed inside the For Loop container.

The Grid Options button in the Variables window toolbar displays the Variable Grid Options dialog box. The Filter section of the dialog box provides two options that we can use to filter the list of variables being displayed in the Variables window. When the Show system variables option is checked, all of the predefined system variables are added to the list. These system variables let us include information about the package, the user executing the package, and the computer the package is running on in the expressions and code created within the package. When the Show variables of all scopes option is checked, all variable regardless of scope are added to this. When this is unchecked, only those variables that belong to the scope of the object selected appear in the designer area.

The Columns section of the dialog box enables us to select the columns displayed in the grid. Three columns are not displayed by default: the Namespace column, the Raise event when variable value changes column, and the Description column. A *namespace* simply provides a way to create logical groupings of variables for easier debugging and maintenance. All of the system variables are in the System namespace. By default, all of the variables we create are in the User namespace. We can change the namespace of these user-defined variables by using the Choose Variable Columns dialog box to display the Namespace column and then editing the namespace in the grid.

Using the Raise event when variable value changes column, we can choose to trigger an event each time the value of a variable changes. We can then configure an event handler that executes each time the value changes. This can be done for both system- and user-defined variables. In fact, this is the only property of the system variables that we can edit in the Variables window grid. We talk more about events and event handlers in the section "Event Handlers."

Expressions

Expressions let us modify the behavior of a package by evaluating conditions and changing properties at run time. Integration Services uses an expression syntax that is similar to that of the C# programming language. This is used to provide strongly typed variables. As was mentioned previously, strong typing is necessary to implement the advanced memory management necessary for top performance.

Literals   *Literals* are used in expressions to represent values that are known at the time the code is written. Literals can be strings, numerics, or Booleans. *String literals* are enclosed in double quotes (""). The following escape sequences can be used in string literals to represent nonprinting characters:

Escape Sequence	Character
\a	Alert
\b	Backspace
\f	Form feed
\n	New line
\r	Carriage return
\t	Horizontal tab
\v	Vertical tab
\"	Double quote
\\	Backslash
\xhhhh	Unicode character in hexadecimal notation

Numeric literals can be expressed as integers, as decimal numbers, or as scientific notation. They can include a negative sign, but not a digit grouping symbol (the comma is the digit grouping symbol when using U.S. regional settings). Numeric literals may include a suffix that specifies the data type to assign to it.

Integer values may use the following suffixes:

Suffix	Description	Integration Services Data Type
None	Integer	DT_I4
U	Unsigned Integer	DT_UI4
L	Long	DT_I8
UL	Unsigned Long	DT_UI8

Real values and scientific notation may use the following suffixes:

Suffix	Description	Integration Services Data Type
None	Numeric	DT_NUMERIC
F	Float	DT_R4
L	Double-precision float	DT_R8

The suffixes are not case-sensitive.

Boolean literals are simply presented as true and false. They do not include double quotes. Boolean literals are not case-sensitive.

Identifiers   Identifiers are used in expressions to represent values that are not known until run time. Identifiers can represent variables. For example:

```
@FileName
@_LoopCounter
@PackageName
```

Identifiers that represent variables are always preceded by an at sign (@). Identifiers can also represent data flow columns. For example:

```
Customer#
AmountWith6PercentTax
```

Identifiers that fit the following rules are called regular identifiers:

▶   The first character is a letter or an underscore (_).

▶   The remaining characters are letters, numbers, an underscore (_), an at sign (@), a dollar sign ($), or a pound sign (#).

The at sign that precedes each variable name is not considered part of the variable name when determining if it is a regular identifier. All of the identifiers in the previous paragraph are *regular identifiers.*

If an identifier does not fit these criteria, it is a *qualified identifier.* This simply means that it must be enclosed in square brackets. For example:

```
@[Continue Processing Flag]
[Customer Name]
[12MonthTotal]
```

The first two are qualified identifiers because they contain spaces. The third is a qualified identifier because it does not start with a letter or an underscore. If a variable name is a qualified identifier, the at sign (@) is placed outside of the square brackets.

If two identifiers within a given scope have the same name, we must provide additional information to allow the package to determine which identifier to use. When two variables have the same name, they must have different namespaces. We can then include the namespace with the variable name to make the reference unique. The name resolution operator, : :, is placed between the scope and the variable name. Whenever the name resolution operator is used, the identifier is always placed in square brackets, even if it is a regular identifier. For example:

```
@[User::UserName]
@[System::UserName]
```

When two data flow columns have the same name, we can include the name of the data flow source or transformation item where each column was created. A period is placed between the item name and the column name. For example:

```
FlatFileSource.CustomerName
DataConversion.CustomerName
```

If either the item name or the column name is not a regular identifier, they must be enclosed in square brackets. In all cases, the period is not enclosed in the brackets. For example:

```
FlatFileSource.[Customer Number]
[Character Map].ContactName
[Derived Column].[12MonthTotal]
```

Operators   The following operators are supported by expressions:

Operator	Description	Example
(data type)	Data type conversion (Cast)	(DT_WSTR)"Acme"
()	Grouping	(4+5) * (4+7)
+	Addition	34 + 25
+	(String) Concatenation	"Sally" + " " + "Jones"
−	Subtraction	592 − 96
−	Negative	−234

(continued)

Operator	Description	Example
*	Multiply	20 * 409
/	Divide	39 / 3
%	Modulo division (provides the remainder of the division)	41 % 4
||	Logical OR	@LoopCount < 5 || @Alldone
&&	Logical AND	@Continue && @ DatalsValid
!	Logical Not	!@InError
|	Bitwise Inclusive OR	@Flags | @MaskVar
^	Bitwise Exclusive OR	@Flags ^ @MaskVar
&	Bitwise AND	@Flags & @MaskVar
~	Bitwise Not	~@MaskVar
==	Equality	@Quantity == @MaxValue
!=	Inequality	@Quantity != @MaxValue
>	Greater Than	@Quantity > @MaxValue
<	Less Than	@Quantity < @MaxValue
>=	Greater Than or Equal To	@Quantity >= @MaxValue
<=	Less Than or Equal To	@Quantity <= @MaxValue
?:	Conditional	@Counter == @MaxCount? @DoneFlag:@ContinueFlag

Functions The following mathematical functions are supported by expressions:

Function	Description	Example	Result
ABS	Returns the absolute value of a numeric expression	ABS(−235)	235
CEILING	Returns the smallest integer that is greater than or equal to a numeric expression	CEILING(37.483)	38
EXP	Returns the exponential of a numeric expression	EXP(4)	54.598150033144236
FLOOR	Returns the largest integer that is less than or equal to a numeric expression	FLOOR(37.483)	37
LN	Returns the natural logarithm of a numeric expression	LN(10)	2.3025850929940459
LOG	Returns the base-10 logarithm of a numeric expression	LOG(20)	1.3010299956639813
POWER	Returns the result of raising a numeric expression to a power	POWER(10,3)	1000
ROUND	Returns the numeric expression rounded to the specified number of decimal places	ROUND(87.3863, 2)	87.39

(continued)

Function	Description	Example	Result
SIGN	Returns −1 if the number is negative	SIGN(−234)	−1
SQUARE	Returns the square of a numeric expression	SQUARE(5)	25
SQRT	Returns the square root of a given numeric expression	SQRT(25)	5

The following string functions are supported by expressions:

Function	Description	Example	Result
CODEPOINT	Returns the Unicode value of the leftmost character of the string expression	CODEPOINT ("Anderson Co.")	65
FINDSTRING	Returns the one-based index of the specified occurrence of a character string within a string expression	FINDSTRING ("ABC XYZ ABC", "ABC", 2)	9
HEX	Returns a string representing the hexadecimal value of an integer expression	HEX(1583)	62F
LEFT	Returns the specified number of characters from the beginning of the string	LEFT ("Anderson Co.", 7)	Anderso
LEN	Returns the number of characters in a string expression	LEN("ABC XYZ ABC")	11
LOWER	Returns the lowercase version of a string expression	LOWER ("Anderson Co.")	anderson co.
LTRIM	Returns a string expression with all of the leading blanks removed	LTRIM (" ABC XYZ ")	ABC XYZ
REPLACE	Returns a string with a set of characters replaced by another set of characters or with an empty string	REPLACE ("ABC XYZ ABC", "ABC", "DEF")	DEF XYZ DEF
REPLICATE	Returns a string copied a specified number of times	REPLICATE ("XYZ", 3)	XYZXYZXYZ
REVERSE	Returns a string expression in reverse order	REVERSE ("ABC XYZ")	ZYX CBA
RIGHT	Returns the specified number of characters from the end of the string	RIGHT ("Anderson Co.", 7)	son Co.
RTRIM	Returns a string expression with all of the trailing blanks removed	RTRIM (" ABC XYZ ")	ABC XYZ
SUBSTRING	Returns the specified portion of a string expression starting at a specified location and including a specified number of characters	SUBSTRING ("Anderson Co.", 3, 6)	derson

(continued)

Function	Description	Example	Result
TOKEN	Parses a string using a specified delimiter and returns the specified delimited occurrence	TOKEN("ABC,LMN,XYZ", ",", 2)	LMN
TOKENCOUNT	Parses a string using a specified delimiter and returns the number of delimited items found	TOKENCOUNT("ABC,LMN,XYZ", ",")	3
TRIM	Returns a string expression with all of the leading and trailing blanks removed	TRIM (" ABC XYZ ")	ABC XYZ
UPPER	Returns the uppercase version of a string expression	UPPER ("Anderson Co.")	ANDERSON CO.

The following date functions are supported by expressions:

Function	Description	Example	Result
DATEADD	Returns a new date based on a set time period added to a specified date	DATEADD("day", 100, (DT_DBTIMESTAMP) "1/1/2011")	2011-04-11 00:00:00
DATEDIFF	Returns the time period between two specified dates	DATEDIFF("day", (DT_DBTIMESTAMP) "1/1/2011", (DT_DBTIMESTAMP) "4/11/2011")	100
DATEPART	Returns an integer representing the selected part of the specified date	DATEPART("day", (DT_DBTIMESTAMP) "4/11/2011")	11
DAY	Returns an integer that represents the day portion of the specified date	DAY((DT_DBTIMESTAMP) "4/11/2011")	11
GETDATE	Returns the current system date and time	GETDATE()	2011-04-11 11:39:43
GETUTCDATE	Returns the current system date in Universal Time Coordinate (UTC) time	GETUTCDATE()	2011-04-11 16:39:43
MONTH	Returns an integer that represents the month portion of the specified date	MONTH((DT_DBTIMESTAMP) "4/11/2011")	4
YEAR	Returns an integer that represents the year portion of the specified date	YEAR((DT_DBTIMESTAMP) "4/11/2011")	2011

The following null functions are supported by expressions:

Function	Description	Example
ISNULL	Returns true if the expression is null; otherwise, returns false	ISNULL(@FileName)
NULL	Returns a null value of the requested data type	NULL(DT_WSTR, 50)
REPLACENULL	Returns the value of the second expression if the value of the first expression is NULL, otherwise returns the value of the first expression	REPLACENULL(@InputValue, @DefaultValue)

Type Casts In some cases, we need to change the data type of a variable or expression to a different data type for use within an expression. This is known as a type cast. The following type casts can be used:

Type Cast	Resulting Data Type
(DT_I1)	One-byte Integer
(DT_I2)	Two-byte Integer
(DT_I4)	Four-byte Integer
(DT_I8)	Eight-byte Integer
(DT_UI1)	Unsigned One-byte Integer
(DT_UI2)	Unsigned Two-byte Integer
(DT_UI4)	Unsigned Four-byte Integer
(DT_UI8)	Unsigned Eight-byte Integer
(DT_R4)	Four-byte Floating Point Number
(DT_R8)	Eight-byte Floating Point Number
(DT_STR, *length, codepage*)	Non-Unicode String with specified length and code page
(DT_WSTR, *length*)	Unicode String with specified length
(DT_DATE)	Date
(DT_BOOL)	Boolean
(DT_NUMERIC, *precision, scale*)	Numeric with specified precision and scale
(DT_DECIMAL, *scale*)	Decimal with specified scale
(DT_CY)	Currency
(DT_GUID)	Globally Unique Identifier (GUID)
(DT_BYTES, *length*)	Binary Data with specified length
(DT_DBDATE)	Date consisting of year, month, and day
(DT_DBTIME)	Time consisting of hour, minute, and second

(*continued*)

Type Cast	Resulting Data Type
(DT_DBTIME2, *scale*)	Time consisting of hour, minute, second, and fractional seconds with the specified scale
(DT_DBTIMESTAMP)	Timestamp consisting of year, month, day, hour, minute, second, and fractional second with a scale of three decimal places
(DT_DBTIMESTAMP2, *scale*)	Timestamp consisting of year, month, day, hour, minute, second, and fractional second with the specified scale
(DT_DBTIMESTAMPOFFSET, *scale*)	Timestamp with a time zone offset consisting of year, month, day, hour, minute, second, and fractional second with the specified scale
(DT_FILETIME)	A 64-bit value representing the 100-nanosecond intervals since January 1, 1601
(DT_IMAGE)	Binary value for an image representation
(DT_TEXT, *codepage*)	Large Non-Unicode String with the specified code page
(DT_NTEXT)	Large Unicode String

Event Handlers

The event handlers within a package enable us to create a control flow that executes in reaction to a certain event. The event could be an error, a warning, or a change to the value of a variable. The event could also be the beginning or the completion of a task within the package.

NOTE

Remember that the Variable Value Changed event is triggered only if you have the Raise Change Event property set to true for one or more variables in the package.

The control flow that we create to respond to an event looks exactly the same as the control flow created for the package as a whole. While the package control flow is executed exactly once each time the package is run, an event handler control flow may be executed many times or not at all. The execution of the event handler control flow depends on what happens during the running of the package. If no error conditions are encountered, the OnError event is never fired. If 20 error conditions are encountered (and this does not terminate the package as a whole), then the OnError event is executed 20 times.

Error handlers are useful for such things as

▶ Checking the state of the host server to make sure it is appropriate for the Integration Services package to execute

▶ Sending an e-mail to the administrator when an error occurs

▶ Doing any necessary cleanup after a process has completed

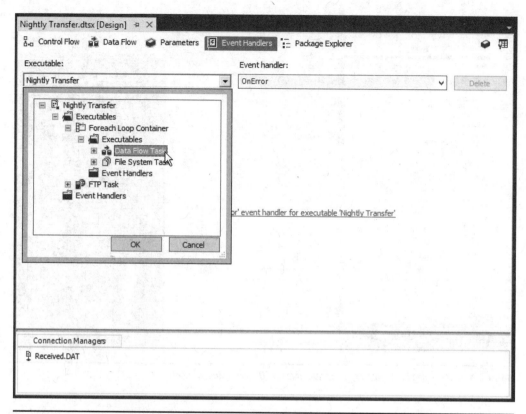

Figure 8-2   *The Event Handlers tab*

To create an event handler, click the Event Handlers tab, shown in Figure 8-2. Use the Executable drop-down list to select an item in the Integration Services package. Use the Event handler drop-down list to select the event. Now click the blue link in the middle of the design area to create an error handler for this event. You can drag and drop items from the SSIS Toolbox to create the functionality for this event handler.

Package Development Tools

The aids to Integration Services package development do not stop with the rich programming environment. Several features help with package creation and testing. These features make Integration Services a truly robust data transformation environment.

Import/Export Wizard

The *Import/Export Wizard* lets us quickly transfer data from one location to another. After we walk through the pages of the wizard to define the data transfer, the wizard

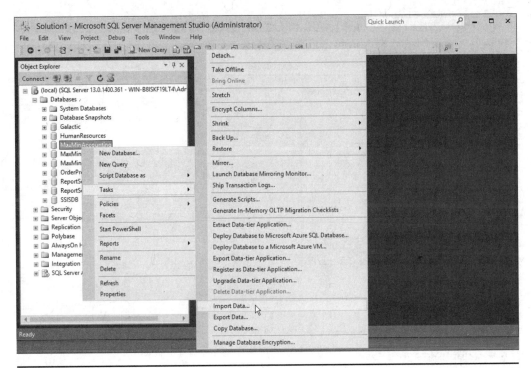

Figure 8-3   *Launching the Import/Export Wizard from the SQL Server Management Studio*

creates an Integration Services package and executes it. The package created by the wizard can also be saved for future use.

To launch the Import/Export Wizard, from SQL Server Data Tools, select Project | SSIS Import and Export Wizard from the Main menu. The Import/Export Wizard can also be launched from the SQL Server Management Studio, as shown in Figure 8-3. To accomplish this, right-click a database entry in the Object Explorer window and select either Tasks | Import Data or Tasks | Export Data from the context menu. The only difference between these two menu items is the fact that the Import Data item defaults the destination to the database that was clicked, while the Export Data item defaults the source to the database that was clicked.

When the wizard is launched from the SQL Server Management Studio, we can choose to save the Integration Services package to a SQL server or to a file for future use. When it is launched from SQL Server Data Tools, the package is automatically saved to the Integration Services project. A saved package can be executed again in the future in its current form, or it can be edited in an Integration Services project to serve as the starting point for a more complex data transformation.

Logging

Because Integration Services packages are, for the most part, designed for unattended operation, it can be extremely important to create a log documenting the execution of the package. This type of execution log can also be helpful for testing and debugging during the creation of the package. We control the logging performed by an Integration Services package using the Configure SSIS Logs dialog box, shown in Figure 8-4.

To display the Configure SSIS Logs dialog box, open an Integration Services package in SQL Server Data Tools and select Logging from the SSIS menu. Use the Providers and Logs tab to determine where the information should be logged. Select the location for the logging from the Provider type drop-down list, and then click Add to create a new log. We can create the following types of logs:

- ► Comma-separated values text file
- ► File to be read by the SQL Profiler
- ► SQL Server Table named sysssislog
- ► Windows Event Log
- ► Extensible Markup Language (XML) text file

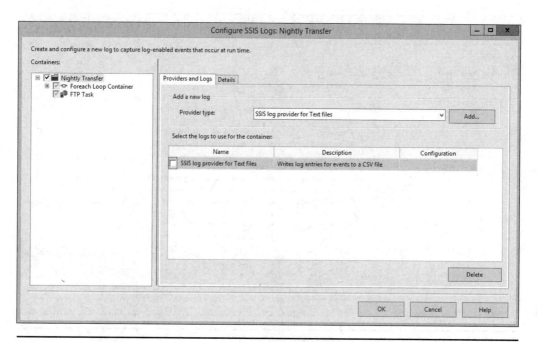

Figure 8-4   *The Providers and Logs tab of the Configure SSIS Logs dialog box*

All of the log types, with the exception of the Windows Event Log, need to be configured to specify exactly where the logged information is to be stored. A Connection Manager is used to determine where each log type will store its entries. Click in the Configuration column to select an existing Connection Manager or create a new one.

In the Containers list, select either the entry for the package itself or an entry for one of the items in the package. Check the check box for an item to enable logging for that item. If a check box is gray, it is being enabled or disabled along with its parent item. You can break this association with the parent by clicking the grayed check box. Once you have enabled logging for an item, click one or more check boxes in the Name column for each of the log types that should be active for that item. Multiple log types can be selected.

Finally, we need to determine which events should be logged for the package or for a package item. On the Details tab, shown in Figure 8-5, check the check boxes for the events that should be logged for this item and any child items that remain associated with it. If no events are checked, only the beginning and ending of an item's execution will be logged.

In addition to the log types discussed, you can view the log entries for a package by using the Log Events window in SQL Server Data Tools. This is located under View | Other Windows in the main menu. Logging must be enabled for the package

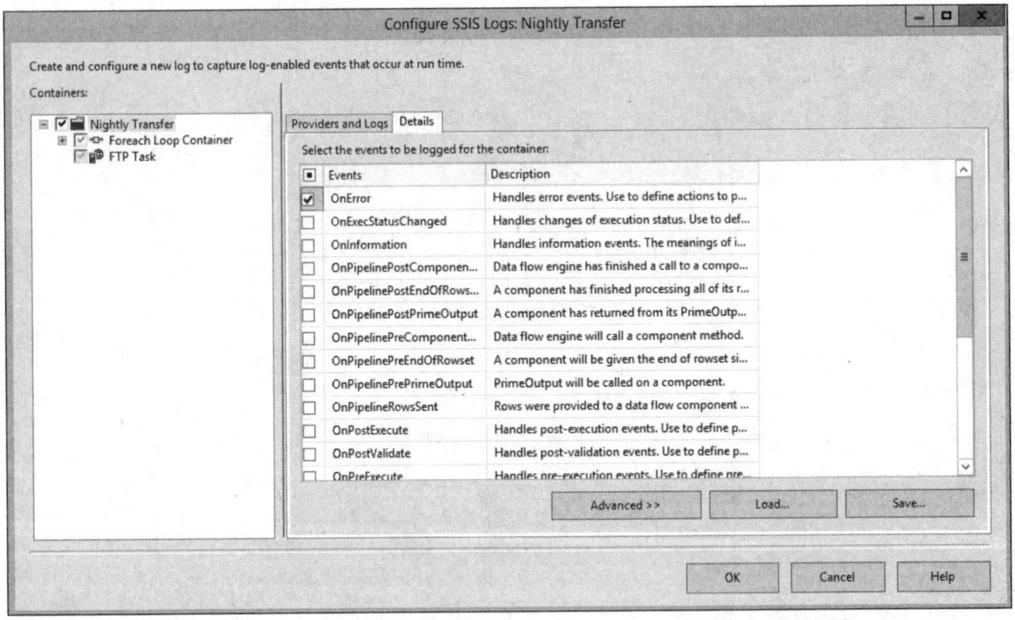

Figure 8-5   *The Details tab of the Configure SSIS Logs dialog box*

or for one or more items in the package before log events are displayed in the Log
Events window. However, you do not need to have any log types enabled for the events
to appear in the Log Events window. The Log Events window is cleared each time you
run the package.

Transactions

As with operations in Transact-SQL (T-SQL), we can use transactions in Integration
Services packages to ensure that our data remains in a consistent state. By using
transactions, we can ensure that a series of items in a package all complete successfully,
or the entire process is rolled back to the state where it was prior to the attempted
changes. We can even use distributed transactions to commit or roll back changes
spread across multiple servers.

Each of the items in the Control Flow SSIS Toolbox and the Integration Services
package itself has a TransactionOption property that determines how it deals with
transactions. This property has three possible settings:

- ▶ **Supported** An item with this property setting joins a transaction if one is
  already active, but it does not initiate a transaction itself. This is the default setting
  for the property.

- ▶ **Required** An item with this property setting joins a transaction if one is already
  active and will initiate a transaction if one is not currently active.

- ▶ **NotSupported** An item with this property setting does not join a transaction
  if one is already active and does not initiate a transaction if one is not
  currently active.

The TransactionOption is set by selecting an item and then modifying this property
in the Properties window. This property is not included in the Editor dialog boxes for
each item.

Consider the sample Integration Services package with the TransactionOption
property settings shown in Figure 8-6. Because the package has its TransactionOption
set to Required, a transaction is created when package execution begins. We call this
Transaction 1, as shown in Figure 8-7. The File Transfer Protocol task participates in
Transaction 1 because its TransactionOption is set to Supported.

The Foreach Loop container does not participate in Transaction 1 because its
TransactionOption is set to NotSupported. The data flow task inside the Foreach Loop
container cannot participate in Transaction 1, even though its TransactionOption is
set to Required. The reason for this is its parent object, the Foreach Loop container,
is not participating in Transaction 1. Instead, because its TransactionOption is set to

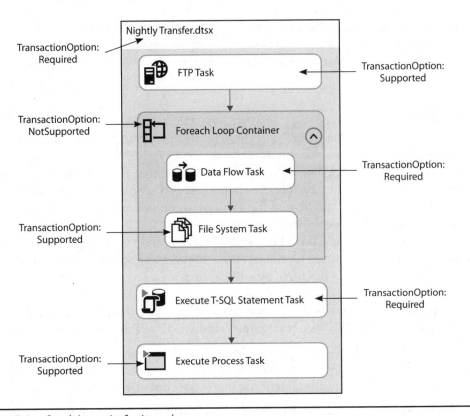

Figure 8-6   *Sample Integration Services package*

Required, it initiates a second transaction called Transaction 2. All items in the data flow task participate in Transaction 2.

If any of the items in the data flow task should fail, all of the data changes within Transaction 2 are rolled back. Also, because Transaction 2 is nested within Transaction 1, all of the data changes within Transaction 1 are rolled back as well. If, on the other hand, all of the items in the data flow task complete successfully, the data changes in Transaction 2 are committed as soon as the data flow task completes. In other words, a rollback of Transaction 2 causes a rollback of Transaction 1, but not the other way around.

The File System task in Figure 8-6 and Figure 8-7 has its TransactionOption set to Supported, but there is no transaction for it to join. It is outside of Transaction 2 and it cannot join Transaction 1 because its parent object is not participating in that transaction. Therefore, the File System task is not a member of any transaction. Its success or failure does not affect either Transaction 1 or Transaction 2.

The Execute T-SQL Statement task has its TransactionOption set to Required. It does not need to create a new transaction, however, because it can join the active

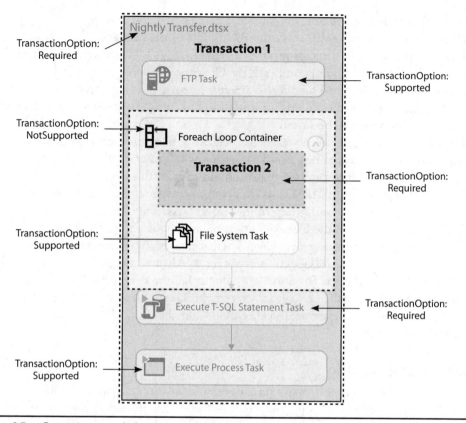

Figure 8-7 *Transactions created when executing the sample Integration Services package*

transaction, Transaction 1. If the Execute T-SQL Statement task should fail, it rolls back all data changes in Transaction 1. As mentioned earlier, the success or failure of the Execute T-SQL Statement task in Transaction 1 has no effect on Transaction 2.

The Execute Process task has its TransactionOption set to Supported. It also joins the active transaction, Transaction 1. Again, its success or failure only affects Transaction 1.

Checkpoints

There are many situations where an Integration Services package could be restarted at some point in the middle of the control flow after a failure, rather than re-executing the entire package from the beginning. Perhaps the first portion of a package deletes an old import text file and uses File Transfer Protocol (FTP) to download a new copy of this import file. If the package fails at some point later in the process, it is probably not necessary to perform the file deletion and download again. Checkpoints provide a mechanism for performing this restart in the middle of the package.

The package includes three properties that let us enable checkpoint restarting. These are the SaveCheckpoints property, the CheckpointFilename property, and the CheckpointUsage property. The *SaveCheckpoints property* is a Boolean flag that enables or disables the saving of checkpoint information. This property must be set to true for checkpoint information to be saved.

The *CheckpointFilename property* lets us specify the filename where checkpoint information is to be saved. When a package executes, information about each successfully completed task and each committed transaction is saved to this checkpoint file. In the event of a package failure, this file is used to determine where the package can be restarted.

The *CheckpointUsage property* determines how the checkpoint file is used when a package is executed. When the CheckpointUsage property is set to Never, the checkpoint file is not used when executing a package. The package is always run from beginning to end. When the CheckpointUsage property is set to Always, the package always reads the checkpoint file and starts from the last point of failure. When the CheckpointUsage property is set to IfExists, the package looks for a checkpoint file and uses it to restart from the last point of failure, if it exists. If a checkpoint file does not exist, the package is run from beginning to end.

Package Debugging

One of the most helpful tools in program development is the capability to pause program execution at a breakpoint and examine the execution state. This feature makes it much easier to pinpoint a problem and fix it. Fortunately, Integration Services provides this functionality.

Setting Breakpoints   We can set a breakpoint on any of the control flow tasks in a package. To accomplish this, right-click the task and select Edit Breakpoints from the context menu. The Set Breakpoints dialog box appears as shown in Figure 8-8. A breakpoint can be set on any of the events triggered by that task. We can use the Hit Count Type and Hit Count columns to determine whether execution pauses every time this event is triggered or only after a hit has occurred multiple times.

In addition to these task event breakpoints, breakpoints can be set on any line of code in the Script task. When execution is paused within a script, we may use the Step Into, Step Over, and Step Out features to move through the script code one line at a time. The step features do not function when paused at a task event breakpoint.

Viewing Package State   While the package execution is paused at a breakpoint, there are several places to see the current execution state of the package. The windows

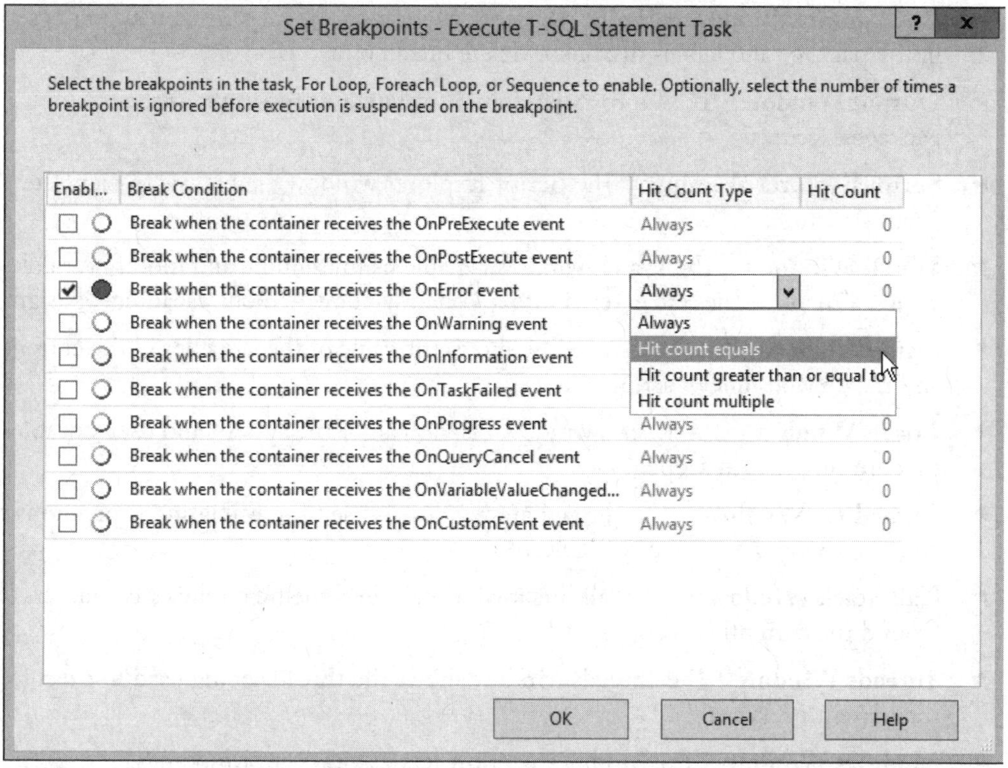

Figure 8-8   *The Set Breakpoints dialog box*

discussed here are opened using the Debug | Windows menu, the View menu, or the Windows Toolbar button.

▶ **Progress Marks**   As the tasks of a package execute, a symbol appears in the upper-right corner of each item to show the current execution status. A yellow circle containing a timer spinner indicates an item that is currently executing. A green circle containing a white checkmark indicates successfully completed execution. A red circle containing a white "X" indicates execution completed with errors. While execution is paused, we can switch between the Control Flow and Data Flow tabs to see the execution status of both.

▶ **Row Counts**   As the data flow tasks of a package execute, the number of rows processed through each data flow is displayed across the data flow arrows.

▶ **Execution Results**   We can switch to the Execution Results tab to see a description of the current execution status in outline form.

▶ **Breakpoints Window** The Breakpoints window shows all of the breakpoints set in the package and lets us disable or delete breakpoints.

▶ **Output Window** The Output window displays status messages as the package executes.

▶ **Script Explorer Window** The Script Explorer window enables us to view the script structure.

▶ **Watch Windows** The Watch windows enable us to examine and modify variable values. Variable names are entered into a Watch window without a leading "@" sign.

▶ **Autos Window** The Autos window shows the value of the variables in the current and the previous line of script code.

▶ **Locals Window** The Locals window displays all of the system and user variables that are currently in scope.

▶ **Immediate Window** The Immediate window is used for evaluating expressions and displaying the value of variables.

▶ **Call Stack Window** The Call Stack window shows the hierarchy of containers around the currently executing task.

▶ **Threads Window** The Threads window shows the threads being used to execute the current package.

▶ **Modules Window** The Modules window lets us view script modules.

▶ **Processes Window** The Processes window shows the currently executing processes.

Several of the debug windows are not used for debugging Integration Services packages. These are the Memory window, the Disassembly window, and the Registers window.

Viewing Data Flow In addition to viewing the doings inside package tasks, it is helpful (perhaps even more helpful) to see what is happening inside the data flow at various steps along the way. We do this by attaching data viewers to the data flow. The data viewer pauses the package execution and enables us to examine the rows in the data flow as it moves from one item to another.

We can attach a data viewer to a data flow from the Data Flow Path Editor dialog box. Open the Data Flow Path Editor dialog box by double-clicking a flow path arrow. The General page of the Data Flow Path Editor dialog box provides general information about this flow path arrow. The Metadata page of this dialog box provides information about the columns in the data flow at that point. This in itself can be helpful when developing and debugging packages. Data viewers are added to the data flow on the Data Viewers page.

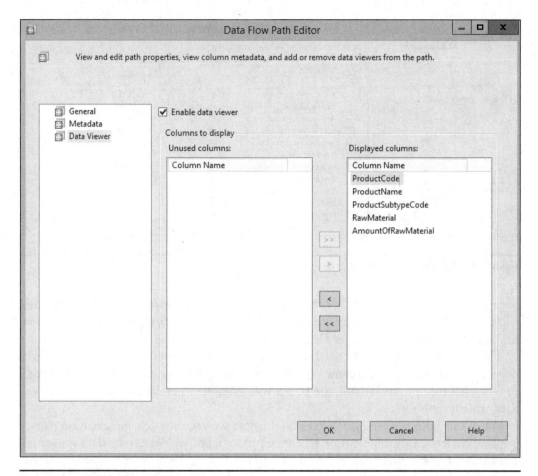

Figure 8-9   *The Data Flow Path Editor dialog box*

On the Data Viewers page of the dialog box, check Enable data viewer to attach a data viewer to the data flow path. By default, all columns in the data flow are displayed in the data viewer. You can change this by moving columns between the Unused columns and the Displayed columns lists. The Data Viewer page of the Data Flow Path Editor dialog box is shown in Figure 8-9.

It is also possible to create a data viewer without opening the Data Flow Path Editor dialog. To do this, right-click a flow path arrow and select Enable Data Viewer from the context menu. This will enable the data viewer with all columns in the data flow. To remove the data viewer, right-click the flow path arrow and select Disable Data Viewer from the context menu.

Data viewers can be placed on multiple flow path arrows in a data flow, if desired. A data viewer icon is placed on the flow path arrow to show that a data viewer has

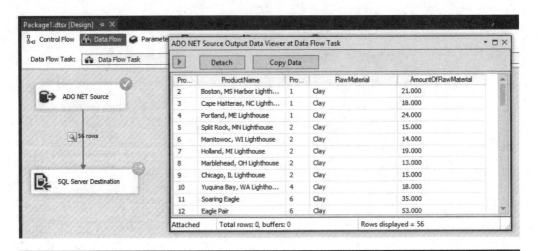

Figure 8-10   *A flow path arrow with a data viewer icon and a data viewer window*

been attached. When the package executes, the package execution pauses whenever the package reaches a data flow with a data viewer attached. A data viewer window appears for each data viewer, as shown in Figure 8-10.

The data viewers show data one buffer at a time. The number of rows in the buffer depends on the number of columns in the data flow at that point and the width of the data in each column. By default, the buffer will contain either 10,000 rows or 10MB of data, whichever is less.

When one buffer of data is loaded into the data viewer, the package execution pauses until we click the Continue button (the green triangle) or we detach the data viewer from that data flow. Data viewers are detached by clicking Detach. When data viewers are detached, the data flow resumes without loading data into the data viewer. Data viewers can be reattached by clicking Attach. We can visually inspect the data in the data viewer or click Copy Data to copy the data to the clipboard for saving or analysis in another application.

Change Data Capture

One of the biggest challenges of the extract, transform, and load (ETL) process is determining which records need to be extracted from the source data and loaded into the data mart. For smaller dimensional tables that are not used to populate slowly changing dimensions, we may choose to truncate the target table and refill it with all of the data from the source with every load. This won't work for some fact tables, large dimensional tables, and slowly changing dimensional tables. In these situations, we need to determine what data has changed since the last extract and only grab those records.

There are several methods for determining which data has changed since the last extract. They include

▶   Adding create and last update fields to the database table

▶   Adding flag fields to indicate when records have been extracted

▶   Creating triggers or stored procedures to replicate changes to change capture tables

All of these approaches add overhead to the transactional system and can even require changes to the front-end systems that create the transactions.

If our source data is coming from a SQL Server 2008 or later database, we have a feature to make this process much easier. That feature is known as *change data capture*. Rather than working from the tables themselves, change data capture uses the SQL transaction log to capture data modifications. These modifications are then written to a set of change data capture tables. Our ETL process can then read data from the change capture tables to update the data mart.

NOTE

Either the Enterprise Edition or the Developer Edition of SQL Server is required for change data capture.

Change Data Capture Architecture

As inserts, updates, and delete transactions occur in a SQL Server database table, they are recorded in both the SQL transaction log and in the table itself. While the table contains the net result of these changes, the SQL transaction log contains a record of the changes themselves. This allows the SQL server to maintain data integrity as the modifications are being made and allows for these modifications to be re-created if a log backup is applied as part of database recovery.

The SQL transaction log, therefore, has just the information we need to determine what data changes need to occur in our data mart. Unfortunately, the SQL transaction log is in a format that can only be used internally by the SQL Server database engine. Change data capture provides us with a utility that can harvest the change information from the SQL transaction log and convert it to a format that can be easily understood and used for other purposes. This utility is run as part of a SQL Agent Job, as shown in Figure 8-11.

The transaction information is converted into a more readily usable format and stored in a *change table*. One change table is created for each table that is being tracked by change data capture. The change tables are created in the cdc schema, which is created specifically for that purpose.

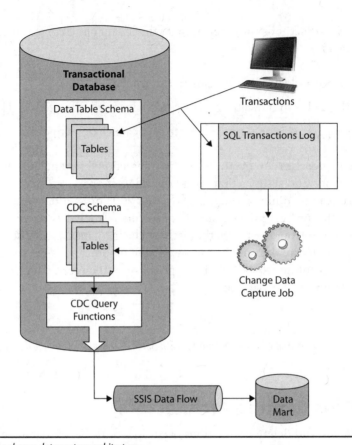

Figure 8-11   *The change data capture architecture*

Change data tracking also provides a method for creating a set of functions to facilitate easy retrieval of the change information from a change table. These functions return a table-valued result containing all of the changes made to a particular table during a specified period. The records in this result set make it possible for a program or an Integration Services package to re-create the changes in another data source, such as a data mart.

Enabling Change Data Capture

Enabling change data capture is a two-step process. This feature must first be enabled for the database as a whole. Once this is done, change data capture must also be enabled for each table individually.

The following system stored procedure will enable change data capture for a specified database:

```
USE OrderProcessingSystem
EXEC sys.sp_cdc_enable_db
```

This example will enable change data capture in the OrderProcessingSystem database.

> **NOTE**
>
> The example here is not meant to be a Learn By Doing exercise. If you do choose to restore the OrderProcessingSystem database and try the commands shown here, you will need to use an Enterprise Edition or Developer Edition of SQL Server 2016. You will also have to run the following before doing any of the other commands:
>
> USE OrderProcessingSystem
> Exec sp_changedbowner 'sa'

In addition to enabling change data capture for each database, it must be enabled for a given table. This is done with a command similar to the following:

```
EXECUTE sys.sp_cdc_enable_table
    @source_schema = N'dbo'
  , @source_name = N'Orders'
  , @role_name = N'cdc_Admin'
  , @supports_net_changes = 1
```

This example will enable change data capture on the dbo.Orders table. The @role_name parameter defines a database role that will be used to establish database rights for the change data capture process. This database role will be created, if it does not already exist in the database.

All Changes vs. Net Changes

As stated, change data capture provides a table-valued function that returns all of the changes made to a table in a given time period. If the same record is updated three times during that time period, the function will return three sets of rows: one set for each change. In some cases, we may care only about the current state of a record at the end of the time period. We may not need to know all of the individual changes along the way.

To support this situation, change data capture has an optional setting to support net changes. When the @supports_net_changes function is set to 1, the change data capture for this particular table will support the net changes feature. This feature provides a second function that returns a single record representing the net effect of the changes made to each record over the given time period.

The Change Table

One change table is created for each table where change data capture has been enabled. The table is named for the schema and table name of the source table as follows:

```
cdc.schemaname_tablename_CT
```

The cdc tables are found in the System Tables folder in SQL Server Management Studio.

The change table has one column that mirrors each column in the source table where changed data is being captured. These columns have the same name and, in most cases, the same data type as the corresponding column in the source table.

The default, as shown in our previous example of the sys.sp_cdc_enable_table stored procedure, is to capture changes for all of the columns in a table. The sys.sp_cdc_enable_table stored procedure has an optional parameter, @captured_column_list, which enables us to capture changes to only selected columns in a table. Enabling change data capture on selected columns would be done as follows:

```
EXECUTE sys.sp_cdc_enable_table
    @source_schema = N'dbo'
  , @source_name = N'Orders'
  , @role_name = N'cdc_Admin'
  , @captured_column_list = N'OrderID,CustomerAccount,Product,SalesPerson'
```

In addition to the columns that mirror the source table, the change table contains several columns of metadata, as follows:

▶ **__$start_lsn** The Log Sequence Number (LSN) assigned to this change. All changes committed within the same transaction will have the same LSN. The LSN shows the order in which transactions occurred.

▶ **__$end_lsn** This column may be utilized in future versions of SQL Server. In SQL Server 2016, it is always NULL.

▶ **__$seqval** A sequence number used to determine the order of changes that are within the same transaction and thus have the same LSN.

▶ **__$operation** The operation that caused the change as follows:

1 – delete
2 – insert
3 – update (values prior to the update)
4 – update (values after the update)

▶ **__$update_mask** A bit map indicating which columns were affected by an update.

The Validity Interval

In addition to creating a SQL Agent Job to capture change data from the SQL transaction log, the sys.sp_cdc_enable_db stored procedure creates a SQL Agent Job to remove old change data from the change tables. This prevents the change tables from growing indefinitely. It also means that there is a limited time period during which change data is available. This time period is known as the *validity interval*. By default, the validity interval is three days.

Loading a Data Mart Table from a Change Data Capture Change Table

In order to utilize the data in the change table, we need to create two Integration Services packages. The first performs the initial load of the data. The second propagates the incremental changes from the source to the destination.

The CDC Initial Load Package

The Integration Services package for performing the initial load consists of three control flow items. An initial CDC Control task marks the starting Log Sequence Number (LSN). Next, a control flow copies all of the records from the source table to the destination table. Finally, a second CDC Control task marks the ending LSN. The CDC initial load package is shown in Figure 8-12.

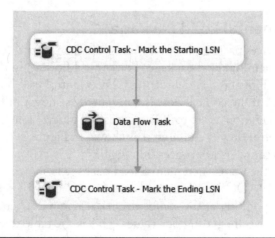

Figure 8-12   *The CDC initial load control flow*

In the CDC Control Task Editor dialog box for the task used to mark the starting LSN, the "SQL Server CDC database ADO.NET connection manager" must be set to an ADO.NET connection manager pointing at the source database. This is the database where change data capture is enabled. The "CDC control operation" must be set to "Mark initial load start," which is the default setting.

The "Variable containing the CDC state" is set to an SSIS package variable that is used to hold the CDC state while the package is running. This variable can be created by clicking the New button next to the "Variable containing the CDC state" drop-down list. The data type of this variable must be String.

The "Automatically store state in database table" option must be checked. The "Connection manager for the database where the state is stored" is set to a connection manager pointing at the database which will contain the CDC state table. This is usually the destination database. Use the "Table to use for storing state" drop-down list to select the CDC state table. You will probably want to use the New button next to this drop-down list to have this table created for you in the specified database. (Click New, and then click Run in the Create New State Table dialog box.)

Finally, the State name contains a string. This string acts as the key for the CDC state information in the cdc_states table. It defaults to be the same as the CDC state variable. The completed CDC Control Task Editor dialog box for the CDC Control task used to mark the starting LSN is shown in Figure 8-13.

The CDC Control task used to mark the ending LSN is configured identically to the CDC Control task used to mark the starting LSN with one exception. The "CDC control operation" is set to "Mark initial load end." The completed package is run once to perform the initial load of the data from source to destination.

The CDC Incremental Load Package

The Integration Services package for performing the incremental load is almost as straightforward as the initial load package. The control flow again consists of a CDC Control task, a Data Flow task, and a second CDC Control task. The CDC Control task at the beginning of the control flow is configured as shown in Figure 8-13 *except* the "CDC control operation" is set to "Get processing range." The CDC Control task at the end of the control flow is configured as shown in Figure 8-13 *except* the "CDC control operation" is set to "Mark processed range."

The data flow for the CDC incremental load package is shown in Figure 8-14. In the CDC Source, the "ADO.NET connection manager" must be set to an ADO.NET connection manager pointing at the source database. The "CDC enabled table" is set to the table from which we are getting our values. This is the table that has change data

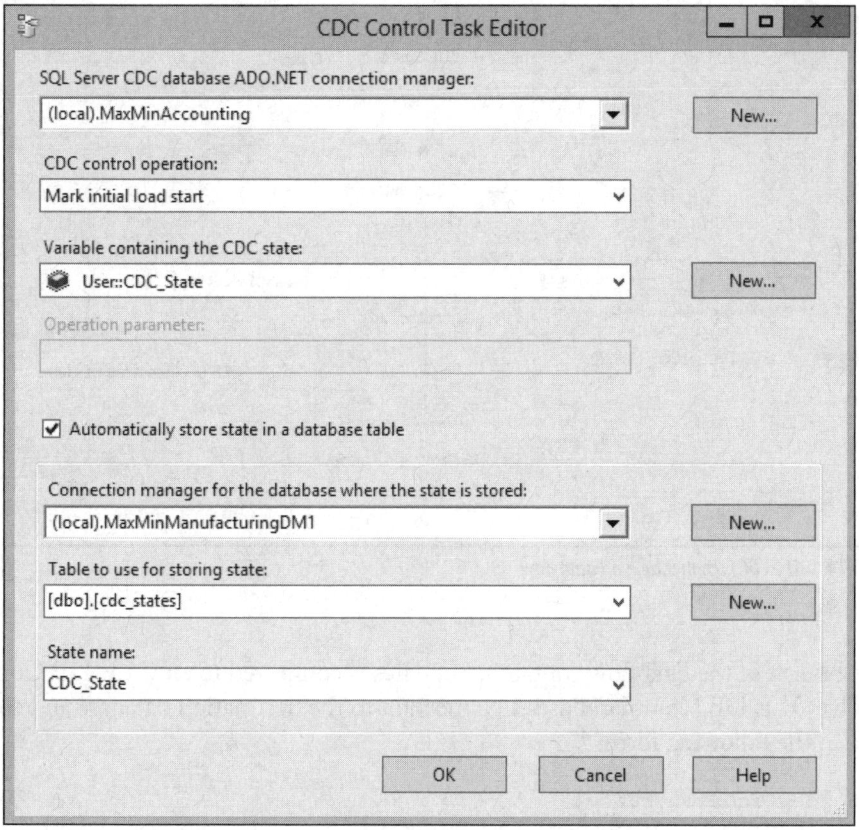

Figure 8-13   *The CDC Control Task Editor dialog box for the starting LSN CDC Control Task*

capture enabled. Selecting this table will also set the "Capture instance" for you. The "CDC processing mode" is set to the desired processing mode. (See the "CDC Source" section of Chapter 7 for more information.) Finally, the "Variable containing the CDC state" is set to the package variable tracking CDC state.

The CDC Splitter item defaults to the correct configuration. It creates three branches to the data flow: one containing rows to be inserted, one containing rows to be updated, and one containing rows to be deleted. The branch of the data flow containing inserts is connected to an OLE DB Destination pointing at the destination table with the fields mapped to insert the new rows appropriately.

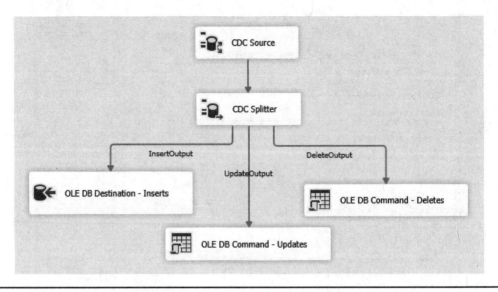

Figure 8-14 *The CDC incremental load data flow*

The branch of the data flow containing updates is connected to an OLE DB Command item. The OLE DB Command uses a connection to the destination database and contains a query in the following form:

```
UPDATE {destination_table}
SET {field_0} = ?,
    {field_1} = ?,
       .
       .
       .
    {field_n} = ?
WHERE {PK_field} = ?
```

Each question mark serves as a placeholder for a parameter value. They are numbered from the beginning of the query to the end starting with Param_0 up to Param_n+1. Param_n+1 is used with the primary key field in the WHERE clause. This is shown in Figure 8-15.

The branch of the data flow containing deletes is connected to another OLE DB Command item. This OLE DB Command also uses a connection to the destination database and contains a query in the following form:

```
DELETE FROM {destination_table}
WHERE {PK_field} = ?
```

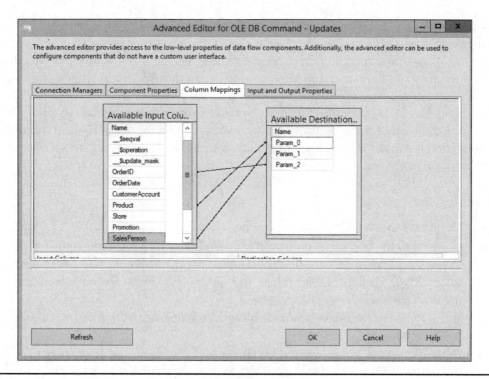

Figure 8-15   *Mapping fields to parameters in the OLE DB Command for updates*

This time, the single question mark parameter is mapped to the primary key field of the destination table.

Loading a Fact Table

Next, we will work through two additional Learn By Doing exercises. We have populated the dimensional tables in the Manufacturing data mart in a previous Learn By Doing exercise. Now we will populate the fact table in this data mart. In fact, we will add a new wrinkle to the business requirements and populate two fact tables.

Learn By Doing: Adding a Second Fact Table to the Manufacturing Data Mart

Features Highlighted

- ▶ Modifying the structure of a data mart database
- ▶ Using multiple fact tables in a single data mart

Business Need The vice president of production at Maximum Miniatures, Incorporated would like to be able to view the current inventory amount and the number of backorders pending for products while analyzing manufacturing production. The inventory and backorder amounts are available in the order processing system.

The inventory and backorder information is added as a second fact table in the data mart. This is done because the inventory information does not relate to all of the same dimensions as the production information. In addition, because the inventory information is populated from a different data source, loading the data mart is easier with two separate fact tables.

Steps

1. Open SQL Server Management Studio.
2. Connect to the SQL server where you created the MaxMinManufacturingDM.
3. Expand the Databases folder, and expand the MaxMinManufacturingDM database folder. Right-click the Tables folder, and select New | Table from the context menu. A Table Designer tab appears.
4. If the Properties window is not visible, select Properties Window from the View menu.
5. In the Properties window, enter **FactInventory** for Name and **Inventory Fact populated from the Order Processing System database** for Description.
6. Add the following columns to the table:

Column Name	Data Type	Allow Nulls
InventoryLevel	Int	No
NumberOnBackorder	Int	No
DateOfInventory	Date	No
ProductCode	Int	No
MaterialKey	Int	No

7. Select the DateOfInventory, Product Code, and MaterialKey entries in the Table Designer. Click the Set Primary Key button on the toolbar.
8. Click the Save toolbar button to save this table design. The InventoryFact table should appear as shown in Figure 8-16.
9. Close SQL Server Management Studio.

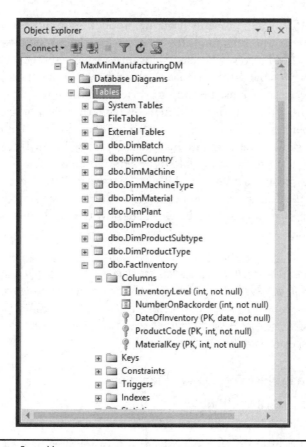

Figure 8-16   *The InventoryFact table*

Learn By Doing: Populating the Fact Tables in the Manufacturing Data Mart

Feature Highlighted

▶   Populating a fact table with Integration Services

Business Need

Obviously, these data marts don't do Maximum Miniatures any good unless they contain facts! Therefore, we need to populate the fact tables. The information for the Manufacturing fact table is in the BatchInfo.csv file. In an actual production environment, this file would probably have the production results for one day or perhaps one week at the most. The Integration Services package that processes this file would be run daily or weekly. However, because we want to have a good deal of sample data to work from, our copy of BatchInfo.csv has three years' worth of data. The design of the Integration Services package used to import this information remains unchanged.

We also have the little issue of one dimension table that has not been populated. This is the DimBatch table. The only source we have for the batch number information is the BatchInfo.csv file. Therefore, we include a data flow in our Integration Services package to populate the dimension table right before the fact table is populated.

We now have a second fact table in this data mart as well: the Inventory fact table. The information for this fact table comes from the order processing database. Our Integration Services package also includes a data flow to handle this.

NOTE

To complete this Learn By Doing activity, you need the BatchInfo.csv file and the Maximum Miniatures Order Processing database. If you have not done so already, go to www.mhprofessional.com and search for the book's web page using the ISBN, which is 9781259641480. Use the "Downloads & Resources" tab to download the Zip file containing the book's material. Follow the instructions within the zipped folders in the Zip file to install the Maximum Miniatures Order Processing database.

Steps to Create a Project Connection Manager

1. Open SQL Server Data Tools.
2. Reopen the MaxMinManufacturingDMLoad project.
3. Open the DimensionLoad.dtsx package, if it is not already open.
4. In the Connections tray, right-click the MaxMinManufacturingDM connection, and select Convert to Project Connection in the context menu. The MaxMinManufacturingDM connection is moved to the Connection Managers folder in the Solution Explorer window. A reference to the project-level MaxMinManufacturingDM connection is placed in the Connections tray. This reference name is preceded by "(project)" to indicate it is a link to a project connection, not a package connection.

NOTE

A project connection can be shared by several packages within the project. A package connection can be promoted to a project connection, as was done in this example. You can also create a project connection directly by right-clicking the Connection Managers folder in the Solution Explorer window and selecting New Connection Manager from the context menu.

Steps to Create the Load DimBatch Data Flow

1. In the Solution Explorer window, right-click the SSIS Packages folder, and select New SSIS Package from the context menu.

2. Right-click the Package1.dtsx entry in the Solution Explorer window, and select Rename from the context menu. Enter **FactLoad.dtsx** for the package name and press ENTER.

3. Drag a Data Flow Task item from the SSIS Toolbox and drop it on the Control Flow tab.

4. Right-click the Data Flow Task item you just created and select Rename from the context menu. Enter **Load DimBatch** and press ENTER. Double-click the Load DimBatch item. This takes you to the Data Flow tab.

5. Right-click in the Connections tray and select New Flat File Connection from the context menu. The Flat File Connection Manager Editor dialog box appears.

6. Enter **BatchInfo.CSV File** for Connection Manager Name. Click Browse. The Open dialog box appears.

7. Select CSV Files (*.csv) in the file type drop-down list in the lower-right corner of the dialog box.

8. Browse to the BatchInfo.csv file that you downloaded from the book's web page. Select this file and click Open to exit the Open dialog box.

9. Check Column names in the first data row, if it is not checked by default.

10. Select Columns in the page selector on the left side of the dialog box. Note the content of the columns being read from the CSV text file.

11. Select Advanced in the page selector.

12. Change the data type for the BatchNumber, MachineNumber, ProductCode, NumberProduced, and NumberRejected columns to four-byte signed integer [DT_I4]. Change the data type for the TimeStarted and TimeStopped columns to database timestamp [DT_DBTIMESTAMP].

13. Click OK to exit the Flat File Connection Manager Editor dialog box.

14. Drag a Flat File Source item from the Other Sources section of the SSIS Toolbox, and drop it on the Data Flow tab.

15. Double-click the Flat File Source item you just created. The Flat File Source Editor dialog box appears.

16. The BatchInfo.csv File data connection should be selected in the Flat File connection manager drop-down list.

17. Select Columns in the page selector on the left side of the dialog box.

18. Uncheck all of the columns in the Available External Columns list except the BatchNumber column.

19. Click OK to exit the Flat File Source Editor dialog box.

20. Drag a Sort item from the Common section of the SSIS Toolbox, and drop it on the Data Flow tab.

21. Click the Flat File Source item. Click the blue data flow arrow, drag it on top of the Sort item, and drop it on this item. This connects the source to the transformation.

22. Double-click the Sort item you just created. The Sort Transformation Editor dialog box appears.

23. Check the box to the left of BatchNumber in the Available Input Columns list.

24. Check Remove rows with duplicate sort values in the lower-left corner of the dialog box. This gives us a distinct list of batch numbers that we can use to populate our dimension table.

25. Click OK to exit the Sort Transformation Editor dialog box.

26. Drag a Derived Column item from the SSIS Toolbox and drop it on the Data Flow tab.

27. Click the Sort item. Click the blue data flow arrow, drag it on top of the Derived Column item, and drop it on this item. This connects the two transformations.

28. Double-click the Derived Column item you just created. The Derived Column Transformation Editor dialog box appears.

29. Enter **BatchName** in the first row under Derived Column Name.

30. Enter the following in the first row under Expression:

    ```
    (DT_WSTR, 50) [BatchNumber]
    ```

31. Click OK to exit the Derived Column Transformation Editor dialog box.

32. Drag a SQL Server Destination item from the Other Destinations section of the SSIS Toolbox, and drop it on the Data Flow tab.

33. Click the Derived Column item. Click the blue data flow arrow, drag it on top of the SQL Server Destination item, and drop it on this item. This connects the transformation to the destination.

34. Double-click the SQL Server Destination item. The SQL Destination Editor dialog box appears.

35. The MaxMinManufacturingDM connection should already be selected in the Connection manager drop-down list. Select [dbo].[DimBatch] from the Use a table or view drop-down list.

36. Click Mappings to view the Mappings page. The columns from the data source (which are Available Input Columns to this data destination item) should be

automatically mapped to the columns in the destination (the Available Destination Columns). The following mappings should be in place:

Available Input Columns		Available Destination Columns
BatchNumber	to	BatchNumber
BatchName	to	BatchName

37. Click OK to exit the SQL Destination Editor dialog box. The Data Flow tab should appear, as shown in Figure 8-17.

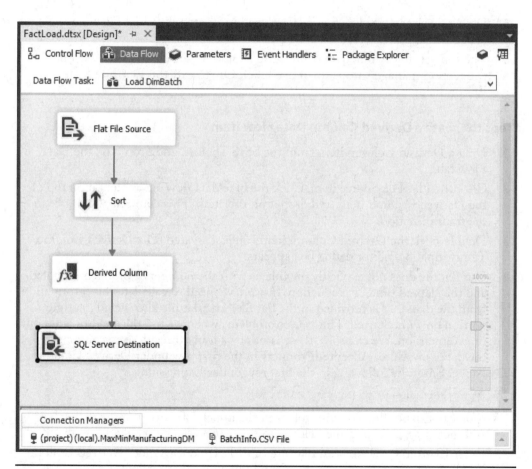

Figure 8-17   *The Data Flow tab for the Load DimBatch Data Flow task*

Steps to Begin Creating the Load ManufacturingFact Data Flow

1. Click the Control Flow tab. Drag another Data Flow Task item onto the Control Flow tab. Rename this new Data Flow Task item **Load ManufacturingFact**.

2. Click the Load DimBatch item. Drag the precedence arrow onto the Load ManufacturingFact item and drop it there. (The DimBatch table must be loaded successfully before the ManufacturingFact table can be loaded.)

3. Double-click the Load ManufacturingFact item. This takes you to the Data Flow tab with Load ManufacturingFact selected in the Data Flow Task drop-down list.

4. Drag a Flat File Source item from the SSIS Toolbox and drop it on the Data Flow tab.

5. Double-click the Flat File Source item you just created. The Flat File Source Editor dialog box appears.

6. The BatchInfo.csv File data connection should be selected in the Flat File connection manager drop-down list. Click OK to exit the Flat File Source Editor dialog box.

Steps to Create a Derived Column Data Flow Item

1. Drag a Derived Column item from the SSIS Toolbox and drop it on the Data Flow tab.

2. Click the Flat File Source item. Click the blue data flow arrow, drag it on top of the Derived Column item, and drop it on this item. This connects the source to the transformation.

3. Double-click the Derived Column item you just created. The Derived Column Transformation Editor dialog box appears.

4. Our flat file does not explicitly provide us with the number of products accepted and the elapsed time of production. Instead, we need to calculate this information from the data that is provided in the flat file. The flat file also includes a time portion on TimeStarted. This causes problems when we use this field to build our time dimension. We can solve these issues by adding three derived columns to the data flow. Enter **AcceptedProducts** in the first row under Derived Column Name. Enter the following in the first row under Expression:

```
[NumberProduced] - [NumberRejected]
```

(You can expand the Columns folder in the upper-left corner of the dialog box and then drag-and-drop the fields onto the expression, if you like.)

5. Enter **ElapsedTimeForManufacture** in the second row under Derived Column Name. Enter the following in the second row under Expression:

```
(DT_NUMERIC,6,2)DATEDIFF("mi", [TimeStarted], [TimeStopped])
```

(You can expand the Date/Time Functions folder in the upper-right corner of the dialog box and then drag-and-drop the DATEDIFF function onto the expression. You can also drag-and-drop the fields onto the expression.)

6. Enter **DateOfManufacture** in the third row under Derived Column Name. Enter the following in the third row under Expression:

```
(DT_DBDATE)SUBSTRING((DT_WSTR,25)[TimeStarted],1,10)
```

This expression converts TimeStarted into a string and selects the first ten characters of that string (the date portion, but not the time portion). This string is then converted a date data type. (You can expand the Type Casts and String Functions folders in the upper-right corner of the dialog box and drag and drop the (DT_WSTR) type cast, SUBSTRING function, and (DT_DBDATE) type cast onto the expression. You can also drag-and-drop the fields onto the expression.)

7. Click OK to exit the Derived Column Transformation Editor dialog box.

Steps to Create Lookup Data Flow Items

1. Drag a Lookup item from the SSIS Toolbox and drop it on the Data Flow tab.
2. Change the name of this item to **Validate Batch Number**.
3. Click the Derived Column item. Click the blue data flow arrow, drag it on top of the Validate Batch Number item, and drop it on this item. This connects the two transformations.
4. Double-click the Validate Batch Number item. The Lookup Transformation Editor dialog box appears.
5. In the Specify how to handle rows with no matching entries drop-down list, select Redirect rows to no match output.
6. Click Connection to view the Connection page.
7. Select [dbo].[DimBatch] from the Use a table or a view drop-down list.
8. Click Columns to view the Columns page.
9. Click BatchNumber in the Available Input Columns list, and drag-and-drop it on BatchNumber in the Available LookupColumns list.
10. Click OK to exit the Lookup Transformation Editor dialog box.
11. Drag another Lookup item from the SSIS Toolbox and drop it on the Data Flow tab.
12. Change the name of this item to **Validate Machine Number**.
13. Click the Validate Batch Number item. Click the blue data flow arrow, drag it on top of the Validate Machine Number item, and drop it on this item. The Input Output Selection dialog box appears.
14. Select Lookup Match Output from the Output drop-down list and click OK.
15. Double-click the Validate Machine Number item. The Lookup Transformation Editor dialog box appears.

16. In the Specify how to handle rows with no matching entries drop-down list, select Redirect rows to no match output.

17. Click Connection to view the Connection page.

18. Select [dbo].[DimMachine] from the Use a table or a view drop-down list.

19. Click Columns to view the Columns page.

20. Click MachineNumber in the Available Input Columns list, and drag-and-drop it on MachineNumber in the Available Lookup Columns list.

21. Click OK to exit the Lookup Transformation Editor dialog box.

22. Repeat Steps 11 through 21 in this "Steps to Create Lookup Data Flow Items" section to add the following Lookup item to the data flow:

Item Name	Table	Available Input Column	Available Lookup Columns
Validate Product	[dbo].[DimProduct]	ProductCode	ProductCode

Steps to Create a SQL Server Data Destination Item

1. Drag a SQL Server Destination item from the SSIS Toolbox and drop it on the Data Flow tab.

2. Click the Validate Product item. Click the blue data flow arrow, drag it on top of the SQL Server Destination item, and drop it on this item. The Input Output Selection dialog box appears.

3. Select Lookup Match Output from the Output drop-down list, and click OK.

4. Double-click the SQL Server Destination item. The SQL Destination Editor dialog box appears.

5. Select [dbo].[FactManufacturing] from the Use a table or view drop-down list.

6. Click Mappings to view the Mappings page. The columns from the data source (which are Available Input Columns to this data destination item) should be automatically mapped to the columns in the destination (the Available Destination Columns). The following mappings should be in place:

Available Input Columns		Available Destination Columns
BatchNumber	to	BatchNumber
MachineNumber	to	MachineNumber
ProductCode	to	ProductCode
AcceptedProducts	to	AcceptedProducts
ElapsedTimeForManufacture	to	ElapsedTimeForManufacture
DateOfManufacture	to	DateOfManufacture

7. Use drag-and-drop to add the following mapping:

Available Input Columns		Available Destination Columns
NumberRejected	to	RejectedProducts

8. Click OK to exit the SQL Destination Editor dialog box.

Steps to Create a Data Destination for the Rows in Error

1. Drag a Union All item from the SSIS Toolbox and drop it on the Data Flow tab.
2. Click the Validate Batch Number item. Click the unattached blue data flow arrow, drag it on top of the Union All item, and drop it on this item. Note that the Lookup No Match Output is connected to the Union All item. This means the unmatched records are going to follow this data flow.
3. Click the Validate Machine Number item. Click the unattached blue data flow arrow, drag it on top of the Union All item, and drop it on this item.
4. Repeat this process with the Validate Product item.
5. Drag a Flat File Destination item from the SSIS Toolbox and drop it on the Data Flow tab.
6. Change the name of this item to **Write Error Records to a Text File**.
7. Click the Union All item. Click the blue data flow arrow, drag it on top of the Write Error Records to a Text File item, and drop it on this item.
8. Double-click the Write Error Records to a Text file item. The Flat File Destination Editor dialog box appears.
9. Click New to create a new Flat File Connection Manager. The Flat File Format dialog box appears.
10. Leave the format set to delimited, and click OK. The Flat File Connection Manager Editor appears.
11. Enter **Error Output** for Connection manager name.
12. Click Browse. The Open dialog box appears.
13. Browse to an appropriate location for this error text file. Enter **MfgInfoErrors.txt** for File name.
14. Click Open to exit the Open dialog box.
15. Check the Column names in the first data row check box.
16. Click OK to exit the Flat File Connection Manager Editor.
17. Click Mappings to view the Mappings page of the Flat File Destination Editor dialog box. Mappings have been created for all columns.
18. Click OK to exit the Flat File Destination Editor dialog box. The Data Flow tab should appear as shown in Figure 8-18.

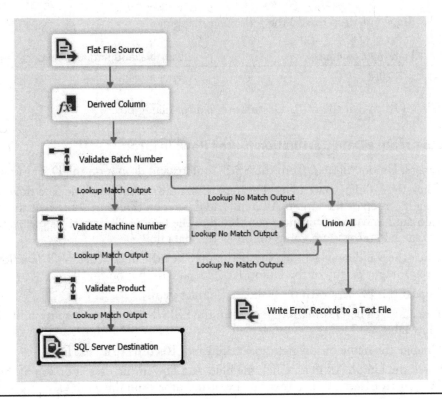

Figure 8-18   *The data flow to load the Manufacturing fact table*

19. Click the background of the design area so none of the items is selected.

20. Hold down CTRL and click the following items in the data flow:

     Validate Batch Number
     Validate Machine Number
     Validate Product
     Union All
     Write Error Records to a Text File

21. Right-click the Validate Batch Number item, and select Group from the context menu. The selected items are all placed inside a grouping in the data flow.

22. Click the ^ in the upper-right corner of the Group box to contract the group.

23. Drag the group so it is between the Derived Column item and the SQL Server Destination item. Position and size the items appropriately.

24. Rename the Group item to **Validate Batch Number, MachineNumber, Product**. The Data Flow should appear similar to Figure 8-19.

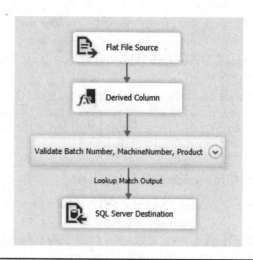

Figure 8-19   *The data flow to load the Manufacturing fact table with the Validation Grouping*

> **NOTE**
>
> *A Group can be used in a control flow or in a data flow to help organize items and improve organization and readability. They do not have any effect on the operation of the SSIS package. You can undo a grouping by right-clicking the group item and selecting Ungroup from the context menu.*

Steps to Begin Creating the InventoryFact Data Flow

1. Click the Control Flow tab. Drag a third Data Flow Task item onto the Control Flow tab. Rename this new Data Flow Task item **Load InventoryFact**. (You do not need to set precedence between the Load InventoryFact item and the other Data Flow Task items. It does not matter when the InventoryFact table is filled relative to the operations being done on the other tables.)

2. Double-click the Load InventoryFact item. This takes you to the Data Flow tab.

3. Right-click in the Connections tray, and select New OLE DB Connection from the context menu. Click New in the Configure OLE DB Connection Manager dialog box to create a new data connection.

4. Enter the name of the server where the Maximum Miniatures Order Processing database is installed in Server name. Select the appropriate method for accessing this server in the Log on to the server section. Enter credentials if necessary. Select OrderProcessingSystem from the Select or enter a database name drop-down list. (If the drop-down list is empty, either your server name or your login credentials are incorrect.) Click OK to return to the Configure OLE DB Connection Manager dialog box. Click OK again to exit this dialog box.

5. Drag an OLE DB Source item from the SSIS Toolbox and drop it on the Data Flow tab.

6. Double-click the OLE DB Source item you just created. The OLE DB Source Editor dialog box appears.

7. Select the OrderProcessingSystem data connection that you just created in the OLE DB connection manager drop-down list. Leave the Data access mode drop-down list set to Table or view. Select [dbo].[Inventory] from the Name of the table or the view drop-down list. Click OK.

Steps to Create a Data Conversion Data Flow Item

1. Drag a Data Conversion item from the SSIS Toolbox and drop it on the Data Flow tab.

2. Click the OLE DB Source item. Click the blue data flow arrow, drag it on top of the Data Conversion item, and drop it on this item.

3. Double-click the Data Conversion item. The Data Conversion Transformation Editor dialog box appears.

4. Check the check box next to Material in the Available Input Columns area.

5. Enter **Material-Unicode** in the Output Alias column.

6. Select Unicode string [DT_WSTR] from the drop-down list in the Data Type column.

7. Check the check box next to InventoryDate in the Available Input Columns area.

8. Enter **InventoryDate-DateType** in the OutputAlias Column for Inventory Date.

9. Select database date [DT_DBDATE] from the drop-down list in the Date Type column.

10. Click OK to exit the Data Conversion Transformation Editor dialog box.

Steps to Create Lookup Data Flow Items

1. Drag a Lookup item from the SSIS Toolbox and drop it on the Data Flow tab.

2. Change the name of this item to **Validate Product**.

3. Click the Data Conversion item. Click the blue data flow arrow, drag it on top of the Validate Product item, and drop it on this item. This connects the source to the transformation.

4. Double-click the Validate Product item. The Lookup Transformation Editor dialog box appears.

5. Select Redirect rows to no match output in the Specify how to handle rows with no matching entries drop-down list.

6. Click Connection to view the Connection page.

7. Select the MaxMinManufacturingDM data connection in the OLE DB connection manager drop-down list.

8. Select [dbo].[DimProduct] from the Use a table or a view drop-down list.

9. Click Columns to view the Columns page.

10. Click Code in the Available Input Columns list and drag-and-drop it on ProductCode in the Available LookupColumns list.

11. Click OK to exit the Lookup Transformation Editor dialog box.

12. Drag a Lookup item from the SSIS Toolbox and drop it on the Data Flow tab.

13. Change the name of this item to **Lookup and Validate Material**.

14. Click the Validate Product item. Click the blue data flow arrow, drag it on top of the Lookup and Validate Material item, and drop it on this item. The Input Output Selection dialog box appears.

15. Select Lookup Match Output from the Output drop-down list. Click OK.

16. Double-click the Lookup and Validate Material item. The Lookup Transformation Editor dialog box appears.

17. Select Redirect rows to no match output in the Specify how to handle rows with no matching entries drop-down list.

18. Click Connection to view the Connection page.

19. Select the MaxMinManufacturingDM data connection in the OLE DB connection manager drop-down list.

20. Select [dbo].[DimMaterial] from the Use a table or a view drop-down list.

21. Click Columns to view the Columns page.

22. Click Material-Unicode in the Available Input Columns list and drag-and-drop it on Material in the Available Lookup Columns list.

23. Check the check box next to MaterialKey in the Available Lookup Columns list.

24. Click OK to exit the Lookup Transformation Editor dialog box.

Steps to Create a Data Destination Data Flow Item

1. Drag a SQL Server Destination item from the SSIS Toolbox and drop it on the Data Flow tab.

2. Click the Lookup and Validate Material item. Click the blue data flow arrow, drag it on top of the SQL Server Destination item, and drop it on this item. The Input Output Selection dialog box appears.

3. Select Lookup Match Output from the Output drop-down list. Click OK.

4. Double-click the SQL Server Destination item. The SQL Destination Editor dialog box appears.

5. Select the MaxMinManufacturingDM data connection in the OLE DB connection manager drop-down list. Select [dbo].[FactInventory] from the Use a table or view drop-down list.

6. Click Mappings to view the Mappings page.

7. Use drag-and-drop to add the following mappings:

Available Input Columns		Available Destination Columns
Code	to	ProductCode
AmountOnHand	to	InventoryLevel
AmountBackordered	to	NumberOnBackorder
InventoryDate-DateType	To	DateOfInventory

8. Click OK to exit the SQL Destination Editor dialog box.

Steps to Create a Data Destination for the Rows in Error

1. Drag a Union All item from the SSIS Toolbox and drop it on the Data Flow tab.

2. Click the Validate Product item. Click the unattached blue data flow arrow, drag it on top of the Union All item, and drop it on this item. Note that the Lookup No Match Output is connected to the Union All item. This means the unmatched records are going to follow this data flow.

3. Click the Lookup and Validate Material item. Click the unattached blue data flow arrow, drag it on top of the Union All item, and drop it on this item.

4. Drag a Flat File Destination item from the SSIS Toolbox and drop it on the Data Flow tab.

5. Change the name of this item to **Write Inventory Error Records to a Text File**.

6. Click the Union All item. Click the blue data flow arrow, drag it on top of the Write Inventory Error Records to a Text File item, and drop it on this item.

7. Double-click the Write Inventory Error Records to a Text File item. The Flat File Destination Editor dialog box appears.

8. Click New to create a new Flat File Connection Manager. The Flat File Format dialog box appears.

9. Leave the format set to delimited, and click OK. The Flat File Connection Manager Editor appears.

10. Enter **Inventory Error Output** for Connection manager name.

11. Click Browse. The Open dialog box appears.

12. Browse to the same folder you selected for the manufacturing error text file. Enter **InvInfoErrors.txt** for File name.

13. Click Open to exit the Open dialog box.

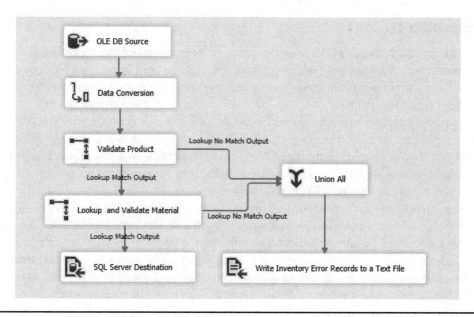

Figure 8-20 *The data flow to load the Inventory fact table*

14. Check the Column names in the first data row check box.
15. Click OK to exit the Flat File Connection Manager Editor.
16. Click Mappings to view the Mappings page of the Flat File Destination Editor dialog box.
17. Click OK to exit the Flat File Destination Editor dialog box. The Data Flow tab should appear as shown in Figure 8-20.
18. Click the Save All button on the toolbar to save the completed package.
19. Click the Start button on the toolbar to execute the completed package. When the execution is complete, click Stop Debugging or the Package Execution Completed link to return to Design mode.
20. Close the project.

Putting Integration Services Packages into Production

Integration Services packages can be executed in SQL Server Data Tools. This is convenient for development and debugging, but it probably is not the way you want to use these packages in a production environment. This section looks at how we deploy packages to our servers and execute those packages once they are there.

Parameters

The Integration Services packages we created in the previous Learn By Doing exercises in this chapter are completely self-contained. We execute the package, and it does its stuff. All of the configuration was done at design time. When we run the package, it requires no further input.

In some situations, however, we may want to have some interaction with the package at run time. For example, a package may be created using databases on a development server, put through quality assurance testing using databases on a test server, and put into production using databases on a production server. It would be nice to move the package through this process without having to open it up in SQL Server Data Tools each time to change the server name. Similarly, server names and data paths change over time as a natural outgrowth of network growth and maintenance. It would be nice to have these items be part of the configuration of the package so they can be managed by an administrator rather than a package developer. This is where parameters come in.

Parameters function much like variables in an SSIS package. The difference is that *parameters* are exposed outside of the package and can have their value set at run time. This allows us to make our packages configurable.

There are two types of parameters. Project parameters are created in the SSIS project and can be used by any of the packages in that project. This is similar to the project connection manager we encountered in the last Learn By Doing exercise. Package parameters exist within a single package.

When a parameter is created, it is given a value. This value is used for the parameter when the package is run in SQL Server Data Tools. This does not serve as a default value for the parameter when the package is deployed to the server. All parameters have a value of blank (or 0 for parameters with numeric data types) when they are deployed to the server. Therefore, values must be respecified for the parameters on the server.

We will see how to create package and project parameters in the next Learn By Doing exercise.

Associating Properties with Parameters

Once a parameter has been created, we can use its value to set properties on various items in our package. This can be done in one of two ways. For an item in the control flow, we can right-click the item and select Parameterize from the context menu. This will display the Parameterize dialog box shown in Figure 8-21.

Using the Property drop-down list at the top of the dialog box, we can select a property from this item. The value of the parameter will then be used for this property each time the package is executed. We can then use the "Create new parameter" and "Use existing parameter" radio buttons to determine whether we

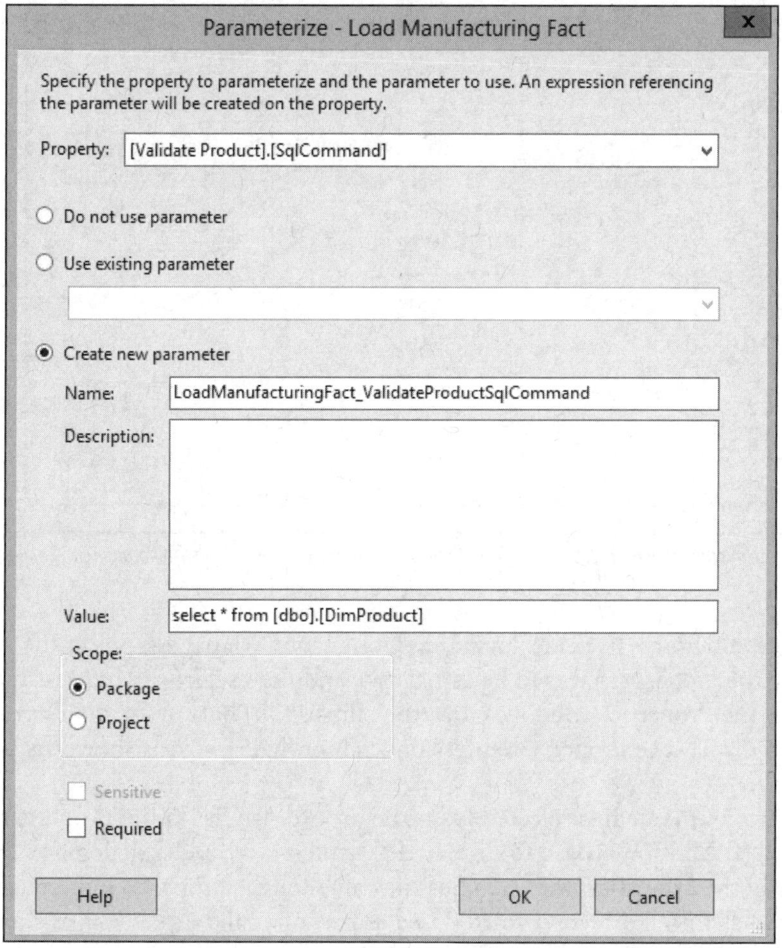

Figure 8-21   *The Parameterize dialog box*

are associating this property with a parameter that has already been created or we are creating a new parameter.

If a new parameter is being created, we can specify its name and description. We can also provide a value for the parameter. Remember that this value will be used as the value of the associated item property any time the package is run within SQL Server Data Tools. Finally, we can specify whether this is a package parameter or a project parameter and whether or not a value is required.

The second method for associating a parameter value with an item property is to use the Expressions property of the item. This can be done for almost any item in

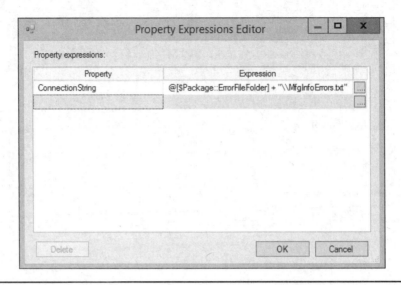

Figure 8-22   *Using the Property Expressions Editor dialog box to associate properties with parameters*

an Integration Services package, including Connection Managers. Select the item containing the property that is to be associated, and then select the Expressions property in the Properties window. Click the ellipsis (...) button for the Expressions property to display the Property Expressions Editor dialog box, as shown in Figure 8-22.

A property of the item is selected from the drop-down list in the Property column. The ellipsis (...) button is used to display the Expression Builder dialog box. Here we can build the expression that supplies the value for the property. This can simply be the parameter itself or the parameter used as part of a valid expression, as shown in Figure 8-23.

The Integration Services Catalog

Integration Services packages can be stored and executed on a server. There is, however, a bit of preparation we must do before this can take place. First, we need to include Integration Services as part of the SQL Server install. After this is done, we also need to create the Integration Services Catalog that will store our packages.

This second step is accomplished using the SQL Server Management Studio. In SSMS, on a server that does not yet have the Integration Services Catalog created, you will see a folder in the Object Explorer window for Integration Services Catalogs with nothing in it. To create the Integration Services Catalog, right-click the Integration

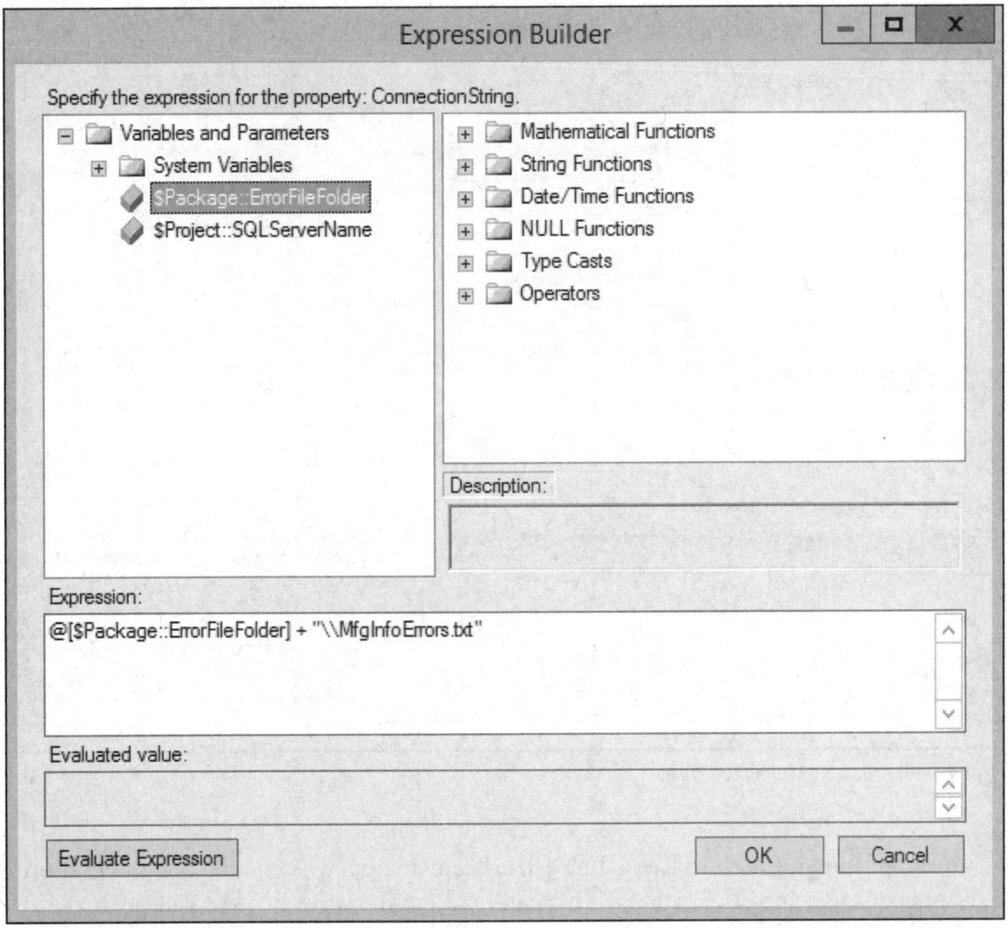

Figure 8-23   *Using a parameter as part of an expression*

Services Catalogs folder and select Create Catalog from the context menu. The Create Catalog dialog box appears, as shown in Figure 8-24.

The operation of the Integration Services Catalog requires Common Language Runtime (CLR) integration to be enabled on this SQL Server instance. CLR integration allows SQL Server code to utilize features of the .NET Framework. Check the box to enable CLR integration if it is not enabled on this SQL Server instance. Also, specify a password to be used to protect the encryption key used by the Integration Services Catalog for storing sensitive information. You will see this in action in the next Learn By Doing exercise.

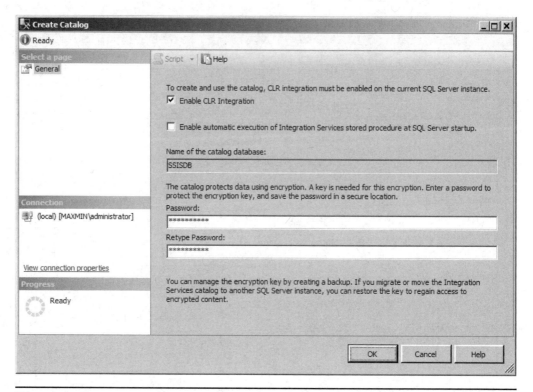

Figure 8-24   *The Create Catalog dialog box*

Once the Integration Services Catalog has been created, we can load our Integration Services packages into the catalog. This can be done in two ways. We can push an Integration Services project and its constituent packages to the catalog from SQL Server Data Tools using the deploy process. Alternatively, we can pull a package to the catalog using the import process.

Deploying SSIS Projects from SQL Server Data Tools

To deploy an Integration Services project from SQL Server Data Tools, right-click the package entry in the Solution Explorer window and select Deploy Package from the context menu. You can also right-click the SSIS project entry in the Solution Explorer window and select Deploy from the context menu. Either of these methods will launch the Integration Services Deployment Wizard and take you to the Introduction page. Clicking Next takes you to the Select Source page of the wizard, as shown in Figure 8-25. The wizard automatically advances to the next page. You can return to the Select Source by clicking Previous if you wish to modify the default settings.

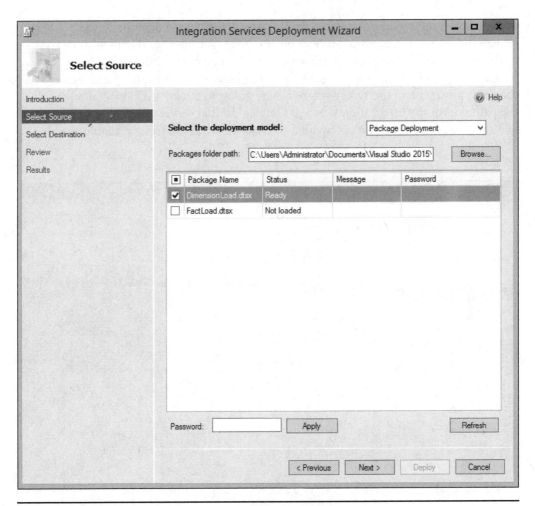

Figure 8-25   *The Select Source page of the Integration Services Deployment Wizard*

On the Select Source page of the wizard, there are two modes of operation. If you launch the wizard from a package entry, the wizard operates in package deployment mode. You can choose to deploy one or more of the SSIS packages in that project. It defaults to deploying the package you right-clicked to launch the wizard.

If you launch the wizard from the project entry, the wizard operates in project deployment mode. It deploys an SSIS project file (with a .ispac file extension) found in the file system or a package that exists in an Integration Services Catalog on another server. This latter functionality makes it easy to take a package deployed on a development or quality assurance server and promote it to the next server along the develop-test-production progression. In this mode, the wizard defaults to the SSIS project file for the Integration Services project you right-clicked to launch the wizard.

As stated previously, the wizard automatically advances from the Select Source page to the Select Destination page as shown in Figure 8-26. On this page, we need to specify the name of the server where we are going to deploy the project along with the path within the Integration Services Catalog on that server where the project will reside. A Browse button is provided to enable us to select from available servers.

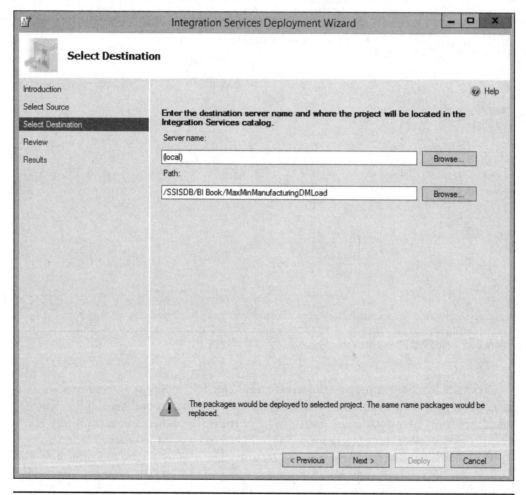

Figure 8-26   *The Select Destination page of the Integration Services Deployment Wizard*

A second Browse button is provided so we can select an existing path within the chosen Integration Services Catalog. We can also specify a new path, which will be created as part of the deployment process.

Clicking Next on the Select Destination page takes you to the Review page of the wizard. Here you can review the choices made and launch the deployment process by clicking Deploy. The results of the deployment are shown on the Results page. You will see this in the Learn By Doing exercise later in this chapter.

Importing Packages into the SSIS Catalog

Importing packages is done from SQL Server Management Studio. In order to import a package, we must first have a folder created in the SSIS Catalog. To do this, launch SQL Server Management Studio and expand the Integration Services Catalogs folder in the Object Explorer window. Right-click the SSISDB entry and select Create Folder from the context menu. In the Create Folder dialog box, specify the folder name and a folder description, if desired, and click OK.

The import process itself is a two-step process. The selected SSIS package must be migrated to an Integration Services project deployment (.ispac) file. Then the project deployment file can be deployed to the server. This is accomplished through two wizards that are executed one after the other for us. The Integration Services Project Conversion Wizard creates the Integration Services project deployment file, and the Integration Services Deployment Wizard (the same wizard we discussed in the previous section) deploys the file to the server.

In the Object Explorer window, expand the folder entry that is to contain the imported package. The folder will contain a Projects folder and an Environments folder by default. Right-click the Projects folder and select Import Packages from the context menu. This launches the Integration Services Project Conversion Wizard and takes you to the Introduction page. Clicking Next takes you to the Locate Packages page of the wizard, as shown in Figure 8-27.

On the Locate Packages page, you select a folder containing Integration Services packages. This can be a folder in the file system or in a previous version of Integration Services. After selecting the appropriate folder, clicking Next takes you to the Select Packages page of the wizard, as shown in Figure 8-28.

The Select Packages page enables you to select one or more packages for import. After checking the packages you would like to import, click Next. This takes you to the Select Destination page of the wizard shown in Figure 8-29. On this page, you specify the path and the file name of the interim Integration Services project deployment file that will be created as part of this process. Remember that this file is only needed by the Integration Services Deployment Wizard, which will run next.

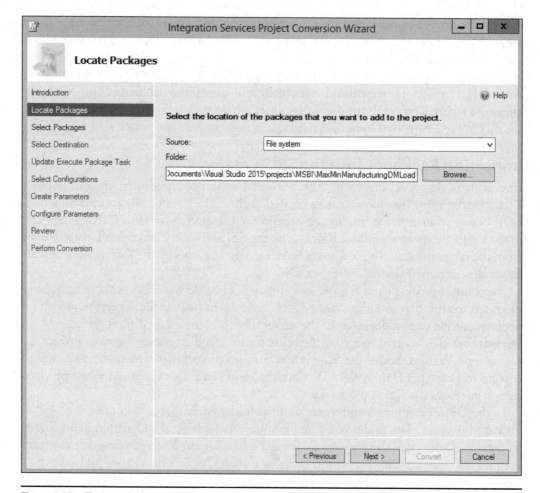

Figure 8-27 *The Locate Packages page of the Integration Services Project Conversion Wizard*

Once the package has been deployed, the Integration Services project deployment file can be deleted.

The next four pages of the wizard pertain to migrating older-version Integration Services packages to the current deploy format. Click Next to move through these pages. The Review page of the wizard allows you to view the decisions made. Click Convert to migrate the package to the Integration Services project deployment file. The progress of the migration is shown on the Results page.

When you click Close on the Results page, the Integration Services Deployment Wizard is automatically launched to complete the deployment. Click Next on the

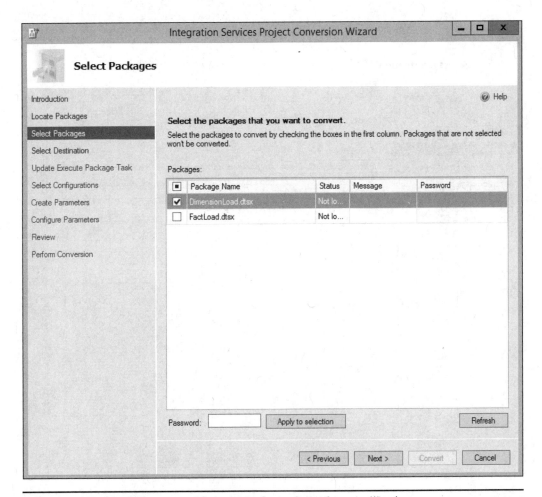

Figure 8-28 *The Select Packages page of the Integration Services Project Conversion Wizard*

Introduction page to move to the Select Destination page. This is shown in Figure 8-26. The folder from which you launched the import process will be selected by default. Click Next to move to the Review page, and click Deploy to complete the process. The status of the deployment will be shown on the Results page. When complete, click Close to exit the wizard.

An entry for the package name that you specified as part of the import process appears in the Projects folder. If it does not appear there, right-click and select Refresh from the context menu. Expanding the package entry reveals a Packages folder, which, in turn, contains the imported package.

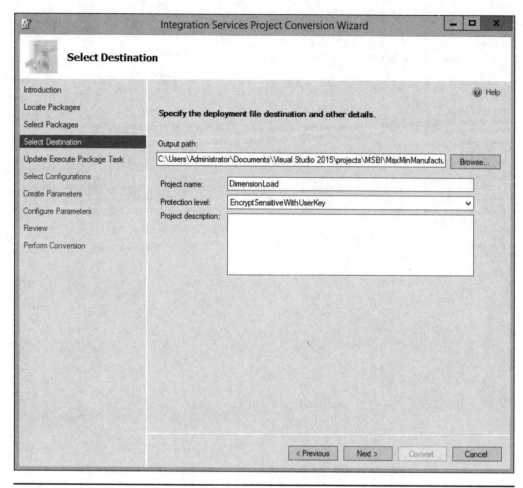

Figure 8-29 *The Select Destination page of the Integration Services Project Conversion Wizard*

Learn By Doing: Deploying the Packages to a Server

Features Highlighted

- ▶ Creating an Integration Services Catalog
- ▶ Creating parameters
- ▶ Deploying packages to a server

Business Need

Now that we have packages created to load data into our manufacturing data mart, we need to put those packages in a production server environment for regular use.

Steps to Create an Integration Services Catalog

1. Open SQL Server Management Studio.
2. Connect to the SQL Server relational database instance that will host your Integration Services Catalog.
3. In the Object Explorer window, right-click the Integration Services Catalogs entry and select Create Catalog from the context menu. The Create Catalog dialog box appears.
4. Check the Enable CLR Integration check box.
5. Enter a password for the SSIS Catalog encryption key.
6. Retype the SSIS Catalog encryption key password.
7. Click OK. The SSIS Catalog, called SSISDB, is created.

Steps to Create a Project Parameter

1. Open SQL Server Data Tools.
2. Reopen the MaxMinManufacturingDMLoad project.
3. In the Solution Explorer window, double-click the Project.params entry. The Project Parameters (Project.params [Design]) tab opens.
4. Click the Add Parameter button in the Project Parameters tab toolbar. An entry for a new parameter is created.
5. In the Name column, change "Parameter" to **SQLServerName**.
6. Select String from the drop-down list in the Data type column.
7. In the Value column, enter the name of the server hosting the MaxMinAccounting and OrderProcessingSystem databases. (This exercise assumes both of these databases are hosted on the same server.)
8. In the Required column, select True from the drop-down list. You have created a Project Parameter.

Steps to Create a Package Parameter

1. In the Solution Explorer window, double-click the entry for FactLoad.dtsx. The FactLoad package design (FactLoad.dtsx [Design]) tab is opened and/or is given focus.
2. Select the Parameters tab.

3. Click the Add Parameter button in the Parameters tab toolbar. An entry for a new parameter is created.

4. In the Name column, change "Parameter" to **ErrorFileFolder**.

5. Select String from the drop-down list in the Data type column.

6. In the Value column, enter the Universal Naming Convention (UNC) path to the folder where the error text files are to be stored.

7. In the Required column, select True from the drop-down list. You have created a package parameter.

Steps to Associate Properties with the ErrorFileFolder Parameter

1. Select the Control Flow tab.

2. Select the Error Output entry in the Connections tray.

3. In the Properties window, select the Expressions item.

4. Click the ellipsis (…) button that appears next to the entry for Expressions. The Property Expressions Editor dialog box appears.

5. Click the blank entry in the Property column. A drop-down list appears.

6. Select ConnectionString from the drop-down list.

7. Click the ellipsis (…) button at the end of the first row. The Expression Builder dialog box appears.

8. Expand the Variables and Parameters entry in the upper-left corner.

9. Drag the $Package::ErrorFileFolder entry and drop it in the Expression area.

10. Type the additional text so the Expression area appears as follows:

```
@[$Package::ErrorFileFolder] + "\\MfgInfoErrors.txt"
```

11. Click Evaluate Expression to make sure the expression is valid. The resulting file path is displayed in the Evaluated value area.

12. Click OK to exit the Expression Builder dialog box.

13. Click OK to exit the Property Expressions Editor dialog box.

14. Select the Inventory Error Output entry in the Connections tray.

15. In the Properties window, select the Expressions item.

16. Click the ellipsis (…) button that appears next to the entry for Expressions. The Property Expressions Editor dialog box appears.

17. Click the blank entry in the Property column. A drop-down list appears.

18. Select ConnectionString from the drop-down list.

19. Click the ellipsis (…) button at the end of the first row. The Expression Builder dialog box appears.

20. Expand the Variables and Parameters entry in the upper-left corner.

21. Drag the $Package::ErrorFileFolder entry, and drop it in the Expression area.

22. Type the additional text so the Expression area appears as follows:

```
@[$Package::ErrorFileFolder] + "\\InvInfoErrors.txt"
```

23. Click Evaluate Expression to make sure the expression is valid. The resulting file path is displayed in the Evaluated value area.

24. Click OK to exit the Expression Builder dialog box.

25. Click OK to exit the Property Expressions Editor dialog box.

Steps to Associate Properties with the SQLServerName Parameter

1. Select the OrderProcessingSystem entry in the Connections tray.

2. In the Properties window, select the Expressions item.

3. Click the ellipsis (…) button that appears next to the entry for Expressions. The Property Expressions Editor dialog box appears.

4. Click the blank entry in the Property column. A drop-down list appears.

5. Select ServerName from the drop-down list.

6. Click the ellipsis (…) button at the end of the first row. The Expression Builder dialog box appears.

7. Expand the Variables and Parameters entry in the upper-left corner.

8. Drag the $Project::SQLServerName entry and drop it in the Expression area.

9. Click OK to exit the Expression Builder dialog box.

10. Click OK to exit the Property Expressions Editor dialog box.

11. In the Solution Explorer window, double-click the entry for DimensionLoad. dtsx. The DimensionLoad package design (DimensionLoad.dtsx [Design]) tab is opened and/or is given focus.

12. Select the MaxMinAccounting entry in the Connections tray.

13. In the Properties window, select the Expressions item.

14. Click the ellipsis (…) button that appears next to the entry for Expressions. The Property Expressions Editor dialog box appears.

15. Click the blank entry in the Property column. A drop-down list appears.

16. Select ServerName from the drop-down list.

17. Click the ellipsis (…) button at the end of the first row. The Expression Builder dialog box appears.

18. Expand the Variables and Parameters entry in the upper-left corner.

19. Drag the $Project::SQLServerName entry, and drop it in the Expression area.

20. Click OK to exit the Expression Builder dialog box.

21. Click OK to exit the Property Expressions Editor dialog box.

22. Click the Save All button on the toolbar to save the project.

Steps to Deploy the Project

1. In the Solution Explorer window, right-click the entry for the MaxMinManufacturingDMLoad project, and select Deploy from the context menu. The Introduction page of the Integration Services Deployment Wizard appears.

2. Click Next. After validating the project, the Select Destination page of the Integration Services Deployment Wizard appears.

3. For Server name, enter the name of the SQL Server where you created the SSIS Catalog (SSISDB) earlier in this Learn By Doing exercise.

4. Click the Browse button next to the Path text box. The Browse for Folder or Project dialog box appears.

5. Click New Folder. The Create New Folder dialog box appears.

6. Enter **BI Book** for Name.

7. Click OK to exit the Create New Folder dialog box.

8. Select the BI Book folder you just created in the Browse for Folder or Project dialog box. Click OK to exit this dialog box.

9. Click Next. The Review page of the Integration Services Deployment Wizard appears.

10. Click Deploy. The two packages in the project will be deployed to the server.

11. Click Close when the deployment is complete.

Steps to Configure the Project

1. Open or return to SQL Server Management Studio.

2. In the Object Explorer window, expand the SSISDB entry under Integration Services Catalogs. You will see the BI Book folder created by our project deployment.

3. Expand the BI Book folder.

4. Expand the Projects folder.

5. Right-click the MaxMinManufacturingDMLoad entry, and select Configure from the context menu. The Configure – MaxMinManufacturingDMLoad dialog box appears.

6. Click the ellipsis (…) button in the SQLServerName row. The Set Parameter Value dialog box appears.

7. In the Edit value text box, enter the name of the SQL Server that is hosting the MaxMinAccounting and OrderProcessingSystem databases.

8. Click OK to exit the Set Parameter Value dialog box.

9. Click the ellipsis (…) button in the ErrorFileFolder row. The Set Parameter Value dialog box appears.

10. In the Edit value text box, enter the UNC path to the folder that should contain the error text files.

11. Click OK to exit the Set Parameter Value dialog box.

12. Click OK to exit the Configure – MaxMinManufacturingDMLoad dialog box.

Managing Packages in the Integration Services Catalog

Once our packages are in the Integration Services Catalog, we can manage them using SQL Server Management Studio. In the last section of the Learn By Doing exercise, you saw how to configure a package on the server. We can also save configuration settings that can be shared by several packages. These settings are saved in an environment.

After looking at environments, we'll take a quick look at setting security for Integration Services packages on the server.

Utilizing Environments

An *environment* is a set of values that can be shared among several packages. This can be useful when a number of packages rely on the same information for their parameters. For example, you may have a number of packages that use one set of servers and file paths when they are undergoing quality assurance testing and another set of servers and file paths when they are in production. We can create one environment called "QA Test" that holds the appropriate parameter settings for a package undergoing quality assurance testing. We can create another environment called "Production" that holds the appropriate parameter settings for a package operating in production.

To create an environment, right-click the Environments folder and select Create Environment from the context menu, as shown in Figure 8-30. This will take you to the Create Environment dialog box. Enter a name and description, as shown in Figure 8-31. Click OK to create the environment.

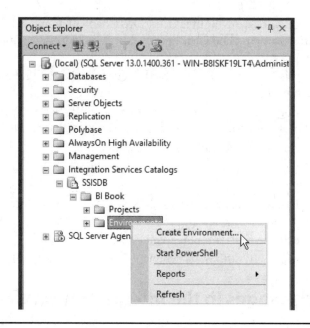

Figure 8-30 *Creating a new environment*

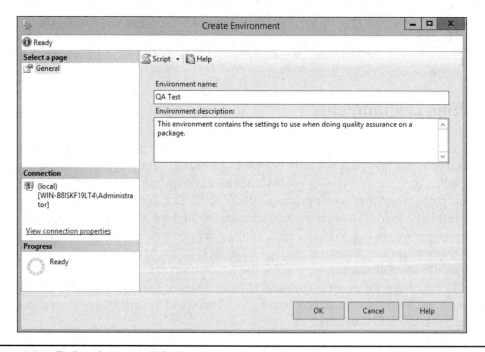

Figure 8-31 *The Create Environment dialog box*

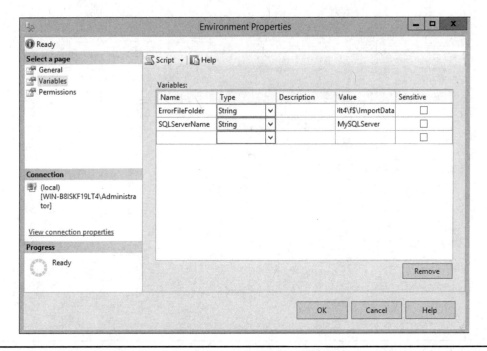

Figure 8-32   *The Variables page of the Environment Properties dialog box*

Once the environment is created, right-click the environment and select Properties from the context menu. This displays the Environment Properties dialog box. Select the Variables page of the dialog box. Create variables to correspond to each of the parameters that should be controlled by this environment. This is shown in Figure 8-32. Once the variables are created, click OK to exit the Environment Properties dialog box.

Environments are associated with projects and packages using the configuration settings. Right-click a project or package and select Configure from the context menu. This displays the Configure dialog box. Select the References page of the dialog box. Add a reference to each of the environments that may be used by this project or package, as shown in Figure 8-33.

Once the references are added, select the Parameters page of the Configure dialog box. Use the ellipsis (…) button for each of the parameters to associate it with a variable in the environments. This is shown in Figure 8-34.

When the package is run from the server, you have an opportunity to select an environment to use for this execution, as shown in Figure 8-35. The values in the selected environment's variables are used for the associated parameters for this execution of the package.

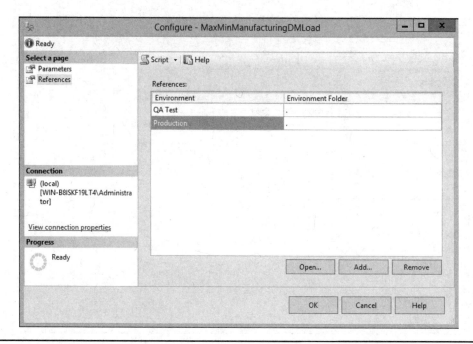

Figure 8-33 *The References page of the Configure dialog box*

Figure 8-34 *The Set Parameter Value dialog box used to associate an environment variable*

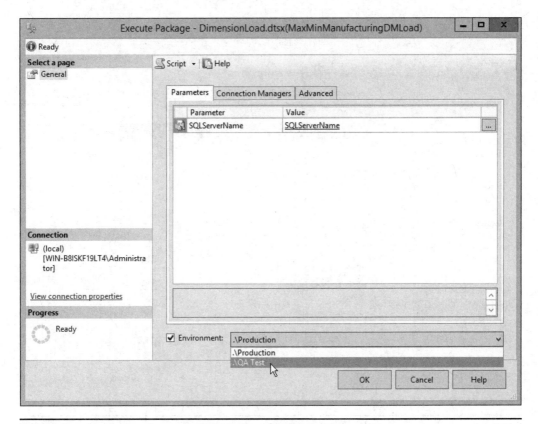

Figure 8-35   *Selecting an environment in the Run Package dialog box*

Setting Permissions

Security for Integration Services packages on the server can be set at the folder and project levels. To modify security settings, right-click a folder or project and select Properties from the context menu. Go to the Permissions page of the Properties dialog box. The Permissions page of a project is shown in Figure 8-36.

The following permissions can be set for projects:

▶ Read

▶ Modify

▶ Execute

▶ Manage Permissions

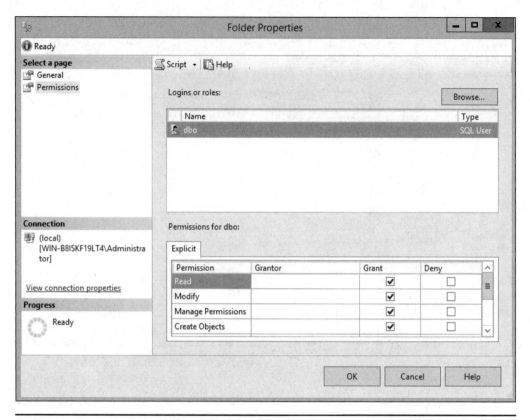

Figure 8-36 *The Permissions page of the Project Properties dialog box*

The following permissions can be set for a folder:

▶ Read

▶ Modify

▶ Manage Permissions

▶ Create Objects

▶ Modify Objects

▶ Execute Objects

▶ Read Objects

▶ Manage Object Permissions

The following permissions can be set for an environment:

▶ Read

▶ Modify

▶ Manage Permissions

Executing Packages from the SSIS Catalog

Now that we have all of the configuration completed, our packages are ready to be run from the server. To execute a package from the server, right-click the package entry in the Object Explorer window and select Execute from the context menu. The Execute Package dialog box appears.

The Execute Package dialog box enables us to make any final changes to the parameter values before the package is executed. If environments are associated with the package, we can select an environment to use for this execution, as shown in Figure 8-35.

NOTE

If you wish to try executing either the DimensionLoad package or the FactLoad package from the server, you will first need to remove the existing data from the tables they populate. If you do not do so, the package execution will fail with duplicate primary key errors—we are attempting to load the same data more than once. Prior to running the DimensionLoad package, truncate the following tables:

DimCountry
DimMachine
DimMachineType
DimMaterial
DimPlant
DimProduct
DimProductSubtype
DimProductType

Prior to running the FactLoad package, truncate the following tables:

DimBatch
FactInventory
FactManufacturing

In the Execute Package dialog box, click OK to begin package execution. When you do this, you will receive a dialog box explaining that package execution has begun and to see execution status you should use the Integration Services Dashboard report. In most cases, you'll want to click Yes to have this report opened for you.

Execution Dashboard Reports

The Integration Services Dashboard reports provide information on the execution of an Integration Services package from the server. An example of a Dashboard report is shown in Figure 8-37. Any text that is blue and underlined provides a drillthrough link to another report that provides additional detail information. For example, the Execution Performance Dashboard report is shown in Figure 8-38. Once you have navigated to a drillthrough report, use the Navigate Backward button in the upper-left corner to return to the parent report.

You can view the Integration Services Dashboard reports at any time by right-clicking any item under Integration Services in the Object Explorer window and selecting from the Reports submenu in the context menu.

Figure 8-37 *The Integration Services Dashboard report*

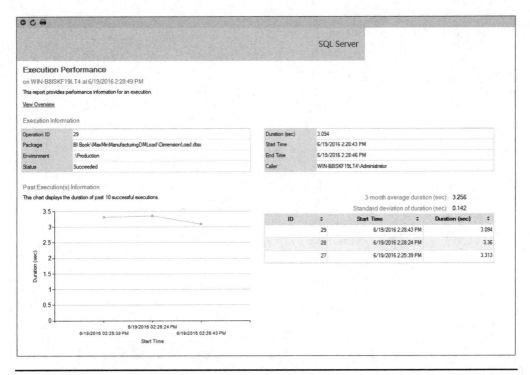

Figure 8-38   *The Execution Performance Dashboard report*

Meanwhile, Back at the BI Semantic Model

As we have seen, there is a great deal of capability and flexibility in Integration Services. We can use Integration Services to cleanse data and load it into our data marts, but that is only the beginning. Now that we have a handle on Integration Services, we can return to looking more in-depth at working with the BI Semantic Model in the next chapter.

Part III

Working with a Tabular BI Semantic Model

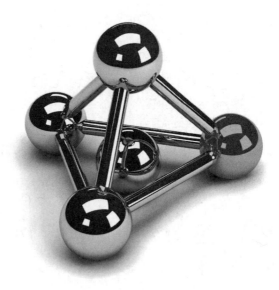

Chapter 9

Setting the Table: Creating a Tabular BI Semantic Model

In This Chapter

- ► **Preparation for Creating Tabular Models**
- ► **Creating a Tabular Model**
- ► **A Second Tabular Model**
- ► **Putting More on the Table**

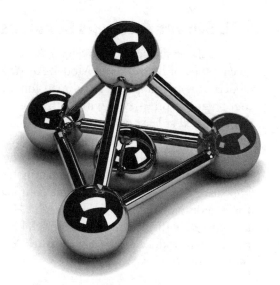

I drink to the general joy o' the whole table.

—*Macbeth, Act iii, Sc. 4,* William Shakespeare

In Chapter 6, we built two data mart structures for our sample company, Maximum Miniatures, Inc. At the same time, we built our first Multidimensional BI Semantic Model: MaxMinSalesDM. In Chapter 11, we will build our second Multidimensional BI Semantic Model—MaxMinManufacturingDM.

Before we get there, however, we are going to take some time to look at the newer of Microsoft's BI Semantic Models, the Tabular model. In this chapter, we will create Tabular models using the same data we put into the MaxMinSalesDM and MaxMinManufacturingDM data marts. In Chapter 10, we will explore the Data Analysis Expressions (DAX) language used by Tabular models.

This parallel between our Tabular model examples and Multidimensional model examples is being done purposefully. It will give you the opportunity to gauge the relative effort in creating Multidimensional and Tabular models. It will also allow you to compare the capabilities of the two types of models.

Preparation for Creating Tabular Models

Before we begin creating Tabular models, we need to do a bit of preparation. As we build the Tabular model, SQL Server Data Tools will be in constant communication with the Analysis Services server to give us immediate feedback on what the data looks like in the model. Therefore, we need to let SQL Server Data Tools know where to find an appropriate Tabular instance of Analysis Services.

SQL Server Analysis Services Tabular Instance

A particular instance of SQL Server Analysis Services 2016 is installed to support a specific type of BI Semantic Model. An Analysis Services instance can support Tabular models or it can support Multidimensional models, but not both. In order for you and your organization to work with both Multidimensional models and Tabular models, you will need at least two instances of Analysis Services. As always, a development or test instance of Analysis Services should be used. Do not use a production instance of Analysis Services when completing the exercises in this book.

It is recommended that the Tabular instance of Analysis Services that hosts your workspace databases be on the same computer where you are running SQL Server Data Tools to design your model. Having this "local" setup will give you the best performance as you work with the data in the model. Having your workspace database on a remote server can introduce delays due to issues with network bandwidth and slow down your design process.

There are also a couple of restrictions when you host your workspace databases on a remote server. You cannot set the Data Backup property to "Backup to Disk." Also, you cannot import data from a PowerPivot workbook using the Import from PowerPivot project template. Both of these items are discussed later.

Managing the Workspace Database

As mentioned previously, SQL Server Data Tools is going to be in constant communication with Analysis Services as we define our Tabular model. In fact, as soon as we create an Analysis Services Tabular project, SQL Server Data Tools creates a workspace database in Analysis Services. This *workspace database* hosts the data in our model to give us a real-time view of the model as we create it.

The location and behavior of the workspace database is controlled by three properties of the Tabular model. These are

- ▶ Workspace Server
- ▶ Workspace Retention
- ▶ Data Backup

Because the values found in these properties are used to instantiate the workspace database as the model is first created, we must provide meaningful default values for these items.

The default values for these properties come from three SQL Server Data Tools options settings. They are

- ▶ **Default workspace server**   The server name found in this option setting is assigned to the model's Workspace Server property, and a workspace database is immediately created on that server. This must be a Tabular instance of SQL Server 2016 Analysis Services. It is recommended that this Tabular instance be running on the same computer where you are executing SQL Server Data Tools for optimum performance.

- ▶ **Workspace database retention after the model is closed**   The selection made for this option is assigned to the model's Workspace Retention property. This determines what happens to the workspace database when the model project is closed in SQL Server Data Tools. The options are

  - ▶ **Keep workspace in memory**   This option keeps the workspace database loaded in the Analysis Services memory space. The model is still available for querying and browsing through the server.

▶ **Keep workspace databases on disk but unload from memory**   This option unloads the workspace database from the Analysis Services memory space. However, it persists a copy of the database on disk. This allows the database to be quickly reloaded into the Analysis Services memory space the next time the model project is opened, without having to reload the data from the data sources. (This option is selected by default.)

▶ **Delete workspace**   This option unloads the workspace database from the Analysis Services memory space and does not persist the database on disk. The next time the model project is opened, the workspace database is re-created and its data is reloaded from the data sources.

▶ **Data backup**   Specifies whether the data is backed up to disk (to an .abf file) each time the model definition is saved. This data backup is used if you cancel the changes made to the model. Therefore, having the backup of the data on disk will make canceling changes go faster. However, creating the backup of the data on disk will increase the time required each time the model is saved. Options are

▶ Keep backup of data on disk.

▶ Do not keep backup of data on disk. (This is selected by default.)

Learn By Doing: Preparing SQL Server Data Tools for Tabular Model Development

Feature Highlighted

▶ Set SQL Server Data Tools default to a Tabular instance of Analysis Services

Business Need
In order for SQL Server Data Tools to function properly as we create Tabular BI Semantic Models, it needs to point to a Tabular instance of Analysis Services by default.

Steps to Set the Default Workspace Server

1. Open SQL Server Data Tools.
2. Select Tools | Options from the main menu. The Options dialog box appears.
3. Scroll down in the pages area until you see the section for Analysis Services Tabular Designers.
4. Expand the Analysis Services entry and select Workspace Database. The Workspace Database page of the Options dialog box appears.

5. For Default workspace server, enter the name of a Tabular instance of SQL Server Analysis Services where you have rights to create databases. (Do *not* perform this or any other Learn By Doing activity on a server used for production operations!)

6. Click Test Connection to make sure you can connect to the Tabular instance of Analysis Services you entered. If the test does not succeed, check the following:

   ▶ The name of the Analysis Services instance is entered correctly. If this is a named instance of Analysis Services, ensure the instance name is included along with the server name.

   ▶ You have the appropriate rights to interact with this instance of Analysis Services.

   ▶ You are entering the name of a Tabular instance of Analysis Services, not a Multidimensional instance of Analysis Services. If you receive an error message telling you the workspace database server is not running in Tabular mode, then you entered the name of a Multidimensional instance of Analysis Services.

   ▶ If you are using a named instance of SQL Server Analysis Services, make sure the SQL Server Browser service is running.

You need to make a successful connection before proceeding with the other activities in this chapter. The Options dialog box is shown in Figure 9-1 with the Default workspace server set to a named instance of Analysis Services called "TABULAR" running on the local computer. The name of your Analysis Services server will likely be something different.

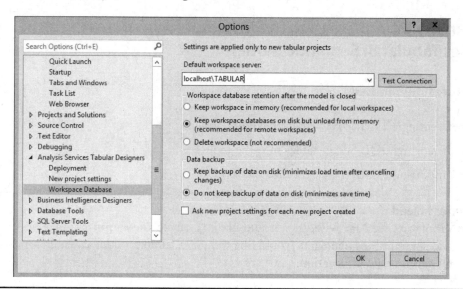

Figure 9-1   *The Workspace Database page of the Options dialog box*

7. We will use the default settings for "Workspace database retention after the model is closed" and "Data backup." Click OK to exit the Options dialog box.

With this, we are ready to begin. Let's create a Tabular model.

Creating a Tabular Model

We are now ready to create our first Tabular model. We will create a Tabular version of the Maximum Miniatures sales data first. We will follow that up by creating a Tabular version of the Maximum Miniatures manufacturing data.

Data Sources for Our Tabular Models

We could certainly create our Tabular models from the MaxMinSalesDM database and the MaxMinManufacturingDM database. In some ways, this might make it easier for us to create neat, clean models for our users to explore. It certainly wouldn't be wrong to create a Tabular model using data that has been copied from transactional systems into a reporting warehouse or relational data mart.

However, for our Learn By Doing exercises, we are going to load our Tabular models directly from the original source systems. That would be the MaxMinAccounting and OrderProcessingSystem databases in SQL Server and the BatchInfo comma-separated value (CSV) text file. This will give you a better feel for what is required when loading transactional data into a Tabular model.

Learn By Doing: Creating the Maximum Miniatures Sales Tabular BI Semantic Model

Features Highlighted

▶ Creating a Tabular BI Semantic Model project
▶ Importing SQL Server tables into the model
▶ Importing a query result set into the model

Business Need

The VP of sales for Max Min, Inc., would like to analyze sales information. The VP of sales and several of his managers would like to have a tabular model available for doing this self-service data exploration.

The VP of sales would like to be able to analyze the following numbers:

▶ Dollar value of products sold

▶ Number of products sold

These numbers should be viewable by

▶ Store

▶ Sales promotion

▶ Product

▶ Day, month, quarter, and year

▶ Customer

▶ Salesperson

Steps to Create the Analysis Services Tabular Project

1. Open SQL Server Data Tools.
2. Click the New Project button in the toolbar.
3. Make sure Business Intelligence | Analysis Services is selected in the Installed Templates area, and then select Analysis Services Tabular Project from the center area.
4. Enter **MaxMinSalesTabular** for Name and set the Location to the appropriate folder. Make sure Create directory for solution is not checked. The New Project dialog box is shown in Figure 9-2.
5. Click OK to exit the New Project dialog box and create the Tabular model project.
6. The Tabular model designer dialog box appears. Ensure SQL Server Data Tools has the correct Workspace server and the Compatibility level is set to SQL Server 2016. Click OK.

NOTE

A blank Model.bim tab should open in the main design area of the SQL Server Data Tools screen. If this does not open, you do not have the Default workspace server option set properly and need to redo the "Learn By Doing: Preparing SQL Server Data Tools for Tabular Model Development" exercise.

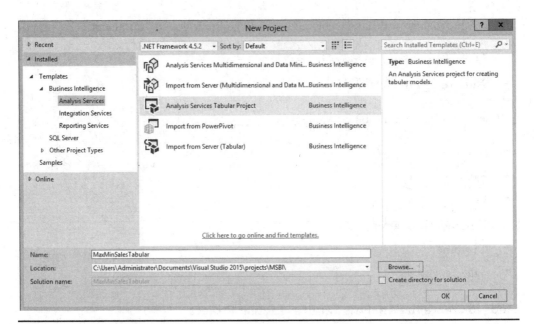

Figure 9-2 *The New Project dialog box creating a Tabular model project*

Steps to Create a Data Source in the Model

1. Select Model | Import From Data Source from the main menu. The Table Import Wizard dialog box appears with the Connect to a Data Source page visible.

2. Scroll through the list and note all of the different types of data sources that may be used to provide data for a Tabular model. Scroll back to the top and ensure the Microsoft SQL Server entry is selected in the Relational Databases section of the list, as shown in Figure 9-3.

3. Click Next. The Connect to a Microsoft SQL Server Database page of the Table Import Wizard appears.

4. In the Server name field, enter the name of the SQL Server relational database server where you restored the OrderProcessingSystem database.

5. Enter the appropriate credentials for accessing this server.

6. Select OrderProcessingSystem from the Database name drop-down list. The Connect to a Microsoft SQL Server Database page of the wizard should appear, as shown in Figure 9-4.

7. Click Next. The Impersonation Information page of the Table Import Wizard appears.

8. Enter a Windows user name and password that can be used to connect to the OrderProcessingSystem database. These credentials will be used when the Analysis Services server imports and refreshes the data in the model. This is shown in Figure 9-5.

Figure 9-3   *The Connect to a Data Source page of the Table Import Wizard*

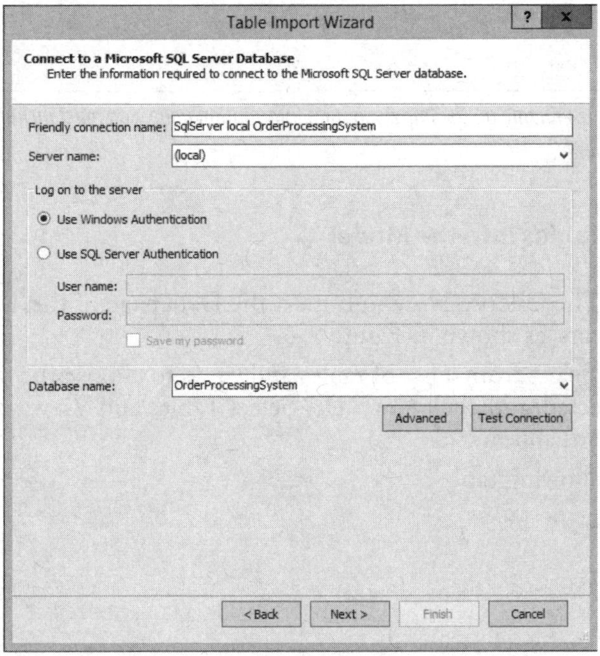

Figure 9-4   *The Connect to a Microsoft SQL Server Database page of the Table Import Wizard*

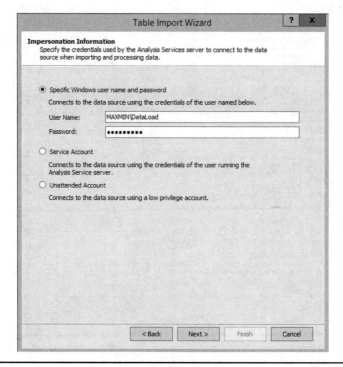

Figure 9-5   *The Impersonation Information page of the Table Import Wizard*

NOTE

If you enter a specific user name on the Impersonation Information page, you must include the domain name along with the user name.

Steps to Import Tables into the Model

1. Click Next. The Choose How to Import the Data page of the Table Import Wizard appears, as shown in Figure 9-6.
2. Ensure the "Select from a list of tables and views to choose the data to import" option is selected, and click Next. The Select Tables and Views page of the Table Import Wizard appears.
3. Check the following tables:
   - ► Customers
   - ► Discounts
   - ► Products
   - ► SalesLocations

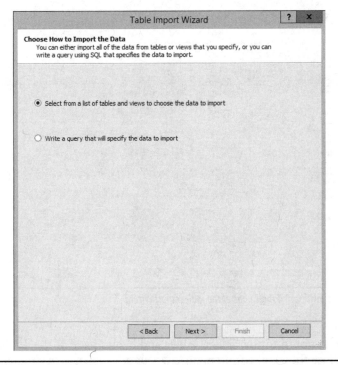

Figure 9-6   *The Choose How to Import the Data page of the Table Import Wizard*

4. Change the Friendly Name for Discounts to **Promotions**.

5. Change the Friendly Name for SalesLocation to **Stores**.

6. Select the Customers row.

7. Click Preview & Filter in the lower-right corner of the dialog box. A new dialog box appears showing the Preview Selected Table page of the Table Import Wizard with the Customers table data.

8. Uncheck the following columns to exclude them from the model:

    ▶ MiddleInitial

    ▶ NumberOfCarsOwned

    ▶ HomeOwnerFlag

    ▶ Married

    ▶ NumberOfChildren

    The Preview Selected Table page of the Table Import Wizard appears, as shown in Figure 9-7.

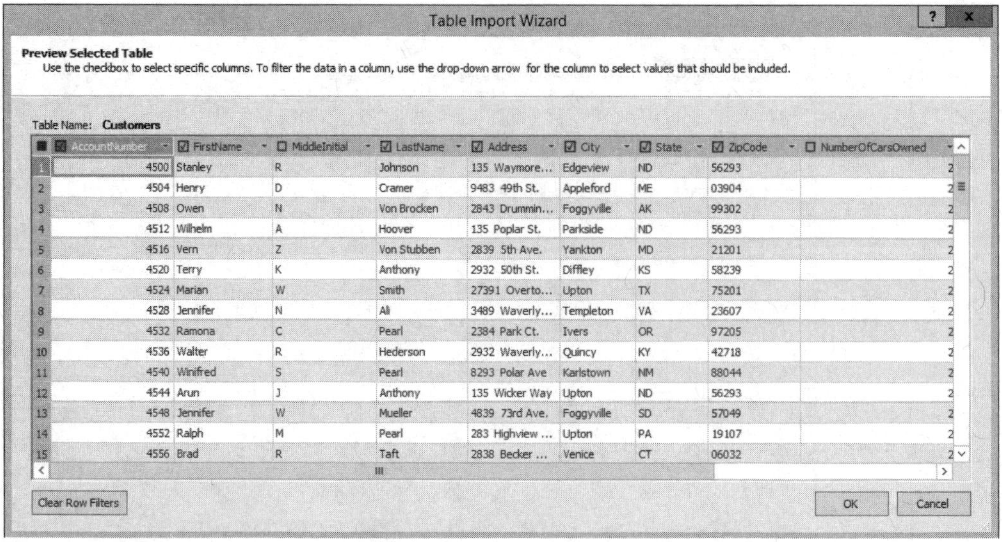

Figure 9-7   *The Preview Selected Table page of the Table Import Wizard*

9. Click OK to return to the Select Tables and Views page of the Table Import Wizard. Note the Applied filters link, which now appears in the Customers row. This link allows us to modify the column filtering for this table.

10. Repeat Steps 6 through 9 to remove the following field from the Products table:

   ▶ TypeCode

   Upon completion of this step, the Select Tables and Views page of the Table Import Wizard will appear similar to Figure 9-8.

11. Click Finish. Data from the selected tables will be imported into the model. Upon completion of the data import, the Importing page of the Table Import Wizard will appear, as shown in Figure 9-9.

12. Click Close. Each imported table will appear as a tab across the bottom of the model design area, as shown in Figure 9-10.

Steps to Import a Query Result Set into the Model

1. We still need to add orders and salespeople to our model. You may recall we set up Salesperson to be a slowly changing dimension. Tabular models do not directly accommodate slowly changing dimensions, so we are going to create a query that will combine this information into a single table in the model. Select Model | Existing Connections from the main menu. The Existing Connections dialog box appears.

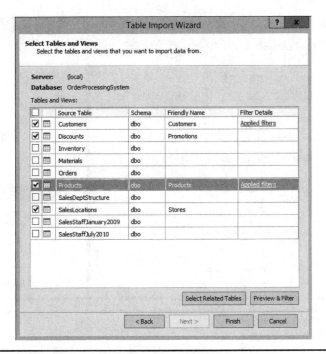

Figure 9-8   *The Select Tables and Views page of the Table Import Wizard*

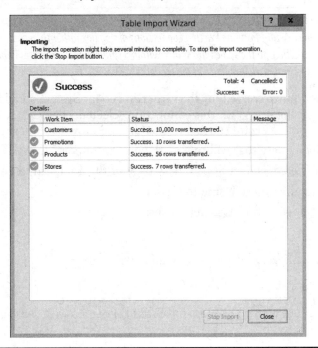

Figure 9-9   *The Importing page of the Table Import Wizard*

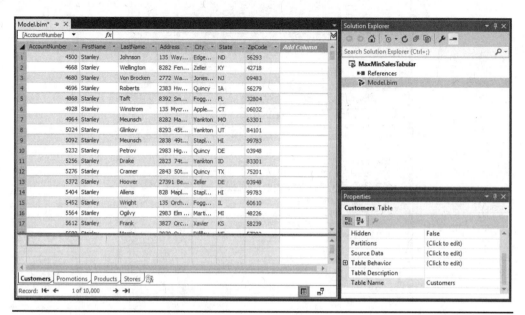

Figure 9-10   *The model with imported data*

NOTE

When going back to pull additional data from a data source already used in a Tabular model, it is important to launch the Table Import Wizard from the Existing Connections dialog box rather than creating a new connection. Creating multiple connections to the same data source within a single model generates unnecessary overhead and causes problems for future maintenance of the model.

2. The connection we created for the OrderProcessingSystem should be the only connection in the list. With this connection selected, click Open. This launches the Table Import Wizard starting at the Choose How to Import the Data page.

3. Select Write a query that will specify the data to import.

4. Click Next. The Specify a SQL Query page of the Table Import Wizard appears.

5. Change Friendly Query Name to **Orders**.

6. Enter the following for SQL Statement:

```
SELECT
    o.*,
    ISNULL(s1.Name, s2.Name) AS SalesPersonName
FROM
    Orders o
LEFT OUTER JOIN
    SalesStaffJanuary2013 s1 ON o.SalesPerson = s1.SalesTerritory
```

```
                              AND o.OrderDate < '7/1/2014'
LEFT OUTER JOIN
   SalesStaffJuly2014 s2 ON o.SalesPerson = s2.SalesTerritory
                              AND o.OrderDate >= '7/1/2014'
```

7. Click Validate to ensure the query was entered correctly. The dialog box should appear, as shown in Figure 9-11.

8. Click Finish. This causes the query to be executed and the resulting data to be imported into the model. The Orders table is fairly large, so this import will take a bit. Still, you should get over 3 million rows imported into the model in a minute or less.

9. Click Close.

Steps to Rename Columns in the Model

1. Click the Customers tab to select the Customers table.

2. Right-click the AccountNumber column heading and select Rename Column from the context menu.

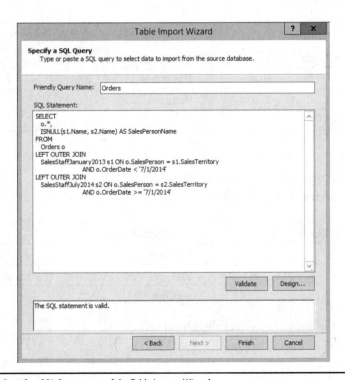

Figure 9-11   *The Specify a SQL Query page of the Table Import Wizard*

3. Replace the column name with **Account Number**.
4. Press ENTER.
5. Repeat Steps 2 through 4 to rename the following columns.

Old Column Name	New Column Name
FirstName	First Name
LastName	Last Name
ZipCode	Zip Code

6. Click the Promotions tab to select the Promotions table.
7. Rename the following columns.

Old Column Name	New Column Name
Code	Promotion Code
Name	Promotion

8. Click the Products tab to select the Products table.
9. Rename the following columns.

Old Column Name	New Column Name
Code	Product Code
Description	Product
TypeDescription	Product Type
RetailPrice	Retail Price

10. Click the Stores tab to select the Stores table.
11. Rename the following columns.

Old Column Name	New Column Name
Code	Store Code
Name	Store
StoreType	Store Type

12. Click the Orders tab to select the Orders table.
13. Rename the following column.

Old Column Name	New Column Name
SalesPersonName	Sales Person

14. Click Save All in the toolbar.

Measures in a Tabular Model

A measure is a quantity that can be aggregated across groups of records. In the Tabular model we just created, the StoreSales and UnitSales fields are quantities we wish to analyze. However, in some client tools, we cannot use those fields by themselves as measures. A field, in and of itself, does not have an aggregation method associated with it.

To create a measure in our Tabular model, we define a formula in the Measure Grid that associates a field with an aggregate function. Once this is in place, the Tabular model knows how to deal with that quantity in grouping situations. The Tabular model uses the measure's aggregate function to quickly calculate aggregations from the data stored in memory.

Learn By Doing: Adding Measures to the Maximum Miniatures Sales Tabular BI Semantic Model

Features Highlighted

▶ Adding measures to the model

▶ Hiding fields in the model

Business Need

We need to continue our work on the MaxMinSalesTabular model to meet the requirements set by the VP of sales.

Steps to Add Measures to the Model

1. Click the Orders tab to select the Orders table.
2. Click the StoreSales column title to select the entire column.
3. Click the sigma (Σ) in the toolbar. Depending on the resolution of your monitor, the sigma may not be visible in the toolbar. You may need to use the drop-down arrow at the end of the toolbar, as shown in Figure 9-12, to find the sigma toolbar button. This creates a measure in the Measure Grid at the bottom of the design area. This is shown in Figure 9-13. (The column has been widened to show the entire column content.)

Figure 9-12 *Locating additional Analysis Services toolbar options*

4. The cell containing the new Sum of StoreSales measure should be selected. In the Properties window, enter **Sales in Dollars** for Measure Name property.
5. Also in the Properties window, select Currency for the Format property.
6. Click the UnitSales column title to select the entire column.
7. Click the sigma in the toolbar to create a measure for this column in the measure grid. The cell containing the new Sum of UnitSales measure should be selected.
8. In the Properties window, enter **Sales in Units** for the Measure Name property.

	Account	Product	Store	Promotion	SalesPerson	StoreSales	UnitSales	Sales Person
1	4504	60	2		6	138.6	4	Eddie
2	4504	60	2		6	138.6	4	Eddie
3	4504	60	2		6	138.6	4	Eddie
4	4504	60	2		6	138.6	4	Eddie
5	4504	60	2		6	138.6	4	Eddie
6	4504	60	2		6	138.6	4	Eddie
7	4504	60	2		6	138.6	4	Eddie
8	4504	60	2		6	138.6	4	Eddie
9	4504	60	2		6	138.6	4	Eddie
10	4504	60	2		6	138.6	4	Eddie
11	4504	60	2		6	138.6	4	Eddie
12	4504	60	2		6	138.6	4	Eddie
13	4504	60	2		6	138.6	4	Eddie
14	4504	60	2		6	138.6	4	Eddie
15	4504	60	2		6	138.6	4	Eddie
16	4504	60	2		6	138.6	4	Eddie
17	4504	60	2		6	138.6	4	Eddie

Model.bim*
[StoreSales] 138.6

Sum of StoreSales: 4856129 46.96...

Customers | Promotions | Products | Stores | **Orders**

Record: 1 of 3,139,401

Figure 9-13 *A column with a sum measure in the Measure Grid*

9. Select Whole Number for the Format property.

10. Select True for the Show Thousands Separator property.

Steps to Hide Columns in the Model

1. Click the OrderID column title to select the entire column.

2. Hold down the SHIFT key and click the UnitSales column title. This will select all of the columns from OrderID to UnitSales. The columns contain foreign key IDs that will be used to create relationships within the model, but should not be exposed to the business user. The StoreSales and UnitSales columns will be exposed through the measures you just created, so these fields should be hidden as well.

3. In the Properties window, set the Hidden property to True. The Orders table will appear similar to Figure 9-14.

4. Click Save All in the toolbar.

Manually Creating a Time Table

We need to add another table to the model to allow us to do time analytics. This table will be the Time table. We will need to manually generate the content of the Time table by creating a calculated table in our model. This is a new feature in SQL Server 2016.

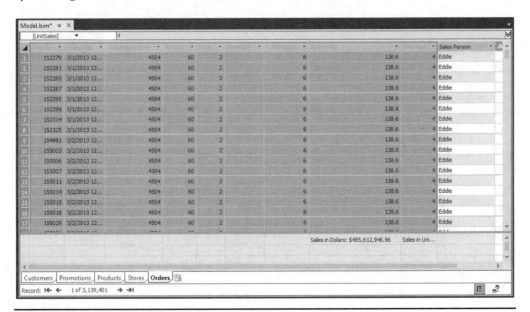

Figure 9-14   *The Orders table with hidden columns*

Learn By Doing: Creating a Calculated Table to Add a Time Table to the Maximum Miniatures Sales Tabular BI Semantic Model

Features Highlighted

► Creating a calculated table

► Using the CALENDAR() function

Business Need

Additional work on the MaxMinSalesTabular model is needed to meet the requirements set by the VP of sales.

Steps to Create a Calculated Table

1. Click the Create a new table button at the right end of the table tabs, as shown in Figure 9-15. (You can also select Table | New Calculated Table from the main menu.)

2. A new calculated table appears and is ready for the entry of a DAX formula to create the table content. Enter the following in the formula bar:

```
=CALENDAR( DATE(2013, 1, 1), DATE(2015, 12, 31)
```

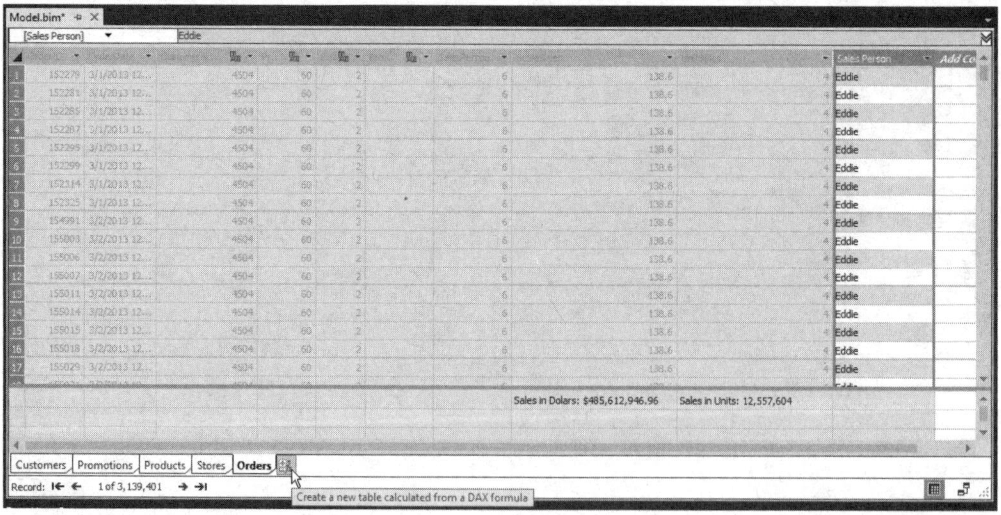

Figure 9-15   *The Create Calculated Table button*

3. Press ENTER. This will cause SQL Server Data Tools to generate a table with dates from 1/1/2013 to 12/31/2015.
4. Right-click the CalculatedTable 1 tab and select Rename from the context menu.
5. Type **Time** and press ENTER.

Steps to Add More Time Columns to the Table

1. Click the Add Column heading.
2. Enter the following expression in the formula bar:

   ```
   =YEAR([Date])
   ```

   and press ENTER.
3. Right-click the Calculated Column 1 heading and select Rename Column from the context menu.
4. Type **Year** and press ENTER.
5. Repeat Steps 1–4 to create additional calculated columns as indicated:

Column Name	Column Formula
Quarter	=YEAR([Date]) & "-" & SWITCH(MONTH([Date]),1,"Q1",2,"Q1",3,"Q1",4,"Q2",5,"Q2",6,"Q2", 7,"Q3",8,"Q3",9,"Q3",10,"Q4",11,"Q4",12,"Q4")
Month	=FORMAT([Date], "MMMM, YYYY")
Month Sort	=FORMAT([Date], "YYYYMM")
Day of Year	=DATEDIFF(DATE(YEAR([Date]), 1, 1), [Date], DAY) + 1
Day of Quarter	=DATEDIFF(DATE(YEAR([Date]), SWITCH(MONTH([Date]), 1, 1, 2, 1, 3, 1, 4, 4, 5, 4, 6, 4, 7, 7, 8, 7, 9, 7, 10, 10, 11, 10, 12, 10), 1), [Date], DAY) + 1
Day of Month	=DAY([Date])
Month of Year	=FORMAT([Date], "MMMM")
Month of Year Sort	=MONTH([Date])
Month of Quarter	=SWITCH(MONTH([Date]), 1, 1, 2, 2, 3, 3, 4, 1, 5, 2, 6, 3, 7, 1, 8, 2, 9, 3, 10, 1, 11, 2, 12, 3)
Quarter of Year	=SWITCH(MONTH([Date]), 1, 1, 2, 1, 3, 1, 4, 2, 5, 2, 6, 2, 7, 3, 8, 3, 9, 3, 10, 4, 11, 4, 12, 4)

When completed, the Time table should appear as shown in Figure 9-16.

6. Make sure the Time table is selected, and then select Table | Date | Mark As Date Table from the main menu. The Mark as Date Table dialog box appears, as shown in Figure 9-17.

	Date	Year	Quarter	Month	Month Sort	Day of Year	Day of Quarter	Day of Month	Month of
1	1/1/2013 12:00:00 AM	2013	2013-Q1	January, 2013	201301	1	1	1	
2	1/2/2013 12:00:00 AM	2013	2013-Q1	January, 2013	201301	2	2	2	
3	1/3/2013 12:00:00 AM	2013	2013-Q1	January, 2013	201301	3	3	3	
4	1/4/2013 12:00:00 AM	2013	2013-Q1	January, 2013	201301	4	4	4	
5	1/5/2013 12:00:00 AM	2013	2013-Q1	January, 2013	201301	5	5	5	
6	1/6/2013 12:00:00 AM	2013	2013-Q1	January, 2013	201301	6	6	6	
7	1/7/2013 12:00:00 AM	2013	2013-Q1	January, 2013	201301	7	7	7	
8	1/8/2013 12:00:00 AM	2013	2013-Q1	January, 2013	201301	8	8	8	
9	1/9/2013 12:00:00 AM	2013	2013-Q1	January, 2013	201301	9	9	9	
10	1/10/2013 12:00:00 AM	2013	2013-Q1	January, 2013	201301	10	10	10	
11	1/11/2013 12:00:00 AM	2013	2013-Q1	January, 2013	201301	11	11	11	
12	1/12/2013 12:00:00 AM	2013	2013-Q1	January, 2013	201301	12	12	12	
13	1/13/2013 12:00:00 AM	2013	2013-Q1	January, 2013	201301	13	13	13	
14	1/14/2013 12:00:00 AM	2013	2013-Q1	January, 2013	201301	14	14	14	

Model.bim*
[Date] *fx* =CALENDAR(DATE(2013, 1, 1), DATE(2015, 12, 31))

Customers | Promotions | Products | Stores | Orders | *fx* **Time**

Record: 1 of 1,095

Figure 9-16   *The calculated Time table*

7. The Date field should be selected as the unique identifier for the table. This is correct. Click OK to exit the Mark as Date Table dialog box.

NOTE

If the incorrect field is selected as the unique identifier for the Date Table, you can select Table | Date | Date Table Settings from the main menu to modify this value.

8. Click Save All in the toolbar.

Mark as Date Table

Select a column to be used as unique identifier for the date table. The selected column must be of the date data type and must contain unique values only.

Date   [Date]

OK   Cancel

Figure 9-17   *The Mark as Date Table dialog box*

The CALENDARAUTO() Function

Instead of using the CALENDAR() function and specifying the begin and end dates for our calendar, we could have used the CALENDARAUTO() function. The CALENDARAUTO () function explores the date values in the model to determine the minimum date value and the maximum date value in the model. It then creates date records from the first day of the year that contains the minimum date value to the last day of the year that contains the maximum date value. If your dates utilize a fiscal calendar, we can specify the month number of the first month of the fiscal year as an optional parameter for this function.

We will create a Time table using the CALENDARAUTO() function later in this chapter.

Relationships and Hierarchies

We now have all of the data we need imported into the MaxMinSalesTabular model. Unfortunately, our model still isn't very useful. We have a collection of tables in our model, but these tables are not related to each other in any way. We can't really query the model in a meaningful way until relationships are created between the tables.

NOTE

If the source database contains foreign key constraints, these are brought into the model as relationships. This was not the case with our source database.

Our users would also like to drill down to view different periods of time. They want to go from viewing a particular year to seeing the data by quarter, by month, or even by day. To facilitate this, we need to create a hierarchy in our Time table.

Learn By Doing: Adding Relationships and a Time Hierarchy to the Maximum Miniatures Sales Tabular BI Semantic Model

Features Highlighted

▶   Using the diagram view

▶   Creating relationships in our model

▶   Creating a time hierarchy

Business Need

A final set of modifications to the MaxMinSalesTabular model is needed to meet the requirements set by the VP of sales.

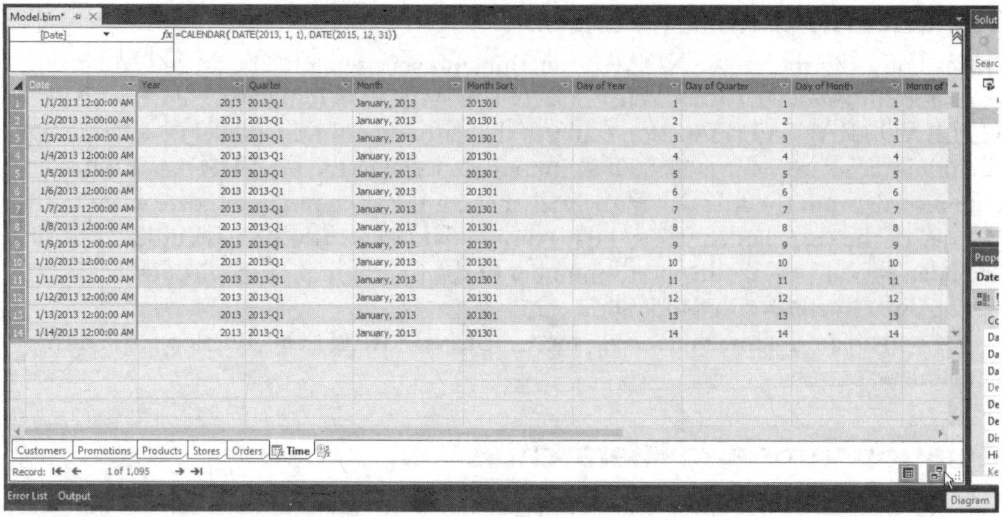

Figure 9-18 *Switching to diagram view*

Steps to Add Relationships to the Model

1. In the lower-right corner of the design area, click the Diagram button as shown in Figure 9-18. The design area will change from grid view to diagram view.

2. The set of controls across the bottom of the diagram view manages our view of the diagram. Use the plus (+)/minus (-) slider to zoom in and out.

3. Click Display to view the display popup menu. The four check boxes control what is displayed in the view. The Reset Layout option resets the view back to the default arrangement.

4. Click Display again to close this menu.

5. Click the Fit to Screen button to view all of the tables.

6. Arrange the tables into a more compact formation. Because the Orders table links to the other five tables, place the Orders table in the middle of the formation with the other five tables around it. You may also want to resize the Customers, Orders, and Time tables so all of the fields are visible.

7. Click the Fit to Screen button again. If you have done a good job of arranging the tables, you should now see a much larger view with all six tables remaining in view. You can experiment with different arrangements to determine what gives you the best layout to work with.

8. Drag the OrderDate field from the Orders table and drop it on the Date field in the Time table, as shown in Figure 9-19. (The OrderDate field is supposed to be grayed out because it is not visible to the business user in the model. This will not

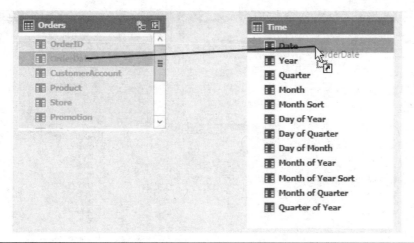

Figure 9-19   *Creating a relationship in the diagram view*

prevent you from completing this step.) If you receive an error dialog box after attempting this step, click OK and try again.

9. Drag the CustomerAccount field from the Orders table and drop it on the Account Number field in the Customers table. This will create a relationship between Orders and Customers.

10. Drag the Product field from the Orders table and drop it on the Product Code field in the Products table.

11. Drag the Store field from the Orders table and drop it on the Store Code field in the Stores table.

12. Drag the Promotion field from the Orders table and drop it on the Promotion Code field in the Promotions table. The diagram should appear similar to Figure 9-20.

Steps to Set the Sort By Columns

The values in the Month and Month of Year fields will not sort correctly. That was why we created the Month Sort and Month of Year Sort fields. We need to set the model to use our sort columns for proper sorting.

1. Click the Month field in the Time table.

2. In the Properties window, select the Sort By Column property. From the drop-down list for this property, select Month Sort.

3. Click the Month of Year field in the Time table.

4. In the Properties window, select the Sort By Column property. From the drop-down list for this property, select Month of Year Sort.

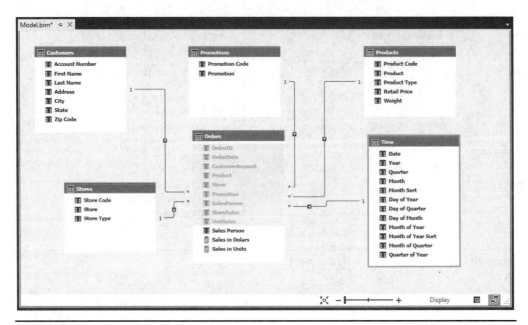

Figure 9-20 *Relationships in the diagram view*

Steps to Create a Hierarchy in the Model

The Time table that we added to the model has a hierarchy rolling up individual dates into months, then quarters, then years. We need to add this hierarchy to our model.

1. Right-click the Year field in the Time table and select Create Hierarchy from the context menu. A new entry called Hierarchy1 is created at the bottom of the table.

2. Change Hierarchy1 to **Date Hierarchy** and press ENTER.

3. Scrolling down, you will see that the Year field was added as the top level of the hierarchy. Drag Quarter and drop it below Year in the hierarchy.

4. Drag Month and drop it below Quarter in the hierarchy.

5. Drag Date and drop it below Month in the hierarchy.

6. The Date, Month, Quarter, and Year fields are exposed through the hierarchy. To avoid confusing the user, we are going to hide these fields and require the user to access them through the hierarchy. Select the Date field.

7. Hold down SHIFT and select Month. This should select four fields.

8. Right-click the selected fields and select Hide from Client Tools in the context menu.

9. The Month Sort and Month of Year Sort fields are used for sorting purposes only and are not needed for any client tool. We will go ahead and hide these

Figure 9-21   *The Time table with the Date hierarchy*

fields as well. Right-click the Month Sort field and select Hide from Client Tools in the context menu. Month Sort is now grayed out in the table.

10. Right-click the Month of Year Sort field and select Hide from Client Tools in the context menu. When sized to show all fields, the Time table appears as shown in Figure 9-21.

11. Click Save All in the toolbar.

Validating the Model Using the Analyze in Excel Feature

We now have all of the requested information assembled in our model with the correct relationships and hierarchies. Next we need to validate the model to ensure things are set up correctly. This is done using the Analyze in Excel feature.

Learn By Doing: Viewing the Model

Feature Highlighted

▶   Using the Analyze in Excel feature

Business Need

We need to validate the data in our MaxMinSalesTabular model.

Viewing the Model

Microsoft Excel 2010 or later must be installed on the computer where you are running SQL Server Data Tools in order for you to use the Analyze in Excel feature demonstrated here. If you do not have Microsoft Excel 2010 installed on this computer, skip this part of the Learn By Doing exercise.

1. Click the Analyze in Excel button in the toolbar (the green Excel icon). The Analyze in Excel dialog box appears, as shown in Figure 9-22.

2. You can use the options in this dialog box to view the model as another user or to select a specific perspective. We'll cover model perspectives in Chapter 14. We'll use the default settings for now. Click OK to continue. Excel will open with our model active in a PivotTable designer.

3. In the PivotTable Fields window, click the Sales in Dollars and Sales in Units measures. Each measure will be selected and placed in the VALUES area of our pivot table.

4. Scroll down to find the Product field in the Products table. Drag the Product field and drop it in the ROWS area.

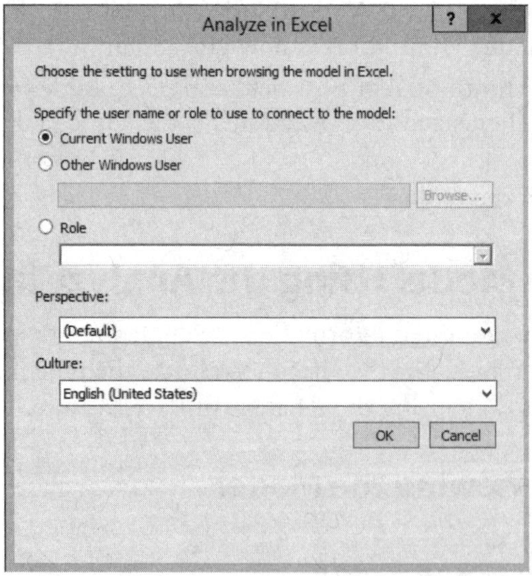

Figure 9-22   *The Analyze in Excel dialog box*

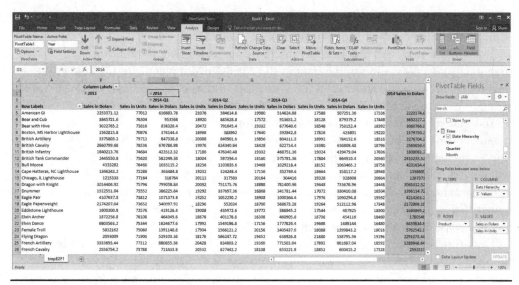

Figure 9-23   *The PivotTable in Excel*

5. Scroll down to find the Date Hierarchy in the Time table. Expand the Date Hierarchy, drag the Year level, and drop it in the COLUMNS area above the Values entry.

6. In the pivot table, click the plus sign next to 2014 to drill down to the quarter level of the hierarchy. Your PivotTable should appear similar to Figure 9-23 with a little sizing.

7. Close Excel. When asked to save changes, click Don't Save.

Congratulations! You have created your first Tabular BI Semantic Model and used the Analyze in Excel feature to show the model can be used for data analysis.

A Second Tabular Model

In our previous work in this chapter, we have seen how quickly a basic Tabular model can be created. We have also seen how quickly and efficiently a Tabular model can deal with fairly large amounts of data. Now let's further explore Tabular model creation by building a model from the MaxMinManufacturingDM database tables.

Data Persistence

When we created the Tabular model for Sales, we noted that we could have used the MaxMinSalesDM data mart as the source for this model. Instead of doing that, we imported the data directly from the line of business systems. This better illustrated some of the capabilities of the Tabular model.

The same is true with the Tabular model we are now going to build for manufacturing. We could use the data in the MaxMinManufacturingDM data mart as our source. However, to show off a few more capabilities of the Tabular model, we are going to use the line of business systems as our data source.

You may recall the data on the processing done by the Maximum Miniatures manufacturing equipment is saved to a comma-separated value (CSV) text file. We can import the data directly from the CSV file into our model for this learning exercise and will have the data from the manufacturing process available for analysis. This works in our situation for one specific reason—we only have a single text file. In a real-world scenario, the manufacturing machinery is going to spit out a text file at the end of every day, or maybe even at the end of each shift.

Each time we load data into a table in our Tabular model, the existing data is dumped from the table and it is loaded from scratch. If we did indeed try to load manufacturing information directly from daily text files, it would mean that we would only have the last day's worth of data to analyze. Each time the current day's text file is loaded, data from any previous days would be lost. Probably not an acceptable scenario for your users.

It will work to continually reload data from a text or XML file, only if the content of that file is always comprehensive. Perhaps the text file contains fairly static list look-up values, like state names and abbreviations. Or perhaps the text file always has a complete list of all customers from your CRM system. In these cases, it is acceptable to completely refresh the table in the model each time. No history is lost in the process.

If, however, your text or XML file contains transactional information, odds are you are going to need to persist that data in a data mart. It won't easily persist across multiple table refreshes in the Tabular model. So, in this exercise we will take advantage of the limitations of our sample data to enable you to try loading data from a text file. When you design your real-world solutions, be sure to take into account the real-world data persistence needs required for your data.

Learn By Doing: Creating the Maximum Miniatures Manufacturing Tabular BI Semantic Model

Features Highlighted

▶ Importing data from a CSV file

▶ Using the Create Relationship dialog box

Business Need

The vice president (VP) of production for Max Min, Inc., wants to analyze the statistics available from the manufacturing automation system using a Tabular model.

Steps to Create the Analysis Services Tabular Project and Import MaxMinAccounting Tables

1. Create an Analysis Services Tabular project called **MaxMinManufacturingTabular**. Use the same settings for the workspace server.

2. Select Model | Import From Data Source from the main menu. The Table Import Wizard dialog box appears with the Connect to a Data Source page visible.

3. Ensure the Microsoft SQL Server entry is selected and click Next.

4. Enter the name of the SQL Server relational database server where you restored the MaxMinAccounting database.

5. Enter the appropriate credentials for accessing this server.

6. Select MaxMinAccounting from the Database name drop-down list.

7. Click Next. The Impersonation Information page of the Table Import Wizard appears.

8. Enter a Windows user name and password that can be used to connect to the MaxMinAccounting database. These credentials will be used when the Analysis Services server imports and refreshes the data in the model.

9. Click Next. The Choose How to Import the Data page of the Table Import Wizard appears.

10. Ensure the Select from a list of tables and views to choose the data to import option is selected, and click Next.

11. Click the check box in the upper corner of the grid to select all of the tables in the database.

12. Enter **Machines** for the Friendly Name of the CapitalAssets table.

13. With the CapitalAssets row selected, click the Preview & Filter button. The Preview Selected Table dialog box appears.

14. Click the drop-down arrow for the AssetType column heading. The sorting and filtering menu box appears.

15. Click (Select All) in the Text Filters area to uncheck all of the items.

16. Check the Molding Machine entry in the Text Filters area. Only records with a value of "Molding Machine" in the AssetType column will be imported for this table. The sorting and filtering menu box appears as in Figure 9-24.

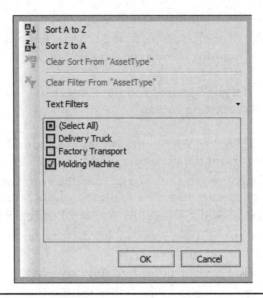

Figure 9-24 *The sorting and filtering menu box*

17. Click OK to exit the sorting and filtering menu box. The filtered data is displayed in the grid.
18. Click the check box in the upper-left corner of the grid to uncheck all columns.
19. Check the following columns:
    - ▶ AssetCode
    - ▶ AssetClass
    - ▶ AssetName
    - ▶ LocationCode
    - ▶ RawMaterial
20. Click OK to exit the Preview Selected Table dialog box.
21. Select the Locations row and click the Preview & Filter button.
22. Click the drop-down arrow for the LocationType column heading. The sorting and filtering menu box appears.
23. Click (Select All) in the Text Filters area to uncheck all of the items.
24. Check the Plant Site entry in the Text Filters area. Only records with a value of "Plant Site" in the LocationType column will be imported for this table.
25. Click OK to exit the sorting and filtering menu box. The filtered data is displayed in the grid.

26. Click the check box in the upper-left corner of the grid to uncheck all columns.

27. Check the following columns:

    ▶ LocationCode

    ▶ LocationName

    ▶ CountryCode

28. Click OK to exit the Preview Selected Table dialog box.

29. Select the Products row and click the Preview & Filter button.

30. Click the check box in the upper-left corner of the grid to uncheck all columns.

31. Check the following columns:

    ▶ ProductCode

    ▶ ProductName

    ▶ ProductSubtypeCode

32. Click OK to exit the Preview Selected Table dialog box.

33. Click Finish. The Importing page will be displayed, and the table data will be imported into the model.

34. When the import is complete, click Close.

35. Click Save All in the toolbar.

Steps to Import the BatchInfo.CVS File

In order to complete this Learn By Doing exercise, you must download and install the Microsoft Access Database Engine 2010 Redistributable, if it is not already installed on your PC. This redistributable includes the software driver used for reading a CSV file. You can download the install for this software driver at www.microsoft.com/en-us/download/details .aspx?id=13255.

1. Select Model | Import from Data Source from the main menu. The Connect to a Data Source page of the Table Import Wizard appears.

2. Scroll down in the list and select Text File.

3. Click Next. The Connect to Flat File page of the Table Import Wizard appears.

4. Enter **BatchInfo.CSV** for Friendly connection name.

5. Click Browse. The Open dialog box appears.

6. In the lower-right corner, change the file type to Comma Separated File (*.csv).

7. Browse to and select the BatchInfo.CSV file, and then click Open.

8. Make sure the Use first row as column headers check box is checked.

9. Click Next. The Impersonation Information page of the Table Import Wizard appears.

10. Enter a Windows user name and password that can be used to access this text file. These credentials will be used when the Analysis Services server imports and refreshes the data in the model.

11. Click Finish. The Importing page will be displayed, and the data from the text file will be imported into the model.

12. When the import is complete, click Close. The data is imported into a table called BatchInfo.

13. Right-click the BatchInfo tab and select Rename from the context menu.

14. Change the name to **Manufacturing Info** and press ENTER.

Steps to Add Relationships to the Model

When we created the MaxMinSalesTabular BI Semantic Model, we created table relationships in the diagram view using drag-and-drop. This time around, we are going to use the Manage Relationships dialog box. Both methods produce exactly the same result, so use whichever works best for you.

1. Select Table | Manage Relationships from the main menu. The Manage Relationships dialog box appears.

2. Click Create. The Create Relationship dialog box appears.

3. Select Manufacturing Info from the Table 1 drop-down list.

4. Select MachineNumber from the Columns list for Table 1.

5. Select Machines from the Table 2 drop-down list. A warning message may appear at the bottom of the dialog box. Our next selection will fix this issue, so ignore the warning message.

6. Select AssetCode from the Columns list for Table 2. The Create Relationship dialog box correctly determines that we are creating a many-to-one relationship with many rows in the Manufacturing Info table linked to one row in the Machines table. It defaulted to having a row selected in the Machines table filter the rows displayed in the Manufacturing Info table. These default decisions are correct. The Create Relationship dialog box appears, as shown in Figure 9-25.

7. Click OK to create the relationship and exit the Create Relationship dialog box.

8. Use the same method to add these relationships:

Table 1	Table 1 Column	Table 2	Table 2 Column
Machines	LocationCode	Locations	LocationCode
Locations	CountryCode	Countries	CountryCode
Manufacturing Info	ProductCode	Products	ProductCode
Products	ProductSubtypeCode	ProductSubtypes	ProductSubtypeCode
ProductSubtypes	ProductTypeCode	ProductTypes	ProductTypeCode

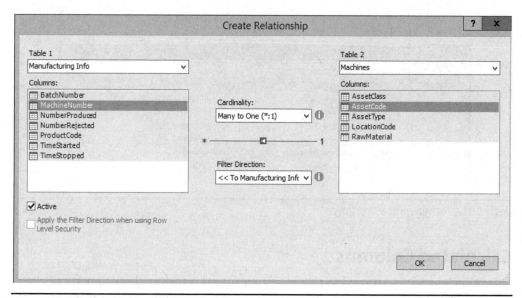

Figure 9-25   *The Create Relationship dialog box*

The Manage Relationships dialog box appears, as shown in Figure 9-26.

9.   Click Close to exit the Manage Relationships dialog box.

10.   Click the tab for the Machines table. Notice two new relationship column icons have shown up in the column headings as indicated in Figure 9-27. The icon next to the AssetCode heading indicates this column is being used as a lookup column. In other words, it is being used as the primary key in the relationship. The icon next to the LocationCode heading indicates this column is being used as a foreign key column in a relationship.

11.   Click Save All in the toolbar.

Active	Table 1	Cardinality	Filter Direction	Table 2
Yes	Locations [CountryCode]	Many to One (*:1)	<< To Locations	Countries [CountryCode]
Yes	Machines [LocationCode]	Many to One (*:1)	<< To Machines	Locations [LocationCode]
Yes	Manufacturing Info [MachineNumber]	Many to One (*:1)	<< To Manufacturing Info	Machines [AssetCode]
Yes	Manufacturing Info [ProductCode]	Many to One (*:1)	<< To Manufacturing Info	Products [ProductCode]
Yes	Products [ProductSubtypeCode]	Many to One (*:1)	<< To Products	ProductSubtypes [ProductSubty...
Yes	ProductSubtypes [ProductTypeCode]	Many to One (*:1)	<< To ProductSubtypes	ProductTypes [ProductTypeCode]

Figure 9-26   *The Manage Relationships dialog box*

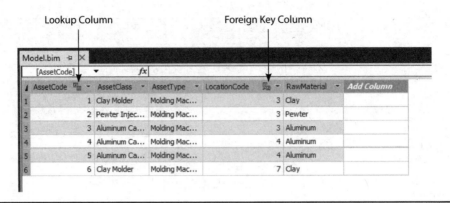

Figure 9-27   *The relationship column icons*

Calculated Columns

One of the quantities we need to provide in our model is the number of products accepted by the quality assurance process. This number is not in the data from our source system. Instead, we need to derive this quantity by creating an arithmetic expression in a calculation. In a Tabular BI Semantic Model, this is done by adding calculated columns to our tables.

Calculated columns are created in a Tabular model in a manner similar to the way calculated columns are added in Excel. A formula is added in an empty cell. As soon as we press ENTER, the formula is evaluated and the resulting value is displayed. What is different about the Tabular model environment is that the formula is automatically spread to all of the rest of the rows in the table (even if there are millions of rows in that table!).

In the Learn By Doing exercises that follow, we will use calculated columns for three different purposes. In the first exercise, we will calculate new quantities and use those quantities to create measures. This is probably the first purpose most of us would think of when it comes to calculated columns, but it is by no means their only use.

We will also create calculated columns to help us define elements for our time-based analysis in the model. We are not creating our own custom Time table for this model, so we need to use calculated columns to determine month, quarter, etc. In the final Learn By Doing exercise in the chapter, we will use calculated columns to assist with the creation of two hierarchies within the model.

So, let's make a calculated effort to learn how to work with calculated columns.

Learn By Doing: Using Calculated Columns

Feature Highlighted

► Creating calculated columns in the model

Business Need

Additional work on the MaxMinManufacturingTabular model is needed to meet the requirements set by the VP of production.

Steps to Add Calculated Columns to the Manufacturing Info Table

1. Select the Manufacturing Info tab and scroll to the right until you see the "Add Column" column heading.
2. Click the cell below the Add Column heading.
3. Type the following formula:

   ```
   =[NumberProduced] - [NumberRejected]
   ```

   As soon as you type the equal sign, the character shows up in the formula area with the text cursor there ready for more.

TIP

Use the chevron button to the right of the formula entry area to expand the formula entry area when entering long formulas.

4. Press ENTER. The formula you entered is evaluated for all of the rows in the table. The column heading is changed to CalculatedColumn1 and a new "Add Column" column is added to the table.
5. In the Properties window, enter **NumberAccepted** for Column Name.
6. Repeat this process to add the following calculated columns to the Manufacturing Info table with the specified column names.

Column Name	Formula
ElapsedTime	=HOUR([TimeStopped] - [TimeStarted]) * 60 + MINUTE([TimeStopped] - [TimeStarted])
Date of Manufacture	=DATEVALUE(FORMAT([TimeStarted], "MM/DD/YYYY"))

NOTE

The formula for the Date of Manufacture calculated column uses the FORMAT() function to convert the date/time value in the TimeStarted field to text without including the time portion. It then uses the DATEVALUE() function to convert that text back to a date/time value. This causes all of the date/time values to have midnight as their time portion, essentially eliminating time from consideration.

Steps to Add Measures and Hide Columns

1. Add measures to the following columns with the specified measure names. Each measure should use the SUM() aggregation. (If you need help with this, see the "Steps to Add Measures to the Model" section earlier in this chapter.) Also, set the Format and Show Thousands Separator properties as shown.

Column Name	Measure Name	Format	Show Thousands Separator
NumberProduced	Total Products	Whole Number	True
NumberRejected	Rejected Products	Whole Number	True
NumberAccepted	Accepted Products	Whole Number	True
ElapsedTime	Elapsed Time For Manufacture	Whole Number	True

2. Hide the following columns in the Manufacturing Info table. (If you need help with this, see the "Steps to Hide Columns in the Model" section earlier in this chapter.)

Column Name
MachineNumber
ProductCode
TimeStarted
TimeStopped
NumberProduced
NumberRejected
NumberAccepted
ElapsedTime

The Manufacturing Info table will appear as shown in Figure 9-28 and Figure 9-29.

3. Click Save All in the toolbar.

Hierarchies Spanning Multiple Tables

When we created the Date Hierarchy, all of the fields that made up the levels of our hierarchy were in the same table. This makes hierarchy creation very easy. It turns out that it is also a requirement in the Tabular model.

This presents a problem for us in the MaxMinManufacturingTabular model. We wish to duplicate the Plant Hierarchy and Product Hierarchy that we created in the

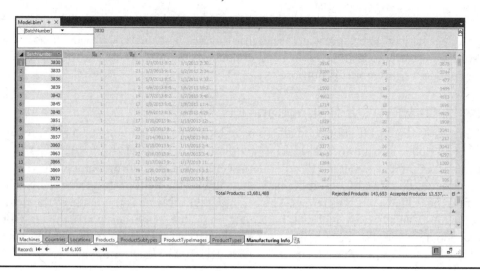

Figure 9-28   *The left eight columns of the Manufacturing Info table*

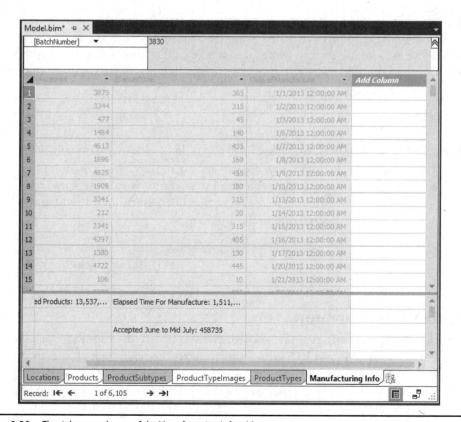

Figure 9-29   *The right two columns of the Manufacturing Info table*

MaxMinManufacturingDM Multidimensional model. The fields needed for those hierarchies happen to be spread across multiple tables. Fortunately, we can consolidate that information into a single table using calculated columns. There are two different functions we can use for this purpose.

The LOOKUPVALUE() Function

The LOOKUPVALUE()function allows us to look up a value in one table, the lookup table, and pull it into another table. In its simplest form, the LOOKUPVALUE() function has three parameters: ResultColumnName, SearchColumnName, and SearchValue. The ResultColumnName is the name of the field in the lookup table where we find the value we wish to return. The SearchColumnName is the name of the field in the lookup table where we will look for a matching value—in other words, the key field of the lookup table. The SearchValue is the value we are looking for in the lookup table.

Here is an example of this form of the LOOKUPVALUE() function:

```
=LOOKUPVALUE(States[StateName], [StateKey], "MN")
```

In this example, we want to return a value from the StateName field of the States table. We are looking for a value of "MN" in the StateKey field of the States table. The value we are looking for can come from a field in the table that is hosting the LOOKUPVALUE() function. For example, we can look for a match to the content of the StateAbbrv field:

```
=LOOKUPVALUE(States[StateName], [StateKey], [StateAbbrv])
```

The LOOKUPVALUE() function can also handle situations where our lookup table has several fields that make up its key. We can specify multiple SearchColumnName and SearchValue pairs as function parameters. For example, we can look up the ItemQuantity from an invoice line item where that line item is uniquely identified by the invoice number and the line number as follows:

```
=LOOKUPVALUE(LineItem[ItemQuantity], [InvoiceNumber], "MM12943",
                                     [LineNumber], 4)
```

The RELATED() Function

The RELATED() function provides us with another way to do a similar type of lookup. The difference is the RELATED() function leverages the relationships already defined in the model (thus, the name). With the LOOKUPVALUE() function, we had to specify the fields that were being matched between the two tables. The RELATED() function, by contrast, uses the relationship defined in the model to determine this link.

The RELATED() function takes a single parameter. That parameter is a fully qualified reference to a field in another table. "Fully qualified" means we need to specify both the name of the table and the name of the field. A relationship must exist in the model between the table that contains the calculated column using the RELATED() function and the table referred to by the fully qualified parameter.

For example, in our model we have a relationship between the Products table and the ProductSubtypes table. The relationship in the model specifies that the ProductSubtypeCode field in the Products table is a foreign key reference to the ProductSubtypeCode field in the ProductSubtypes table. Because of this relationship, we can create the following calculated column in the Products table:

```
=RELATED(ProductSubtypes[ProductSubtypeName])
```

This returns the content of the ProductSubtypeName field in the ProductSubtypes table that is related to the given row in the Product table.

Because the RELATED() function leverages an existing relationship within the model, it will perform better than the LOOKUPVALUE() function, which is creating an ad hoc relationship on-the-fly. This is especially true when you are working with values in large tables. That being said, there may be times when you need to utilize the ad hoc capabilities of the LOOKUPVALUE() function.

Let's try out these functions to create the hierarchies in the MaxMinManufacturingTabular model.

Learn By Doing: Using the LOOKUPVALUE() and RELATED() Functions

Features Highlighted

- ▶ Using the LOOKUPVALUE() function
- ▶ Using the RELATED() function

Business Need

A final set of modifications to the MaxMinManufacturingTabular model is needed to meet the requirements set by the VP of production.

NOTE

Because of the relationships that exist in the model, it would be proper to use the RELATED() function for all of the calculated columns in this Learn By Doing exercise. We are using the LOOKUPVALUE() function here to allow you to gain some familiarity with both of these functions.

Steps to Create Calculated Columns Using the LOOKUPVALUE() Function

1. Select the Locations table.
2. Add the following calculated column:

Column Name	Formula
CountryName	=LOOKUPVALUE(Countries[CountryName], [CountryCode], [CountryCode])

3. Select the Machines table.
4. Add the following calculated columns:

Column Name	Formula
LocationName	=LOOKUPVALUE(Locations[LocationName], [LocationCode], [LocationCode])
CountryName	=LOOKUPVALUE(Locations[CountryName], [LocationCode], [LocationCode])

Steps to Create Calculated Columns Using the RELATED() Function

1. Select the ProductSubtypes table.
2. Add the following calculated column:

Column Name	Formula
ProductTypeName	=RELATED(ProductTypes[ProductTypeName])

3. Select the Products table.
4. Add the following calculated columns:

Column Name	Formula
ProductSubtypeName	=RELATED(ProductSubtypes[ProductSubtypeName])
ProductTypeName	=RELATED(ProductSubtypes[ProductTypeName])

Steps to Create Hierarchies in the Model

1. Click the Diagram button in the lower-right corner of the design area.
2. Rearrange the tables in the diagram, if you wish.
3. Locate the Machines table.
4. Right-click the RawMaterial field and select Create Hierarchy from the context menu.

5. Change Hierarchy1 to **Material Hierarchy** and press ENTER.

6. Scrolling down, you will see that the RawMaterial field was added as the top level of the hierarchy. Right-click this entry and select Rename from the context menu.

7. Type **Material** and press ENTER.

8. Drag AssetClass and drop it below Material (RawMaterial) in the hierarchy.

9. Rename AssetClass to **Machine Type** in the hierarchy.

10. Drag AssetName and drop it below Machine Type (AssetClass) in the hierarchy.

11. Rename AssetName to **Machine**.

12. Right-click CountryName and select Create Hierarchy from the context menu.

13. Change Hierarchy1 to **Plant Hierarchy** and press ENTER.

14. Rename CountryName to **Country** in the hierarchy.

15. Drag LocationName and drop it below Country (CountryName) in the hierarchy.

16. Rename LocationName to **Plant** in the hierarchy.

17. Drag AssetName and drop it below Plant (LocationName) in the hierarchy.

18. Rename AssetName to **Machine**.

19. Select AssetCode.

20. Hold down the SHIFT key and click CountryName. The seven fields in the table should be selected.

21. Right-click these fields and select Hide from Client Tools in the context menu. The Machines table should appear, as shown in Figure 9-30.

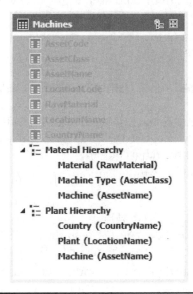

Figure 9-30 *The Machines table with hierarchies*

22. Because the location and country information is now exposed through the Plant Hierarchy, we do not need to expose the Locations and Countries tables to the end user. Right-click the heading of the Locations table and select Hide from Client Tools from the context menu. The entire table will be grayed out.

23. Right-click the heading of the Countries table and select Hide from Client Tools from the context menu.

24. Locate the Products table.

25. Create a hierarchy named **Product Hierarchy** using the following fields:

Field Name	Name in Hierarchy
ProductTypeName	Product Type
ProductSubtypeName	Product Subtype
ProductName	Product

26. Hide the following fields in the Products table:
ProductCode
ProductName
ProductSubtypeCode
ProductSubtypeName
ProductTypeName

27. Because the product subtype and product type information is now exposed through the Product Hierarchy, we do not need to expose the ProductSubtypes and ProductTypes tables to the end user. Right-click the heading of the ProductSubtypes table and select Hide from Client Tools from the context menu.

28. Right-click the heading of the ProductTypes table and select Hide from Client Tools from the context menu.

Steps to Create a Calculated Table Using CALENDARAUTO()

1. Switch to Grid view, and then click the Create a new table button at the right end of the table tabs. A new calculated table appears and is ready for the entry of a DAX formula to create the table content.

2. Enter the following in the formula bar:

```
=CALENDARAUTO()
```

3. Press ENTER. The CALENDARAUTO() function determines the earliest date in the model is 1/1/2013 and the latest date in the model is 12/31/2015. Therefore, it generates a table with rows from January 1, 2013 to December 31, 2015.

4. Right-click the CalculatedTable 1 tab and select Rename from the context menu.

5. Type **Time** and press ENTER.

6. Click the Add Column heading.
7. Enter the following expression in the formula bar:

   ```
   =FORMAT([Date], "YYYY-MM")
   ```

8. Right-click the Calculated Column 1 heading and select Rename Column from the context menu.
9. Type **Month** and press ENTER.
10. Repeat Steps 6–9 to create additional calculated columns as indicated:

Column Name	Column Formula
Quarter	=YEAR([Date]) & "-" & SWITCH(MONTH([Date]), 1, "Q1", 2, "Q1", 3, "Q1", 4, "Q2", 5, "Q2", 6, "Q2", 7 , "Q3", 8, "Q3", 9, "Q3", 10, "Q4", 11, "Q4", 12, "Q4")
Year	=YEAR([Date])

11. Switch to Diagram view.
12. Rearrange the tables so you can see both the Manufacturing Info table and the Time table.
13. Drag the Date of Manufacture field from the Manufacturing Info table and drop it on the Date field in the Time table. This will create a relationship between the two tables.
14. Right-click the Date of Manufacture field in the Manufacturing Info table and select Hide from Client Tools in the context menu.
15. Create a hierarchy named **Date Hierarchy** in the Time table using the following fields:

Field Name	Name in Hierarchy
Year	Year
Quarter	Quarter
Month	Month
Date	Date

16. Hide the following fields in the Time table:
    Date
    Month
    Quarter
    Year
    Your model should appear similar to Figure 9-31.
17. Click Save All in the toolbar.

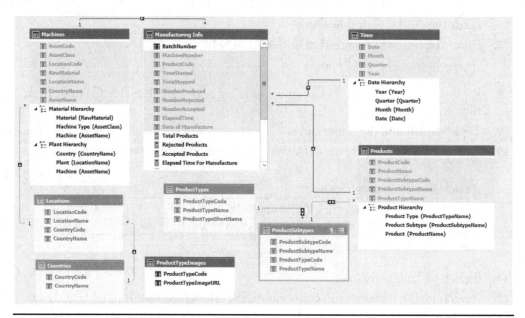

Figure 9-31   *The completed MaxMinManufacturingTabular model*

Putting More on the Table

We have created two Tabular models. We have seen how quickly these models can be created and how effectively they can deal with large sets of data. In the next chapter we will explore a few more features in the Tabular model and explore more of the DAX query language.

The table has been set. Let's dig in!

Chapter 10

A Fancy Table: Tabular BI Semantic Model Advanced Features

In This Chapter

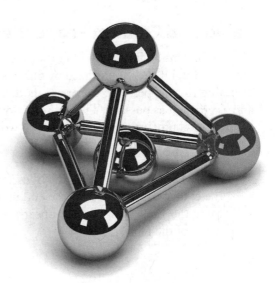

I don't set a fancy table, but the kitchen's awful homey.

—Anthony Perkins as Norman Bates in *Psycho*

In Chapter 9, we created two Tabular BI Semantic Models. We saw that Tabular models are quick and easy to create. Even so, they provide a powerful analysis environment.

In this chapter, we add to our Tabular models as we look at some of the more advanced features of this architecture. Next, we look at the DAX language. In Chapter 9, we used DAX functions to define measures and to create the members of our time hierarchy in the MaxMinManufacturingTabular model. In this chapter, we examine DAX functions that assist us with more sophisticated time analytics.

Finally, we deploy our model to a "production" environment. Even though the workspace database provides a fully functioning Tabular model, this is not a database we want to expose to our end users. Instead, we will deploy the models to a secure production environment for general use.

Without further ado, let's take our simple table and make it fancy!

Enhancing Our Tabular Model

One of the main reasons we utilize BI Semantic Models is to capture an organization's business logic in a central location. This allows for business rules to be used in a consistent manner across reporting and analysis tasks. Once this business logic is collected in the model, we need to make it quick and easy to use. In the next few sections of this chapter, we look at ways to do just that.

Table and Column Properties

Our BI Semantic Models, whether they are Tabular models or Multidimensional models, are only useful if they are utilized by our business decision makers. One of the keys to having this happen is to make our models as well organized, as self-documenting, and as efficient as possible. The Tabular model provides a number of table-level and column-level properties we can utilize to work toward these goals.

Those properties are

▶ **Table Description** The Table Description property provides an explanation of the content of the table for the end user. In the Microsoft Tabular model query tools, the Table Description appears as a ToolTip when the user hovers over the name of the table.

▶ **Description**   The Description property of a column provides an explanation of the content of the column. The property does not apply to hierarchy members based on the column. In the Microsoft Tabular model query tools, the Column Description appears as a ToolTip when the user hovers over the name of the column.

▶ **Row Identifier**   The Row Identifier property signifies the column that serves as the primary key for that table. The values in this column must be unique. Only one column in a table can be set as the Row Identifier.

▶ **Default Label**   The Default Label property identifies a column to serve as the default value for each row in the table. The value in this column is then used by client tools as a label or heading for the row. Only one column in a table can be set as the Default Label.

▶ **Default Image**   The Default Image property identifies an image column to serve as the default image for each row in the table. The image is then used by client tools as a representation for the row. Only one column in a table can be set as the Default Image.

▶ **Default Field Set/Table Detail Position**   The Default Field Set/Table Detail Position properties determine which columns should be included as the default detail columns for this table. In a client tool, when the table is selected, the default columns are placed in the visualization being created. Default Field Set is a property of the table. Table Detail Position is a property of a column. Each property provides access to the same Default Field Set dialog box used to select which fields are default fields and what order they should appear in the client tool.

▶ **Data Format/Format**   The Data Format/Format property applies formatting to a set of values. A column has a Data Format property. A measure has a Format property.

Adding Images to a Tabular Model

One capability unique to the Tabular BI Semantic Model is the ability to have images in the model. It can be beneficial in a number of situations to have images associated with the rows in a table. You could have a picture of each employee in a personnel table, an illustration of each item in a product table, or a map of each sales territory in the sales region table.

Client tools that support images can then display these pictures, illustrations, or maps along with data being analyzed. As noted in the prior section, you can use the Default Image property to identify an image column. The client tool will then display that image with each row.

Images Stored in a Table

Images can be utilized in two different ways. The first method utilizes images stored as binary large objects (BLOBs) in the database table. Images stored in this manner are imported right into the model along with the rest of the data in the table.

Images pulled into the model in this way may take up large amounts of memory. They may negatively affect the performance and the capacity of the model. Having the images in the model does, however, ensure those images are always available with the model data.

After the table containing the images is imported into the model, the BLOB field appears as a binary data field. We must change the data type of the field to Image. We can also identify the field as a Default Image, if desired.

Images Referenced as URLs

Images can also be accessed through URLs stored in a field. The images, of course, must be available on a web server for this architecture to be used. That web server must be accessible to any client tool that will explore the model.

This architecture makes it very easy to update an image. The new image file simply replaces the old one on the web server. In addition, the same image can be referenced from multiple tables in multiple models. This makes storage much more efficient.

To use URLs to reference images, we create a string field in the source table. This string field contains the URL for each image. Each row can contain a different URL so each row points to a unique image. Alternatively, several rows can contain the same URL so groups of rows point to the same image.

The URL field is imported into the model along with the other fields. Once the table is imported, we must change the data type of the URL field to Image URL. We can also identify the field as a Default Image, if desired.

Learn By Doing: Enhancing the Maximum Miniatures Manufacturing Tabular BI Semantic Model

Features Highlighted

▶ Setting model properties to improve user friendliness

▶ Adding images to a model

Business Need The VP of production for Max Min, Inc., would like to have an image in the model to identify each product type. In addition, we need to provide a well-organized and self-documenting reporting model.

Steps to Set Table and Column Properties

1. Open SQL Server Data Tools.
2. Open the MaxMinManufacturingTabular model.
3. Change to the grid view of the model if it opens in diagram view.
4. Click the Machines table tab.
5. In the Properties window, enter **This table contains the Material/MachineType hierarchy and the Plant/Country hierarchy** for Table Description.
6. Click the Default Field Set property. An ellipsis (…) button appears.
7. Click the ellipsis button. The Default Field Set dialog box appears.
8. Select the AssetClass field in the Fields in the table area and click Add.
9. Select the AssetName field in the Fields in the table area and click Add. The Default Field Set dialog box appears, as shown in Figure 10-1.

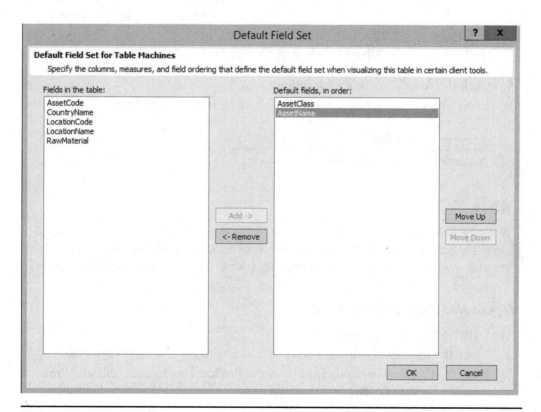

Figure 10-1   *The Default Field Set dialog box*

10. Click OK to exit the Default Field Set dialog box.

11. Right-click the AssetCode column heading and select Freeze Columns. The AssetCode column becomes the leftmost column in the grid and will stay on the screen when scrolling the grid to the right. (This does not help the user of the model, but it can help us by keeping the unique identifier for each row in view as we work with the data in the table.)

12. With the AssetCode column still selected, change the following property settings in the Properties window:

Property	Value
Description	The unique identifier for each machine
Row Identifier	true

13. Click the AssetName column heading.

14. In the Properties window, change the following property settings:

Property	Value
Description	The make and model of the manufacturing machine

15. Click the AssetClass column heading.

16. In the Properties window, change the following property settings:

Property	Value
Description	The machine type

NOTE

We have set these properties for a single table within our model. We are not going to take the space to provide step-by-step instructions to do this for the remaining tables in this model and in the MaxMinSalesTabular model. Feel free to take that task as a homework assignment if you would like further practice working with these properties.

Steps to Add Images to the Model

1. Switch to the diagram view.

2. Move the ProductTypeImages table so it is next to the ProductTypes table.

3. Drag the ProductTypeCode field from the ProductTypeImages table and drop it on the ProductTypeCode field in the ProductTypes table. This will create a relationship between these two tables.

4. Right-click the existing relationship line between the ProductTypes table and the ProductSubtypes table, and select Edit Relationships from the context menu.
5. Select To Both Tables from the Filter Direction drop-down list.
6. Click OK.
7. Right-click the existing relationship line between the ProductSubtypes table and the Products table, and select Edit Relationships from the context menu.
8. Select To Both Tables from the Filter Direction drop-down list.
9. Click OK.
10. Click Save All.

Advanced Relationships and Filtering

If you look closely at the diagram, you will see SQL Server Data Tools correctly identified the relationship between the ProductTypeImages and the ProductTypes as a one-to-one relationship. For every product type record in the ProductTypes table there is one and only one record in the ProductTypeImages table containing the image for that product type. The converse is also true: for every product type image record in the ProductTypeImages table there is one and only one record in the ProductTypes table.

Because this is a one-to-one relationship, SQL Server Data Tools set this relationship for bidirectional filtering by default. We, in turn, modified two additional relationships in the product information chain to use bidirectional filtering. We did this because users will actually see and make selections from the Products table. We want that selection to transfer up the chain to ProductSubtypes on to ProductTypes and finally to ProductTypeImages. Also, if we make a selection from the ProductTypeImages table, we want that selection to transfer down the chain to ProductTypes on to ProductSubtypes and finally to Products. (Any filtering on Products, wherever it is initiated, also filters the Manufacturing Info table.)

In addition to one-to-one relationships, and one-to-many relationships, Tabular models also support many-to-many relationships. The one-to-one relationship and many-to-many relationship along with the bidirectional filtering capability are new features in SQL Server 2016.

Parent/Child Relationships

The one-to-one relationship we just saw is one example of a special type of relationship. Another type of special relationship is the *parent/child relationship*. This is built on a table that contains a self-referential relationship. An employee table that contains a supervisor field is a good example. Figure 10-2 shows a table with a Supervisor field. The Supervisor field contains the employee number of the person to whom the employee reports. This field is a foreign key field that points back to the same table.

Employees

EmpNum	Name	Position	Supervisor
129	Sandra	Team Leader	239
235	Eva	Developer	129
239	Peter	Development Manager	303
293	Maya	CEO	
303	Frank	IT Director	470
470	Tia	CFO	293
487	Juan	System Administrator	303

Figure 10-2   *An employee table with a self-referential field*

A parent/child dimension creates its own hierarchy. Each step from child to parent creates another level in that hierarchy. What is unique about this is there are an undetermined number of levels to the hierarchy. The number of hierarchy levels depends on the number of links in the parent/child chain you are following.

In the Employee dimension shown in Figure 10-2, we can start at Eva, the developer, and follow the chain of supervisors up to Maya, the CEO. There are six levels to the hierarchy along this path. If, however, we start at Juan, the system administrator, and follow the chain of supervisors up to Maya, there are four levels to the hierarchy. (Not saying that system administrators are more important than developers. That's just the way this company happens to be structured!)

When a table containing the records shown in Figure 10-2 is imported into a Tabular model, we use three DAX functions to turn the parent/child relationship into a hierarchy.

PATH(PrimaryKeyField, ParentForeignKeyField)

The PATH() function uses the primary key field and the parent foreign key field to traverse up the parent/child relationship. As it does, it builds a list of each of the primary key values it encounters along the way. The primary key values are delimited by the "|" character.

In the structure shown in Figure 10-2, we could use the following PATH() function:

```
=PATH([EmpNum], [Supervisor])
```

In the record for Eva, this function returns the following path:

```
293|470|303|239|129|235
```

This path results because Eva is employee number 235 and Eva's supervisor is employee number 129—Sandra. Sandra's supervisor is employee number 239—Peter. Peter's supervisor is employee number 303—Frank. Frank's supervisor is employee number 470—Tia. Tia's supervisor is employee number 293—Maya. Maya is the CEO, so her supervisor field is empty.

PATHITEM(PathField, PathLevel)

The PATHITEM() function extracts one of the primary key values from the delimited list created by the PATH() function. To use the PATHITEM() function, a calculated field must first be created using the PATH() function. The "path field" can then be referenced as the first parameter (PathField) of the PATHITEM() function.

The value extracted from the list is determined by the second parameter (PathLevel) of the PATHITEM() function. A PathLevel value of 1 extracts the leftmost primary key value in the path. A PathLevel of 2 extracts the primary key value that is second from the left, and so on.

If we use the PATH() function to create a calculated field called SupervisorPath for our structure in Figure 10-2, we can then use the following PATHITEM() function:

```
=PATHITEM ([SupervisorPath], 3)
```

In the record for Eva, this function returns the following foreign key value:

```
303
```

This is the third item from the left in the list created by the PATH() function.

PATHITEMREVERSE(PathField, PathLevel)

The PATHITEMREVERSE() function works the same as the PATHITEM() function except it starts from the rightmost item in the path. Again, using our example from Figure 10-2, the following PATHITEMREVERSE() function:

```
=PATHITEMREVERSE([SupervisorPath], 3)
```

would return the following foreign key value in the Eva record:

```
239
```

This is the third item from the right in the list created by the PATH() function.

PATHCONTAINS(PathField, Item)

The PATHCONTAINS() function determines if a given item is contained somewhere along the specified path. It returns true if the item was found along this path and false if it was not. Continuing with our example from Figure 10-2, we can use this function to determine if employee number 129 is in the supervisory path:

```
=PATHCONTAINS([SupervisorPath], 129)
```

This function will return true for the path in the Eva record and false for the path in the Peter record.

PATHLENGTH(PathField)

The PATHLENGTH() function returns a count of the number of items in a given path. The following expression:

```
=PATHLENGTH([SupervisorPath])
```

returns:

```
6
```

in the record for Eva.

LOOKUPVALUE(ReturnValueField, PrimaryKeyField, PrimaryKeyValue)

In most cases, finding the primary key value at a certain level in the parent/child relationship is not enough. In our example here, we probably want to know the name of the supervisor or their position. We do this with the LOOKUPVALUE() function we encountered in Chapter 9.

Again, using the sample from Figure 10-2, we use the following expression to get the name of the person at the third level in the relationship:

```
=LOOKUPVALUE ([Name], [EmpNum], PATHITEM ([SupervisorPath], 3))
```

In the record for Eva, this function returns:

```
Frank
```

because Frank is the name corresponding to the employee number found at the third level of the path.

Creating a Parent/Child Hierarchy

Using the LOOKUPVALUE() function and the PATHITEM() function together as shown in the preceding example, we create a calculated column for each possible level of the parent/child relationship. This does require that we know the maximum number of levels that are possible in the parent/child relationship. The resulting table in the model is shown in Figure 10-3.

Many of the calculated columns will have blank values for some records. This is expected based on that record's level in the parent/child relationship. A record will have values for the calculated column showing its level in the hierarchy and for all levels above that level. It will be blank for all levels in the hierarchy below its level.

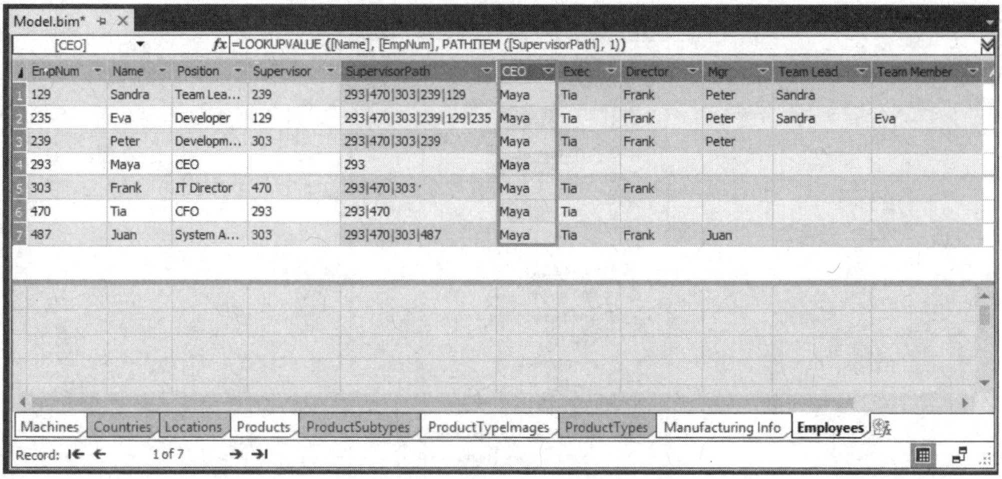

EmpNum	Name	Position	Supervisor	SupervisorPath	CEO	Exec	Director	Mgr	Team Lead	Team Member
129	Sandra	Team Lea...	239	293|470|303|239|129	Maya	Tia	Frank	Peter	Sandra	
235	Eva	Developer	129	293|470|303|239|129|235	Maya	Tia	Frank	Peter	Sandra	Eva
239	Peter	Developm...	303	293|470|303|239	Maya	Tia	Frank	Peter		
293	Maya	CEO		293	Maya					
303	Frank	IT Director	470	293|470|303	Maya	Tia	Frank			
470	Tia	CFO	293	293|470	Maya	Tia				
487	Juan	System A...	303	293|470|303|487	Maya	Tia	Frank	Juan		

Figure 10-3 *A parent/child relationship table in a Tabular model*

Finally, we use these calculated columns to create a hierarchy within our model. This is shown in Figure 10-4. This hierarchy allows aggregations to provide the appropriate values at any desired level.

Multiple Relationships Between the Same Tables

In some cases, we can have multiple relationships between two of our tables in the model. This occurs most often between the Time table and a table that records the dates of several steps in a multi-step process. For instance, an order may have an order date and a delivery date. With a Tabular model, we can define these multiple relationships, but only one of the relationships can be active. This is shown in Figure 10-5.

This figure shows relationships between both the OrderDate and the DeliveryDate in the Orders table and the Time table. The active relationship is shown as a solid line. The inactive relationship is shown as a dashed line. The active relationship is used with any RELATED() functions defined between the two tables. Therefore, the content of a calculated column using a RELATED() function can change depending on which relationship is active.

You can modify the active status of a relationship using the Active property in the Properties window or in the Edit Relationship dialog box. This is shown in Figure 10-6. You must set the currently active relationship as inactive before you can set another relationship as active.

Figure 10-4 *The hierarchy created from the parent/child relationship*

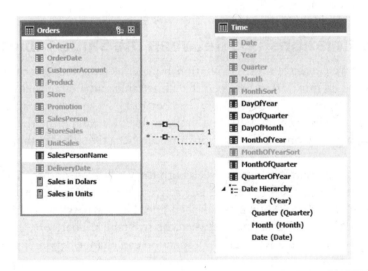

Figure 10-5 *Multiple relationships between two tables*

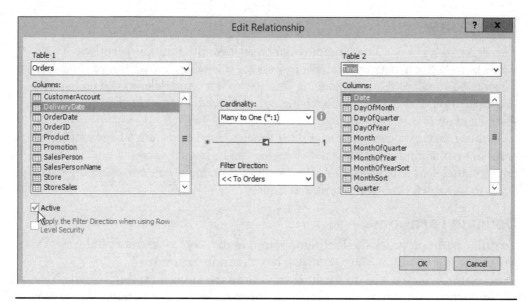

Figure 10-6 *Modifying the active status of a relationship*

USERRELATIONSHIP() Function

You can also use code to instruct Analysis Services to make a particular relationship the active relationship temporarily, for the execution of a DAX expression. This is done using the USERRELATIONSHIP() function. This function takes two columns as its parameters. Analysis Services will then make the relationship identified by these two columns the active relationship for the duration of the DAX expression containing the USERELATIONSHIP() function.

For example:

```
=CALCULATE(SUM('Orders'[StoreSales]),
            USERELATIONSHIP('Orders'[DeliveryDate], 'Time'[Date]))
```

will make the relationship between the DeliveryDate column in the Orders table and the Date column in the Time table the active relationship for the duration of the SUM aggregation.

> **NOTE**
>
> *As an alternative, you can take the content of a table that functions solely as a reference or lookup table and import it into two or more different tables in the model. Each copy of the reference table can then be related to a different field in your main table. This eliminates the existence of multiple relationships between the same two tables.*

Partitions

The larger tables in our Tabular model can be divided into multiple partitions. This allows us to better manage the refresh process for this table. The partitions should be constructed so values that are changing (inserts, updates, and deletes) will end up in a single partition. Values that are not changing, usually values from further back in time, should end up in other partitions.

In this manner, we can cut down on the time required to refresh a large table. The partitions containing data that is not changing can be loaded once and not touched during subsequent data loads. Only the partition containing new and changing data needs to be loaded each time a refresh is done.

Defining Partitions

To define partitions, click the Partitions button in the toolbar when in Grid view. This will display the Partition Manager dialog box shown in Figure 10-7.

Select the table you wish to partition from the Table drop-down list. Use the New button or the Copy button to define new partitions. Give each partition a descriptive name. You can populate each partition from a different relational database table.

Alternatively, you can use WHERE clauses to divide the content of a single relational database table amongst several partitions. This is done by using the Query Editor button to change to the Query Editor and adding a WHERE clause to each query. With either method, multiple tables or WHERE clauses, all of the partitions in a single table must utilize the same connection.

Processing Partitions

To load data for a selected partition rather than an entire table, use the Process Partitions option on the toolbar, as shown in Figure 10-8. This will display the Process Partitions dialog box shown in Figure 10-9.

The Process Partitions dialog box enables you to choose one or more partitions to be refreshed. Once you click OK, the selected partitions are refreshed. The refresh status and the number of rows loaded are shown in the Data Processing dialog box, as shown in Figure 10-10.

Perspectives

Not all of your users need to utilize all of the information in your model. To make the model more user friendly for those users, it would be helpful to limit their view of the model. This is done by creating one or more perspectives within the model.

A perspective limits the tables, fields, and measures that can be seen by the user. These limits correspond to the needs of a particular set of business users. This allows a decision maker to focus on what they care about to make efficient use of the model.

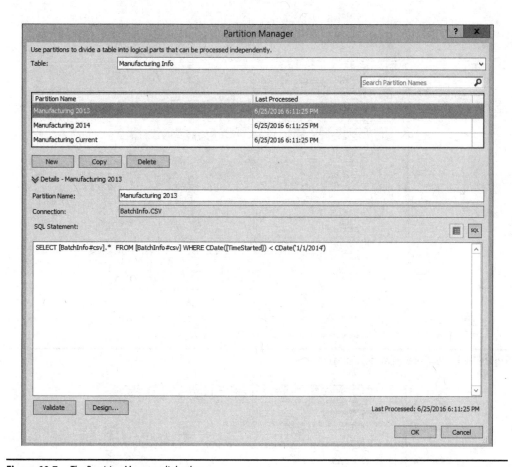

Figure 10-7   *The Partition Manager dialog box*

Creating Perspectives

Perspectives are created by clicking the Perspectives button in the toolbar. This will display the Perspectives dialog box, shown in Figure 10-11. Clicking the New Perspective button creates a column for a new perspective. Rename the new perspective, and then select items that should be visible through this perspective.

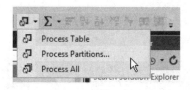

Figure 10-8   *The Process Partitions option*

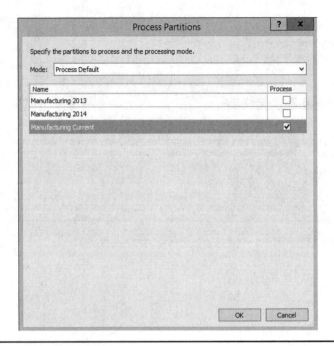

Figure 10-9   *The Process Partitions dialog box*

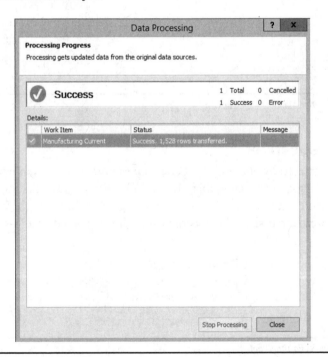

Figure 10-10   *The Data Processing dialog box*

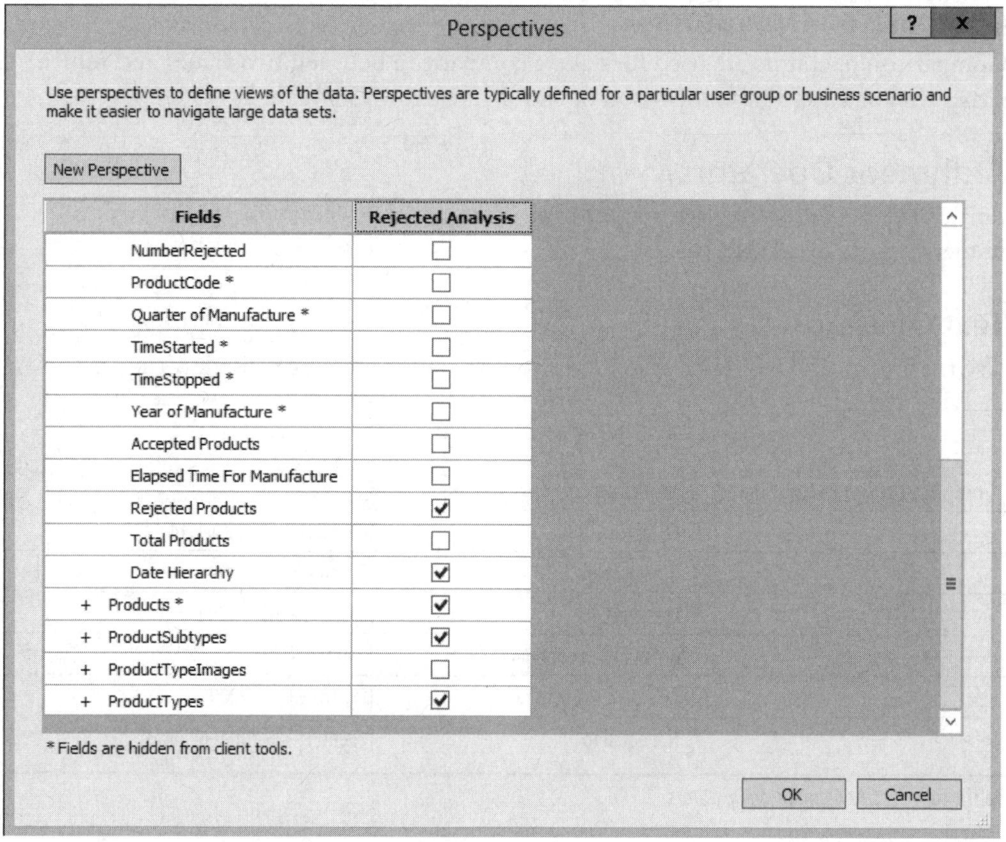

Figure 10-11 *The Perspectives dialog box*

DAX Expressions

Entire books could be written, and have been written, about the DAX language. We encountered some DAX expressions in Chapter 9 and earlier in this chapter. In this section, we take a closer look at the DAX language.

The power of the DAX language comes from functions. Almost all DAX expressions will include at least one DAX function. Therefore, the majority of this section will be about DAX functions. Before we get to that, let's make sure we all understand the very basics—DAX operators.

DAX Operators

DAX operators can be divided into four categories: comparison operators, arithmetic operators, text operator, and logic operators.

Comparison Operators

Comparison operators are used to make a comparison between two values and return either true or false. The comparison operators are shown in Table 10-1.

Arithmetic Operators

Arithmetic operators are used to perform mathematical calculations and provide a numeric result. See Table 10-2.

Text Operator

Use the ampersand (&) to concatenate two text values, creating a single string as shown in Table 10-3.

Comparison Operator	Meaning	Example
=	Equal to	[Product] = "Soaring Eagle"
>	Greater than	[Revenue] > 10000
<	Less than	[Cost Of Sales] < 5000
>=	Greater than or equal to	[Rating] >= 1
<=	Less than or equal to	[Expenses] <= 2000
<>	Not equal to	[Country] <> "United States"

Table 10-1 *DAX Comparison Operators*

Arithmetic Operator	Meaning	Example
+	Addition	[Cost Of Sales] + [Expenses]
−	Subtraction or sign	[Revenue] − [Cost Of Sales]
*	Multiplication	−1 * [Expenses]
/	Division	[Cost Of Sales] / [Revenue]
^	Exponentiation	8 ^ 2

Table 10-2 *DAX Arithmetic Operators*

Text Operator	Meaning	Example
&	Concatenate	[Month Name] & " " & [Year]

Table 10-3 *DAX Text Operator*

Logical Operator	Meaning	Example
&&	Creates an AND condition between two logical expressions. Both expressions must evaluate to true in order for this to return true; otherwise, false is returned.	([Country] = "Germany") && ([Year] = 2015)
||	Creates an OR condition between two logical expressions. If either expression evaluates to true, then true is returned; both values have to return false in order for the result to be false.	([City] = "Chicago") || ([City] = "Dallas")
NOT	Reverses the logical meaning of an expression	NOT ([City] = "Chicago")

Table 10-4   *DAX Logical Operators*

Logical Operators

Logical operators are used to combine multiple conditional expressions into a single logical result. The logical operators are shown in Table 10-4.

The Context for Measures and Calculated Columns

As we turn our attention to DAX functions used in calculated columns and, more importantly, to measures, it is essential to understand the context in which these calculations occur. A solid understanding of this is needed in order to create the appropriate expression for the calculation desired. This context changes depending on where and how you are creating the expression.

The Default Context for Calculated Columns

For calculated columns, the default context of the calculation is the row itself. In Chapter 9, we created a calculated column to give us the number of accepted products using the following expression:

```
[NumberProduced] - [NumberRejected]
```

This expression is evaluated for each row in the table. As this is done, the values for NumberProduced and NumberRejected from each row are used to create a result for that row. We saw this in the previous chapter in Figure 9-28.

The Default Context for Measures

Measures are not created as a table row. Instead, they are created below the table in the Measure Grid. This difference in location provides a reminder of the measure's context.

The default context for a measure is the entire table. For this reason, we must utilize aggregate functions when creating measures. We need to give the model a way to take values from multiple rows in the table and calculate a single result. We saw this in the previous chapter in Figure 9-13.

Aggregate Functions in Calculated Columns

While aggregate functions are required in measures, they can also be used in calculated columns. The default context for an aggregate function is the entire table (see Figure 10-12). When evaluating the expression for the row indicated by the large white arrow, the SUM() function adds together the values in the NumberProduced column from all of the rows in the table to get the total of 725.

NOTE

If you add the calculated column shown in Figure 10-12 to the Manufacturing Info table in your model, you will get a result much larger than 725. Figure 10-12 and those that follow are using a simplified version of the Manufacturing Info data for clarity and simplicity of illustration. Also, in the name of clarity and simplicity, the text and illustrations will use the Date Of Manufacture field in the Manufacturing Info table. When actually creating measures later in this chapter, we will use the related Time table and its Time Hierarchy for our date references.

This difference in default context can be useful. We can calculate things such as percent of total. This is done using the following expression:

```
=[NumberProduced] / SUM([NumberProduced])
```

as shown in Figure 10-13.

Manufacturing Info   =SUM([NumberProduced])

Date Of Manufacture	Product Code	Machine Number	Number Produced	Calculated Column1
1/1/2009	11	1	100	725
1/1/2009	11	2	50	725
1/1/2009	12	1	200	725
1/2/2009	11	1	150	725
1/2/2009	12	1	125	725
1/3/2009	11	1	75	725
1/3/2009	11	2	25	725

Figure 10-12 *An aggregate function in a calculated column*

Manufacturing Info

=[NumberProduced] / SUM([NumberProduced])   100/ 725 = .1379

Date Of Manufacture	Product Code	Machine Number	Number Produced	Calculated Column1
1/1/2009	11	1	100	13.79%
1/1/2009	11	2	50	6.90%
1/1/2009	12	1	200	27.59%
1/2/2009	11	1	150	20.69%
1/2/2009	12	1	125	17.24%
1/3/2009	11	1	75	10.34%
1/3/2009	11	2	25	3.45%

Figure 10-13 *Calculating percent of total*

The first reference to the NumberProduced column is in the default context of the calculated column so, when evaluating the value for the row indicated by the large white arrow, it will return the value for the NumberProduced column in that row. The second reference to the NumberProduced column is in the default context of the aggregate function, so the result of the aggregate function will be the sum of all the values in the NumberProduced column for all the rows. When we take the first and divide it by the second, and then format as a percentage, we get the percent of total.

Filtering Aggregates

Being able to use aggregate functions to produce values across the entire table is useful in some circumstances, as we just saw. However, in many situations, we want to use aggregate functions on a subset of the rows in the table. We, along with our end users, can create these subsets in a couple of different ways. First, we can use functions to modify the context of an aggregation. Second, our end users can filter the data as they perform their analysis using a front-end tool.

CALCULATE(Expression, Filter1, Filter2, …)

We first explore modifying the context of an aggregate by using functions. This is a two-step process. First, we use one function to create a framework for applying filters. Then, we add one or more filters.

The function that creates the framework is the CALCULATE() function. The CALCULATE() function provides a mechanism for executing an expression in a context other than its default context. The first parameter is a valid DAX expression. The second and following parameters are DAX filters. The DAX expression is executed

Manufacturing Info

Date Of Manufacture	Product Code	Machine Number	Number Produced
1/1/2013	11	1	100
1/1/2013	11	2	50
1/1/2013	12	1	200
1/2/2013	11	1	150
1/2/2013	12	1	125
1/3/2013	11	1	75
1/3/2013	11	2	25
			725

Total Products:=CALCULATE(SUM([NumberProduced]))

Figure 10-14 *The CALCULATE() function with no filter parameters*

in the context resulting from the application of the filters. This resulting context is a table whose rows all satisfy the filter conditions. The filter parameters are optional.

Let's look at what happens when we use the CALCULATE() function in a measure without any filter parameters. We can wrap the CALCULATE() function around the SUM() function and take the sum of the NumberProduced as follows:

```
Total Produced:=CALCULATE(SUM([NumberProduced]))
```

The result is shown in Figure 10-14. The CALCULATE() function by itself does not change the context of the aggregation. The result is the sum of the NumberProduced column for the entire table.

Now let's add a filter to the expression for this measure. We will sum the number produced for product code 11, which is the product named Soaring Eagle. Here is the DAX expression:

```
Total Produced Soaring Eagle:=CALCULATE(SUM([NumberProduced]),
                        'Manufacturing Info'[ProductCode]=11)
```

Because this is a measure, we need to fully qualify our reference to the ProductCode column even though this measure is being defined in the Manufacturing Info table. We need to specify the table name in single quotes along with the column name in square brackets. The context of this measure is now just those rows where ProductCode=11, as shown in Figure 10-15. The top of the figure shows the values for our measures when they are queried using a pivot table in Excel. The lower portion of the figure shows how the data is filtered and aggregated to create that result.

What happens, now, when users come along and start using our model? Users may make use of front-end tools such as pivot tables in Excel to examine the data in the

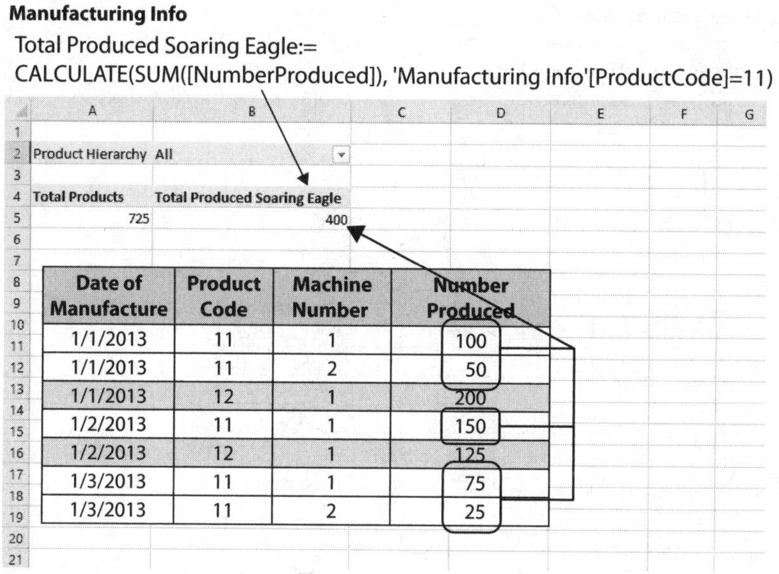

Manufacturing Info

Total Produced Soaring Eagle:=
CALCULATE(SUM([NumberProduced]), 'Manufacturing Info'[ProductCode]=11)

Figure 10-15 *The CALCULATE() function with a filter parameter*

model. As part of that process, users will create their own filters in the front-end tool to view the data in the model in a certain way. What happens when a user specifies a filter that interferes with the filter contained in our measure? Suppose the user specifies a filter such that only rows where ProductCode=12 are included in the result set. Figure 10-16 shows this situation. In this case, the user filter removes rows for all products except ProductCode=12. When our measure tries to aggregate an amount for rows where ProductCode=11, it doesn't find any in context being used for the aggregation. Consequently, it return a blank value.

Fortunately, DAX provides a couple of functions that can help us out in this situation: the ALL() function and the ALLEXCEPT() function.

ALL(TableNameOrTableFieldReference1, TableFieldReference2, …)

The ALL() function creates an alternative result set or table for our aggregate function to use as its context when it is calculating a value. The function creates the alternative context by essentially overriding specific user-created filters that are in place at the time the measure expression is evaluated. A specific example will make this easier to understand.

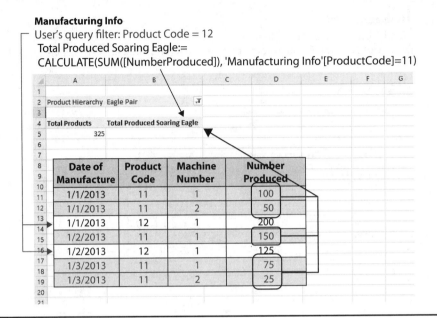

Figure 10-16 *A user filter interfering with our filter in the measure*

In this example, we have created a measure called "Total Produced All Dates." This measure returns the sum of the number of products produced across all dates in the dataset. To prevent any user-created filters from getting in the way of this calculation, we are going to add the ALL() function as a filter within the CALCULATE() function. The syntax for our measure is:

```
Total Produced All Dates:=CALCULATE(SUM([NumberProduced]),
                    ALL('Manufacturing Info'[Date of Manufacture]))
```

The ALL() function requires at least one parameter. In our example, the parameter is the Date of Manufacture column in the Manufacturing Info table. Essentially, this expression says that when calculating this measure, ignore *all* filters that might be in place on 'Manufacturing Info'[Date of Manufacture]. Instead, use *all* of the rows available when any filters on this particular column are disregarded.

Figure 10-17 shows the result. Even though the user has filtered out rows where Date of Manufacture is 1/2/2013 and 1/3/2013, these rows are included when calculating the value of our measure. The context for the aggregation created by the ALL() function within the CALCULATE() function includes all rows that would otherwise have been filtered out by the user's Date of Manufacture filter.

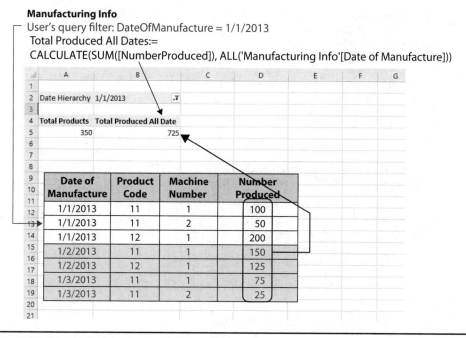

Manufacturing Info
User's query filter: DateOfManufacture = 1/1/2013
Total Produced All Dates:=
CALCULATE(SUM([NumberProduced]), ALL('Manufacturing Info'[Date of Manufacture]))

Figure 10-17 *Using the ALL() function to override user filtering*

NOTE

Things are a bit more complex in our actual model if we use the Time table and its Date Hierarchy. To completely eliminate any filtering on date in our measure, we would have to provide an ALL() function with multiple parameters—each parameter referencing a different level of the Date Hierarchy. The syntax for this DAX expression would be:

```
Total Produced All Dates:=CALCULATE(SUM([NumberProduced]),
                ALL('Time'[Date],
                    'Time'[Month],
                    'Time'[Quarter],
                    'Time'[Year]))
```

Now suppose our user adds a second filter criteria, this time selecting only those products where ProductCode=12. Our measure is set up to ignore all filters on the Date of Manufacture column but include filters on any other columns. In this case, our measure would produce the result shown in Figure 10-18.

The ALL() function can have one or more parameters. Each parameter is a table reference or a reference to a specific field in a table. The ALL() function builds the new aggregation context table, ignoring filters on each and every field or table specified as a parameter.

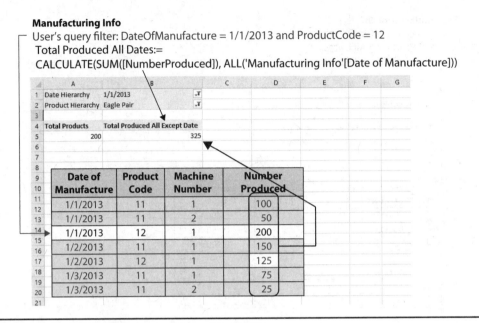

Manufacturing Info
User's query filter: DateOfManufacture = 1/1/2013 and ProductCode = 12
Total Produced All Dates:=
CALCULATE(SUM([NumberProduced]), ALL('Manufacturing Info'[Date of Manufacture]))

	A	B	C	D	E	F	G
1	Date Hierarchy	1/1/2013					
2	Product Hierarchy	Eagle Pair					
3							
4	Total Products	Total Produced All Except Date					
5	200	325					
6							
7							
8							

Date of Manufacture	Product Code	Machine Number	Number Produced
1/1/2013	11	1	100
1/1/2013	11	2	50
1/1/2013	12	1	200
1/2/2013	11	1	150
1/2/2013	12	1	125
1/3/2013	11	1	75
1/3/2013	11	2	25

Figure 10-18 *The ALL() function reacting to two user filter conditions*

ALLEXCEPT(TableName, TableFieldReference1, TableFieldReference2, ...)

Whereas the ALL() function enables us to specify a field or table and instructs the aggregation to ignore all filters on that field or table, the ALLEXCEPT() function enables us to specify a field or table and instructs the aggregate to ignore all filters except for those on that field or table. The first parameter of this function, TableName, specifies the name of the table whose rows we are filtering. The second parameter, and subsequent parameters, specify a table or field whose filters are exceptions and will apply to the aggregation context.

Figure 10-19 shows an example of a measure using the ALLEXCEPT() function. In this case, our measure is ignoring all filters except for those that apply to Date of Manufacture. The syntax for this measure is:

```
Total Produced All Except Date:=CALCULATE(SUM([NumberProduced]),
    ALLEXCEPT('Manufacturing Info', 'Manufacturing Info'[Date of
Manufacture]))
```

In Figure 10-19, the filter on ProductCode is ignored, but the filter on Date of Manufacture is applied when calculating the measure result.

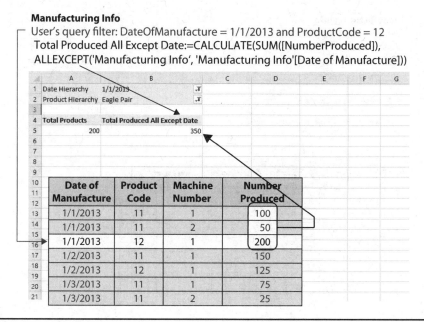

Manufacturing Info
User's query filter: DateOfManufacture = 1/1/2013 and ProductCode = 12
Total Produced All Except Date:=CALCULATE(SUM([NumberProduced]),
ALLEXCEPT('Manufacturing Info', 'Manufacturing Info'[Date of Manufacture]))

Figure 10-19 *Using the ALLEXCEPT() function to override user filtering*

Combining Filters

Let's return briefly to our original filtering example, the Total Produced Soaring Eagle measure. For that measure, we wanted to show the total produced for the Soaring Eagle product. Figure 10-16 shows how the user's filtering can get in the way of the filtering in our measure. To overcome this, we can improve our measure by combining two filters in the CALCULATE() statement to get exactly what we want. The syntax for this improved measure is:

```
Total Producted Soaring Eagle:=CALCULATE(SUM([NumberProduced]),
                    ALL('Manufacturing Info'[ProductCode]),
                    'Manufacturing Info'[ProductCode]=11)
```

Because we are using the ALL() function with reference to the ProductCode column, our measure calculation context starts out ignoring the user's filter on ProductCode and including all of the rows no matter what their product code might be. Then, we can set our filter ProductCode=11 inside the calculation context to include only those rows for Soaring Eagle (ProductCode 11). The result of this new measure expression is shown in Figure 10-20.

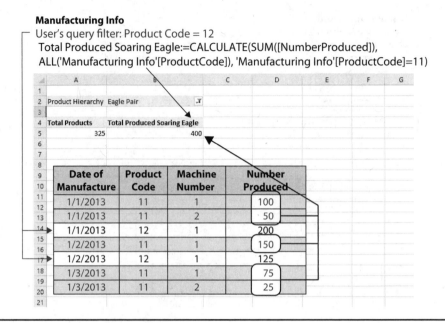

Figure 10-20 *Combining multiple filters in a CALCULATE() function*

Table-Valued Functions

In the next section of this chapter, we are going to look at the aggregate functions available in the DAX language. Before we do that, however, we need to look at another group of DAX functions—those that return a table. These table-valued functions are used as input to some types of aggregate functions, thus our need to consider the table-valued functions first.

A table-valued function takes a table as its input. It applies a filter to that table or in some other way manipulates the rows in that table and, in turn, produces a table as its output. That resulting table cannot be displayed directly. It can only be used as the input to another function that requires a table as one of its input parameters.

FILTER(TableExpression, Filter)

The FILTER() function applies a filter to a table to create a new table from the resulting subset of the initial table. The Filter is a Boolean expression that is evaluated for each row in the specified table. Rows where the Boolean expression evaluates to true are included in the resulting table.

The following example creates a table of all the rows in the Manufacturing Info table that have 500 or more products produced:

```
FILTER('Manufacturing Info', [NumberProduced] >= 500)
```

RELATEDTABLE(TableExpression)

The RELATEDTABLE() function is similar to the RELATED() function we saw in Chapter 9. It makes use of a one-to-many relationship between the table where the function is used and the table specified by the TableExpression parameter. The RELATED() function takes a foreign key and uses the relationship to find the record containing the matching primary key. The RELATEDTABLE() function takes a primary key and uses the relationship to find all the rows containing a matching foreign key. Where the RELATED() function works from the "many" side of the relationship to find the "one," the RELATEDTABLE() function works from the "one" side of the relationship to find the "many." Note that the TableExpression can be a table in the model or it can be the resultset from another table-valued function.

The following example can be used in the Products table to create a table of all the rows in the Manufacturing Info table related to each product:

```
RELATEDTABLE('Manufacturing Info')
```

As we will see in the next section of this chapter, we can then use the table that results from the RELATEDTABLE() function as a parameter to an aggregate function. This enables us to sum a field or count rows in a related table.

CALCULATETABLE(TableExpression, Filter1, Filter2)

The CALCULATETABLE() function is almost identical to the RELATEDTABLE() function. Even though the word "RELATED" is not present in the name of the function, the CALCULATETABLE() function utilizes any relationship that exists between the table where the function is used and the table specified by the TableExpression parameter. The only difference is the CALCULATETABLE() function allows you to add filters by specifying additional filter parameters. Note that the TableExpression can be a table in the model or it can be the resultset from another table-valued function.

The following example can be used in the Products table to create a table of all the rows in the Manufacturing Info table related to each product where the MachineNumber is 1:

```
CALCULATETABLE('Manufacturing Info',
                    'Manufacturing Info'[MachineNumber] = 1)
```

Additional Filter and Table Functions

DAX includes a number of additional filter and table functions enabling us to create exactly the context needed for our analysis. More information on these functions is available through the Microsoft Developer Network (MSDN) online. These are shown in Table 10-5.

Syntax	Result
ADDMISSINGITEMS(ShowAllColumn[, ShowAllColumn]..., Table, GroupingColumn [, GroupingColumn]...[, FilterTable]...)	Adds combinations of items from multiple columns that are not present in a table
ALLNONBLANKROW(TableOrColumn)	Using the parent table of a relationship, this function returns all rows excluding the blank row or all distinct values in a column excluding the blank row. It disregards any context filter that might be in place.
ALLSELECTED(TableOrColumn)	Removes all context filters from columns and rows in the current query
CROSSFILTER(Column1, Column2, Direction)	Specifies the cross-filtering direction to be used for an existing relationship in a calculation
DISTINCT(Column)	Returns a one-column table containing the distinct values from a specified column
EARLIER(Column, EvaluationLevel))	Returns the current value of the specified column in an outer evaluation pass of the column
EARLIEST(Column)	Returns the current value of the specified column in an outer evaluation pass of the column. This function is similar to the EARLIER() function, but allows for the specification of one additional level of recursion.
FILTERS(Column)	Returns the values that are directly applied as filters to the specified column
HASONEFILTER(Column)	Returns true when there is only one directly filtered value on the specified column, otherwise false
HASONEVALUE(Column)	Returns true when the specified column contains only one distinct value, otherwise false
ISCROSSFILTERED(Column)	Returns true when the specified column or another column in the same or a related table is being filtered, otherwise false
ISFILTERED(Column)	Returns true when the specified column is being filtered directly, otherwise false
KEEPFILTERS(Expression)	Modifies how filters are applied within a CALCULATE() or CALCULATETABLE() function
SUBSTITUTEINDEX(Table, IndexColumn, IndexColumnsTable, [OrderBy, [Order], ...)	Returns a table representing a left semi-join between two specified tables
VALUES(TableOrColumn)	Returns a one-column table containing the distinct values from the specified table or column

Table 10-5   *Additional Filter and Table Functions*

Aggregate Functions

Now that you know a bit about table-valued functions, let's take a look at some of the basic aggregate functions available in the DAX language. The aggregate functions come in several varieties. Standard aggregate functions calculate their aggregation on a field found in the table where they are used.

Aggregate functions with an "X" appended to their name require a table as their first parameter. (This is where the FILTER(), RELATEDTABLE(), and CALCULATETABLE() functions come into play.) These "X" functions calculate their aggregation in the context of the table passed as that first parameter. The standard and "X" aggregate functions are able to perform aggregations on fields with numeric and date types only.

Aggregate functions with an "A" appended to their name will work with additional types of data. They will work with Boolean values and with text values. When working with Boolean values, true is considered to be 1 and false is considered to be 0. A text value is always considered to be 0.

The final types of aggregate functions have an "AX" appended to their function name. These functions combine the characteristics of both the "X" and "A" aggregate functions. They require a table as their first parameter and calculate in the context of that table. They handle Boolean and text values as described earlier.

You should be aware of the fact that there is a performance difference between the various types of aggregate functions. Aggregate functions that use a field as their only parameter are able to use the data model very efficiently to obtain their results. Aggregate functions that allow an expression as one of their parameters (those ending in "X") must be evaluated row by row and can be slower when working with large tables.

AVERAGE(Field)

Calculates the mean of the values in the specified field. Works with numeric and date types only.

Example:

```
=AVERAGE([Accepted Products])
```

AVERAGEA(Field)

Calculates the mean of the values in the specified field. Handles Boolean and text data types as well as numeric and date data types.

Example:

```
=AVERAGEA([Accepted Products])
```

AVERAGEX(Table, Expression)

Calculates the mean of the values yielded by the expression in the context of the specified table.

Example:

```
=AVERAGEX(RELATEDTABLE('Manufacturing Info'),
                        'Manufacturing Info'[Accepted Products])
```

CONCATENATEX(Table, Field, [Delimiter])

Concatenates string values from multiple rows in a table.

Example:

```
=CONCATENATEX('Products',[ProductName], ", ")
```

COUNT(Field)

Counts the number of rows in which the specified field contains a numeric or date value.

Example:

```
=COUNT([Accepted Products])
```

COUNTA(Field)

Counts the number of rows in which the specified field contains a value.

Example:

```
=COUNTA([Accepted Products])
```

COUNTAX(Table, Expression)

Counts the number of rows in which the expression yields a value in the context of the specified table.

Example:

```
=COUNTAX(RELATEDTABLE('Manufacturing Info'),
                        'Manufacturing Info'[Accepted Products])
```

COUNTBLANK(Field)

Counts the number of rows in which the specified field is blank. If no rows have a blank value, a blank is returned by the function.

Example:

```
=COUNTBLANK([NumberRejected])
```

COUNTROWS(Table)

Counts the number of rows in the specified table.
    Example:

```
=COUNTROWS(RELATEDTABLE('Manufacturing Info'))
```

COUNTX(Table, Expression)

Counts the number of rows in which the expression yields a numeric or date value in the context of the specified table.
    Example:

```
=COUNTX(RELATEDTABLE('Manufacturing Info'),
                      'Manufacturing Info'[Accepted Products])
```

DISTINCTCOUNT(Field)

Counts the number of distinct values in the specified field.
    Example:

```
=DISTINCTCOUNT([ProductTypeName])
```

GEOMEAN(Field)

Returns the geometric mean of the values in the specified field. Works with numeric and date types only.
    Example:

```
=GEOMEAN([Accepted Products])
```

GEOMEANX(Table, Expression)

Returns the geometric mean of the values yielded by the expression in the context of the specified table.
    Example:

```
=GEOMEANX(RELATEDTABLE('Manufacturing Info'),
                       'Manufacturing Info'[Accepted Products])
```

MAX(Field)

Returns the maximum of the values in the specified field. Works with numeric and date types only.

Example:

```
=MAX([Accepted Products])
```

MAXA(Field)

Returns the maximum of the values in the specified field. Handles Boolean and text data types as well as numeric and date data types.

Example:

```
=MAXA([Accepted Products])
```

MAXX(Table, Expression)

Returns the maximum of the values yielded by the expression in the context of the specified table.

Example:

```
=MAXX(RELATEDTABLE('Manufacturing Info'),
                    'Manufacturing Info'[Accepted Products])
```

MEDIAN(Field)

Returns the median of the values in the specified field. Works with numeric and date types only.

Example:

```
=MEDIAN([Accepted Products])
```

MEDIANX(Table, Expression)

Returns the median of the values yielded by the expression in the context of the specified table.

Example:

```
=MEDIANX(RELATEDTABLE('Manufacturing Info'),
                      'Manufacturing Info'[Accepted Products])
```

MIN(Field)

Returns the minimum of the values in the specified field. Works with numeric and date types only.

Example:

```
=MIN([Accepted Products])
```

MINA(Field)

Returns the minimum of the values in the specified field. Handles Boolean and text data types as well as numeric and date data types.

Example:

```
=MINA([Accepted Products])
```

MINX(Table, Expression)

Returns the minimum of the values yielded by the expression in the context of the specified table.

Example:

```
=MINX(RELATEDTABLE('Manufacturing Info'),
                    'Manufacturing Info'[Accepted Products])
```

PRODUCT(Field)

Multiplies the values in the specified field.

Example:

```
=PRODUCT([Multiples])
```

PRODUCTX(Table, Expression)

Multiplies the values yielded by the expression in the context of the specified table.

Example:

```
=PRODUCTX(RELATEDTABLE('Multiples Table'),
                    'Multiples Table'[Multiples])
```

SUM(Field)

Calculates the total of the values in the specified field.

Example:

```
=SUM([Accepted Products])
```

SUMX(Table, Expression)

Calculates the total of the values yielded by the expression in the context of the specified table.

Example:

```
=SUMX(RELATEDTABLE('Manufacturing Info'),
                        'Manufacturing Info'[Accepted Products])
```

DAX Functions for Time Analytics

One of the reasons we create a model is to capture time analytics within the model. We do this in a Tabular model through the use of DAX functions. Here is a basic overview of a few of the time analytic functions available to us.

The DAX time analytics functions work with a standard Gregorian calendar year. They can also work with your organization's fiscal year, if that year is based on Gregorian calendar months. All you need to do is specify the year-end date for that fiscal calendar. If your organization uses a week-based fiscal calendar, such as those used in retail or manufacturing, you will need to use more complex DAX expressions to create your own custom time analytics.

CLOSINGBALANCEMONTH(Expression, Dates, Filter)
CLOSINGBALANCEQUARTER(Expression, Dates, Filter)
CLOSINGBALANCEYEAR(Expression, Dates, Filter, YearEndDate)

The CLOSINGBALANCE*period*() functions enable us to perform calculations with semi-additive measures. A semi-additive dimension may be summed across certain slicers but not across others. Inventory levels are the classic example. The sum of the inventory amounts for each product yields the total number of products in the warehouse. However, the sum of the first three months' inventory amounts does not give the inventory amount at the end of the first quarter. It is the inventory amount for the last month of the quarter, the "closing balance for the quarter," that is the inventory amount for the quarter.

The CLOSINGBALANCE*period*() functions provide a way to find these end-of-period amounts. Three different periods are supported. There are functions for end of month, end of quarter, and end of year.

The Expression parameter must return a numeric value. This is the quantity we want to find the closing balance for. In the example discussed earlier, this would be the number of products in the warehouse.

The Dates parameter must be one of the following:

- A reference to a field containing date/time values
- A table-valued function call that returns a table with a single column of dates
- A Boolean expression that defines a single-column table of date/time values

This field is used to determine which numeric quantity is the one for the end of the period. The Filter parameter is optional. It is a filter expression used to modify the context of the function.

Example:

```
=CLOSINGBALANCEMONTH(SUM('Inventory Info'[InventoryLevel]), 'Time'[Date])
```

DATEADD(Dates, NumberOfIntervals, Interval)

The DATEADD() function starts with a given date and adds a set number of time intervals—years, months, etc.—to it to produce a new date. The number of intervals may be either positive to move forward in time or negative to move backward in time. Valid values for interval are

- Year
- Quarter
- Month
- Day

Interval should not be enclosed in quotes.

```
=DATEADD('Manufacturing Info'[Date of Manufacture], 1, year)
```

DATESBETWEEN(Dates, StartDate, EndDate)

The DATESBETWEEN() function returns a table with a single column that contains all of the dates between the start date and the end date.

```
Accepted June to Mid July:=CALCULATE(SUM('Manufacturing Info'[NumberAccepted]),
        DATESBETWEEN('Manufacturing Info'[Date of Manufacture],
        DATE(2014,6,1), DATE(2014,7,15))
```

DATESINPERIOD(Dates, StartDate, NumberOfIntervals, Interval)

The DATESINPERIOD() function works similar to the DATESBETWEEN() function in that it returns a table with a single column of dates. However, DATESINPERIOD() uses the number of time intervals relative to a starting date to calculate the date range. Valid values for interval are

▶ Year

▶ Quarter

▶ Month

▶ Day

Interval should not be enclosed in quotes.

```
Accepted for Past 3 Weeks:=CALCULATE(SUM('Manufacturing Info'[NumberAccepted]),
        DATESINPERIOD('Manufacturing Info'[Date of Manufacture],
        DATE(2014,6,1), -21, day)
```

DATESMTD(Dates)
DATESQTD(Dates)
DATESYTD(Dates, [YearEndDate])

In the discussion of the CLOSINGBALANCE*period*() functions, one possibility for the second parameter was a table-valued function returning a single column of dates. The DATES*period*() functions do just that. Given a column containing dates, these functions return a table of dates up to and including the current date in the context. There are functions for month to date, quarter to date, and year to date.

The Dates parameter must be one of the following:

▶ A reference to a field containing date/time values

▶ A table-valued function call that returns a table with a single column of dates

▶ A Boolean expression that defines a single-column table of date/time values

For example, suppose the DATESMTD() function is called in a column containing a reference to January 15, 2009. January 15, 2009 becomes the context for the function call. The function would return a table with rows for January 1, 2009 through January 15, 2009.

```
=CALCULATE(SUM('Manufacturing Info'[NumberAccepted]),
  ALLEXCEPT('Manufacturing Info', 'Manufacturing Info'[ProductCode]),
  DATESYTD('Manufacturing Info'[Date of Manufacture]))
```

ENDOFMONTH(Dates)
ENDOFQUARTER(Dates)
ENDOFYEAR(Dates)

The ENDOF*period*() functions return a single column, single row table containing the last date in the month, quarter, or year in the given context. This allows you to easily find the last date in a period without doing a lot of fancy date calculations. Those of you that have had to do those date calculations know how nice these functions are to have in the arsenal.

Example:

```
=ENDOFMONTH('Manufacturing Info'[Date of Manufacture])
```

FIRSTDATE(Dates)

The FIRSTDATE() function returns a single-column, single-row table containing the first date in the current context.

Example:

```
=FIRSTDATE('Manufacturing Info'[Date of Manufacture])
```

LASTDATE(Dates)

The LASTDATE() function returns a single-column, single-row table containing the last date in the current context.

Example:

```
=LASTDATE('Manufacturing Info'[Date of Manufacture])
```

NEXTDAY(Dates)
NEXTMONTH(Dates)
NEXTQUARTER(Dates)
NEXTYEAR(Dates)

The NEXT*period* functions return a table containing all of the dates within the next period in the current context.

Example:

```
=CALCULATE(SUM('Manufacturing Info'[NumberProduced]),
                          NEXTMONTH('Manufacturing Info'[Date])
```

OPENINGBALANCEMONTH(Expression, Dates [, Filter])
OPENINGBALANCEQUARTER(Expression, Dates [, Filter])
OPENINGBALANCEYEAR(Expression, Dates [, Filter])

The OPENINGBALANCE*period* functions evaluate the given expression on the first day of the specified period.

Example:

```
=OPENINGBALANCEQUARTER(SUMX('Manufacturing Info',
   'Manufacturing Info'[NumberProduced] - 'Manufacturing Info'[NumberRejected),
   'Manufacturing Info'[Date of Manufacture])
```

PARALLELPERIOD(Dates, NumPeriods, Period)

The PARALLELPERIOD() function also returns a table of dates. It takes the dates passed as the first parameter and shifts those dates by the specified number of periods. The PARALLELPERIOD() function always returns all of the dates in the specified period. For example, if the Dates parameter contains dates from June 10, 2011 through June 20, 2011, the NumPeriods is −1, and the Period parameter is month, the PARALLELPERIOD() function will return a table of dates from June 1, 2010 to June 30, 2010.

The Dates parameter must be one of the following:

▶ A reference to a field containing date/time values

▶ A table-valued function call that returns a table with a single column of dates

▶ A Boolean expression that defines a single-column table of date/time values

A period can be any of the following:

▶ Month

▶ Quarter

▶ Year

The period value is not put in quotes.

Example:

```
=CALCULATE(SUM('Manufacturing Info'[NumberAccepted]),
  ALLEXCEPT('Manufacturing Info', 'Manufacturing Info'[ProductCode]),
  PARALLELPERIOD('Manufacturing Info'[Date of Manufacture], -1, month))
```

PREVIOUSDAY(Dates)
PREVIOUSMONTH(Dates)
PREVIOUSQUARTER(Dates)
PREVIOUSYEAR(Dates)

The PREVIOUS*period* functions return a table containing all of the dates within the previous period in the current context.

Example:

```
=CALCULATE(SUM('Manufacturing Info'[NumberProduced]),
             PREVIOUSMONTH('Manufacturing Info'[Date of Manufacture]))
```

SAMEPERIODLASTYEAR(Dates)

The SAMEPERIODLASTYEAR() function is similar to a call to the PARALLELPERIOD() function with the NumPeriods parameter set to −1 and the Periods parameter set to year. The difference is the SAMEPERIODLASTYEAR() function returns one and only one date in the output table for each date in the Dates parameter. It does not fill in the entire period as the PARALLELPERIOD() function does.

The Dates parameter must be one of the following:

► A reference to a field containing date/time values

► A table-valued function call that returns a table with a single column of dates

► A Boolean expression that defines a single-column table of date/time values

Example:

```
=CALCULATE(SUM('Manufacturing Info'[NumberAccepted]),
  ALLEXCEPT('Manufacturing Info', 'Manufacturing Info'[ProductCode]),
  SAMEPERIODLASTYEAR('Manufacturing Info'[Date of Manufacture]))
```

STARTOFMONTH(Dates)
STARTOFQUARTER(Dates)
STARTOFYEAR(Dates)

The STARTOF*period*() functions return a single-column, single-row table containing the first date in the month, quarter, or year in the given context. This allows you to easily find the first date in a period.

Example:

```
=STARTOFMONTH('Manufacturing Info'[Date of Manufacture])
```

TOTALMTD(Expression, Dates, Filter)
TOTALQTD(Expression, Dates, Filter)
TOTALYTD(Expression, Dates, Filter,[YearEndDate])

The TOTAL*period*() functions enable us to total a numeric quantity to get a period-to-date value. There are functions for month to date, quarter to date, and year to date. The Expression parameter must return a numeric value.

The Dates parameter must be one of the following:

▶ A reference to a field containing date/time values

▶ A table-valued function call that returns a table with a single column of dates

▶ A Boolean expression that defines a single-column table of date/time values

The Filter parameter is optional. It is a filter expression used to modify the context of the function.

Example:

```
=TOTALYTD(SUM('Manufacturing Info'[NumberAccepted]),
   'Manufacturing Info'[Date of Manufacture])
```

Additional DAX Functions

Along with the workhorse functions we've covered so far, DAX has a number of other functions that aid us in producing exactly the values we and our users need. We take a quick look at those functions here.

Date and Time Functions

The date functions in DAX allow us to manipulate date/time data types. Shown in Table 10-6.

Informational Functions

The informational functions in DAX tell us something about a column, an expression, or the environment in which we are working. Shown in Table 10-7.

Logical Functions

The logical functions in DAX allow us to perform true/false decision making in our expressions. Shown in Table 10-8.

Text Functions

The text functions in DAX allow us to manipulate textual data. Shown in Table 10-9.

Grouping and Set Functions

The grouping and set functions in DAX allow us to create and manipulate tables as sets of rows. Shown in Table 10-10.

Math and Trigonometric Functions

The math and trigonometric functions in DAX allow us to do complex mathematical calculations. Shown in Table 10-11.

Statistical Functions

The statistical functions enable us to add statistical analysis to our DAX expressions. Shown in Table 10-12.

Putting DAX Functions to Use

Now that you have been introduced to some of the basic DAX concepts and functionality, we look at two ways to put DAX, and the calculations it creates, to use. First, we examine the process for creating KPIs in a Tabular model. Second, we see how to create security roles.

Creating a Key Performance Indicator

As we have stated previously, one of the goals of our models is to capture business logic within the model. A key performance indicator (KPI) is an excellent way to accomplish

Syntax	Result
DATE(Year, Month, Day)	Returns a date/time data type value with the specified year, month, and day
DATEDIFF(StartDate, EndDate, Interval)	Returns the number of intervals between two dates where interval can be: ► Year ► Quarter ► Month ► Week ► Day ► Hour ► Minute ► Second
DATEVALUE(DateText)	Converts a textual representation of a date into a date/time data type value
DAY(DateTime)	Returns the day of the month of the specified date
EDATE(StartDate, NumberOfMonths)	Returns the date that is the specified number of months before or after the given date
EOMONTH(StartDate, NumberOfMonths)	Returns the date that is the last day of the month before or after the given date
HOUR(DateTime)	Returns the hour portion of the specified date/time
MINUTE(DateTime)	Returns the minute portion of the specified date/time
MONTH(DateTime)	Returns the month portion of the specified date/time
NOW()	Returns a date/time data type value with the current date and time
SECOND(DateTime)	Returns the seconds portion of the specified date/time
TIME(Hour, Minute, Second)	Returns a date/time data type value with the specified hour, minute, and second
TIMEVALUE(TimeText)	Converts a textual representation of a time into a date/time data type value
TODAY()	Returns the current date as a date/time data type
WEEKDAY(DateTime, ReturnType)	Returns the day of the week number of the specified date/time. ReturnType may be: ► 1—week begins on Sunday with Sunday as day 1 and Saturday as day 7 ► 2—week begins on Monday with Monday as day 1 and Sunday as day 7 ► 3—week begins on Monday with Monday as day 0 and Sunday as day 6
WEEKNUM(DateTime, ReturnType)	Returns the week number in the current year for the specified date/time. ReturnType may be: ► 1—weeks begin on Sunday ► 2—weeks begin on Monday
YEAR(DateTime)	Returns the year portion of the specified date/time
YEARFRAC(StartDate, EndDate [, Basis])	Returns the number of whole days between the two dates. Basis may be: ► 0—US (NASD) 30/360 ► 1—Actual/Actual ► 2—Actual/360 ► 3—Actual/365 ► 4—European 30/360

Table 10-6   *DAX Date and Time Functions*

Syntax	Result
CONTAINS(Table, Column, Value [, Column, Value]...)	Returns true if the specified values exist or are contained in those specified columns
CUSTOMDATA()	Returns the content of the CustomData property in the connection string
ISBLANK(Value)	Returns true if the specified value is blank, otherwise false
ISERROR(Value)	Returns true if the specified value is in error, otherwise false
ISEVEN(Number)	Returns true if the specified number is even, otherwise false
ISLOGICAL(Value)	Returns true if the specified value is a logical data type
ISNONTEXT(Value)	Returns true if the specified value is not textual
ISNUMBER(Value)	Returns true if the specified value is numeric
ISONORAFTER(ScalarExpression1, ScalarExpression2 [, SortOrder [, ScalarExpression3, ScalarExpression4 [, SortOrder]], ...)	Compares each pair of scalar values based on the sort order specified or ascending if no sort order is specified. If each pair of values is in the designated sort order, the function returns true, otherwise false.
ISTEXT(Value)	Returns true if the specified value is textual
USERNAME	Returns the domain name and user name for the credentials used to connect to Analysis Services

Table 10-7 *DAX Informational Functions*

Syntax	Result
AND(LogicalExpression, LogicalExpression)	Returns true if both logical expressions are true, otherwise false
FALSE()	Returns false
IF(LogicalExpression, Expression1, Expression2)	Returns the content of expression 1 if the logical expression is true, otherwise returns the content of expression 2
IFERROR(Expression1, Expression2)	If expression 1 is in error, returns the content of expression 2, otherwise returns the content of expression 1
NOT(LogicalExpression)	Returns the opposite of the logical expression
OR(LogicalExpression, LogicalExpression)	Returns true if either logical expression is true, otherwise false
SWITCH(Expression, Value1, Result1 [, Value2, Result2]...[, ElseResult])	If the expression evaluates to value 1, then result 1 is returned. If the expression evaluates to value 2, then result 2 is returned. If the expression does not match any of the specified values, the else result is returned.
TRUE()	Returns true

Table 10-8 *DAX Logical Functions*

Syntax	Result
BLANK()	Returns a blank textual value
CODE(String)	Returns the numeric ANSI or Macintosh character set code for the first character in the string
CONCATENATE(String1, String2)	Returns the concatenation of the two strings
EXACT(String1, String2)	Returns true if the two strings are exactly the same
FIND(Search, Target [, [StartPosition] [, NotFound]])	Returns the starting position of the search text within the target text, optionally beginning at the starting position. If the search text is not found, the NotFound value is returned, if it has been specified. FIND() is case-sensitive.
FIXED(Number, Decimals, NoCommas)	Rounds a number to the specified number of decimals and returns the result as a textual value
FORMAT(Value, FormatString)	Formats the specified value according to the format string and returns the result as a textual value
LEFT(String, NumCharacters)	Returns the specified number of characters from the left of the string
LEN(String)	Returns the length of the string
LOWER(String)	Converts the string to all lowercase text
MID(String, StartPosition, NumCharacters)	Returns the specified number of characters from the string starting at the specified location
REPLACE(OldString, StartPosition, NumCharacters, NewString)	Replaces the specified number of characters in the old string at the starting position with the content of the new string
REPT(String, Repetitions)	Creates a new string by concatenating the specified string with itself the given number of repetitions
RIGHT(String, NumCharacters)	Returns the specified number of characters from the right of the string
SEARCH(Search, Target [, [StartPosition] [, NotFound]])	Returns the starting position of the search text within the target text, optionally beginning at the starting position. If the search text is not found, the NotFound value is returned, if it has been specified. SEARCH() is case-insensitive and accent-sensitive.
SUBSTITUTE(Target, OldString, NewString, InstanceNum)	Replaces the specified instance of the old string with the new string within the target text
TRIM(String)	Removes all spaces from the string except for single spaces between words
UPPER(String)	Converts the string to all uppercase text
VALUE(String)	Converts the string to a numeric value

Table 10-9   *DAX Text Functions*

Syntax	Result
EXCEPT(Table1, Table2)	Returns the rows of table 1 that do not appear in table 2
GROUPBY(Table, [GroupByColumn1] [, GroupByColumn2]... [, Name, Expression]...)	Groups the rows of the specified table on the given values creating new aggregated rows as specified. This function does not do an implicit CALCULATE on each aggregation expression.
INTERSECT(Table1, Table2)	Returns the rows present in both table 1 and table 2, retaining duplicates
ISEMPTY(Table)	Returns true if the table is empty, otherwise false
NATURALINNERJOIN(LeftTable, RightTable)	Performs an inner join of the two tables based on columns with the same name in both tables
NATURALLEFTOUTERJOIN(LeftTable, RightTable)	Performs a left outer join of the two tables based on columns with the same name in both tables
SUMMARIZE(Table, [GroupByColumn1] [, GroupByColumn2]... [, Name, Expression]...)	Groups the rows of the specified table on the given values creating new aggregated rows as specified. This function does an implicit CALCULATE on each aggregation expression.
SUMMARIZECOLUMNS(GroupByColumn1 [GroupByColumn2]...,[FilterTable]..., [Name, Expression]...)	Groups the rows on the given values within the specified filter context, creating new aggregate rows as specified
UNION(Table1, Table2 [, Table3]...)	Creates a union of the specified tables

Table 10-10 *DAX Grouping and Set Functions*

Syntax	Result
ABS(Number)	Returns the absolute value of a number
ACOS(Number)	Returns the arccosine of a number in radians
ACOSH(Number)	Returns the inverse hyperbolic cosine of a number
ASIN(Number)	Returns the arcsine of a number in radians
ASINH(Number)	Returns the inverse hyperbolic sine of a number
ATAN(Number)	Returns the arctangent of a number in radians
ATANH(Number)	Returns the inverse hyperbolic tangent of a number
CEILING(Number, Significance)	Rounds the number up to the nearest integer or the nearest multiple of the significance
COMBIN(NumberOfItems, NumberInEachCombination)	Returns the number of combinations for a given number of items
COMBINA(NumberOfItems, NumberInEachCombination)	Returns the number of combinations for a given number of items with repetitions

Table 10-11 *DAX Math and Trigonometric Functions (continued)*

Syntax	Result
COS(Number)	Returns the cosine of a given number in radians
COSH(Number)	Returns the hyperbolic cosine of a given number
CURRENCY(Number)	Returns the given number as a currency data type
DEGREES(Angle)	Returns the angle in radians converted to degrees
DIVIDE(Numerator, Denominator [, AlternateResult])	Returns the numerator divided by the denominator or an optional alternate result if there is a divide-by-zero error
EVEN(Number)	Returns the number rounded up to the nearest even integer
EXP(Number)	Returns e raised to the power of the given number
FACT(Number)	Returns the factorial of a number
FLOOR(Number, Significance)	Rounds the number down to the nearest multiple of the significance
GCD(Integer, Integer, …)	Returns the greatest common divisor of the integers specified
INT(Number)	Returns the number rounded down to the nearest integer
ISO.CEILING(Number, Significance)	An ISO-compatible version of the CEILING function
LCM(Integer, Integer, …)	Returns the least common multiple of the integers specified
LN(Number)	Returns the natural logarithm of a number
LOG(Number, base)	Returns the logarithm of a number using the specified base
LOG10(Number)	Returns the base-10 logarithm of a number
MROUND(Number, Multiple)	Returns the number rounded to the desired multiple
ODD(Number)	Returns the number rounded up to the nearest odd number
PI()	Returns the value of pi to 15 digits
POWER(Number, Power)	Returns a number raised to the specified power
QUOTIENT(Numerator, Denominator)	Returns the integer portion of the numerator divided by the denominator
RADIANS(Angle)	Returns the angle converted from degrees to radians
RAND()	Returns a random number greater than or equal to 0 and less than 1
RANDBETWEEN(LowerLimit, UpperLimit)	Returns a random number between the lower limit and the upper limit
ROUND(Number, NumberOfDigits)	Returns the number rounded to the specified number of digits to the right of the decimal point
ROUNDDOWN(Number, NumberOfDigits)	Returns the number rounded down to the specified number of digits to the right of the decimal point
ROUNDUP(Number, NumberOfDigits)	Returns the number rounded up to the specified number of digits to the right of the decimal point

Table 10-11   *DAX Math and Trigonometric Functions (continued)*

Syntax	Result
SIGN(Number)	Returns 1 if the number is positive, 0 if the number is zero, or −1 if the number is negative
SIN(Number)	Returns the sine of a given number in radians
SINH(Number)	Returns the hyperbolic sine of a given number
SQRT(Number)	Returns the square root of a given number
TAN(Number)	Returns the tangent of a given number in radians
TANH(Number)	Returns the hyperbolic tangent of a given number
TRUNC(Number)	Returns the integer portion of a number

Table 10-11   *DAX Math and Trigonometric Functions*

Syntax	Meaning
BETA.DIST(X, Alpha, Beta, Cumulative, [A], [B])	Returns the beta distribution
BETA.INV(Probability, Alpha, Beta, [A], [B])	Returns the inverse of the BETA.DIST() function
CHISQ.INV(Probability, DegreesOfFreedom)	Returns the inverse of the left-tailed probability of the chi-squared distribution
CHISQ.INV.RT(Probability, DegreesOfFreedom)	Returns the inverse of the right-tailed probability of the chi-squared distribution
CONFIDENCE.NORM(Alpha, StandardDeviation, SampleSize)	Returns the Confidence.Norm
CONFIDENCE.T(Alpha, StandardDeviation, SampleSize)	Returns the confidence interval for a population mean, using a Student's t distribution
EXPON.DIST(X, Lambda, Cumulative)	Returns the exponential distribution
PERCENTILE.EXC(Column, K)	Returns the k-th percentile of values in a range, where k is in the range 0..1, exclusive
PERCENTILE.INC(Column, K)	Returns the k-th percentile of values in a range, where k is in the range 0..1, inclusive
PERCENTILEX.EXC(Table, Expression, K)	Returns the percentile number of an expression evaluated for each row in a table, where k is in the range 0..1, exclusive
PERCENTILEX.INC(Table, Expression, K)	Returns the percentile number of an expression evaluated for each row in a table, where k is in the range 0..1, inclusive
POISSON.DIST(X, Mean, Cumulative)	Returns the Poisson distribution
RANK.EQ(Value, Column [, Order])	Returns the ranking of a number in a list of numbers
RANKX(Table, Expression [, Value [, Order [, Ties]]])	Returns the ranking of a number in a list of numbers for each row
STDEV.P(Column)	Returns the standard deviation of the entire population
STDEV.S(Column)	Returns the standard deviation of a sample population

Table 10-12   *DAX Statistical Functions (continued)*

Syntax	Meaning
STDEVX.P(Table, Expression)	Returns the standard deviation of the entire population for the specified table
STDEVX.S(Table, Expression)	Returns the standard deviation of a sample population for the specified table
SQRTPI(Number)	Returns the square root of (number * pi)
VAR.P(Column)	Returns the variance of the entire population
VAR.S(Column)	Returns the variance of a sample population
VARX.P(Table, Expression)	Returns the variance of the entire population for the specified table
VARX.S(Table, Expression)	Returns the variance of a sample population for the specified table
XIPR(Table, Values, Dates [, Guess])	Returns the internal rate of return for a schedule of cash flows that is not necessarily periodic
XNPV(Table, Values, Dates, Rate)	Returns the present value for a schedule of cash flows that is not necessarily periodic

Table 10-12 *DAX Statistical Functions*

this goal. The key performance indicator takes a measure and adds a target along with information on how to interpret the measure's performance against that target.

KPIs in a Tabular model include the following information:

▶ The measure the KPI is based upon

▶ A target value, either defined by another measure or entered as a constant value

▶ Threshold values

▶ An icon style

▶ Descriptions of the value, the status, the target, and the KPI itself

To create a KPI in a Tabular model, select an existing measure in the grid view of the model. With the measure selected, click the Create KPI button in the toolbar as shown in Figure 10-21. You may need to click the drop-down arrow at the end of the toolbar to find additional toolbar buttons in order to get to the KPI button. Clicking the KPI button will open the Key Performance Indicator dialog box.

Either click Absolute value and type in the target value for this measure, or leave Measure selected and pick the Measure that defines the target value from the drop-down list. Next, set the values to denote the transitions between the red, yellow, and green areas for the KPI. Also select how many thresholds there should be and how they

Figure 10-21 *The Create KPI button in the toolbar*

should be arranged—red to yellow to green, green to yellow to red, red to yellow to green to yellow to red, or green to yellow to red to yellow to green.

Select the style of icon you would like the KPI to use. Finally, fill in the desired description text for each of these items as desired. Simple as that. The Create KPI dialog box is shown in Figure 10-22. We will give this a try in the Learn By Doing exercise later in this chapter.

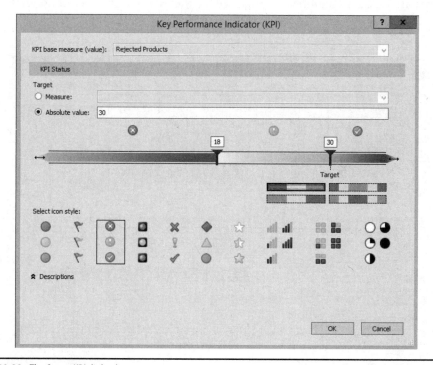

Figure 10-22 *The Create KPI dialog box*

Quick Launch (Ctrl+Q)
Perspective
<Default>
Roles

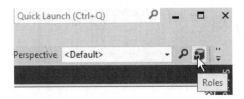

Figure 10-23 *The Roles button in the toolbar*

Role-Based Security

In many cases, we may want to limit the access certain individuals or groups have within a Tabular model. This is done by creating one or more roles within the model. A role is created by clicking the Roles button in the toolbar, as shown in Figure 10-23. This displays the Role Manager dialog box.

Using the Role Manager dialog box, we can define new security roles within the Tabular model. For each role, we can use DAX expressions to filter the rows of a given table that are visible to members of this role. In the example shown in Figure 10-24,

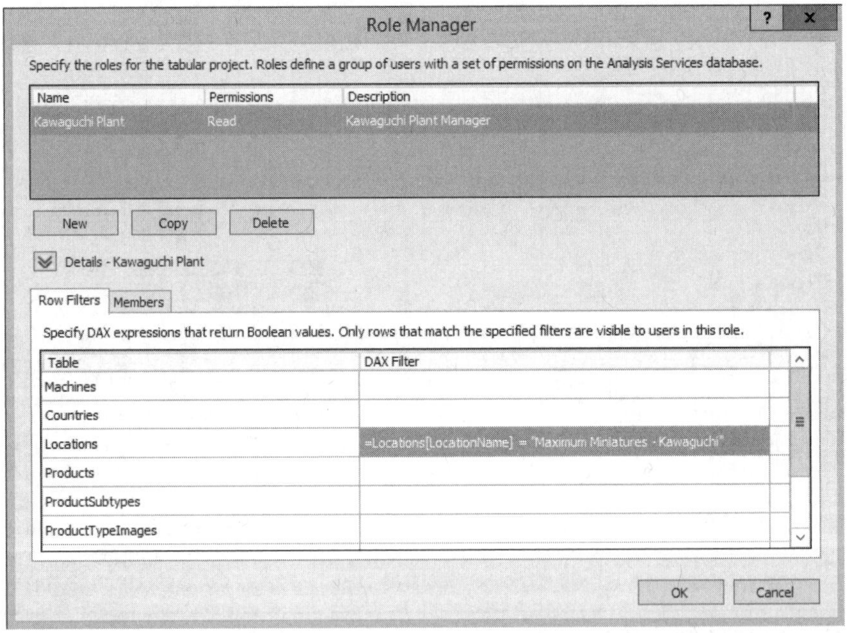

Role Manager
Specify the roles for the tabular project. Roles define a group of users with a set of permissions on the Analysis Services database.
Name
Permissions
Description
Kawaguchi Plant
Read
Kawaguchi Plant Manager
New
Copy
Delete
Details - Kawaguchi Plant
Row Filters
Members
Specify DAX expressions that return Boolean values. Only rows that match the specified filters are visible to users in this role.
Table
DAX Filter
Machines
Countries
Locations
=Locations[LocationName] = "Maximum Miniatures - Kawaguchi"
Products
ProductSubtypes
ProductTypeImages
OK
Cancel

Figure 10-24 *The Role Manager dialog box*

the members of the Kawaguchi Plant role can only see rows in the Locations table where the LocationName is "Maximum Miniatures - Kawaguchi."

The Members tab of the Role Manager dialog box enables us to specify Active Directory users or Active Directory groups that are members of a particular role.

Variables in the Tabular Model

Another new feature in the Tabular model in SQL Server 2016 is the use of variables within DAX expressions. Before variables, we had two options for creating complex business calculations. We could create multiple intermediate measures in a table, ultimately combining those intermediate measures into a final measure that produced the number we actually wanted to see. Alternatively, we could create a highly complex, multiply nested calculation to produce the desired result. Neither situation was ideal. Now we have variables to help handle this complexity.

Declaring DAX Variables and Assigning a Value

Variables are declared within a DAX expression using the var function. DAX variables are not strongly typed. Instead, they take on the type of the content assigned to them. The variable can hold either a scalar value (text, date/time, numeric, etc.) or a table.

Because DAX variables receive their type from the value assigned to them, DAX variables are declared and assigned a value at the same time. The format is:

```
VAR <variable name> = <expression>
```

For example:

```
VAR LastYearTotalProduced = CALCULATE([Total Products],
      SAMEPERIODLASTYEAR('Manufacturing Info'[Date of Manufacture]))
```

Note in the example that the expression used to define the value of the variable is dependent on the context. The SAMEPERIODLASTYEAR() function is going to return a different set of dates depending on what period the user is looking at. It is important to understand the value of the variable is not calculated only once when it is first defined in the model. It is part of a dynamic calculation that is being reevaluated each time the context of the expression changes.

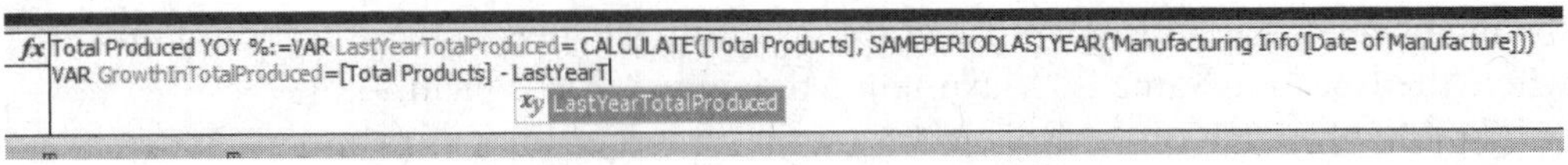

```
fx Total Produced YOY %:=VAR LastYearTotalProduced= CALCULATE([Total Products], SAMEPERIODLASTYEAR('Manufacturing Info'[Date of Manufacture]))
   VAR GrowthInTotalProduced=[Total Products] -LastYearT|
                                    xy  LastYearTotalProduced
```

Figure 10-25   *A DAX variable in auto-complete*

Using a DAX Variable

Once our variable has been declared, we can use it in other locations in our DAX expression. For example, we can use the LastYearTotalProduced variable in the initialization of another variable as follows:

```
VAR GrowthInTotalProduced=[Total Products] - LastYearTotalProduced
```

SQL Server Data Tools is even smart enough to recognize the variable and include it in the context-sensitive auto-complete, as shown in Figure 10-25.

Using Return in a Measure

Up to this point, our measures have consisted of a single DAX function. Now there may have been other functions nested within that function, but there was always a single outer DAX function. Whatever value was returned by this outermost function became the value of the measure.

When using DAX variables, our measure code looks more like a function written in C# or a stored procedure written in T-SQL. Similar to those two situations, we need a way to specify what is to be used as the final value for the C# function or the T-SQL stored procedure. As with those constructs, we use a return to specify our final result. The return includes an expression which is evaluated to determine the ultimate value for the measure.

In the example we have been building in this section, this is the statement that would return the final year over year growth calculation:

```
return IF([Total Products]<>0, DIVIDE(GrowthInTotalProduced,
                                       LastYearTotalProduced))
```

Deploying a Tabular Model

In the beginning of Chapter 9, we discussed the fact that any time you have a Tabular model open in SQL Server Data Tools, it creates a workspace database on the specified Tabular instance of SQL Server Analysis Services. It may be tempting to have users access this workspace database from a front-end tool for their analysis needs. However, there are several problems with this approach.

First, because the workspace database is an extension of the development environment, it should not be placed on a production server. It should reside on a workstation or a development server that is not generally available to your users. Second, the names assigned to workspace databases are long and cumbersome. Finally, a given workspace database exists on the Analysis Services server only when the associated Tabular model is open for modification in SQL Server Data Tools. In most cases, depending on configuration settings, as soon as the model project is closed, the workspace database disappears—a situation most users won't put up with.

When we are ready for users to access a Tabular model, we need to use the deploy process to create an instance of that model on a staging or production Analysis Services server. We will look at two different mechanisms for deploying a Tabular model to an Analysis Services server: deploying from SQL Server Data Tools and deploying through the Deployment Wizard.

Deploying from SQL Server Data Tools

The first deployment mechanism we will look at is through SQL Server Data Tools. This deployment mechanism is best for putting your model onto a testing or staging server.

Deployment Configuration

Before deploying, we must specify the name and location of the Analysis Services database where the model will reside. This is done in the Properties dialog box for the project, as shown in Figure 10-26.

We can set the following properties for the model in the server environment:

▶ **Processing Option** Determines the type of processing the model receives after it is deployed. Options are Full, Do Not Process, or Default.

▶ **Transactional Deployment** Determines whether the deployment process is completed as a single transaction. If not transactional, completed portions of the deployment will persist on the server even if a subsequent step in the deployment fails.

▶ **Server** The name of a Tabular instance of SQL Server Analysis Services.

▶ **Edition** The edition of SQL Server this model is targeted for. Options are

   ▶ Developer

   ▶ Enterprise

   ▶ Business Intelligence

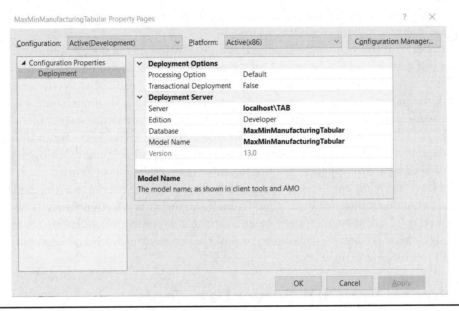

Figure 10-26 *The Properties dialog box for a Tabular model project*

- ▶ Enterprise: Core-Based Licensing
- ▶ Evaluation
- ▶ Standard
- ▶ **Database** The name of the Analysis Services database where this model will be deployed.
- ▶ **Model Name** The name of the model shown in client tools when connecting to it.
- ▶ **Version** This is a read-only property showing the version of the SQL Server Analysis Services instance.

Completing the Deployment

Once the deployment configuration is set, we can complete the deployment to the Analysis Services server. This is done using the Deploy dialog box, which can be launched from the Deploy menu choice on the Build menu. It can also be done by selecting Deploy from the context menu for the project in the Solution Explorer window.

This will initiate the deploy process. If the model has been set to process automatically as part of the deployment process, the status of that processing will be shown on the Deploy dialog box, as in Figure 10-27.

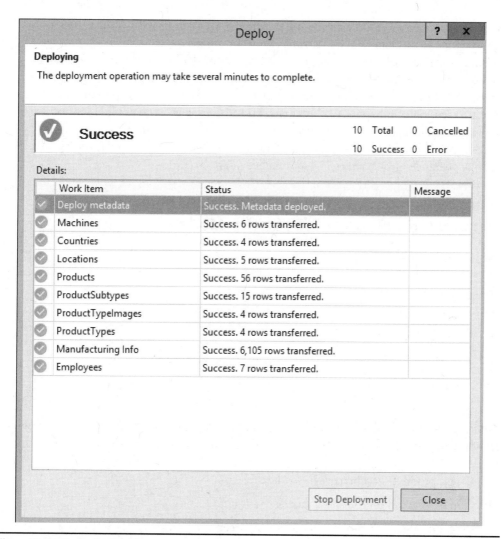

Figure 10-27 *The Deploy dialog box*

Deploying from the Analysis Services Deployment Wizard

Many times, we do not have access to the production instance of Analysis Services from our development SQL Server Data Tools environment. It may also be the case that a production deployment must be done by a database administrator. In cases such as these, we need to create a deployment script that can be transported to another machine or to another person in order to complete the deployment process. This is where the Analysis Services Deployment Wizard comes into play.

The process for deploying Tabular models and for deploying multidimensional models using the Analysis Services Deployment Wizard is exactly the same. This process is covered in the "Deploying from the Analysis Services Deployment Wizard" section of Chapter 12. The instructions there cover the deployment of a multidimensional model to a multidimensional instance of SQL Server Analysis Services. You can follow those same instructions to deploy your Tabular model to a Tabular instance of SQL Server Analysis Services.

Learn By Doing: Enhancing the Maximum Miniatures Manufacturing Tabular BI Semantic Model

Features Highlighted

- ▶ Using DAX functions
- ▶ Adding time analytics to a model
- ▶ Using DAX variables
- ▶ Creating a KPI
- ▶ Deploying a model

Business Need The VP of production for Max Min, Inc. has asked for the following additions to the MaxMinManufacturingTabular model:

- ▶ Total products accepted year-to-date
- ▶ Total accepted on the same day last year
- ▶ Total produced year over year growth percent
- ▶ A KPI of products rejected as a percentage of total products

The VP also wants to begin using the model as soon as possible.

Steps to Add Measures to the Model

1. Open SQL Server Data Tools.
2. Open the MaxMinManufacturingTabular model.
3. Change to the grid view of the model, if it opens in diagram view.

4. Click the Manufacturing Info tab.
5. Click the cell immediately below the Accepted Products measure in the Measure Grid.
6. Type the following in the formula bar at the top of the screen:

```
Accepted Products YTD:=CALCULATE([Accepted Products], DATESYTD('Time'[Date]))
```

7. Press ENTER.
8. In the Properties window, set Format to Whole Number.
9. In the Properties window, set Show Thousands Separator to true.
10. Click the cell immediately below the Accepted Products YTD measure.
11. Type the following in the formula bar at the top of the screen:

```
Accepted Products Last Year:=CALCULATE([Accepted Products],
                            SAMEPERIODLASTYEAR('Time'[Date]))
```

12. Press ENTER.
13. In the Properties window, set Format to Whole Number.
14. In the Properties window, set Show Thousands Separator to true.

Steps to Use DAX Variables to Create a Measure in the Model

1. Click the cell immediately below the Total Products measure in the Measure Grid.
2. Type the following in the formula bar at the top of the screen:

```
Total Produced YOY %:=VAR LastYearTotalProduced= CALCULATE([Total Products],
        SAMEPERIODLASTYEAR('Time'[Date]))
```

3. Click the double down arrow to the right of the formula bar to expand the formula entry area to be multiple lines.
4. Hold down SHIFT and press ENTER. This will take your cursor to a new line in the formula entry area without causing SQL Server Data Tools to try to evaluate the measure expression.
5. Type the following on the second line of the formula entry area:

```
VAR GrowthInTotalProduced=[Total Products] - LastYearTotalProduced
```

6. Hold down SHIFT and press ENTER.
7. Type the following on the third line of the formula entry area:

```
return IF([Total Products]<>0, DIVIDE(GrowthInTotalProduced,
                                LastYearTotalProduced))
```

```
Total Produced YOY %:= VAR LastYearTotalProduced = CALCULATE([Total Products], SAMEPERIODLASTYEAR('Time'[Date]))
VAR GrowthInTotalProduced = [Total Products] - LastYearTotalProduced
return IF([Total Products]<>0, DIVIDE(GrowthInTotalProduced, LastYearTotalProduced))
```

Figure 10-28 *Using DAX variables in a measure definition*

The formula entry area should appear as shown in Figure 10-28.

8. Press ENTER.

9. In the Properties window, set Format to Percentage.

Steps to Add a KPI to the Model

1. Click the cell below Rejected Products in the Measure Grid.

2. Enter the following formula:

```
Percent Rejected:=SUM([NumberRejected]) / SUM([NumberProduced])
```

3. Press ENTER.

4. In the Properties window, set Format to Percentage.

5. With the newly created Percent Rejected measure still selected, click the Create KPI button in the toolbar. The Key Performance Indicator (KPI) dialog box appears.

6. Click the Absolute value radio button.

7. Replace "100" with **.0102**.

8. Find the group of four color bars in the lower-right corner of the KPI Status area. Click the bar with green on the left, yellow in the middle, and red on the right, as shown in Figure 10-29.

9. Again in the KPI Status area, click the double-headed arrow at the far-right end of the color bar. Drag the double-headed arrow to the left slightly. This will shift the position of the two threshold indicators on the color bar.

10. Click the double-headed arrow at the far-left end of the color bar and drag it slightly to the left. You may also need to click the two black slider bars on the color bar and drag them Repeat this process until the color bar appears, as shown in Figure 10-30.

11. Replace "0.0001" with **0.0104**.

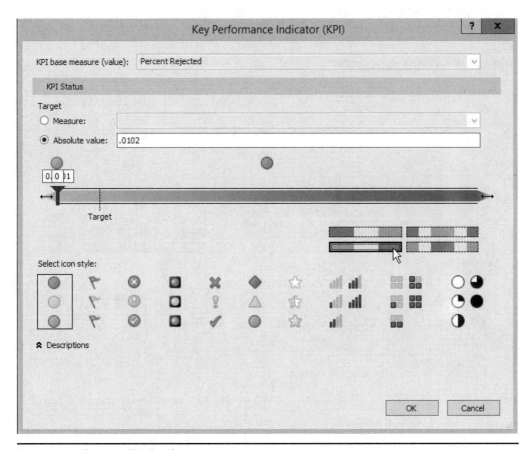

Figure 10-29 *Choosing a KPI color scheme*

12. Press TAB. The entry area containing "0.0104" moves to the right.
13. Replace "0" with **0.0102**.
14. Press TAB, and then use the double-headed arrows at the ends of the color bar to again have it divided into three roughly equal sections—one-third green, one-third yellow, and one-third red.
15. In the Select icon style area, click the set of icons with the red diamond/yellow triangle/green circle.
16. Click OK to exit the Key Performance Indicator (KPI) dialog box.

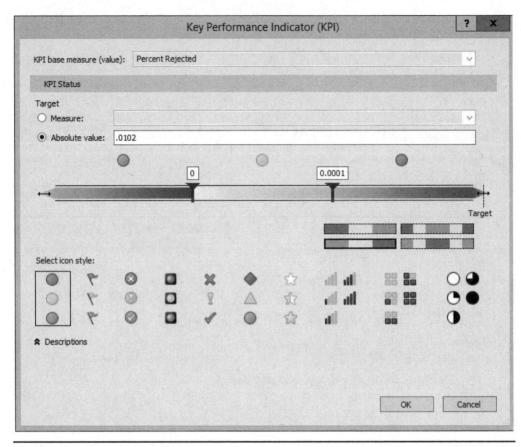

Figure 10-30 *Adjusting the threshold points on the color bar*

Steps to Deploy the MaxMinManufacturingTabular Model

1. Select Project | MaxMinManufacturingTabular Properties from the main menu. (The menu choice may just say "Properties" depending on what is selected at the time.) The MaxMinManufacturingTabular Property Pages dialog box appears.

2. For the Server property, enter the name of a Tabular instance of SQL Server Analysis Services where you have rights to create databases. (Do *not* perform this or any other Learn By Doing activity on a server used for production operations!)

3. For the Database property, enter **Max Min Manufacturing**.

4. For the Model Name property, enter **Max Min Manufacturing**.

5. Click OK to exit the MaxMinManufacturingTabular Property Pages dialog box.

6. Select Build | Deploy MaxMinManufacturingTabular from the main menu. The Deploy dialog box appears.

7. Enter the impersonation credentials password for each connection, if prompted, and click OK.

8. When the deploy and processing complete, click Close to exit the Deploy dialog box.

Steps to Deploy the MaxMinSalesTabular Model

1. Click Save All in the toolbar.

2. Close the MaxMinManufacturingTabular solution and open the MaxMinSalesTabular solution.

3. Select Project | MaxMinSalesTabular Properties from the main menu. (The menu choice may just say "Properties" depending on what is selected at the time.) The MaxMinSalesTabular Property Pages dialog box appears.

4. For the Server property, enter the name of a Tabular instance of SQL Server Analysis Services where you have rights to create databases. (Do *not* perform this or any other Learn By Doing activity on a server used for production operations!)

5. For the Database property, enter **Max Min Sales**.

6. For the Model Name property, enter **Max Min Sales**.

7. Click OK to exit the MaxMinSalesTabular Property Pages dialog box.

8. Select Build | Deploy MaxMinSalesTabular from the main menu. The Deploy dialog box appears.

9. Enter the impersonation credentials password for each connection, if prompted, and click OK.

10. When the deploy and processing complete, click Close to exit the Deploy dialog box.

11. Close SQL Server Data Tools.

Another Model Awaits

We have seen the simplicity and capability of the Tabular BI Semantic Model. Now it's time to look at the other model in the SQL Server Analysis Services bag of tricks—the Multidimensional BI Semantic Model. In the next four chapters, we see how Multidimensional models differ and how they are similar to Tabular models.

Part IV

Working with a Multidimensional BI Semantic Model

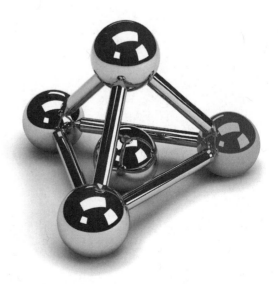

Chapter 11

Cubism: Measures and Dimensions

In This Chapter

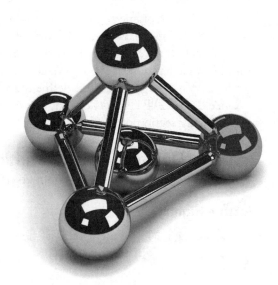

There is a fifth dimension beyond those known to man. It is a dimension vast as space and timeless as infinity.

Introduction to *The Twilight Zone*
—Rod Serling

We have looked at the basics of cubes, with their measures, dimensions, and attributes. We also examined the means of getting information from transactional and other data sources into our data marts. We have implemented the Tabular BI Semantic Model. Now it's time to travel to another dimension and work with the Multidimensional BI Semantic Model.

The Multidimensional BI Semantic Model lets us group measures together. It also enables us to create different types of dimensions. This classification and differentiation make it easier for users to analyze the data in our cubes. It also makes the cubes easier for us to manage.

Building a Multidimensional BI Semantic Model

In Chapter 6, we created two data mart structures for our sample company, Maximum Miniatures, Inc. We called these the Manufacturing data mart and the Sales data mart. These data marts serve as repositories for business information that is not available elsewhere from a single source. In this chapter, we will look at working with the Manufacturing data mart to create a Multidimensional BI Semantic Model.

Creating a Cube

We will define an online analytical processing (OLAP) cube on top of the Manufacturing data mart relational database. In Chapter 6, we defined one OLAP cube at the same time we created the Sales data mart relational database. This time around, we approach things from a different direction. We already have the Manufacturing data mart relational database. What we need to do is define our OLAP cube on top of that existing database.

Once the OLAP cube is defined, we use it to help us learn more about measures in the following section of this book.

Learn By Doing: Building a Multidimensional BI Semantic Model for the Manufacturing Data Mart

Feature Highlighted

▶   Creating a Multidimensional BI Semantic Model on top of an existing data mart

Business Need   The vice president of production wants to perform multidimensional analysis on the information in the Manufacturing data mart. To enable him to do that, we need to define an OLAP cube on top of that database.

Steps to Create the Project and Data Source

1. Open SQL Server Data Tools.
2. Click the New Project button on the toolbar.
3. Select Business Intelligence | Analysis Services in the Installed Templates area, and then select Analysis Services Multidimensional and Data Mining Project from the templates.
4. Enter **MaxMinManufacturingDM** for the Name and set the Location to the appropriate folder.
5. Click OK to create the project.
6. Right-click the Data Sources folder in the Solution Explorer window, and select New Data Source from the context menu. The Data Source Wizard appears.
7. Click Next on the Welcome page. The "Select how to define the connection" page appears.
8. Select the MaxMinManufacturingDM data connection you previously created, and click Next. The Impersonation Information page appears.

NOTE

Analysis Services needs to access the data mart relational database to populate and update the information in the OLAP cube. This is done using the information in the data connection selected in Step 8. The Analysis Services updates run as a background process. This can be an issue if the data connection specifies Windows Authentication or if the connection is to a file-based database, such as Microsoft Access. In these situations, Analysis Services needs to know what Windows credentials to use when accessing the data source. In other words, Analysis Services needs to impersonate a Windows identity while accessing the data.

9. On the Impersonation Information page, if you are using Windows Authentication in your data connection, select Use a specific Windows user name and password, and then enter a valid Windows user name and password for database access. If you entered a specific SQL Server login in the data connection, you do not need to worry about impersonation. (If you cannot remember how the data connection was configured, select Use a specific Windows user name and password, and then enter valid Windows credentials, just to be on the safe side.) Click Next. The Completing the Wizard page appears.
10. Enter **Max Min Manufacturing DM** for Data Source Name, if it is not already there. Click Finish.

Steps to Create the Data Source View

1. Right-click the Data Source Views folder in the Solution Explorer window, and select New Data Source View from the context menu. The Data Source View Wizard appears.

NOTE

A data source view enables us to specify the subset of the tables and their fields from the data source that should be included in the OLAP cube. We can also define table relationships and calculated fields that do not exist in the underlying database. In this case, we are accessing a data mart that was architected with the cube in mind. Therefore, we use all of the tables and fields in the data mart database and we do not need to specify additional relationships. However, we do use the data source view to define three calculated fields that let us easily create a time dimension hierarchy from the single datetime field that exists in the fact table.

2. Click Next on the Welcome page. The Select a Data Source page appears.

3. The Max Min Manufacturing DM data source that you just created should be selected. Click Next. The Name Matching page appears.

4. This page appears because we do not have foreign key constraints defined in our database. We will allow the wizard to create logical foreign keys in the data source view. Leave the "Create logical relationships by matching columns" check box checked. Also, leave the "Same name as primary key" option selected.

5. Click Next. The Select Tables and Views page appears.

6. Move all of the dimension and fact tables to the Included objects list. (Remember, there are two fact tables now.) Click Next. The Completing the Wizard page appears.

7. Enter **Max Min Manufacturing DM** for Name, if it is not already there. Click Finish. The Data Source View Design tab appears.

NOTE

The Data Source View Design tab shows a diagram of the data source view we just created. This looks similar to a database diagram. This is to be expected because a data source view is simply a view into the underlying database. The data source view gives us the chance to add items that are required by, or remove items that are irrelevant to, the cube we are creating.

8. Find the FactManufacturing table in the data source view diagram. Right-click the title bar of this table, and select New Named Calculation from the context menu. The Create Named Calculation dialog box appears.

9. Enter **YearOfManufacture** for Column Name.

10. Enter the following for Expression:

```
CONVERT(char(4), YEAR(DateOfManufacture))
```

This creates a character field containing the year corresponding to the date of manufacture.

NOTE

The data source view is interacting with the underlying database to create the named calculation. Therefore, the expression language of that database must be used to define the expression. In this case, the underlying database is SQL Server, so the expression language is T-SQL. The expression is evaluated by sending this SELECT statement to the underlying database:

```
SELECT {Table Name in Data Source View}.*,
{Named Calculation Expression} AS {Named Calculation Name}
FROM {Table in Data Source} AS {Table Name in Data Source View}
```

For the named calculation we are creating here, the SELECT statement would be:

```
SELECT FactManufacturing.*,
CONVERT (char(4), YEAR(DateOfManufacture)) AS YearOfManufacture
FROM FactManufacturing AS FactManufacturing
```

Any T-SQL expression that is valid in this context, including subqueries (when explicitly surrounded by parentheses), is valid as a named calculation.

11. Click OK to exit the Create Named Calculation dialog box.

12. Create a second named calculation called **QuarterOfManufacture** with the following expression to contain the year and quarter corresponding to the date of manufacture:

```
CONVERT(char(4), YEAR(DateOfManufacture)) +
CASE
WHEN MONTH(DateOfManufacture) BETWEEN 1 AND 3 THEN 'Q1'
WHEN MONTH(DateOfManufacture) BETWEEN 4 AND 6 THEN 'Q2'
WHEN MONTH(DateOfManufacture) BETWEEN 7 AND 9 THEN 'Q3'
ELSE 'Q4'
END
```

13. Create a third named calculation called **MonthOfManufacture** with the following expression to contain the year and month corresponding to the date of manufacture:

```
CONVERT(char(4), YEAR(DateOfManufacture)) +
RIGHT('0'+CONVERT(varchar(2), MONTH(DateOfManufacture)),2)
```

14. Create **YearOfInventory**, **QuarterOfInventory**, and **MonthOfInventory** named calculations in the FactInventory table. Use the same T-SQL expressions, substituting DateOfInventory for DateOfManufacture. When completed (and with a little rearranging), the Data Source View Design tab should appear similar to Figure 11-1.

15. Click Save All on the toolbar, and then close the Max Min Manufacturing DM.dsv tab.

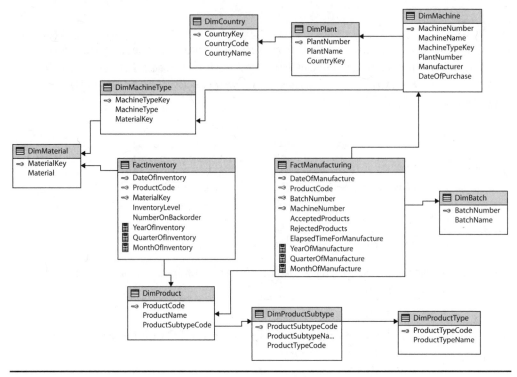

Figure 11-1   *The Data Source View Design tab for the Max Min Manufacturing DM data source view*

Steps to Create the Cube

1. Right-click the Cubes folder in the Solution Explorer window, and select New Cube from the context menu. The Cube Wizard appears.

2. Click Next on the Welcome page. The Select Creation Method page appears.

3. Use existing tables should be selected by default. Click Next. The Select Measure Group Tables page appears.

4. The Max Min Manufacturing DM data source view that you just created should be selected. Check FactManufacturing in the Measure group tables area. We initially leave the measures in the FactInventory table out of the cube and add them in at a later time.

5. Click Next. The Select Measures page appears.

6. The wizard should have found and checked all of the measure fields in the FactManufacturing table. The wizard also added a field called Fact Manufacturing Count, which counts the number of records. This does not provide us with any useful information in this data mart, so you should uncheck the Fact Manufacturing Count field.

7. Click Next. The Select New Dimensions page appears.

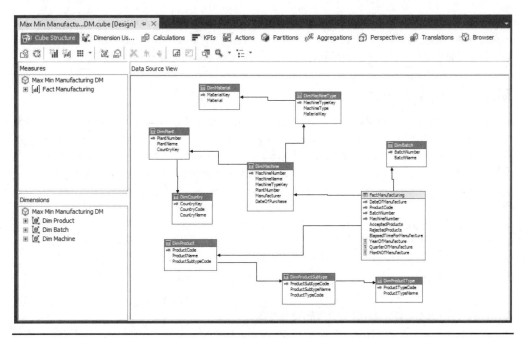

Figure 11-2   *SQL Server Data Tools window after the Cube Wizard completes*

8. The wizard should have found all of the tables related to the FactManufacturing table in the data source view. It should also have created hierarchies for the Dim Product and Dim Machine dimensions. Uncheck both FactManufacturing entries.

9. Click Next. The Completing the Wizard page appears.

10. Enter **Max Min Manufacturing DM** for Cube Name, if it is not already there. Click Finish. The Cube Design tab appears. SQL Server Data Tools windows should appear similar to Figure 11-2.

11. Click the Save All button on the toolbar.

You will notice the wizard did not create our time dimension for us. We will manually create the time dimension later in this chapter.

Measures

Now that we have a real live cube in captivity, we can study its basic parts and look at some of its more advanced features. We begin with measures. Measures provide the actual information that the users of our cubes are interested in. *Measures* are the bits of numerical data that we need to aggregate. As we saw in the Cube Wizard, measures come from the fields in the fact tables in the data mart.

The Multidimensional BI Semantic Model provides us with a number of features for managing measures. We can even create new measures that don't exist in the data mart. We can also control the aggregation of the measures along our dimensions.

Measure Groups

In the Multidimensional BI Semantic Model, measures do not exist on their own inside cubes. Instead, they are clustered together and managed in groupings. These groupings are called measure groups. Each *measure group* in a cube corresponds to a table in the data source view. This table is the measure group's source for its measure data. The measure group is said to be bound to this table. Each record in the table becomes a different member of the measure group.

In the Max Min Manufacturing DM cube created by the Cube Wizard, there is a single measure group called Fact Manufacturing. This measure group contains the Accepted Products, Rejected Products, and Elapsed Time for Manufacture measures. This measure group is bound to the FactManufacturing table in the data source view.

Measure Groups and Dimensions

Previously, we discussed how dimensions are used to aggregate measures. For this aggregation to take place, the dimensions in a cube must be somehow related to the measures. When we created our data marts, this was done using a foreign key field in the measure or fact table that linked to primary key fields of our dimension tables. In the cube itself, we do the same thing by creating relationships between the measure groups and the dimensions.

At first, this may seem a bit strange. As we have discussed cubes conceptually in previous chapters, we have always talked about measures being related to dimensions, with no talk of measure groups. When we query the data from our cubes, we use dimensions as if they were directly related to measures. However, if you consider the underlying architecture, this makes perfect sense.

In our data mart, we have multiple measures in a single record of our fact table. In the Manufacturing data mart, the Accepted Products, Rejected Products, and Elapsed Time for Manufacture measures are present in each record. The record also contains the foreign key fields linking it to the lowest-level dimension tables in each of the hierarchies. Again, in the Manufacturing data mart, these are DimProduct, DimBatch, and DimMachine (along with the time dimension that will be created virtually from the DateOfManufacture field).

All of the measures in the FactManufacturing record (a single row of data) depend on all of the foreign key fields in that record. Therefore, if a given Accepted Products measure and Rejected Products measure reside in the same record, it is impossible for them to relate to two different records in the DimProduct table (see Figure 11-3). Only

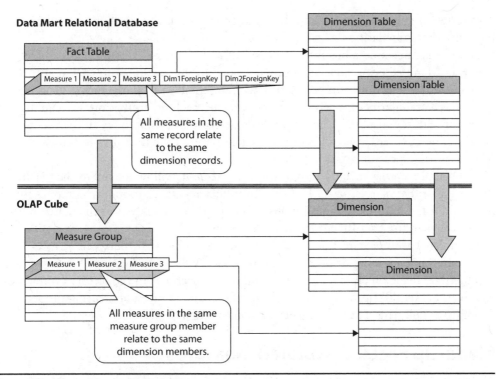

Figure 11-3 *Measure groups and dimensions*

one foreign key field in their record can be used to link to the DimProduct table, so they must both link to the same product. That's the way well-normalized relational databases work.

We just said that measure groups correspond to a table in the data source view. Just as all of the measures in a record in the fact table must relate to the same dimension table records, it follows that all of the measures in a given measure group must relate to the same members in the cube dimensions.

We look at the technique for creating relationships between measure groups and dimensions in the section "Role Playing Dimensions."

Granularity

The lowest level of a particular dimension hierarchy that is related to a given measure group determines the granularity of that measure group for that dimension. Analysis can only be done on a measure along a certain dimension down to the granularity of its measure group for that dimension. Because measures are related to dimensions through their measure group, all of the measures in a measure group have the same granularity.

Two different measure groups (and their constituent measures) in the same cube can have different granularity.

All of this can sound a bit like double-speak, so let's look at a couple of examples. The Fact Manufacturing measure group is related to the machine dimension at the lowest level, the machine number level. Therefore, the Fact Manufacturing measure group has a granularity of machine number for the machine dimension. We can drill down through the machine hierarchy from material to machine type, all the way to the machine number level, and get information for all of the measures in the Fact Manufacturing measure group.

The Fact Inventory measure group, once we create it, will be related to the machine dimension at the material level. The Fact Inventory measure group has a granularity of material for the machine dimension. We can only perform analysis at the material level for measures in the Fact Inventory measure group.

Granularity is important for the analysis, but remember that there will be facts with some values missing or null. Not all materials in the complete list of dimension members are made on all machine types and on all machines in the factory on the same day. SQL Server 2016 Analysis Services continues the tradition of assuring proper handling of null data started by earlier versions of Analysis Services.

Made-Up Facts: Calculated Measures

The underlying data sources for our cubes may not contain all of the information we want to make available for our users. In many cases, we need to use the available data to calculate new measures that our users require. Perhaps the list price, discount amount, and sales tax amount need to be added together to determine the actual total of a sale. Perhaps we want to divide the number of rejected products by the total number of products manufactured to get the percentage of rejects produced. We can create this information using calculated measures.

A *calculated measure* is part of a measure group. It functions in the same manner as any other measure in the group. The only difference is this: Instead of coming directly from a field in the underlying data source, a calculated measure is defined by an expression. These expressions are created using a language known as Multidimensional Expression Language (MDX) script. Remember that when we created named calculations in a data source view, we used the language of the underlying data source. In our case, it was T-SQL. It would certainly be easier if we could use the same language here to define calculated measures. Unfortunately, that is not the case. *MDX* is a special language with features designed to handle the advanced mathematics and formulas required by OLAP analysis. MDX also includes features for navigating through the dimensions and hierarchies of OLAP cubes. These features are not found in T-SQL, so we need to use MDX script.

In the "Learn By Doing" section for measures and measure groups, we create some straightforward calculated measures. These calculated measures do not require an in-depth knowledge of the MDX script language. We get into the details of MDX script in Chapter 13.

The definition of a calculated measure is stored in the OLAP cube itself. The actual values that result from a calculated measure are not calculated, however, until a query containing that calculated measure is executed. The results of that calculation are then cached in the cube. The cached value is delivered to any subsequent users requesting the same calculation.

Creating Calculated Measures

Calculated measures are managed on the Calculations tab of the Cube Design tab. A new calculated measure is created by clicking the New Calculated Member toolbar button, shown in Figure 11-4. This opens the Calculated Member form view, shown in Figure 11-5.

The name of the calculated measure is entered in Name. If the name contains one or more spaces, it must be enclosed in square brackets. Likewise, if the name contains one or more of the following characters:

```
! @ # $ % ^ & * ( ) – + = / ? : ; " ' { } \ < >,
```

it must be enclosed in square brackets.

Thus far, we have talked of calculated measures. However, it is possible to calculate members for dimensions as well. In fact, both calculated measures and calculated dimension members are referred to as calculated members, which is why the entry form is called the Calculated Member form. To specify that we are creating a calculated measure, Measures must be selected from the Parent hierarchy drop-down list.

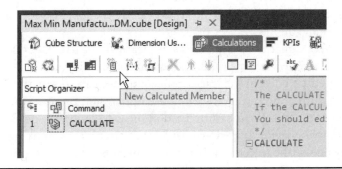

Figure 11-4   *Creating a new calculation on the Calculations tab*

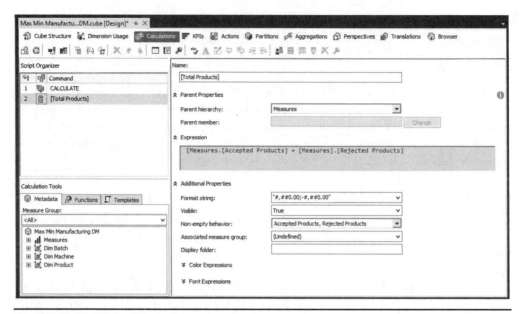

Figure 11-5 *The Calculated Member form view*

The actual definition of the calculated measure is entered in Expression. As mentioned earlier, this expression uses the MDX script language. The expression can be typed by hand, or it can be built using the existing measures, MDX script functions, and templates found in the Calculation Tools window. This window can be seen in the lower-left area of Figure 11-5.

The Format string drop-down list enables us to select the formatting to be applied to the calculation results. We can either select from one of the numeric formatting strings in the drop-down list or type in a custom format string. In most cases, one of the formatting strings from the drop-down list can do the job. The format string must be enclosed in double quotes.

As we study MDX queries in Chapter 14, we learn about MDX queries that ask for only non-empty values from a measure. Rather than evaluating a calculated measure expression repeatedly to determine if it is non-empty, we can specify the conditions under which the calculation can produce a non-empty result. In most cases, this depends on whether one or more of the measures used in the calculation is non-empty.

The Non-empty behavior drop-down list lets us select one or more measures in the cube. If any one of the selected measures is non-empty, the expression is executed

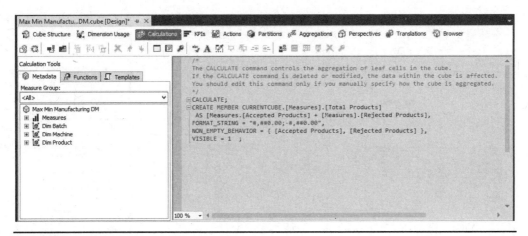

Figure 11-6   *The Script view*

to determine whether the resulting calculated measure is non-empty. When all of the selected measures are empty, the calculated measure is assumed to be empty without ever executing the expression.

In addition to the form view shown in Figure 11-5, we can look at the underlying MDX script that completely defines the calculated measure. This is shown in Figure 11-6. Again, we explore the MDX script language more completely to understand this code in Chapter 13.

We can use the measures in a cube in the expressions that define calculated measures in that cube. We can also use calculated measures in the expressions that define other calculated measures. This lets us break up complex calculations into much simpler building blocks that are easier to create and maintain.

It Doesn't Add Up: Measure Aggregates Other Than Sum

We have already discussed how measures are aggregated along dimension hierarchies. By default, the Sum aggregate function is used for each measure. Measures that use the Sum function for their aggregation are *additive measures.*

In some cases, however, things just don't add up. In other words, there may be some measures that should not be summed along dimension hierarchies. For example, taking the sum of an average results in a number that is total nonsense. Instead, we always want to recalculate the average from the granular data. In other situations, we may want

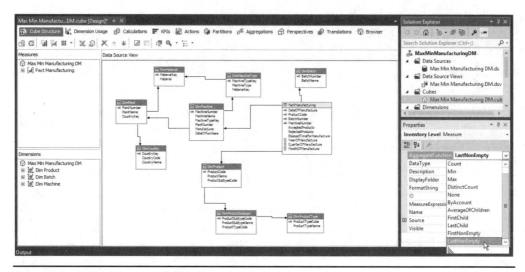

Figure 11-7 *Setting the aggregate function for a measure*

to use the maximum or minimum value for a measure along a dimension, rather than taking the sum. These measures are *nonadditive measures*.

The aggregate function used by a particular measure is controlled by the Aggregate property from that measure. Select the measure in the Measures window of the Cube Structure tab, and then use the Properties window to set the AggregateFunction property for this measure. This is shown in Figure 11-7.

Semiadditive Measures

Certain measures may be added along all dimensions except for the time dimension. For example, the inventory level measure can be added along the product dimension. The sum of the inventory amounts for each product yields the total number of products in the warehouse. However, the sum of the first three months' inventory amounts does not give the inventory amount at the end of the first quarter. This is shown in Figure 11-8.

Measures such as inventory level are said to be semiadditive. These measures must use a *semiadditive aggregation* to achieve the proper results when aggregating. Measures that use a semiadditive aggregation must be related to a time dimension.

Semiadditive measures require the Enterprise Edition or Developer Edition of SQL Server Analysis Services 2016. Semiadditive measures are not supported by the Standard Edition or other editions.

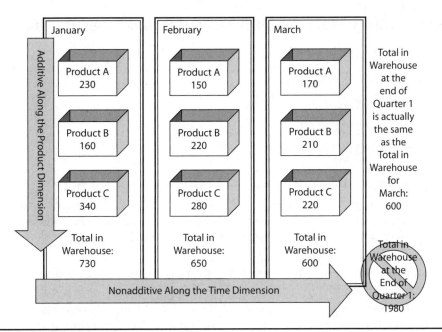

Figure 11-8   *Inventory level is a semiadditive measure.*

Aggregate Functions

Analysis Services provides a number of aggregate functions for use with measures in an OLAP cube.

Function	Additivity	Result
AverageOfChildren	Semiadditive	The average of all non-empty child members.
ByAccount	Semiadditive	Uses the aggregate function specified by an account dimension in the cube. If the cube does not include an account dimension, this aggregate function works the same as the None aggregate function.
Count	Additive	A count of the number of child members.
DistinctCount	Nonadditive	A count of the number of unique child members.
FirstChild	Semiadditive	The value of the first child member.
FirstNonEmpty	Semiadditive	The value of the first non-empty child member.
LastChild	Semiadditive	The value of the last child member.
LastNonEmpty	Semiadditive	The value of the last non-empty child member.
Max	Semiadditive	The greatest value of all child members.
Min	Semiadditive	The least value of all child members.
None	Nonadditive	No aggregation is done.
Sum	Additive	The sum of all child members. This is the default aggregate function for a measure.

Learn By Doing: Working with Measures and Measure Groups

Features Highlighted

- ▶ Adding formatting to a measure
- ▶ Adding a measure group to a cube
- ▶ Setting the aggregation function for a measure
- ▶ Creating calculated measures

Business Need   We have not yet completed the vice president of production's change request for inventory and backorder information in the Max Min Manufacturing DM cube. We added a table for this information into the data mart and we populated that table from the Order Processing database. We now need to add these measures to the cube in a new measure group.

Once the inventory level measure is added to the cube, we need to specify the correct aggregate function for this measure. As noted earlier, inventory level is not additive. The inventory level for a given period is not the sum of the inventory levels within the period. Instead, inventory level is semiadditive. The inventory level for a given period is the inventory level at the end of that period.

In addition, the vice president of production has come up with another change. He would like to see not only the number of accepted products produced and the number of rejected products produced, but also the total number of products produced. This, of course, is the sum of the number of accepted products, plus the number of rejected products. He also wants to see the number of rejected products produced as a percentage of the total number of products produced. We can implement these requests using calculated measures.

Steps to Finalize the Measures

1. Open SQL Server Data Tools.
2. Open the MaxMinManufacturingDM project.
3. In the Solution Explorer window, double-click the entry for Max Min Manufacturing DM.cube to display the Cube Design tab, if it is not already visible.
4. Expand the Fact Manufacturing measure group in the Measures window.
5. Select the Accepted Products measure.
6. In the Properties window, select Standard from the FormatString drop-down list.
7. Select the Rejected Products measure in the Measures window.
8. In the Properties window, select Standard from the FormatString drop-down list.

9. Select the Elapsed Time For Manufacture measure in the Measures window.

10. In the Properties window, select Standard from the FormatString drop-down list.

11. Right-click in the Measures window, and select New Measure Group from the context menu. The New Measure Group dialog box appears.

12. Select FactInventory from the Select a table from the data source view list, and click OK to exit the New Measure Group dialog box. The FactInventory table is added to the cube, and the Fact Inventory measure group appears in the Measures window.

NOTE

A red, wavy line may appear under the entry for the Fact Inventory measure group in the Measures window. This error notification occurs because we have not related this new measure group to any dimensions. We take care of this in a later Learn By Doing exercise titled "Relating Dimensions in the Max Min Manufacturing DM Cube."

13. Expand the Fact Inventory measure group in the Measures window.

14. Select the Inventory Level measure.

15. If you are using an edition of SQL Server 2016 other than the Enterprise Edition or Developer Edition, skip to Step 16. In the Properties window, select LastNonEmpty from the drop-down list for the AggregateFunction property. The LastNonEmpty aggregate function is now used when aggregating this measure.

NOTE

The Enterprise Edition or Developer Edition of SQL Server 2016 is required by the LastNonEmpty aggregate function. If you are not using one of these editions, ignore Step 15 and Step 18, as well as the aggregate numbers that result from these measures. If you use the LastNonEmpty aggregate function with the Standard Edition or other edition of SQL Server 2016, you will receive an error when you try to deploy the cube definition to the server.

16. In the Properties window, select Standard from the FormatString drop-down list.

17. Select the Number On Backorder measure in the Measures window.

18. If you are using an edition of SQL Server 2016 other than the Enterprise Edition or Developer Edition, skip to Step 19. In the Properties window, select LastNonEmpty from the drop-down list for the AggregateFunction property.

19. In the Properties window, select Standard from the FormatString drop-down list.

20. Right-click the Fact Inventory Count measure in the Measures window, and select Delete from the context menu. The Delete Objects dialog box appears.

21. Click OK to confirm the deletion. The Cube Design tab should appear similar to Figure 11-9.

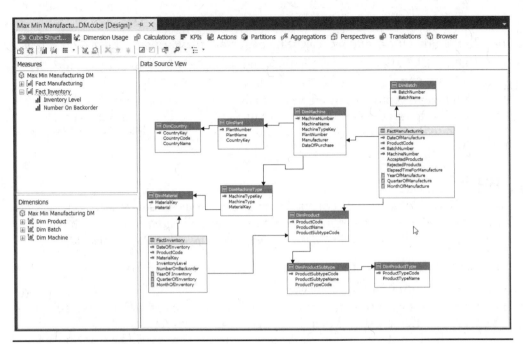

Figure 11-9 *The Max Min Manufacturing DM cube with the Fact Inventory measure group*

NOTE

A count of the number of members in the measure group is automatically created when a new measure group is created. In this case, a count of the number of inventory entries is not a helpful measure, so it can be deleted.

Steps to Add Calculations to the Cube

1. Select the Calculations tab of the Cube Design tab to create calculated measures.
2. Click the New Calculated Member button on the Calculations tab toolbar. The Calculated Member form view appears.
3. Enter [**Total Products**] for Name. Enter the following for Expression:

   ```
   [Accepted Products] + [Rejected Products]
   ```
4. Select Standard from the Format string drop-down list.
5. Check the Accepted Products and Rejected Products measures in the Non-empty behavior selection window, and click OK.
6. Click the New Calculated Member button on the Calculations tab toolbar. The Calculated Member form returns to the default values.

7. Enter [**Percent Rejected**] for Name. Enter the following for Expression:

   ```
   [Rejected Products] / [Total Products]
   ```

8. Select Percent from the Format string drop-down list.

9. Check the Accepted Products and Rejected Products measures in the Non-empty behavior selection window, and click OK.

10. Click the Save All button on the toolbar.

Dimensions

After taking a good look at measures, let's move on to another part of the OLAP cube—namely, the dimensions. As we have seen, dimensions are what give cubes their true analytical power. They enable us to slice and dice the measures in the cube until we find the meaningful business intelligence hidden among all of the numbers. Dimensions provide understandable phrases in business language to define what may be cryptic in a transactional database system.

Just as there is more to measures than initially meets the eye, dimensions, too, come in a number of different varieties. We will examine their various classifications and capabilities, but first, let's look at the way dimensions are related to measure groups.

Managing Dimensions

Dimensions are managed using the Dimension Design tab. To display this tab, double-click a dimension in the Solution Explorer window. The Dimension Design tab is shown in Figure 11-10 displaying the Dim Product dimension. We will create the Product Hierarchy shown in the figure in the next Learn By Doing exercise.

The Dimension Design tab includes the entire structure of the dimension. The Dim Product dimension in Figure 11-10 has a three-level hierarchy. The Dimension Design tab contains information about all three levels: the product level, the product subtype level, and the product type level.

The left-hand column of the Dimension Design tab shows all of the attributes for the entire dimension. The center column shows the structure of the dimension hierarchy. The right-hand column shows the tables from the data source view that define this dimension.

Notice the blue squiggly under the dimension name. This indicates the development environment has some dimensional design suggestions to make. Hover over the squiggle to view these suggestions. We will look at implementing some of this advice in the following Learn By Doing exercise.

We will begin working with dimensions by creating a time dimension in the Max Min Manufacturing DM cube. We will also create hierarchies for two of our dimensions.

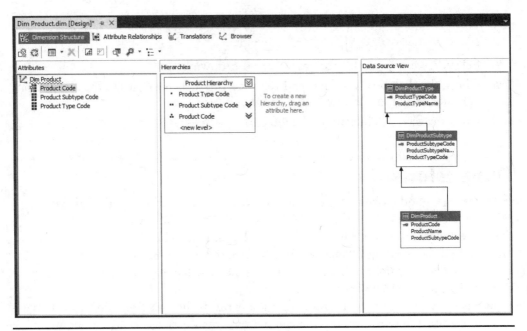

Figure 11-10 *The Dimension Design tab with the Dim Product dimension*

Finally, we will do some additional clean-up to make our dimensions easier to use when we start to query data from the Max Min Manufacturing DM cube.

Learn By Doing: Cleaning Up the Dimensions in the Max Min Manufacturing DM Cube

Features Highlighted

▶ Creating a time dimension

▶ Creating dimensional hierarchies

▶ Hiding unneeded attribute hierarchies

Business Need   We need to have the dimensions in the Max Min Manufacturing DM cube related to the measure groups to perform any meaningful analysis on this cube.

Steps to Create a Time Dimension
1. Open SQL Server Data Tools.
2. Open the MaxMinManufacturingDM project.

3. Right-click the Dimensions entry in the Solution Explorer window, and select New Dimension from the context menu. The Dimension Wizard dialog box appears.

4. Click Next on the Welcome page. The Select Creation Method page of the wizard appears.

5. Leave the Use an existing table item selected and click Next. The Specify Source Information page appears.

6. The Max Min Manufacturing DM data source view is already selected. Select FactManufacturing from the Main table drop-down list. Even though this is a fact table, it is also the table that contains the date information, so it will serve double duty.

7. DateOfManufacture is selected as the first Key column, which is correct. However, the other columns selected in the Key columns area do not apply to our time dimension. Click on each and select the blank entry from each of the drop-down lists so DateOfManufacture is the only key column selected.

8. Select DateOfManufacture from the Name column drop-down list. The Specify Source Information page of the wizard should appear, as shown in Figure 11-11.

9. Click Next. The Select Related Tables page appears.

10. Uncheck all items in the Related tables area.

11. Click Next. The Select Dimension Attributes page appears.

12. Uncheck Product Code, Batch Number, and Machine Number.

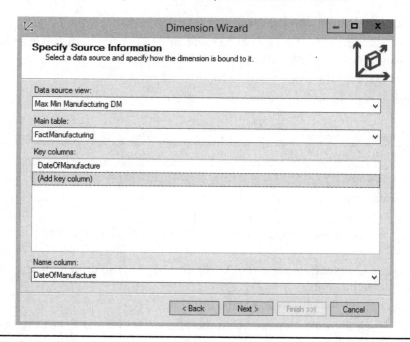

Figure 11-11 *Creating the Time dimension*

13. Leave Date Of Manufacture checked and also check Year Of Manufacture, Quarter Of Manufacture, and Month Of Manufacture.

14. Click in the Attribute Type column across from Date Of Manufacture.

15. Click the drop-down arrow.

16. Expand the Date entry.

17. Expand the Calendar entry.

18. Select Date and click OK.

19. Click in the Attribute Type column across from Year Of Manufacture.

20. Click the drop-down arrow.

21. Expand the Date entry.

22. Expand the Calendar entry.

23. Select Year and click OK.

24. Repeat Steps 19–23 for Quarter Of Manufacture, selecting Quarter.

25. Repeat Steps 19–23 for Month Of Manufacture, selecting Month.

26. Click Next. The Completing the Wizard page appears.

27. Change the name to **Dim Time**.

28. Click Finish. The Dimension Design tab appears with the Dim Time dimension.

Steps to Create Dimension Hierarchies

1. Right-click the entry for Date of Manufacture in the Attributes area, and select Rename from the context menu.

2. Enter **Date** for the name of this attribute, and press ENTER.

3. Repeat Steps 1 and 2 to rename the other attributes as follows:

Old Name	New Name
Month Of Manufacture	Month
Quarter Of Manufacture	Quarter
Year Of Manufacture	Year

4. Drag the Year item from the Attributes column, and drop it in the Hierarchies area.

5. Drag the Quarter item from the Attributes column, and drop it on <new level> in the Hierarchies area.

6. Repeat Step 5 for Month and Date.

7. Right-click the word "Hierarchy" in the Hierarchies area, and select Rename from the context menu.

8. Enter **Date Hierarchy** and press ENTER.

9. Click Date in the Attributes area. Hold down SHIFT and click Year in the Attributes area. All four attributes should be selected.

10. In the Properties window, change the AttributeHierarchyVisible property to False.

NOTE

These attributes can show up individually in the dimension as their own attribute hierarchies, as well as members of the Date Hierarchy we just created. This gets a bit confusing for the user querying data from the cube. To cut down on this confusion, we told the individual attribute hierarchies to be hidden. Only the Date Hierarchy will be visible to the user.

---

11. Click the Attribute Relationships tab. Note the Date is related to the other three items, but the relationship structure does not mirror the hierarchy we just created.

12. Select the Month and drop it on the Quarter.

13. Select the Quarter and drop it on the Year.

14. Right-click each of the relationship arrows, and select Relationship Type | Rigid from the context menu. The Attribute Relationships tab should appear as shown in Figure 11-12.

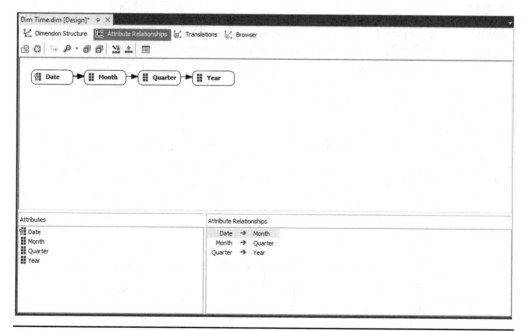

Figure 11-12 *The Attribute Relationships tab*

NOTE

A flexible attribute relationship may change between full processes of the dimension. A rigid attribute relationship does not change. For example, 8/1/2016 will always be in August 2016. It is a rigid relationship. Attribute relationships default to flexible. They should be set to rigid wherever appropriate to increase cube processing efficiency.

15. Click the Save All button on the toolbar.

16. Close the Dim Time dimension tab.

17. In the Solution Explorer window, double-click the Dim Machine dimension entry. The Dim Machine dimension tab appears.

18. Right-click the Country Key attribute in the Attributes area and select Rename from the context menu.

19. Type **Country** and press ENTER.

20. Click the NameColumn property in the Properties window.

21. Click the ellipsis (…) button. The Name Column dialog box appears.

22. In the Source column area, click CountryName.

23. Click OK to exit the Name Column dialog box.

NOTE

The Name column property of an attribute determines what value will be displayed for this attribute. In this case, the CountryCode is used to uniquely identify a member of the Country attribute. However, the CountryName is what is shown to the user as they use the Country attribute in a query.

24. Repeat Steps 18–23 to modify the other attributes in the Dim Machine dimension as follows:

Old Name	New Name	Name Column – Source Column
Machine Number	Machine	MachineName
Machine Type Key	Machine Type	MachineType
Material Key	Material	Material
Plant Number	Plant	PlantName

25. Create a new hierarchy and name it **Material Hierarchy**. This hierarchy should have the following levels:
Material
Machine Type
Machine

26. Create a second hierarchy and name it **Plant Hierarchy**. This hierarchy should have the following levels:
Country
Plant
Machine

27. Set the AttributeHierarchyVisible property for all of the attributes to False.

28. Select the Attribute Relationships tab.

29. Change all of the relationship types to rigid.

30. Click the Save All button on the toolbar.

31. Close the Dim Machine dimension tab.

32. In the Solution Explorer window, double-click the Dim Product dimension entry. The Dim Product dimension tab appears.

33. Rename and set the Source Column for the following attributes:

Old Name	New Name	Name Column – Source Column
Product Code	Product	ProductName
Product Subtype Code	Product Subtype	ProductSubtypeName
Product Type Code	Product Type	ProductTypeName

34. Create a new hierarchy and name it **Product Hierarchy**. This hierarchy should have the following levels:
Product Type
Product Subtype
Product

35. Set the AttributeHierarchyVisible property for all of the attributes to False.

36. Select the Attribute Relationships tab.

37. Change all of the relationship types to rigid.

38. Click the Save All button on the toolbar.

39. Close the Dim Product dimension tab.

Relating Dimensions to Measure Groups

In the previous Learn By Doing activity, we got our dimensional structure in shape. However, we still have one issue with the Dim Time dimension we created. This dimension is not related to either of the measure groups. A dimension must be related to a measure group before we can use it to analyze data from the cube.

We can solve this situation right now with another Learn By Doing activity.

Learn By Doing: Relating Dimensions in the Max Min Manufacturing DM Cube

Feature Highlighted

▶ Relating dimensions to measure groups

Business Need We need to have the Dim Time dimension in the Max Min Manufacturing DM cube related to the measure groups to perform any meaningful analysis on this cube.

Steps to Relate Dimensions to Measure Groups

1. Double-click the entry for Max Min Manufacturing DM.cube to display the Cube Design tab.
2. Select the Dimension Usage tab of the Cube Design tab.
3. Right-click in the empty area of the tab and select Add Cube Dimension. The Add Cube Dimension dialog box appears.
4. Select the Dim Time dimension, and click OK.
5. The Dim Time dimension is added to the cube. SQL Server Data Tools figures out how to relate the Dim Time dimension to the Fact Manufacturing group. (Not too difficult, considering they are both defined from the same table.) We will need to relate the Fact Inventory group ourselves.
6. Click the entry in the Fact Inventory column and the Dim Time row. An ellipsis (…) button appears.
7. Click the ellipsis button. The Define Relationship dialog box appears.
8. Select Regular in the Select relationship type drop-down list. We are specifying that the Dim Time dimension relates to the Fact Inventory measure group as a regular dimension.
9. Select Date from the Granularity attribute drop-down list. This is the attribute in the dimension that defines the granularity of the dimension for this measure group. We can either select the primary key of the table that defines the dimension or we can select one of the attribute fields in this table.
10. In the Relationship grid, select DateOfInventory from the drop-down list under Measure Group Columns. This creates a relationship between the DateOfManufacture column in the table that defines the dimension and the DateOfInventory column in the table that defines the measure group.
11. Click OK to exit the Define Relationship dialog box. Once completed, the Dimension Usage tab should appear as shown in Figure 11-13.
12. Click the Save All button on the toolbar.

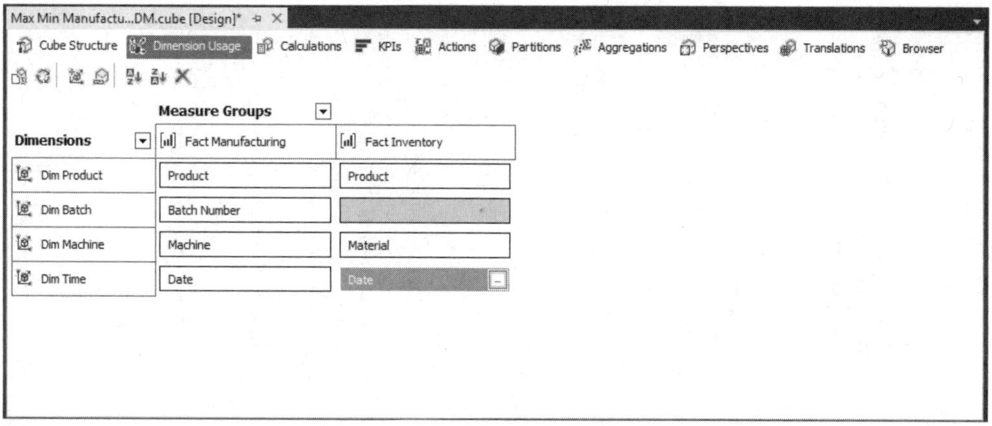

Figure 11-13   *The Dimension Usage tab of the Max Min Manufacturing DM cube*

Types of Dimensions

Dimensions can be placed in a number of classifications. These classifications tell us something about the way a dimension is created and managed. They can also shed some light on how a dimension is utilized.

Fact Dimensions

In most cases, the information used to populate a dimension resides in a dimension table. DimProduct and DimMachine are examples from our Manufacturing data mart. However, when we created the Dim Time dimension, we used data from the DateOfManufacture field and the YearOfManufacture, QuarterOfManufacture, and MonthOfManufacture named calculations in the FactManufacturing table.

Dimensions created from attributes in a fact table are known as *fact dimensions*. They are also known in the "biz" as degenerate dimensions. (This seems like a highly prejudicial name, if you ask me.)

The most common use of fact dimensions is a situation where the business users would like access to a detail-level business key, such as a transaction number, that is unique for each record in the fact table. If we created a dimension table for this data, it would have as many rows as the fact table itself. Instead, in these situations, we can create a fact dimension and avoid all of the data redundancy.

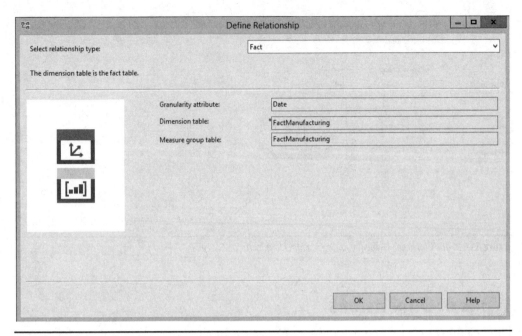

Figure 11-14   *The Define Relationship dialog box for a fact dimension*

Fact dimensions follow a few simple rules in Analysis Services:

▶   At most, one fact dimension can be in a measure group.

▶   A fact dimension must be defined by one and only one measure group.

▶   A fact dimension can have a fact relationship with only one measure group. It can, however, have a regular relationship with additional measure groups.

The Define Relationship dialog box for a fact dimension is shown in Figure 11-14.

Parent/Child Dimensions

A *parent/child dimension* is built on a table that contains a self-referential relationship. We discussed parent/child relationships and saw how they are handled in the Tabular models in Chapter 10. (See Figure 10-2.)

When a table, such as the Employee table in Figure 10-2, is used to define a dimension, the Supervisor field becomes an attribute. This is a special type of attribute known as a *parent attribute*. A parent attribute is created by right-clicking an attribute in the Attributes column of the Dimension Design tab and selecting Set Attribute Usage | Parent from the context menu.

A parent/child dimension creates its own hierarchy. Each step from child to parent creates another level in that hierarchy. What is unique about this is there are an undetermined number of levels to the hierarchy. The number of hierarchy levels depends on the number of links in the parent/child chain you are following.

Role Playing Dimensions

A *role playing dimension* is a dimension that is related to the same measure group multiple times. Each relationship represents a different role the dimension plays relative to the measure group. One of the best examples of this is a time dimension and a sales measure group. The time dimension is related to the sales measure group once for the date of the sale, another time for the date of shipment, and a third time for the date of payment. In this case, the time dimension plays three different roles—date of sale, date of shipment, and date of payment—relative to the sales measure group.

To create a role playing dimension, add the dimension to the Dimension Usage tab multiple times. Each instance of the dimension should be renamed to reflect one of the roles it is playing for this measure group. Then, create a relationship between each instance of the dimension and the measure group.

Reference Dimensions

A reference dimension is not related directly to the measure group. Instead, a *reference dimension* is related to another regular dimension, which is, in turn, related to the measure group. This is referred to as the intermediate dimension. Reference dimensions are created by selecting Referenced from the Select relationship type drop-down list in the Define Relationship dialog box.

Data Mining Dimensions

We can include information discovered by data mining algorithms in our cubes for analysis. This is done through the creation of data mining dimensions. *Data mining dimensions* are created by selecting Data Mining from the Select relationship type drop-down list in the Define Relationship dialog box.

Many-to-Many Dimensions

Many-to-many dimensions, as the name implies, support many-to-many relationships between dimension members and measure group members. For example, if an e-commerce site allows an order to have multiple ship-to addresses, there is a many-to-many relationship. An order can have multiple addresses and, of course, an address can be used by more than one order.

In a relational database, a many-to-many relationship is implemented by creating an intermediate linking table. When a many-to-many relationship is implemented in an Analysis Services cube, the intermediate linking table becomes an intermediate fact table. Many-to-many dimensions are created by selecting Many-to-Many from the Select relationship type drop-down list in the Define Relationship dialog box.

Slowly Changing Dimensions

For our cubes to provide meaningful information from year to year, we need to have dimensions whose members are fairly constant. If the dimensions are changing drastically month to month, our analysis across the time dimension becomes worthless. Therefore, we need mainly static dimensions.

Some dimensions, however, change over time. Salespeople move from one sales territory to another. The corporate organizational chart changes as employees are promoted or resign. These are known as Slowly Changing Dimensions (SCDs).

SCDs come in many varieties with the most common being Type 1, Type 2, and Type 3, as defined by the Business Intelligence community. Not exciting names, but they didn't ask for my input, so it's what we are stuck with! Anyway, let's look at what differentiates each of these three common types of SCD.

Type 1 Slowly Changing Dimensions

When a dimension is implemented as a Type 1 SCD, we don't keep track of its history as it changes. The members of the dimension represent the way things are right now. With a *Type 1 SCD*, it is impossible to go back and determine the state of the dimension members at any time in the past.

In actuality, all dimensions in Analysis Services cubes are allowed to change. Some dimensions track that change so a previous state of that dimension's members can be reconstructed during analysis. These are the Type 2 SCD and Type 3 SCD, which we discuss in the sections "Type 2 Slowly Changing Dimensions" and "Type 3 Slowly Changing Dimensions." If a dimension does not track this change, it is a Type 1 SCD. In most cases, the majority of the dimensions in your cubes are going to be Type 1 SCD.

Let's consider a situation where we have four salespeople—Jackie, Andy, Sam, and Mollie—in four sales territories: A, B, C, and D. (All right, so maybe my naming isn't always that creative either!) Figure 11-15 shows the situation in May. Jackie is in sales territory A, Andy is in sales territory B, Sam is in sales territory C, and Mollie is in sales territory D. The figure reflects the fact that the four salespeople are expected to remain in their territories through the rest of the year.

Now, let's suppose at the beginning of July, Mollie is promoted to sales manager. Andy is moved to Mollie's former sales territory (sales territory D), and a new salesperson, Pat, is hired to take over Andy's former territory (sales territory B). The state of the

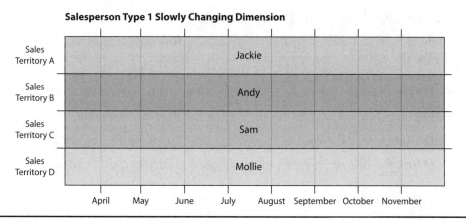

Figure 11-15 *The state of the salesperson Type 1 SCD in May*

salesperson dimension after the shuffling is shown in Figure 11-16. Because this is a Type 1 SCD, we do not track any history. We just overwrite the previous dimension information with the current dimension information.

If we perform analysis on sales information using this cube, it will look like Andy has always been in sales territory D and Pat has always been in sales territory B. This is true if we look at sales measures for June or if we look at sales information for October. The history is lost.

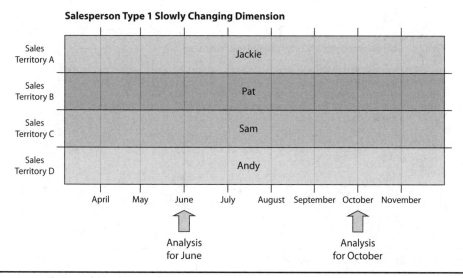

Figure 11-16 *The state of the salesperson Type 1 SCD after July*

Type 2 Slowly Changing Dimensions

When a dimension is implemented as a *Type 2 SCD*, four supplementary attributes are added to the dimension to track the history of that dimension. These four attributes are

▶ **SCD Original ID**   The unique identifier from the transactional system

▶ **SCD Start Date**   The date this dimension member became active

▶ **SCD End Date**   The date this dimension member ceased being active

▶ **SCD Status**   The current state of this dimension member, either active or inactive

Let's return to our salesperson dimension example. Figure 11-17 shows the state of the dimension in May. Three of the four new fields are shown in the figure: Start Date, End Date, and Status. Because none of the dimension members has an end date filled in, they are expected to remain active indefinitely into the future.

After the changes to the sales territories occur at the beginning of July, you can see how the new fields are used to track both the previous state and the current state of the sales territory assignments. This is shown in Figure 11-18. Now, by using the Start Date and End Date attributes, when we perform analysis for June, we see how the salespeople were arranged in June. When we do analysis for October, we see how the salespeople were arranged in October. When we want to find the current state of the dimension, we can use the Status attribute to quickly locate the active members rather than doing a lot of date comparisons.

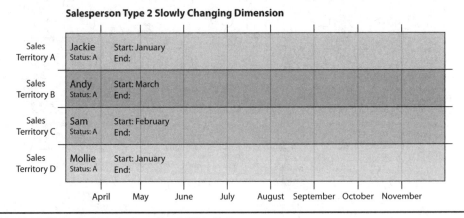

Figure 11-17   *The state of the salesperson Type 2 SCD in May*

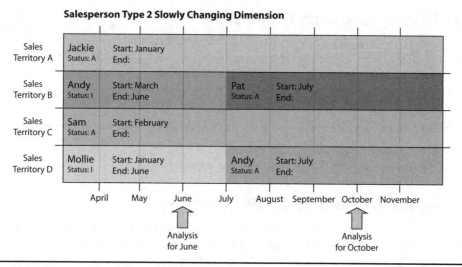

Figure 11-18 *The state of the salesperson Type 2 SCD after July*

The Original ID attribute holds a unique identifier that was used as the primary key for the dimension members in the original transactional system. This is used to help tie fact information coming from the transactional system to the appropriate dimension member. This Original ID cannot be used as the primary key in our dimension. Because a salesperson can appear in the dimension more than once, the Original ID associated with that salesperson would appear more than once. Therefore, we need to create an alternate key to be used as the primary key to prevent duplicate key violations.

In the Type 1 SCD example, each employee can only appear once in the Salesperson dimension. Therefore, the salesperson's Original ID can be used as the primary. This is not the case with the Type 2 SCD.

In the Type 2 SCD, a salesperson can appear in the dimension more than once. You can see this with Andy in Figure 11-18. Andy has two dimension members: the member with an effective start date in March and the member with the effective start date in July. If we defined a primary key using the Original ID, we would receive an error when we tried to insert the second entry into this dimension. When the alternate key is used as the primary key, there are no run-time errors because the alternate key is unique to each record in the dimension.

When we use the alternate key as the primary key, we also have to use it in the foreign key fields in the fact tables. That way, we can tell which measures are linked to Andy when he was in sales territory B and which measures are linked to Andy when he was in sales territory D.

Type 3 Slowly Changing Dimensions

A Type 3 SCD is similar to a Type 2 SCD with one exception. A Type 3 SCD does not track the entire history of the dimension members. Instead, a *Type 3 SCD* tracks only the current state and the original state of a dimension member.

A Type 3 SCD is implemented using two additional attributes:

▶ **SCD Start Date**   The date the current state of this dimension member became active

▶ **SCD Initial Value**   The original state of this attribute

Loading the Max Min Sales DM Data Mart

In addition to the Manufacturing data mart, we created another data mart back in Chapter 6. This is the Sales data mart. You will recall that we created both the database schema for the data mart and the OLAP cube definition at the same time using the Cube Wizard.

The cube we created for the Sales data mart includes an SCD to track the salespeople as they moved from job to job. You can see how we load data into an SCD by looking at the MaxMinSalesDMLoad project we use to populate the Sales data mart. We use this project to populate the MaxMinSalesDM database in Chapter 12.

You Are Special

In this chapter, we looked deeper into what makes an OLAP cube in a Multidimensional BI Semantic Model tick. We examined the cube's basic parts: measures and dimensions. In Chapter 12, we move from the basics to what makes Microsoft SQL Server Analysis Services such an outstanding tool. We examine many of the special features available to us as we work with our OLAP cubes.

Bells and Whistles: Special Features of OLAP Cubes

In This Chapter

- ▶ **Where No Cube Has Gone Before**
- ▶ **Additional Cube Features**
- ▶ **More Sophisticated Scripting**

I do not like poems that resemble hay compressed into a geometrically perfect cube.

—Yevgeny Yevtushenko

Thus far, we have created two data marts for our sample company, Maximum Miniatures, Incorporated. Both data marts are full of data. We also have an online analytical processing (OLAP) cube built on top of each of these data marts. You may think our work is almost done. On the contrary, it is just beginning!

We have data sitting in data marts in relational databases. We have cube definitions that exist as Extensible Markup Language (XML) definition documents in our development environments. What we do not have are multidimensional cubes filled with preprocessed aggregates waiting to help us create business intelligence. (In case you forgot after reading the first few chapters, that is why we are here.)

We begin by taking care of this very issue. We can deploy our cubes to SQL Server Analysis Services databases. We can then begin querying aggregates from the cubes and see benefit from our labors.

Once the cubes are deployed, we examine many of the special features available in these OLAP cubes. We move between SQL Server Data Tools and the SQL Server Management Studio to view the data and try out the development tools at our disposal.

Where No Cube Has Gone Before

We begin this chapter by taking our cubes where they have not gone before: to a Multidimensional SQL Server Analysis Services server. Up to this point, when we have worked with dimensions and measures, it has been as definitions in SQL Server Data Tools. This environment is great for creating and refining these objects. Unfortunately, dimensions and measures cannot do much when they only exist here. To put them to work, we must deploy them to an Analysis Services server.

Our Analysis Services projects in SQL Server Data Tools contain several properties that control deployment of the content of a project. Once these properties are set correctly, deploying the project content is a snap. All it takes is one selection from a context menu.

Alternatively, we can turn the entire definition of the project into an XML for Analysis (XML/A) script. This is done using the Analysis Services Deployment Wizard. As the script is generated by the Deployment Wizard, we have the ability to change some of the configuration information, such as server names and credentials, so the scripts function on different servers. Your environment may require slightly different configurations for development, quality assurance, and production. Once the script is generated with the appropriate configuration settings, it can be loaded into a SQL Server Management Studio query window and executed on an Analysis Services server.

Deploying and Processing

We need to complete two steps before our cubes become useful. First, we need to deploy the structures to the Analysis Services database. Second, we need to process those structures in the Analysis Services database.

Deploying

Deploying is the first step to creating a useful Analysis Services structure. When we *deploy* an Analysis Services project, we move that project's definition from the development environment to a server environment. In a development environment, the developer is the only one who has access to the objects in a project. In the server environment, those objects are exposed to any users with the appropriate access rights.

The objects in a project cannot reside on an Analysis Services server on their own. They must be contained within an Analysis Services database. The name of the database is specified in the project definition. If the specified database is not present, it is created as part of the deployment process.

Deploying a project results in an exact copy of that project's measures and dimensions on the server. Deploying a project does not result in any members being placed in those dimensions or any facts being placed in those measures. For this to happen, we need to process the Analysis Services database.

Processing

Processing is the procedure that pumps the database full of the good stuff. When an Analysis Services database is processed, it reads data from its data source. Dimensions are populated with members. Measures are populated with facts. Then the aggregates for all the combinations within the dimensional hierarchy are calculated.

Dimensions are processed first. Data is read from the dimension tables in the data source and used to create dimension members. After all of the dimension members are loaded, map files that contain all of the possible dimension and hierarchy member combinations are created. These map files are used for calculating aggregates.

Measures are processed after the dimension processing is complete. Data is read from the fact tables in the data source and used to create measures. The map files are used to ensure that aggregations are created for the entire cube.

When processing is complete, the Analysis Services database is ready for analysis to begin.

Deploying from SQL Server Data Tools

We first look at the steps necessary to deploy from SQL Server Data Tools. This method is certainly the most straightforward of our two options. However, as we see shortly, it does not provide the flexibility of the Analysis Services Deployment Wizard.

We begin with an Analysis Services project in SQL Server Data Tools. Several properties of this project must be set before the deployment can take place. These properties are found on the Deployment page of the Project Property Pages dialog box, shown in Figure 12-1.

Let's go through the properties starting at the bottom of the dialog box and working our way to the top. The *Database property* is the name of an Analysis Services database. This database is created on the server, if it does not already exist there. The *Server property* contains the name of a Multidimensional SQL Server Analysis Services server instance where the project is to be deployed.

The *Server Mode property* controls how the project is deployed; either all of the project is deployed or only the changed objects are deployed. The *Transactional Deployment property* determines whether the project is deployed as a single transaction or as multiple transactions. When this property is set to True, the project is deployed as a single transaction. If the project is deployed as multiple transactions, the deploying is done in one transaction and each processing operation done as part of the deployment is done in its own transaction.

The *Processing Option parameter* establishes what cube processing is done as part of the deployment. If Default is selected, the deployment includes whatever processing is necessary to bring the deployed objects to a fully processed state. If Do Not Process is selected, no processing is done. If Full is selected, all of the data is deleted from the deployed objects and all values are reloaded or recalculated.

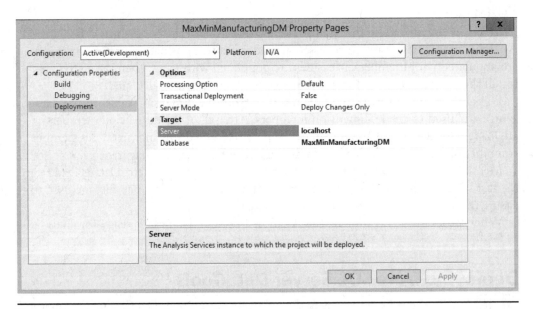

Figure 12-1   *The Project Property Pages dialog box*

The information entered on the Deployment page of the Project Property Pages dialog box is stored in two different configuration files. These files are located in the bin folder inside of the folder created for your project. The configuration settings are stored in the {*project name*}.deploymentoptions file. The deployment target settings are stored in the {*projectname*}.deploymenttargets file. Note that the bin folder and these deployment files are created as part of the deployment process so they will not be present until you have tried to deploy the project.

Once the properties on the Deployment page are set, we can perform the actual deployment. This can be done by selecting Build | Deploy {*project name*} from the Main menu or by right-clicking the project entry in the Solution Explorer window and selecting Deploy from the context menu. The progress of the deployment is displayed in the Output window and the Deployment Progress window, as shown in Figure 12-2.

SQL Server Data Tools begins the deployment by creating a script. This script contains commands to create the specified Analysis Services database, if necessary, and to create each of the objects in the project. If a processing option is selected for the project, the script also includes commands to process each object. This script is then executed on the specified server. We see what one of these scripts looks like in the next section of this book.

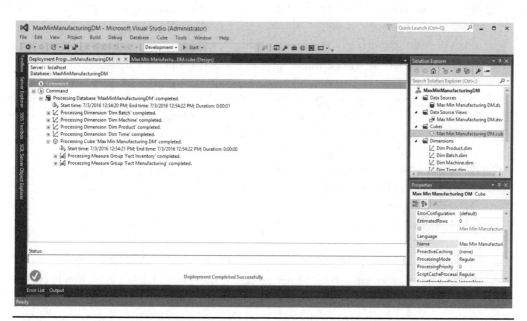

Figure 12-2   *Deploying an Analysis Services project from SQL Server Data Tools*

Learn By Doing: Deploying the MaxMinManufacturingDM Project Using SQL Server Data Tools

Features Highlighted

▶ Deploying an Analysis Services project using SQL Server Data Tools

▶ Using the Browse window in the SQL Server Management Studio to browse the content of a cube

Business Need   To have an OLAP cube we can finally put to use, we must deploy and process this project.

Steps to Deploy from SSDT

1. Open SQL Server Data Tools.

2. Open the MaxMinManufacturingDM project.

3. Select Project | MaxMinManufacturingDM Properties from the Main menu. The MaxMinManufacturingDM Property Pages dialog box appears.

4. For the Server property on the Deployment page, enter the name of a test or development server running a Multidimensional instance of SQL Server 2016 Analysis Services. (Do *not* perform this or any other Learn by Doing activity on a server used for production operations!)

5. MaxMinManufacturingDM should already be entered for Database.

6. Click OK to exit the MaxMinManufacturingDM Property Pages dialog box.

7. Select Build | Deploy MaxMinManufacturingDM from the Main menu. Provide a set of credentials for completing this deployment, if prompted to do so. Monitor the progress of the deployment in the Output and Deployment Progress windows until the Deployment Completed Successfully message appears.

8. Close the Deployment Progress tab.

9. To prove that we actually did something, we use SQL Server Management Studio to browse the cube in our newly created Analysis Services database. Open SQL Server Management Studio.

10. Select Analysis Services for Server type, and connect to the Analysis Services server where you deployed the project.

11. Expand the Databases folder under this server in the Object Explorer window.

12. Expand the entry for the MaxMinManufacturingDM database, and then expand the Cubes folder under this database.

13. Right-click the Max Min Manufacturing DM cube, and select Browse from the context menu. You see a Browse window, as shown in Figure 12-3.

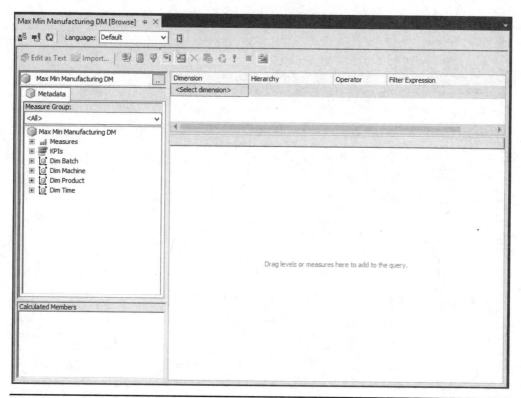

Figure 12-3   *The Browse window in SQL Server Management Studio*

14. Expand the Measures entry in the Metadata area of the Browse window. Drag the Total Products calculated member, and drop it on "Drag levels or measures here to add to the query." You see the total products calculated for the entire cube.

15. Expand the Dim Product entry in the Metadata area of the Browse window. Expand the Product Hierarchy entry beneath it. Drag the Product Type level, and drop it to the left of the Total Products column in the main area of the Browse window. You see the total products calculation spread across each of the product types.

16. Expand the Dim Time entry in the Metadata area of the Browse window. Expand the Date Hierarchy entry beneath it. Drag the Month level, and drop it between the Product Type and Total Products columns. You see the total products calculation spread across the product types and months of the year. This is shown in Figure 12-4.

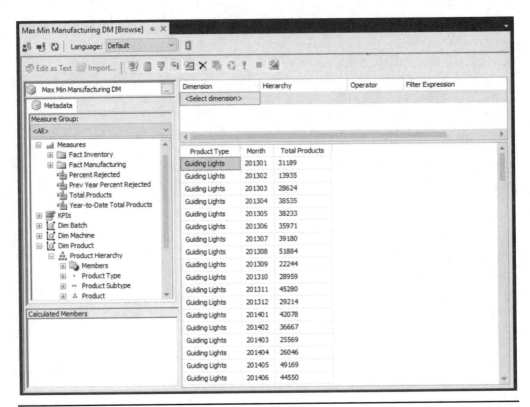

Figure 12-4   *Browsing the Max Min Manufacturing DM cube*

17. Drag the Year level, and drop it between the Product Type and Month columns. This is shown in Figure 12-5.

NOTE

We are able to skip levels in the hierarchy when we use the Browse window. In this example, we use the Year and Month levels of the Dim Time dimension without using the Quarter level.

18. Drag the Month heading off the query result until the mouse pointer includes an *X*, as shown in Figure 12-6. Drop the heading any time the mouse pointer includes the *X*, and this dimension is then removed from the query.

19. Continue to experiment with the Browse window as long as you like.

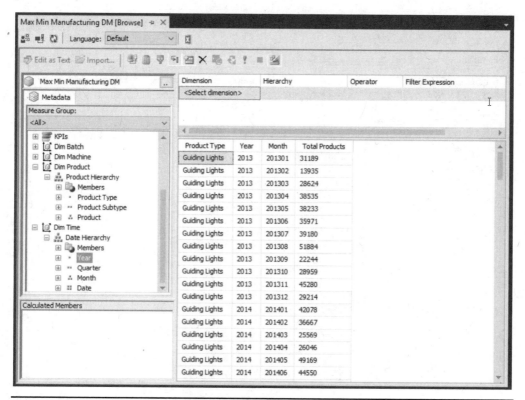

Figure 12-5   *Two levels from the Dim Time dimension in the Browse window*

Congratulations! You have just created and browsed your first multidimensional model. SQL Server 2016 greatly simplifies the creation of multidimensional models, but it still takes some work. Don't worry: This gets easier and goes faster each time you repeat the process from here on.

NOTE

We have loaded the detail-level data into our cube, but we have not yet created the preprocessed aggregates we have been talking about. We are able to get relatively quick results in the Browse window because the amount of data in our cube is relatively small. We discuss how to control the aggregation setting for the cube and create preprocessed aggregates in the "Aggregation Design" section of this chapter. Completing the aggregation design is essential to creating a cube that provides aggregated measures efficiently.

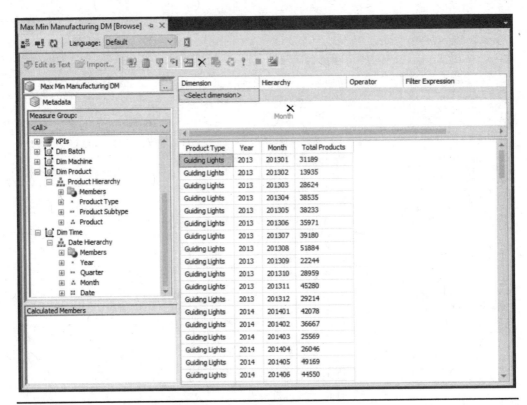

Figure 12-6 *Dragging an item out of the Browse window results area*

Deploying from the Analysis Services Deployment Wizard

Deploying the Analysis Services project from SQL Server Data Tools works well when we have access to the target Analysis Services server. At times, however, this may not be the case. And, at other times, we need to make changes to the configuration of the project when it is moved from the development environment into production. Fortunately, we have a second method for deploying that handles both of these needs: deploying from the Analysis Services Deployment Wizard.

The Analysis Services Deployment Wizard can deploy a project directly to a server, just like SQL Server Data Tools. However, it can also examine the definition of a project and create a JSON script for a Tabular model deployment or an XML/A script for a multidimensional model deployment. These scripts can re-create the model on a server. The JSON or XML/A script is written to a file. It is up to us to execute that file on the server to complete the deployment.

To use the wizard, we need to develop an Analysis Services project in SQL Server Data Tools. Once the project is developed, we need to perform a build operation on the project to create the files necessary for the wizard. This is done by selecting Build | Build {*project name*} from the Main menu. Once the project builds successfully, it is ready to deploy.

The wizard is a stand-alone program, separate from SQL Server Data Tools. The Analysis Services Deployment Wizard is launched from the Start screen. In the Microsoft SQL Server 2016 group, find the Deployment Wizard entry. Note, there is also an Integration Services Deployment Wizard application. The Analysis Services Deployment Wizard has an icon that includes a yellow cube. When you launch the Deployment Wizard, make sure it says "Analysis Services Deployment Wizard" across the top of the dialog box.

After the welcome page, the wizard prompts you for the path and name of an Analysis Services database file on the Specify Source Analysis Services Database page, shown in Figure 12-7. This database file is created when we build the Analysis Services project.

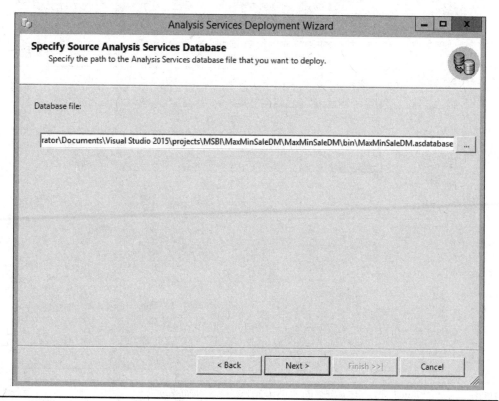

Figure 12-7   *The Specify Source Analysis Services Database page of the Analysis Services Deployment Wizard*

It has a file extension of .asdatabase and is located in the bin folder inside of the folder created for your project (for example, C:\...\Myproject\bin\MyAnalSrvcsProj .asdatabase).

The Installation Target page, shown in Figure 12-8, asks for the Analysis Services server and Analysis Services database this project is to be deployed to. Remember, the wizard does not perform the deployment; it only creates a script for the deploy step. Therefore, the wizard does not need access to the server you specify.

The Specify Options for Partitions and Roles page enables us to determine how partitions and security entities are to be handled by the deployment. We discuss partitions in the section "Partitions" in this chapter. We discuss security in Chapter 13. This page asks us to specify whether existing objects are overwritten or retained. Therefore, it only applies to situations where we are deploying updates to an existing database. The Specify Options for Partitions and Roles page is shown in Figure 12-9.

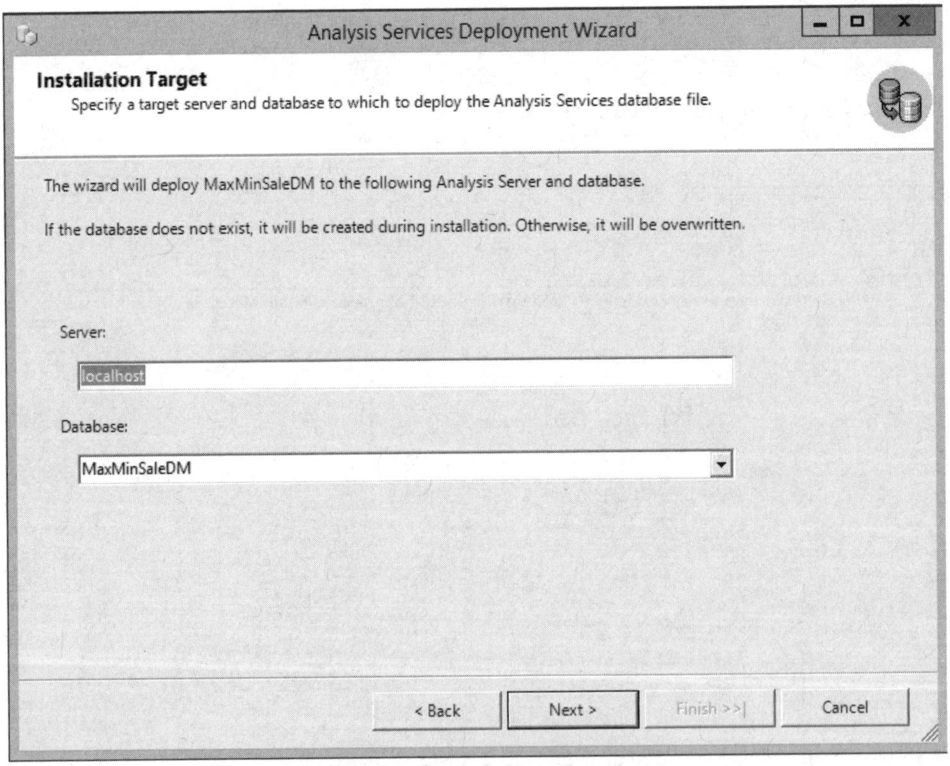

Figure 12-8 *The Installation Target page of the Analysis Services Deployment Wizard*

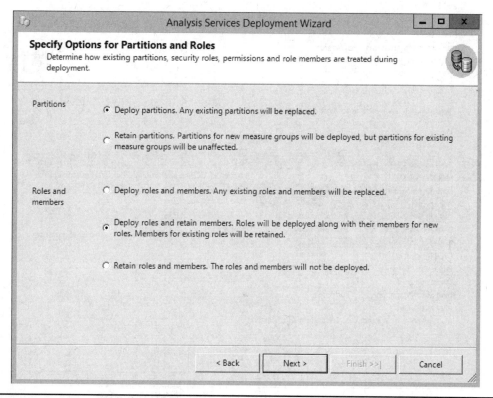

Figure 12-9   *The Specify Options for Partitions and Roles page of the Analysis Services Deployment Wizard*

The Specify Configuration Properties page, shown in Figure 12-10, collects a number of pieces of configuration information. First, it lets us specify whether the configuration and optimization settings for existing objects are retained or overwritten. Next, it enables us to modify the connection strings used by the data sources in this project. This may be necessary as projects are moved from a development environment to a production environment. We can also configure the impersonation settings, error log file locations, and the path to the database file being created.

The Data Source Impersonation Information entry specifies the Windows credentials that are to be impersonated by this data source while accessing the underlying database. The Default Data Source Impersonation Information entry specifies the Windows credentials that are impersonated if the data source's impersonation is set to default. Somewhere in this chain, we need an actual set of credentials to use during data processing. For this reason, you may need to select the service account for either the Data Source Impersonation Information or the Default Data Source Impersonation Information to deploy and process the script correctly.

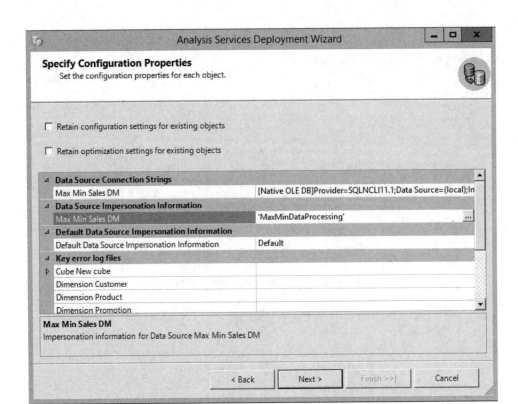

Figure 12-10   *The Specify Configuration Properties page of the Analysis Services Deployment Wizard*

The Select Processing Options page lets us select the type of processing we would like to occur as part of the deployment. It also enables us to configure the writeback options. We discuss writeback in the section "Writeback." This page also lets us choose whether the processing is done in one transaction or in multiple transactions. This page is shown in Figure 12-11.

The Confirm Deployment page, shown in Figure 12-12, is where we start the deployment process, either deploying to a server or creating a deployment script. The Create deployment script check box enables us to create a deployment script, rather than having the wizard deploy directly to the server. We need to specify the path and name if the script file option is selected.

Clicking Next on the Confirm Deployment page causes the wizard either to deploy the project to the server or to create the deployment script. Once either of these processes is completed, the page appears similar to Figure 12-13. The Deploying database page is followed by the Deployment Complete page, which confirms the deployment process, or at least the script generation, is complete.

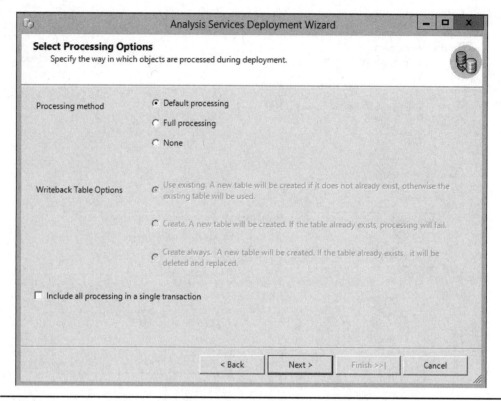

Figure 12-11   *The Select Processing Options page of the Analysis Services Deployment Wizard*

If a script is generated by the wizard, we need to execute that script on the appropriate instance, multidimensional or Tabular, of SQL Server 2016 Analysis Services. If the server is not directly connected to the development environment where it was created, the script file can be copied and transferred as needed. When the script is in a location that can be accessed by the Analysis Services server, it can be opened and executed in SQL Server Management Studio.

After starting SQL Server Management Studio, select File | Open | File from the Main menu or use the Open File button on the toolbar to load the deployment script. Loading the script causes the SQL Server Management Studio to open a query window and prompts you to connect to an Analysis Services server, if you are not already connected to one. Once the script is loaded and this connection is made, SQL Server Management Studio appears, similar to Figure 12-14.

Execute the script by selecting Query | Execute from the main menu. The script creates all of the items in your project and performs processing as you instructed in the Deployment Wizard. When the script is completed, you see the "Query executed successfully" message below the Query window.

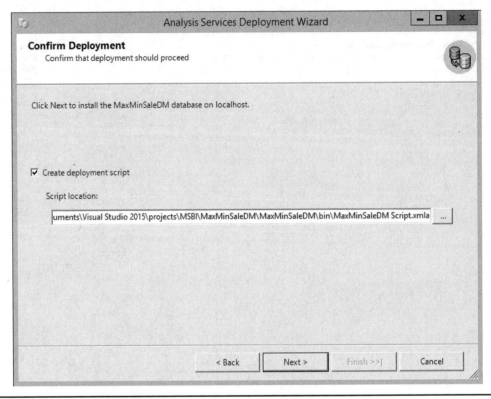

Learn By Doing: Deploying the MaxMinSalesDM Project Using the Analysis Services Deployment Wizard

Feature Highlighted

▶ Deploying an Analysis Services project using the Analysis Services Deployment Wizard

Business Need   To have a second OLAP cube ready to go, we must deploy and process the MaxMinSalesDM project.

NOTE

You need to either execute the MaxMinSalesDMLoad Integration Services package or restore the MaxMinSalesDM database from the materials provided for this book. If you do not, your cube will not contain data after processing.

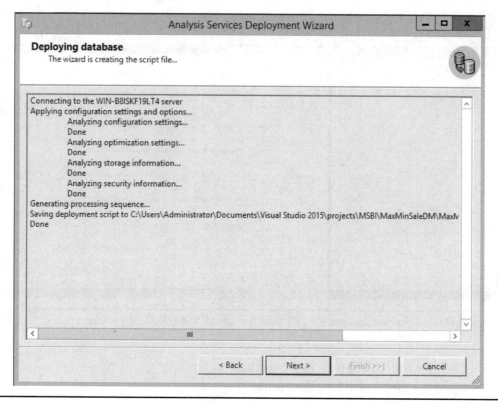

Figure 12-13 *The Deploying database page of the Analysis Services Deployment Wizard*

Steps to Make Additional Changes to the Model

1. Open SQL Server Data Tools.
2. Open the MaxMinSalesDM project.
3. Open the MaxMinSalesDM.dsv data source view.
4. Right-click anywhere in the unoccupied area of the data source view diagram, and select Refresh from the context menu. This will determine the differences between the structures in the data source view and the underlying relational tables. The Refresh Data Source View dialog box appears, listing these differences. These are the fields we manually added to the tables near the end of Chapter 6. We need to manually add these changes into the appropriate dimensions.
5. Click OK to incorporate these changes into the data source view. If you receive an error message, click OK.

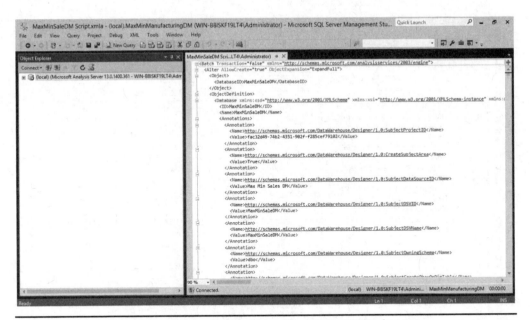

Figure 12-14   *The Deployment Script loaded in a SQL Server Management Studio XML/A Query window*

6. Click the Save All button on the toolbar.
7. Close the data source view design tab.
8. Open the Customer dimension.
9. In the Data Source View pane of the Customer dimension design tab, select the PK_Customer field.
10. Drag it to the Attributes pane.
11. Repeat this process with the Address, City, State, ZipCode, HomeOwner, MaritalStatus, NumCarsOwned, and NumChildrenAtHome fields.
12. In the Attributes pane, rename the PK Customer attribute to **Account Num**.
13. With Account Num still selected, change the OrderBy property in the Properties window to Key.
14. Click the Save All button on the toolbar.
15. Close the Customer design tab.
16. Open the Product dimension.
17. Drag the RetailPrice and Weight fields from the Data Source View pane to the Attributes pane.
18. Click the Save All button on the toolbar.
19. Close the Product design tab.

20. Repeat Steps 16–19 to add the Sales_Person_Territory field to the Sales Person dimension.

21. Repeat Steps 16–19 to add the Store_Type field to the Store dimension.

22. Select Build | Build MaxMinSalesDM from the Main menu.

23. Click the Save All button on the toolbar.

24. Close SQL Server Data Tools.

Steps to Create the Deployment Script

1. Launch the Analysis Services Deployment Wizard from the Start menu. The Analysis Services Deployment Wizard Welcome page appears.

2. Click Next on the Welcome page. The Specify Source Analysis Services Database page of the wizard appears.

3. Click the ellipsis button (…). The Open dialog box appears.

4. Browse to the location of the bin directory under the MaxMinSalesDM project. Select the MaxMinSalesDM.asdatabase file and click Open. Click Next. The Installation Target page of the wizard appears.

5. For the Server property, enter the name of a test or development server running a Multidimensional instance of SQL Server 2016 Analysis Services. (Do *not* perform this or any other Learn by Doing activity on a server used for production operations!)

6. MaxMinSalesDM should already be entered for Database. Click Next. The Specify Options for Partitions and Roles page of the wizard appears.

7. Leave the default settings on this page. Click Next. The Specify Configuration Properties page of the wizard appears.

8. Click the words "Default Data Source Impersonation Information" under Default Data Source Impersonation Information. An ellipsis (…) button appears. Click the ellipsis button. The Impersonation Information dialog box appears.

9. Select Use a specific Windows user name and password. Enter the User name and Password for an account that has administrative rights on the selected Analysis Services server. Click OK.

10. Click Next. The Select Processing Options page of the wizard appears.

11. For Processing method, select None.

12. Click Next. The Confirm Deployment page of the wizard appears.

13. Check Create deployment script. Click the ellipsis (…) button. The Save As dialog box appears. Browse to a folder that is accessible from the test or development Analysis Services server you are using. Enter **MaxMinSalesDM Script.xmla** for File name. Click Save, and then click Next. The Deploying database page of the wizard appears as the wizard creates the deployment script.

14. When the script creation is done, click Next. The Deployment Complete page of the wizard appears. Click Finish.

Steps to Execute the Deployment Script

1. Open SQL Server Management Studio and connect to a multidimensional instance of Analysis Services.

2. Click the Open File button on the toolbar. The Open File dialog box appears.

3. Browse to the location where you created the MaxMinSalesDM Script.xmla file. Select this file and click Open. The script is loaded into an XML/A Query window.

4. If prompted, enter the server name and appropriate credentials for the Analysis Services server, and then click Connect.

5. Select Query | Execute from the main menu. SQL Server Management Studio executes the script and creates the MaxMinSalesDM Analysis Services database.

6. When the Query has completed executing, right-click the Databases folder entry in the Object Explorer window, and select Refresh from the context menu. The MaxMinSalesDM database appears in the Object Explorer window.

7. Expand the MaxMinSalesDM database and the Data Sources folder.

8. Double-click the Max Min Sales DM data source. The Data Source Properties dialog box appears.

9. Click the Impersonation Info item to select it. Click the ellipsis (...) button. The Impersonation Information dialog box appears.

10. Enter the password for this user name and click OK.

11. Click OK to exit the Data Source Properties dialog box.

12. Right-click the MaxMinSalesDM database and select Process from the context menu. The Process Database dialog box appears.

13. Click OK to begin processing the database.

14. Click Close when processing is complete. Feel free to browse the MaxMinSales cube, just as we did with the Max Min Manufacturing DM cube.

NOTE

We have loaded the detail-level data into our cube, but we have not yet created the preprocessed aggregates we have been talking about. We are able to get relatively quick results in the Browse window because the amount of data in our cube is relatively small. We discuss how to control the aggregation setting for the cube and create preprocessed aggregates in the "Aggregation Design" section of this chapter. Completing the aggregation design is essential to creating a cube that provides aggregated measures efficiently.

Additional Cube Features

Throughout the past few chapters, we have learned how to create and, most recently, deploy Analysis Services cubes. I know you are all ready to rush off and create data marts and cubes to start analyzing your own data. This is when I need to be like the miracle knife salesperson on late-night TV and say, "But wait, there's more!"

SQL Server 2016 offers a number of special features in its OLAP cubes. These features enable us to provide our users with more meaningful, better organized, and more secure business intelligence. Space does not permit a detailed examination of each of these features. Instead, the goal here is to give you a basic understanding of each item so you can do additional exploration on your own. SQL Server 2016 has online documentation called Books Online. Refer to this documentation for a more detailed explanation.

Linked Objects

Depending on the intricacy of your organization and its data processing structure, you may end up creating a number of different Analysis Services cubes from a number of different data sources. Odds are there will be measures in two or three different cubes that a user wants to analyze together. We could solve this problem by duplicating the measures in several cubes. Duplicating data is not a great option, especially if we are preprocessing hundreds of thousands, or even millions, of aggregate values in each cube. Fortunately, we have a better alternative: using linked objects.

By linking objects, we can take measures and their related dimensions from one cube and allow them to be referenced through another cube. This solves our problem without creating maintenance nightmares. Once created, these linked measures and dimensions look to the end user like any other measure or dimension in the cube.

Creating a Linked Measure

Linked objects are created on the Cube Structure tab of the Cube Design tab in SQL Server Data Tools. We open the project for the cube that will contain the linked objects. Right-click in the Measures or Dimensions area, and select New Linked Object from the context menu, as shown in Figure 12-15, to launch the Linked Object Wizard.

After the introductory page, the Select a Data Source page of the wizard is displayed. Here, we can select an existing Analysis Service data source, if one exists, or create a new data source using the New Data Source button. If the New Data Source button is clicked, the Data Source Wizard appears. This wizard walks us through the creation of a new data source as we have done previously. The only difference is we are creating a connection to an Analysis Services database, rather than to a transactional database.

Once a data source is created, we are returned to the Linked Object Wizard. Clicking Next takes us to the Select Objects page of the wizard. On this page, we can select the dimensions and measures we want to utilize from this cube to link back into the cube open in SQL Server Data Tools. This is shown in Figure 12-16.

The next page of the wizard lets us review our selections and complete the process. After we click Finish, the selected items are added to the cube definition open in SQL Server Data Tools, as shown in Figure 12-17. The linked items appear in the Measures

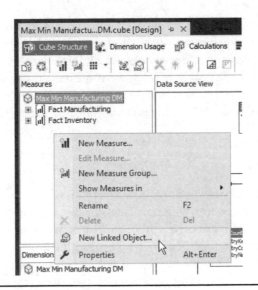

Figure 12-15 *Creating a linked object*

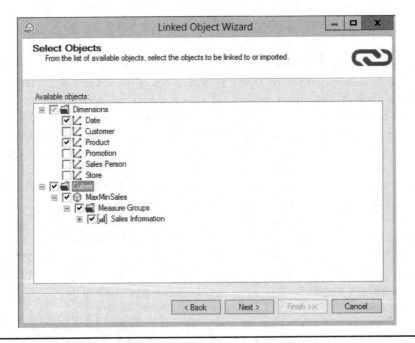

Figure 12-16 *The Select Objects page of the Linked Object Wizard*

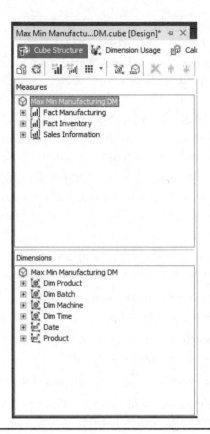

Figure 12-17 *A cube definition with linked objects*

and Dimensions areas with a chain link added to their icons. These items must still be maintained through their original cube. This is why the source tables for these dimensions are not added to the Data Source View in this cube.

The Business Intelligence Wizard

A number of complex business intelligence concepts can be applied to cubes in SQL Server 2016 Analysis Services. SQL Server Data Tools wraps a number of these concepts into the Business Intelligence Wizard. You can think of this as being eight wizards wrapped into one.

The Business Intelligence Wizard enables us to do any of the following:

▶ **Define time intelligence**   Adds time-related calculated measures to the cube. This includes period-to-date calculations, rolling averages, and period-over-period growth.

▶ **Define account intelligence**   Identifies a dimension and its attributes that define a chart of accounts. Once the chart of accounts is defined, additional calculated values can be created using the account definition.

▶ **Define dimension intelligence**   Identifies a dimension and its attributes as being of a certain type, such as products, customers, rates, time, and so forth. Once the dimension type is defined, additional calculated values can be created using the dimension definition.

▶ **Specify a unary operator**   Specifies the operator to be used instead of the default aggregation in a dimension with a parent-child hierarchy.

▶ **Create a custom member formula**   Creates a calculation to be used instead of the default aggregation in a hierarchy.

▶ **Specify attribute ordering**   Specifies how the members of a particular attribute are to be sorted. The default order is by name.

▶ **Define semiadditive behavior**   Defines the semiadditive behavior of a measure.

▶ **Define currency conversion**   Defines the rules for converting currency and analyzing other multinational information.

The Business Intelligence Wizard is launched by clicking the Add Business Intelligence button on the Cube Structure tab of the Cube Design tab toolbar or by right-clicking a cube or a dimension in the Solution Explorer window and selecting Add Business Intelligence from the context menu. This is shown in Figure 12-18.

Key Performance Indicators

A key performance indicator (KPI) lets us define a simple, graphic method for analyzing business intelligence that is important to our organization. *KPIs* are meant to enable a decision maker to monitor a number of key aspects of the organization's operations at a single glance. KPIs are often used as part of a concept called a digital dashboard.

The *digital dashboard* is modeled after the dashboard in your car: On the car's dashboard, a number of gauges and lights enable you to easily monitor the status of your car's operation. When you want to know what speed you are traveling at, you don't need to wade through an output of the tire's rotational speed over the past few minutes or

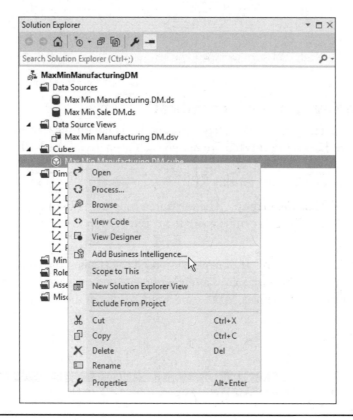

Figure 12-18 *Launching the Business Intelligence Wizard*

perform a calculation to determine the tire's circumference. All of the intelligence is built into the dashboard. You simply look down at the speedometer, and the needle tells you what your speed is.

The same is true with the digital dashboard. The decision maker doesn't need to plow though voluminous reports or crunch numbers in a spreadsheet to determine how the organization is doing against specified goals. This business intelligence is in the digital dashboard. A set of electronic gauges and other symbols provides the necessary status information at a single glance.

In SQL Server 2016 Analysis Services, a KPI can reflect five different status levels:

▶   Very Good

▶   Good

- ▶ Fair
- ▶ Bad
- ▶ Very Bad

Creating a Key Performance Indicator

Key performance indicators are created using the KPIs tab on the Cube Design tab shown in Figure 12-19. On this tab, we define each property of the KPI:

- ▶ **Name**   A unique name for this KPI.
- ▶ **Associated Measure Group**   The measure group being used to calculate the values for this KPI. This can be a single measure group in the cube or all measure groups in the cube.
- ▶ **Value Expression**   An MDX expression used to calculate the current value of the KPI. This may be as simple as a single measure or a calculated member from the cube, or it may be a complex MDX expression looking at the interaction of several measures.

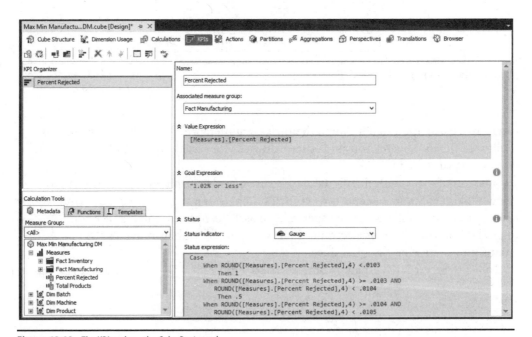

Figure 12-19   *The KPIs tab on the Cube Design tab*

▶ **Goal Expression**   An MDX expression used to express the current goal for the KPI. If the goal is a set value, this is a constant value. In other cases, the goal may need to reflect cyclic trends or it may need to vary, depending on dimensional members. The goal could even come from a dimensional attribute. For example, the production goal for each product could be an attribute in the product dimension.

▶ **Status Indicator**   The graphical representation to be used with this KPI. SQL Server Data Tools and its KPI viewer support nine different graphics. Be aware, however: The graphics available to the user depend heavily on the client tool being used to browse and analyze the cube.

▶ **Status Expression**   An MDX expression used to translate the current value of the KPI into a graphic representation. As noted previously, the KPI can support five different status levels. These equate to five different numeric values: 1 for Very Good, 0.5 for Good, 0 for Fair, –0.5 for Bad, and –1 for Very Bad. The MDX expression must calculate the appropriate value for each status.

Beyond these required items, we can define the following to give the KPI additional functionality:

▶ **Trend Indicator**   The graphical representation to be used when expressing the direction in which the KPI value is trending. SQL Server Data Tools and its KPI viewer support four different graphics. As with the Status Indicator, the graphics available to the user depend heavily on the client tool being used to browse and analyze the cube.

▶ **Trend Expression**   An MDX expression used to translate the trend of the KPI value into a graphic representation. The KPI supports five trend states: 1 for an upward trend, 0.5 for a mildly upward trend, 0 for a flat trend, –0.5 for a mildly downward trend, and –1 for a downward trend. The MDX expression must calculate the appropriate value for each trend situation.

▶ **Display Folder**   The grouping folder for this KPI. This property can be used to collect KPIs into groupings. KPIs that are related can be placed in the same display folder. The client tool used to browse and analyze the cube should then present all of the KPIs in a display folder as a single grouping.

▶ **Parent KPI**   The KPI that serves as a rollup for this and other child KPIs. KPIs can be created in a hierarchical structure, where one KPI displays the status of a rollup value and its child KPIs display the status of the more detailed indicators that make up this value.

▶ **Current Time Member** An MDX expression defining the current time member. We discuss the concept of a current member of a dimension in Chapter 13.

▶ **Weight** An MDX expression that expresses the emphasis given to this KPI relative to other KPIs in the group. This expression usually returns a numeric value.

▶ **Description** A textual description of the KPI.

Key Performance Indicators and Client Software

We can define KPIs in our cubes and even suggest the graphics we would like used to present those KPIs. However, it is up to the client software used to browse and analyze the cube to display the KPI. Therefore, the client software must not only have the same graphics available, but also honor our suggested graphic for each KPI for the KPIs to appear as we designed them.

You should look at the capabilities of the client tools being used in your organization before spending a lot of time defining KPIs. Make sure KPIs are supported, and determine which parts of the KPI definition the client tools can utilize.

Learn By Doing: Adding a KPI to the Max Min Manufacturing DM Cube

Feature Highlighted

▶ Defining a key performance indicator

Business Need Maximum Miniatures is contemplating the creation of a digital dashboard using KPIs. An initial KPI should be created showing the status of the Percent Rejected calculated measure. This KPI will be used as part of a proof-of-concept project.

The Percent Rejected KPI should reflect the status as follows:

▶ Values less than 1.03 percent should get a Very Good status.

▶ Values greater than or equal to 1.03 percent but less than 1.04 percent should get a Good status.

▶ Values greater than or equal to 1.04 percent but less than 1.05 percent should get a Fair status.

▶ Values greater than or equal to 1.05 percent but less than 1.06 percent should get a Bad status.

▶ Values greater than or equal to 1.06 percent should get a Very Bad status.

Steps to Create a KPI in the Model

1. Open SQL Server Data Tools.
2. Open the MaxMinManufacturingDM project.
3. Double-click the entry for Max Min Manufacturing DM.cube in the Solution Explorer window. The Cube Design tab appears.
4. Select the KPIs tab. Click the New KPI button on the KPIs tab toolbar.
5. Enter **Percent Rejected** for Name.
6. Select Fact Manufacturing from the Associated measure group drop-down list.
7. Enter the following for Value Expression:

```
[Measures].[Percent Rejected]
```

8. Enter the following for Goal Expression:

```
"1.02% or less"
```

9. Leave Status indicator set to the default of Gauge.
10. Enter the following MDX expression for Status Expression:

```
Case
    When ROUND([Measures].[Percent Rejected],4) <.0103
        Then 1
    When ROUND([Measures].[Percent Rejected],4) >= .0103 AND
        ROUND([Measures].[Percent Rejected],4) < .0104
        Then .5
    When ROUND([Measures].[Percent Rejected],4) >= .0104 AND
        ROUND([Measures].[Percent Rejected],4) < .0105
        Then 0
    When ROUND([Measures].[Percent Rejected],4) >= .0105 AND
        ROUND([Measures].[Percent Rejected],4) < .0106
        Then -.5
    Else -1
End
```

We discuss MDX expressions in detail in Chapter 13.

11. Click the Save All button on the toolbar. The KPIs tab should appear similar to Figure 12-19.
12. We now want to use SQL Server Data Tools's KPI browser to look at the result of our efforts. To do this, we need to deploy these modifications to the Analysis Services database. Select Build | Deploy MaxMinManufacturingDM from the Main menu.
13. Enter the appropriate credentials, if prompted for them.
14. When the Deployment Completed Successfully message appears, close the Deployment Progress tab.
15. Click the Browser View button on the KPIs tab toolbar, as shown in Figure 12-20. The KPI browser appears.

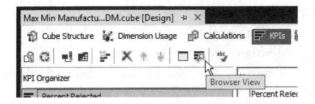

Figure 12-20 *The Browser View toolbar button*

The KPI browser shows us the Percent Rejected KPI we just created, as shown in Figure 12-21. The value shown represents the value for the Percent Rejected calculated measure across the entire cube. Our KPI translates this value to a status of Bad (between the red and yellow areas on the gauge).

The upper portion of the KPI browser allows us to filter the information we are sending to the KPI. We use the filter to look at the KPI for some specific dates of production, rather than across the entire cube.

16. Click the cell containing <Select dimension> in the upper portion of the KPI browser. A dimension drop-down list appears. Select Dim Time from this drop-down list. (If <Select dimension> does not appear in the upper portion of the KPI browser, click the Reconnect button on the toolbar of the KPIs tab.)

17. Click the cell immediately below the Hierarchy heading. The hierarchy drop-down list appears. Select Date Hierarchy from this drop-down list.

18. Click the cell immediately below the Filter Expression heading. The Filter Expression drop-down window control appears. Click the down arrow to display the drop-down window.

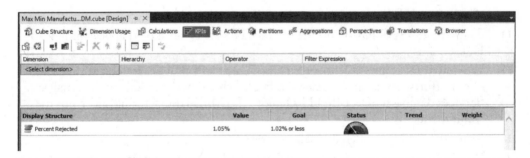

Figure 12-21 *The KPI browser with the Percent Rejected KPI for the entire cube*

19. Expand the All entry in the drop-down window. Next, expand the 2013 entry, the 2013Q1 entry, and the 201301 entry. Check 2013-01-02 and click OK.

20. Click anywhere on the KPI browser so the Filter Expression cell loses focus. This causes the KPI to refresh. The KPI browser now has a value of 1.04 percent, which translates to a status of Fair (straight up in the yellow), as shown in Figure 12-22.

21. Try this process again for the following dates:

Date	Value	Status
2013-01-07	1.06%	Very Bad
2013-01-17	1.03%	Good
2013-01-29	1.02%	Very Good

Be sure to uncheck one date before checking another to see the results described here. Also, remember to click anywhere on the KPI browser so the Filter Expression cell loses focus in order to see the result of each change to the filter value.

22. You can experiment with additional analysis. Try adding a second filter to see the KPI for a single product or a single product type.

Actions

Actions allow the OLAP cubes to "reach out and touch someone." They enable us to define commands, statements, and directives that are to be executed outside of the cube. In fact, Actions are designed to be executed outside of the Analysis Services environment altogether.

Actions are instructions that are defined and stored inside the cube itself. They are linked to certain objects in the cube. When the user is browsing a certain object

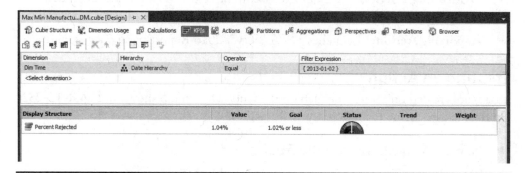

Figure 12-22 *The KPI browser with the Percent Rejected KPI for January 2, 2013*

in the client software, that software can look for any Actions related to the object. These Actions are then displayed to the user as menu items or Action buttons on the client screen. The user can select one of these Actions to launch separate, but related, applications or interfaces to accomplish related tasks.

For example, suppose a user is browsing a cube that analyzes changing stock prices. This cube may include an action for navigating to a website that contains up-to-the-minute market analysis. If the stock symbol for the company is stored as an attribute in the cube, the Action could pass this along as a parameter in the Uniform Resource Locator (URL).

In another case, a user may be browsing a cube that contains information on purchasing. The cube could include an Action that would launch the organization's document management system and take the user to the folder containing scanned copies of the hardcopy purchase orders. Then, when a questionable purchase is spotted, the user can launch the document management program and examine the paper trail for the purchase.

Types of Actions

Three different types of Actions are available:

- **Action**   The generic Action type, which has a number of subtypes:
  - **Dataset**   Retrieves a dataset.
  - **Proprietary**   A proprietary action defined by the client software.
  - **Rowset**   Retrieves a rowset.
  - **Statement**   Runs an OLE DB command.
  - **URL**   Displays a page in a browser.
- **Drillthrough Action**   Defines a dataset to be returned as a drillthrough to a more detailed level.
- **Reporting Action**   Launches a SQL Server 2016 Reporting Services report.

Creating an Action

Actions are created on the Actions tab on the Cube Design tab shown in Figure 12-23. On this tab, we define each property of the action:

- **Name**   A unique name for this Action.
- **Target type**   The type of object with which this Action is associated.

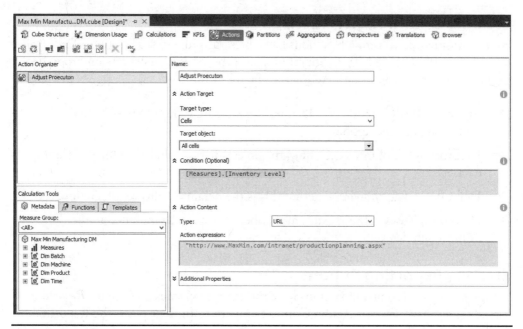

Figure 12-23 *The Actions tab on the Cube Design tab*

- ▶ **Target object**   The specific objects of the selected Target type to which this Action is associated.

- ▶ **Condition**   An MDX expression defining a condition that would further limit the objects to which this Action is associated.

- ▶ **Type**   The type of Action (Dataset, Proprietary, Rowset, Statement, or URL).

- ▶ **Action expression**   The command that is executed to carry out the Action.

- ▶ **Invocation**   How the command is executed: Batch, Interactive, On Open.

- ▶ **Application**   The application used to carry out the Action.

- ▶ **Description**   A description of the Action.

- ▶ **Caption**   A caption for this Action.

- ▶ **Caption is MDX**   A flag showing whether the caption is a string constant or an MDX expression to be evaluated.

Creating Drillthrough Actions

For the most part, Drillthrough Actions have the same properties as Actions. *Drillthrough Actions* do not have Target Type, Target Object, Type, or Action expression properties. In their place, the Drillthrough Action has the following:

► **Measure Group Members** Defines the measure groups to which this drillthrough action applies.

► **Drillthrough Columns** Defines the objects to be included in the drillthrough dataset.

► **Default** A flag showing whether this is the default Drillthrough Action.

► **Maximum Rows** The maximum number of rows to be included in the drillthrough dataset.

Creating Reporting Actions

For the most part, Reporting Actions have the same properties as Actions. *Reporting Actions* do not have Type or Action Content properties. In their place, the Reporting Action has the following:

► **Server name** The name of the report server.

► **Report path** The path to the report server.

► **Report format** The format of the report to be returned (HTML, Excel, PDF).

► **Parameters** The parameter values to be passed to the report.

Actions and Client Software

We can define Actions in our cubes. However, it is up to the client software used to browse and analyze the cube to display and implement the Action. You should look at the capabilities of the client tools being used in your organization before spending a lot of time defining Actions. Make sure Actions are supported, and determine which parts of the Action definition the client tools can utilize.

Partitions

We have deployed and processed our cubes to databases on the SQL Server Analysis Services server. We now have, as we have seen, cubes full of information that can be browsed and analyzed. What we have not discussed up to this point is exactly how and where the information in the databases is stored. Let's take care of that deficiency right now.

Measure Groups and Partitions

When we created the measure groups in our cubes, SQL Server Data Tools created something else for us behind the scenes. It created one partition for each of our measure groups. These partitions are where all of the measure group information is stored. We can view the partitions defined in a cube by using the Partitions tab on the Cube Design tab, as shown in Figure 12-24.

In Figure 12-24, you can see the partitions that were created for each of the measure groups in the Max Min Manufacturing DM cube. The partitions were given the same name as the measure group they are tied to. The *Source column* on this tab tells us where each partition, and therefore each measure group, gets its fact data. Each partition is tied to a fact table in the data mart. The *Aggregation Design column* tells us how each partition is configured for storing aggregate data.

Multiple Partitions for a Measure Group

Although we start out with one partition for each measure group, that does not mean we have to keep it that way. We can assign a number of partitions to a single measure group. Each partition has its own data source table. The Standard Edition of SQL Server 2016 allows us to create up to three partitions per measure group. The Enterprise Edition and Developer Edition support this feature without a limitation on the number of partitions per measure group.

This is similar to the concept of partitioned views on the relational side of SQL Server. With partitioned views, we distribute the data from what would be a large table among a number of smaller tables, as shown in Figure 12-25. Sales data from 2012 is in

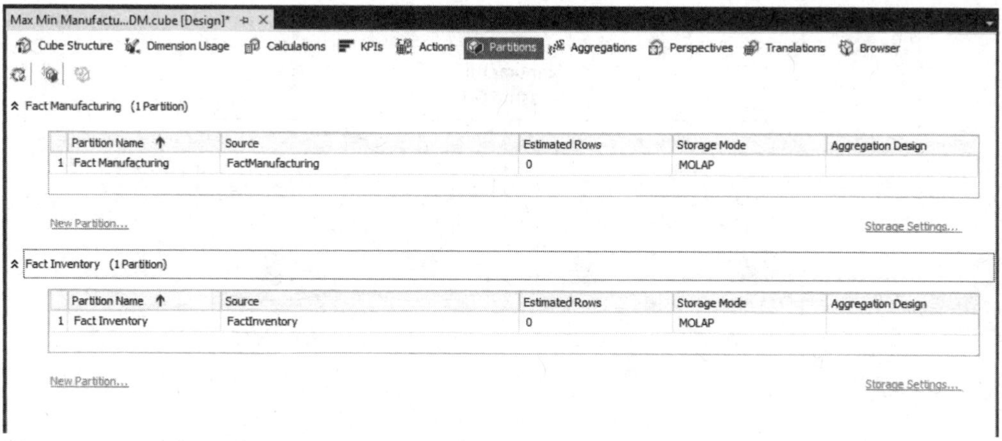

Figure 12-24 *The Partitions tab on the Cube Design tab*

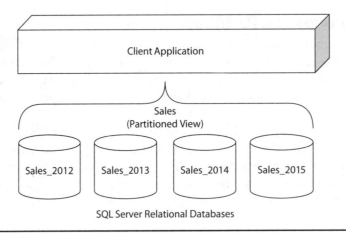

Figure 12-25 *A partitioned view*

one table. Sales data from 2013 is in another table, and so on. These tables are presented to the client application as if they were a single table by combining them together in a partitioned view. This is done for ease of management and for better performance.

We can essentially do the same thing with partitions and measure groups, as shown in Figure 12-26. Our data can be divided among a number of tables. These tables could

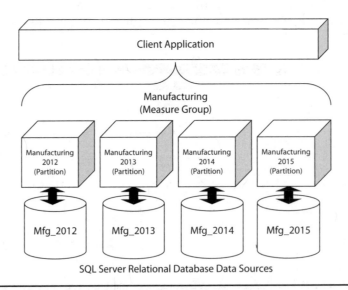

Figure 12-26 *A measure group with multiple partitions from multiple relational tables*

be in the same data source or in different data sources. Because they can be in different data sources, the tables could even be on different database servers. We can define multiple partitions, each one pulling data from one of the data source tables. These multiple partitions are then brought together in a single measure group.

As with a partitioned view in a relational database, all of the partitions combined in a single measure group must have the same structure. They must have the same measures and the same relationships to dimensions. If the measures and dimensional relationships don't match, we cannot make the partitions into a single measure group.

It is also possible to create multiple partitions from a single table. We may want to do this because our source data works just fine in a single table, but we can better manage it as a number of separate partitions in Analysis Services. This is appropriate for larger tables where only the newer data in the table is changing. This is shown in Figure 12-27.

We do this by creating a number of views in the relational database or named queries in the data source view. You can think of named queries as equivalent to views. They are defined in the data source view of a cube. We try creating a few named queries in the section "Learn By Doing: Creating Multiple Partitions from a Single Table." Each view or named query becomes the data source for a single partition. The partitions are joined together again by the measure group.

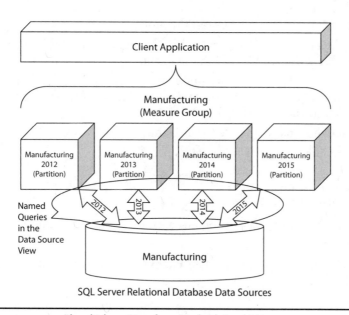

Figure 12-27 *A measure group with multiple partitions from a single relational table*

Any time we use multiple partitions in a single measure group, but especially when using named queries with a single table, we must be careful not to get the same data in two partitions. If this occurs, the information in our measure group will be incorrect. To prevent this, it is important to strictly define the criteria for membership in each view or named query. In many cases, dividing data by time is wise, as is shown in Figures 12-25, 12-26, and 12-27.

Learn By Doing: Creating Multiple Partitions from a Single Table

Features Highlighted

▶   Creating named queries in a data source view

▶   Creating multiple partitions for a single measure group

Business Need   To better manage the Fact Manufacturing information in Analysis Services, this measure group should utilize three partitions. One partition should contain data from 2013, one partition should contain data from 2014, and one partition should contain data from 2015.

Steps to Create Named Queries in the Data Source View

1. Open SQL Server Data Tools.
2. Open the MaxMinManufacturingDM project.
3. Double-click the entry for the Max Min Manufacturing DM.dsv data source view. The Data Source View Design tab appears.
4. Right-click any place there isn't a table in the data source diagram area. Select New Named Query from the context menu. The Create Named Query dialog box appears, as shown in Figure 12-28.
5. Enter **FactManufacturing_2013** for Name.
6. Enter the following query in the SQL pane:

```
SELECT *
FROM FactManufacturing
WHERE YEAR(DateOfManufacture) = 2013
```

The Create Named Query dialog box appears, as shown in Figure 12-29.

7. Click OK.
8. Create a second named query called **FactManufacturing_2014**, which includes only 2014 data.

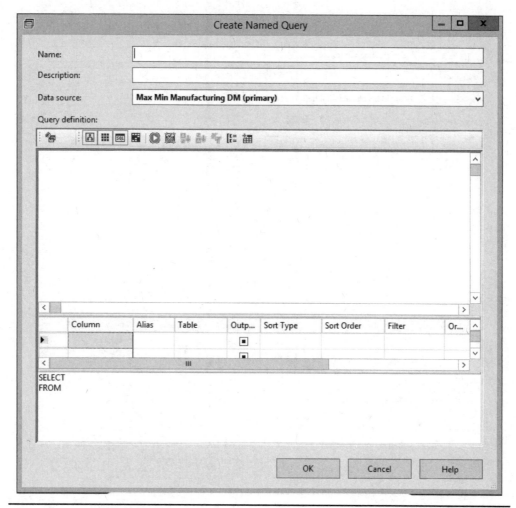

Figure 12-28 *Creating a new named query*

9. Create a third named query called **FactManufacturing_Current** using the following query:

```
SELECT *
FROM FactManufacturing
WHERE YEAR(DateOfManufacture) > 2014
```

Obviously, some annual maintenance is required at the beginning of each year. At least, by keeping our final named query open-ended, using > 2014 rather than = 2015, we do not run the risk of leaving out data.

10. Click the Save All button on the toolbar, and close the Data Source View Design tab.

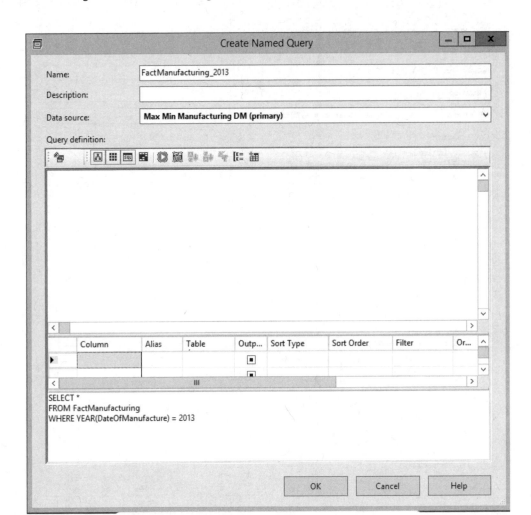

Figure 12-29 *The FactManufacturing_2013 Named Query definition*

Steps to Add Partitions to the Cube

1. Double-click the entry for Max Min Manufacturing DM.cube in the Solution Explorer window. The Cube Design tab appears.

2. Select the Partitions tab.

3. Click the New Partition link or the New Partition button on the Partitions tab toolbar. The Welcome page of the Partition Wizard dialog box appears.

4. Click Next on the Welcome page. The Specify Source Information page of the wizard appears. Select the Fact Manufacturing measure group and the Max Min

Manufacturing DM data source view if they are not already selected. Click the Find Tables button, and check FactManufacturing_2013 in the Available tables list.

5. Click Next. The Restrict Rows page of the wizard appears. Here, we can further filter the rows in the selected table or named query to ensure no overlap exists between partitions. Our named queries are structured such that no overlap occurs, so we do not need to specify a filter here.

6. Click Next. The Processing and Storage Locations page of the wizard appears. This page enables us to specify which Analysis Services server is to be used to calculate the aggregates and where the resulting data should be stored. You can see, if we needed a great deal of computing power to calculate a large set of aggregates, we could have a separate server for calculating each partition! If we needed a large amount of storage space, we could have a separate drive system to store the data from each partition! We don't have those types of requirements, so we can leave the defaults.

7. Click Next. The Completing the Wizard page appears. This page lets us choose when and how to design aggregations. We discuss the Aggregation Design Wizard later in this chapter. For now, select Design aggregations later.

8. Click Finish. The new partition appears under the Fact Manufacturing measure group.

9. Repeat Steps 3–8 for the FactManufacturing_2014 named query.

10. Repeat Steps 3–8 for the FactManufacturing_Current named query.

11. Right-click the original Fact Manufacturing partition, and select Delete from the context menu. The Delete Objects dialog box appears.

12. Click OK to confirm the deletion. Click the Save All button on the toolbar. The Partitions tab should appear as shown in Figure 12-30.

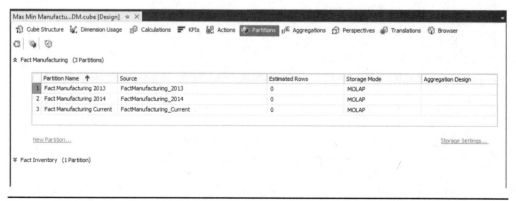

Figure 12-30 *The Fact Manufacturing measure group with three partitions*

Partitions and Storage Options

In Chapter 4, we discussed the different types of OLAP architectures: Relational OLAP (ROLAP), Multidimensional OLAP (MOLAP), and Hybrid OLAP (HOLAP). Refer to Figure 4-4 if you need a refresher. We are now going to discuss these storage options with regard to our partitions.

As we have said, the aggregates in our partitions are going to be preprocessed. Once the preprocessing is completed, all of that data needs to be stored somewhere. SQL Server 2016 Analysis Services provides us with a number of options here, enabling us to select the best mix of query speed versus data latency.

If we click the Storage Settings link or the Storage Settings button on the Partitions tab toolbar, we see the Partition Storage Settings dialog box, as shown in Figure 12-31. This dialog box presents a continuum of storage choices on the Standard Setting slider. These are preconfigured storage options that Analysis Services makes available to us. You can also create your own custom storage settings, but leave that alone for the moment.

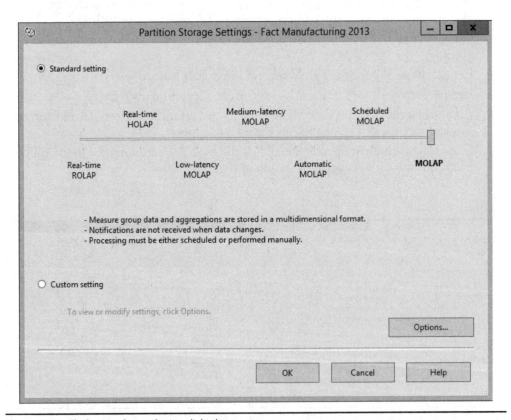

Figure 12-31 *The Partition Storage Settings dialog box*

The options on the left side of the slider represent the lowest latency but the slowest query speed. The options on the right side of the slider represent the highest latency but the fastest query speed. We need to determine the best choice for each partition.

The predefined options control the following characteristics:

▶ **Storage location for the detail data and the preprocessed aggregates** The detail data and preprocessed aggregates can be stored in one of the following three ways:

    ▶ **ROLAP** The detail data and the preprocessed aggregates are both stored in a relational format.

    ▶ **HOLAP** The detail data is stored in a relational format and the aggregates are stored in a multidimensional format.

    ▶ **MOLAP** The detail data and the preprocessed aggregates are both stored in a multidimensional format.

▶ **How Analysis Services finds out a data source has changed** Analysis Services can discover data source changes in the following ways:

    ▶ **SQL Server Notification** The SQL Server relational database engine notifies Analysis Services when changes are made to a data source table. When the partition is linked to a view or a named query, we must specify a SQL table that will cause the notification when it is changed. This is known as a *tracking table.*

    ▶ **Client Initiated Notification** The client software that is responsible for updating the relational data source sends a NotifyTableChangeCommand to Analysis Services to let it know that data has been changed. Of course, this only works if the data source is modified exclusively through this client software.

    ▶ **Scheduled Polling** Analysis Services periodically runs a query to determine if the data has changed. This query must return a single value that is compared with the value saved from the previous query execution. This value could be the MAX() of an identity field in the fact table that catches adds, but not edits and deletes. This could also be a MAX() of a last updated date/time stamp, which would catch inserts and edits, but still miss deletes.

▶ **Enable Proactive Caching** Whether proactive caching is used. This feature requires the Enterprise Edition or Developer Edition of SQL Server 2016. (See Chapter 4 for more information on proactive caching.)

▶ **Silence Interval** The length of time the data must go without a change before processing begins. The thinking here is that data updates often come in bursts. We don't want to start processing the cube if another ten data changes are coming down the pike. We can wait until things settle down and then start processing.

▶ **Silence Override Interval**   The length of time we wait for a silence interval before we go ahead and initiate processing without one. This prevents the data in the cube from getting too old while waiting for the data changes to die down.

▶ **Drop Outdated Cache Latency**   This is the maximum amount of time we permit outdated aggregates to live in the proactive cache while we are waiting for processing to complete. When this time period is reached, the cache is dropped and querying is directed to the relational data source.

▶ **Update Cache Periodically**   This is a schedule for updating the proactive cache, even if we have not received a notification that it is out-of-date. This is often used when no notification mechanism is in place.

Let's look at each of the predefined settings in a bit more detail.

Real-Time ROLAP   All detail data and aggregates are queried directly from the relational data source. No notification is necessary. No proactive caching is used. This may result in slow query performance, but data is always current.

This setting is best for data that is changing frequently, leaving no time for cube processing, and that must always be up-to-date.

Real-Time HOLAP   Detail data remains in the relational data source. Aggregates are in multidimensional storage. When Analysis Services is notified that the aggregates are out-of-date, it processes the cube. It does not wait for a silence interval. While the aggregates are out-of-date or being processed, queries are sent directly to the relational data source. No proactive cache is used. This provides better performance for queries when the aggregates are up-to-date, but reverts to slow performance while processing.

This setting is best for data that is also changing frequently, but provides some intervals for processing.

Low-Latency MOLAP   Detail data and aggregates are in multidimensional storage. When Analysis Services is notified that the aggregates are out-of-date, it waits for a silence interval of ten seconds before beginning processing. It uses a silence override interval of ten minutes. While the cube is processing, queries are sent to a proactive cache. If processing takes longer than 30 minutes, the proactive cache is dropped and queries are sent directly to the relational data source. This provides fast query response, unless processing takes longer than 30 minutes. Maximum latency is 30 minutes.

This setting is best in situations where query performance is important but data must remain fairly current.

Medium-Latency MOLAP   Detail data and aggregates are in multidimensional storage. When Analysis Services is notified that the aggregates are out-of-date, it waits for a silence interval of ten seconds before it starts processing. It uses a silence override interval of ten minutes. While the cube is processing, queries are sent to a proactive cache. If processing takes longer than four hours, the proactive cache is dropped and queries are sent directly to the relational data source. This provides fast query response, unless processing takes longer than four hours. Maximum latency is four hours.

This setting is best in situations where query performance is important and a bit more latency can be tolerated.

Automatic MOLAP   Detail data and aggregates are in multidimensional storage. When Analysis Services is notified that the aggregates are out-of-date, it waits for a silence interval of ten seconds before it starts processing. It uses a silence override interval of ten minutes. While the cube is processing, queries are sent to a proactive cache. The proactive cache is not dropped, no matter how long processing takes. This provides fast query response at all times, but it can lead to a large latency if processing is long-running.

This setting is best in situations where query performance is the most important factor and a potentially large latency can be tolerated.

Scheduled MOLAP   Detail data and aggregates are in multidimensional storage. Analysis Services does not receive notification of data source changes. Instead, it processes automatically every 24 hours. While the cube is processing, queries are sent to a proactive cache. The proactive cache is not dropped, no matter how long processing takes. This provides fast query response at all times, but it has a maximum latency of 24 hours, plus the time required for processing.

This setting is typically used in situations where a notification mechanism is not available or where data updates occur nightly.

MOLAP   Detail data and aggregates are in multidimensional storage. Analysis Services does not receive notification of data source changes. Instead, processing is initiated manually by an administrator. No proactive caching is used, so queries cannot be run while processing is occurring.

This setting is typically used in situations where data is changing rarely or for development and testing environments.

Learn By Doing: Setting Storage Options for a Cube Partition

Features Highlighted

▶   Setting storage options for a cube

▶   Enabling SQL Notification when using named queries

Business Need Before we put the Max Min Manufacturing DM cube into production, we need to revise the storage settings so it keeps itself up-to-date without having to be manually processed. The vice president of production at Maximum Miniatures has asked that this cube have a maximum latency of four hours.

NOTE

The Enterprise Edition or Developer Edition of SQL Server 2016 is required for proactive caching. If you are not using one of these editions, skip Step 7 of this Learn By Doing exercise. If you use proactive caching with the Standard Edition or another edition of SQL Server 2016, you will receive an error when you try to deploy the cube definition to the server.

Steps to Set Storage Options for the Cube Partitions

1. Open SQL Server Data Tools.
2. Open the MaxMinManufacturingDM project.
3. Double-click the entry for Max Min Manufacturing DM.cube in the Solution Explorer window. The Cube Design tab appears.
4. Select the Partitions tab.
5. Select the Fact Manufacturing 2013 partition.
6. Click the Storage Settings link or the Storage Settings button on the Partitions tab toolbar. The Partition Storage Settings – Fact Manufacturing 2013 dialog box appears.
7. Move the slider to the Medium-latency MOLAP setting. Note the warning message at the bottom of the screen telling us that the default notification method does not work with a named query as a data source.
8. Click the Options button. The Storage Options dialog box appears, as shown in Figure 12-32.
9. Select the Notifications tab.
10. Check Specify tracking tables. This lets us specify a table whose changes cause changes to our named queries. In other words, when this table changes, the data in our named queries changes and the cube needs to be processed.
11. Click the ellipsis (…) button to the right. The Relational Objects dialog box appears.
12. Check the box next to the FactManufacturing table. Changes to this table cause the SQL Server relational database engine to notify Analysis Services that the cube must be processed.
13. Click OK to exit the Relational Objects dialog box. The Notifications tab of the Storage Options dialog box should appear, as shown in Figure 12-33.
14. Click OK to exit the Storage Options dialog box. Click OK to exit the Partition Storage Settings dialog box.
15. Repeat Steps 5–14 for the Fact Manufacturing 2014 partition.

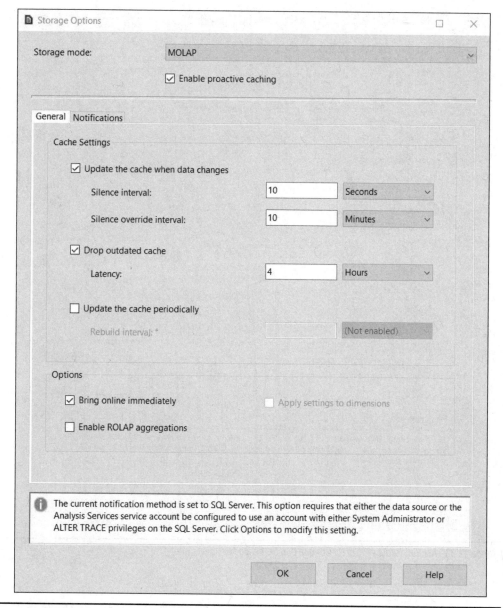

Figure 12-32 *The General tab of the Storage Options dialog box*

16. Repeat Steps 5–14 for the Fact Manufacturing Current partition.
17. Click the Save All button on the toolbar.
18. Select Build | Deploy MaxMinManufacturingDM from the Main menu. Close the deploy tab when the processing is complete. The cube is deployed to the server and processed.

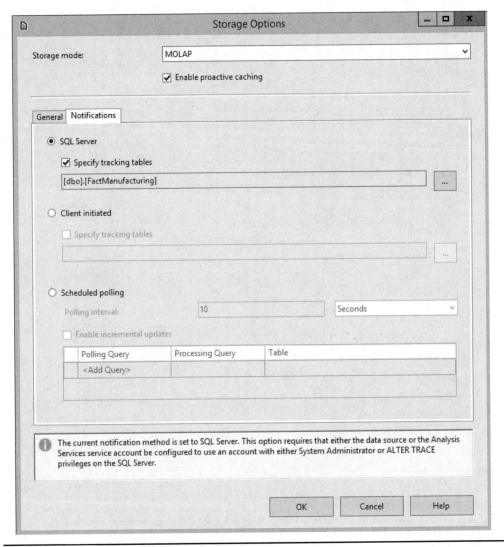

Figure 12-33 *The Notifications tab of the Storage Options dialog box*

19. Now let's test our notification mechanism. Select the Browser tab on the Cube Design tab.

20. Expand the Measures entry, drag the Total Products calculated member, and drop it in the "Drag levels or measures here to add to the query" area. The total should be 10,296,577.

21. Open SQL Server Management Studio (leave SQL Server Data Tools open as well) and connect to the SQL Server database engine hosting the MaxMinManufacturingDM relational database.

22. Expand the items in the Object Explorer window until you can see the FactManufacturing table in the MaxMinManufacturingDM database.

23. Right-click the FactManufacturing table, and select Edit Top 200 Rows from the context menu.

24. Change the AcceptedProducts field at the top of the grid from 3875 to 4875.

25. Move your cursor off the modified row and wait about a minute.

26. Return to SQL Server Data Tools.

27. Click the Execute Query button on the Browser tab toolbar. If everything is working properly, the total should change to 10,297,577.

28. Go back to SQL Server Management Studio and change the AcceptedProducts field back to 3875.

29. Move your cursor off the modified row, and then close the SQL Server Management Studio.

Writeback

Many times, while a user is analyzing data in a cube, they discover data that needs to be adjusted for one reason or another. It may be too time-consuming to make the change in the data source and then wait for it to be processed into the cube. Also, in some situations, business reasons may make it impossible to make the adjustment in the data source. This is where writeback comes in.

Writeback enables us to make adjusting entries to the cube data. These entries are stored in a special table that is added to the data source. This table then shows up as an additional partition in the measure group. The adjusting entries are incorporated into queries from this measure group in the same way that data from all of the other partitions is combined.

Writeback is enabled by right-clicking a partition on the Partitions tab and selecting Writeback Settings on the context menu. This displays the Enable Writeback dialog box shown in Figure 12-34. We can specify the name of the writeback table being created and the data source it is created in. We can also specify the storage mode used for the writeback data.

Once writeback is enabled, the writeback partition can be seen on the Partitions tab, as shown in Figure 12-35. Clicking Writeback Settings on the context menu of the writeback partition when writeback is enabled lets you disable this feature.

As with a number of other cube features, the client software used to browse and analyze the cube must support writeback for this feature to be put to use. Microsoft's Office Tools, Excel 2000 and newer all support this writeback function.

Enable Writeback - Fact Manufacturing
Specify the writeback table to be used to store the changes to the data of the measure group.
Table name:
WriteTable_Fact Manufacturing
Data source:
Max Min Manufacturing DM
New...
Storage mode:
MOLAP
OK
Cancel
Help

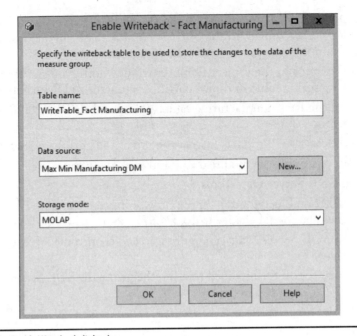

Figure 12-34 *The Enable Writeback dialog box*

Aggregation Design

Previously, we discussed preprocessing all of the aggregates in a cube and putting the results in a multidimensional storage. This is a bit of an overstatement. In fact, Analysis Services determines a pattern of aggregates within the partition that strikes a balance between storage requirements and query speed. This is called an *aggregation design.*

Max Min Manufactu...DM.cube [Design]*
Cube Structure
Dimension Usage
Calculations
KPIs
Actions
Partitions
Aggregations
Perspectives
Translations
Browser
Fact Manufacturing (4 Partitions)
Partition Name
Source
Estimated Rows
Storage Mode
Aggregation Design
1 Fact Manufacturing 2013
FactManufacturing_2013
0
MOLAP
2 Fact Manufacturing 2014
FactManufacturing_2014
0
MOLAP
3 Fact Manufacturing Current
FactManufacturing_Current
0
MOLAP
4 WriteTable_Fact Manufact...
WriteTable_Fact Manufacturing [Max Min Manufacturing DM]
0
MOLAP
New Partition...
Storage Settings...
Fact Inventory (1 Partition)

Figure 12-35 *The Partition tab with a writeback partition*

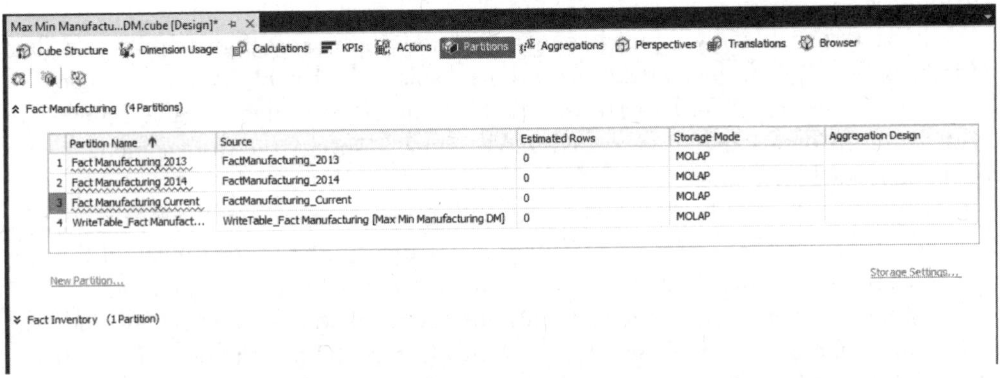

This process determines key aggregates and then calculates and stores them. Other aggregations are calculated from the key aggregates at the time a query is submitted.

Aggregations can be designed in two different ways: based on usage or manually. With usage-based aggregation design, the Usage-Based Optimization Wizard uses information from the Analysis Services query log to determine the best aggregation design for a partition. When aggregations are designed manually, the Aggregation Design Wizard guides us through the manual design process. Both wizards are launched from the Aggregations tab on the Cube Design tab.

Manual Aggregation Design

Here, we look at a few of the screens from the Aggregation Design Wizard. After the Welcome page, the wizard allows you to select which partitions within a measure group you wish to work with. The next page of the wizard is the Review Aggregation Usage page, shown in Figure 12-36.

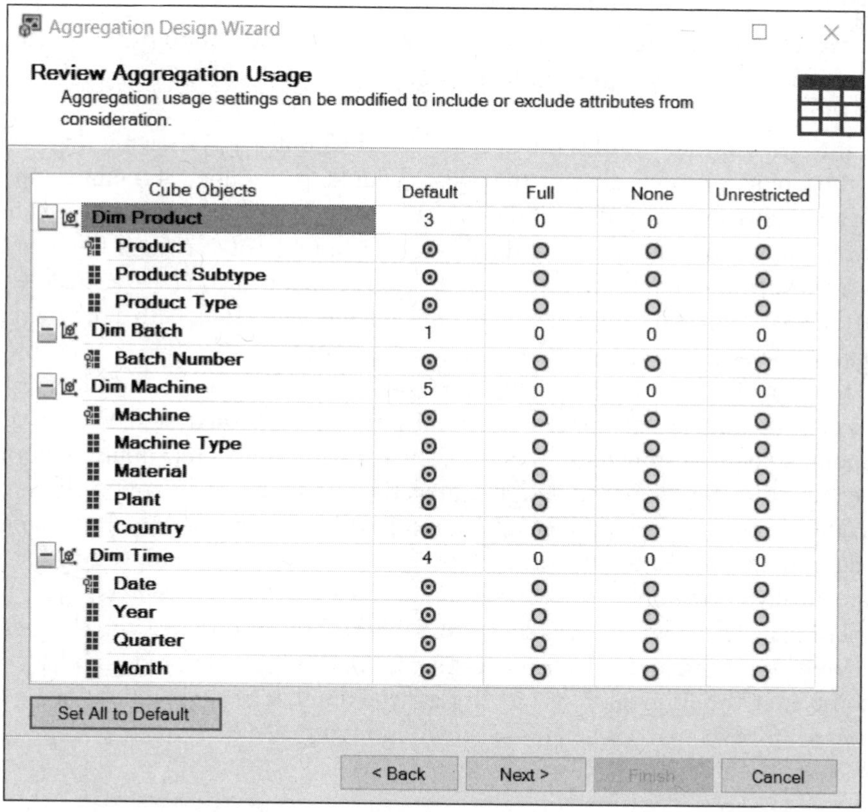

Cube Objects	Default	Full	None	Unrestricted
Dim Product	3	0	0	0
Product	◉	○	○	○
Product Subtype	◉	○	○	○
Product Type	◉	○	○	○
Dim Batch	1	0	0	0
Batch Number	◉	○	○	○
Dim Machine	5	0	0	0
Machine	◉	○	○	○
Machine Type	◉	○	○	○
Material	◉	○	○	○
Plant	◉	○	○	○
Country	◉	○	○	○
Dim Time	4	0	0	0
Date	◉	○	○	○
Year	◉	○	○	○
Quarter	◉	○	○	○
Month	◉	○	○	○

Figure 12-36 *The Review Aggregation Usage page of the Aggregation Design Wizard*

As we have discussed previously, the dimensional attributes in the cube are used to slice and dice the fact data during analysis. It is the various combinations of these attributes that define the multitude of aggregations that could be created in advance. The aggregation designer looks at each attribute in the cube and makes a determination on how it should be used for preprocessed aggregations. The Review Aggregation Usage page of the wizard allows us to make that determination for the aggregation designer by selecting one of the following:

► **Default**   The default aggregation rule is used for this dimensional attribute.

► **Full**   Every preprocessed aggregate must include either this attribute or a lower attribute in the same hierarchy. This forces every precalculated aggregate to be sliced by this dimensional attribute. This should not be selected for dimensional attributes that have a large number of members.

► **None**   None of the preprocessed aggregates will include this attribute. It will be ignored when designing preprocessed aggregates.

► **Unrestricted**   No restrictions are placed on the consideration of this attribute for use when designing preprocessed aggregates.

The next page of the wizard is the Specify Object Counts page, shown in Figure 12-37. When the Count button is clicked, the wizard counts the number of members in each of the dimensions, including the fact dimension. If you are working with a large cube and do not want to wait for the wizard to do all of this counting, you can enter the member counts manually. You may also want to manually enter counts if you have a small set of data in the cube for testing, but know that a much larger set of data with a different count distribution will be processed into the cube at a later date.

The following page is the Set Aggregation Options page. This is shown in Figure 12-38. On this page, we tell the wizard how to optimize the aggregation design. We can specify a maximum amount of storage we want to allow for aggregates, a maximum performance gain we require, or choose not to design aggregations at all. A fourth option allows the optimization process to run until we tell it to stop. With this last option, the optimizer continues running until it has the best solution or until you get tired of waiting for it and stop it manually. As the optimizer runs, it shows you a graph of its progress.

The last page of the wizard enables us to either deploy and process the changes immediately or save them for later processing. Once the aggregation design has been completed, the Aggregations tab displays the number of aggregations being preprocessed for each partition. This is shown in Figure 12-39.

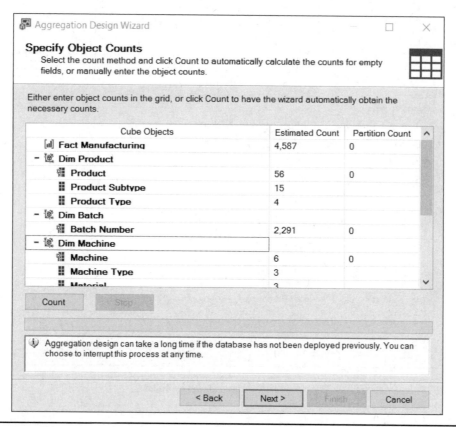

Figure 12-37 *The Specify Object Counts page of the Aggregation Design Wizard*

Be sure to complete the aggregation design before putting your cubes into production to ensure you get the query performance you expect.

Perspectives

In real life, many objects look different, depending on how you look at them—depending on your perspective. In the same way, we can define different perspectives so our cubes look different to different users. By using perspectives, we can provide our users with what they need and not overwhelm them with things they don't. The Enterprise Edition or Developer Edition of SQL Server 2016 is required to use perspectives.

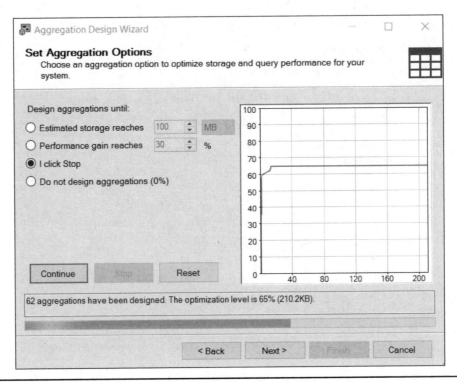

Figure 12-38 *The Set Aggregation Options page of the Aggregation Design Wizard*

Figure 12-39 *The Aggregations tab with the aggregation design completed*

Creating Perspectives

Perspectives are created on the *Perspectives tab*. This tab lists all of the items in our cube, as shown in Figure 12-40. We can then determine which items are visible in each perspective.

New perspectives are added by clicking the New Perspective button on the Perspectives tab toolbar. Each perspective is given a unique name to identify it. When the perspective is first created, it includes all of the items in the cube. We can remove (uncheck) the items that are not needed or that should not be viewed by people who are going to use that perspective to access the cube.

Figure 12-40 shows two perspectives in the Max Min Manufacturing DM cube. The Inventory Monitoring perspective is for users who will be looking at the Inventory Fact measures. They do not need access to the Fact Manufacturing measures or other items that apply only to those measures. The Highlevel Mfg Info perspective is for users who are only interested in the KPI and the two calculated members we have created in our cube. Therefore, only those items and the dimensions are included in this perspective.

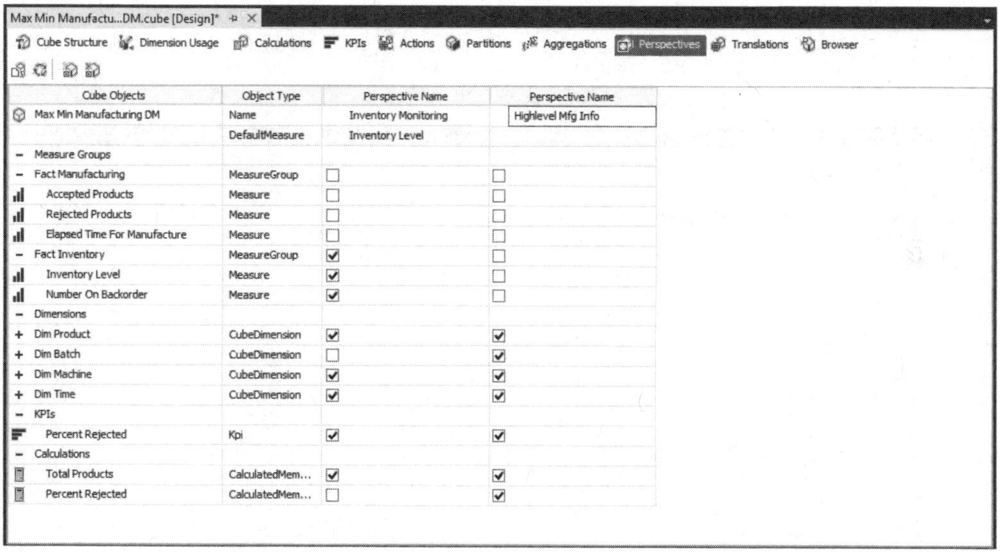

Figure 12-40 *The Perspectives tab*

Translations

We live in a global society. More and more, we are required to work internationally to get things done. Business intelligence is certainly no exception to this trend.

To help this along, Analysis Services provides us with the means to localize the metadata contained in our cubes. This is done using the *Translations tab*. The Translations tab is shown in Figure 12-41.

Creating Translations

New translations are created by clicking the New Translation button on the Translations tab toolbar. First, we must pick the language for the translation. The Select Language dialog box, shown in Figure 12-42, enables us to select the language and country designation for this translation. Next, we can fill in the appropriate translation for each of the metadata items in the cube.

The translations entered in the Translations tab only apply to metadata in the cubes, not to the data in each of the dimensions. To implement multilingual support for the dimensional members, each dimension must have an attribute for each language supported. These attributes then contain the appropriate translations for each member.

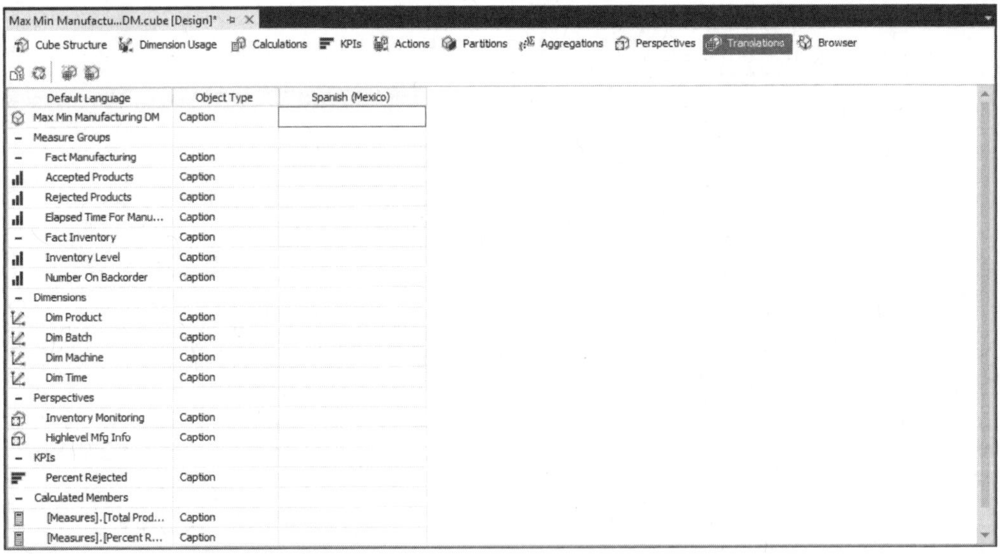

Figure 12-41 *The Translations tab*

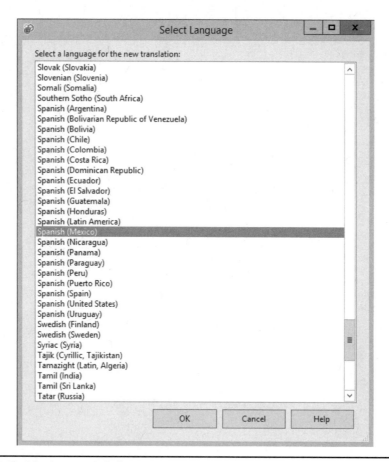

Figure 12-42 *The Select Language dialog box*

More Sophisticated Scripting

We have used some basic scripting to define objects in Chapters 11 and 12. In Chapter 13, we add to your ability to write MDX script expressions. As a result, we enhance your ability to manipulate and analyze the information in your OLAP cubes.

Chapter 13

Writing a New Script: MDX Scripting

In This Chapter

- ► **Terms and Concepts**
- ► **Putting MDX Scripting to Work**
- ► **Extracting Data from Cubes**

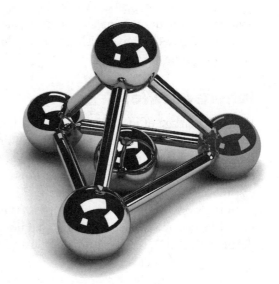

The world is a stage and most of us are desperately unrehearsed.

—Sean O'Casey, playwright

We have already used some basic MDX script expressions to create calculated members in Chapter 11 and to define key performance indicators (KPIs) and Actions in Chapter 12. To complete these tasks, we used the basics of MDX scripting. You probably need to employ more complex MDX scripts to meet the needs of your organization. Thus, we have Chapter 13.

In this chapter, we work to get a handle on the power of MDX scripts. We see how they can be used to perform powerful analysis on your organization's information. In addition to data analysis, we use MDX scripts to set up security restrictions on a cube.

Terms and Concepts

Before we begin doing all of this good stuff, we need to cover some basics. Up to this point, we have looked at cube concepts and definitions with the goal of cube creation and population. Now we need to shift gears a bit and look at the concepts and definitions required for extracting and analyzing the information residing in our cubes.

Let's use an analogy from the relational database world. When we are defining and populating a relational database, we need to know about normalization, constraints, and foreign keys. When we are querying data from a relational database, we need to know about INNER and OUTER JOINS, ORDER BY, and GROUP BY.

As we move to extracting and analyzing information in the cube, we need to learn how to move through our dimensional hierarchies to address a particular location or set of locations in the cube. We need to know how to select a particular measure and combine that with other measures in complex calculations. In short, we need to know how to navigate our cubes without getting lost or, worse yet, without returning utter nonsense to our users.

Where Are We?

We live in an age of many electronic wonders: computers, of course, but also cell phones, digital cameras, and global positioning satellite (GPS) receivers. With a GPS receiver, we can tell exactly where we are on the planet to within a few feet, perhaps even to within a few inches! The question is this: Will we men now be too stubborn to consult our GPS receivers for directions?

In the world of online analytical processing (OLAP) cubes, we need the equivalent of a GPS system. We need a means to uniquely specify any location within a cube. Fortunately, MDX scripting provides just such a mechanism.

Cells

The first question might be: Just what are we trying to locate? The answer is: We are trying to locate cells. Fortunately, we do not need a microscope to find these cells. (I never was very good at biology.) These cells are located right inside of our cubes.

Figure 13-1 shows a simplified version of our Max Min Manufacturing DM cube with three dimensions: Dim Machine, Dim Product, and Dim Time. The dimensions divide the cube up into smaller sections. These are cells.

In our cubes, cells contain the values for our measures. In Figure 13-1, the highlighted cell contains the measures for the Woodland Creatures product type produced on the Clay Molder machine type for all of 2014. We can see that 951,959 products were accepted while 10,143 products were rejected and 89,720 minutes were spent in this manufacturing process. If cells contain the measures in a cube, then it is important that we know how to properly address them.

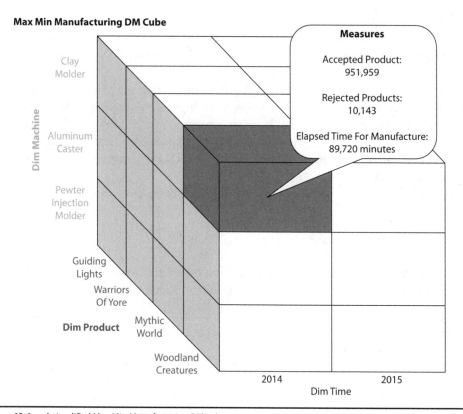

Figure 13-1   *A simplified Max Min Manufacturing DM cube*

Identifying the location of a cell in a cube is similar to identifying the location of a point on a three-dimensional graph. On a 3D graph, we specify the value from each axis (or dimension) that corresponds to the point's location along that axis. Our cube works the same way. We specify the member from each dimension that identifies the cell's location along that dimension. So the cell in Figure 13-1 has a location of

```
[Clay Molder], [Woodland Creatures], [2014]
```

NOTE

Identifiers in MDX—member names, dimension names, hierarchy levels, and so forth—must be enclosed in square brackets ([ ]) when they contain a space or other special character or start with a numeral. Because we often have one or more spaces in our identifiers and they often start with numerals, it is a good idea to always enclose identifiers in square brackets, whether they need them or not. This saves trouble down the road.

Tuples

The cell location we came up with from Figure 13-1 has a special name. It is a tuple (pronounced *to-pull*). A *tuple* is a list of dimension members with one member present from each dimension.

In our example from Figure 13-1, and in most of the examples in this chapter, we are going to look at three dimensions. Therefore, our tuples have three members. We are using three dimensions because this is easier for you to grasp and for me to illustrate. (I haven't yet mastered drawing in four-dimensional space!) Just don't fall into the trap of thinking all tuples have three members. A cube with 100 dimensions would have a tuple that includes 100 members.

In MDX expressions, tuples are enclosed in parentheses. So our tuple from Figure 13-1 becomes

```
([Clay Molder], [Woodland Creatures], [2014])
```

You can think of it this way: The information between the parentheses, no matter if it is three members or a hundred members, points to a single cell.

NOTE

MDX expressions are not case-sensitive. The tuple
```
([clay molder], [woodland creatures], [2014])
```
is also valid.

Levels

You are probably thinking: What's the big deal about locating cells? Creating tuples seems pretty straightforward. Well, it would be except for one little detail. Many of our dimensions contain hierarchies. We have to take those hierarchies into account as we create our tuples.

Figure 13-2 shows the structure and the members of the Dim Product hierarchy in the Max Min Manufacturing DM cube. In this hierarchy, we created three levels: the product type, the product subtype, and the product. In addition to the levels we defined, Analysis Services automatically adds another level at the top of the dimension. In Figure 13-2, this upper level is given the same name as the dimension itself: Dim Product. The upper level always contains a single element called All. This element contains all of the dimension members from the lower levels.

Suppose we want to specify the location of the cell containing measures for the Dragon with Knight product. Figure 13-3 shows the path we must follow from the

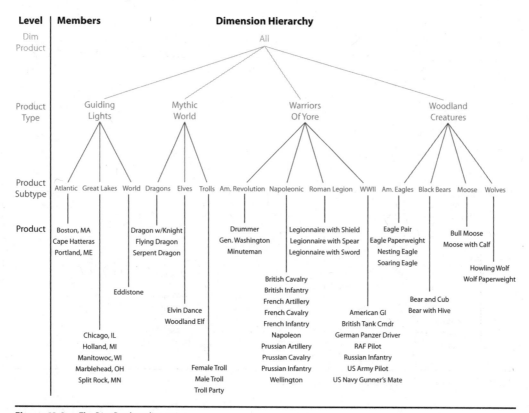

Figure 13-2   *The Dim Product dimension*

highest level of the dimension to reach this product at the lowest level. To specify this location in a tuple, start with the name of the dimension. Then follow the path from the top of the hierarchy to the bottom, including every member we pass along the way.

What we end up with is this:

```
[Dim Product].[All].[Mythic World].[Dragons].[Dragon with Knight]
```

Of course, dimensions with more hierarchy levels are going to have longer expressions. We do not always want to retrieve measures at the lowest level of a hierarchy. We may want to see figures for a product subtype or even a product type. Figure 13-4 shows this situation. Here, we want measures for the World War II product subtype. Again,

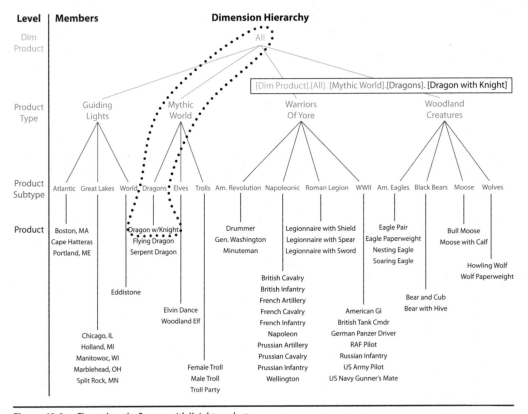

Figure 13-3   *The path to the Dragon with Knight product*

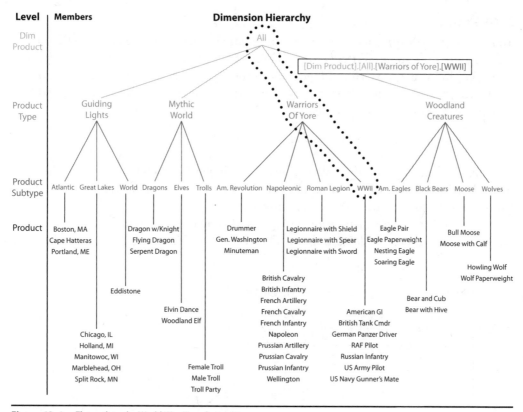

Figure 13-4   *The path to the World War II product subtype*

we start with the name of the dimension, and then follow the path until we get to the desired member. We do not have to go all the way to the bottom of the tree. The correct expression from Figure 13-4 is

```
[Dim Product].[All].[Warriors Of Yore].[World War II]
```

NOTE

The figures use the abbreviation for World War II (WWII) because of the need to fit in a large amount of information. The data in our cube uses the longer form of the name. Therefore, the examples in the text will use the longer form as well.

Shortcuts

You can see these expressions tend to get long rather quickly. Fortunately, MDX scripting provides some shortcuts for us. Figure 13-5 illustrates one of these shortcuts. Instead of following the chain of members all the way down, we specify the name of the dimension, as before, but then add the name of the hierarchy level we are interested in and, finally, the member of that hierarchy. So, the expression becomes

```
[Dim Product].[Product Subtype].[World War II]
```

Using this shortcut, it is possible to specify any dimension member with only three items. In a hierarchy with a large number of levels, this can save a lot of typing. However, this is not the only way we can save keystrokes.

It is possible to leave out additional pieces of this path. We can drop the name of the dimension, the dimension level, or both. The key is this: We always have to end up with

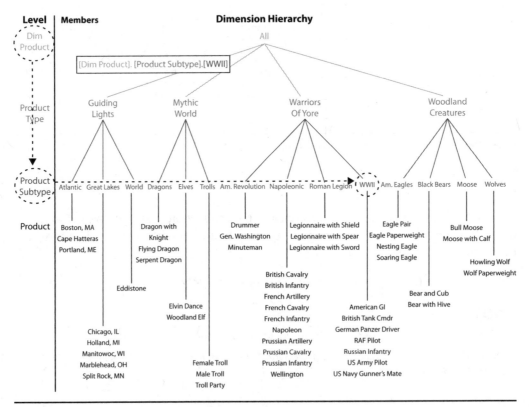

Figure 13-5   *A shortcut path to the World War II product subtype*

an unambiguous location in the dimension. In our Max Min Manufacturing DM cube, any of the following expressions are valid references to the World War II member:

```
[Product Subtype].[World War II]
[Dim Product].[World War II]
[World War II]
```

Because World War II is a unique member name across all levels of all dimensions in our cube, that's all we need to uniquely identify the dimension member.

Even if we are using our original method from Figure 13-3 and Figure 13-4, we can take some shortcuts. First, we can leave out the All member. Thus, our expression from Figure 13-3 becomes

```
[Dim Product].[Mythic World].[Dragons].[Dragon with Knight]
```

The name of the dimension can be removed as well:

```
[Mythic World].[Dragons].[Dragon with Knight]
```

We can also trim off members from the top of the hierarchy, so this still works:

```
[Dragons].[Dragon with Knight]
```

The one thing we cannot do is drop members out of the middle of the path. Therefore, this expression will not work:

```
[Mythic World].[Dragon with Knight]
```

Expression Errors

If we inadvertently enter an expression for a dimension member that is incorrect, we do not receive an error message. Instead, we end up with nothing for this dimension. The tuple that included the errant dimension is not included in the final result.

This is both a benefit and a problem. It is a benefit because an invalid path expression does not bring everything to a screeching halt. It is a problem because our expression may return information that appears good, but is missing something we expected!

Default Members

Now that we know how to specify expressions for hierarchical dimensions, let's go back to building tuples. Figure 13-6 shows a more complex, but still watered-down, representation of the Max Min Manufacturing DM cube. This cube includes two-level hierarchies on all three of its dimensions.

Max Min Manufacturing DM Cube

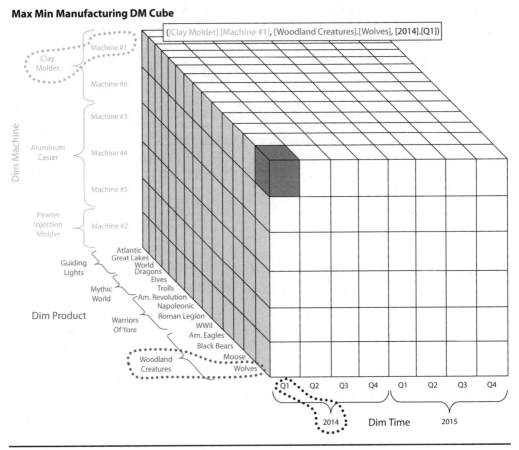

Figure 13-6 *A more complex version of the Max Min Manufacturing DM cube*

Figure 13-6 has one cell highlighted in the cube. The tuple identifying this location is also shown in the figure. Here we are using a shortcut and omitting the dimension names from our path expressions. We could even shorten this up a bit more:

```
([Machine #1], [Wolves], [2014].[Q1])
```

As the dimension members are shown in the figure, we could *not* use the following:

```
([Machine #1], [Wolves], [Q1])
```

There is a Q1 member under 2014 and under 2015, so this last path expression would result in an ambiguous reference.

NOTE

In the actual Max Min Manufacturing DM cube we created, we use the form 2014Q1 for quarters and 201401 for months, so there is no problem with ambiguous references, even if we use only a single member name.

What happens if we leave one of the dimensions out of a tuple? Figure 13-7 shows the result. The tuple in this figure includes a member from the Dim Product dimension and the Dim Time dimension. It does not include a member from the Dim Machine dimension.

In this situation, Analysis Services supplies the member for the missing dimension. It does this by using the default member. In this case, the *default member* for the

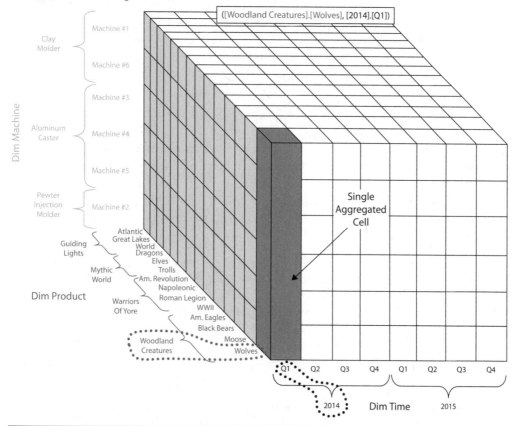

Figure 13-7   *A tuple with one dimension omitted*

Dim Machine dimension is All. (The All member is not shown in the dimensional hierarchies in Figure 13-7, but it is there at the top of each hierarchy by default.) The path expression shown in Figure 13-7 is the equivalent of

```
([Dim Machine].[All], [Woodland Creatures].[Wolves], [2014].[Q1])
```

Each dimension in the cube has a default member. In almost all cases, the All member is most appropriate for the default member. For some dimensions, however, a different member makes more sense. For instance, it may be reasonable to have the Dim Time dimension default to the current year or current quarter. We set the default member of the Dim Time dimension in the Max Min Manufacturing DM cube to 2015 in our next Learn By Doing activity.

The result of this tuple in Figure 13-7 is not six cells. Instead, it is a single cell. This cell contains aggregates of each measure for the first quarter of 2014 for Wolves that were produced on any of the machines. The cell is an aggregate, but it is still a single cell—a single number for each measure in the cube.

Indeed, tuples, as we have seen them expressed so far, can only return a single cell from the cube. Next, we see how to return multiple cells.

Sets

Figure 13-8 shows another aggregate cell in our simplified Max Min Manufacturing DM cube. This cell contains aggregates of each measure for 2014 for Woodland Creatures produced on any of the machines. Suppose, instead of a single aggregate cell, we want to see the measures from all of the individual cells at the lower levels of the hierarchy.

What we want is the *set* of cells shown in Figure 13-9. To do this, we need to use a group of tuples to specify each of the cells in our set. We express this set of tuples as follows:

```
{([American Eagles], [2014].[Q1]), ([American Eagles], [2014].[Q2]),
([American Eagles], [2014].[Q3]), ([American Eagles], [2014].[Q4]),
([Black Bears], [2014].[Q1]), ([Black Bears], [2014].[Q2]),
([Black Bears], [2014].[Q3]), ([Black Bears], [2014].[Q4]),
([Moose], [2014].[Q1]), ([Moose], [2014].[Q2]),
([Moose], [2014].[Q3]), ([Moose], [2014].[Q4]),
([Wolves], [2014].[Q1]), ([Wolves], [2014].[Q2]),
([Wolves], [2014].[Q3]), ([Wolves], [2014].[Q4])}
```

Note the curly brackets ({ }) surrounding the entire set in addition to the parentheses around each tuple.

Max Min Manufacturing DM Cube

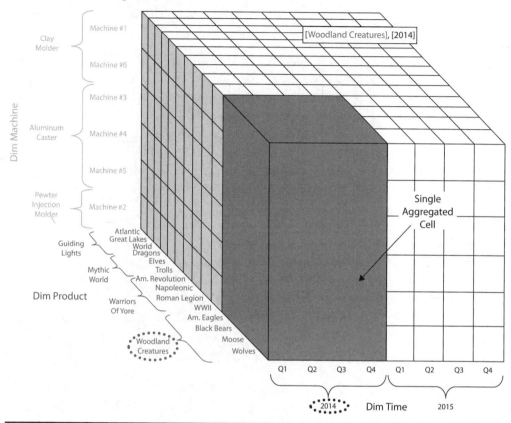

Figure 13-8   *Another aggregate cell in the Max Min Manufacturing DM cube*

This notation gets the job done, but it is inefficient. Let's look at another way to specify a set that requires fewer keystrokes.

Range Operator

Excel is another Microsoft product that deals with cells. This program has a special syntax for specifying a range of cells. This is the colon (:) operator. To specify cells A1 through A15, for example, we enter A1:A15 in an Excel expression.

The same is true in Analysis Services. We can use the colon operator to specify a range of members in a tuple. To specify the set shown in Figure 13-9, we can use the range operator as follows:

```
([American Eagles]:[Wolves], [2014].[Q1]:[2014].[Q4])
```

Max Min Manufacturing DM Cube

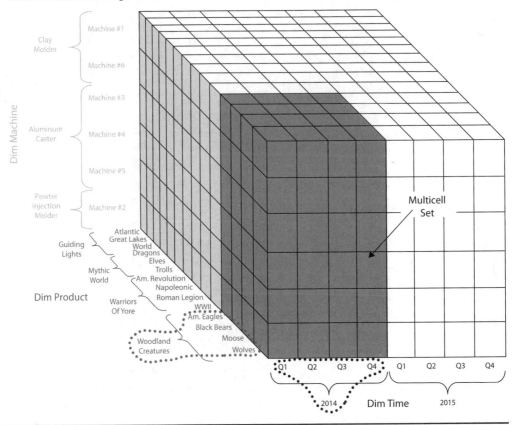

Figure 13-9 *A multicell set*

This may not be quite as self-documenting as the set notation, but it is more efficient. Of course, some groupings cannot be specified by a range. One such grouping is shown in Figure 13-10. Because these cells are not contiguous, we cannot use a range. We can also combine ranges and sets, as shown in Figure 13-11.

Name Attributes

When we set up the MaxMinManufacturingDM data mart relational database, we used integer key fields to identify members in the dimensions. The foreign key relationships we created in the data mart are all based on these integer keys. When the OLAP cube was created on top of this data mart, the integer keys were used as the unique identifiers for our members.

Max Min Manufacturing DM Cube

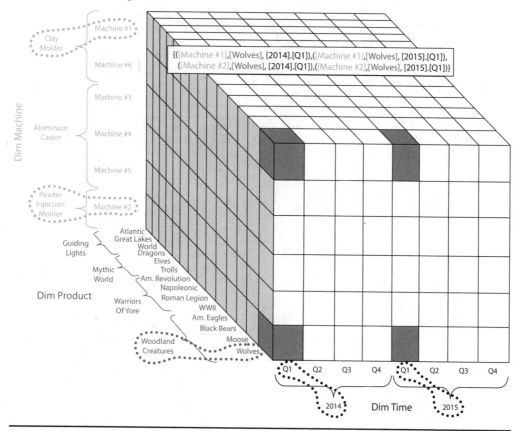

Figure 13-10 *A cell group requiring a set*

This is not convenient. We don't want our users to have to remember that the Wolf Paperweight is product 21 and the plant in Mumbai is plant 6. As a matter of fact, we would not like to have to remember this stuff either. Fortunately, we and our users don't have to.

In addition to having integer key fields in our relational data mart, we have text fields that contain names for each member value. The text fields became attributes in our OLAP cube. In Chapter 11, we told Analysis Services which attribute contains the name for each dimension hierarchy for most of our dimensions. We now make sure that our dimension members are sorted by the names rather than the integer keys.

Max Min Manufacturing DM Cube

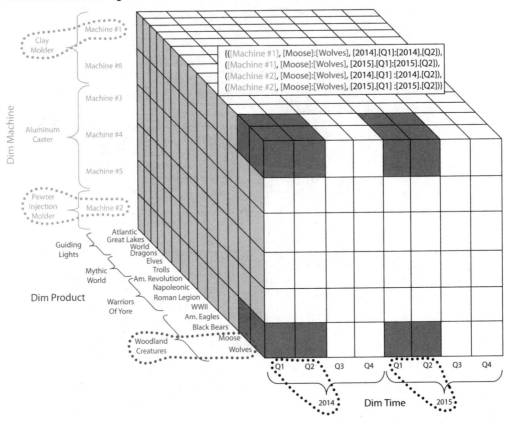

```
{([Machine #1], [Moose]:[Wolves], [2014].[Q1]:[2014].[Q2]),
 ([Machine #1], [Moose]:[Wolves], [2015].[Q1]:[2015].[Q2]),
 ([Machine #2], [Moose]:[Wolves], [2014].[Q1] :[2014].[Q2]),
 ([Machine #2], [Moose]:[Wolves], [2015].[Q1] :[2015].[Q2])}
```

Figure 13-11 *A cell group using a set with ranges*

At times, we may need to reference a member by its key value rather than its name. We can do this by putting an ampersand (&) in front of the member key. For example:

```
[Dim Product].[Product].&[21]
```

is the same as

```
[Dim Product].[Product].[Wolf Paperweight]
```

Learn By Doing: Default Members and the OrderBy Property

Features Highlighted

▶ Set a default member

▶ Sort attributes by name, not key

Business Need   To make it easier for our users to query the Max Min Manufacturing DM cube, we can set the default member for our Dim Time dimension to 2015. We also make sure attributes sort as the user expects, by name rather than by key.

Steps to Set Dimension Characteristics

1. Open SQL Server Data Tools.
2. Open the MaxMinManufacturingDM.sln solution.
3. Double-click the Dim Time.dim dimension in the Solution Explorer. The Dimension Design tab appears.
4. Select the Year entry in the Attributes area.
5. In the Properties Window, click the DefaultMember property. An ellipsis (…) button appears. Click the ellipsis button. The Set Default Member dialog box appears.
6. Select "Enter an MDX expression that specifies the default member."
7. Enter **[Dim Time].&[2015]**. The Set Default Member dialog box appears, as shown in Figure 13-12.
8. Click OK to exit the Set Default Member dialog box.
9. Click the Save All button on the toolbar.
10. Close the Dimension Design tab.
11. Double-click the Dim Product.dim dimension in the Solution Explorer. The Dimension Design tab appears.
12. Select the Product Subtype entry in the Attributes area.
13. In the Properties window, select Name from the OrderBy drop-down list.
14. Select the Product Type entry in the Attributes area.
15. In the Properties window, select Name from the OrderBy drop-down list.

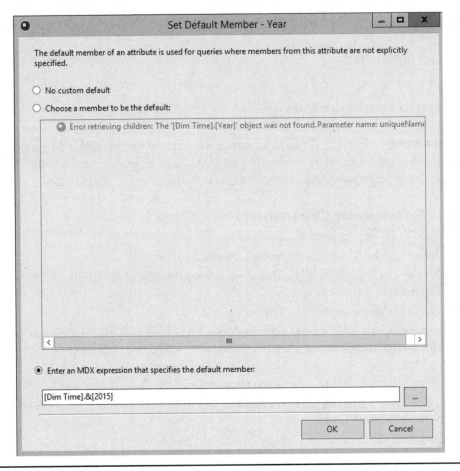

Figure 13-12 *The Set Default Member dialog box*

16. Select the Product entry in the Attributes area.
17. Again, in the Properties window, select Name from the OrderBy drop-down list. The Dimension Design tab should appear as shown in Figure 13-13.
18. Click the Save All button on the toolbar.
19. Close the Dimension Design tab.
20. Double-click the Dim Machine.dim dimension in the Solution Explorer. The Dimension Design tab appears.

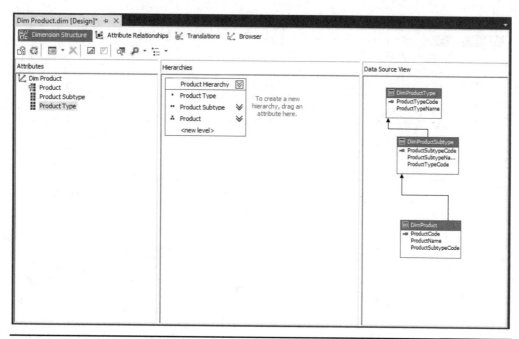

Figure 13-13   *The Dim Product dimension*

21. Set the OrderBy property for the following items in the Attributes area:

Item	OrderBy
Country	Name
Machine	Name
Machine Type	Name
Material	Name
Plant	Name

The Dimension Design tab should appear as shown in Figure 13-14.

22. Click the Save All button on the toolbar.
23. Close the Dimension Design tab.
24. Double-click the Dim Batch.dim dimension in the Solution Explorer. The Dimension Design tab appears.

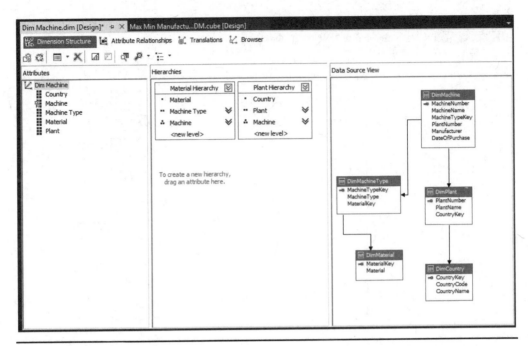

Figure 13-14 *The Dim Machine dimension*

25. Set the NameColumn property and the OrderBy property for the following item in the Attributes area:

Item	NameColumn	OrderBy
Batch Number	BatchName	Name

The Dimension Design tab should appear as shown in Figure 13-15.

26. Click the Save All button on the toolbar.
27. Close the Dimension Design tab.
28. Select Build | Deploy MaxMinManufacturingDM from the Main menu.
29. Enter the appropriate credentials, if you are prompted to do so.
30. Close the Deployment progress tab when the cube processing is complete.

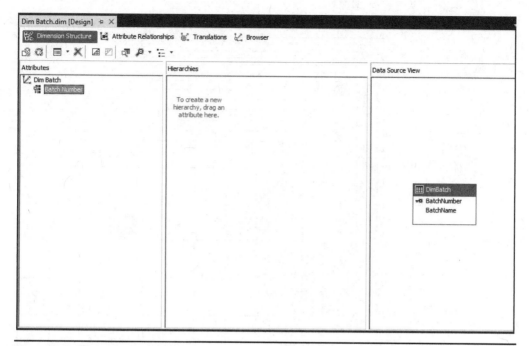

Figure 13-15 *The Dim Batch dimension*

Getting There from Here

We now know how to address any cell or group of cells in the cube. This type of absolute navigation is important as we move toward being able to manipulate and extract information from our cubes. We need to master one other skill, which is the skill of relative navigation. *Relative navigation* is the capability to start from a given location and move to another location based on that starting point.

For example, suppose we are examining measures for Wolves produced on Machine #6 in Q1, 2015. This is the Current Cell in Figure 13-16. We may want to look at those same measures from one year ago. This is designated as the Comparison Cell in the figure. We need to know how to find the position of the Comparison Cell relative to the Current Cell.

Of course, we could do this using the absolute navigation we already know. We know the tuple for the Comparison Cell is

```
([Machine #6], [Wolves], [2014].[Q1])
```

Max Min Manufacturing DM Cube

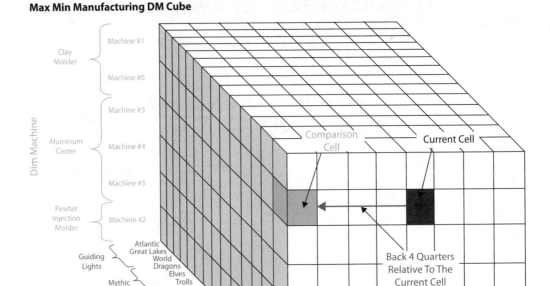

Figure 13-16 *Comparing measures from two cells using relative location*

This works fine until we move on to look at the measures for Q2, 2015. Now we have to figure out the tuple for the Comparison Cell all over again. Perhaps we are looking at measures in a set of cells—say Q1, 2015 through Q4, 2015. Now it becomes even more tedious to manually determine the tuples for all of the Comparison Cells.

Even more helpful would be a way to identify one cell by its relative position to another cell. Fortunately, MDX scripting provides a way for us to do this: through the use of MDX functions. But, before we look at functions that help us determine the tuple for the Comparison Cell, we need a function that helps us determine the tuple for the Current Cell.

The Starting Point: The CurrentMember Function

Like any other cell, the Current Cell can be identified by a tuple. This tuple contains the current member from each hierarchy in the cube. But how can we determine what those current members are?

The answer is through the use of the CurrentMember function. For example, we can use the following expression to find out the current member of the Time Hierarchy dimension:

```
[Dim Time].CurrentMember
```

In the example in Figure 13-16, this expression would return the [2015].[Q1] member.

As with any function, the CurrentMember function takes input and returns output. In MDX expressions, the function's input is whatever precedes the function. In this case, that input is the [Dim Time] hierarchy. In fact, the CurrentMember function requires either a hierarchy or a dimension as its input. This makes sense because only hierarchies and dimensions have members.

The *CurrentMember function* returns a member. The CurrentMember function does not return a string containing the name of the member. Instead, it returns a reference to the member itself. This distinction is important as we begin to apply other MDX functions to the result returned by the CurrentMember function.

Function	Input	Output	Description
CurrentMember	Hierarchy or Dimension	Member	Returns the current member of the specified hierarchy or dimension

Relative Position Within a Hierarchy Level: The Lag, Lead, NextMember, and PrevMember Functions

A number of MDX functions enable us to select a member relative to a specified member within the same hierarchy. These are shown in Figure 13-17. Assuming the [Dim Time].CurrentMember is [2015].[Q1], the expressions corresponding to the figure are shown here:

Expression	Resulting Member
[Dim Time].CurrentMember.Lag(4)	[2014].[Q1]
[Dim Time].CurrentMember.Lead(-4)	[2014].[Q1]
[Dim Time].CurrentMember.PrevMember	[2014].[Q4]
[Dim Time].CurrentMember.NextMember	[2015].[Q2]
[Dim Time].CurrentMember.Lead(3)	[2015].[Q4]
[Dim Time].CurrentMember.Lag(-3)	[2015].[Q4]

Max Min Manufacturing DM Cube

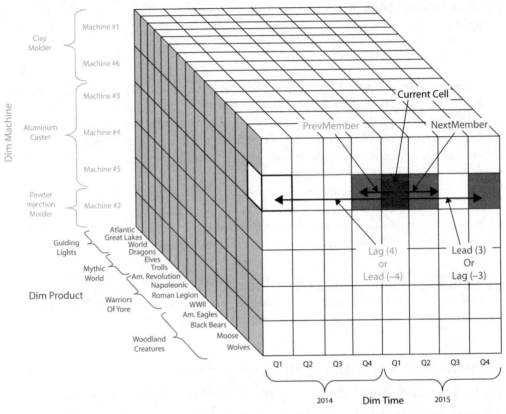

Figure 13-17 *Comparing measures from two cells using relative location*

As you can see, the PrevMember function takes us to the member immediately preceding the current member. The NextMember function takes us to the member immediately after the current member. These functions are useful for looking at the way measures are trending from one period to the next.

The Lag and Lead functions require an additional parameter. This is an integer representing the number of members to lag or lead. This second parameter is passed in parentheses immediately after the function name.

The *Lag function* moves us backward by the specified number of members. The *Lead function* moves us forward by the specified number of members. Using a negative integer for the number of members parameter reverses the natural direction of each function.

Function	Input	Output	Description
Lag(N)	Member, *N* = number of members	Member	Returns the member that is *N before* the specified member. (A negative value for *N* reverses the direction of the function.)
Lead(N)	Member, *N* = number of members	Member	Returns the member that is *N after* the specified member. (A negative value for *N* reverses the direction of the function.)
NextMember	Member	Member	Returns the member that is immediately after the specified member.
PrevMember	Member	Member	Returns the member that is immediately before the specified member.

Immediate Relative Position Between Hierarchy Levels: The Children, FirstChild, FirstSibling, LastChild, LastSibling, Parent, and Siblings Functions

Just as we may want to move across a hierarchy level, we may want to move up and down between hierarchy levels. A number of MDX functions can help us here as well. We begin by looking at the functions that deal with the immediate family in the hierarchy, and then look at functions that return more distant relations.

The functions dealing with immediate relatives are shown in Figure 13-18. Assuming the [Dim Product].CurrentMember is [Roman Legion], the expressions corresponding to the figure are shown here:

Expression	Resulting Member(s)
[Dim Product].CurrentMember.Children	[Legionnaire with Shield], [Legionnaire with Spear], [Legionnaire with Sword]
[Dim Product].CurrentMember.FirstChild	[Legionnaire with Shield]
[Dim Product].CurrentMember.FirstSibling	[Am. Revolution]
[Dim Product].CurrentMember.LastChild	[Legionnaire with Sword]
[Dim Product].CurrentMember.LastSibling	[WWII]
[Dim Product].CurrentMember.Parent	[Warriors Of Yore]
[Dim Product].CurrentMember.Siblings	[Am. Revolution], [Napoleonic], [Roman Legion], [WWII]

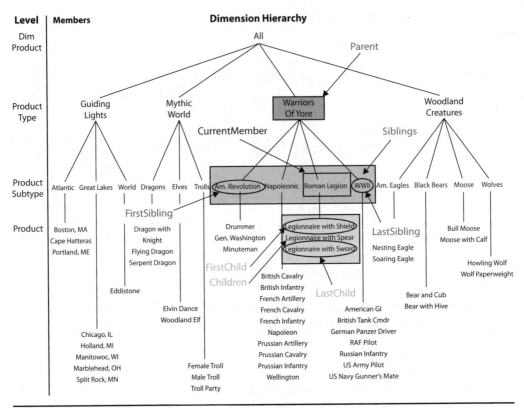

Figure 13-18 *MDX immediate relative position functions within the same hierarchy*

Most of the functions are self-explanatory, but a word about the Siblings function may be helpful. If you look at the list of members returned by the Siblings function, you see that the Roman Legion member is included. This is true even though Roman Legion is the current member when we call the function. The member itself is always included in a list of its siblings.

Function	Input	Output	Description
Children	Member	Set	Returns the set of members from the hierarchy level immediately below the specified member that is related directly to the specified member
FirstChild	Member	Member	Returns the first member from the hierarchy level immediately below the specified member that is related directly to the specified member
FirstSibling	Member	Member	Returns the first member that shares the same parent with the specified member

(continued)

Function	Input	Output	Description
LastChild	Member	Member	Returns the last member from the hierarchy level immediately below the specified member that is related directly to the specified member
LastSibling	Member	Member	Returns the last member that shares the same parent with the specified member
Parent	Member	Member	Returns the member from the hierarchy level immediately above the specified member that is related directly to the specified member
Siblings	Member	Set	Returns the set of members that shares the same parent with the specified member

Distant Relative Position Between Hierarchy Levels: The Ancestor, Cousin, and Descendants Functions

In addition to the functions that return the close relatives of a member, a number of MDX functions let us select more distant relatives. These are shown in Figure 13-19. The expressions corresponding to the figure are shown here:

Expression	Resulting Member
Ancestor([2013].[Q3].[Jul], [Dim Time] .[Year]) or Ancestor ([2013].[Q3].[Jul], 2)	[2013]
Cousin([2013].[Q2].[Apr], [2013].[Q4])	[2013].[Q4].[Oct]
Descendants([2015], [Month]) or Descendants([2015], 2)	[2015].[Q1].[Jan], [2015].[Q1].[Feb], [2015].[Q1].[Mar], [2015].[Q2].[Apr], [2015].[Q2].[May], [2015].[Q2].[Jun], [2015].[Q3].[Jul], [2015].[Q3].[Aug], [2015].[Q3].[Sep], [2015].[Q4].[Oct], [2015].[Q4].[Nov], [2015].[Q4].[Dec]

The Ancestor function returns the parent, grandparent, great-grandparent, and so forth of the specified member. The Ancestor function requires two parameters, both of which must be placed within the parentheses. The first parameter is the member that serves as the starting point for the function. The second parameter is either the hierarchy level where the ancestor is to be found or an integer specifying the number of levels to move upward to find the ancestor.

The Cousin function finds the equivalent member at the same level of the hierarchy but down a different branch of the hierarchy structure. For example, January is the first month of Q1. Its cousins would be the first months in the other three quarters of the year—namely, April, July, and October. Likewise, Q2 is the second quarter in 2013. Its

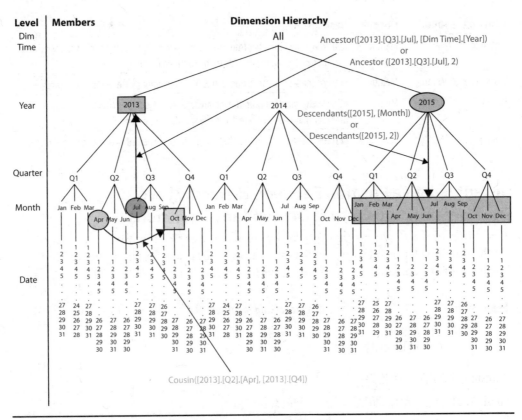

Figure 13-19 *MDX distant relative position functions within the same hierarchy*

cousins would be Q2, 2014 and Q2, 2015. Obviously, this is extremely helpful when we are trying to compare like periods in the time dimension.

The Cousin function requires two parameters, both of which must be placed within the parentheses. The first parameter is the member whose cousin is to be found. The second parameter is a member at a higher level in the hierarchy under which the cousin is to be found.

The Descendants function returns the children, grandchildren, great-grandchildren, and so forth of the specified member. The Descendants function requires two parameters, both of which must be placed within the parentheses. The first parameter is the member that serves as the starting point for the function. The second parameter is either the hierarchy level where the descendants are to be found or an integer specifying the number of levels to move downward to find the descendants.

Function	Input	Output	Description
Ancestor	Member, Hierarchy Level or number of levels to go up	Member	Returns the member that is a parent, grandparent, and so forth of the specified member at the specified level
Cousin	Member, Member	Member	Returns the member that is in the same sibling position as the specified member
Descendants	Member, Hierarchy Level or number of levels to go down	Set	Returns a set of members that are the children, grandchildren, and so forth of the specified member

Putting MDX Scripting to Work

Now that you have a basic understanding of MDX scripting, we can take a look at how it is used in Analysis Services. We do this by completing a Learn By Doing exercise, which defines a security role in an Analysis Services database. Along the way, we utilize MDX functions to get the job done.

Cube Security

In Chapter 12, we saw how to create perspectives that can divide a cube into more manageable pieces for our users. Perspectives are helpful for organizing information in a cube, but they do not limit users' access to only those items in a particular perspective. To secure portions of a cube from unwanted access, we need to use security roles.

Security roles enable us to restrict or permit access to items within the cube, measures, dimensions, and dimensional members. We can also allow or prevent users from doing certain administrative tasks, such as processing the cube or viewing the definition of its structure. The roles are associated with Windows logins and Windows groups to provide access to the cube information.

Learn By Doing: Setting Security Within an OLAP Cube

Features Highlighted

► Creating a security role

► Using an MDX expression to limit access to cube members

Business Need   Maximum Miniatures would like to provide access to the Max Min Manufacturing DM cube to the plant manager at the Kawaguchi plant. The plant manager should be given access to the Total Products and Percent Rejected calculated members, but none of the other measures in the cube. This plant only produces products from the Guiding Lights and Woodland Creatures product types. Therefore, access should be limited to these two product types.

Steps

1. Open SQL Server Data Tools.

2. Open the MaxMinManufacturingDM project.

3. Right-click the Roles folder in the Solution Explorer window, and select New Role from the context menu. The Role Design tab and a Role.role entry in the Solution Explorer window appear.

4. Right-click the Role.role entry in the Solution Explorer window and select Rename from the context menu.

5. Enter **Kawaguchi Plant.role** and press ENTER.

6. A dialog box appears asking if you want to change the object name as well. Click Yes.

7. On the General tab of the Role Design tab, enter an appropriate description for Role Description.

8. The items under "Set the database permissions for this role" determine whether members of this role can perform these administrative tasks or read the definition of the cube. Uncheck any of these check boxes that are checked by default. The General tab of the Role Design tab is shown in Figure 13-20.

9. Select the Membership tab. This is the place where the Kawaguchi plant manager's Windows login would be added to this role. If you have a test Windows login that you can use for testing this role, click Add and add the login to the role. Otherwise, move on to Step 10. The Membership tab of the Role Design tab is shown in Figure 13-21.

10. Select the Data Sources tab. Here, we control the access to each data source. Select Read from the Access drop-down list for the Max Min Manufacturing DM data source. We do not want this role to be able to read the definition of the data source, so leave Read Definition unchecked. The Data Sources tab of the Role Design tab is shown in Figure 13-22.

11. Select the Cubes tab. Select Read from the Access drop-down list for the Max Min Manufacturing DM cube. We do not need to allow drillthrough or rights to process this cube, so do not make any changes to these two items. The Cubes tab of the Role Design tab is shown in Figure 13-23.

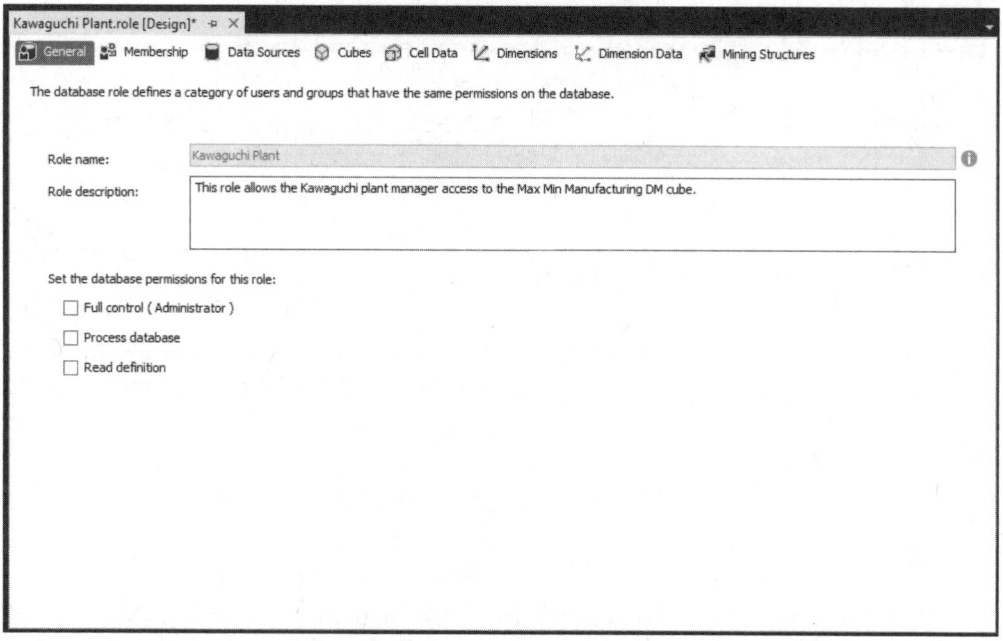

Figure 13-20 *The General tab of the Role Design tab*

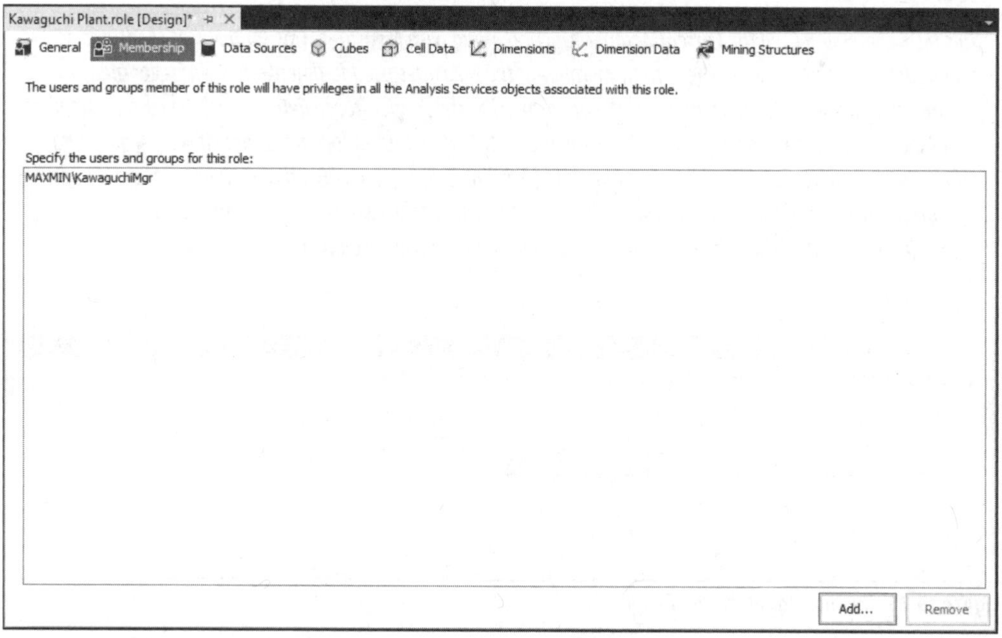

Figure 13-21 *The Membership tab of the Role Design tab*

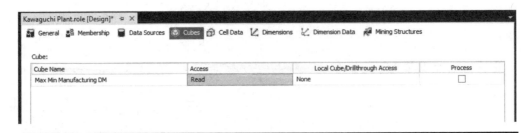

Figure 13-22 *The Data Sources tab of the Role Design tab*

12. Select the Cell Data tab. This is where we restrict access to the measures in the cube cells. Make sure the Max Min Manufacturing DM cube is selected at the top of the tab.

13. Check Enable read permissions.

14. Enter the following MDX expression for Allow reading of cube content:

```
[Measures].CurrentMember IS [Measures].[Total Products] OR
[Measures].CurrentMember IS [Measures].[Percent Rejected]
```

When creating expressions here, you can click the button next to Edit MDX to use the MDX Builder dialog box for assistance in building your MDX expressions. The Cell Data tab of the Role Design tab should appear as shown in Figure 13-24.

NOTE

This MDX expression used the CurrentMember function along with Measures. This syntax uses Measures as a pseudodimension in the cube. The current member of the Measures pseudodimension is whatever measure we are trying to query information from. We are also using the IS operator to determine if the current member is the specified member. The expression here will return true and, thus, allow access only if we are querying information from the Total Products measure or the Percent Rejected measure. If any other measure is queried, the current member of the measure will not be equal to either of the two we have specified and the MDX expression will return false. When the MDX expression is false, access is denied.

Figure 13-23 *The Cubes tab of the Role Design tab*

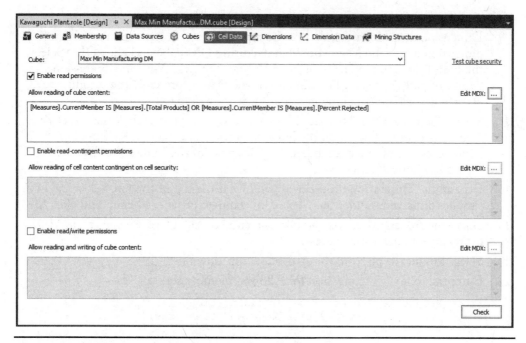

Figure 13-24 *The Cell Data tab of the Role Design tab*

15. Select the Dimensions tab. On this tab, we set the access rights for the
     dimensions. Leave the Access drop-down lists set to Read for all of the dimensions.
     Do not allow this role to read the definitions or process any of the dimensions.
     The Dimensions tab of the Role Design tab is shown in Figure 13-25.

16. Select the Dimension Data tab. This is the place to limit access to members of
     a particular dimension. The Basic tab enables us to use the brute-force method

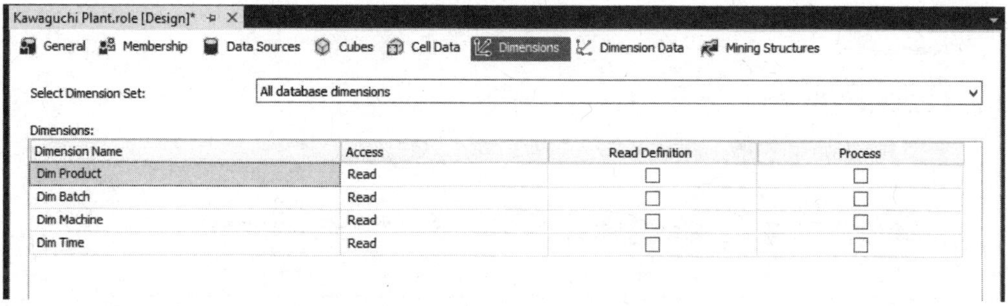

Figure 13-25 *The Dimensions tab of the Role Design tab*

and check or uncheck dimension members to determine access. Expand the Dimension drop-down window at the top of the tab. Select the Dim Machine dimension under the Max Min Manufacturing DM cube and click OK. (Select the Dim Machine dimension in the cube, not the Dim Machine dimension definition in the project. The dimension you want is probably the second occurrence of Dim Machine in the drop-down window.)

17. Select Plant from the Attribute Hierarchy drop-down list. Click the Deselect all members radio button on the left side of the tab. Check the Maximum Miniatures—Kawaguchi member. The Basic tab of the Dimension Data tab is shown in Figure 13-26.

18. Expand the Dimension drop-down window at the top of the tab. Select the Dim Product dimension under the Max Min Manufacturing DM cube, and click OK.

19. Select the Advanced tab on the Dimension Data tab. Here, we can create MDX expressions to determine access.

20. Select Product Type from the Attribute drop-down list.

21. Enter the following expression for Allowed member set:

```
{[Dim Product].[Product Type].[Guiding Lights],
[Dim Product].[Product Type].[Woodland Creatures]}
```

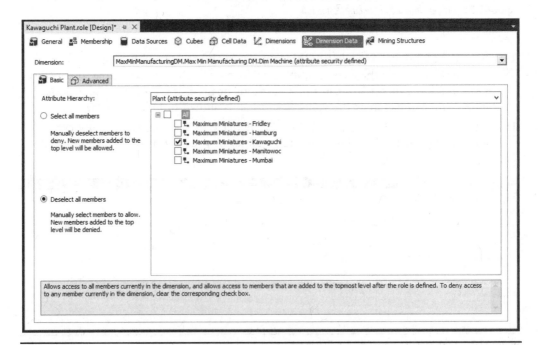

Figure 13-26 *The Basic tab of the Dimension Data tab of the Role Design tab*

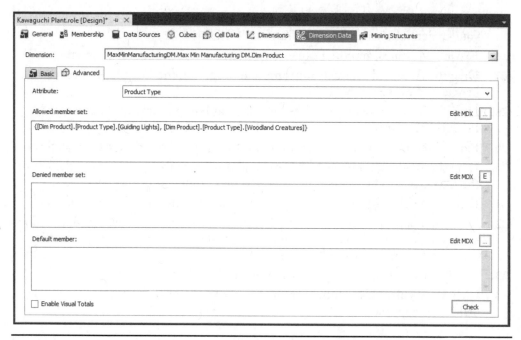

Figure 13-27 *The Advanced tab of the Dimension Data tab for the Dim Product dimension*

Here, we have created a set containing the two allowed members. The Advanced tab of the Dimension Data tab should now appear as shown in Figure 13-27.

NOTE

As shown in Figure 13-27, a user in the Kawaguchi Plant role will be able to see the totals for product types when the query result is at the All level of the Product Hierarchy. Only when the user drills down to the Product Type level of the hierarchy will they be limited to just the totals for the Guiding Lights and Woodland Creatures product types. If you would like to limit the user to seeing totals for only the allowed members no matter what level of the hierarchy is being queried, check the Enable Visual Totals check box.

22. Select the Mining Structures tab. We do not have any data mining structures defined in this cube, so we do not need to make any entries here. Click the Save All button on the toolbar. Close the Role Design tab.

23. Select Build | Deploy MaxMinManufacturingDM from the Main menu to deploy the changes to the Analysis Services server.

24. Next, we use the Browser tab to test our security settings. Double-click the entry for Max Min Manufacturing DM.cube in the Solution Explorer window. The Cube Design tab appears.

25. Select the Browser tab on the Cube Design tab. You are browsing the cube with your credentials, which have administration rights.

26. Expand Measures, and then expand the Fact Manufacturing measure group.

27. Drag the Accepted Products measure, and drop it on the Drag levels or measures here to add to the query target.

28. Drag the Total Products calculated member and drop it next to the Accepted Products measures.

29. Expand the Dim Product dimension, and then expand the Product Hierarchy.

30. Drag the Product Type hierarchy level and drop it on the query area to the left of the Accepted Products column. Notice all four product types are present.

31. Expand the Dim Machine dimension, and then expand the Plant Hierarchy.

32. Drag the Plant hierarchy level, and drop it on the query area between the Product Type and Accepted Products columns. Notice there are three plants present at least once in the query result.

33. The Browser tab appears as shown in Figure 13-28.

34. Click the Change User button on the Browser tab toolbar. The Security Context dialog box appears.

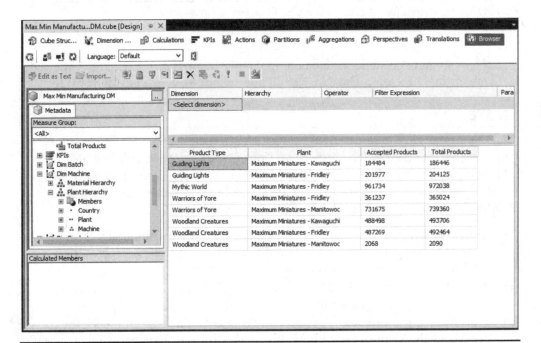

Figure 13-28 *The Browser tab using administrative credentials*

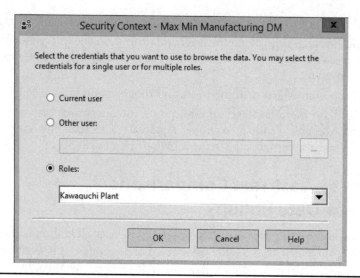

Figure 13-29 *The Security Context dialog box*

35. Select the Roles radio button. In the Roles drop-down window, check the Kawaguchi Plant Role. (The All Roles item is also checked.) Click OK to exit the drop-down window. The Security Context dialog box appears, as shown in Figure 13-29.

36. Click OK to exit the Security Context dialog box. The Browser tab resets. A message under the Browser tab toolbar informs us that we are browsing while using the credentials of the Kawaguchi Plant security role.

37. We can build the same query as we did before. Expand Measures, and then expand the Fact Manufacturing measure group. All of the measures still appear in this list. However, watch what happens when we try to query from a restricted measure.

38. Drag the Accepted Products measure and drop it on the Drag levels or measures here to add to the query target. We receive a (null) result because our security role does not allow querying from this measure.

39. Drag the Total Products calculated member and drop it next to the Accepted Products measures. Our security role does allow querying from this calculated member, so we do receive our results.

NOTE

You may recall that the Total Products calculated member is the sum of the Accepted Products measure and the Rejected Products measure. Even though our security role does not provide access to these two measures, the calculated member still works. This lets us provide a user with calculated members without having to expose the underlying data.

40. Expand the Dim Product dimension, and then expand the Product Hierarchy.
41. Drag the Product Type hierarchy level and drop it on the query area to the left of the Accepted Products column. As our security role stipulates, only two product types are present.
42. Expand the Dim Machine dimension, and then expand the Plant Hierarchy.
43. Drag the Plant hierarchy level and drop it on the query area between the Product Type and Accepted Products columns. Again, as expected, only one plant is present. The Browser tab appears, as shown in Figure 13-30.

This Year–to–Last Year Comparisons and Year-to-Date Rollups

Two bits of business intelligence are often requested by users. The first is the comparison of a value from this year with the same value from one year ago. It is a natural desire to know how the organization is doing versus where it was one year ago. In many cases, this is also a telling statistic, providing beneficial insight into the organization's health and performance.

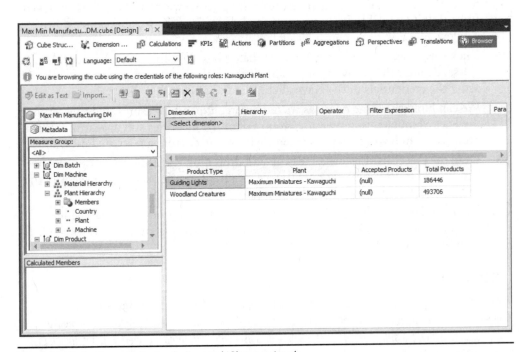

Figure 13-30 *The Browser tab using the Kawaguchi Plant security role*

The second bit of business intelligence that is often requested is the year-to-date total. Monthly and quarterly figures are fine, but users also want to know the grand totals as we move through the year. If the year-to-date numbers are not monitored, the year-end figures could be a big surprise to management, which is usually not a good thing!

In this section, we add two calculated members to the Max Min Manufacturing DM cube. One calculated member returns the Percent Rejected from the previous year. The other calculated member returns the year-to-date amount for the Total Products calculated member. To create these calculated members, we use three new functions: ParallelPeriod, YTD, and SUM.

The ParallelPeriod Function

The *ParallelPeriod function* returns the member from the time dimension that corresponds to a specified member. For example, if we ask for the time dimension member parallel to Q1, 2015 from one year earlier, we would get Q1, 2014. If we ask for the time dimension member parallel to August 2014 from one year earlier, we would get August 2013.

The ParallelPeriod function has the following format:

```
ParallelPeriod(TimeHierarchyLevel, NumberOfPeriodsBack,
    TimeDimensionMember)
```

TimeHierarchyLevel is the level in the Time Dimension Hierarchy that we are using to move backward. The most common hierarchy level to use here is the year level. *NumberOfPeriodsBack* is the number of the TimeHierarchyLevels to move backward. *TimeDimensionMember* is the Time Dimension Member that serves as the starting point.

Consider the following example:

```
ParallelPeriod([Date Hierarchy].[Year], 1,
                        [Date Hierarchy].[Month].[201503])
```

This function starts at the March 2015 member and moves backward one year to return the March 2014 member. In this example:

```
ParallelPeriod([Date Hierarchy].[Quarter], 1,
                        [Date Hierarchy].[Month].[201509])
```

the function starts at the September 2015 member and moves backward one quarter to return the June 2015 member.

The YTD Function

The *YTD function* returns a set of members from a time hierarchy level that represents the beginning of the year, up to and including the specified member. If the specified member is Q3, 2015, the members Q1, 2015, Q2, 2015, and Q3, 2015 are returned in the set. If the specified member is April 2015, the members January 2015, February 2015, March 2015, and April 2015 are returned in the set.

The YTD function has the following format:

```
YTD(TimeDimensionMember)
```

TimeDimensionMember is a member from the time dimension. For example:

```
YTD([Date Hierarchy].[Month].[201503])
```

returns a set of [201501], [201502], and [201503].

The SUM Function

The *SUM function* adds together the values in a set of measures to create an aggregate value. The SUM function has the following format:

```
SUM(SetOfMeasures)
```

SetOfMeasures is a set of measures. For example:

```
SUM({([201504], [Measure].[Total Products]),
                 ([201505], [Measure].[Total Products])})
```

adds the total products produced in April 2015 to the total products produced in May 2015.

Learn By Doing: Time-Based Analytics

Features Highlighted

▶ Creating a calculated member to return a value from the previous year

▶ Creating a calculated member to return a year-to-date value

Business Need   To make analysis easier, the vice president of production would like to have calculated members for the Percent Rejected in the parallel period of the previous year and for the Year-To-Date Total Products produced.

Steps to Create Calculated Members

1. Open SQL Server Data Tools.
2. Open the MaxMinManufacturingDM project.
3. Double-click the Max Min Manufacturing DM.cube in the Solution Explorer. The Cube Design tab appears.
4. Select the Calculations tab.
5. Click the New Calculated Member button on the Calculations tab toolbar. A blank Calculated Members form appears.
6. Enter **[Prev Year Percent Rejected]** for Name.
7. Enter the following for Expression:

```
(ParallelPeriod([Date Hierarchy].[Year], 1,
[Date Hierarchy].CurrentMember), [Measures].[Percent Rejected])
```

8. Select Percent from the Format string drop-down list.
9. Check the Accepted Products and Rejected Products measures in the Non-empty behavior selection window, and click OK. The Calculations tab should appear as shown in Figure 13-31.

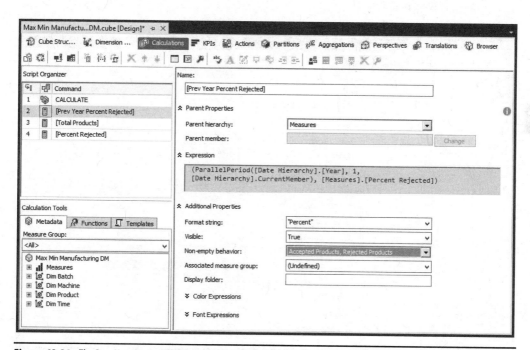

Figure 13-31 *The Prev Year Percent Rejected calculated measure*

10. Click the New Calculated Member button on the Calculations tab toolbar to add a second calculated member.

11. Enter **[Year-To-Date Total Products]** for Name.

12. Enter the following for Expression:

```
SUM(YTD([Date Hierarchy].CurrentMember),
[Measures].[Total Products])
```

13. Select Standard from the Format string drop-down list.

14. Check the Accepted Products and Rejected Products measures in the Non-empty behavior selection window, and click OK. The Calculations tab will appear as shown in Figure 13-32.

15. Click the Save All button on the toolbar.

16. Select Build | Deploy MaxMinManufacturingDM from the Main menu. The cube definition is deployed to the Analysis Services server.

17. When the deployment is complete, select the Browser tab.

18. If dimensions and measures are still on the browser from the previous Learn By Doing exercise, click the Reconnect button on the Browser tab toolbar.

19. Click the Change User button on the Browser tab toolbar. The Security Context dialog box appears.

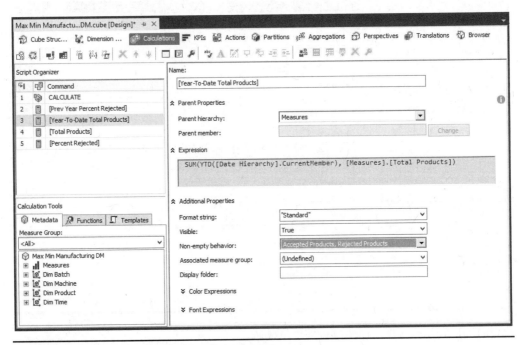

Figure 13-32 *The Year-To-Date Total Products calculated measure*

20. Select Current user and click OK.

21. Expand the Dim Time dimension and the Date Hierarchy.

22. Drag the Year hierarchy level and drop it on the Drag levels or measures here to add to the query target. The column will be added, but no data will appear. This is because we do not yet have any measures added to our query.

23. Expand Measures. Drag the Percent Rejected calculated member and drop it to the right of the Year column.

24. Drag the Prev Year Percent Rejected calculated member and drop it to the right of the Percent Rejected calculated member.

25. Drag the Total Products calculated member and drop it to the right of the two calculated members already in the browser.

26. Drag the Year-To-Date Total Products calculated member and drop it with the other three.

27. Drag the Quarter hierarchy level and drop it between the Year and Percent Rejected columns of the query.

28. You can try adding other levels of the Date Hierarchy to the query as well to confirm the calculations are working as they should. The Browser tab appears similar to Figure 13-33.

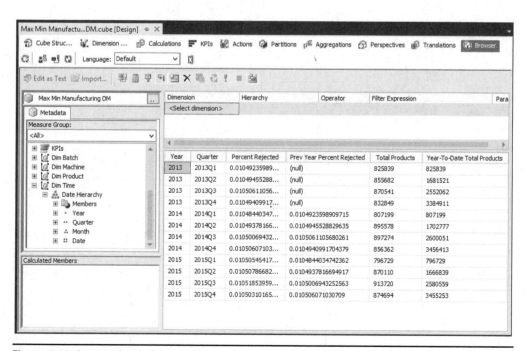

Figure 13-33 *Browsing the calculated members*

Extracting Data from Cubes

Up to this point, we have been concentrating on building our OLAP cubes. Here, at the end of this last Learn By Doing exercise, we can begin to see some of the potential for getting data out of these cubes and analyzing it to gain business intelligence. In the next chapter, we concentrate on this aspect of Analysis Services as we explore MDX queries.

Chapter 14

Pulling It Out and Building It Up: MDX Queries

In This Chapter

► **The MDX SELECT Statement**
► **Additional MDX Syntax**
► **Feel the Power**

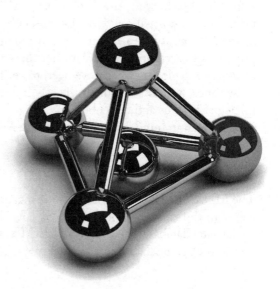

I've never been convinced that experience is linear, circular, or even random. It just is. I try to put it in some kind of order to extract meaning from it, to bring meaning to it.

—Toni Cade Bambara
U.S. fiction writer

W e now turn our attention from building and maintaining online analytical processing (OLAP) cubes in a Multidimensional BI Semantic Model to extracting the information resting within them. After all, this is the whole reason these cubes exist. To do this extraction, we utilize MDX queries. As a reminder, MDX stands for Multidimensional Expression Language.

We have been looking at MDX expressions since Chapter 11. In this chapter, we look at MDX statements. An MDX statement, specifically the *SELECT statement*, provides the mechanism for querying information. We look at other MDX statements in addition to the SELECT statement. These statements enable us to manipulate the data in an OLAP cube.

Many visual tools are available for extracting information from a cube. We worked with one of these when we used the Browser tab in SQL Server Data Tools in Chapter 12. This tool enables us to drag-and-drop dimensions and measures to pull data from the cube. Of course, SQL Server Data Tools is one big visual tool for defining and managing OLAP cubes (among other things).

Why, when we have such capable tools for defining cubes and extracting their information, do we need to learn anything about MDX statements? The answer is this: It creates character, and helps build strong bones and muscles. Well, perhaps not. The real answer is: It gives us a deeper understanding of how these visual tools operate. After all, SQL Server Data Tools creates MDX statements behind the scenes to perform the information extraction and cube management activities we ask of it.

In addition, at times, it is more convenient and, perhaps, even faster to use an MDX statement to accomplish a goal, rather than using a visual interface. When we are first creating or deploying a cube, we need to verify that everything is set up correctly. At these times, we want to look at the raw information and not have a visual tool adding layers between us and the cube.

With that in mind, let's begin with the MDX SELECT statement.

The MDX SELECT Statement

The MDX SELECT statement is our means of extracting information from OLAP cubes. In the same way the T-SQL SELECT statement produces a result set from a relational database, the MDX SELECT statement produces a result set from a multidimensional database. The first major difference between the two statements is the *T-SQL SELECT statement* returns rows and columns, while the *MDX SELECT statement* returns a multidimensional result set that can contain rows and columns, but it also can contain things called pages, sections, and chapters. More on that in the "Additional Dimensions" section of this chapter.

The other difference between the T-SQL SELECT statement and the MDX SELECT statement is the MDX SELECT statement is easier. That may be hard for many of you relational database jockeys to believe, but it is true. Just work through this section and see if you don't agree.

When I say "work through this section," I mean it. This section is not labeled "Learn By Doing," but it might as well be. You can gain a better understanding if you read this in front of a running copy of SQL Server Management Studio and try out each query as you go. By the time you're done, you'll agree this multidimensional analysis is no trouble at all.

The Basic MDX SELECT Statement

We begin with the most basic MDX SELECT statement and gradually add complexity. When we are done, you should have a good understanding of the statement and be ready for almost any data analysis challenge. We begin with some brief instructions for opening an MDX Query window so you can play along at home.

Opening a SQL Server Management Studio MDX Query Window

To open a SQL Server Management Studio MDX Query window pointing to the Max Min Manufacturing DM cube, do the following:

1. Open SQL Server Management Studio.
2. Connect to the Analysis Services server hosting the MaxMinManufacturingDM database.
3. Expand the entry for this server in the Object Explorer window, and then expand the Databases Folder under this server.
4. Right-click the entry for the MaxMinManufacturingDM database, and select New Query | MDX from the context menu. The MDX Query window displays, as shown in Figure 14-1.
5. The Cube drop-down list shows the cubes and perspectives available in the MaxMinManufacturingDM database. If you created a perspective in your version of the Max Min Manufacturing DM cube, be sure the full cube is selected in this drop-down list, not a perspective.

NOTE

*You can save your entries in the SQL Server Management Studio Query window by selecting the Save button on the toolbar or by selecting File | Save **filename** from the Main menu.*

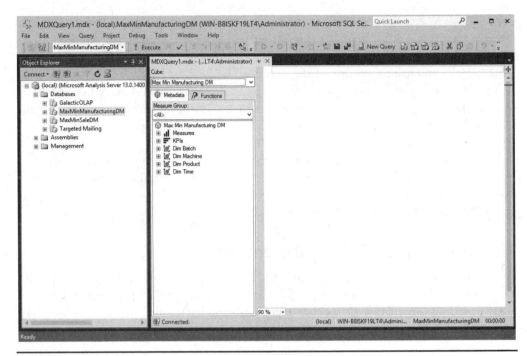

Figure 14-1   *SQL Server Management Studio with an MDX Query window*

The Very Basics

We begin with the most basic MDX SELECT statement possible:

```
SELECT FROM [Cube Name]
```

For example:

```
SELECT FROM [Max Min Manufacturing DM]
```

SELECT identifies this as a SELECT statement. The FROM clause identifies the cube or partition the information is selected from. This is known as the cube context for the SELECT statement. The result of this SELECT statement is shown in Figure 14-2.

NOTE

*You can type **SELECT FROM** in the Query window, and then drag the name of the cube from the Metadata tab and drop it after the word "FROM" in the Query window. If you do this, make sure you unhighlight the cube name before executing the query. If any text is highlighted in the Query window, only that text is executed. This means you can have several query statements in the Query window at the same time and highlight the single query you want to execute. To execute the query, click the Execute button on the toolbar or press F5.*

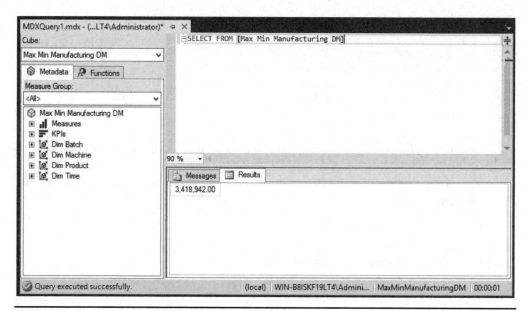

Figure 14-2 *The most basic MDX SELECT statement*

When a SELECT statement executes, it creates a set of tuples and then returns the value of one or more measures for each of those tuples. Remember that a tuple must contain one member from each dimension in the cube. This includes one of the measures in the cube that is considered part of the Measures dimension. A tuple from the Max Min Manufacturing DM cube includes the following dimensions:

```
(Dim Batch Hierarchy Member,
Dim Machine Hierarchy Member,
Dim Product Hierarchy Member,
Dim Time Hierarchy Member,
Measures Member)
```

In our basic MDX SELECT statement, we are not specifying the members of any dimensions to be included in the result. As we learned in Chapter 13, when a member is not explicitly specified for a dimension, the default member is used. Therefore, our query must be using the default members for all of the dimensions, including the Measures dimension, to get the result.

The tuple that defines our result is

```
([Dim Batch].[Batch Number].DefaultMember,
[Dim Machine].[Material Hierarchy].DefaultMember,
[Dim Product].[Product Hierarchy].DefaultMember,
[Dim Time].[Time Hierarchy].DefaultMember,
[Measures].DefaultMember)
```

The default member for most of the dimensions is All. Recall that we set the default member for the Time dimension to 2015. The default member for the Measures dimension is the first measure we defined—namely, the Accepted Products measure. So, the equivalent tuple is

```
([Dim Batch].[Batch Number].[All],
[Dim Machine].[Material Hierarchy].[All],
[Dim Product].[Product Hierarchy].[All],
[Dim Time].[Date Hierarchy].[2015],
[Measures].[Accepted Products])
```

By executing our basic MDX SELECT statement, we learned that for all batches, all materials, and all products for the year 2015, a total of 3,418,942 products were accepted.

Query Dimensions

As you might expect, we need to be able to specify members other than the default members in our MDX SELECT statements for those statements to be of much interest. We do this by including query dimensions. An MDX SELECT statement with one query dimension has the following format:

```
SELECT {set of dimension members} ON COLUMNS
FROM [Cube Name]
```

For example:

```
SELECT { [Guiding Lights],
         [Mythic World],
         [Warriors Of Yore],
         [Woodland Creatures] } ON COLUMNS
FROM [Max Min Manufacturing DM]
```

Remember that a set is enclosed in curly brackets ({ }). The results of this statement are shown in Figure 14-3.

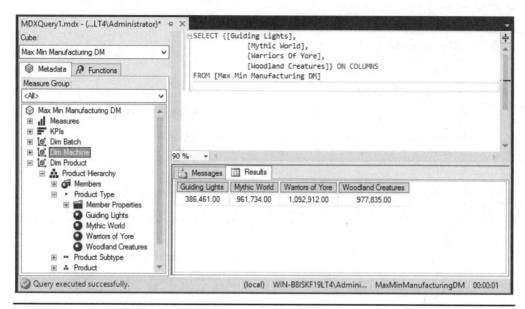

Figure 14-3 *An MDX SELECT statement with a query dimension*

> **NOTE**
>
> *As with the cube name, you can locate the dimension members in the Metadata tab and then drag-and-drop them into the query. If you do this, the query designer will use the key value to identify the dimension member rather than the name. Spaces, tabs, and new lines can be used interchangeably in MDX queries. The new lines are used in the code listing and figures to display the SELECT statements conveniently in the space allowed. Also, the query editor does syntax checking via Intellisense to give you cues if your query is not in proper form.*

If you are paying attention, you realize we can save ourselves some typing and enter this query as follows:

```
SELECT [Product Type].Members ON COLUMNS
FROM [Max Min Manufacturing DM]
```

This gives us the same result but with the All member thrown in as well. When a set of members is specified in this manner, the curly brackets are optional. (The All member will be a part of the result set only if you type the MDX query exactly as shown. If you drag the members of the hierarchy from the Metadata tab, as described in the note, the All member will not be included.)

Figure 14-4 illustrates how the COLUMNS query dimension is used to create the result set of the SELECT statement. A tuple is created using each member of the COLUMNS query dimension. A value is then retrieved for the member of the Measures dimension in each tuple.

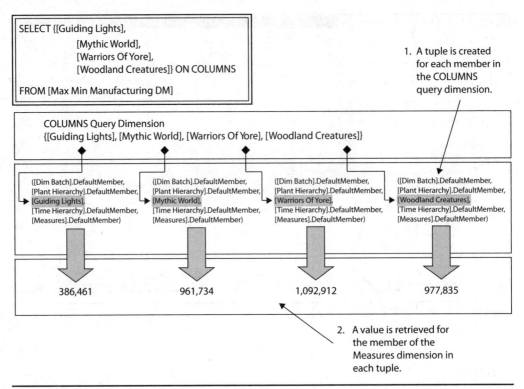

Figure 14-4 *Creating a result with a COLUMNS query dimension*

NOTE

The All member of the dimension is included in the query result but is not included in the figures in order to simplify the diagrams.

Let's add a second query dimension to our MDX SELECT statement. With two query dimensions, the MDX SELECT statement has the following format:

```
SELECT {set of dimension members} ON COLUMNS,
       {set of dimension members} ON ROWS
FROM [Cube Name]
```

For example:

```
SELECT [Product Type].Members ON COLUMNS,
       [Year].Members ON ROWS
FROM [Max Min Manufacturing DM]
```

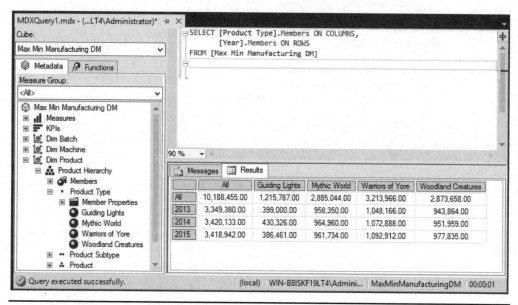

Figure 14-5   *An MDX SELECT statement with two query dimensions*

The results of this statement are shown in Figure 14-5.

Figure 14-6 illustrates how the COLUMNS query dimension and the ROWS query dimension are used to create the result set of the SELECT statement. A tuple is created combining each member of the COLUMNS query dimension with each member of the ROWS query dimension. A value is then retrieved for the member of the Measures dimension in each tuple. We can go beyond two query dimensions in an MDX SELECT statement, but we save that discussion for the section "Additional Dimensions."

Because Measures is considered another dimension of our cube, we can use a set of dimension members for a query dimension. For example:

```
SELECT {[Measures].[Accepted Products], [Measures].[Total Products]}
                                          ON COLUMNS,
       [Year].Members ON ROWS
FROM [Max Min Manufacturing DM]
```

This MDX SELECT statement uses a set containing the Accepted Products measure and the Total Products calculated member for the COLUMNS query dimension. The result is shown in Figure 14-7. We end up with the total of all accepted products and the total of all production for each year.

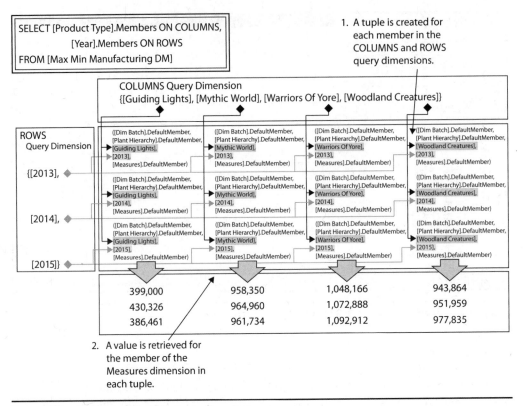

Figure 14-6   *Creating a result with two query dimensions*

Slicer

Using members of the Measures dimension in a query dimension is one way to view different measures in the result set. Using a slicer is another. When using a *slicer*, the MDX SELECT statement has the following format:

```
SELECT {set of dimension members} ON COLUMNS,
       {set of dimension members} ON ROWS
FROM [Cube Name]
WHERE [Measures dimension member]
```

For example:

```
SELECT [Product Type].Members ON COLUMNS,
       [Year].Members ON ROWS
FROM [Max Min Manufacturing DM]
WHERE [Measures].[Total Products]
```

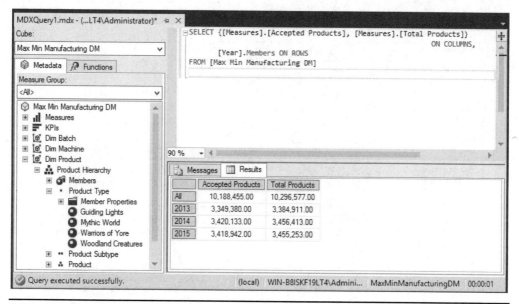

Figure 14-7 *Measures dimension members in the COLUMNS query dimension*

The results of this statement are shown in Figure 14-8. Remember that the default measure is Accepted Products. Now in this result set, we get the total products for each product type for each year.

In addition to specifying the measure used in the result set, we can use the slicer to do a bit more. We can specify dimension members to use in place of our default members for dimensions not included in the query dimensions. The format for this type of MDX SELECT statement is

```
SELECT {set of dimension members} ON COLUMNS,
       {set of dimension members} ON ROWS
FROM [Cube Name]
WHERE ([Measures dimension member], [dimension member])
```

The WHERE clause now contains a tuple, rather than a single Measures dimension member. This tuple can include as many dimension members as you like. The rule is this: A dimension can only appear in one place in the MDX SELECT statement: either on one of the query dimensions or in the slicer.

This sounds confusing, but an example clears things up. Suppose we want to see the total products for our product types for each of the years in the cube, but we only want to see those numbers as they pertain to the Maximum Miniatures plant in

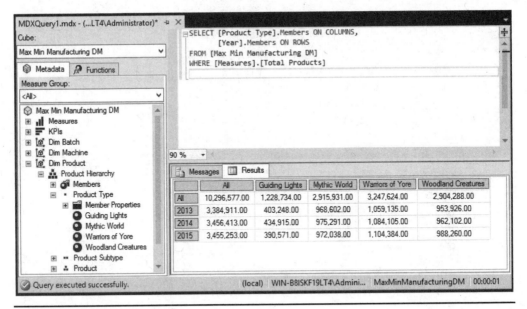

Figure 14-8   *An MDX SELECT statement with a slicer*

Fridley (Plant #3). We can use the following MDX SELECT statement to get this information:

```
SELECT [Product Type].Members ON COLUMNS,
       [Year].Members ON ROWS
FROM [Max Min Manufacturing DM]
WHERE ([Measures].[Total Products], [Plant].&[3])
```

The result of this query is shown in Figure 14-9.

Figure 14-10 illustrates how the tuple in the slicer affects the result set. Each member of the COLUMNS query dimension is combined with each member of the ROWS query dimension. These combinations are then combined with the members of the slicer tuple. The default member is used for any dimension not represented in the COLUMNS query dimension, the ROWS query dimension, or the slicer tuple.

Filtering with the FILTER Function

Many times, as we are creating MDX SELECT statements, the set of members we want to see on a dimension is dependent on the content of the data. For example, the production manager at Maximum Miniatures may want to see the number of accepted products manufactured for those products that had an increase in their backorder

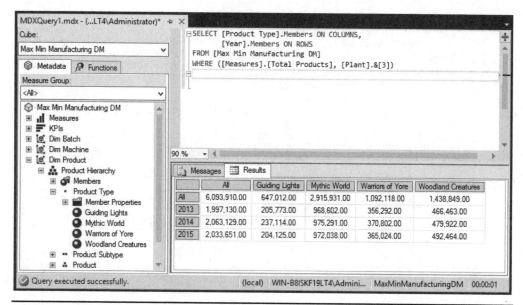

Figure 14-9   *An MDX SELECT statement with a tuple in the slicer*

amounts during the month. The production manager does not want to see all of the products in the dimension, only those with a higher amount on backorder. It is not possible to manually type a set of products to satisfy this query from month to month. A product that may have an increasing backorder from May to June may not be in that same state from June to July. It all depends on the data.

Fortunately, the *FILTER function*, which is an MDX function, lets us determine the content of a set using a condition expression. The FILTER function starts with a set of members as a parameter. Then it removes members from the set that do not satisfy the condition expression. Let's see if we can come up with a FILTER condition that can satisfy the production manager. We can compare the backorder amounts for November 2015 and December 2015.

If you switch to the Functions tab, you find the FILTER function in the Set folder because it returns a set. Drag the FILTER function and drop it on the Query window to use it as the content of one of the query dimensions. You see the following:

```
FILTER ( «Set», «Search Condition» )
```

The syntax tells us we need to supply the FILTER function with two parameters: a set and a search condition.

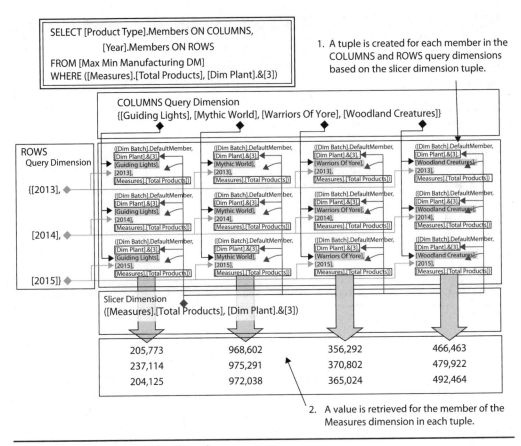

Figure 14-10   *Creating a result with a slicer tuple*

To satisfy the production manager's requirements, the set should be all members of the Product dimension at the product level. The FILTER function then removes those products that do not meet the search condition. The expression [Product].Members provides a list of all products.

For the search condition, we use an expression comparing two values with a Boolean operator. The values we are creating come from two tuples. The first tuple is composed of the December 2015 member of the Month hierarchy along with the Accepted Products measure. The second tuple is composed of the November 2015 member of the Month hierarchy along with the Accepted Products measure.

These two tuples are evaluated by including each member of the set of Products (the first parameter of the function) one at a time. The function evaluates

```
([Product].[American GI], [Month].[201512],
                    [Measures].[Number On Backorder]) <
([Product].[American GI], [Month].[201511],
                    [Measures].[Number On Backorder])
```

and then it evaluates

```
([Product].[Bear and Cub], [Month].[201512],
                    [Measures].[Number On Backorder]) <
([Product].[Bear and Cub], [Month].[201511],
                    [Measures].[Number On Backorder])
```

Any members of the set of products that result in an expression evaluating to true are included in the set returned as the FILTER function's result. The result is then used by the SELECT statement to create columns. The MDX SELECT statement and its result are shown in Figure 14-11.

Note that a number of products show "(null)" for the number of accepted products in December 2015. This occurs because this product was not manufactured in December 2015. No data exists to report for this measure in this timeframe, which probably explains why the number of backorders increased for these products!

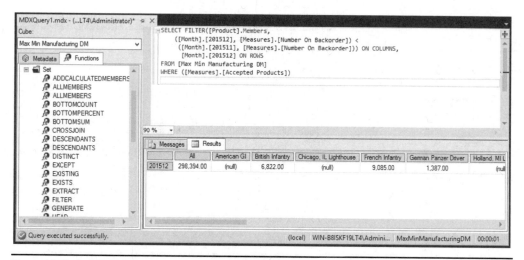

Figure 14-11 *An MDX SELECT statement using the FILTER function*

The NON EMPTY Statement

In the sample query in Figure 14-11, the data for many of the products was (null). These cells in our results set are really empty. The "(null)" string is put there as a placeholder so we can tell the difference between an empty cell and a cell that might happen to contain an empty string ("").

In many situations, we are interested only in the items that actually have data. We want to see only the non-empty cells in our result. We can achieve this by adding the NON EMPTY clause at the beginning of any query dimension statement. This is shown in Figure 14-12.

Additional Tools for Querying

We have now covered the basics of the MDX SELECT statement. You have seen how to quickly assemble dimensions, hierarchies, and measures to analyze the cube data and discover business intelligence (BI). However, a few more tools can help take the query process one step further.

The WITH Statement

In the previous section, we used the FILTER function to create the desired set for one of our query dimensions. But there may be times when the desired set cannot be defined by an expression in a FILTER function. Perhaps we want to look at the production of American World War II figures. There is nothing that lets us create this set using a filter (at least, not a straightforward filter). We need to build this set manually.

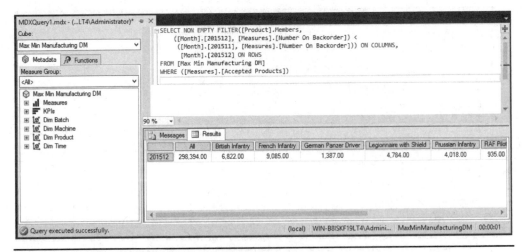

Figure 14-12 *An MDX SELECT statement with a NON EMPTY statement*

Rather than putting this manually created set in the MDX SELECT statement itself, we can use the WITH statement to define a *named set*. Once the named set is defined, it can be used in the MDX SELECT statement. The format for a WITH statement creating a named set is

```
WITH SET [named set name] AS
{set definition}
```

Here is the WITH statement and an MDX SELECT statement that uses it:

```
WITH SET [American WWII Figures] AS
{[American GI], [US Army Pilot], [US Navy Gunner's Mate]}

SELECT {[American WWII Figures]} ON COLUMNS,
       [Year].Members ON ROWS
FROM [Max Min Manufacturing DM]
WHERE [Measures].[Total Products]
```

The results are shown in Figure 14-13.

The main advantage of the named set is to keep your MDX SELECT statements neat, easily understandable, and self-documenting. The named set is also reusable. As we saw in Figure 14-3, even a simple query can look rather complex when a large set is specified right in one of the query dimensions. Named sets provide a way to avoid these complex statements by splitting things up.

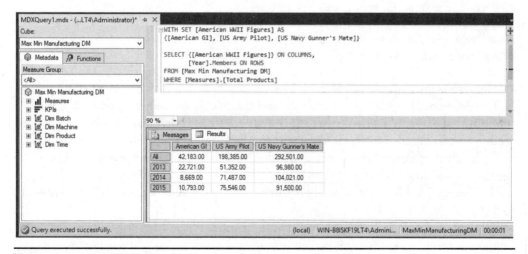

Figure 14-13 *An MDX SELECT statement using a named set*

We can also use the WITH statement to define temporary calculated members. These can be members of one of our dimensional hierarchies or members of the Measures dimension. The format for a WITH statement that defines a temporary calculated member is

```
WITH
  MEMBER [parent member].[calculated member name] AS
    {member definition}
```

Let's expand on our American World War II Figures set and create calculated members that create rollups for each nationality in the World War II product subtype.
Here is the code:

```
WITH
  MEMBER [World War II].[American Figures] AS
    [American GI]+[US Army Pilot]+[US Navy Gunner's Mate]
  MEMBER [World War II].[British Figures] AS
    [British Tank Commander]+[RAF Pilot]
  MEMBER [World War II].[Russian Figures] AS
    [Russian Infantry]+[Russian Tank Commander]
  MEMBER [World War II].[German Figures] AS
    [German Panzer Driver]

SELECT {[American Figures],
          [British Figures],
          [Russian Figures],
          [German Figures]} ON COLUMNS,
        [Year].Members ON ROWS
FROM [Max Min Manufacturing DM]
WHERE [Measures].[Total Products]
```

The results are shown in Figure 14-14.

The difference between the named set and the calculated member can seem a bit subtle at first glance. The named set is just that—a set of individual members. When we used the set in Figure 14-13, each of the individual members appeared in the result set.

Each calculated member is a new individual member that is composed of the aggregation of information from other members. When the calculated members are used in Figure 14-14, only the newly defined calculated members, not their constituent parts, appear in the result set.

While we are at it, let's define a temporary member of the Measures dimension. Suppose we want to know what percentage of total products our members of the

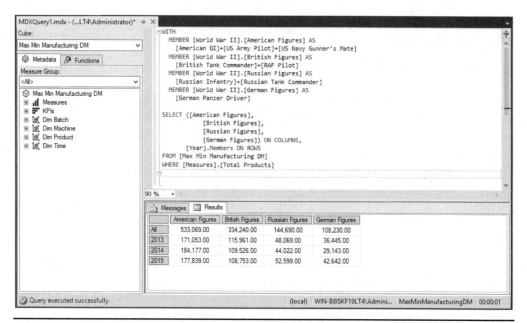

Figure 14-14 *An MDX SELECT statement using temporary calculated members*

product hierarchy accounted for. We can define a temporary calculated member of the
Measures dimension and use it as follows:

```
WITH
  MEMBER [Measures].[Percent Of Parent] AS
     CStr(ROUND((([Product Hierarchy].CurrentMember,
                      [Measures].[Total Products])*100/
        ([Product Hierarchy].CurrentMember.Parent,
                      [Measures].[Total Products]),2) )+"%"
SELECT [Product Type].Members ON COLUMNS,
  [Year].Members ON ROWS
FROM [Max Min Manufacturing DM]
WHERE [Measures].[Percent Of Parent]
```

The expression used to define the temporary calculated member is somewhat complex:
It consists of two tuples. The first tuple:

```
([Product Hierarchy].CurrentMember, [Measures].[Total Products])
```

returns the value of the total products measure for the current member of the product dimension. The second tuple:

```
([Product Hierarchy].CurrentMember.Parent,[Measures].[Total Products])
```

returns the value of the total products measure for the parent of the current member of the product dimension. We multiply the total products value from the current member by 100, and then divide it by the total products value from the parent member. The resulting decimal number is rounded to two decimal places and converted to a string. Finally, we concatenate the percent sign on the end. There you have it.

The results are shown in Figure 14-15. Note, we get a divide-by-zero error for the All products column, but we can ignore this and analyze the valid data for each product.

CROSSJOIN

Up to this point, our MDX SELECT statements have been limited to one dimension on each query dimension. Given that they are called query dimensions, it does make sense that would be the case. However, at times, we would like to break what seems an obvious correlation and put two dimensions on a single query dimension. Fortunately, MDX provides a way to do just that. (Of course it does; otherwise, I wouldn't have brought it up!)

We use the *CROSSJOIN function* to combine sets from two dimensions into a single joined set. This joined set can then be placed on a query dimension. If you are familiar with the cross join in T-SQL, you have a pretty good idea how this is going to work.

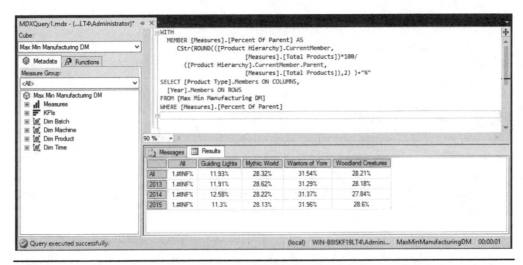

Figure 14-15 *An MDX SELECT statement using a temporary calculated member of the Measures dimension*

Our new set is going to be made out of tuples, which combine every member of one set with every member of the other set.

If you switch to the Functions tab, you find the CROSSJOIN function in the Set folder because it returns a set. Drag the CROSSJOIN function and drop it on the Query window. You see the following:

```
CROSSJOIN( <<Set1>>, <<Set2>> )
```

The syntax tells us we need to supply the CROSSJOIN function with two parameters: both sets. Let's look at an example.

Suppose we want to see the total products by product type, by plant, by year. We have three dimensions to work with. Here is what it looks like using the CROSSJOIN function:

```
SELECT CROSSJOIN([Product Type].Members,
                             [Plant].Members) ON COLUMNS,
       [Year].Members ON ROWS
FROM [Max Min Manufacturing DM]
WHERE [Measures].[Total Products]
```

In this query, we are taking all of the members of the product type hierarchy and cross-joining them to all of the members in the plant hierarchy. With four product types plus the All member and five plants plus the All member, we end up with 30 tuples in the cross-joined set and 30 columns in the result set. The result is shown in Figure 14-16.

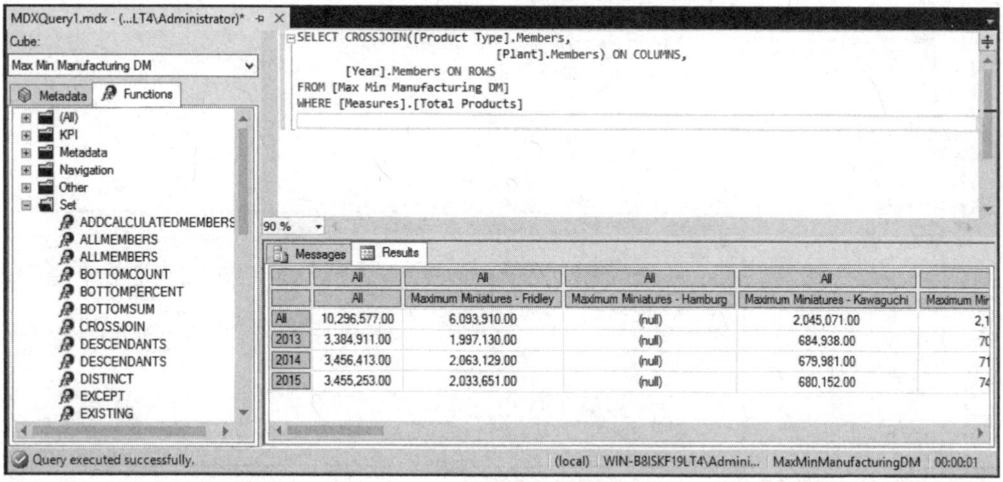

Figure 14-16 *An MDX SELECT statement using the CROSSJOIN function*

If you look at the result set in Figure 14-16, you see a number of (null) entries. This indicates a particular product type was not manufactured at a particular plant during that year. For example, there have never been any products from the Guiding Lights product type manufactured at the Hamburg plant.

Let's make our result set easier to analyze by eliminating columns with null values in every row. Again, we do that by adding the NON EMPTY statement to the MDX SELECT statement. With the NON EMPTY keyword included, our query looks like this:

```
SELECT NON EMPTY CROSSJOIN([Product Type].Members,
                            [Plant].Members) ON COLUMNS,
     [Year].Members ON ROWS
FROM [Max Min Manufacturing DM]
WHERE [Measures].[Total Products]
```

The results, with the empty columns removed, are shown in Figure 14-17.

As an alternative to the CROSSJOIN function, we can use the "*" crossjoin operator. The following query provides the same result as the query shown in Figure 14-17:

```
SELECT NON EMPTY { [Product Type].Members *
                            [Plant].Members} ON COLUMNS,
     [Year].Members ON ROWS
FROM [Max Min Manufacturing DM]
WHERE [Measures].[Total Products]
```

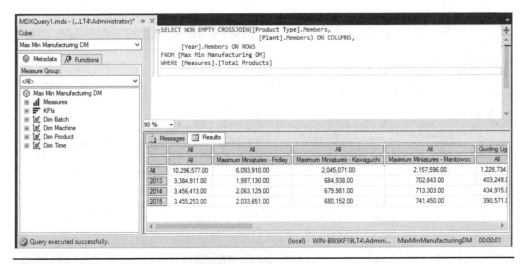

Figure 14-17 *An MDX SELECT statement using the NON EMPTY keyword*

TOPCOUNT/BOTTOMCOUNT

Often during analysis, we want to see the highest or the lowest values for a given measure. Of course, we can manually scan the rows and columns of numbers to make this determination. However, the more information we need to sift through, the more this becomes an arduous and error-prone task. Instead, we should have our MDX SELECT query do this analysis for us.

This is where the TOPCOUNT and BOTTOMCOUNT functions come in. These functions return the select set of the members with the highest or lowest values for a specified measure. The TOPCOUNT and BOTTOMCOUNT functions are found in the Set folder because they each return a set. Drag the TOPCOUNT function and drop it on the Query window. You see the following:

```
TOPCOUNT( <<Set>>, <<Count>>[, <<Numeric Expression>>])
```

The first parameter is the set we are to select from. The second parameter is the number of members to include in our result set. The third parameter is the numeric expression, usually a measure, which is used to rank the set members before taking the requested number of members off the top. The syntax of the BOTTOMCOUNT function is identical to that of the TOPCOUNT function. The only difference, of course, is the BOTTOMCOUNT function is pulling from the bottom of the ranking rather than the top.

Let's begin by looking for the five products we have manufactured the most in 2015. To accomplish this, we use the TOPCOUNT function in the following query:

```
SELECT TOPCOUNT([Product].Members, 5,
        [Measures].[Total Products]) ON COLUMNS
FROM [Max Min Manufacturing DM]
```

The results are shown in Figure 14-18. Note that we now have only five products in the result set, including the All member, but the products are in their ranking order.

To find the three machines that have manufactured the least amount of product in 2015, we can use the following query:

```
SELECT BOTTOMCOUNT([Machine].Members, 3,
            [Measures].[Total Products]) ON COLUMNS
FROM [Max Min Manufacturing DM]
```

The results are shown in Figure 14-19.

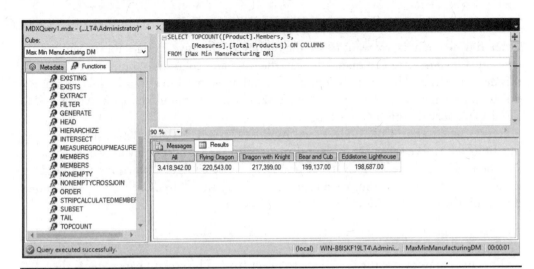

Figure 14-18 *An MDX SELECT statement using the TOPCOUNT function*

Remember that the TOPCOUNT and BOTTOMCOUNT functions simply create a set to use in one of the query dimensions. Let's look at another example to illustrate this point:

```
SELECT TOPCOUNT([Product].Members, 5,
          [Measures].[Total Products]) ON COLUMNS,
     [Year].[2014] ON ROWS
FROM [Max Min Manufacturing DM]
```

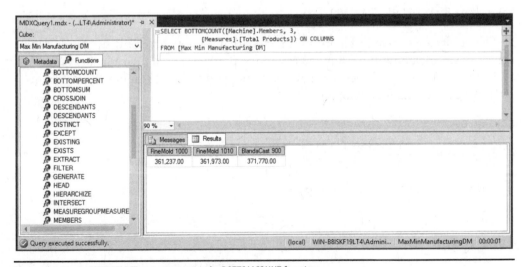

Figure 14-19 *An MDX SELECT statement using the BOTTOMCOUNT function*

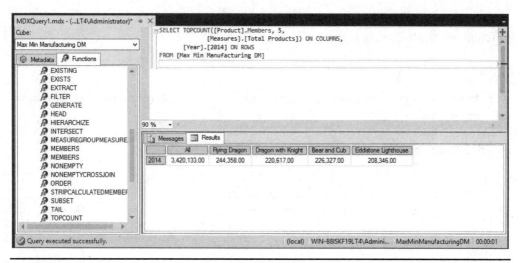

Figure 14-20 *An MDX SELECT statement using the TOPCOUNT function along with a ROWS query dimension*

The results are shown in Figure 14-20.

At first, a problem seems to exist with the result set shown in Figure 14-20. The products do not appear in the proper rank order. Maximum Miniatures made more Bear and Cub than Dragon with Knight, yet Dragon with Knight is second in the result set and Bear and Cub is third. We need to look at exactly what our MDX SELECT statement is doing.

The TOPCOUNT function executes first to create the set for the COLUMNS query dimension. Because we have not specified a member of the Time dimension, the function uses the default member of 2015. It finds the five products with the largest production in 2015. Using this set of five products for the COLUMNS query dimension, the SELECT statement combines it with the 2014 member from the ROWS query dimension to get the total products for our five products in 2014. Dragon with Knight production may have exceeded Bear and Cub production in 2015, but it did not in 2014. As with most computer code, you usually get exactly what you ask for. The trick is asking for the correct thing!

Aggregates

We have looked at aggregate functions with respect to the rollup done for hierarchy members in the cube. MDX also offers aggregation functions that may be used for creating calculations in MDX SELECT statements. We examine two of these functions here.

First, the SUM function adds the values of a numeric expression for all of the members in a set. The format of the SUM function is

```
SUM( <<Set>> [, <<Numeric Expression>>] )
```

Second, the COUNT function counts the number of items in a set. The COUNT function has the following format:

```
COUNT( <<Set>> [, EXCLUDEEMPTY | INCLUDEEMPTY] )
```

The optional second parameter to the COUNT function determines whether empty cells are counted.

Let's use these two aggregate functions to calculate the average amount produced per month for each product. We use the following query:

```
WITH
        MEMBER [Measures].[Avg per Month] AS
        'ROUND(Sum(Descendants([Date Hierarchy].CurrentMember, [Date]),
                                        [Measures].[Total Products]) /
        Count(Descendants([Date Hierarchy].CurrentMember, [Date]))),0)'

SELECT [Year].Members ON COLUMNS,
        [Product Type].Members ON ROWS
FROM [Max Min Manufacturing DM]
WHERE [Measures].[Avg per Month]
```

In our temporary calculated member, we first find the descendants of the current time hierarchy member at the day level. We then take the SUM of the Total Products measure to determine the number produced for this time period. We also take the COUNT of the number of days in the current time hierarchy member. We can then divide the sum of the total products produced by the count of the number of days in the time period to get the average produced per day. Wrap it in a ROUND function to get rid of the fraction amount. We also are required to enclose the entire expression in single quotes. The results are shown in Figure 14-21.

NOTE

MDX also includes a DISTINCTCOUNT function that has the same structure and function as the COUNT function. The difference is the DISTINCTCOUNT function counts multiple occurrences of a member in the set only once. The DISTINCTCOUNT function can have a very detrimental effect on performance. It is often a good idea to put a measure requiring a DISTINCTCOUNT by itself in its own measure group.

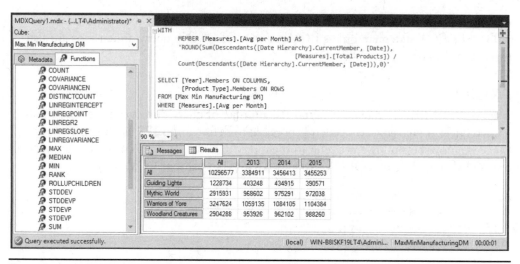

Figure 14-21 *An MDX SELECT statement using SUM and COUNT aggregates*

Additional Dimensions

To this point, we have worked only with the COLUMNS and ROWS query dimensions. We did hint that more dimensions were possible. Indeed, though it is hard for our brains to visualize in more than three dimensions, Analysis Services can provide many more.

Pages, Sections, and Chapters

Five named query dimensions are supported by the MDX SELECT statement. They are

- ► COLUMNS
- ► ROWS
- ► PAGES
- ► SECTIONS
- ► CHAPTERS

These query dimensions must be used in the order they are presented here. You cannot have a ROWS query dimension in your MDX SELECT statement unless a COLUMNS query dimension is also present. You cannot have a PAGES query dimension in your MDX SELECT statement unless ROWS and COLUMNS query dimensions are also present, and so on.

AXIS(*n*)

The MDX SELECT statement supports a number of query dimensions beyond the five named query dimensions. Indeed, it is possible to define up to 128 query dimensions. Once we move beyond five, we refer to the query dimensions as AXIS(*n*). In fact, we can use AXIS(0) in place of COLUMNS and AXIS(1) in place of ROWS, like so:

```
SELECT [Product Type].Members ON AXIS(0),
       [Year].Members ON AXIS(1)
FROM [Max Min Manufacturing DM]
WHERE [Measures].[Total Products]
```

The results are shown in Figure 14-22.
This can be shortened even further to simply ON 0 and ON 1 like this:

```
SELECT [Product Type].Members ON 0,
       [Year].Members ON 1
FROM [Max Min Manufacturing DM]
WHERE [Measures].[Total Products]
```

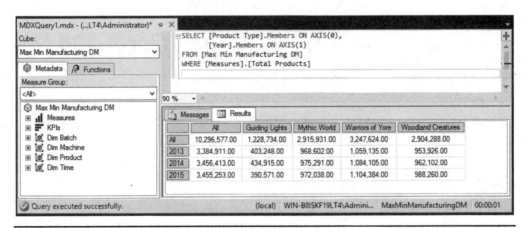

Figure 14-22 *An MDX SELECT statement using AXIS(0) and AXIS(1)*

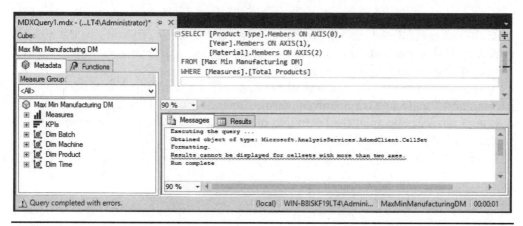

Figure 14-23 *A front-end Query window error when trying to use three query dimensions*

Unfortunately, the Query window in SQL Server Management Studio does not display more than two query dimensions. When we try, we receive an error message, as shown in Figure 14-23. This is an error from the front-end Query window, not from the Analysis Services server. Other front-end tools allow for more dimensions in our queries.

Additional MDX Syntax

Up to this point in the chapter, we have looked at the ins and outs of the MDX SELECT statement. This statement is extremely important to cube analysis. For the remainder of this chapter, we touch on some additional MDX that is useful in both the MDX SELECT statement and in MDX syntax scripts.

Operators

First, we take a look at the operators available in MDX.

Comment

Item	Description
/*...*/	Multiline comment
--	Single-line comment
//	Single-line comment

If you save your MDX queries for use by others or for your own reuse later, documenting what the query is for and exactly what it returns is important. With some of the more intricate MDX statements, it is not always easy to decipher the statement's purpose. A comment or two can be a lifesaver in these situations.

Multiline comments can span several lines and are not terminated until a */ is encountered. Single-line comments are terminated at the end of the line. Any of the comment types can begin at the beginning or in the middle of a line. Comments are completely ignored during MDX processing.

Here is an example of all three types of comments:

```
/* This is an MDX SELECT statement from the
   "Delivering Business Intelligence with SQL
   Server 2016" book. */
SELECT [Product Type].Members ON COLUMNS, -- the COLUMNS dimension
       [Year].Members ON ROWS              // the ROWS dimension
FROM [Max Min Manufacturing DM]
WHERE [Measures].[Total Products]          /* The slicer */
```

Numeric

Item	Description
+	Positive
+	Addition
−	Negative
−	Subtraction
*	Multiplication
/	Division

The numeric operators function as we would expect.

String

Item	Description
+	Concatenation

String concatenation is performed with the plus (+) sign, as in T-SQL.

Logical

Item	Description
<	Less than
<=	Less than or equal to
<>	Not equal to
=	Equal
>	Greater than
>=	Greater than or equal to
AND	Logical and
IS	Tuple equality
NOT	Logical not
OR	Logical or
XOR	Logical exclusive or

The logical operators perform as expected.

Set

Item	Description
–	Except
*	Crossjoin
+	Union
:	Range

The except (–) and union (+) operators only work with sets from the same dimension. The crossjoin (*) operator requires two sets from different dimensions. The Range operator was covered in Chapter 13. The crossjoin operator functions in the same manner as the CROSSJOIN function covered in the section "CROSSJOIN" in this chapter.

If Set 1 is

```
{[Bear and Cub], [Bear with Hive], [Bull Moose]}
```

and Set 2 is

```
{[Bull Moose], [Eagle Pair], [Howling Wolf]}
```

then

```
[Set 1] - [Set 2]
```

is

```
{[Bear and Cub], [Bear with Hive]}
```

In other words, it is the members in Set 1 that are not in Set 2.

```
[Set 1] + [Set 2]
```

is

```
{[Bear and Cub], [Bear with Hive], [Bull Moose],
                 [Eagle Pair], [Howling Wolf]}
```

Items found in both sets appear only once in the resulting concatenated set.

Functions

We look at some additional MDX functions that may be of use.

Dimensional

These functions return a dimension, a hierarchy, or a level.

Dimension   Returns the dimension to which the given object belongs.

```
[Bear and Cub].Dimension
```

returns

```
[Dim Product]
```

Hierarchy   Returns the hierarchy to which the given object belongs.

```
[Bear and Cub].Hierarchy
```

returns

```
[Product Hierarchy]
```

Level   Returns the level to which the given object belongs.

```
[Bear and Cub].Level
```

returns

```
[Product]
```

Logical

These functions return either true or false.

IsAncestor(member1, member2)   Returns true if *member1* is an ancestor of *member2*.

```
IsAncestor([Woodland Creatures], [Bear and Cub])
```

returns true.

IsEmpty(MDXexpression)   Returns true if *MDXexpression* results in an empty cell.

```
IsEmpty(([Warriors Of Yore],[Maximum Miniatures—Mumbai]))
```

returns true because the cell represented by this tuple has no data.

IsGeneration(member1, numeric expression)   Returns true if *member1* is a member of the generation represented by *numeric expression*. The lowest level, or leaf level, of a hierarchy is level 0.

```
IsGeneration([Black Bears],1)
```

returns true.

IsLeaf(member1)   Returns true if *member1* is at the lowest level of its hierarchy.

```
IsLeaf ([Bear and Cub])
```

returns true.

IsSibling(member1, member2)   Returns true if *member1* is a sibling of *member2*.

```
IsSibling ([Bear and Cub], [Bear with Hive])
```

returns true.

IIF(logical expression, expression1, expression2)   The IIF function may return a type, logical, set, dimensional, and so on. The IIF function is here because it requires a logical expression as its first parameter. Therefore, the IIF function is a likely place to find one of these other logical expressions.

If the *logical expression* evaluates to true, *expression1*, the second parameter, is evaluated and the result returned by the IIF function. If the *logical expression* evaluates to false, *expression2*, the third parameter, is evaluated and the result returned. For example:

```
IIF(IsLeaf([Product Hierarchy].CurrentMember),
    [Product Hierarchy].CurrentMember,
    [Product Hierarchy].CurrentMember.FirstChild)
```

In this example, if the current member of the product hierarchy is a leaf member, the current member of the product hierarchy is returned. This is the content of the second parameter passed to the IIF function. If the current member of the product hierarchy is not a leaf member, the first child of the current member of the product hierarchy is returned. This is the content of the third parameter passed to the IIF function.

Member

These functions return a member.

ClosingPeriod(level, member)   Returns the member at the level of *level* that represents the last item in the period occupied by *member*.

```
ClosingPeriod([Month], [2015Q3])
```

returns [201509], the last month member in Q3, 2015.

Item(n)   Returns the *n*th member of the tuple. Note that the index is zero-based.

```
([2014], [Bear and Cub], [Clay]).Item(1)
```

returns [Bear and Cub].

OpeningPeriod(level, member)   Returns the member at the level of *level* that represents the first item in the period occupied by *member*.

```
OpeningPeriod([Month], [2015Q3])
```

returns [201507], the first month member in Q3, 2015.

The AGGREGATE Function

When we used the SUM function to aggregate values to calculate the average production per month, we forced an aggregation on the rollup. All of the items were added together to create the aggregate. In some cases, this may not have been appropriate.

If we were working with sales figures, we could have inadvertently added in return amounts that should have been subtracted. If we were working with financial data, we could have added in credits that should have been subtracted. (In these days of Sarbanes-Oxley, that can get a company in real trouble, real fast!)

Instead of forcing an aggregation by using a function like the SUM function, we can use the AGGREGATE function. The AGGREGATE function works just like the SUM function, with one major exception. The *AGGREGATE function* uses the default aggregation operator for a measure, rather than forcing one on it. This helps ensure the data resulting from an aggregation is correct.

Data Analysis

MDX provides a number of numerical functions to assist in the analysis of OLAP cube data. We do not have space here to treat each in detail. We'll provide a list of these functions here to make you aware of their existence. Then, if you or one of your users has need of a particular type of data or statistical analysis, you can track down the details for the function or functions that fit the bill.

Function	Description
Covariance	Returns the population covariance of two series evaluated over a set, using the biased population formula.
CovarianceN	Returns the sample covariance of two series evaluated over a set, using the unbiased population formula.
LinRegIntercept	Calculates the linear regression of a set and returns the value of b in the regression line $y = ax + b$.
LinRegPoint	Calculates the linear regression of a set and returns the value of y in the regression line $y = ax + b$.
LinRegR2	Calculates the linear regression of a set and returns R2 (the coefficient of determination).
LinRegSlope	Calculates the linear regression of a set and returns the value of a in the regression line $y = ax + b$.

Function	Description
LinRegVariance	Calculates the linear regression of a set and returns the variance associated with the regression line $y = ax + b$.
LookupCube	Returns the value of an MDX expression evaluated over another specified cube in the same database.
Max	Returns the maximum value of a numeric expression evaluated over a set.
Median	Returns the median value of a numeric expression evaluated over a set.
Min	Returns the minimum value of a numeric expression evaluated over a set.
Stddev, Stdev	Returns the sample standard deviation of a numeric expression evaluated over a set, using the unbiased population formula.
StddevP, StdevP	Returns the population standard deviation of a numeric expression evaluated over a set, using the biased population formula.
Var, Variance	Returns the sample variance of a numeric expression evaluated over a set, using the unbiased population formula.
VarP, VarianceP	Returns the population variance of a numeric expression evaluated over a set, using the biased population formula.

Feel the Power

Thus far in this book, we have examined a tool for moving data into our data marts, SQL Server Integration Services, and a tool for hosting data models, SQL Server Analysis Services. In the next chapters, we look at a Microsoft tool that combines these capabilities into a single package. This tool also includes data visualization capabilities. In short, it does it all.

The tool is Power BI. Its purpose is to provide an easy-to-use, all-inclusive tool for power users to create their own business intelligence through self-directed analysis. So, let's move on and power up.

Part V

Modeling and Visualizing with Power BI

Chapter 15

Power to the People: Loading Data with Power BI

In This Chapter

- ▶ **The Power BI Architecture**
- ▶ **Getting Started with Power BI: Gathering Data**
- ▶ **Transforming Data During the Data Import**
- ▶ **Parameters**
- ▶ **Delivering the Power**

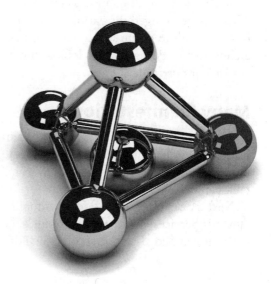

If you give a man a fish he is hungry again in an hour. If you teach him to catch a fish you do him a good turn.

—Anne Isabella Thackeray Ritchie
English author

We have spent the past six chapters working with SQL Server Analysis Services and the two types of BI Semantic Models it supports: Tabular and Multidimensional. Prior to that, we spent two chapters with SQL Server Integration Services learning its capabilities for loading and cleansing data. These are environments used primarily by data professionals to create an enterprise-level data infrastructure.

We change our focus now from tools designed for data professionals to a tool designed for business users, a tool designed to give power users the ability to create their own self-service business intelligence. That tool is Power BI.

Because of its mission to facilitate self-service business intelligence, Power BI must provide all of the capabilities of the data professional's SQL Server toolset. Power BI combines many of the data extract and transform capabilities of SQL Server Integration Services with the Tabular modeling capabilities of SQL Server Analysis Services. It also includes the data reporting and visualization features of SQL Server Reporting Services that we will see in Chapter 17.

The Power BI Architecture

The capabilities that are now brought together under the name Power BI have shown up in a number of different places as parts of different tools and with different names. Microsoft rearranged the various pieces as it worked to find the right platform for business users to create self-service business intelligence. Before we explore the current architecture of Power BI, let's look at these past manifestations—all of which are still available for use today.

Many Manifestations

Tabular data modeling made its debut as an add-in to Excel called Power Pivot. This was the environment where we first saw the speed and ease-of-design that in-memory processing made possible. Data could be queried from Power Pivot models using pivot tables and pivot charts in Excel.

Next, Power View was added as a tool for visualizing data from Power Pivot and Analysis Services–based Tabular models. Power View was part of the SharePoint environment and also showed up as an add-in to Excel. With Power View, the focus is on creating presentation-ready visualizations from the very first click. You'll see this is still true when working on visualizations in Power BI.

Power Query arrived next as an Excel add-in. Power Query provided a mechanism for extracting data from a wide variety of data sources and cleansing that data before it was loaded into the data model. Power Query provides a straightforward user interface for creating these data extract and cleansing routines. This continues in Power BI.

The resulting content produced by these tools has had various homes. It could be saved and distributed in an Excel file. It could be stored in a library in SharePoint or uploaded to a special area in Office 365.

Power BI Desktop

Now all of these parts and pieces have come together in a single tool called Power BI Desktop. This tool allows a user to create their own business intelligence environment by gathering data from a variety of sources and loading it directly into a data model. Visualizations may then be created from that data model in the same workspace.

The tool that started life as Power Query now creates queries in Power BI Desktop. However, these queries do more than just select the data from the data sources. The queries in Power BI Desktop transform the data so it is ready to be loaded directly into a data model.

The tool formerly known as Power Pivot now manages data models in Power BI Desktop. These models continue to use the same architecture as the Tabular Models created for Analysis Services. In fact, Power BI data models use the same DAX language that we studied in Chapters 9 and 10. Finally, two tools that use the same language!

Last, but not least, the tool once known as Power View now creates visualizations as part of the Power BI Desktop. The visualization tool has grown and matured. Many new visualizations have been added, along with the ability to create and add your own. Two things that have not changed are the ease of use and the ability to create highly interactive, presentation-ready content with just a few clicks.

PowerBI.com

The content created in Power BI Desktop is published to PowerBI.com. Once the content is on PowerBI.com, it can be explored online in several different ways. Users can interact with existing visualizations or use a browser-based, Power BI Desktop–like interface to manipulate the model and create new visualizations. Users can also query the data using a natural language interface called Q & A. Content from the PowerBI. com site can also be shared with others and embedded in your own custom applications.

Each user obtains their own login to access PowerBI.com. This access is free within certain limitations. Check the PowerBI.com site for information on the current limitations on free access. Even if you need more capacity than the free access allows, the subscription access is currently just US$9.99 per month. Again, consult the PowerBI.com website to determine the current subscription cost and terms.

NOTE

You may notice when you enter "powerbi.com" in your browser address bar that you are actually forwarded to "powerbi.microsoft.com" with the appropriate language added on the end. For simplicity, I will refer to this site as PowerBI.com in this book.

Power BI Content on Premises

In addition to publishing to PowerBI.com, you have a couple of other options when you wish to share your Power BI content with others. While PowerBI.com provides a home for your content in the cloud, there are—or soon will be, depending on when you are reading this—two tools that will host Power BI content on your own servers. These tools are Pyramid Analytics and SQL Server Reporting Services.

Pyramid Analytics

Pyramid Analytics provides a browser-based environment for creating visualizations from SQL Server Analysis Services models. It provides a very capable environment for IT staff to create reports and dashboards. It can also be used by business users to create their own self-service analytics.

In addition to facilitating the creation and storage of these visualizations, the Pyramid Analytics server provides a place where you can deploy and consume Power BI content. The models and visualizations created by the Power BI Desktop can be deployed to a Pyramid Analytics server on your network. That content can then be shared throughout your organization.

SQL Server Reporting Services

At the time of this writing, the Microsoft BI development team has stated a commitment to hosting Power BI content in the Reporting Services web portal. This has been promised in an early service pack for SQL Server 2016. Similar to the functionality currently available in Pyramid Analytics, this would allow you to share Power BI content on premises through your Reporting Services server.

Currently, you can store your Power BI files on the web portal, but when you open them, the Power BI Desktop development environment starts up on your desktop. This does allow you to store multiple types of report content—paginated reports, mobile reports, Power BI reports—all in one location. However, starting up Power BI Desktop is certainly not the way you want your end users to interact with visualizations.

Those of you reading this a few months from now, or perhaps over a year from now, will have to determine if this promised capability has indeed become a reality.

Power BI Mobile

Content placed on the PowerBI.com site can be viewed and interacted with using any modern browser. Those looking for a richer experience on a mobile device can download the Power BI native mobile app for your particular phone operating environment. The mobile app allows you to interact with the data in addition to simply viewing the content.

Constant Improvement

As Microsoft has embraced cloud-based computing, it has moved toward shorter and shorter delivery cycles. Power BI has been one of the environments that has benefited the most from this change in philosophy. Fixes—as well as new features and visualizations—are available monthly. You will want to get in the habit of downloading the latest and greatest version of Power BI Desktop and the Power BI mobile app often to stay current and to take advantage of the latest and greatest.

Obtaining the Power BI Desktop Software

The Power BI Desktop software is available as a free download from Microsoft. The easiest way to locate the download page is to go to:

```
www.powerbi.com
```

using any modern browser. At the top of the main page of the PowerBI.com site, you will see a menu. Select Products | Power BI Desktop. This will take you to the Power BI Desktop page.

On the Power BI Desktop page, click Download. This will begin the download of the installation file. Run this file and follow the instructions to install the Power BI Desktop software on your computer. You may also be asked for your contact information so Microsoft can send you additional information on Power BI.

The Power BI Data Engine

Power BI uses the same data engine as the SQL Server Analysis Services Tabular model. As we discussed in Chapter 9, this data engine gets its speed from the fact that it loads all of the data in the model into memory and accesses it there when performing analysis in response to user queries. The data engine can usually load multiple millions of rows of data into memory because of highly effective data compression algorithms.

Once the data is loaded into memory, it can be searched, aggregated, and otherwise manipulated much faster than data which must be read from a hard drive each time it is needed. The results are a data model that is simple and easy to maintain and yet very fast even when dealing with large amounts of data. A win-win all the way around.

Getting Started with Power BI: Gathering Data

As we discussed at the beginning of this book, business intelligence is all about getting the right data to the right people at the right time to facilitate effective decision making. Therefore, the first thing we need to do in any business intelligence operation is gather the data. Before we do that, let's take a quick look at the Power BI Desktop environment.

The Start Dialog Box

When you start up Power BI Desktop, the first thing you'll see is the Start dialog box. This provides a jumping-off point for finding the latest Power BI updates, connecting with Power BI resources, opening an existing Power BI report, or beginning a new Power BI report project. The Power BI Start dialog box is shown in Figure 15-1.

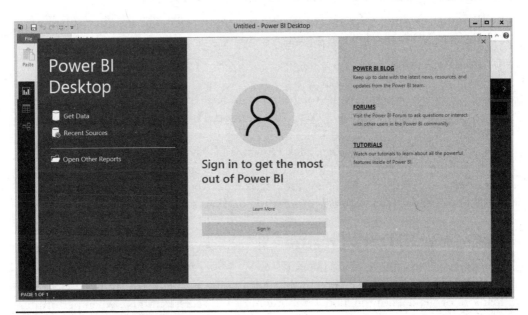

Figure 15-1 *The Power BI Start dialog box*

The right side of the dialog box provides links for getting the latest information on Power BI. You can also follow these links to download the latest version of the Power BI tools to stay up-to-date. Clicking the Learn More about Power BI link in the center of the dialog box takes you directly to the PowerBI.com website. The Sign in button will sign you in to PowerBI.com without your having to open the website in a browser window. Once signed in, you'll be ready to publish content to PowerBI.com at any time.

Recently opened Power BI files will be listed on the left side of the dialog box. In addition, the folder icon on the left side will enable you to browse and find the existing Power BI report file you want to work with. Power BI content is stored in a file with a .pbix extension. As with files produced by many Microsoft products these days, the pbix file is actually a zip file containing a number of other files that work together to define the data queries, data model, and data visualizations that make up a Power BI report.

Get Data

The remaining two buttons on the left side of the dialog box allow us to begin a new Power BI report by doing what we have already established is the first vital step: Get Data. We use the Recent Sources button to gather new data from a data source we have connected to in the past. The Get Data button enables us to make a brand-new data connection.

While the Start dialog box makes it easy to begin the data gathering process, we are not required to come to this dialog box every time we want to add data to a model. There are also Get Data and Recent Sources buttons on the Home tab of the Power BI Desktop ribbon. Both the Get Data button on the Start dialog box and the Get Data button on the ribbon take us to the same starting place, the Get Data dialog box, shown in Figure 15-2.

Data Sources

As you can see from Figure 15-2, Power BI can pull data from a wealth of sources. In fact, new data sources are being added each month. As you scroll down the list of supported sources, you will probably see a few marked as "(Beta)." These data sources are so new they haven't gone through the entire testing process yet. You are welcome to try them out and help Microsoft make sure they are ready for production use.

Because the list of supported data sources is ever changing, I won't try to explain every data source here. The truth is, if you don't know what a particular data source is for, you probably don't need it. Conversely, if you recognize the name of a given data source because you've heard it talked about around your organization, it is probably something you will need to use.

Power BI data sources fall into several categories. The lists in each category are not all-inclusive. The list of Power BI data sources is shown in Table 15-1.

Figure 15-2   *The Get Data dialog box*

Data Source Category	Examples
Databases	Most popular database systems are covered. Examples include: ▶ SQL Server Relational Databases ▶ SQL Server Analysis Services Databases ▶ Oracle ▶ MySQL ▶ IBM DB2 ▶ Teradata
Files	Both structured and free-form files can be used as data sources. Some examples include: ▶ Excel ▶ CSV ▶ XML ▶ JSON ▶ Text

Table 15-1   *Types of Power BI Data Sources (continued)*

Data Source Category	Examples
Azure	If your data is stored on Microsoft Azure, the odds are good you will be able to load that data into a Power BI model. Some examples: ▶ Azure SQL Database ▶ Azure Marketplace ▶ Azure HDInsight ▶ Azure Blob Storage ▶ Azure Data Lake Store
Online Services	Extract data from cloud-based services for your own analysis. Examples include: ▶ Microsoft Exchange Online ▶ Dynamics CRM Online ▶ Facebook ▶ Salesforce ▶ GitHub ▶ MailChimp ▶ Quickbooks Online
Standard Drivers	Power BI provides support for several data access standards. Some examples include: ▶ OData Feed ▶ ODBC
File Systems	You can use a file system as a data source with information about the files it contains as the data. Some examples: ▶ Windows File System ▶ Hadoop File System (HDFS)
Websites	Scrape web page content for information or analyze website usage statistics. Examples include: ▶ Web pages ▶ Google Analytics ▶ Webtrends
SharePoint	Load data from SharePoint both on premises and in the cloud. Some examples: ▶ SharePoint List ▶ SharePoint Folder ▶ SharePoint Online List
Other	Popular data sources that don't fit into any of the preceding categories: ▶ Microsoft Exchange ▶ Active Directory ▶ R Script

Table 15-1   *Types of Power BI Data Sources*

Creating Your First Power BI Content

We're going to put one of those data sources to use and create your first Power BI model. We will pull in data from the MaxMinSalesDM database we created back in Chapter 4 (and should have populated at the beginning of Chapter 12). If you have not created and populated this database, you can restore the database from the backup found in the supporting materials for this book. As always, do not use a production SQL Server instance to host your training data.

Learn By Doing: Creating the Max Min Sales Data Model in Power BI

Features Highlighted

▶ Bringing in data from SQL Server tables

▶ Building a basic column chart

▶ Creating a slicer

Business Need   The VP of sales for Max Min, Inc., would like to use Power BI for self-service analytics. Analysis will be based on sales in U.S. dollars and sales in number of units. He wants to create his own data model so he can add data and measures on his own in the future. However, he wants to get the data into the model in the most straightforward way possible.

Steps to Bring the MaxMinSalesDM Data into a Power BI Model

1. Open Power BI Desktop. The Start dialog box appears.
2. Click Get Data. The Get Data dialog box appears.
3. Select SQL Server Database, as shown in Figure 15-3.
4. Click Connect. The SQL Server Database connection dialog box appears.
5. For Server, type the name of the SQL Server instance hosting the MaxMinSalesDM database. You can type **(local)** if the SQL Server instance is running on the same machine where you are executing Power BI Desktop.
6. For Database, type **MaxMinSalesDM**. The SQL Server Database Connection dialog box should appear similar to Figure 15-4.
7. Ensure the Import option is selected and click OK. The Access a SQL Server Database dialog box appears.
8. If the Access a SQL Server Database dialog box appears, make sure the Use my current credentials option is selected and click Connect.
9. If an Encryption Support dialog box appears, click OK.

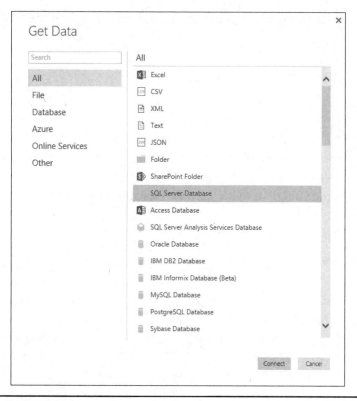

Figure 15-3   *The Get Data dialog box*

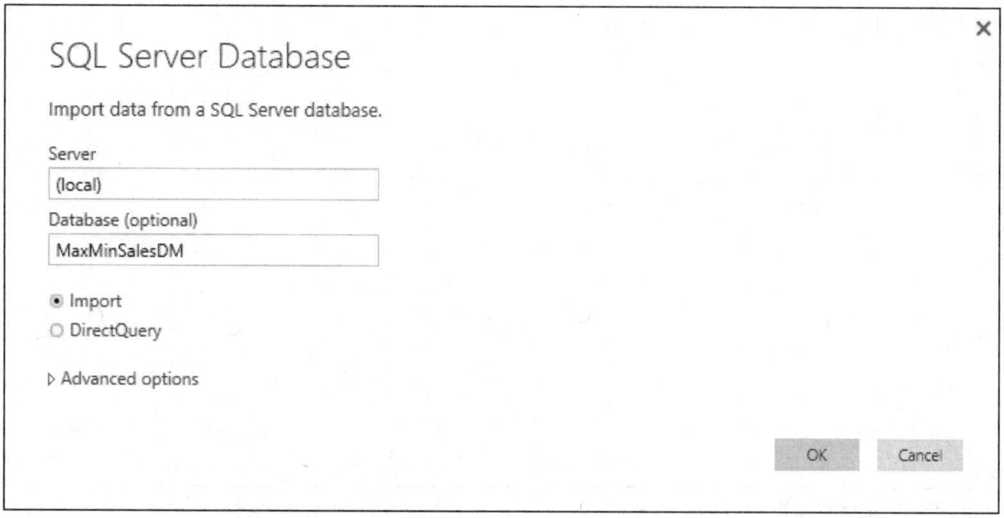

Figure 15-4   *The SQL Server Database Connection dialog box*

10. The Navigator dialog box appears. Check the box for each of the following tables:

Customer

Date

Product

Promotion

Sales_Information

Sales_Person

Store

The Navigator dialog box will appear as shown in Figure 15-5.

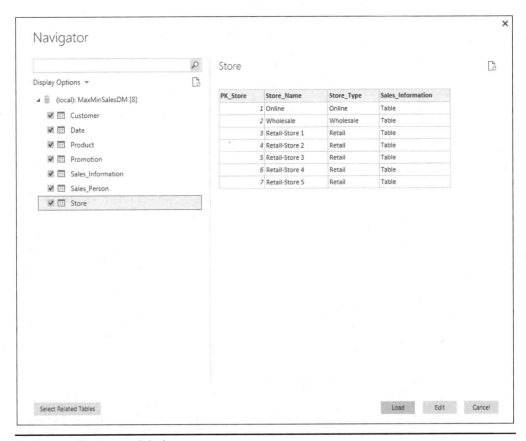

Figure 15-5   *The Navigator dialog box*

11. Click Load. The data from the selected tables is loaded into the Power BI data model. Once the data load is complete, you will be taken to the Report page of Power BI Desktop.

12. Click the button for the Relationships page on the left side of the window, as shown in Figure 15-6.

    With some rearranging, the Relationships page appears as shown in Figure 15-7. The relationships in the model were created from relationships (foreign key constraints) that exist in the MaxMinSalesDM database. Each of the lookup tables (Customer, Date, Product, Promotion, Sales_Person, and Store) has a relationship to the main data table (Sales_Information).

    We will talk more about relationships in the model later in this chapter.

13. Click the button for the Data page on the left side of the window. (The Data button is right above the Relationships button.) You see the data in the Customer table.

14. Click on any of the table names in the Fields on the right side of the window, as shown in Figure 15-8. You will see the data loaded into the model for that table.

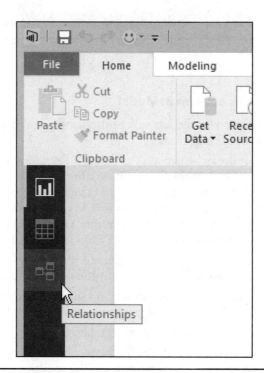

Figure 15-6 *The button for the Relationships page*

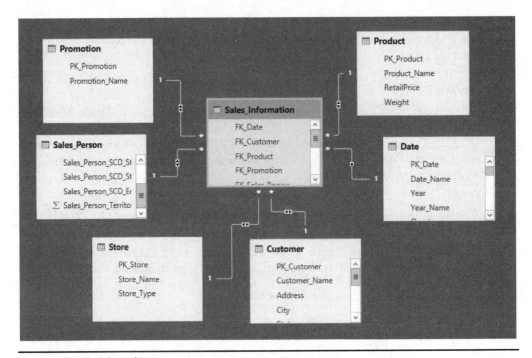

Figure 15-7 *The Relationships page*

Steps to Visualize Data in a Power BI Model

1. Click the Report button on the left side of the window (above the Data button). You see the blank report layout area.

2. In the Fields area on the right, expand the Sales_Information table and scroll so you can see all of the fields in the Sales_Information table, as shown in Figure 15-9. Note the Greek letter sigma next to several of the fields in the Sales_Information table. This signifies the model knows how to add up the values for these fields across multiple records in the table. For example, we can get the total Sales_in_Dollars for a customer or get the total Sales_in_Units for a particular month.

3. Click the check box next to Sales_in_Dollars in the Fields area. A bar chart showing the total sales in dollars across all of the data in the model is displayed.

4. Click the Page View button on the ribbon and select Actual Size from the drop-down menu. The bar chart is now bigger and easier to read.

5. In the Fields area, expand the Sales_Person table.

6. Click the check box next to Sales_Person_Name. You may need to make the Fields area wider or hover over the item to see the tooltip to determine which one to select.

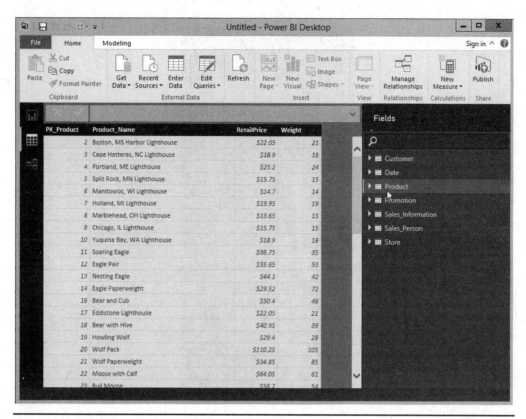

Figure 15-8   *The Data page*

7. Click somewhere in the report layout area that is outside of the chart so the chart is no longer selected.

8. Scroll up in the Fields area and expand the Date table.

9. Click the check box next to Year_Name. A table of the data in the Year_Name field is created.

10. Drag this table so it is on the right side of the report layout area near the top.

11. In the Visualizations area, click the Slicer button, as shown in Figure 15-10. The Year_Name table is now a slicer. A slicer filters the values on the report page by what is selected. Note that having no items selected in the slicer is the same as having all items selected in the slicer.

12. Use the sizing handles to remove the whitespace surrounding the year names in the slicer as shown in Figure 15-11.

13. Arrange the two items on the report, as shown in Figure 15-12.

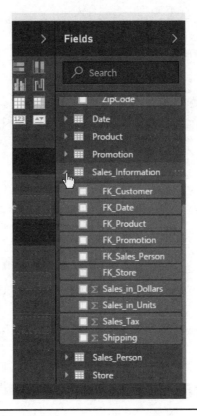

Figure 15-9   *The Fields area on the Report page*

Figure 15-10   *The Slicer button in the Visualizations area*

Figure 15-11 *Sizing the slicer*

14. Click the Calendar 2015 entry in the slicer. The chart shows sales for each salesperson in calendar year 2015.

15. Click the Calendar 2014 entry in the slicer. The chart shows sales for 2014. Note that by default the chart is sorted by Sales_in_Dollars descending. When we use the slicer to switch the data from one year to another, the sort order changes according to who were the top sellers in that year.

16. Hold down CTRL and click Calendar 2015. The chart now shows the combined sales results for calendar year 2014 and calendar year 2015.

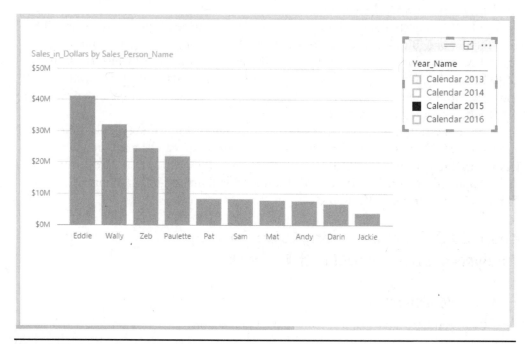

Figure 15-12 *A Power BI report with slicer*

17. Click the Save button at the top of the window. The Save As dialog box appears. Navigate to the location where you would like to save the content created in this chapter and the next.

18. Create a new folder called **PowerBI**. Double-click the PowerBI folder to navigate into it.

19. Enter **Max Min Sales Information** for File name.

20. Click Save.

Congratulations. You've built your first interactive Power BI report.

Using Live Connection

In the previous Learn By Doing exercise, you saw how to quickly create a data model and a visualization using Power BI. In case you weren't aware, we imported and analyzed over 3 million rows of sales data. It took only a few minutes and a few clicks!

Next we are going to look at a way to start visualizing data even faster. This method is going to take advantage of the fact that we already have a data model built from our MaxMinManufacturing data and residing on a SQL Server Analysis Server instance. Instead of pulling the data into a new model, we will have Power BI query the existing model. This is known as Live Connection.

The Live Connection mode knows how to take advantage of the inherent capabilities of a Tabular or Multidimensional model. Instead of querying its own data model to get the data it needs for visualizations, Power BI knows how to efficiently interact with the SQL Server Analysis Services instance to get the data it needs. With Live Connection mode, we allow Power BI to serve as a highly capable data visualization and exploration tool for data residing in enterprise-level data models.

Live Connection is only available when connecting to Tabular and Multidimensional models on SQL Server Analysis Services. Live Connection can be used on a limited basis with Tabular models in SQL Server Analysis Services 2016 Standard Edition. It is fully supported in both Tabular and Multidimensional models in SQL Server Analysis Services 2016 Enterprise Edition.

Learn By Doing: Connecting to an Existing Analysis Services Model with Power BI

Features Highlighted

▶ Connecting to a data source using Live Connection

▶ Using drilldown in a bar chart

▶ Viewing the data underlying a chart

Business Need   The VP of manufacturing for Max Min, Inc., would like to use Power BI for self-service data visualizations. He wants to use Power BI reports to explore the manufacturing data, but he does not want to have to create his own data models.

Steps to Create Live Connection to the MaxMinManufacturing Tabular Model

1. Click the File tab of the menu and select New from the menu. The Start dialog box appears.
2. Click Get Data. The Get Data dialog box appears.
3. Select SQL Server Analysis Services Database and click Connect. The SQL Server Analysis Services Database connection dialog box appears.
4. For Server, type the name of the SQL Server Analysis Services Tabular instance hosting the MaxMinManufacturing Tabular model.
5. For Database, type **Max Min Manufacturing**.
6. Select the Connect live option.
7. Click OK. The Navigator dialog box appears.
8. Any perspectives defined within the data model as well as an entry for the data model as a whole are displayed in the Navigator dialog box when operating in this mode. Select MaxMinManufacturing.
9. Click OK. You immediately see the Report page with the tables in the selected model visible in the Fields area.

Steps to Explore the Data Using Drilldown

1. Expand the Manufacturing Info table in the Fields area.
2. Click the check box next to Total Products in the Fields area. A column chart showing the total products produced across all of the data in the model is displayed.
3. Scroll down in the fields area and expand the Time table.
4. Click the check box next to Date Hierarchy. The column chart shows the total produced for each of the three years in the data model.
5. Hover over the 2013 column. The detail information for this column appears in a tooltip, as shown in Figure 15-13.
6. Because we chose to add the entire Date Hierarchy to the visualization, our column chart has drilldown enabled. Right-click the 2013 column and select Drill Down from the context menu, as shown in Figure 15-14. You see the Total Products for the four quarters of 2013.
7. Right-click the 2013-Q3 column and select Drill Down from the context menu. You see the Total Products for each month in the third quarter of 2013.

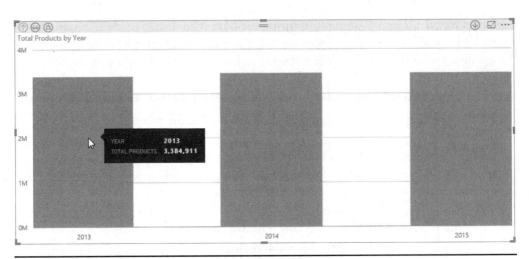

Figure 15-13 *Tooltip showing detail information*

8. Click the 2013-08 column. The selected column retains its color while the color fades on the other two columns. This draws special attention to the selected column. We will see in Chapter 16 how clicking on a chart item causes additional interactions with other visualizations on the report.

9. Click the 2013-08 column again to have all the columns return to the same color intensity.

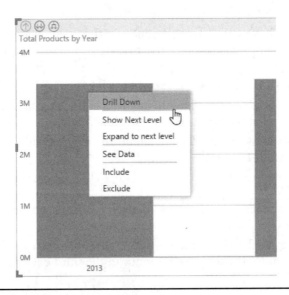

Figure 15-14 *Selecting Drill Down from the context menu*

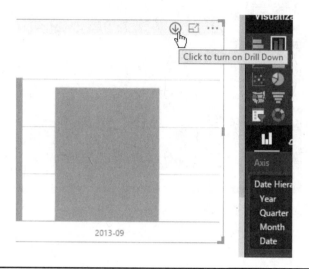

Figure 15-15 *Turning on single-click drilldown*

10. We can change the chart so a click causes a drilldown action rather than a highlight action. Click the single down arrow in the upper-right corner of the chart, as shown in Figure 15-15. The arrow changes from dark on light background to light on dark background. This indicates single-click drilldown has been activated.

11. Once again, click the 2013-08 column. This time you see the Total Products for each day in August 2013.

12. Right-click one of the columns and select See Data from the context menu. The detail data for each column appears at the bottom of the report area, as shown in Figure 15-16.

13. Click the button in the upper-right corner of the report area to pivot the windows, as shown in Figure 15-17. The chart and the detail data window will appear side by side.

14. Right-click one of the columns and select Drill Up from the context menu. You see the Total Products for each month in the third quarter of 2013.

15. Click the button to pivot the windows again and they appear top to bottom again.

16. Click Back to Report in the upper-left corner of the report area to remove the detail data window.

17. Click the Drill Up arrow in the upper-left corner of the chart, as shown in Figure 15-18. You see the Total Products for each quarter of 2013.

18. Click the Drill Up arrow again. You see the Total Products for each year.

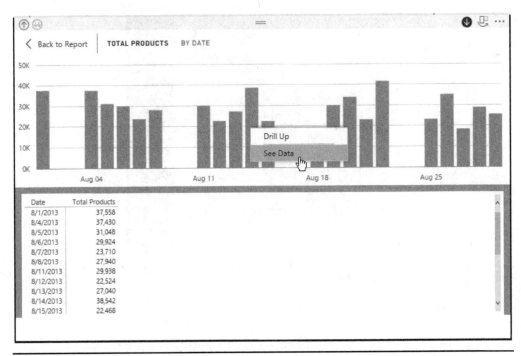

Figure 15-16 *Viewing detail data with a chart*

19. In addition to drilling down to the next level for a single column, we can drill down to the next level for all columns at once. Right-click one of the columns and select Expand All from the context menu. You see the Total Products for all quarters of all years in the data model.

20. Click the Drill all to the next level double down arrow in the upper-left corner of the chart, as shown in Figure 15-19. You see the Total Products for all months of all years in the data model.

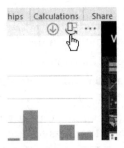

Figure 15-17 *Changing the report windows to be side by side*

Figure 15-18 *The Drill Up button*

21. Click Save in the upper-left corner of the Power BI window. The Save As dialog box appears.
22. Enter **Max Min Manufacturing Live Connection** for File name.
23. Click Save.

Connection Types and Direct Query

In our first two Learn By Doing exercises, we used two different types of connections to access our data. Let's review the characteristics of these connection types. We'll also discuss a third connection type, Direct Query.

Import

With the model we created in the first Learn By Doing exercise, we used the Import method to access the data for the model. That meant the data was loaded and stored within the Power BI model at the time the model was created. The original source for that data, the MaxMinSalesDM database, is not accessed again until we choose to update the data contained in the model. This allows Power BI to keep the model data in memory when it is being queried so we get that great performance we discussed earlier in this chapter.

Once we had the data loaded into the Power BI model, we saw how additional structure was added. Relationships were automatically created within the Power BI model. The ability to quickly aggregate quantities across a number of records was added. These additions, which make up the structure of the data model, were created in and stored as part of the Power BI model itself.

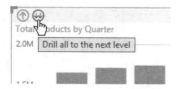

Figure 15-19 *The Drill All to the Next Level button*

To summarize, when using Import mode, the data and the model structure are both stored within the Power BI model. This is represented by the bottom row in Figure 15-20. The big advantage of Import mode is the speed gained from use of the in-memory model versus the query performance of whatever might be providing the underlying data. In the remainder of this chapter, we will also discover features that allow us to manipulate the data as it is imported into the Power BI model. The major disadvantage of Import mode is the data is refreshed from the data source on a periodic basis. That means the data can be out-of-date. Also, there is some model downtime required each time the data is being reloaded.

Live Connection

With the model we created in the second Learn By Doing exercise, we used the Live Connection method to access the data for the model. Live Connection only works with Tabular and Multidimensional data models stored in SQL Server Analysis Services. In our case, it was a Tabular model. With Live Connection, we didn't load any data into our Power BI model. Instead, Power BI queried the Tabular model whenever it needed data.

Further, we didn't create any model structure within Power BI. Any definition as to how we aggregate values or what tables are related to each other, etc., comes from the underlying Tabular model. It is all prepared for us ahead of time by some nice model developer—in this case it was us working on Learn By Doing exercises in earlier chapters!

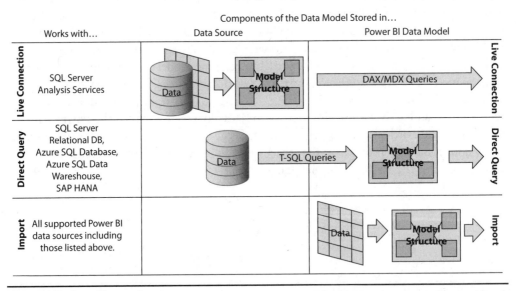

Figure 15-20 *Power BI connection types*

In short, the Live Connection mode depends entirely on the data and the model structure stored in the data source. This is represented by the top row in Figure 15-20. The advantage of Live Connection mode is we can quickly take advantage of a preexisting enterprise-level model. We don't have to duplicate the effort that went into creating that model. Also, multiple users can access the same data model, again saving on duplication of effort. The disadvantage of Live Connection is we do not have the opportunity to add our own content to the model definition. We can perform self-service data exploration using the existing data model, but we can't create truly self-service business intelligence.

Direct Query

As alluded to earlier, there is a third path when it comes to Power BI connection types. This is Direct Query. As you might have guessed (or as you might have seen in Figure 15-20), Direct Query is in between the functionality of Live Connection and Import.

Like Live Connection mode, Direct Query leaves the data residing in the data source. It does not import the data into the Power BI model. Instead, it queries the data from the source when it is needed. In this case, T-SQL queries are constructed behind the scenes to pull the required data from the database. This means we are always getting live, up-to-date data for our analysis. The disadvantage is we may experience poorer performance, especially if we are querying and aggregating large amounts of data.

Like Import mode, the model structure is maintained within the Power BI model. That means we have control over that structure and can shape it however we like. We can do truly self-service business intelligence.

Direct Query mode is supported by:

- ► SQL Server relational databases
- ► Azure SQL Database
- ► Azure SQL Data Warehouse
- ► SAP HANA

Transforming Data During the Data Import

We are going to turn our focus back to features supported by a Power BI model operating in Import mode: namely, the ability to make changes to the structure and content of the data as it is being imported into the Power BI model. This enables us to transform the data into a format that is better suited for our analysis. It also gives us a way to deal with problem data before it makes it into our Power BI models.

This in-flight data manipulation is made possible by the Power BI Query Editor.

The Power BI Query Editor

The name Query Editor might give you visions of a blank text edit window and mountains of intricate syntax to learn in order to manipulate data. Despite the odd name, the Power BI Query Editor is an easy-to-use, drag-and-drop tool. There is a text edit mode available behind the scenes for advanced operations, but you may never have to use it.

So far, we have created two Power BI models through two Learn By Doing exercises without having to utilize the Query Editor. The model using Live Connection mode didn't require the Query Editor because Live Connection does not load any data into the model. When we created our first model, we were able to take all of the data as-is from the data mart and put it into Power BI. That is an unusual situation in the real world.

Usually, as we create a Power BI model, there will be certain fields in a source table we will not want to bring into our model. Data in the source table will be the wrong data type or in the wrong format. Certain invalid data values will need to be changed or removed. We may even have data that is organized in multiple columns that needs to be unpivoted into multiple rows. All of this can be done very easily using the Query Editor.

Query Editor Layout

The Query Editor has four parts, as shown in Figure 15-21. The left side of the Query Editor shows the queries that have been created for the current Power BI model. The queries are named after the data sources on which they operate. If you like, you can right-click a query and rename it to make it easier to determine its purpose later on.

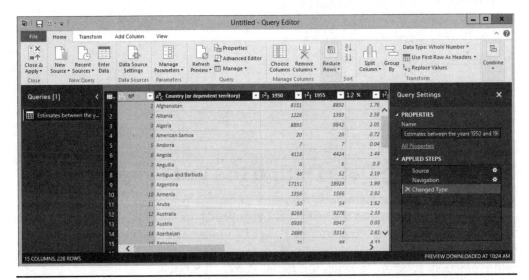

Figure 15-21 *The Power BI Query Editor*

The right side of the Query Editor shows each of the steps that have been applied to the data within the selected query. Each applied step builds upon the next. If we change the name of a column in one step, then we can refer to that column by the new column name in the next step.

The center section of the Query Editor shows the status of the data after the application of the selected step. By default, the last step in the list of Applied Steps is selected. Therefore, most of the time the center section shows what the data looks like after all of the steps in the query are applied.

We can, however, select a different step in the Applied Steps list. When we do this, the center section shows us what the data looks like when all of the steps are applied up to and including the selected step. Essentially, we can go back through the steps of the query to see how the application of each step affected the data. We can even drag a step and drop it in a new location if we need to change the order in which the steps are applied. We can also right-click and rename a step if we want to give the step a more descriptive name.

Some of the steps in the Applied Steps list include a cog icon in the upper-left corner of the step. If you click on this icon, you will see a dialog box with information about the decisions made during the creation of that step. We can change that information if the step was not configured properly.

The column headings in the center section contain both the name of the column and the data type currently assigned to that column. This is shown in Figure 15-22. The cluster of symbols on the left side of the column heading indicates the data type. "ABC" indicates a text data type, "123" indicates an integer data type, "1.2" indicates a decimal data type, and so on.

Across the top of the Query Editor is the ribbon. The ribbon contains all of the data manipulations we use to create the steps in the query. We will walk through the operation of each of these data manipulations later in this chapter. Before we do that, let's use the Query Editor to bring some data into a new Power BI model.

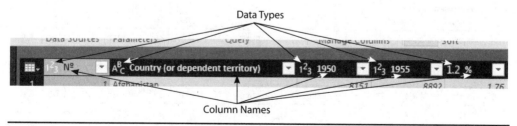

Figure 15-22 *Column names and data types in the Query Editor*

A New Sample: World Population

In order to explore some of the features of the Power BI Query Editor, we are going to depart from our Maximum Miniatures, Inc. examples and look at some real-world data. We start with population information from 1950 to 2015 for each country in the world. To obtain this data we are going to do what we all do these days when we need information, look to the Internet.

For our example, we are going to use information from Wikipedia. As with all information found on the Internet, make certain your information source is trustworthy before using the data for analysis. The world population information we find on Wikipedia will suit our purposes just fine. If you want to take this information and use it for hard-core analysis, you can do more vetting of the data.

The Starting Point and the Destination

Wikipedia features two tables of world population data organized by country by year. The first covers 1950 to 1980 in 5-year intervals. The second is from 1985 to 2015, also in 5-year intervals. The tables have the format shown in Table 15-2.

The population figures in the table are in millions, except the world population numbers which are in billions.

This format is great for humans to read and interpret. However, it would be very difficult to analyze if it were put into a model this way. What we need in our model is a format as shown in Table 15-3.

When we report numbers in a Power BI report, automatic scaling to thousands or millions is done for us. In order for this automatic scaling to work properly, our data in the model must have all scaling removed. You will also notice that we want to remove the values from the "World" totals line. Our data model only needs the population numbers for the individual countries. The Power BI reports will handle the totaling for us. We will also remove the percent growth columns as these are not needed for our analysis.

No.	Country (or Dependent Territory)	1950	1955	%	1960	%	1965	%	1970	%	1975	%	1980	%
1	Afghanistan	8,151	8,892	1.76	9,830	2.03	10,998	2.27	12,431	2.48	14,133	2.60	15,045	1.26
2	Albania	1,228	1,393	2.56	1,624	3,12	1,884	3.02	2,157	2.74	2,402	2.17	2,672	2.16
~	~	~	~	~	~	~	~	~	~	~	~	~	~	~
227	Zimbabwe	2,854	3,410	3,62	4,001	3.31	4,686	3.16	5,515	3.31	6,342	2.83	7,170	2.49
	World	2,557	2,782	1.7	3,043	1.81	3,350	1.94	3,712	2.07	4,089	1.95	1,451	1.71

Table 15-2   *Source Format of the World Population Information*

Country (or Dependent Territory)	Year	Population
Afghanistan	1950	8,151,000
Afghanistan	1955	8,892,000
Afghanistan	1960	9,830,000
~	~	~
Zimbabwe	1970	5,515,000
Zimbabwe	1975	6,342,000
Zimbabwe	1980	7,170,000

Table 15-3   *Desired Model Format for the World Population Information*

Learn By Doing: Loading World Population Data from the Internet

Features Highlighted

- ▶ Connecting to a Web data source
- ▶ Using the Query Editor to manipulate the data prior to loading in the model

Business Need   We will be analyzing world population, Gross Domestic Product (GDP), and world CO_2 emissions from the late 20th century to the present using Power BI. We will begin by obtaining population information by country for that time period from the Internet.

Steps to Create a Connection to Web Data Source

1. Click the File tab of the menu and select New from the menu. The Start dialog box appears.
2. Click Get Data. The Get Data dialog box appears.
3. Select Other from the category list on the left, and then select Web.
4. Click Connect. The From Web connection dialog box appears.
5. Enter the following URL:

   ```
   http://en.wikipedia.org/wiki/List_of_countries_by_past_and_future_
   population
   ```

6. Click OK. Power BI will connect to this web page and look for any tables on the page. You will see the Navigator dialog box with entries for the entire web page document and four tables within that document.

7. Check the box next to Estimates between the years 1950 and 1980(In Thousands) [edit]. You see a sample of the data in this table, which should have the same structure as Table 15-2.

8. Click Edit. (The Load button is very tempting with its bright yellow color. Be sure you click Edit instead.) You see the Query Editor with the information from the population table loaded. This is shown in Figure 15-21. In addition to connecting to the web page and navigating to the desired table, you will see Power BI automatically added a step to change the data type of some of the fields as they were imported.

Steps to Transform the Data in the Query Editor

1. The Nº column should be selected, but click the Nº column heading to make sure.

2. On the Home tab of the ribbon, click Remove Columns. The Nº column is removed.

3. Click the % column heading to select that column. Don't be confused by the data type indicator in the column heading. This particular column heading looks a bit strange because it includes the "1.2" that indicates it is a decimal data type and the "%" that is the actual name of the column.

4. Scroll the data view to the right.

5. Hold down CTRL and select the %2 column. Both the % and %2 columns are selected.

6. Continue to hold down CTRL and select %3, %4, %5, and %6. Scroll right as needed.

7. On the Home tab of the ribbon, click Remove Columns. All of the selected columns are removed.

8. Click the drop-down arrow in the Country (or dependent territory) column. The sorting and filtering drop-down appears.

9. Scroll down to find "World" in the list of countries and dependent territories.

10. Uncheck the entry for World as shown in Figure 15-23.

11. Click OK to exit the sorting and filtering drop-down. The row with the world totals is removed from the data.

12. Click the 1950 column heading.

13. Scroll right, hold down SHIFT, and click the 1980 column heading. The columns from 1950 through 1980 are selected.

14. On the Transform tab of the ribbon, select Unpivot Columns as shown in Figure 15-24. The columns are unpivoted to create rows with new columns called Attribute and Value. The items in the Attribute column were the column names before the pivot. The figures in the Value column were the contents of those columns before the pivot.

15. Click the Attribute column heading so the Attribute column is selected on its own.

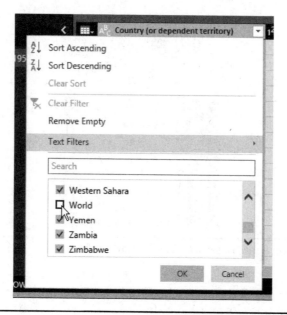

Figure 15-23 *The Sorting and Filtering drop-down*

16. Right-click the Attribute column heading and select Rename from the context menu.
17. Type **Year** and press ENTER.
18. Right-click the Value column heading and select Rename from the context menu.
19. Type **Population** and press ENTER.
20. On the Transform tab of the ribbon, select Standard | Multiply, as shown in Figure 15-25. The Multiply dialog box appears.
21. Type **1000** for Value.
22. Click OK. The Population numbers are multiplied by 1000 to show their true magnitude.

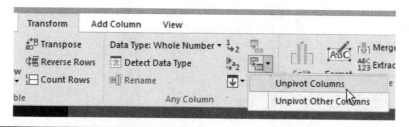

Figure 15-24 *The Unpivot button on the Transform tab of the ribbon*

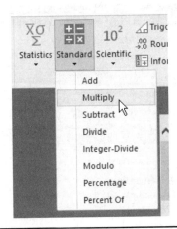

Figure 15-25 *The Standard | Multiply button on the Transform tab of the ribbon*

23. Click the data type indicator in the Population column, as shown in Figure 15-26. The data type drop-down list appears.

24. Select Whole Number. The data type of the Population column is changed to whole number.

25. On the right, under Properties, replace the content of Name with **Population 1950-1980**.

26. On the Home tab of the ribbon, click Close & Apply. The data is pulled from the web page, the transformations are applied, and the transformed data is loaded into the data model.

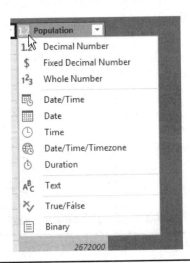

Figure 15-26 *The Data Type drop-down list*

Steps to Verify the Data

1. On the Home tab of the ribbon, click Page View | Actual Size.

2. In the Fields area on the Report page of Power BI Desktop, check the box for Population. A column chart is created.

3. In the Visualizations area, click the Stacked bar chart icon. The chart is changed to a bar chart.

4. In the Fields area, check the box for Country. At the moment, this is a meaningless number because it is totaling the population for each country across all of the years in the data model.

5. Click anywhere in the report layout area outside of the chart. The chart is unselected.

6. In the Fields area, check the box for Year. A table listing the Years is created.

7. In the Visualizations area, click Slicer. The Year table is converted to a slicer.

8. Drag the Year slicer to the upper-right corner of the layout area and size it to remove the whitespace.

9. Select the bar chart and size it to fill most of the rest of the layout area.

10. Try selecting individual years to view the result. Your report should appear similar to Figure 15-27.

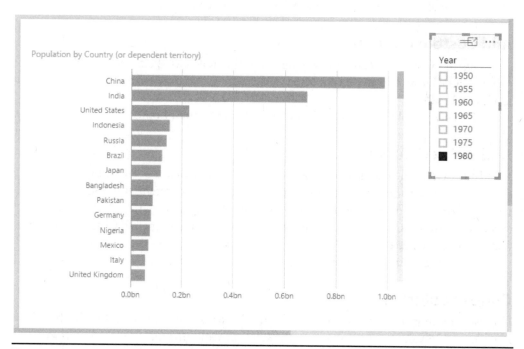

Figure 15-27 *An initial Population by Country report*

11. Click Save.
12. If necessary, navigate to the PowerBI folder you created previously.
13. Enter **Population-GDP-CO2 by Country** for File name.
14. Click Save.

Transformations

The previous Learn By Doing exercise gave you a taste of the power and flexibility of the Query Editor. That data load would have been much more difficult, if not impossible, in SQL Server Integration Services. Now let's take a look at all the transformations the Query Editor provides. The transformations are spread across several tabs of the Query Editor ribbon. In fact, some of the transformations appear on more than one tab of the ribbon. We'll note where on the ribbon each transformation can be found. In addition, many of the transformations can be found in the context menu when you right-click on a column heading.

Certain transformations provide information to the person creating the query but don't add content to the query. These are noted as "informational only." When an informational only transformation is used, the result is displayed to the user. Once the user has noted the information, the transformation should be deleted using the Applied Steps area to allow for the continuation of the query creation.

Add Custom Column

Add Custom Column creates a new column in the table based on a custom DAX formula. The custom formula is defined in the Add Custom Column dialog box, shown in Figure 15-28.

Add Custom Column is on the Add Column tab of the ribbon.

Add Index Column

Add Index Column creates a new column in the table with a sequential number for each row based on the current sort order of the rows. The sequential numbering starts with 0 by default. You can specify to have the numbering start with 1. You can also specify a custom starting value and a custom increment using the Add Index Column dialog box shown in Figure 15-29.

Add Index Column is on the Add Column tab of the ribbon.

Choose Columns

Choose Columns displays a dialog box where the set of columns to endure in the table is selected. Only columns checked on the Choose Columns dialog box, shown in Figure 15-30, stay in the table after this transformation is applied.

Choose Columns is on the Home tab of the ribbon.

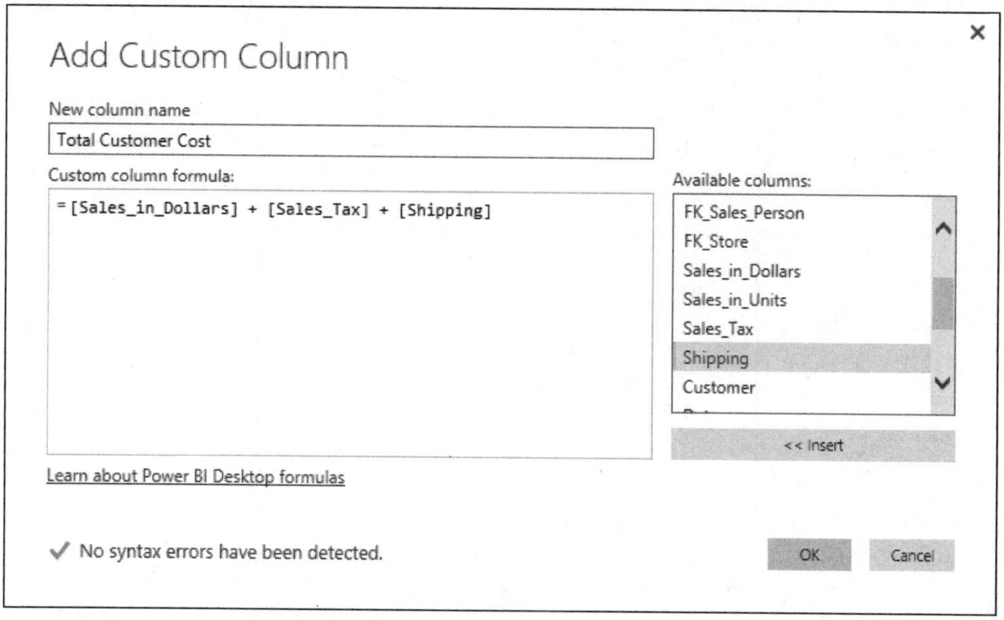

Add Custom Column

New column name

Total Customer Cost

Custom column formula:

`=[Sales_in_Dollars] + [Sales_Tax] + [Shipping]`

Available columns:

FK_Sales_Person
FK_Store
Sales_in_Dollars
Sales_in_Units
Sales_Tax
Shipping
Customer

<< Insert

Learn about Power BI Desktop formulas

✓ No syntax errors have been detected.

OK   Cancel

Figure 15-28 *The Add Custom Column dialog box*

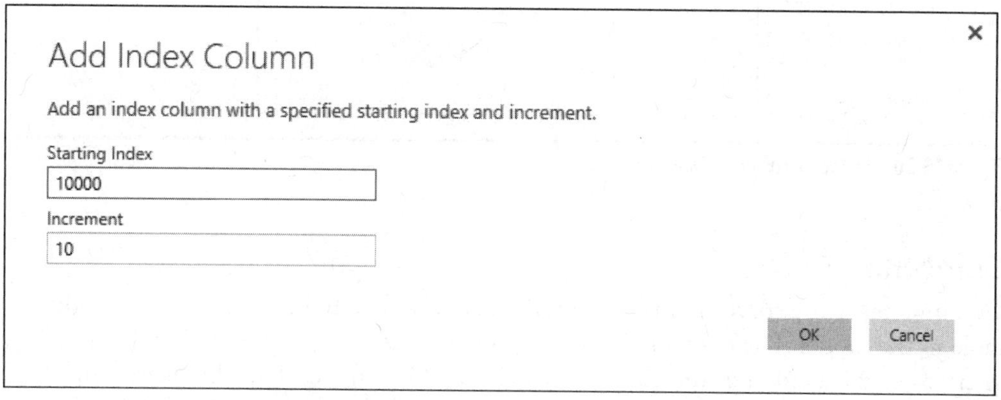

Add Index Column

Add an index column with a specified starting index and increment.

Starting Index

10000

Increment

10

OK   Cancel

Figure 15-29 *The Add Index Column dialog box*

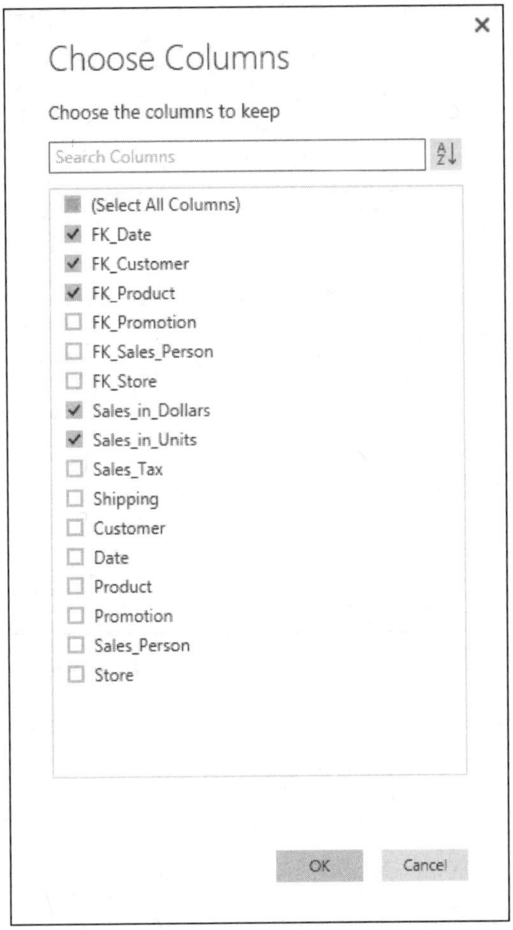

Figure 15-30 *The Choose Columns dialog box*

Combine

Combine takes the content of two or more queries and combines them into a single table in the model. The content of one or more queries can be appended to an initial query to create a union of the queries involved. If this is done, all of the queries involved must have the identical structure. The append is defined with the Append dialog box shown in Figure 15-31. Alternately, two queries can be joined using one of several join options. The join condition is defined in the Merge dialog box, shown in Figure 15-32. The final Combine option merges all of the binary values in a column into a single binary.

Combine is on the Home tab of the ribbon. If you have Power BI Desktop maximized on a wide screen, you may see Append Queries, Merge Queries, and Combine Binaries displayed as separate buttons in a section of the Home tab of the ribbon labeled "Combined."

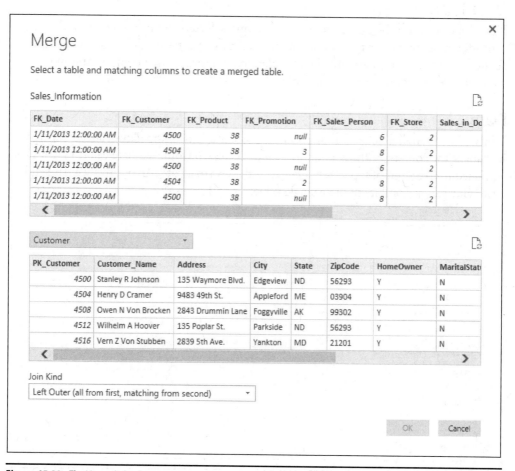

Figure 15-31 *The Append dialog box*

Merge

Select a table and matching columns to create a merged table.

Sales_Information

FK_Date	FK_Customer	FK_Product	FK_Promotion	FK_Sales_Person	FK_Store	Sales_in_Do
1/11/2013 12:00:00 AM	4500	38	*null*	6	2	
1/11/2013 12:00:00 AM	4504	38	3	8	2	
1/11/2013 12:00:00 AM	4500	38	*null*	6	2	
1/11/2013 12:00:00 AM	4504	38	2	8	2	
1/11/2013 12:00:00 AM	4500	38	*null*	8	2	

Customer

PK_Customer	Customer_Name	Address	City	State	ZipCode	HomeOwner	MaritalStat
4500	Stanley R Johnson	135 Waymore Blvd.	Edgeview	ND	56293	Y	N
4504	Henry D Cramer	9483 49th St.	Appleford	ME	03904	Y	N
4508	Owen N Von Brocken	2843 Drummin Lane	Foggyville	AK	99302	Y	N
4512	Wilhelm A Hoover	135 Poplar St.	Parkside	ND	56293	Y	N
4516	Vern Z Von Stubben	2839 5th Ave.	Yankton	MD	21201	Y	N

Join Kind

Left Outer (all from first, matching from second)

Figure 15-32 *The Merge dialog box*

Conditional Column

Conditional Column defines a new column in the table based on one or more conditional expressions. This enables the value of the new column to be determined by the content of one or more existing columns in that row. The conditional expressions are defined using the Add Conditional Column dialog box, shown in Figure 15-33.

Conditional Column is on the Add Column tab of the ribbon.

Count Rows

Count Rows simply counts the number of rows satisfying the current query and displays the result. Count Rows is informational only. Count Rows is on the Transform tab of the ribbon.

Data Type

Data Type specifies the data type of the currently selected column or columns. Use the drop-down list on either the Home tab or the Transform tab of the ribbon to set the desired data type. Alternatively, click the data type indicator in a column heading to select the desired data type for that column.

Date

When Date is applied to a column containing values of any of the date-related data types, it changes the content of the column to a value calculated from that date value. When Date is applied to a column of type Text, it converts the text to a date. Alternatively, a date and a time value can be combined into a single value.

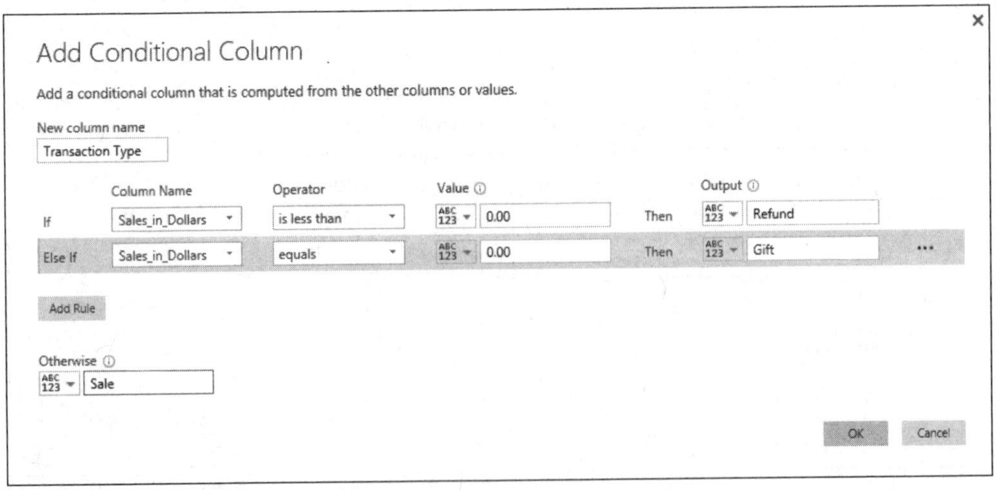

Figure 15-33 *The Add Conditional Column dialog box*

The following values can be calculated from a date-related data type:

Age	The amount of time between the current system date and time and the value in the row
Date Only	Removes any time portion of the value
Year | Year	The year portion of the value
Year | Start of Year	The first day of the year containing the value
Year | End of Year	The last day of the year containing the value
Month | Month	The month portion of the value as a number
Month | Start of Month	The first day of the month containing the value
Month | End of Month	The last day of the month containing the value
Month | Days in Month	The number of days in the month containing the value
Month | Name of Month	The name of the month containing the value
Quarter | Quarter of Year	The quarter containing the value as a number
Quarter | Start of Quarter	The first day of the quarter containing the value
Quarter | End of Quarter	The last day of the quarter containing the value
Week | Week of Year	The number of the week containing the value within that year
Week | Week of Month	The number of the week containing the value within that month
Week | Start of Week	The first day of the week containing the value
Week | End of Week	The last day of the week containing the value
Day | Day	The day portion of the value as a number
Day | Day of Week	The number of the day specified by the value within that week
Day | Day of Year	The number of the day specified by the value within that year
Day | Start of Day	The earliest time within the day containing the value
Day | End of Day	The latest time within the day containing the value
Day | Day Name	The name of the day containing the value
Earliest	The earliest value in the column—informational only
Latest	The latest value in the column—informational only

Date is on the Transform tab and the Add Column tab of the ribbon. When Date is selected from the Add Column tab of the ribbon, it creates a new column to hold the resulting values. When Date is selected from the Transform tab of the ribbon, the resulting values replace the values in the current column.

Detect Data Type

Detect Data Type examines the content of the selected column and determines the data type. It then changes the data type of the column to that data type. Detect Data Type is on the Transform tab of the ribbon.

Duplicate Column

Duplicate Column creates a new column in the query from the content of an existing column. Duplicate Column is on the Add Column tab of the ribbon.

Duration

Duration takes an age and translates it to various durations. The possible durations are:

▶ Days

▶ Hours

▶ Minutes

▶ Seconds

▶ Total Years

▶ Total Days

▶ Total Hours

▶ Total Minutes

▶ Total Seconds

Duration will also multiply an age by a value or divide an age by a value. Alternatively, Duration will perform statistical analysis on an age. The statistical analysis is informational only. Available statistics include:

▶ Sum

▶ Minimum

▶ Maximum

▶ Median

▶ Average

Duration is on the Transform tab and the Add Column tab of the ribbon. When Duration is selected from the Add Column tab of the ribbon, it creates a new column to hold the resulting values. When Duration is selected from the Transform tab of the ribbon, the resulting values replace the values in the current column.

Extract

Extract creates a new column from either the length of the value in the selected column or from a set number of characters from the beginning, end, or a range in the middle of the value in the selected column. If a range is selected, the starting index and number

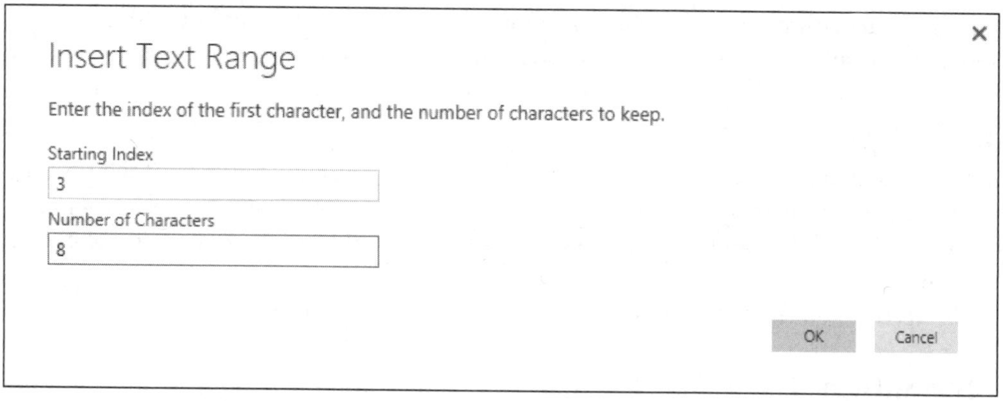

Figure 15-34 *The Insert Text Range dialog box*

of characters to extract are specified using the Insert Text Range dialog box, shown in Figure 15-34.

Extract is on the Transform tab and the Add Column tab of the ribbon. When Extract is selected from the Add Column tab of the ribbon, it creates a new column to hold the resulting values. When Extract is selected from the Transform tab of the ribbon, the resulting values replace the values in the current column.

Fill

Fill inserts the selected values into any empty cells either above or below the selected cell in the table. Fill is on the Transform tab of the ribbon.

Format

Format applies formatting to text in a given column. Valid formats are:

▶ Lower Case

▶ Upper Case

▶ Capitalize Each Word

▶ Trim (Remove leading and trailing whitespace)

▶ Clean (Remove non-printable characters)

▶ Add Prefix

▶ Add Suffix

Format is on the Transform tab and the Add Column tab of the ribbon. When Format is selected from the Add Column tab of the ribbon, it creates a new column to hold the resulting values. When Format is selected from the Transform tab of the ribbon, the resulting values replace the values in the current column.

Group By

Group By aggregates multiple rows into single rows using grouping criteria. Each column to be included in the result must either be part of the group by or must be derived from an aggregation. The grouping criteria are created using the Group By dialog box, shown in Figure 15-35.

Group By is on the Home tab and the Transform tab of the ribbon.

Information

Information creates a new column, noting whether the value in the selected column is even or odd or indicating the sign of the value in the selected column. When indicating the sign, 1 means positive, −1 means negative, and 0 means the value was 0.

Information is on the Transform tab and the Add Column tab of the ribbon. When Information is selected from the Add Column tab of the ribbon, it creates a new column to hold the resulting values. When Information is selected from the Transform tab of the ribbon, the resulting values replace the values in the current column.

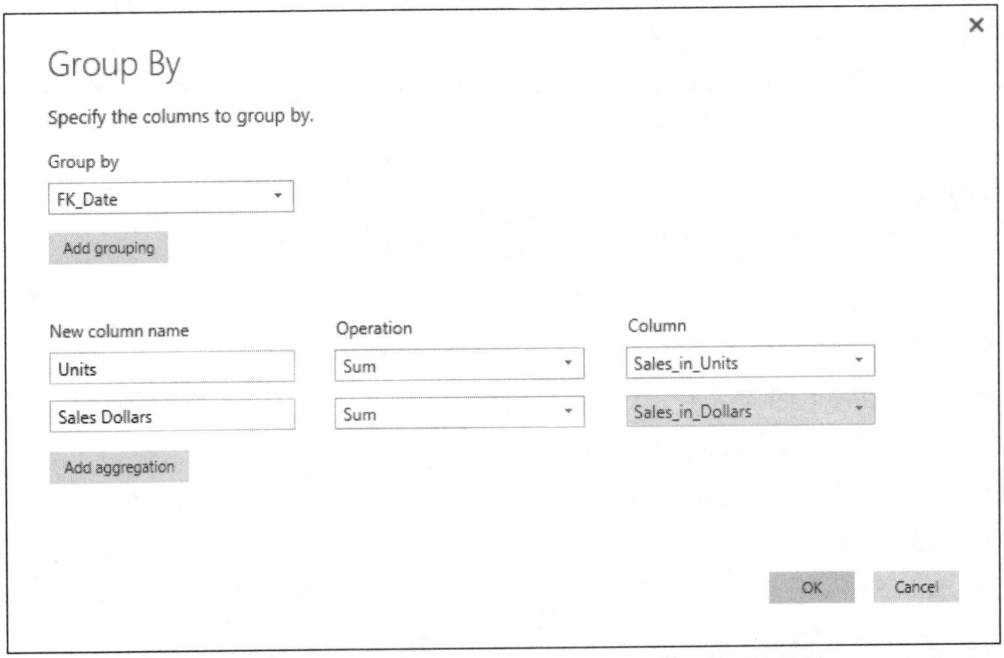

Figure 15-35 *The Group By dialog box*

Keep Rows

Keep Rows specifies rows to keep in the data set. We can use any of the following to specify which rows to keep:

▶ Keep Top Rows

▶ Keep Bottom Rows

▶ Keep Range of Rows

▶ Keep Duplicates

▶ Keep Errors

The Keep Range of Rows dialog box, shown in Figure 15-36, is used when specifying a range of rows to keep.

Keep Rows is on the Home tab of the ribbon.

Merge Columns

Merge Columns joins the content of two columns into a new column. A separator can be specified for insertion between the two values. The Merged Columns dialog box is used to define the new column, as shown in Figure 15-37.

Merge Columns is on the Transform tab and the Add Column tab of the ribbon. When Merge Columns is selected from the Add Column tab of the ribbon, it creates a new column to hold the resulting values. When Merge Columns is selected from the Transform tab of the ribbon, the resulting values replace the values in the current column.

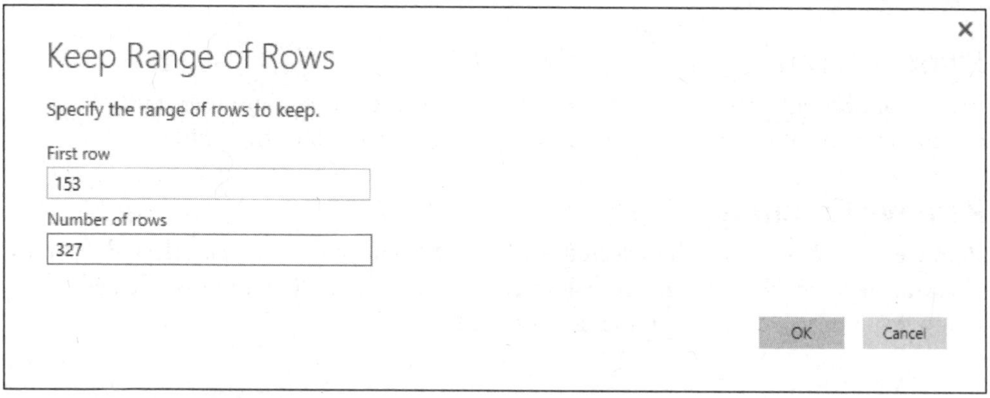

Figure 15-36 *The Keep Range of Rows dialog box*

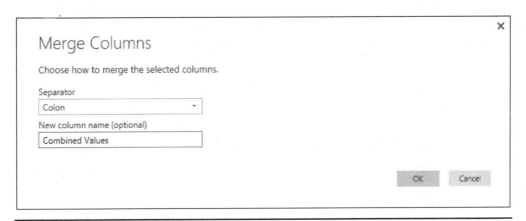

Figure 15-37   *The Merge Columns dialog box*

Move

Move changes the position of the selected column to the left, to the right, to the beginning of the table, or to the end of the table. Move is on the Transform tab of the ribbon.

Parse

Parse interprets the selected column as either an XML or JSON structure. The contents are parsed and placed as an embedded table in a new column. Parse is on the Transform tab and the Add Column tab of the ribbon. When Parse is selected from the Add Column tab of the ribbon, it creates a new column to hold the resulting values. When Parse is selected from the Transform tab of the ribbon, the resulting values replace the values in the current column.

Pivot Column

Pivot Column takes values in a selected column and converts them into multiple columns in the table. Pivot Column is on the Transform tab of the ribbon.

Remove Columns

Remove Columns deletes the selected columns, if Remove Columns is selected. Remove Columns deletes the non-selected columns if Remove Other Columns is selected. Remove Columns is on the Home tab of the ribbon.

Remove Rows

Remove Rows specifies rows to remove from the data set. We can use any of the following to specify which rows to remove:

- ▶ Remove Top Rows
- ▶ Remove Bottom Rows
- ▶ Remove Alternate Rows
- ▶ Remove Duplicates
- ▶ Remove Blank Rows
- ▶ Remove Errors

The Remove Alternate Rows dialog box, shown in Figure 15-38, is used when specifying an alternating pattern of rows to remove.

Remove Rows is on the Home tab of the ribbon.

Rename

Rename enables the entry of a new name for a column. Rename is found on the Transform tab of the ribbon.

Replace Errors

Replace Errors substitutes a specified value for error values in the selected column. The replacement value is specified on the Replace Errors dialog box, shown in Figure 15-39.

Replace Errors is on the Transform tab of the ribbon.

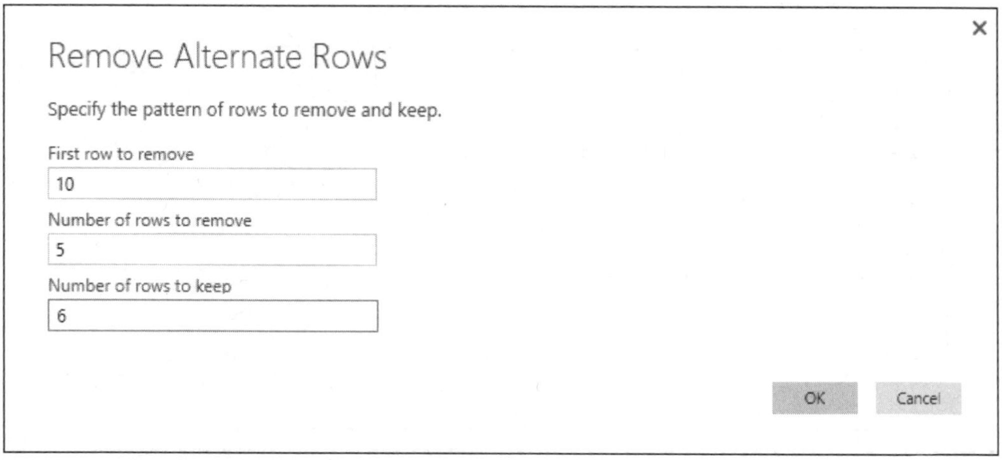

Figure 15-38 *The Remove Alternate Rows dialog box*

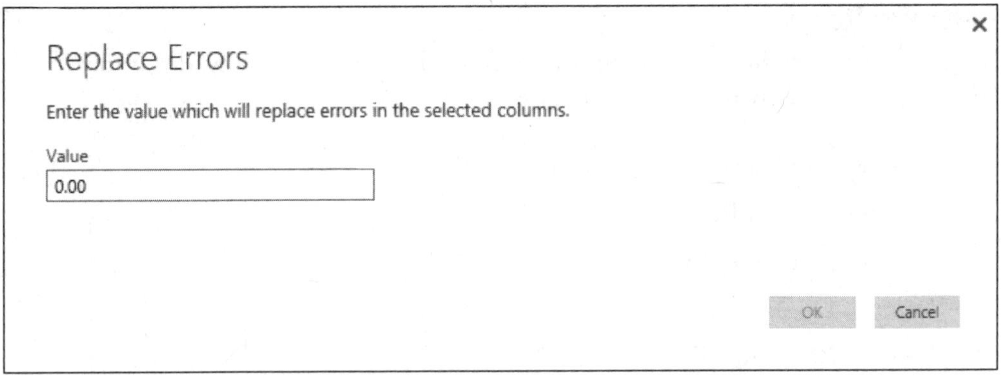

Figure 15-39 *The Replace Errors dialog box*

Replace Values

Replace Values substitutes a specified value for another specified value in the selected column. The values are entered on the Replace Values dialog box shown in Figure 15-40. Replace Values is on the Home tab and the Transform tab of the ribbon.

Reverse Rows

Reverse Rows reverses the order of the rows in the table. Reverse Rows is on the Transform tab of the ribbon.

Rounding

Rounding removes some or all of the decimal portion of a value. Round Up moves the value up to the closest integer. Round Down moves the value down to the closest integer.

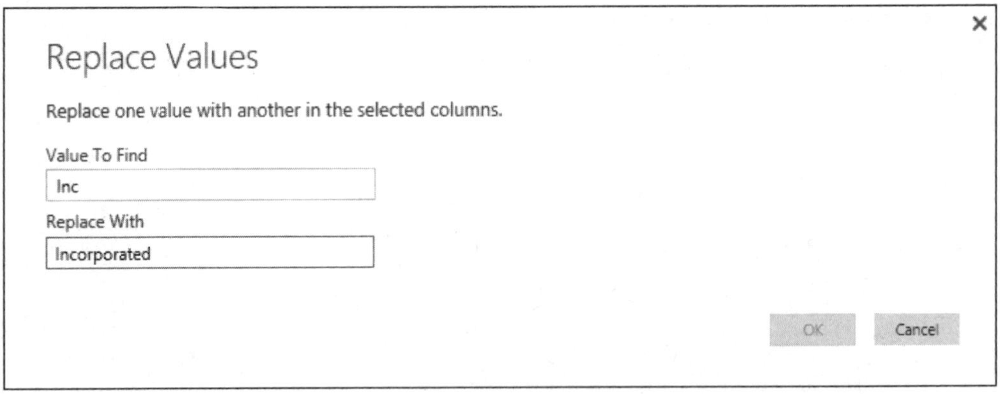

Figure 15-40 *The Replace Values dialog box*

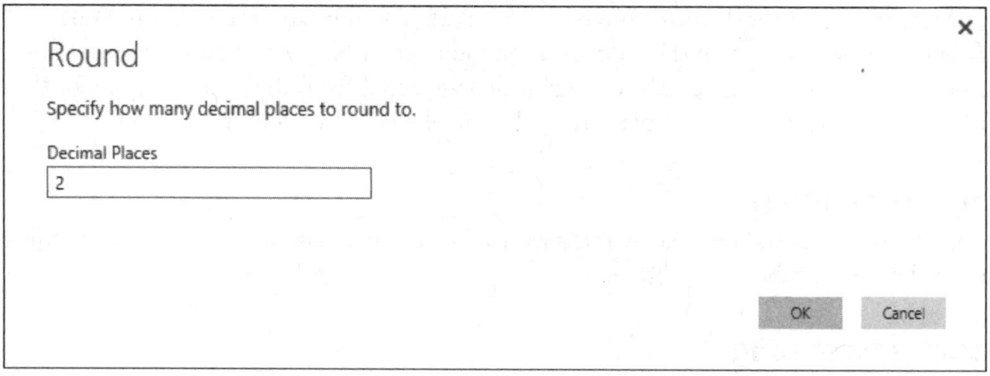

Figure 15-41 *The Round dialog box*

Round . . . performs rounding to the specified decimal place. The Round dialog box, shown in Figure 15-41, is used to specify the number of decimal places to round to.

Rounding is on the Transform tab and the Add Column Tab of the ribbon. When Rounding is selected from the Add Column tab of the ribbon, it creates a new column to hold the resulting values. When Rounding is selected from the Transform tab of the ribbon, the resulting values replace the values in the current column.

Run R Script

Run R Script executes a script written in R to transform the data. You must have the R engine installed in order to use this transformation. Run R Script is on the Transform tab of the ribbon.

Scientific

Scientific applies one of the following scientific operations to the values in a numeric column replacing the value with the result:

- Absolute Value
- Power
- Square Root
- Exponent
- Logarithm
- Factorial

Scientific is on the Transform tab and the Add Column tab of the ribbon. When Scientific is selected from the Add Column tab of the ribbon, it creates a new column to hold the resulting values. When Scientific is selected from the Transform tab of the ribbon, the resulting values replace the values in the current column.

Sort Ascending

Sort Ascending sorts the table by the selected column in ascending order. Sort Ascending is on the Home tab of the ribbon.

Sort Descending

Sort Descending sorts the table by the selected column in descending order. Sort Descending is on the Home tab of the ribbon.

Split Column

Split Column parses the text content of a selected column and splits it into two or more new columns. The text can be split by specifying a delimiter or by specifying a number of characters at which to create breaks. The Split Column by Delimiter dialog box, shown in Figure 15-42, is used when a delimiter is to be specified.

Split Column is on the Home tab and the Transform tab of the ribbon.

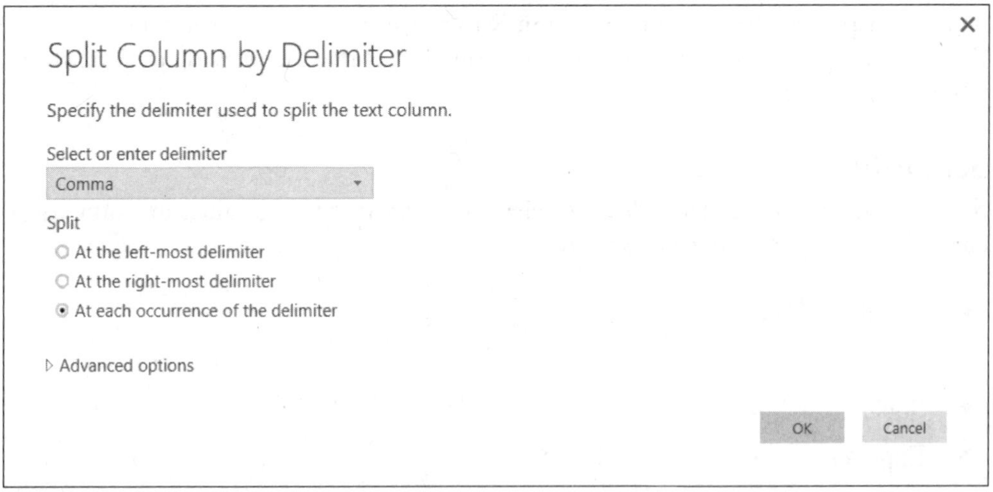

Figure 15-42 *The Split Column by Delimiter dialog box*

Standard

Standard applies one of the following standard mathematical operations to the values in a numeric column, replacing the value with the result:

▶ Add

▶ Multiply

▶ Divide

▶ Integer-Divide

▶ Modulo

▶ Percentage

▶ Percent Of

Standard is on the Transform tab and the Add Column tab of the ribbon. When Standard is selected from the Add Column tab of the ribbon, it creates a new column to hold the resulting values. When Standard is selected from the Transform tab of the ribbon, the resulting values replace the values in the current column.

Statistics

Statistics performs one of the following statistical analyses on the selected column:

▶ Sum

▶ Minimum

▶ Maximum

▶ Median

▶ Average

▶ Standard Deviation

▶ Count Values

▶ Count Distinct Values

The statistical analysis is informational only.

Statistics is on the Transform tab and the Add Column tab of the ribbon. When Statistics is selected from the Add Column tab of the ribbon, it creates a new column to hold the resulting values. When Statistics is selected from the Transform tab of the ribbon, the resulting values replace the values in the current column.

Structured Column

Structured Column works with a column that contains a nested data structure such as a table, a list, or a record. When the Expand option is used, it extracts data from the nested data and promotes it to the parent query result. When Aggregate is used, it performs statistical analysis (average, maximum, etc.) on the nested data.

Structured Column is on the Transform tab of the ribbon. If you have Power BI Desktop maximized on a wide screen, you may see Expand and Aggregate displayed as separate buttons in a section of the Transform tab of the ribbon labeled "Structured Column."

Time

When Time is applied to a column containing time-related values, it changes the content of the column to a value calculated from the time value. When Time is applied to a column of type Text, it converts the text to a time value. Alternatively, a date and a time value can be combined into a single value.

The following values can be calculated from a time-related data type:

Time Only	Removes any date portion of the value
Local Time	Changes the values to local time
Hour | Hour	The hour portion of the value as a number
Hour | Start of Hour	The minute and second of the hour containing the value
Hour | End of Hour	The last minute and second of the hour containing the value
Minute	The minute portion of the value as a number
Second	The second portion of the value as a number
Earliest	The earliest value in the column—informational only
Latest	The latest value in the column—informational only

Time is on the Transform tab and the Add Column tab of the ribbon. When Time is selected from the Add Column tab of the ribbon, it creates a new column to hold the resulting values. When Time is selected from the Transform tab of the ribbon, the resulting values replace the values in the current column.

Transpose

Transpose changes the query result to treat all rows as columns and all columns as rows. Transpose is on the Transform tab of the ribbon.

Trigonometry

Trigonometry applies one of the following trigonometric operations to the values in a numeric column, replacing the value with the result:

- ▶ Sine
- ▶ Cosine
- ▶ Tangent
- ▶ Arcsine
- ▶ Arccosine
- ▶ Arctangent

Trigonometry is on the Transform tab and the Add Column tab of the ribbon. When Trigonometry is selected from the Add Column tab of the ribbon, it creates a new column to hold the resulting values. When Trigonometry is selected from the Transform tab of the ribbon, the resulting values replace the values in the current column.

Unpivot Columns

Unpivot Columns takes values in a selected set of columns and converts them into a single column in the table. Unpivot Columns is on the Transform tab of the ribbon.

Use First Row As Headers

Use First Row As Headers takes the first row of data in the query result and promotes these values to the names of the columns in the query result. In doing so, the first row of data is removed from the result set. Use First Row As Headers also has an option to perform the opposite operation, taking the names of the columns and adding them as the first row of data in the query result.

Use First Row As Headers is on the Home tab and the Transform tab of the ribbon.

Advanced Editor and Power Query Formula Language

In the Learn By Doing: Loading World Population Data from the Internet exercise, we saw how easy it is to create queries to manipulate and cleanse the data as it is loaded into a Power BI data model. In the "Transformations" section of this chapter, we saw the broad range of transformations that are available for us to use. The Query Editor is a good example of a well-designed user interface that makes a complex task simpler.

However, as was mentioned earlier in this chapter, there is a text-based language lurking behind the scenes. The formal name of this language is the Query Formula Language. The informal name is "M," which comes from Mashup Query Language. That is, after all, what we are doing—creating data mashups.

You can view the Query Formula Language by clicking Advanced Editor on the View tab of the ribbon. This displays the Advanced Editor dialog box, shown in Figure 15-43. There is one line in the text for each applied step in your query. The context is very straightforward. It isn't difficult to determine which text defines which step.

You can use the Advanced Editor to make a quick change to the data query process without having to work through the user interface. The Advanced Editor is most useful, however, when something has changed in a data source that breaks the query used to extract data from that data source. Using the Advanced Editor, you may be able to get the query back into a valid state rather than starting all over again.

Learn By Doing: Completing the Population, GDP, and CO$_2$ Data Model

Features Highlighted

▶ Adding a second table from an existing data source

▶ Combining queries

▶ Importing CSV and Excel files

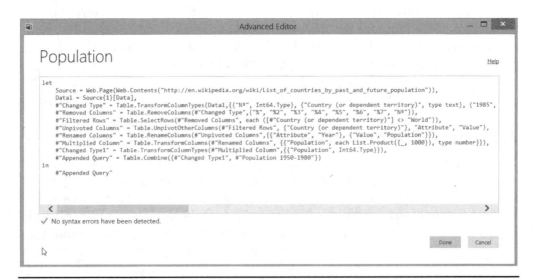

Figure 15-43 *The Advanced Editor with Query Formula Language*

Business Need   We need to complete the data import for our World Population, GDP, and CO_2 model.

Steps to Create a Connection to Web Data Source

1. On the Home tab of the ribbon, click Recent Sources. The Recent Sources drop-down appears.

2. Select the entry that begins "http://en.wikipedia.org/wiki/List_of_countries_by_ ..."The Navigator dialog box appears with entries for the entire web page document and the four tables in that document.

3. Check the box next to Estimates between the years 1985 and 2015(In Thousands) [edit]. You see a sample of the data in this table.

4. Click Edit. (Again, the Load button is very tempting with its bright yellow color. Be sure you click Edit instead.) You see the Query Editor with the information from the population table loaded. Power BI automatically created steps to connect to the web page, load the data from the table, and change the data type of some of the fields as they were imported.

Steps to Transform the Data in the Query Editor

1. The Nº column should be selected, but click the Nº column heading to make sure.

2. Hold down CTRL and select %, %2, %3, %4, %5, %6, and %7. Scroll right as needed.

3. On the Home tab of the ribbon, click Remove Columns. All of the selected columns are removed.

4. Click the drop-down arrow in the Country (or dependent territory) column. The sorting and filtering drop-down appears.

5. Scroll down to find "World" in the list of countries and dependent territories.

6. Uncheck the entry for World.

7. Click OK to exit the sorting and filtering drop-down. The row with the world totals is removed from the data.

8. Click the 1985 column heading.

9. Scroll right, hold down SHIFT, and click the 2015 column heading. The columns from 1985 through 2015 are selected.

10. On the Transform tab of the ribbon, select Unpivot Columns. The columns are unpivoted to create rows with new columns called Attribute and Value. The items in the Attribute column were the column names before the pivot. The figures in the Value column were the contents of those columns before the pivot.

11. Click the Attribute column heading so the Attribute column is selected on its own.

12. Right-click the Attribute column heading and select Rename from the context menu.

13. Type **Year** and press ENTER.

14. Right-click the Value column heading and select Rename from the context menu.

15. Type **Population** and press ENTER.

16. On the Transform tab of the ribbon, select Standard | Multiply. The Multiply dialog box appears.

17. Type **1000** for Value.

18. Click OK. The Population numbers are multiplied by 1000 to show their true magnitude.

19. Click the data type indicator in the Population column. The data type drop-down list appears.

20. Select Whole Number. The data type of the Population column is changed to whole number.

21. On the right under Properties, replace the content of Name with **Population** and press ENTER.

22. On the Home tab of the ribbon, click Combine. If you do not see Combine on the ribbon, click Append Queries.

23. If you clicked Combine, select Append Queries from the Combine drop-down list. The Append dialog box appears.

24. From the Table to append drop-down list, select Population 1950–1980.

25. Click OK. The data we imported into the Population 1950–1980 table is appended to our current Population query.

26. On the Home tab of the ribbon, click Close & Apply. The data is pulled from the web page, the transformations are applied, the 1950–1980 data is appended, and the result is loaded into the data model. Note, the data visualization is not impacted by the changes made to the data model, so it will be unchanged.

Steps to Load the GDP from the Excel File

1. Click Get Data. The Get Data dialog box appears.

2. Select Excel and click Connect. The Open dialog box appears.

3. Navigate to the location where you saved the "GDP in Current US Dollars.xlsx" file.

4. Select the "GDP in Current US Dollars.xlsx" file and click Open. The Navigator appears showing entries for the two spreadsheet tabs in the Excel workbook.

5. Check the entry for the Data tab and click Edit. (Again, be sure you don't click Load.)

6. On the Home tab of the ribbon, click Use First Row As Headers. The first row of data becomes the headings for the columns.

7. On the Home tab of the ribbon, click Choose Columns. The Choose Columns dialog box appears with a list of the columns.

8. Click (Select All Columns) to uncheck all of the items in the list.

9. We only want GDP figures for those years that are present in our Population table. Check the following columns:

   ▶ Country Name

   ▶ 1960

   ▶ 1965

   ▶ 1970

   ▶ 1975

   ▶ 1980

   ▶ 1985

   ▶ 1990

   ▶ 1995

   ▶ 2000

   ▶ 2005

   ▶ 2010

10. Click OK. Only the selected columns remain.

11. We need to replace the "`..`" entries in the table with a null value. Click the 1960 column heading.

12. Hold down SHIFT and click the 2010 column heading to select all of the columns from 1960 to 2010.

13. On the Home tab of the ribbon, click Replace Values. The Replace Values dialog box appears.

14. Enter `..` for Value To Find. We want to leave Replace With blank.

15. Click OK.

16. On the Transform tab of the ribbon, select Unpivot Columns.

17. Click the Attribute column to select that column by itself.

18. Right-click the Attribute column and select Rename from the context menu.

19. Type **Year** and press ENTER.

20. Right-click the Value column and select Rename from the context menu.

21. Type **GDP** and press ENTER.
22. Click the data type indicator in the GDP column. The data type drop-down list appears.
23. Click Whole Number.
24. On the right under Properties, replace the content of Name with **GDP Data** and press ENTER.
25. On the Home tab of the ribbon, click Close & Apply. The data is pulled from the Excel file, the transformations are applied, and the result is loaded into the data model.

Steps to Load the CO_2 Data from the Excel File

1. Click Get Data. The Get Data dialog box appears.
2. Select CSV and click Connect. The Open dialog box appears.
3. Navigate to the location where you saved the "CO2 Emissions in kt.csv" file.
4. Select the "CO2 Emissions in kt.csv" file and click Open. The CO2 Emissions in kt.csv preview screen appears.
5. Click Edit.
6. On the Home tab of the ribbon, click Use First Row As Headers. The first row of data becomes the headings for the columns.
7. On the Home tab of the ribbon, click Choose Columns. The Choose Columns dialog box appears with a list of the columns.
8. Click (Select All Columns) to uncheck all of the items in the list.
9. We only want GDP figures for those years that are present in our Population table. Check the following columns:

   ▶ Country Name
   ▶ 1960
   ▶ 1965
   ▶ 1970
   ▶ 1975
   ▶ 1980
   ▶ 1985
   ▶ 1990
   ▶ 1995
   ▶ 2000
   ▶ 2005
   ▶ 2010

10. Click OK. Only the selected columns remain.

11. We need to replace the ".." entries in the table with a null value. Click the 1960 column heading.

12. Hold down SHIFT and click the 2010 column heading to select all of the columns from 1960 to 2010.

13. On the Home tab of the ribbon, click Replace Values. The Replace Values dialog box appears.

14. Enter .. for Value To Find. We want to leave Replace With blank.

15. Click OK.

16. On the Transform tab of the ribbon, select Unpivot Columns.

17. Click the Attribute column to select that column by itself.

18. Right-click the Attribute column and select Rename from the context menu.

19. Type **Year** and press ENTER.

20. Right-click the Value column and select Rename from the context menu.

21. Type **CO2 Level** and press ENTER.

22. Click the data type indicator in the GDP column. The data type drop-down list appears.

23. Click Whole Number.

24. On the Home tab of the ribbon, click Close & Apply. The data is pulled from the Excel file, the transformations are applied, and the result is loaded into the data model.

25. Click Save.

Parameters

Next we examine one of the newest features of Power BI. Namely, the ability to add parameters to a Power BI model. Parameters allow us to collect user input in a very structured manner, and then use that input within the data model.

Parameters are not meant to facilitate interactivity like a slicer or a report filter. In Power BI, parameters function more like the entries in a configuration file. Power BI parameters enable us to change some aspects of the Power BI model in reaction to the environment where the model is operating.

The values specified for the parameters are used when data is loaded into the model. Usually, the model is loaded infrequently—at most just once at the beginning of an interactive data session. Therefore, we are not going to use parameters as part of our routine when exploring the data.

NOTE

As of this writing, Power BI parameters can be entered when working with the model in Power BI Desktop. They cannot be entered once the model is published to PowerBI.com.

Putting Parameters to Use

Power BI parameters have two main uses within our data model. First, we can use parameters as part of the connection information when connecting to a data source. For example, we can set up a parameter to hold a database server name or a file path. The connection configuration can then be changed to use these parameter values. In this way, we can change a model to move from using a development server to using a production server without going into the model and making modifications.

Parameters can also be used when we filter the rows in a table within the data model. Again, keep in mind this particular filtering comes into play only when the data is loaded into the model. This is not the filtering that occurs each time we interact with a visualization on a report.

Let's make this parameter concept a bit more concrete with a Learn By Doing exercise.

Learn By Doing: Using Power BI Parameters

Features Highlighted

▶ Adding a parameter to connection information

▶ Adding a parameter to a table filter

Business Need   We need to provide a straightforward method to change the SQL Server database instance name from the development instance to the production instance.

Steps to Create Two Parameters

1. Click the File tab in the ribbon. The drop-down menu appears.
2. Click Open and navigate to the folder containing the "Max Min Sales Information.pbix" file. Select this file and click Open. The Max Min Sales Information model opens.
3. Click Edit Queries on the Home tab of the ribbon. The Query Editor appears.
4. Click Manage Parameters on the Home tab of the ribbon in the Query Editor. The Parameters dialog box appears.
5. Click the New link to create a new parameter.
6. Replace Parameter1 with **SQL Server Instance** for Name.
7. For Description, type:

```
The instance of SQL Server hosting the MaxMinSalesDM database.
```

8. Select Text from the Type drop-down list.

9. For Current Value, type the name of the SQL Server instance hosting the MaxMinSalesDM database.

10. Click the New link to create another new parameter.

11. Replace Parameter1 with **Store Number** for Name.

12. For Description, type:

    ```
    The store number where the purchase was made.
    ```

13. Select Decimal Number from the Type drop-down list.

14. Select List of values from the Allowed Values drop-down list.

15. In the Allowed Values list enter:

    ```
    1
    2
    3
    4
    5
    6
    7
    ```

16. Select 1 from the Default Value drop-down list.

17. Select 1 from the Current Value drop-down list. The Parameters dialog box should appear, as shown in Figure 15-44.

18. Click OK to exit the Parameters dialog box. The two parameters will appear in the Queries list, as shown in Figure 15-45.

Steps to Parameterize the Connection

1. Click Data Source Settings in the Home tab of the ribbon. The Data Source Settings dialog box appears.

2. MaxMinSalesDM is the only data source we are using for this model so it is selected. Click Change Source. The SQL Server Database dialog box appears.

3. Click the drop-down under Server and select Parameter, as shown in Figure 15-46.

4. Use the larger drop-down to select the desired parameter. In this case, the SQL Server Instance parameter will be selected by default because it is the only parameter we have defined with a text data type. The SQL Server Database dialog box appears, as shown in Figure 15-47.

5. Click OK to exit the SQL Server Database dialog box.

6. Click Close to exit the Data Source Settings dialog box. Verify your credentials, if necessary.

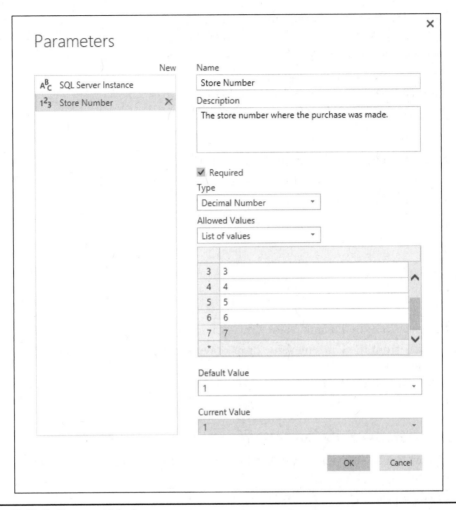

Figure 15-44 *The Parameters dialog box*

Steps to Parameterize a Filter

1. In the Queries area, select Sales_Information.
2. Scroll right until the FK_Store column is visible.
3. Click the drop-down arrow in the FK_Store column heading. The Sort and Filter drop-down appears.
4. Select Number Filters | Equals. The Filter Rows dialog box appears.
5. Click the drop-down to the right of equal sign.

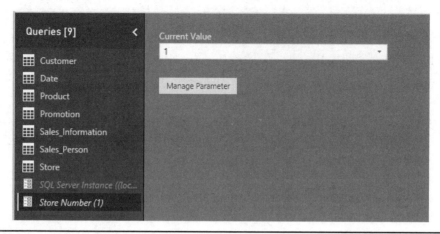

Figure 15-45 *Parameters in the Queries list*

6. Select Parameter from the drop-down list, as shown in Figure 15-48.

7. Use the larger drop-down to select the desired parameter. In this case, the Store Number parameter will be selected by default because it is the only parameter we have defined with a numeric data type. The Filter Rows dialog box appears, as shown in Figure 15-49.

8. Click OK to exit the Filter Rows dialog box.

9. Scroll down in the Sales_Information query result. You will see the table content has been reloaded and had been filtered to only include store number 1. Any analysis we do will be analysis just for sales through store number 1.

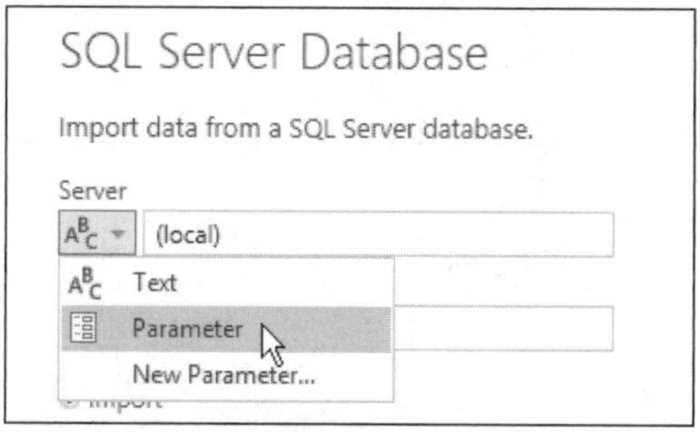

Figure 15-46 *Using a Parameter for the server name in the connection*

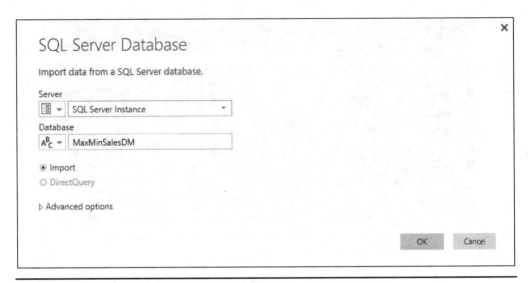

Figure 15-47   *The SQL Server Database dialog box with a parameter specifying the Server*

10. Click Close & Apply to exit the Query Editor.

11. After the data has reloaded, you will see our column chart has changed. It is showing sales by salesperson for the selected year or years, but only for sales through store number 1.

12. To change the parameter and load data for a different store number into the model, click the drop-down arrow below Edit Queries and select Edit Parameters. The Enter Parameters dialog box appears.

13. From the Store Number drop-down list, select 3. The Enter Parameters dialog box appears, as shown in Figure 15-50.

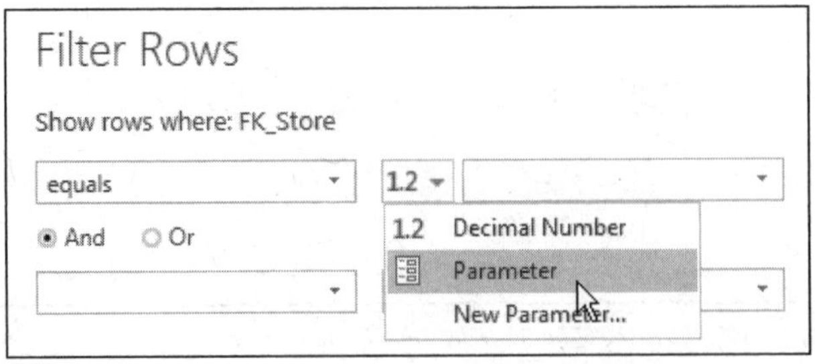

Figure 15-48   *Selecting a Parameter to use in a row filter*

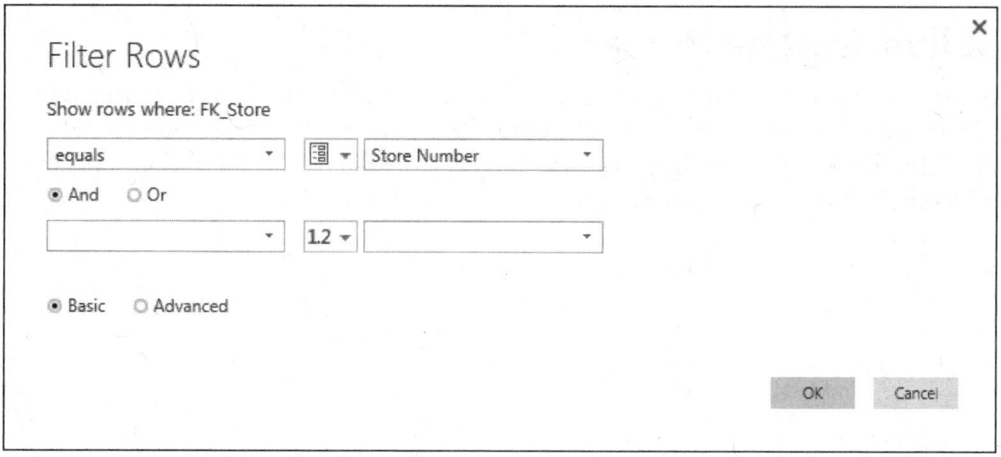

Figure 15-49 *The Filter Rows dialog box using a filter*

14. Click OK to exit the Enter Parameters dialog box. You will see a message telling you that your query has changed and these changes have not been applied.

15. Click Apply Changes. The data is reloaded into the Sales_Information table. This will take a bit of time, so you can see this is not the primary way we want to apply filters while doing data exploration and analysis. Once the data load is complete, you see the sales through store number 3.

16. Click Save.

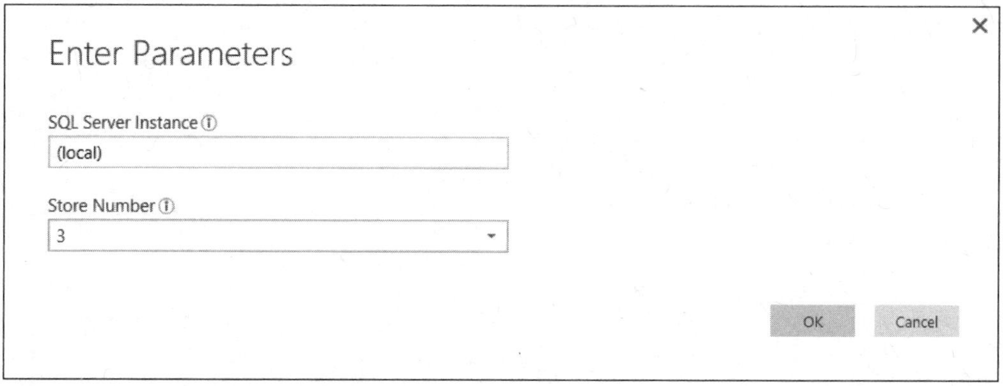

Figure 15-50 *The Enter Parameters dialog box*

Delivering the Power

In this chapter, we focused on getting the data into our Power BI models. In the next chapter, we will concentrate on visualizing that data. We will refine our data models, review the DAX expression language, and then explore the data visualizations available in Power BI. Finally, we will publish our model to PowerBI.com.

Chapter 16

I Can See Clearly Now: Data Visualization with Power BI Reporting

In This Chapter

- ▶ **Enhancing Power BI Data Models**
- ▶ **Power BI Data Visualizations**
- ▶ **DAX Calculations**
- ▶ **Additional Power BI Features**
- ▶ **PowerBI.com**
- ▶ **Special Delivery**

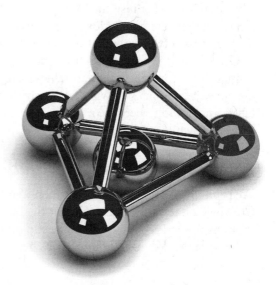

The main thing I love about street photography is that you find answers you don't see in fashion shows. You find information for readers so they can visualize themselves.

—Bill Cunningham
American Photographer

I n this chapter, we turn our attention to visualizing data with Power BI. We briefly saw Power BI charting in action in Chapter 15. We saw the way presentation-ready charts appear with just a few mouse clicks. Here we dive deeper into those visualization capabilities.

We also take time in this chapter to add content to our Power BI data models. The data we need has been pulled into the Max Min Sales Information model and the Population-GDP-CO2 by Country model. Now we need to add relationships, hierarchies, and measures to get the most from our data. We end the chapter looking at sharing our Power BI reports with others by publishing them to PowerBI.com and interacting with them there.

Enhancing Power BI Data Models

Using the Power BI Query Editor we were able to pull data into our data models. We were able to manipulate that data to get it looking just the way we needed it to before loading it into our data models. Even with all of this manipulation, we still need to do some work within the data models to maximize the effectiveness of our data exploration in Power BI.

In our Population-GDP-CO2 by Country model, we can analyze the data in one table at a time to get insights into population growth or changes in CO_2 output. However, there are no relationships between our tables. Therefore, we cannot look for relationships between population growth and changes in CO_2 output.

Our Max Min Sales Information model automatically carried forward the relationships from the data mart tables. This model does not, however, contain any hierarchy definitions. We will see shortly that a number of hierarchies exist in these tables. In addition, there are a few properties we can set to provide a more satisfying experience while working with our models.

Relationships and Intermediate Tables

We begin by creating relationships between the tables in our Population-GDP-CO2 by Country model. Looking at the tables in our models, there are two obvious relationships we need to have in place in order to do effective data exploration across multiple tables. We need relationships between the Year columns in the tables. We need

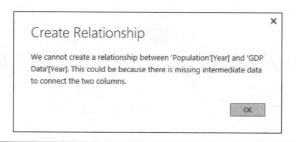

Figure 16-1   *The Create Relationship Error Message dialog box*

to be able to compare the Population in given years with the gross domestic product (GDP) or carbon dioxide (CO_2) emissions in those same years. Likewise, we need relationships between the Country columns in the tables. We should be able to compare the Population for a given country with the GDP or CO_2 emissions for that country.

It is tempting to simply drag the Year field from the Population table and drop it on the Year field in the GDP Data table. Unfortunately, Power BI Desktop will not create this relationship. When we try, we get the message shown in Figure 16-1.

The message is a bit cryptic. What it is telling us is that we are trying to create a many-to-many relationship and Power BI can't deal with this situation. The problem is there are multiple records in both tables that have the same value. There are multiple records for 1960 in the Population table—one for each country—and multiple records for 1960 in the GDP Data table—again one for each country. See Figure 16-2.

What we need to do, as the error message suggests somewhat indirectly, is create an intermediate table. This intermediate table will have one record for each year. We will also create an intermediate table for countries with one record for each country. Once we have the intermediate tables built, we can create several one-to-many relationships as shown in Figure 16-3.

Population

Country (or dependent territory)	Year	Population
Ireland	1960	2833000
Morocco	1960	12424000
Oman	1960	602000
Ireland	1965	2877000
Morocco	1965	14067000
Oman	1965	682000

GDP Data

Country Name	Year	GDP
Ireland	1960	193932975
Morocco	1960	2037154689
Oman	1960	44234654
Ireland	1965	2945704143
Morocco	1965	2948325264
Oman	1965	63279972

Figure 16-2   *Attempting a many-to-many relationship for Year*

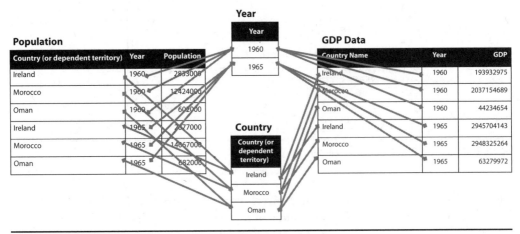

Figure 16-3   *Implementing many-to-many relationships with an intermediate table*

To prevent confusion as we work with the data model, we will hide the Year and Country fields in the initial tables. Only the Year field in the Year intermediate table and the Country (or dependent territory) field in the Country table will be visible in the data model as we work with it to create visualizations. When we select a year in the Year intermediate table, it will filter all of the other tables for that year. When we select a country in the Country intermediate table, it will filter all of the other tables for that country. This is shown in Figure 16-4.

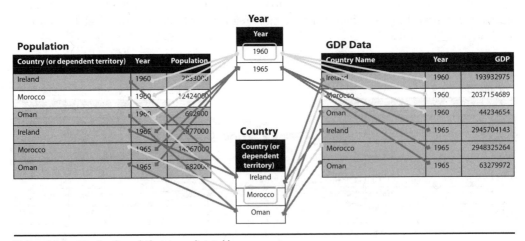

Figure 16-4   *Filtering through the intermediate tables*

> **NOTE**
>
> *This Learn By Doing exercise requires data from another database. Before completing this exercise, you will need to restore the CountryInfo database to your SQL Server. Follow the instructions in the Zip file containing the supporting information for this book to complete the restore process.*

Learn By Doing: Completing the Population-GDP-CO2 by Country Data Model

Features Highlighted

▶ Add intermediate tables to facilitate many-to-many relationships

▶ Hide columns and tables

Business Need   We need to complete the Population-GDP-CO2 by Country Power BI data model in order to begin using it to create visualizations.

Steps to Create the Year Intermediate Table

1. Open Power BI Desktop. The Start dialog box appears.
2. Click "Population-GDP-CO2 by Country.pbix" on the left side of the dialog box. The Population-GDP-CO2 by Country Power BI file opens.
3. Click the Data button on the left side of the window.
4. Click Enter Data on the Home tab of the ribbon. The Create Table dialog box appears.
5. In row 1 under Column1, type **1950** and press ENTER.
6. In row 2 under Column1, type **1955** and press ENTER.
7. In row 3 under Column1, type **1960** and press ENTER.
8. Continue this process until you have rows for every five years from 1950 to 2015.
9. Replace "Table1" with **Year** for Name at the bottom of the dialog box. The Create Table dialog box appears as shown in Figure 16-5.
10. Click Load. The Year table is created in the data model.
11. Select the Year table in the Fields area.
12. Right-click the Column1 column heading and select Rename from the context menu.
13. Type **Year** and press ENTER.
14. In the Default Summarization drop-down list in the Modeling tab of the ribbon, select Do Not Summarize.

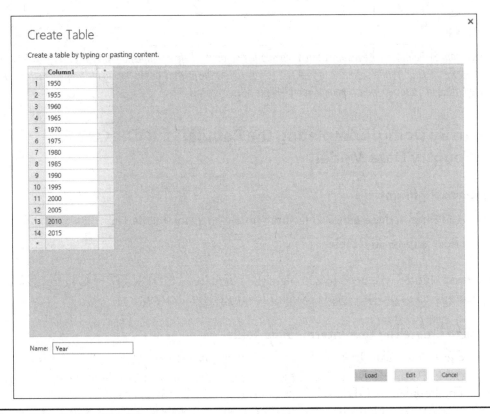

Figure 16-5 *The Create Table dialog box*

Steps to Create the Country Intermediate Table   Each of the tables we imported has slightly different names for some countries and territories. We certainly could have taken the time to add more Replace Values operations in the import queries to bring each set of countries into a consistent naming convention. Rather than taking the time to do that in these exercises, we will be using multiple fields in the Countries table. Each field is adapted to the country naming used in a particular data table. Also, country and territory names tend to be a bit fluid. You may need to update the content of the PopulationTableCntry/Terr field to synchronize it with the current naming in the Wikipedia table before bringing the Countries table into the model.

1. Click Get Data on the Home tab of the ribbon. The Get Data dialog box appears.
2. Select SQL Server Database and click Connect. The SQL Server Database dialog box appears.

3. Enter the name of the SQL Server instance hosting the CountryInfo database for Server.

4. Enter **CountryInfo** for Database.

5. Click OK. The Navigator appears.

6. Check Countries and click Load. The Countries table is added to the model.

7. Right-click the Countries entry in the Fields area and select Rename from the context menu.

8. Type **Country** and press ENTER.

Steps to Create Relationships in the Model

1. On the left side of the window, select Relationships. The Relationships view of the model appears.

2. In the Population table, click Country (or dependent territory) and drop it on PopulationTableCntry/Terr in the Country table. An active, one-to-many relationship that filters in both directions is created. (Note the double arrow in the middle of the line created to represent the relationship.)

3. In the GDP Data table, click Country Name and drop it on GDPCntry/Terr in the Country table. An active, one-to-many relationship that filters in both directions is created.

4. In the CO2 Emissions in kt table, click Country Name and drop it on CO2TableCntry/Terr in the Country table. An active, one-to-many relationship that filters in both directions is created.

5. In the Population table, click Year and drop it on Year in the Year table. An active, one-to-many relationship that filters in both directions is created.

6. In the GDP Data table, click Year and drop it on Year in the Year table. An inactive, one-to-many relationship that filters from the Year table to the GDP Data table is created. This new link is inactive because there is already an active path from Population to GDP Data through Country. If this path were active, there would be a second active path from Population to GDP Data. The Power BI model will not support this. We will fix this issue in a moment.

7. In the CO2 Emissions in kt table, click Year and drop it on Year in the Year table. Another inactive, one-to-many relationship that filters in from the Year table to the GDP Data table is created. Again, this is inactive to avoid having two active paths from Population to CO2 Emissions in kt. The problem is our first four relationships filter in both directions. We don't need the bidirectional filtering for these relationships.

8. Let's change these relationships to single-direction filtering. Double-click the relationship line from the Population table to the Country table. The Edit Relationship dialog box appears.

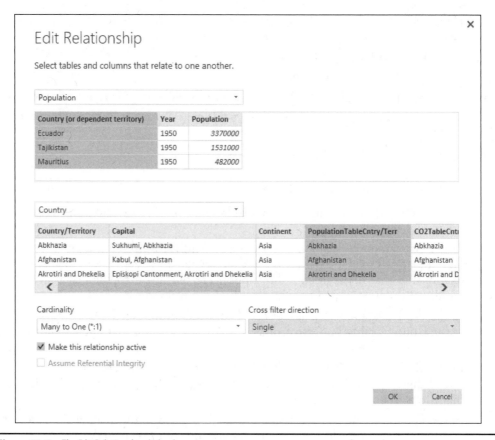

Figure 16-6 *The Edit Relationship dialog box*

9. Change the Cross filter direction drop-down list to Single. The Edit Relationship dialog box appears as shown in Figure 16-6.

10. Click OK to exit the Edit Relationship dialog box.

11. As an alternative to double-clicking each link, we can use the Manage Relationships dialog to make these same changes. Click Manage Relationships on the Home tab of the ribbon. The Manage Relationship dialog box appears as shown in Figure 16-7.

12. Select the relationship from CO2 Emissions in kt (Country Name) to Country (CO2TableCntry/Terr).

13. Click Edit. The Edit Relationship dialog box appears.

14. Change the Cross filter direction drop-down list to Single.

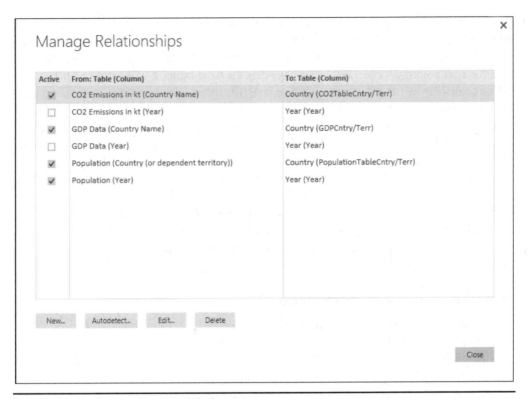

Figure 16-7   *The Manage Relationships dialog box*

15. Click OK to exit the Edit Relationship dialog box.
16. Repeat Steps 12–15 to change the following relationships to single:

From: Table (Column)	To: Table (Column)
GDP Data (Country Name)	Country (GDPCntry/Terr)
Population (Year)	Year (Year)

17. Check the box next to the relationship from CO2 Emissions in kt (Year) to Year (Year) to make this relationship active.
18. Check the box next to the relationship from GDP Data (Year) to Year (Year) to make this relationship active. These relationships were created with single-direction cross-filtering, so that property does not need to be changed.
19. Click Close to exit the Manage Relationships dialog box.

Notice the small arrows on the relationship connections all go from the Country table to the other tables or from the Year table to the other tables. Therefore, when we select a country in the Country table, it will filter the other tables to display just the data for that country. When we select a year in the Year table, it will filter the other tables to display just the data from that year. With the single-direction cross-filtering, there is no problem having all of the relationships active.

With the filtering working in this manner, we don't want to select countries and years in the tables containing the data. They should only be selected in the intermediate tables. Therefore, let's hide the Year- and Country-related fields in the data tables. Likewise, when filtering, we don't want the special linking fields in the Country table selected (PopulationTableCntry/Terr, GDPCntry/Terr, CO2TableCntry/Terr). In addition, the data from the Population 1950-1980 table was appended to the Population table. Therefore, we do not want to use the Population 1950-1980 table in our reporting. To simplify our model, we will hide that table, too. We will also add a bit of formatting to the data.

Steps to Do the Final Model Clean-Up

1. Right-click the heading of the Population 1950-1980 table and select Hide in Report View from the context menu. The table is grayed out.
2. Right-click the Country (or dependent territory) field in the Population table.
3. Select Hide in Report View from the context menu.
4. Right-click the Year field in the Population table.
5. Select Hide in Report View from the context menu.
6. Right-click the Country Name field in the CO2 Emissions in kt table.
7. Select Hide in Report View from the context menu.
8. Right-click the Year field in the CO2 Emissions in kt table.
9. Select Hide in Report View from the context menu.
10. We can also hide fields while viewing the model through the Data view. Click the Data button on the left side of the window. Power BI Desktop switches to Data view.
11. Select the GDP Data table in the Fields area.
12. Right-click the Country Name column heading and select Hide in Report View from the context menu.
13. Right-click the Year column heading and select Hide in Report View from the context menu.
14. Select the Country table in the Fields area on the right.
15. Right-click the PopulationTableCntry/Terr column heading and select Hide in Report View from the context menu.

16. Right-click the CO2TableCntry/Terr column heading and select Hide in Report View from the context menu.

17. Right-click the GDPCntry/Terr column heading and select Hide in Report View from the context menu.

18. Click Save.

19. Close Power BI Desktop.

Formatting and Categories

We switch now from the Population-GDP-CO2 by Country model to the Max Min Sales Information model. This model already had relationships defined, so we don't have to worry about that. What we do need to do in this model is take care of some formatting and naming. The Power BI data models should be as friendly and familiar as possible as we are exploring the data.

We will also assign data categories to several fields in the Customer table. These categories tell Power BI how to use these columns during reporting. For example, we will assign the State or Province category to the State field. This tells Power BI it can use this field to assign values to a location on a map.

The categories shown in Table 16-1 can be assigned to fields within a Power BI data model.

Data Category
Address
Barcode
City
Continent
Country/Region
County
Image URL
Latitude
Longitude
Place
Postal Code
State or Province
Web URL

Table 16-1   *Power BI Data Categories*

Learn By Doing:
Completing the Max Min Sales Information Data Model

Features Highlighted

- ▶ Rename fields to user friendly names
- ▶ Specifying a Sort By column
- ▶ Setting the Data Category
- ▶ Formatting fields

Business Need   We need to complete the Max Min Sales Information Power BI data model in order to begin using it to create visualizations.

Steps to Clean Up the Customer Table

1. Start up Power BI Desktop. The Start dialog appears.
2. Click Max Min Sales Information.pbix on the left side of the dialog box. The Max Min Sales Information Power BI file opens displaying the Sales_in_Dollars by Sales_Person_Name report.
3. On the left side of the window, select Data. The Data view of the model appears.
4. Select the Customer table in the Fields area, if it is not selected by default.
5. The PK_Customer field is used for creating relationships in the model, but does not provide any value as we analyze the data. Right-click the PK_Customer heading and select Hide in Report View from the context menu.
6. Right-click the Customer_Name heading and select Rename from the context menu.
7. Type **Customer** and press ENTER.
8. Click the Address heading.
9. On the Modeling tab of the ribbon, select Address from the Data Category drop-down list.
10. Click the City heading.
11. On the Modeling tab of the ribbon, select City from the Data Category drop-down list.
12. Click the State heading.
13. On the Modeling tab of the ribbon, select State or Province from the Data Category drop-down list.
14. Click the ZipCode heading.

15. On the Modeling tab of the ribbon, select Postal Code from the Data Category drop-down list.

16. Right-click the ZipCode heading and select Rename from the context menu.

17. Type **Zip Code** and press ENTER.

18. Right-click the Homeowner heading and select Rename from the context menu.

19. Type **Home Owner?** and press ENTER.

20. Right-click the MaritalStatus heading and select Rename from the context menu.

21. Type **Married?** and press ENTER.

22. Right-click the NumCarsOwned heading and select Rename from the context menu.

23. Type **Number of Cars Owned** and press ENTER.

24. On the Modeling tab of the ribbon, select Average from the Default Summarization drop-down list.

25. Right-click the NumChildrenAtHome heading and select Rename from the context menu.

26. Type **Number of Children at Home** and press ENTER.

27. On the Modeling tab of the ribbon, select Average from the Default Summarization drop-down list.

Steps to Clean Up the Date Table   In the Date table, there is a human-readable version of each field and a sortable version of each field. We will hide the sortable version of the field while renaming and setting the Sort By property for the human-readable version of the field.

1. Select the Date table in the Fields area.

2. Right-click the PK_Date heading and select Rename from the context menu.

3. Type **Date** and press ENTER.

4. In the Format drop-down list on the Modeling tab of the ribbon, select Date Time | 3/14/2001 (M/d/yyyy).

5. Right-click the Date_Name heading and select Rename from the context menu.

6. Type **Long Date Name** and press ENTER.

7. Right-click the Year heading and select Rename from the context menu.

8. Type **YearSort** and press ENTER.

9. Right-click the YearSort heading and select Hide in Report View from the context menu.

10. Right-click the Year_Name heading and select Rename from the context menu.

11. Type **Year** and press ENTER.
12. Click the Sort By Column button on the Modeling tab of the ribbon.
13. Select YearSort from the menu.
14. Right-click the Quarter heading and select Rename from the context menu. (Scroll right when needed throughout these instructions.)
15. Type **QtrSort** and press ENTER.
16. Right-click the QtrSort heading and select Hide in Report View from the context menu.
17. Right-click the Quarter_Name heading and select Rename from the context menu.
18. Type **Quarter** and press ENTER.
19. Click the Sort By Column button.
20. Select QtrSort from the menu.
21. Right-click the Month heading and select Rename from the context menu.
22. Type **MnSort** and press ENTER.
23. Right-click the MnSort heading and select Hide in Report View from the context menu.
24. Right-click the Month_Name heading and select Rename from the context menu.
25. Type **Month** and press ENTER.
26. Click the Sort By Column button.
27. Select MnSort from the menu.
28. Right-click the Day_Of_Year heading and select Hide in Report View from the context menu.
29. Right-click the Day_Of_Year_Name heading and select Rename from the context menu.
30. Type **Day of Year** and press ENTER.
31. Click the Sort By Column button.
32. Select Day_Of_Year from the menu.
33. Right-click the Day_Of_Quarter heading and select Hide in Report View from the context menu.
34. Right-click the Day_Of_Quarter_Name heading and select Rename from the context menu.
35. Type **Day of Quarter** and press ENTER.
36. Click the Sort By Column button.
37. Select Day_Of_Quarter from the menu.
38. Right-click the Day_Of_Month heading and select Hide in Report View from the context menu.

39. Right-click the Day_Of_Month_Name heading and select Rename from the context menu.
40. Type **Day of Month** and press ENTER.
41. Click the Sort By Column button.
42. Select Day_Of_Month from the menu.
43. Right-click the Month_Of_Year heading and select Hide in Report View from the context menu.
44. Right-click the Month_Of_Year_Name heading and select Rename from the context menu.
45. Type **Month of Year** and press ENTER.
46. Click the Sort By Column button.
47. Select Month_Of_Year from the menu.
48. Right-click the Month_Of_Quarter heading and select Hide in Report View from the context menu.
49. Right-click the Month_Of_Quarter_Name heading and select Rename from the context menu.
50. Type **Month of Quarter** and press ENTER.
51. Click the Sort By Column button.
52. Select Month_Of_Quarter from the menu.
53. Right-click the Quarter_Of_Year heading and select Hide in Report View from the context menu.
54. Right-click the Quarter_Of_Year_Name heading and select Rename from the context menu.
55. Type **Quarter of Year** and press ENTER.
56. Click the Sort By Column button.
57. Select Quarter_Of_Year from the menu.

Steps to Clean Up the Product and Promotion Tables

1. Select the Product table in the Fields area.
2. The PK_Product field is used for creating relationships in the model, but does not provide any value as we analyze the data. Right-click the PK_Product heading and select Hide in Report View from the context menu.
3. Right-click the Product_Name heading and select Rename from the context menu.
4. Type **Product** and press ENTER.
5. Click the RetailPrice heading and select Rename from the context menu.
6. Type **Retail Price** and press ENTER.

7. In the Format drop-down list on the Modeling tab of the ribbon, select Currency | $ English (United States).

8. In the Default Summarization drop-down list on the Modeling tab of the ribbon, select Average.

9. Click the Weight heading.

10. In the Default Summarization drop-down list on the Modeling tab of the ribbon, select Average.

11. Select the Promotion table in the Fields area.

12. The PK_Promotion field is used for creating relationships in the model, but does not provide any value as we analyze the data. Right-click the PK_Promotion heading and select Hide in Report View from the context menu.

13. Right-click the Promotion_Name heading and select Rename from the context menu.

14. Type **Promotion** and press ENTER.

Steps to Clean Up the Sales_Information Table   We will rename the Sales_Information table itself to get rid of the underscore character. We will also hide all of the foreign key fields used to link this table to the other tables in the model. Finally, we will delete the Sales_Tax and Shipping columns, which do not contain any data.

1. In the Fields area, right-click the Sales_Information table and select Rename from the context menu.

2. Type **Sales Information** and press ENTER.

3. Right-click the FK_Date heading and select Hide in Report View from the context menu.

4. Repeat Step 3 to hide the following fields:

    ▶ FK_Customer

    ▶ FK_Product

    ▶ FK_Promotion

    ▶ FK_Sales_Person

    ▶ FK_Store

5. Right-click the Sales_in_Dollars heading and select Rename from the context menu.

6. Type **Sales in US Dollars** and press ENTER.

7. In the Format drop-down list on the Modeling tab of the ribbon, select Currency | $ English (United States).

8. Right-click the Sales_in_Units heading and select Rename from the context menu.

9. Type **Sales in Units** and press ENTER.

10. Right-click the Sales_Tax heading and select Delete from the context menu. The Delete Column dialog box appears.

11. Click Delete.
12. Right-click the Shipping heading and select Delete from the context menu. The Delete Column dialog box appears.
13. Click Delete.

Steps to Clean Up the Sales_Person and Store Tables

1. In the Fields area, right-click the Sales_Person table and select Rename from the context menu.
2. Type **Sales Person** and press ENTER.
3. Select the Sales Person table in the Fields area.
4. Right-click PK_Sales_Person and select Hide in Report View from the context menu.
5. Right-click Sales_Person_Name and select Rename from the context menu.
6. Type **Sales Person** and press ENTER.
7. Right-click Sales_Person_SCD_Original_ID and select Hide in Report View from the context menu.
8. Right-click Sales_Person_SCD_Status and select Rename from the context menu.
9. Type **Status** and press ENTER.
10. Right-click Sales_Person_SCD_Start_Date and select Rename from the context menu.
11. Type **Sales Person Start Date** and press ENTER.
12. In the Format drop-down list on the Modeling tab of the ribbon, select Date Time | 3/14/2001 (M/d/yyyy).
13. Right-click Sales_Person_SCD_End_Date and select Rename from the context menu.
14. Type **Sales Person End Date** and press ENTER.
15. In the Format drop-down list on the Modeling tab of the ribbon, select Date Time | 3/14/2001 (M/d/yyyy).
16. Right-click Sales_Person_Territory and select Rename from the context menu.
17. Type **Sales Territory** and press ENTER.
18. In the Default Summarization drop-down list in the Modeling tab of the ribbon, select Do Not Summarize.
19. Select the Store table in the Fields area.
20. Right-click PK_Store and select Hide in Report View from the context menu.
21. Right-click Store_Name and select Rename from the context menu.
22. Type **Store** and press ENTER.
23. Right-click Store_Type and select Rename from the context menu.
24. Type **Store Type** and press ENTER.
25. Click Save.

Hierarchies

In Chapter 15, we saw how the hierarchies in the Max Min Manufacturing DM Tabular model, accessed through Live Connect, allowed users to drill down into the data. We want to create the same capability in the Max Min Sales Information data model. Therefore, we will add several hierarchies to this model.

Although it may seem a bit counterintuitive, the hierarchies are not added in the Data view. Instead, they are added in the Report view. Apparently, Microsoft is recognizing that hierarchies are intimately tied to the drilldown you can do within your reports. Therefore, managing hierarchies is more a reporting task than a data task.

Whether you view hierarchy management as a part of data modeling or as a part of reporting, it is vital to getting the most insight from our data. With that in mind, we switch to the Report view to create hierarchies. Once those are in place, we shift gears and explore the visualizations available in Power BI.

Learn By Doing: Adding Hierarchies to the Max Min Sales Information Data Model

Feature Highlighted

▶   Creating hierarchies

Business Need   We are still working to complete the Max Min Sales Information Power BI data model in order to begin using it to create visualizations.

Steps to Add Hierarchies

1. On the left side of the window, select Report. The Report view of the model appears.
2. In the Fields area, expand the entry for the Customer table.
3. Right-click the entry for the State field. (You can also click the ellipsis (…) button to see the same context menu.)
4. Select New hierarchy from the context menu. A new hierarchy called State Hierarchy is created. The State field is set as the highest level in the hierarchy.
5. Right-click the State Hierarchy entry and select Rename from the context menu.
6. Type **Geographic Hierarchy** and press ENTER. The hierarchy moves so it is in the correct sort order among the fields in the Customer table.
7. Select the City field and drop it on top of the Geographic Hierarchy entry. City is added as a lower level of the hierarchy.

8. Select the Customer field and drop it on top of the Geographic Hierarchy entry. Customer is added as a lower level of the hierarchy. The Fields area should appear as shown in Figure 16-8.

9. Collapse the entry for the Customer table.

10. Expand the entry for the Date table.

11. Select the Quarter field and drop it on top of the Year field. A new hierarchy is created called Year Hierarchy with Year as the highest level and Quarter as the lowest level.

12. Right-click the Year Hierarchy and select Rename from the context menu.

13. Type **Date Hierarchy** and press ENTER.

14. Select the Month field and drop it on top of the Date Hierarchy entry. Month is added as a lower level of the hierarchy.

15. Select the Date field and drop it on top of the Date Hierarchy entry. Date is added as a lower level of the hierarchy.

16. Collapse the Date Hierarchy entry. We are doing this to make it easier to correctly complete the following steps.

17. Right-click the Year field entry (the Year field entry not in the Date Hierarchy) and select Hide from the context menu.

Figure 16-8   *The Geographic hierarchy in the Customer table*

18. Repeat Step 17 for the Quarter, Month, and Date fields.
19. Now, if we want to use Year, Quarter, Month, or Date in our report, we must access them through the Date Hierarchy.
20. Collapse the entry for the Date table.
21. Expand the entry for the Store table.
22. Select the Store field and drop it on top of the Store Type field. A new hierarchy called Store Type Hierarchy is created.
23. Right-click the Store field entry that is not part of the hierarchy and select Hide from the context menu.
24. Right-click the Store Type field entry that is not part of the hierarchy and select Hide from the context menu.

    We are now ready to dig into Power BI data visualizations.
25. Click Save.

Power BI Data Visualizations

We dabbled with Power BI visualizations in order to validate our data models in Chapter 15. Now it is time to dive in to visualizations in earnest. Power BI offers a rich set of visualizations, all with the same presentation-ready quality in just a few clicks.

We begin by talking through some of the basic visualizations. Then we kick up the interactivity and explore mapping. We will end this section looking at other visual elements.

We've worked hard to build our Power BI data models. Now we let the data tell its story through Power BI visualizations.

Basic Visualization

Learn By Doing: Using Table and Matrix Visualizations

Features Highlighted

▶   Renaming report tabs

▶   Using a table visualization

▶   Working with a matrix visualization

Business Need   We would like to add a second visualization to our Max Min Sales Information Power BI model. This visualization should show sales in dollars for each of the West Coast states (AK, CA, HI, OR, WA) for 2013, 2014, and 2015. This data is going to be used to verify certain sales reporting, so exact numbers are required.

Change the Store Number Parameter

1. Change the Store Number parameter to 2. If you don't recall how to do this, follow Steps 12 through 16 of the Steps to Parameterize a Filter section of the Learn By Doing: Using Power BI Parameters in Chapter 15.

Steps to Name a Tab and Create a New Tab

1. Select Report on the left side of the window if you do not see a report. The report in Page 1 appears.
2. Right-click the Page 1 tab and select Rename Page from the context menu.
3. Type **Sales by Sales Person** and press ENTER.
4. Click the yellow tab containing the plus sign to add a new report page.
5. Right-click the new page and select Rename Page from the context menu.
6. Type **West Coast Sales** and press ENTER.
7. From the Page View drop-down list on the Home tab of the ribbon, select Actual Size.

Steps to Create the Table and Matrix Visualizations

1. In the Fields area, scroll down and expand Sales Information.
2. Check the box for Sales in US Dollars. A column chart appears on the report page.
3. In the Fields area, scroll up and expand Customer.
4. Check the box for State. A column is added to the chart for each state.
5. In the Visualizations area, select the Table visualization as shown in Figure 16-9. The column chart becomes a table of values.
6. In the Fields area, expand Date.
7. Expand the Date Hierarchy and check the box for Year. Year is added to the table.
8. In the Visualizations area, select the Matrix visualization.
9. In the area below Visualizations, click the Date Hierarchy/Year entry and drop it on Columns | Drag data fields here as shown in Figure 16-10. The Years are pivoted to become columns in the matrix layout.
10. Scroll down in the area below the Visualizations so the entire Filters area is visible.
11. Click the entry for State(All). The State filter options area appears.

Figure 16-9   *Selecting the Table visualization*

Figure 16-10 *Moving fields to the Columns area*

12. Scroll through the list and check the boxes for the following states:

  ► AK

  ► CA

  ► HI

  ► OR

  ► WA

13. Use the sizing handles to size the matrix appropriately. The visualization should appear as shown in Figure 16-11.

14. Click Save.

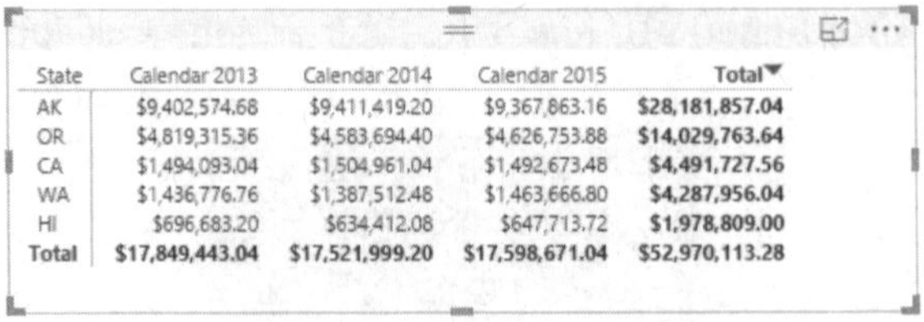

State	Calendar 2013	Calendar 2014	Calendar 2015	Total▼
AK	$9,402,574.68	$9,411,419.20	$9,367,863.16	$28,181,857.04
OR	$4,819,315.36	$4,583,694.40	$4,626,753.88	$14,029,763.64
CA	$1,494,093.04	$1,504,961.04	$1,492,673.48	$4,491,727.56
WA	$1,436,776.76	$1,387,512.48	$1,463,666.80	$4,287,956.04
HI	$696,683.20	$634,412.08	$647,713.72	$1,978,809.00
Total	$17,849,443.04	$17,521,999.20	$17,598,671.04	$52,970,113.28

Figure 16-11 *The West Coast Sales report*

Learn By Doing: Using Card and Multi-row Card Visualizations

Features Highlighted

▶   View a card visualization

▶   Working with a multi-row card visualization

▶   Formatting a visualization

▶   Changing the sort order

Business Need   We need a way to view contact information for customers in a given state.

Steps to Create the Card Visualizations

1.   Click the yellow tab containing the plus sign to add a new report page.
2.   Right-click the new page and select Rename Page from the context menu.
3.   Type **Customer Info** and press ENTER.
4.   From the Page View drop-down list on the Home tab of the ribbon, select Actual Size.
5.   In the Fields area, expand the Customer table and check the Customer field.
6.   In the Visualizations area, select the Card visualization. The Card visualization displays a single value. Therefore, it has to provide an aggregation to the data—in this case, showing a count of the number of customers.
7.   In the Visualizations area, select the Multi-row Card visualization. The visualization changes to a scrolling list with one card layout for each customer.
8.   In the Fields area, check the Address field. The address is added to each customer card.
9.   Add the following fields to the visualization:

   ▶   City

   ▶   State

   ▶   Zip Code

   ▶   Home Owner?

   ▶   Married?

   ▶   Number of Cars

   ▶   Number of Children at Home

Steps to Format and Sort the Card Visualizations

1. Select the Format tab below the Visualizations area.
2. Expand the Data labels area.
3. Click the Color drop-down.
4. Select the gold color shown in Figure 16-12.
5. Expand the Card area.
6. From the Outline drop-down list, select Bottom only.
7. From the Outline color drop-down list, choose your favorite yellow color.
8. Use the Bar thickness slider bar to set the thickness to 10.
9. Expand the Title area.
10. Toggle the Title switch to On.
11. In the Title Text area, type **Customer Information** and press ENTER.
12. Click the report layout area outside of the multi-row card visualization to unselect it.
13. In the Fields area, check the State field.
14. In the Visualizations area, select Slicer.
15. Click the top of the slicer and drag it beside the multi-row card.
16. Select a state in the slicer to view the customers in that state.
17. Click the ellipsis (…) button in the upper-right corner of the multi-row card visualization.
18. Select Sort By City from the pop-up menu. The customer cards are sorted by city.
19. Click the ellipsis button and click the sort order indicator next to the Sort By City item to sort by city in the reverse order. The multi-row card visualization appears similar to Figure 16-13.
20. Click Save.

Figure 16-12 *Selecting a data label color*

Figure 16-13   *The Customer Info report*

Learn By Doing: Using Pie and Donut Charts

Features Highlighted

▶   Working with pie charts and donut charts

▶   Formatting labels

Business Need   We need to explore the proportion of sales by number of units for each of the sales promotions.

Steps to Create the Pie Chart and Donut Chart Visualizations

1. Click the yellow tab containing the plus sign to add a new report page.
2. Right-click the new page and select Rename Page from the context menu.
3. Type **Sales Units by Promotion** and press ENTER.
4. From the Page View drop-down list on the Home tab of the ribbon, select Actual Size.
5. In the Fields area, scroll down to the Sales Information table and check the Sales In Units field.
6. In the Fields area, expand the Promotion table and select the Promotion field.
7. In the Visualizations area, select Pie chart. A pie chart is created.
8. Select the Format tab under Visualizations.
9. Expand the Detail Labels area.

10. Use the Text Size slider to set the text size to 22 pt.
11. Expand the Title area.
12. Use the Text Size slider to set the text size to 25 pt.
13. Use the sizing handles to make the pie chart large enough so all of the labels are displayed in full.
14. In the Visualizations area, select Donut chart. The visualization appears as shown in Figure 16-14.
15. Click Save.

Learn By Doing: Creating a Gauge

Features Highlighted

▶ Working with a gauge visualization

▶ Beginning a page and a visualization from the ribbon

Business Need We would like to compare unit sales for a given month against a sales goal. The monthly sales goal is 250,000 units.

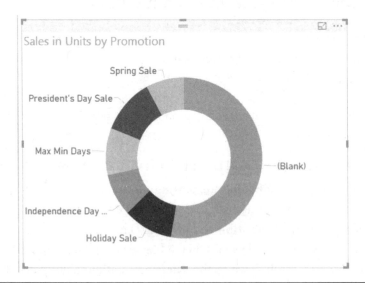

Figure 16-14 *The Sales in Units by Promotion report*

Steps to Create the Gauge Visualizations

1. On the Home page of the ribbon, click the drop-down arrow on the New Page button.

2. Select Blank Page from the drop-down menu to add a new report page.

3. Right-click the new page and select Rename Page from the context menu.

4. Type **Sales Units Gauge** and press ENTER.

5. From the Page View drop-down list on the Home tab of the ribbon, select Actual Size.

6. On the Home tab of the ribbon, click New Visual. A placeholder for a new visual is created.

7. In the Fields area, check Sales in Units.

8. In the Visualizations area, select Gauge. A gauge showing the total sales in units across all time is created.

9. Select the gauge and use the sizing handles to make it larger.

10. On the Home tab of the ribbon, click New Visual. A placeholder for a new visual is created.

11. In the Visualizations area, select Slicer. The placeholder becomes an empty slicer.

12. In the Fields area, check Month from the Date Hierarchy.

13. Drag the slicer up to the right of the gauge and size appropriately.

14. Select January 2013 in the slicer.

15. Select the gauge, and then select the Format tab under Visualizations.

16. Expand the Gauge axis area.

17. For Min, type **200000** and click in the Max entry area. The left end of the gauge scale is set to 200K.

18. For Max, type **300000** and click in the Target entry area. The right end of the gauge scale is set to 300K.

19. For Target, type **250000**. After a moment, a target line is created at 250K.

20. Expand Data labels.

21. From the Display units drop-down list, select Thousands.

22. For Text Size, type **17**.

23. Expand Callout Value.

24. From the Display units drop-down list, select Thousands.

25. Expand Data colors.

26. From the Target drop-down, select the darkest red color.

27. Expand Title.

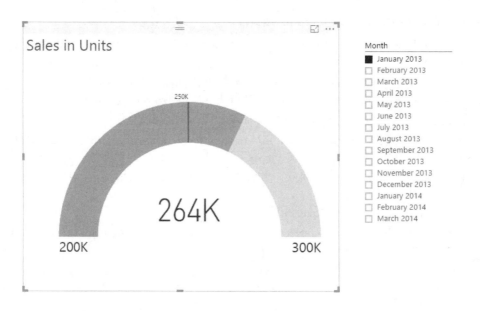

Figure 16-15   *The Sales Unit Gauge report*

28. For Text Size, type **19**. The report should appear as shown in Figure 16-15.
29. Select different months from the slicer and note the sales performance against the goal.
30. Click Save.

High Interactivity

Now that we have worked with much of the basic visualization in Power BI, let's add in more interactivity. We saw how the slicer allows us to quickly change our visualization to analyze different values. Power BI has additional features to provide us even more interactivity. We create charts that interact with one another and even charts that change themselves.

Learn By Doing: Interactivity Between Charts

Features Highlighted

► Working with alignment
► Creating cascading slicers

▶ Using one chart to interact with another

▶ Controlling interactivity

Business Need   We want to compare the population by year for a selected country/territory with the CO2 levels by year for the same period. The values should be on separate column charts with the columns aligned. To make country selection easier, we should select a continent first and then choose a country from the selected continent.

NOTE

This Learn By Doing exercise requires the "Globe Background.jpg" file. Before completing this exercise, you will need to copy this file to a location where it can be accessed by Power BI Desktop. Follow the instructions in the Zip file containing the supporting information for this book to complete this process.

Steps to Create the Chart Visualization

1. If it is not open, open the Population-GDP-CO2 by Country.pbix file in Power BI Desktop.
2. On the Report screen, right-click the Page 1 tab and select Rename Page from the context menu.
3. Type **Population by Country** and press ENTER.
4. Click the yellow tab containing the plus sign to add a new report page.
5. Right-click the new page and select Rename Page from the context menu.
6. Type **Population/CO2 Comparison** and press ENTER.
7. In the Fields area, check the Population field in the Population table.
8. In the Fields area, check the Year field in the Year table.
9. From the Fields area, select the Year field and drop it in the Filters area on Page level filters | Drag data fields here.
10. In the Show items when the value: drop-down list, select "is greater than or equal to."
11. In the box immediately below, type **1960**.
12. Be sure the And option is selected. In the drop-down list below the And option, select "is less than or equal to."
13. In the box below this drop-down list, type **2010** and press ENTER. The Page level filters area should appear as shown in Figure 16-16.
14. Select the Population by Year column chart you created on the report.
15. Select the Format tab under Visualizations.
16. Expand Title.
17. Enter **15** for Text Size.

Figure 16-16 *The Page level filters area*

18. Scroll down and expand General.

19. Enter **950** for Width.

20. Click the Population by Year column chart again to give it focus. It should remain selected.

21. Press CTRL-C.

22. Press CTRL-V. A copy of the chart is pasted on top of the existing chart.

23. Drag the new chart below the existing chart.

24. Select the Fields tab in the area below Visualizations.

25. We are going to add the CO2 Level to the new chart. From the list of tables and fields in the Fields area, select CO2 Level from the CO2 Emissions in kt table and drop it on top of Population as shown in Figure 16-17.

26. Under Value where we just dropped the CO2 Level field, click the "X" next to Population to remove it from the chart.

27. Hold down CTRL and select the Population by Year chart. Both charts should now be selected. We want to make sure the two charts are exactly aligned for comparison.

28. On the Visual Tools | Format tab of the ribbon, click Align.

Figure 16-17 *Adding a field in an existing chart*

29. Select Align Left from the drop-down list.
30. On the Home tab of the ribbon, click New Visual.
31. In the Visualizations area, select Slicer.
32. In the Fields area, check Continent in the Country table.
33. Use the sizing handles to size the Continent slicer appropriately.
34. On the Home tab of the ribbon, click New Visual.
35. In the Visualizations area, select Slicer.
36. In the Fields area, check Country/Territory.
37. Size and position the Country/Territory slicer appropriately.
38. Select Europe in the Continent slicer.
39. Select Denmark in the Country/Territory slicer. The charts are now showing information for Denmark. However, the Continent slicer is being filtered by the Country/Territory slicer and only showing Europe. This makes it difficult to select a country on another continent.
40. Select the Clear selections option at the top of the Continent slicer and the Country/Territory slicer as shown in Figure 16-18.
41. Select Asia in the Continent slicer.
42. Select Japan.
43. In the CO2 Level by Year chart, click the column for 2010. This not only highlights the column for 2010 in the CO2 Level by Year chart, but also highlights the column for 2010 in the Population by Year table.

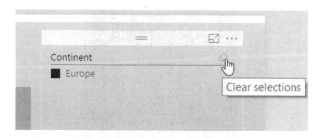

Figure 16-18 *Turning off filtering option for a visualization*

44. Click somewhere in the report layout area where there is no visualization present. This allows us to define properties for the report as a whole.
45. Select the Format tab.
46. Expand Page Background.
47. Click Add Image. The Open File dialog box appears.
48. Navigate to the location where you saved the Globe Background.jpg image file.
49. Select this image file and click Open. The image is loaded as a background image for the entire report. The report appears as shown in Figure 16-19.
50. Click Save.

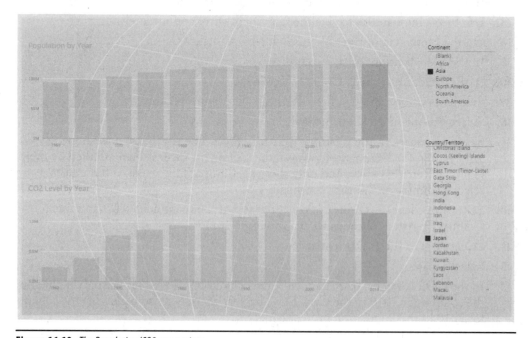

Figure 16-19 *The Population/CO2 comparison*

Learn By Doing: Creating a Scatter Chart

Features Highlighted

▶ Working with a scatter chart

▶ Using the play axis

Business Need   We would like to compare Population, GDP, and CO2 Emissions for members of the Group of Eight nations from 1960 to 2010.

Steps to Create the Scatter Chart Visualization

1. Click the yellow tab containing the plus sign to add a new report page.
2. Right-click the new page and select Rename Page from the context menu.
3. Type **Group of 8 Analysis** and press ENTER.
4. In the Fields area, check the Population field.
5. In the Visualizations area, select Scatter chart. The visualization becomes a scatter chart with Population as the Y-axis.
6. In the Fields area, check the GDP field in the GDP Data table. This becomes the X-axis of the scatter chart.
7. In the Fields area, check the CO2 Level field. The size of each visualization will represent the CO2 level.
8. In the Fields area, check the Country/Territory field and drop it on Legend | Drag data fields here. One circle visualization will be created on the chart for each country/territory.
9. Scroll down until you can see Play Axis | Drag data fields here.
10. In the Fields area, select the Year field and drop it on Play axis | Drag data fields here.
11. Scroll down again to see the Visual level filters.
12. Click the Year(All) entry.
13. In the Show items when the value: drop-down list, select "is greater than or equal to."
14. In the box immediately below, type **1960**.
15. Be sure the And option is selected. In the drop-down list below the And option, select "is less than or equal to."
16. In the box below this drop-down list, type **2010** and press ENTER.
17. Select the GroupOf8Member field and drop it in the Visual level filters area.
18. Click the GroupOf8Member(All) entry.
19. Check the True item. Only countries who are members of the Group of Eight will be included in the visualization.

20. Use the sizing handles to make the scatter chart as large as the report page.
21. Click the play button in the lower-left corner of the scatter chart. Watch the visualizations change as the play axis moves from 1960 to 2010.
22. Once the visualization is done playing, click the 2000 line on the play timeline.
23. Hover over the circle for Japan to view the detail information. The scatter chart should appear as shown in Figure 16-20.
24. Click Save.

Mapping

Data visualization across a geographic or geometric space can be very enlightening. Relationships between data points not readily apparent when viewing information organized alphabetically by country name can be immediately obvious when data is presented on a map. These days, there is no excuse for avoiding geographic presentations.

Let's see just how easy it can be.

Learn By Doing: Creating a Map

Feature Highlighted

▶ Working with a filled map

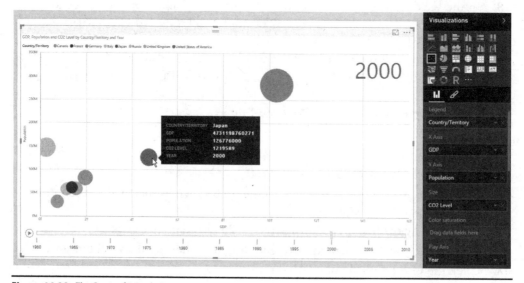

Figure 16-20   *The Group of 8 Analysis report*

Business Need   We would like to view population represented geographically for a selected year.

Steps to Create the Map Visualization

1. Click the yellow tab containing the plus sign to add a new report page.
2. Right-click the new page and select Rename Page from the context menu.
3. Type **World Population Map** and press ENTER.
4. In the Fields area, check the Population field.
5. In the Visualizations area, select Filled map.
6. In the Fields area, check the Country/Territory field.
7. Use the sizing handles to size the map to cover the left three-quarters of the report layout area.
8. Use the scroll wheel on your mouse or a pinch movement on a touch screen to zoom in or zoom out on the map as needed.
9. On the Home tab of the ribbon, click New Visual.
10. In the Visualizations area, select Slicer.
11. In the Fields area, check the Year field.
12. Try selecting various years in the slicer and view the population distribution. The color differences are subtle, but you can hover over each country to see the growth in population. The map should appear as shown in Figure 16-21.
13. Click Save.

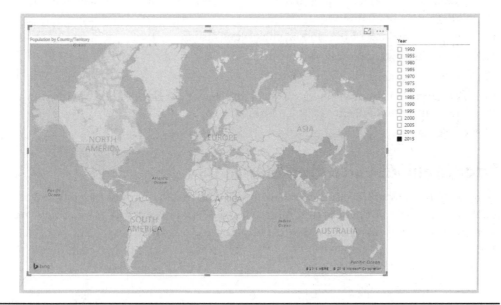

Figure 16-21 *The World Population Map report*

Learn By Doing: Creating a Bubble Map

Feature Highlighted

▶   Working with a bubble map

Business Need   We would like to view GDP and CO2 emissions represented geographically for a selected year.

Steps to Create the Bubble Map Visualization

1. Click the yellow tab containing the plus sign to add a new report page.
2. Right-click the new page and select Rename Page from the context menu.
3. Type **GDP and CO2 Map** and press ENTER.
4. In the Fields area, check the GDP field.
5. In the Visualizations area, select Map. (It is the globe icon.)
6. In the Fields area, check the Country/Territory field.
7. Use the sizing handles to size the map to cover the left three-quarters of the report layout area.
8. Use the scroll wheel on your mouse or a pinch movement on a touch screen to zoom in or zoom out on the map as needed.
9. In the Fields area, click the CO2 Level field and drop it on Color saturation | Drag data fields here. Now the size of each bubble represents the GDP and the shading of the bubble represents the CO2 Level—the darker the shading, the higher the CO2 emissions.
10. On the Home tab of the ribbon, click New Visual.
11. In the Visualizations area, select Slicer.
12. In the Fields area, check the Year field.
13. Try selecting various years in the slicer and view the GDP and CO2 emissions. The map should appear as shown in Figure 16-22.
14. Click Save.

Additional Visualization Elements

There are still a few entries in the Visualizations area that we have not used. We won't touch on every flavor of bar chart, column chart, line graph, and area graph. There are, however, a couple of items that are worth bringing to your attention.

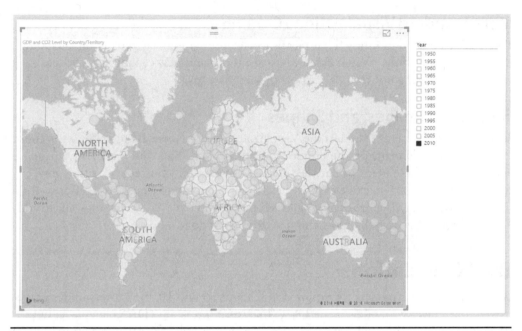

Figure 16-22 *The GDP and CO2 Map report*

R

In among all of the icons in the Visualizations area, there is a big, blue capital R. This item launches the R script editor. Using this tool you can utilize R visualizations within Power BI reports.

The R language is a statistical analysis language that facilitates high-powered data analysis and predictive analytics. Features of the R language are being incorporated into a number of Microsoft products after Microsoft's purchase of Revolution Analytics.

Custom Visualizations

Another unique icon in the Visualizations area is the ellipsis (...) button. Clicking this icon enables you to import custom visualizations into Power BI Desktop. Microsoft has published the interface allowing others to contribute visualizations to the Power BI ecosystem.

Those custom visualizations can be found online and downloaded for inclusion in your reporting. Microsoft makes no warranty of these custom visualizations. As with anything downloaded on the Internet for execution on your computer, be sure you trust the source of the custom visualization. Verify the visualization is both safe and accurate before using in a production environment.

More Standard Visualizations Coming

Power BI is updated monthly. That means the feature set is always changing, including the set of visualizations. Watch for new visualizations and new capabilities of those visualizations rolling out from Microsoft on a regular basis.

Text Boxes, Images, and Shapes

In addition to the items found in the Visualizations area, Power BI provides a few more visual reporting elements on the Home tab of the ribbon. These are Text Box, Image, and Shape. Use these items to put the finishing touches on your reports with logos, headers, and footers. You can even use these items to annotate your visualizations.

Remember, your visualizations should tell the story. However, when you want to add a little window dressing, the tools are there for you to do it.

DAX Calculations

As with the Tabular models we explored in Chapters 9 and 10, the expression language used in our Power BI models is the Data Analysis Expressions (DAX) language. DAX provides an extremely capable platform for creating business calculations within our models. These calculations enable our data models to provide even greater insight.

The DAX language relies heavily on functions that are strung together to create DAX expressions. This is very similar to the way expressions are created in Excel. If you are comfortable creating expressions in Excel, you should be comfortable creating expressions with DAX.

For an in-depth look at DAX and DAX functions, please see Chapter 10. Here, we will see how to utilize DAX functions to create calculated columns and measures in our data models.

Calculated Column: Order Weight

We begin by creating a calculated column. A calculated column has a value for each and every row in the data model. For this example, we are going to create a new column in the Sales Information table showing the total weight for each order line. We do this by taking the number of units and multiplying it by the weight of the product in that order line.

We have one issue we need to overcome before we can accomplish this calculation. The Sales in Units field is present in the Sales Information table and the product key is present in the Sales information table, but the product weight is not. We will need to look up the weight of the product in the Product table using the product key. Fortunately, DAX has a function to do just that.

Learn By Doing: Creating a Calculated Column

Features Highlighted

▶ Creating calculated columns

▶ Using the RELATED() function

Business Need   We would like determine the weight for each order line in the Sales Information table.

Steps to Create a Calculated Column

1. Open the Max Min Sales Information.pbix file in Power BI Desktop.
2. Click Data on the left to go to the Data screen.
3. Select Sales Information in the Fields area on the right. You see the data in the Sales Information table.
4. On the Home tab in the ribbon, click the drop-down arrow under New Measure and select New Column. (You can also select New Column from the Modeling tab in the ribbon.) A new column is created, and the formula bar appears ready for you to enter the formula for that column.
5. Delete the "Column =" text and type the following in the formula bar:

```
Product Wt = RELATED('Product'[Weight])
```

   The text to the left of the equal sign becomes the name of the new column.
6. Press ENTER. After a few moments a new column called Product Wt will be added to the Sales Information table. The Weight will be brought into the new column from the Product table based on the existing relationship between the two tables.
7. Our goal was to have the total weight for the order line, not just the weight of an individual product. Let's add a second calculated column for this calculation. On the Home tab in the ribbon, click the drop-down arrow under New Measure and select New Column.
8. Delete the "Column =" text and type the following in the formula bar:

```
Order Product Wt = 'Sales Information'[Sales in Units] *
                        'Sales Information'[Product Wt]
```

   When completed, the formula bar and the Sales Information table appear as shown in Figure 16-23.
9. Click Save.

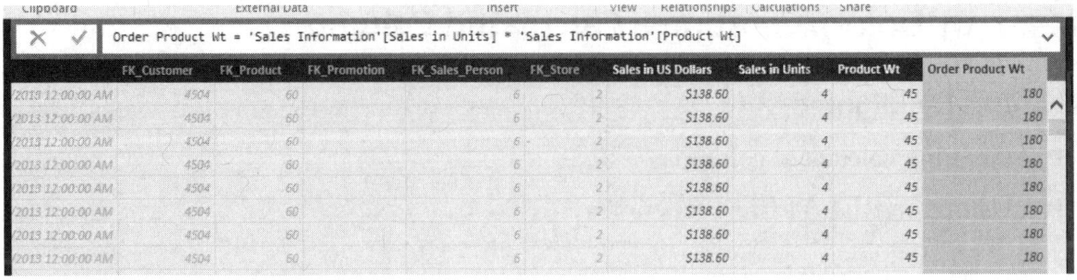

Figure 16-23 *The Order Product Wt calculated column*

Time Analytics

Where calculated columns provide one value for each row encountered, measures deal with multiple rows at the same time. Measures use aggregate functions to sum (or count, or average, etc.) numbers in multiple records to get a single result. We need measures to do any type of meaningful analysis.

The Power BI data model creates some default measures for us by default. Any column with a numeric value will be automatically set up to be summed across multiple records. We can choose to use a different aggregate for the default measure for a given column by using the Default Summarization drop-down list on the Modeling tab of the ribbon. We can even use this drop-down list to tell Power BI not to create a default option for a given numeric column. We do this for columns such as identification numbers or years that do not result in any meaningful value when aggregated.

We define our own measures in a Power BI data model to go beyond the default aggregations created for us. We can use the wealth of the DAX expression language to create highly complex formulas for executing business calculations. One of the most powerful uses of DAX functions within measures is to create time analytics.

Time analytics enable us to easily make comparisons of values across time. How do sales this month compare to the same month last year? What were the total sales to date as of this time last year?

In the following Learn By Doing Exercise, we will create three measures using time analytics. We will then use those measures in two reports to see them at work.

Learn By Doing: Creating Measures with Time Analytics

Features Highlighted

► Creating measures

► Working with time analytics

► Using the KPI visualization

Business Need   We would like to add measures to our Power BI model to easily compare sales in a given period with sales in the same period last year. We would also like to see year-to-date sales and compare that with year-to-date sales for the same period last year.

Steps to Create the Time Analytics Measures

1. On the Home tab of the ribbon, click the top portion of the New Measure button. The formula bar appears ready for you to enter the formula for the new measure.

2. Delete the "Measure =" text and type the following in the formula bar and press ENTER:

```
Sales in US Dollars Last Year = CALCULATE(
                    SUM('Sales Information'[Sales in US Dollars]),
                            SAMEPERIODLASTYEAR('Date'[Date]))
```

   The text to the left of the equal sign becomes the name of the new measure. The DAX expression to the right of the equal sign says to calculate the sum of the Sales in US Dollars column for the set of dates that represents the same period last year. Refer to Chapter 10 for more detailed information on DAX expressions.

3. On the Home tab of the ribbon, click the top portion of the New Measure button.

4. Delete the "Measure =" text and type the following in the formula bar:

```
Sales YTD = TOTALYTD(SUM('Sales Information'[Sales in US Dollars]),
                                        'Date'[Date])
```

5. Add a third measure using the following expression:

```
Sales LY YTD = CALCULATE(SUM('Sales Information'[Sales in US Dollars]),
                PARALLELPERIOD(DATESYTD('Date'[Date]), -12, MONTH))
```

Steps to Create the YOY Comparison Report

1. Select Report on the left side of Power BI Desktop.

2. Click the yellow tab containing the plus sign to add a new report page.

3. Right-click the new page and select Rename Page from the context menu.

4. Type **YOY Comparison** and press ENTER.

5. From the Page View drop-down list on the Home page of the ribbon, select Actual Size.

6. In the Fields area, check the Sales in US Dollars field.

7. In the Fields area, check the Sales in US Dollars Last Year measure.

8. Check the Date Hierarchy. We see a column chart with columns for current year sales and columns for last year sales.

9. Click the ellipsis (…) button in the upper-right corner of the column chart and select Sort By Year from the menu.

10. Click the down arrow in the upper-right corner of the column chart to turn on drilldown.

11. Click the bar for Calendar 2014. The chart drills into the four quarters of 2014.

12. Click the bar for Quarter 3, 2014. Your report appears as shown in Figure 16-24. The chart drills into the three months of that quarter. Notice how our Sales in US Dollars Last Year measure adapts to the level we are at in the drilldown, displaying year or quarter or month values as appropriate.

13. Click Save.

Steps to Create the YTD KPI Report

1. Click the yellow tab containing the plus sign to add a new report page.

2. Right-click the new page and select Rename Page from the context menu.

3. Type **YTD KPI** and press ENTER.

4. From the Page View drop-down list on the Home page of the ribbon, select Actual Size.

5. In the Fields area, check the Sales YTD Measure.

6. In the Visualizations area, select KPI.

7. In the Fields area, select Month under the Date Hierarchy and drop it on Trend Axis | Drag data fields here.

8. In the Fields area, select the Sales LY YTD measure and drop it on Target goals | Drag data fields here.

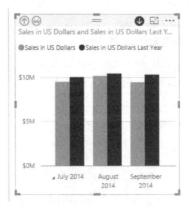

Figure 16-24 *The YOY Comparison report*

9. In the Visual level filters area, click Month(All).

10. Check the boxes for the 12 months in 2014 (January 2014–December 2014). The KPI now show sales performance against last year's sales. We are 0.37% ahead of last year.

11. In the Home tab of the ribbon, click New Visual.

12. In the Visualizations area, select Slicer.

13. In the Fields area, check the box for the Product field.

14. Drag the slicer up beside the KPI visualization.

15. Select "Boston, MS Harbor Lighthouse" in the list of products in the slicer. We can see that this product is 9.77% behind last year's year-to-date sales as shown in Figure 16-25.

16. Click Save.

Context Override: Percent of Total

As we saw in the last reports, one of the best things about measures is they know what context they live in. If the report groups by year, the measure groups by year. If the report is filtered by a product selected in a slicer, then the measure is filtered by that slicer. This makes measures very powerful and yet very easy to use.

There are times, however, when we want our measures to get out of the context box and aggregate on a broader basis. Calculating the percent of total is one of the best examples of this situation. We want to know how much of the total sales this particular

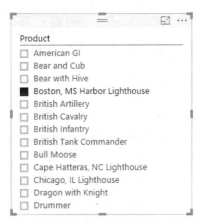

Figure 16-25 *The YTD KPI report*

grouping accounted for. In order to calculate that percentage, we need a way for our measure to get out of its grouping constraints to calculate the sum of the whole thing. Once we know the whole, we can divide to get the percent of total.

DAX offers a function to override aspects of a measure's context to get the totals we are looking for. In the following example we use the ALL() function to utilize all of the values from the specified table without regard for any filtering, slicing, or grouping that might be in place. Again, for an in-depth look at context in DAX expressions and DAX expressions that modify context, see Chapter 10.

Learn By Doing: Creating a Measure to Override Context

Features Highlighted

▶ Creating a measure to override context

▶ Additional work with the matrix

Business Need We would like to easily report on the percentage each salesperson contributes to total sales in dollars.

Steps to Create a Measure with a Context Override

1. Select Data on the left side of Power BI Desktop.
2. On the Home tab of the ribbon, click the top portion of the New Measure button.
3. Delete the "Measure =" text and type the following in the formula bar:

```
Sales Person % = SUM('Sales Information'[Sales in US Dollars])  /
                CALCULATE(SUM('Sales Information'[Sales in US Dollars]),
                                                ALL('Sales Person'))
```

4. Select any one of the other measures in the Fields area, and then select the Sales Person % measure again. This process causes things to refresh within the data model.
5. On the Modeling tab of the ribbon, select Percentage from the Format drop-down list.

Steps to Create the Percent of Sales Report

1. Select Report on the left side of Power BI Desktop.
2. Click the yellow tab containing the plus sign to add a new report page.
3. Right-click the new page and select Rename Page from the context menu.
4. Type **Percent of Sales** and press ENTER.

Year Sales Person	Calendar 2013 Sales in US Dollars	Sales Person %	Calendar 2014 Sales in US Dollars	Sales Person %	Calendar 2015 Sales in US Dollars	Sales Person %	Total Sales in US Dollars▼	Sales Person %
Eddie	$41,440,393.76	34.37 %	$40,570,907.04	34.42 %	$41,063,088.04	34.40 %	$123,074,388.84	34.40 %
Zeb	$24,760,478.40	20.54 %	$24,135,855.36	20.48 %	$24,430,335.64	20.47 %	$73,326,669.40	20.49 %
Paulette	$22,011,142.64	18.26 %	$21,490,567.08	18.23 %	$21,831,492.72	18.29 %	$65,333,202.44	18.26 %
Briggette	$32,346,351.64	26.83 %	$16,108,599.72	13.67 %			$48,454,951.36	13.54 %
Wally			$15,569,984.52	13.21 %	$32,028,196.52	26.83 %	$47,598,181.04	13.30 %
Total	$120,558,366.44	100.00 %	$117,875,913.72	100.00 %	$119,353,112.92	100.00 %	$357,787,393.08	100.00 %

Figure 16-26 *The Percent of Sales report*

5. From the Page View drop-down list on the Home page of the ribbon, select Actual Size.

6. In the Fields area, check the Sales in US Dollars field.

7. In the Fields area, check the Sales Person field.

8. In the Visualizations area, select Matrix.

9. In the Fields area, select Year and drop it on Columns | Drag data fields here.

10. In the Fields area, check the Sales Person % measure.

11. Resize the matrix as needed. Your report should appear as shown in Figure 16-26.

12. Click Save.

Additional Power BI Features

Power BI offers a couple more features to complete your reports and data models. These features enable you to secure the data in your model and make it as user friendly as possible. They also make it possible to share modeling content and move it from one format to another.

Roles

Roles are a new feature in Power BI. Without roles, the Power BI security story was all or nothing. Either we let someone see everything in the model or we had to lock them out of the entire model altogether.

With roles, we can allow access to certain aspects of our data model while limiting access to other areas. This is done by defining DAX expressions that determine what a given security role can see and what it cannot. We can set these limits on one table within the model or create a restriction on each one of the tables in the model.

When you click the Manage Roles button on the Modeling tab of the ribbon, you see the Manage roles dialog box. Add and remove roles using the Create and Delete buttons on the left. Once a role is created, you can rename it and set up its filters.

To add a filter to a role, click the ellipsis (…) button next to the table you want to filter. From the pop-up menu you can choose Add filter. You will then select the field in the table you want to use to create the filtering expression. Figure 16-27 shows the Sales Region 8 role with a filter to display only rows from the Sales Person table where Sales Territory is set to 8.

We can test a role using the View As Roles button on the Modeling tab of the ribbon. Clicking this button displays the View as roles dialog box. We can select our new Sales Region 8 role as shown in Figure 16-28. Once we click OK, we are interacting with the data as if we are a member of that role. For instance, if we view the Percent of Sales while functioning as a member of the Sales Region 8 report, we will only see data for Briggette and Wally as shown in Figure 16-29. These are the only two salespeople who

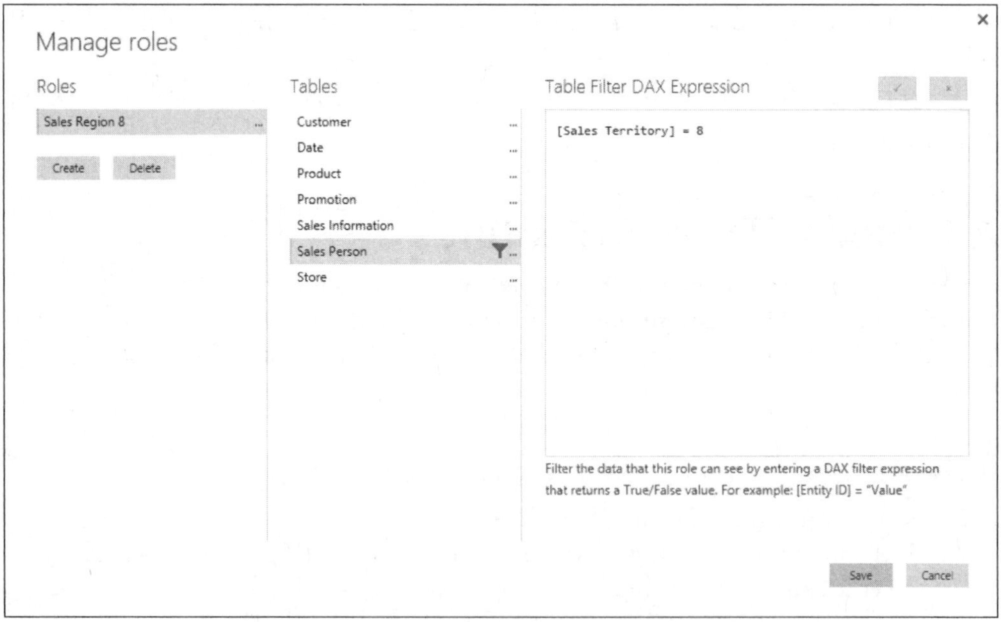

Figure 16-27 *The Sales Region 8 role*

Figure 16-28 *The View as roles dialog box*

have sold in Sales Region 8. To stop viewing the data as a member of the selected role, click the Stop viewing button.

The roles come into play when we publish our Power BI content and allow others to have access. At that point, we can assign those other users to a role when we give them rights to see the published content. Those users will then be limited by the rights granted to the role.

Synonyms

The PowerBI.com website includes a feature called Power Q&A. This is a natural-language query engine allowing users to ask for information from your Power BI data

	Now viewing report as: Sales Region 8		Stop viewing						

Year	Calendar 2013		Calendar 2014		Calendar 2015		Total	
Sales Person	Sales in US Dollars	Sales Person %	Sales in US Dollars	Sales Person %	Sales in US Dollars	Sales Person %	Sales in US Dollars	Sales Person %
Briggette	$32,346,351.64	100.00 %	$16,108,599.72	50.85 %			$48,454,951.36	50.45 %
Wally			$15,569,984.52	49.15 %	$32,028,196.52	100.00 %	$47,598,181.04	49.55 %
Total	$32,346,351.64	100.00 %	$31,678,584.24	100.00 %	$32,028,196.52	100.00 %	$96,053,132.40	100.00 %

Figure 16-29 *Viewing the Percent of Sales report through the Sales Region 8 role*

model by typing English sentences rather than using a query language or a drag-and-drop user interface. In order to make this feature easier to use, Power BI provides a mechanism to define synonyms for the tables and fields in your data model.

The synonym interface is accessed from the Relationships page of Power BI Desktop. Click the Synonyms button on the Modeling page of the ribbon to activate the Synonyms pane. Once this pane is open, it will show entries for the selected table and all of its fields, calculated columns, and measures. You can type a comma-separated list of other names your users are likely to use when referring to this object.

For example, in the Sales Information table, we may have users refer to the Sales YTD measure as "Sales Year-To-Date," "YTD Sales," or "Year-To-Date Sales" instead. These synonyms are shown in Figure 16-30. With these synonyms in place, our users will have much better success with the Power Q&A interface.

Import and Export

Power BI is designed to be a self-service data environment. Even though that may be the case, there are still times we want to share some of what we have created or load content created elsewhere. This can be done by importing Excel workbook contents and through the use of Power BI templates.

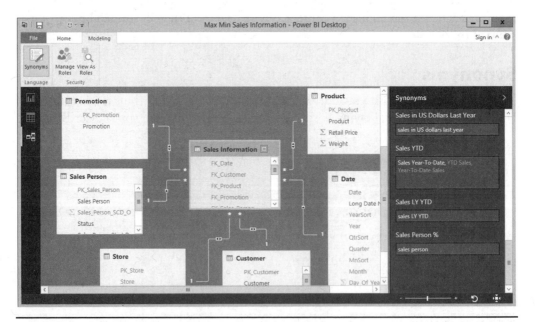

Figure 16-30 *The Synonyms pane*

Excel Workbook Content

If you have content created using the Power Query, Power Pivot, or Power View add-ons in Microsoft Excel, you can import that into Power BI Desktop. Select File | Import | Excel Workbook Contents to bring these items into Power BI Desktop. Once imported, you can work with these items within Power BI Desktop.

Power BI Templates

A Power BI template is a specially created version of your Power BI content stored in a file with a .pbit extension. The template contains all of the content created within a Power BI Desktop file. However, it is in a file format not designed to be opened directly, but intended to be imported by others as a starting point or an assist with their projects.

To create a Power BI template, build out your data model and reports in Power BI Desktop to the point where you would like to provide them to others. Next select File | Export | Power BI Template. Then name your template and choose the location where you would like to save the new .pbit file.

When someone would like to utilize your template file, they select File | Import | Power BI Template. They will receive all of your content to build upon.

PowerBI.com

When you have refined your Power BI content and are ready to share it with others, it is time to publish your content. When published, Power BI content is sent to PowerBI.com. The PowerBI.com website, run by Microsoft, is the place to share your content in a secure, controlled environment.

Signing In to PowerBI.com

In order to publish and maintain content on PowerBI.com, you need to have a PowerBI.com account. PowerBI.com accounts are available free of charge through the PowerBI.com website. If certain usage limits are exceeded, there is a charge for using PowerBI.com. Currently that charge is $9.95 per month.

Publishing

Once you have your PowerBI.com account, publishing through Power BI Desktop is straightforward. Follow these steps:

1. Click Publish on the Home tab of the ribbon.
2. If you are not currently signed in to PowerBI.com, you will be prompted to do so.

3. Once signed in, you will be asked where you want to deploy your content as shown in Figure 16-31.
4. Select the desired destination for your content and click Publish.

That's all there is to it. Once the publish process is complete, you will see a dialog box telling you your publication was successful.

Manipulating Online

When you sign on to PowerBI.com to work with your published content, things should look pretty familiar. We can access the reports created in Power BI Desktop. All of the animation and interactivity we saw in Power BI Desktop is available through the web interface as shown in Figure 16-32.

If you want to make changes to reports, you can do so right online. You can modify the content of the reports using a development environment almost identical to Power BI Desktop. This is shown in Figure 16-33. You can also access the data model and start from scratch creating new reports.

Dashboards and Reports

When you have a visualization in a report that works well, you can pin that visualization to a Power BI dashboard. Simply click Pin Live Page at the top of the visualization. Doing so will display the Pin to dashboard dialog box shown in Figure 16-34.

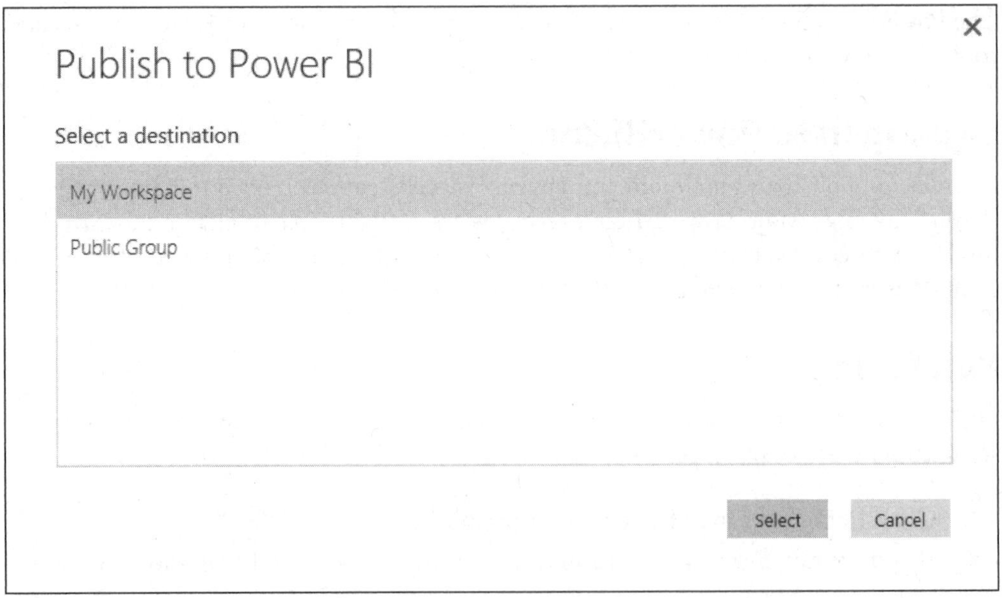

Figure 16-31 *Selecting a PowerBI.com destination*

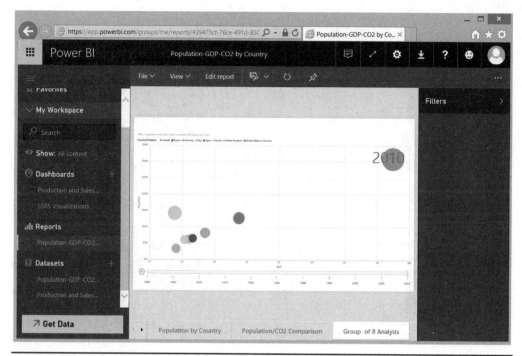

Figure 16-32 *Viewing a report on PowerBI.com*

Refreshing Data Online

Eventually, you will want to load new data into the data models loaded on PowerBI.com. This is not a problem if the data was taken from a public source somewhere in the cloud. It is also pretty straightforward if the data source resides on Microsoft Azure.

Things get a bit more complicated if the data source is on one of your organization's private servers. This is where the On-premises Gateway comes in.

The On-premises Gateway

The On-premises Gateway provides a secure conduit from your on-premises data sources to data consumers in the cloud like Power BI data models. Once in place, the On-premises Gateway provides a safe path for your Power BI data models to refresh their data either on a scheduled basis or on demand. The On-premises Gateway will also support Live Connect access to on-premises SQL Server Analysis Services instances and Direct Query access to SQL Server relational instances and to SQL Server Analysis Services.

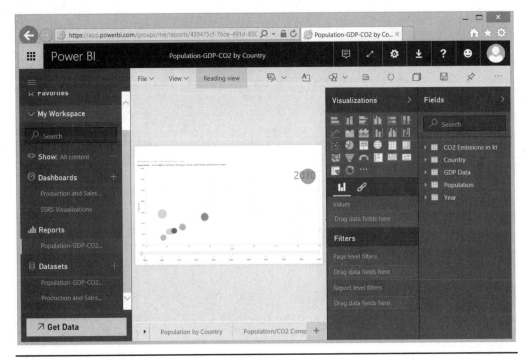

Figure 16-33 *Modifying a report on PowerBI.com*

Figure 16-34 *Pin to dashboard dialog box*

The On-premises Gateway operates on the server infrastructure at an organization and is usually maintained by the IT department. It is set up to be shared by all applications at that organization needing to move data to the Microsoft cloud. A personal version, the Power BI Gateway - Personal, is also available. The personal version operates from a workstation rather than a server. As the name implies, it is intended for personal, not organization-wide, use.

On-premises Power BI Publishing

Some organizations are not comfortable with data being published to the cloud. If this is the case with your organization, there are options for sharing Power BI content on-premises. One of those solutions is a reality. Another of those solutions, as of this writing, will be along real soon.

Pyramid Analytics, as part of its third-party business analytics solution, has the ability to host Power BI content on their on-premises servers. This capability enables you to publish your Power BI Desktop content to your own server. Others within your organization can then interact with the content you created. All that, and your data never has to leave the confines of your building.

The Microsoft SQL Server Reporting Services development team has promised similar support in the Reporting Services web portal. That capability was not part of the SQL Server 2016 release. It is supposed to ship as part of a follow-on service pack. Perhaps that has already become a reality by the time you are reading this. We shall see.

Special Delivery

We saw at the end of this chapter that Power BI has an infrastructure for sharing content with others. What about models built with the Tabular and Multidimensional models? How are they sent out into the world to share the knowledge within them and make good things happen?

In Chapter 17, we look at some of the tools provided by Microsoft for delivering the data in these models to end users and sharing business insights all around.

Part VI

Delivering

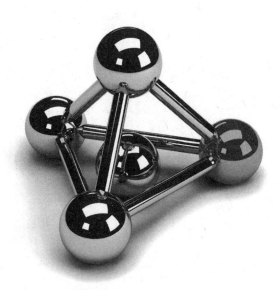

Chapter 17

Special Delivery: Microsoft Business Intelligence Client Tools

In This Chapter

▶ **Front-End BI Tools from Microsoft**
▶ **Reporting Services**
▶ **Reporting Services Paginated Reports**
▶ **Excel**
▶ **PerformancePoint Services in SharePoint**
▶ **Putting It All Together**

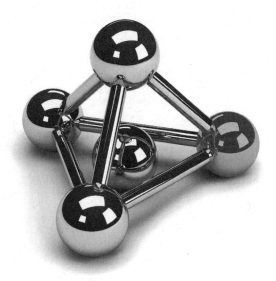

The two most engaging powers of an author are to make new things familiar, and familiar things new.

—Samuel Johnson

I n the preceding chapters of this book, we discovered ways to create business intelligence (BI). We saw the BI Semantic Models and Power BI dissect and analyze data. This dissection and analysis results in the foundational and feedback information needed for business intelligence.

Creating this information is only half the battle. As we discussed in Chapter 1, delivering business intelligence to decision makers in a timely manner is as important as creating that intelligence in the first place. The name of this book begins with the word "delivering" for just that reason.

We talked a bit about delivery at the end of Chapter 16 when we discussed PowerBI. com. In this chapter and the next, we examine the tools provided by Microsoft for delivering business intelligence. These are the tools that consume our BI Semantic Models and provide usable business information to our users. In this chapter, we review various Microsoft tools that utilize BI Semantic Models to put business intelligence in the hands of decision makers. In Chapter 18, we work at ways to integrate business intelligence into custom applications.

Front-End BI Tools from Microsoft

Microsoft provides a rich set of front-end tools for delivering business intelligence to end users. We have already seen Power BI, which functions as a hybrid between a tool that creates business intelligence content and a tool that delivers that content to the users. Here are a few more Microsoft tools that get the content visualized and out the door. They include:

▶ Reporting Services Paginated Report

▶ Reporting Services Mobile Report

▶ Reporting Services Key Performance Indicator

▶ Excel PivotTable

▶ Excel PowerPivot

▶ SharePoint PerformancePoint Services

It is great to know that as we create these robust Tabular and Multidimensional BI Semantic Models, there is a wide array of capable tools for delivering model content to the business user.

Some might say Microsoft is providing too many tools, making it difficult to know what tool to use when. This decision making is not helped by the fact that the capabilities of each tool overlap. We can create something that looks and performs like a dashboard in Reporting Services, or the Excel PivotTable Wizard, or SharePoint PerformancePoint Services.

It would be great if we could try all of the front-end tools and see which one works the best for a particular need. You may not have the time and resources to do that with your organization's business needs. Here, however, we have the luxury of already having a number of data models built. That makes it easier for us to try a bit of them all and gain a working familiarity with each tool.

You may not have access to all the tools covered in this chapter. That's all right. If you don't have a test SharePoint installation, skip over the sections on SharePoint-related environments. Try out the environments you do have and pick your favorites for each particular type of task.

Selecting a Front-End BI Tool

In addition to the test drive you can give each of these tools in this chapter, here are some guidelines for selecting front-end tools.

What Can Be Supported in Your Organization?

First, you need to make an honest determination of what can be adequately supported by the IT infrastructure in your organization. If your organization has a larger IT infrastructure, then it is feasible to support a number of these tools, using them in a more specialized manner. Reporting Services is used for paginated and mobile reports. PerformancePoint is used for dashboards. Excel and Power BI are used for ad hoc data exploration. Each front-end tool has its own group within the IT department to support it.

We'll call this the socket set approach. Think of the person with the 200-piece socket set in the big rolling toolbox. Need to tighten a bolt with the 1/4-inch head? There is a 1/4-inch socket for that. Need to loosen a bolt with a 1/2-inch head? Well, then we put away the 1/4-inch socket and get out the 1/2-inch socket for that.

It costs money to buy the 200-piece socket set. It also costs money for the infrastructure for all of those pieces to be properly stored and stay usable. In this case, it takes a big toolbox with lots of little drawers. It also takes the appropriate training to know how and when to use each specialized tool. (Well, maybe it doesn't take specialized training to know the difference between a 1/4-inch socket and a 1/2-inch socket, but throw in a torque wrench, a cone wrench, and a spoke wrench and the analogy holds...mostly.)

While it might be fun to know and work with all of the tools listed, if your organization has an IT department that consists of just a few people, that may not be the best approach. You will probably achieve better results and higher end-user satisfaction supporting a few tools that you know well.

We might call this the adjustable wrench approach. (I could have called this the monkey wrench approach, but throwing a monkey wrench into a process has negative connotations, so we'll go with adjustable wrench.) We select one tool, an adjustable wrench, that will do a good job tightening a bolt with a 1/4-inch head or loosening a bolt with a 1/2-inch head. The tool is flexible, we can keep it in a pocket, and we know how to use it.

Who Will Be the Primary Developers?

Nowadays, we need to consider who will be using the BI tools we select. We can no longer assume BI will be delivered by a group of techie report developers. It could just as easily be a group of business decision makers doing their own exploration of the data.

More technical users, like those report developers, will want a tool that has a broad range of capabilities to allow them to present the data exactly the way they want it to look. A tool like Reporting Services is a good fit for this group. Less technical users, like the business decision makers, will want a tool that is easy to use and allows them to concentrate on the data rather than on the tool. The Excel PivotTable Wizard, Power View, and Power BI are probably better choices for this group.

Does the Tool Provide the Necessary Capabilities in an Efficient Manner to Fulfill Current and Likely Future Needs?

While many of the Microsoft front-end BI tools are flexible, they all have their limits. There are things you can do with Reporting Services that cannot be accomplished in Power BI. Conversely, there are things that can be done very rapidly in Power BI that take much longer to accomplish in Reporting Services.

Going back to our wrench analogy, there are some situations where an adjustable wrench will work, but it is not quite as optimal as a socket set. There are also some situations where an adjustable wrench will not fit, but a socket wrench will work just fine. In those cases, we need to spend the money for the specialized tool and learn how to use it.

This is probably the trickiest question of the three. It is hard to predict what capabilities our business users will need in the future. It may even be hard to know all of their current needs when we are at the initial tool selection stage of a project. Still, we need to make the best determinations we can with the information available.

A Bit of Knowledge Is a Big Help

The key to selecting one or more front-end BI tools for your organization is having some knowledge of the users' needs and capabilities along with some knowledge of the features of each BI tool. I can't really help you in determining the needs and capabilities of your users. You'll have to determine that. What I hope to do in this chapter, however, is help you get to know enough about the capabilities of each of the tools to do some intelligent decision making.

Reporting Services

Reporting Services is a report authoring and report management environment built into SQL Server. Beginning with SQL Server 2016, the Reporting Services environment supports two different types of reports—paginated and mobile. Paginated reports are designed to be viewed and interacted with on a full-size computer screen. Their layout can be very finely controlled to produce exactly the desired output. Also, as the name implies, they provide for easy printing in a paginated form.

Mobile reports are designed to be viewed and interacted with on a tablet or smartphone. When creating mobile reports, we specify what the layout will look like on various footprints, so we control how the report reacts to various size devices. What we give up in the mobile environment is full control over every aspect of the visualization.

Both paginated reports and mobile reports are hosted by the Reporting Services web portal. The web portal is a complete, enterprise-wide report management and distribution service. Reporting Services enables us to securely distribute reports throughout an organization using an existing intranet infrastructure, and it provides for the integration of reports with both desktop and web-based applications. The Reporting Services web portal also supports the creation of Key Performance Indicators (KPIs) that are displayed as part of the web portal interface.

The following section provides an introduction to Reporting Services and its many capabilities. For a more in-depth and comprehensive exploration of Reporting Services, I recommend *Microsoft SQL Server 2016 Reporting Services* by . . . well, me . . . also available from McGraw-Hill Professional.

Reporting Services Paginated Reports

Since before the invention of computers, the primary method for sharing business intelligence has been the printed report. This is slowly changing as tools that allow interactive exploration of a BI Semantic Model become easier to use and more widely available. Still, in the business intelligence world, the paginated (printable) report is still a staple. That being the case, it is important to have a capable and easy-to-use reporting environment at our disposal. Reporting Services and its paginated reports fit that bill.

Reporting Services is a bridge between static, paper reports and interactive data exploration tools with its ability to play both roles. In addition to creating reports for printing, Reporting Services permits users to interact with reports, drilling down from summary to detail information, navigating to related reports, and even jumping to related websites. To use Reporting Services to its fullest extent, we need to create reports that encourage user interaction.

Reporting Services enables both developers and users to create reports. It offers two report authoring tools: the Report Builder and the Report Designer. The tools are very similar, with the main difference being the user interface. The *Report Builder* is geared toward those who are most comfortable in an environment that resembles the Microsoft Office tools. Report Builder utilizes the ribbon-style interface. Creating a report in Report Builder feels a bit like creating a document in Word or a spreadsheet in Excel.

The *Report Designer* environment is part of SQL Server Data Tools. It is a great fit for those who are comfortable working in SQL Server Data Tools, as I trust most of you are by now. For that reason, the sample reports in this chapter will be created using the Report Designer. There is no difference between reports produced by the Report Builder and those produced by the Report Designer.

Paginated Report Structure

A paginated report project can contain a number of reports. Each report contains two distinct sets of instructions that determine what the report will contain. The first is the *data definition,* which controls where the data for the report comes from and what information is to be selected from that data. The second set of instructions is the *report layout,* which controls how the information is presented on the screen or on paper. Both of these sets of instructions are stored using the Report Definition Language (RDL).

Figure 17-1 shows this report structure in a little more detail.

Data Definition

The data definition contains two parts: the data source and the dataset. The *data source* is the same as we have seen used in Multidimensional BI Semantic Model projects: It is the set of instructions the report needs to gain access to a data source that provides data for the report. The *data source definition* can be created right inside the report definition, or it can be created externally and shared by a number of reports. In most cases, report management is easier when we use external shared data sources.

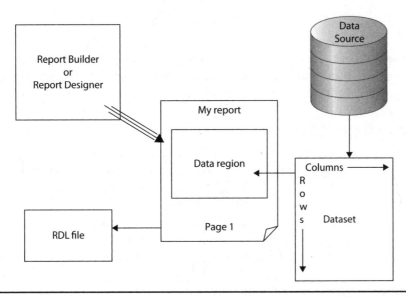

Figure 17-1   *Report structure*

When the report is executing, it uses the data source instructions to gain access to the data source. It then extracts information from the data source into a new format that can be used by the report. This new format is called a *dataset*. A report may contain multiple datasets from the same data source or even multiple datasets from multiple data sources.

The content of the dataset is defined using a tool called the Query Designer. The *Query Designer* helps us build a database query. The database query may be in T-SQL for querying relational data or MDX for querying Tabular and Multidimensional data. The query provides instructions to the data source, telling it what data we want selected for our report. The query is stored in the report as part of the data definition.

The data selected by the query into the dataset consists of rows and columns. The rows correspond to the records the query selects from the data source. The columns correspond to the fields the query selects from the data source. (Reporting Services does not support hierarchical result sets, so MDX query results are flattened into a single table of rows and columns.) Information on the fields to be selected into the dataset is stored in the report as part of the data definition. Only the information on what the fields are to be called and the type of data they are to hold is stored in the report definition. The actual data is not stored in the report definition, but instead, is selected from the data source each time the report is run.

NOTE

Reporting Services does have capabilities to cache report data so that reports can be created from the cache rather than the data source. However, by default, Reporting Services always queries the underlying data sources each time a report is run.

Paginated Report Layout

The data the report has extracted into a dataset is not of much use to us unless we have some way of presenting it to the user. We need to specify which fields go in which locations on the screen or on paper. We also need to add things such as titles, headings, and page numbers. All of this forms the report layout.

In most cases, our report layout will include one or more special areas that interact with the dataset. This special area is known as a data region. A *data region* displays all the rows in the dataset by repeating a section of the report layout for each row.

Report Definition Language

The information in the data definition and the report layout are stored using the Report Definition Language (RDL). *RDL* is an Extensible Markup Language (XML) standard designed by Microsoft specifically for storing report definitions. This includes the data source instructions, the query information that defines the datasets, and the report layout. When we create a report in the Report Designer, it is saved in a file with a .rdl extension.

Paginated Report Delivery

We have discussed how a report is created by the report author. What we have not discussed is where that report will reside after it is created. To make a report available throughout the organization, that report is deployed to a report server. Once on the report server, the report may be executed by a user through the web portal. It may be sent in response to a web service request that came, not from a user, but from another program. It may also be e-mailed to a user who has a subscription to that report.

NOTE

A report server can also be configured to operate in SharePoint Integrated mode. In this case, SharePoint provides the user interface for executing reports.

The Web Portal

One way for users to request a report from the report server is through the web portal. Reports deployed to the report server are organized into folders. The web portal allows users to browse through these folders to find the report they need. They can also search the report titles and descriptions to locate a report.

Security can be applied to folders and to individual reports on the report server. With this security, the site administrator can create security roles for the users who will be accessing the site. These security roles control which folders and reports a user is allowed to access. This ensures that when exploring the report server using the web portal, users only see the reports and folders they should.

In the web portal, reports are always displayed using the Hypertext Markup Language (HTML) format. Starting in SQL Server 2016 Reporting Services, the default is HTML5. Once a report has been displayed as an HTML page, the user can then export it into any of the other available formats.

Subscription Delivery

If the users do not want to go to the report, Reporting Services can make the report go to them. In other words, users do not necessarily need to come to the web portal to receive a report. They can have the report delivered to them through a subscription service. The web portal enables users to locate a report on the site and then subscribe to it so it will be delivered to them in the future.

When users subscribe to a report, they provide an e-mail address to which the report is to be delivered, whether as the body of the e-mail, as an e-mail attachment, or as a URL link to the report. Users can specify the format for the report at the time they create their subscription.

The site administrator can also set up report subscriptions. These function like a mass mailing, using a list of e-mail addresses. Rather than requiring each user to access the web portal to create their own subscription, the site administrator can create one subscription that is delivered to every user in the list.

Web Service Interface

In addition to delivering reports to humans, either at their request or on a subscription basis, the report server can deliver reports to other software applications. This is done through a series of web services. A program calls a web service on the report server, requesting a particular report in a particular format. The completed report is returned to the program that originated the request as the response to the web service request.

We see an example of this in Chapter 18.

Data Regions

In this section, we create a paginated report with Reporting Services. This is an introduction to Reporting Services paginated reports to give you a feel for their capabilities. To really explore the depth and breadth of Reporting Services paginated reports, you will want to work with other reference materials (such as my book mentioned earlier).

Paginated reports are created using a drag-and-drop approach. Report items are taken from the Toolbox window in Report Designer or the ribbon in Report Builder and placed on the report. The function of some of these report items is not hard to figure out: text boxes contain text; images display image files. Other report items are more complex and vital to the workings of Reporting Services reports.

As mentioned earlier, there are special report items designed specifically for working with datasets. These special report items are called data regions. *Data regions* are able to work with multiple records from a dataset. The data region reads a record from the dataset, creates a portion of the report using the data found in that record, and then moves on to the next record. It does this until all the records from the dataset have been processed.

The tablix is one of these data regions. However, you will not find the tablix in the Toolbox or on the ribbon. Instead, the tablix data region is created through the use of three different templates that are found in the Toolbox. These templates control the default look and behavior of the resulting tablix. The three templates are the table, the matrix, and the list. (The name "tablix" comes from the combination of "table" and "matrix"—but maybe you guessed that already.) It should be noted that the templates specify the initial state of a tablix added to a report. They do not limit what can be done with the tablix after it exists in the report layout.

The Table Template for the Tablix

The *table template* creates the traditional-style report with rows and columns. *Rows* are created from the records in the dataset and can be grouped within the tablix as well. *Columns* are created from the fields in the dataset. The table template produces a predefined set of columns and an unknown number of rows; the number of rows depends on the content of the dataset.

The table template creates what is called a *banded report* in some other report authoring environments. The *detail bands* in these reports correspond to the detail rows in the table. The *summary bands* in these reports correspond to the header and footer rows in the table.

The tablix that results from the table template includes a tablix header and footer. The tablix header often contains column headings for the tablix. The tablix footer often contains the grand totals for the entire tablix.

In addition to the tablix header and footer, the tablix data region can include multiple group headers and footers. The group headers often contain the information to identify a grouping. The group footers usually contain totals for the group. Drilldown can be defined in a report so the detail content of a group can be initially hidden and only made visible when the user drills down into the detail for that group.

The Matrix Template for the Tablix

The *matrix template* does not create a banded report, but it does create what is known as a pivot table or a crosstab report. The matrix template creates both rows and columns based on the content of the dataset. The resulting tablix has groupings on both rows and columns. Drilldown can be defined for both rows and columns.

The data cells created by the matrix template always contain aggregate data. Therefore, the data in the cells is numeric. Because of this, the matrix mirrors the fact and dimension structure of a Multidimensional BI Semantic Model cube and works well for displaying cube data.

The List Template for the Tablix

The *list template* does not deal in columns and rows at all. Instead, the list template provides a freeform layout area that is repeated for each record in the dataset. This layout may produce a whole section, perhaps a whole page or more, for each record in the dataset. This makes it a good choice for creating a report that is meant to resemble a form.

The Chart Data Region

The *chart* report item is a data region like the tablix, which means the chart can process multiple records from a dataset. The tablix enables you to place other report items in a row, a column, or a list area that is repeated for every record in the dataset. The chart, on the other hand, uses the records in a dataset to create visuals such as bars, lines, or pie wedges. You cannot place other report items inside a chart item.

The Map Data Region

The *map* report item is a data region used for presenting geographic and geometric data. We can shade areas on a map to represent data elements associated with a particular country, state, province, or other geographic region. The map report item also allows us to place symbols on a map to represent data or simply show location.

We can utilize SQL Server's geographic data type to define our own shapes such as our organization's sales regions or service areas. We can utilize SQL Server's geometric data type to create our representation of an office floor plan or a warehouse layout. By feeding these geographic and geometric data types into a map data region, we can incorporate these custom representations into our reports and overlay them with additional data, such as sales by region or inventory level by warehouse location.

Using Data Regions

Each data region item has a property called DataSetName. This property contains the name of the dataset used by the data region. In most cases, the Report Designer sets this automatically. This property is set to the dataset of the first field placed in the data region.

In many cases, a report includes a single data region to create the body of the report. In other cases, multiple data regions are combined on a single report. This mix and match has no limit. Perhaps a chart data region containing a line graph and a tablix data region containing detail information are placed on the same report. We can mix and match to our hearts' content.

Creating a Reporting Services Paginated Report

In this Learn By Doing exercise, we will create a paginated report using Reporting Services. This exercise will give you a taste of the paginated report creation process. It is in no way a comprehensive look at the features of Reporting Services paginated reports.

If you have a Reporting Services report server available to you, you can deploy the paginated report created here and utilize it in the Learn By Doing exercises in Chapter 18. Remember, don't use a production server for completing training exercises. Even if you do not have a Reporting Services report server, you can still create and preview the report in SQL Server Data Tools.

Learn By Doing: Creating a Paginated Report with a Matrix

Features Highlighted

- ► Using the matrix template
- ► Using aggregate functions
- ► Enabling drilldown
- ► Formatting report items

Business Need The Maximum Miniatures Marketing Department would like to analyze wholesale sales for each store over time. The marketing department wants to be able to select a year and view the quarters within the selected year. They would like to be able to drill down to the month level within a quarter. They would also like to be able to drill down to specific products within a store. In addition to the sales dollar amount, they would like to see the sales as a percent of total sales for the quarter.

We use the Max Min Sales DM Tabular model as the data source for this report.

Steps to Create a Report Server Project

1. Open SQL Server Data Tools.
2. Click the New Project button on the toolbar. The New Project dialog box appears.
3. In the Installed Templates area, select Reporting Services under Business Intelligence.
4. Select Report Server Project in the center of the dialog box.
5. Enter **MaxMinReports** for Name and set the Location to the appropriate folder. This will be the only project in this solution, so leave Create directory for solution unchecked.
6. Click OK to create the project.

Steps to Create a Shared Data Source

1. Right-click the Shared Data Sources folder in the Solution Explorer window and select Add New Data Source from the context menu. The Shared Data Source Properties dialog box appears.
2. Enter **MaxMinSales** for Name.
3. Select Microsoft SQL Server Analysis Services from the Type drop-down list.
4. Click Edit. The Connection Properties dialog box appears.
5. Enter the name of the Analysis Services server hosting the Max Min Sales model for Server name.
6. From the Select or enter a database name drop-down list, select Max Min Sales. The Connection Properties dialog box appears, as shown in Figure 17-2.
7. Click OK to exit the Connection Properties dialog box.
8. Click OK to exit the Shared Data Source Properties dialog box. The shared data source is created.

Steps to Create a New Report with a Dataset

1. Right-click the Reports folder in the Solution Explorer window and select Add | New Item. (Selecting Add New Report launches the Report Wizard, which we are not using for this report.) The Add New Item dialog box appears.
2. Select Report in the center area. Enter **Wholesale Sales By Month Report** for Name.
3. Click Add. The Report Design tab appears.
4. In the Report Data window, select New | Data Source from the toolbar. The Data Source Properties dialog box appears.

NOTE

If the Report Data window is not visible, select View | Report Data from the main menu.

Figure 17-2 *The Connection Properties dialog box*

5. Enter **MaxMinSales** for Name.
6. Select the Use shared data source reference option.
7. Select the MaxMinSales shared data source from the drop-down list. The Data Source Properties dialog box is shown in Figure 17-3.
8. Click OK to exit the Data Source Properties dialog box.
9. Right-click the MaxMinSales data source you just created in the Report Data window and select Add Dataset from the context menu. The Dataset Properties dialog box appears.
10. Enter **WholesaleSales** for Name.
11. Click Query Designer. The MDX Query Designer window appears.
12. Expand Measures and the Orders folder, and then drag the Sales in Dollars measure onto the query area (the area labeled Drag levels or measures here to add to the query). The query executes.
13. Expand the Time table, and then expand Date Hierarchy. Drag the Quarter and Month members of this hierarchy onto the query area.
14. Expand the Stores table and drag the Store attribute onto the query area.
15. Expand the Products table and drag the Product attribute onto the query area.

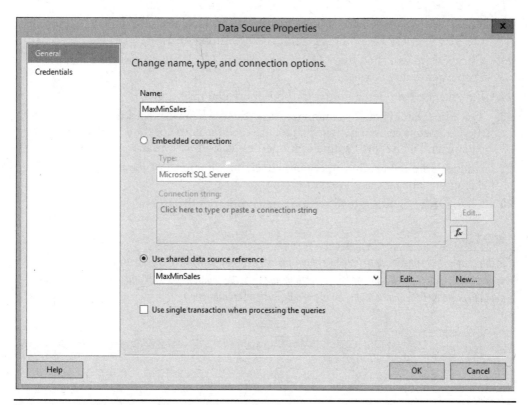

Figure 17-3 *The Data Source Properties dialog box*

16. Because our business requirements were for wholesale sales only, we need to add a filter to the query to include only wholesale customers (account numbers below 5000). In the filter pane (directly above the query pane), click the cell labeled <Select Dimension>. From the drop-down list, select Customers.

17. For Hierarchy, select Account Number.

18. For Operator, select Range (Inclusive).

19. For Filter Expression, create a range from 4500 to 4996.

20. We need to add a second filter to allow the user to select the year being viewed. In the second row in the Filter pane, click the cell labeled <Select Dimension>. From the drop-down list, select Time.

21. For Hierarchy, select Date Hierarchy.

22. For Operator, select Equal.

23. For Filter Expression, select 2015.

24. Check the box in the second row of the Parameters column. This will allow the user to select a year when the report is run.

25. The query executes again to apply the filters. With columns expanded appropriately, the MDX Query Designer appears, as shown in Figure 17-4.

26. Click OK to exit the Query Designer window. Click OK to exit the Dataset Properties dialog box.

27. Expand the Parameters folder in the Report Data window.

28. The TimeDateHierarchy parameter was created when we placed the check mark in the Parameters column in Step 24. Double-click the entry for the TimeDateHierarchy parameter. The Report Parameter Properties dialog box appears.

29. Uncheck the Allow multiple values check box. The Report Parameter Properties dialog box appears, as shown in Figure 17-5.

30. Click OK to exit the Report Parameter Properties dialog box.

NOTE

In this example, we queried data from one of our Tabular BI Semantic Models. We can use a similar approach to connect to a Multidimensional instance of SQL Server Analysis Services and query data from our Multidimensional BI Semantic Model for use in a Reporting Services report.

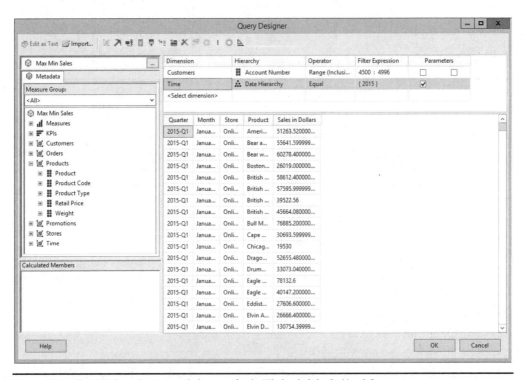

Figure 17-4 *The MDX Query Designer with the query for the Wholesale Sales By Month Report*

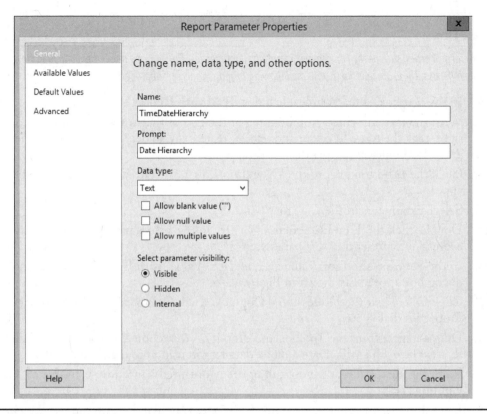

Figure 17-5   *The Report Parameter Properties dialog box*

Steps to Create the Report Layout

1. Click the report design area to activate the Report menu, and then select Report | Report Properties from the main menu. The Report Properties dialog box appears.
2. Select Landscape for Orientation.
3. Click OK.
4. Drag a text box from the Toolbox and drop it on the report body layout area.
5. Using the toolbar or the Properties window, modify the properties of the text box as follows:

Property	Value
Font: FontSize	16pt
Font: FontWeight	Bold
Location: Left	0in
Location: Top	0in
Size: Width	6in
Size: Height	0.375in

> **NOTE**
>
> *Several properties, such as the Font property, contain subproperties. The property must be expanded to view the subproperties. These are referred to with the following format: Property: Subproperty.*

6. In the text box, enter **Wholesale Sales By Month Report** - .

7. With the text edit cursor still blinking at the end of the string you just entered, right-click the text edit cursor and select Create Placeholder from the context menu. The Placeholder Properties dialog box appears.

8. Click the *fx* button next to the Value drop-down list. The Expression dialog box appears.

9. Select Parameters in the Category pane.

10. Double-click the TimeDateHierarchy entry in the Values pane. This will create an expression representing this parameter.

11. In the Set expression for: Value area, replace "Value" with Label. The Expression dialog box appears, as shown in Figure 17-6.

12. Click OK to exit the Expression dialog box. Click OK to exit the Placeholder Properties dialog box.

13. Drag a matrix from the Toolbox and drop it on the report body layout area below the text box. This will create a tablix data region using the matrix template.

14. From the Report Data window, drag the Month field and drop it in the Columns cell.

15. In addition to dragging fields from the Report Data window, we can use the pop-up field picker to select fields. Hover over the Rows cell until the field picker icon appears, as shown in Figure 17-7.

16. Click the field picker icon to display the pop-up field list. Select the Product field from the field list.

17. Select the Sales_in_Dollars field in the Data cell.

18. Drag the Quarter field and drop it on the line forming the top of the Month cell.

19. Drag the Store field and drop it on the line forming the left side of the Product cell. The report layout should appear, as shown in Figure 17-8.

Steps to Enable Drilldown

1. As requested in the business needs, we are going to enable drilldown in this report. Click the drop-down arrow for the Month group in the Column Groups area at the bottom of the screen. Select Group Properties from the drop-down menu. The Group Properties dialog box appears.

2. Select the Visibility page.

3. Select the Hide option under the When the report is initially run prompt.

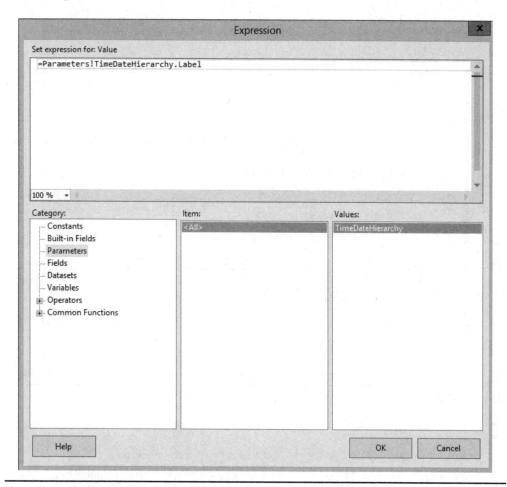

Figure 17-6   *The Expression dialog box with a Parameter expression*

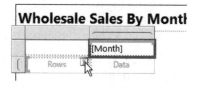

Figure 17-7   *The field picker*

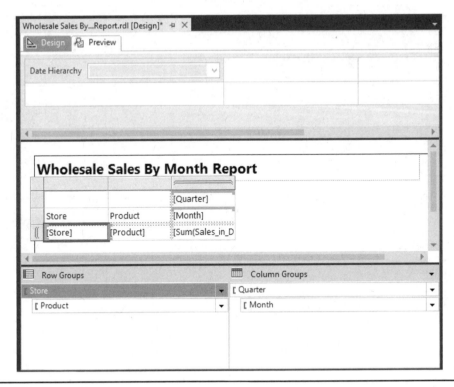

Figure 17-8 *The report layout*

4. Check the Display can be toggled by this report item check box.
5. Select Quarter from the drop-down list. The Group Properties dialog box appears, as shown in Figure 17-9.
6. Click OK to exit the Group Properties dialog box.
7. Click the drop-down arrow for the Product group in the Row Groups area. Select Group Properties from the menu. The Group Properties dialog box appears.
8. Select the Visibility page.
9. Select the Hide option under the When the report is initially run prompt.
10. Check the Display can be toggled by this report item check box.
11. Select Store from the drop-down list.
12. Click OK to exit the Group Properties dialog box.
13. Click the Preview tab. The report appears, as shown in Figure 17-10.

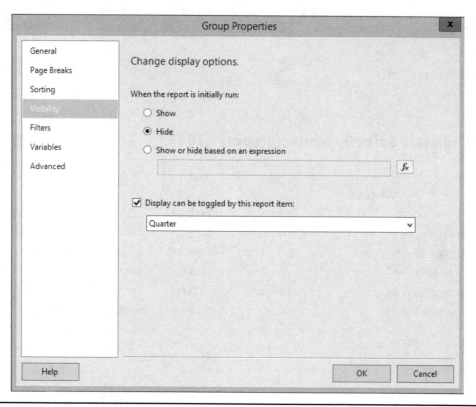

Figure 17-9   *The Group Properties dialog box*

Steps to Accomplish Additional Report Formatting

1. Click the Design tab. Let's make a few changes to improve the looks and readability of the matrix.

NOTE

When selecting cells in a tablix, click near the outside of the cell to avoid entering text edit mode within the cell.

2. Select the cell containing the Sum of the Sales_in_Dollars field (the detail cell for the matrix). Set the following properties in the Properties window:

Property	Value
Format	C
Size: Width	1.5 in

The "C" value provides currency formatting for the number in this cell.

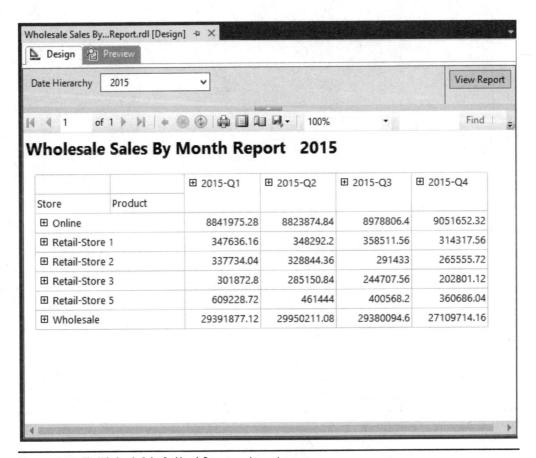

Figure 17-10 *The Wholesale Sales By Month Report preview—in progress*

3. Select the cell containing the Quarter field. Set the following properties in the Properties window:

Property	Value
BackgroundColor	CornflowerBlue
Font: FontWeight	Bold
TextAlign	Right

4. Select the cell containing the Month field. Use the toolbar buttons to set the font weight to bold, the background color to PowderBlue, and the alignment to align right. (Hint: Click the More colors link to select the color by name.)

5. Select the cell containing the Store field. (Not the Store heading.) Use the toolbar buttons to set the font weight to bold and the background color to CornflowerBlue.

6. Select the cell containing the Product field. Use the toolbar buttons to set the font weight to bold and the background color to PowderBlue.

Steps to Add a Calculated Column

1. Right-click the detail cell. Select Tablix: Insert Row | Inside Group - Below. A new detail cell is created below the existing detail cell.

2. Right-click the new detail cell and select Textbox: Expression from the context menu. The Expression dialog box appears.

3. Enter the following expression:

```
=Sum(Fields!Sales_in_Dollars.Value) /
            Sum(Fields!Sales_in_Dollars.Value, "Quarter")
```

> **NOTE**
>
> *The first Sum aggregate function in this expression adds all the sales for the current detail cell. This aggregate function determines what items to add based on the scope of the cell it is in. When no items are expanded in the matrix, the scope of each cell is the quarter column and product row the cell is in. When we pass a second parameter to the aggregate function, we explicitly specify the scope of the function. In this case, we require the second Sum aggregate function to always add sales for the current quarter column grouping. This enables us to calculate the total for the column to complete the percent of total calculation.*

4. Click OK to exit the Expression dialog box. You will see "<<Expr>>" as a placeholder for the expression.

5. Click to the right of the <<Expr>> placeholder in the new detail cell until you see the blinking edit cursor in the cell.

6. Enter a space followed by **of quarter** in the cell after the placeholder.

7. Click the <<Expr>> placeholder until it is highlighted.

8. Right-click the <<Expr>> placeholder and select Placeholder Properties from the context menu. The Placeholder Properties dialog box appears.

9. Select the Number page.

10. Select Percentage from the Category list.

11. Select the Font page.

12. Check the Bold check box.

13. Click OK to exit the Placeholder Properties dialog box.

> **NOTE**
>
> *We changed the numeric formatting and the font weight for just the expression portion of the cell content as represented by the placeholder. We did not change the formatting of the text after the placeholder.*

14. Click elsewhere to unselect this cell, and then click this cell again. Now the entire cell is selected, rather than just one portion of the content.

15. Use the toolbar buttons to set the alignment to align right.

16. Drag the right side of the report layout area (report body) as far left as possible.

17. Select the Preview tab. Your report appears, as shown in Figure 17-11.

18. Try expanding the quarter columns and the store rows. Click the Save All button on the toolbar when you are done exploring the report.

Reporting Services Mobile Reports

New in SQL Server 2016 Reporting Services is the ability to create reports specifically targeted to mobile devices. This is known as *adaptive design*. With adaptive design, we create several layouts of our content. Each layout is adapted to a specific footprint. The renderer then chooses which layout to use based on the size of the area available each time the content is rendered.

Wholesale Sales By Month Report   2015

Store	Product	2015-Q1	2015-Q2	2015-Q3	2015-Q4
⊞ Online		$8,841,975.28	$8,823,874.84	$8,978,806.40	$9,051,652.32
		22.20% of quarter	21.95% of quarter	22.64% of quarter	24.26% of quarter
⊞ Retail-Store 1		$347,636.16	$348,292.20	$358,511.56	$314,317.56
		0.87% of quarter	0.87% of quarter	0.90% of quarter	0.84% of quarter
⊞ Retail-Store 2		$337,734.04	$328,844.36	$291,433.00	$265,555.72
		0.85% of quarter	0.82% of quarter	0.73% of quarter	0.71% of quarter
⊞ Retail-Store 3		$301,872.80	$285,150.84	$244,707.56	$202,801.12
		0.76% of quarter	0.71% of quarter	0.62% of quarter	0.54% of quarter
⊞ Retail-Store 5		$609,228.72	$461,444.00	$400,568.20	$360,686.04
		1.53% of quarter	1.15% of quarter	1.01% of quarter	0.97% of quarter
⊞ Wholesale		$29,391,877.12	$29,950,211.08	$29,380,094.60	$27,109,714.16
		73.79% of quarter	74.51% of quarter	74.09% of quarter	72.67% of quarter

Figure 17-11   *The Wholesale Sales By Month Report preview—completed*

When designing a mobile report, we create layouts for three different display footprints:

▶ Master (full-size screen)
▶ Tablet
▶ Phone

The renderer for mobile reports selects the layout appropriate to the environment each time the report is rendered.

Some of you may be cringing right now as you think about creating three different versions of the layout for every report. If the authoring technique for creating mobile reports was the same as that used to create Reporting Services paginated, you would have a right to be skeptical. However, the goals for these two environments are different, so the report authoring technique is different as well. Give it a try, and I think you will agree it is a breeze to create different layouts of the same report to cater to different footprints.

Mobile Report Publisher

Reporting Services mobile reports are created with a tool called Mobile Report Publisher. Mobile Report Publisher provides a way to quickly and easily create and manage the three layouts created for every report. Its innovative design and ease of use make it a fun tool to work with.

Mobile Report Publisher is available as a free download from Microsoft. You will need to download and install Mobile Report Publisher if you wish to complete the Learn By Doing exercise in this section. You can use the Download button in the header of the Reporting Services web portal, shown in Figure 17-12, to locate and download Mobile Report Publisher. You will need to have a Reporting Services native mode web portal installation available to you to complete the Learn By Doing exercise in this section.

Shared Datasets

Reporting Services mobile reports have a very similar structure to Reporting Services paginated reports. They are made up of data sources, datasets, and report layouts, as shown in Figure 17-13. We have already talked about the fact that paginated reports have a single layout while mobile reports have three layouts for adaptive rendering. The other difference is how the parts and pieces are stored.

Mobile reports do not have a mechanism for storing their own dataset definitions. Instead, they must utilize dataset definitions stored in a separate location. These datasets are created using Report Builder. Consequently, you will need Report Builder available

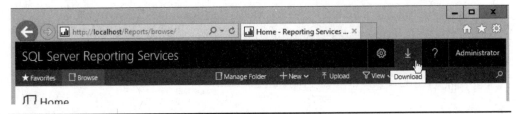

Figure 17-12   *The Reporting Services web portal Download button*

to complete the following Learn By Doing exercise. Report Builder is available as a free download from Microsoft. You can use the Download button in the header of the Reporting Services web portal, shown in Figure 17-12, to locate and download Report Builder.

Creating a Reporting Services Mobile Report

In this Learn By Doing exercise, we will create a mobile report using Reporting Services. This exercise will give you a taste of the mobile report creation process. As with the paginated reports, this is in no way a comprehensive look at the features of Reporting Services mobile reports.

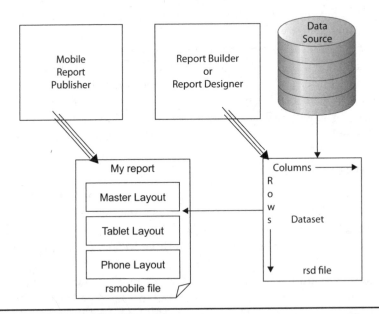

Figure 17-13   *Reporting Services mobile report structure*

Learn By Doing: Creating a Mobile Report

Features Highlighted

▶ Creating a shared dataset

▶ Authoring a mobile report

Business Need   The Maximum Miniatures production manager would like to see production information on his smartphone. He would like to select a product type and see the number accepted and rejected products of each product subtype.

NOTE

Report Builder, Mobile Report Publisher, and a Reporting Services native mode web portal instance are required to complete this Learn By Doing exercise. Remember, don't use a production server for completing training exercises.

Steps to Create a Shared Dataset

1. In your browser, navigate to an instance of the Reporting Services web portal.
2. In the home folder, select New | Folder from the web portal menu. The New Folder dialog box appears.
3. Type **Max Min Reports** for Name, and click Create.
4. Click the entry for the Max Min Reports folder to navigate into that folder.
5. Select New | Folder from the web portal menu. The New Folder dialog box appears.
6. Type **Datasets** for Name, and click Create.
7. Select New | Folder from the web portal menu. The New Folder dialog box appears.
8. Type **Data Sources** for Name, and click Create.
9. Click the entry for the Data Sources folder to navigate into that folder.
10. Select New | Data Source from the web portal menu. The New Data Source page appears.
11. Enter **MaxMinManufacturing** for Name.
12. In the Type drop-down list, select Microsoft SQL Server Analysis Services.
13. Enter the following for Connection string:

    ```
    Data Source={SSAS_Instance};Initial Catalog="Max Min Manufacturing"
    ```

    where *{SSAS_Instance}* is the name of the SQL Server Analysis Services instance where you deployed the MaxMinManufacturing Tabular model.
14. In the Credentials area, select the Using the following credentials option.
15. Enter the appropriate credentials for connecting to this Analysis Services instance.

16. Click Test Connection. If you do not receive the "Connected successfully" message, verify the server instance name and the credentials being used.

17. When the connection tests successfully, click Create.

18. Select New | Dataset from the web portal menu. You will receive a message asking if you would like to run Report Builder.

19. Click the appropriate response to allow this action. The New Report or Dataset dialog box appears with New Dataset preselected.

20. We need to select a data source to use when creating our dataset. Click the Browse other data sources link at the bottom of the dialog box. The Select Data Source dialog box appears.

21. Double-click the Max Min Reports folder.

22. Double-click the Data Sources folder.

23. Select the MaxMinManufacturing data source, and click Open.

24. With the MaxMinManufacturing data source highlighted, click Create.

25. If you are prompted for credentials, enter the appropriate credentials to connect to the MaxMinManufacturing Tabular model and click OK. The query dialog box appears.

26. Expand Measures and the Manufacturing Info folder, and then drag the Accepted Products measure onto the query area. The query executes.

27. Expand the Products table and the Product Hierarchy, and then drag the Product Type attribute onto the query area. This dataset will populate a lookup list of the valid product types. We needed to include the Accepted Products measure in the query in order to generate a result set. The query dialog box appears, as shown in Figure 17-14.

28. Click Save in the upper-left corner of the window. The Save As Dataset dialog box appears.

29. Enter **ProductTypeLookup** for Name.

30. Navigate to the Max Min Reports/Datasets folder.

31. Click OK to exit the Save As Dataset dialog box.

32. Click the File tab of the ribbon and select New from the popup menu. The New Report or Dataset dialog box appears.

33. Select New Dataset.

34. Select the MaxMinManufacturing data source.

35. Click Create. The query dialog box appears.

36. Expand Measures and the Manufacturing Info folder, and then drag the Accepted Products measure onto the query area. The query executes.

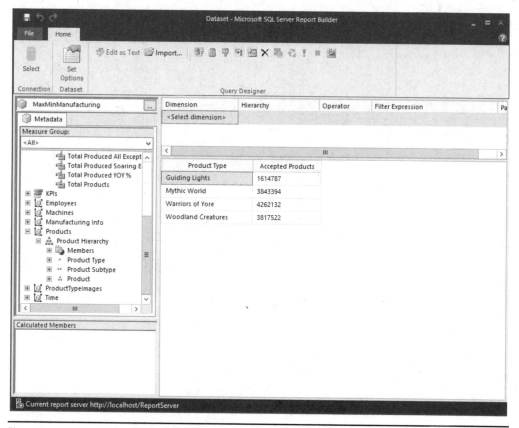

Figure 17-14   *The ProductTypeLookup dataset query*

37. Expand the Products table and the Product Hierarchy, and then drag the Product Type attribute onto the query area.

38. Expand the Machines table and the Plant Hierarchy, and then drag the Plant member of this hierarchy onto the query area. This dataset will populate a lookup list of the valid plants. The query dialog box appears, as shown in Figure 17-15.

39. Click Save in the upper-left corner of the window. The Save As Dataset dialog box appears.

40. Enter **PlantLookup** for Name.

41. Navigate to the Max Min Reports/Datasets folder.

42. Click OK to exit the Save As Dataset dialog box.

43. Click the File tab of the ribbon and select New from the popup menu. The New Report or Dataset dialog box appears.

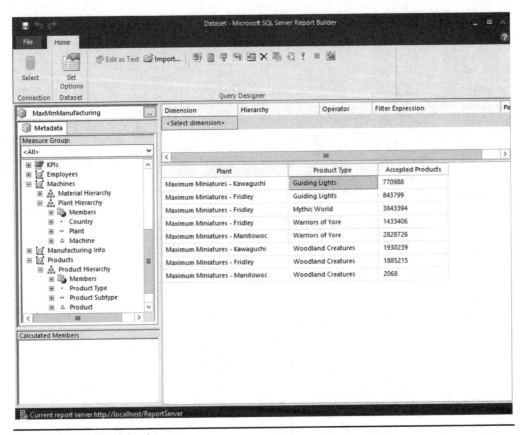

Figure 17-15   *The PlantLookup dataset query*

44. Select New Dataset.

45. Select the MaxMinManufacturing data source.

46. Click Create. The query dialog box appears.

47. Expand Measures and the Manufacturing Info folder, and then drag the Accepted Products measure onto the query area. The query executes.

48. Drag the Rejected Products measure onto the query area.

49. Expand the Machines table and the Plant Hierarchy, and then drag the Plant member of this hierarchy onto the query area.

50. Expand the Products table and the Product Hierarchy, and then drag the Product Type attribute onto the query area.

51. Drag the Product Subtype attribute onto the query area. The query should appear, as shown in Figure 17-16.

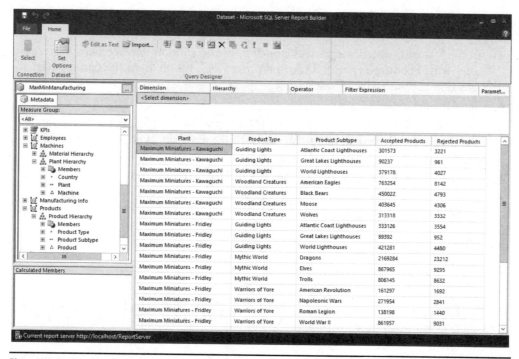

Figure 17-16 *The ManufacturingAnalysis dataset query*

52. Click Save in the upper-left corner of the window. The Save As Dataset dialog box appears.
53. Enter **ManufacturingAnalysis** for Name.
54. Navigate to the Max Min Reports/Datasets folder.
55. Click OK to exit the Save As Dataset dialog box.
56. Close the Report Builder query dialog box.

Steps to Create the Mobile Report Layout

1. Select New | Mobile Report from the web portal menu. You will receive a message asking if you would like to run Mobile Report Publisher.
2. Click the appropriate response to allow this action. Mobile Report Publisher appears with the Layout tab selected.
3. In the Report elements area on the left, under the Navigators heading, click the Selection list and drag it to the upper-left corner of the layout grid. This creates Selection list 1 on the layout grid.

4. Use the sizing handle in the lower-right corner of Selection list 1 to make it one square tall and five squares wide, as shown in Figure 17-17.

5. In the Visual Properties area at the bottom of the window, replace Selection list 1 with **Product Type** for Title and press TAB. This changes the name of the selection list to Product Type.

6. Set Allow multiselect to On.

7. In the Report elements area under the Navigators heading, click the Selection list and drag it to the first square to the right of the Product Type selection list. This creates Selection list 2 on the layout grid.

8. Size Selection list 2 to be one square tall and five squares wide.

9. In the Visual Properties area at the bottom of the window, set the following properties of Selection list 2:

Property	Value
Title	Plant
Allow Multiselect	On

10. In the Report elements area, click the Category chart and drag it to the left-most unoccupied square directly under the Product Type selection list. This creates Category chart 1 on the layout grid.

11. Size Category chart 1 to fill the remainder of the layout grid (four squares tall and ten squares wide).

12. In the Visual Properties area at the bottom of the window, set the following properties of Category chart 1:

Property	Value
Title	Manufacturing
Number format	General
Show legend	On

Your layout should appear as shown in Figure 17-18.

Figure 17-17 *Sizing the Selection list*

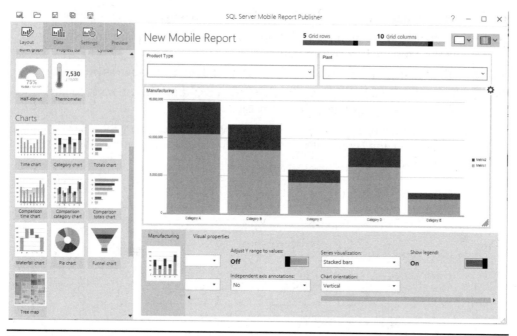

Figure 17-18 *The mobile report Master layout*

13. Use the Layouts drop-down list, shown in Figure 17-19, to select the Tablet layout. The Tablet layout appears. Notice also that only the three report elements included in the Master layout are now available in the Report elements area.

14. In the Report elements area, click the Product Type selection list and drop it in the upper-left square.

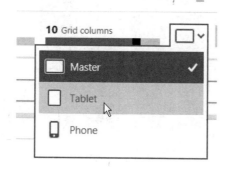

Figure 17-19 *The Layouts drop-down list*

15. Size the Product Type selection list so it is one square tall and six squares wide.

16. Select the Plant selection list and drop it in the left-most square immediately below the Product Type selection list.

17. Size the Plant selection list so it is one square tall and six squares wide.

18. Select the Manufacturing category chart and drop it in the left-most square immediately below the Plant Selection List.

19. Size the Manufacturing category chart to cover the remainder of the layout (six squares tall and six squares wide). Your layout should appear as shown in Figure 17-20.

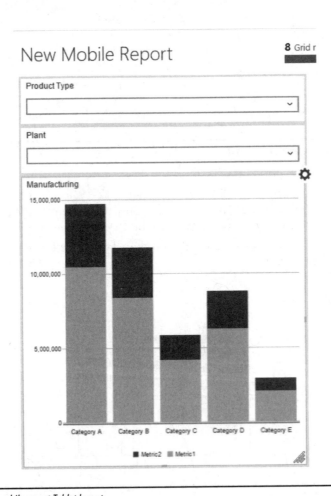

Figure 17-20 *The mobile report Tablet layout*

20. Select Phone from the Layouts drop-down list.
21. Place the report elements on the Phone layout to match Figure 17-21.
22. Click the Save mobile report button in the upper-left corner of the window. The Save mobile report as dialog box appears.
23. Click Save to server. The Save mobile report as dialog box appears.
24. Replace New report name with **Manufacturing Mobile Report**.
25. Click Browse. The content of the Home folder of the web portal appears.
26. Click Max Min Reports.
27. Click Choose folder.
28. Click Save.

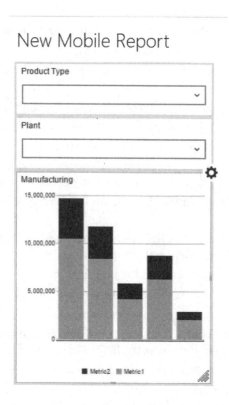

Figure 17-21 *The mobile report Phone layout*

Steps to Add Data to the Report

1. Select the Data tab in the upper-left corner. You can see Mobile Report Publisher created two simulated tables to populate our controls while we created the layout. We now replace those simulated tables with the data from the shared datasets.

2. Click Add data. The Add data dialog box appears.

3. Click Report server. If you have not previously connected to a report server, the Connect to a server dialog box appears. If the Add data from server dialog box appears, skip to Step 8.

4. For server address, enter the URL for the Reporting Services web portal where you saved the shared datasets. You do not need to enter the "http://" portion of the URL.

5. Uncheck Use secure connection if your web portal instance does not support an https connection.

6. Enter appropriate credentials, if necessary.

7. Click Connect. The Add data from server dialog box appears.

8. Click the appropriate server connection item.

9. Click Max Min Reports, if you are not in this folder already.

10. Click Datasets.

11. Click ManufacturingAnalysis. After a moment, you will return to the Data tab of the Manufacturing Mobile Report with the new dataset added.

12. Select the Manufacturing report element on the left.

13. In the properties area across the bottom of the screen, select ManufacturingAnalysis in the drop-down list for the dataset portion of Series name field.

14. Select Product_Subtype in the drop-down list for the field portion of the Series name field.

15. In the drop-down list for the field portion of the Main series, check both Accepted_Products and Rejected_Products.

16. Click Add data. The Add data dialog box appears.

17. Click Report server. The Add data from server dialog box appears.

18. Click the appropriate server connection item.

19. Click PlantLookup. After a moment, you will return to the Data tab of the Manufacturing Mobile Report with the new dataset added.

20. Select the Plant report element on the left.

21. In the properties area across the bottom of the screen, select PlantLookup in the drop-down list for the dataset portion of Keys.

22. Select Plant in the drop-down list for the field portion of Keys.

23. Select Plant in the drop-down list for the field portion of Labels.

24. Under Filter these datasets when a selection is made, check ManufacturingAnalysis.
25. Ensure Plant is selected in the drop-down list next to ManufacturingAnalysis.
26. Click Add data. The Add data dialog box appears.
27. Click Report server. The Add data from server dialog box appears.
28. Click the appropriate server connection item.
29. Click ProductTypeLookup. After a moment, you will return to the Data tab of the Manufacturing Mobile Report with the new dataset added.
30. Select the Product Type report element on the left.
31. In the properties area across the bottom of the screen, select ProductTypeLookup in the drop-down list for the dataset portion of Keys.
32. Ensure Product_Type is selected in the drop-down list for the field portion of Keys. Ensure Product_Type is selected in the drop-down list for the field portion of Labels.
33. Under Filter these datasets when a selection is made, check ManufacturingAnalysis.
34. Select Product_Type from the drop-down list next to ManufacturingAnalysis.
35. Also check PlantLookup.
36. Ensure Product_type is selected in the drop-down list next to PlantLookup.
37. Select the Plant report element.
38. Click the Options button next to the Keys property drop-down lists in the properties area at the bottom of the window. You may need to scroll right to see this button. The Options popup appears.
39. Check the Filtered by: Product Type check box.
40. Click Done. The Data tab appears, as shown in Figure 17-22.
41. Click Save mobile report.

Steps to Preview the Mobile Report

1. Click Preview. Because we last had the Phone layout selected, the preview of the phone layout appears.
2. Select Mythic World in the Product Type drop-down list.
3. Click outside the drop-down list to close it.
4. Expand the Plant drop-down list. Only one plant, Fridley, manufactures the Mythic World product type. Select the Fridley plant. The Phone preview appears, as shown in Figure 17-23.
5. Click the left arrow in the upper left of the window to exit preview mode.
6. Select the Layout tab.
7. Select the Master layout.

Figure 17-22 *The Manufacturing Mobile report Data tab*

8. Click Preview.
9. Select Guiding Lights and Warriors of Yore from the Product Type drop-down list.
10. Select the Kawaguchi and Manitowoc plants from the Plant drop-down list. The Master preview appears, as shown in Figure 17-24.
11. Click Save mobile report.
12. Close the Mobile Report Publisher.

Reporting Services Key Performance Indicators

Also new in SQL Server 2016 Reporting Services is the ability to create Key Performance Indicators (KPIs) right within the Reporting Services web portal. Using these KPIs, we can create a dashboard for our organizations in the same interface where users come to execute reports. This means users can gain information about the performance of key metrics without having to execute a single report.

As with mobile reports, the web portal KPIs rely on shared datasets for their data. We can even use the same shared dataset to populate a mobile report and a KPI should they have the right data overlap. That is, after all, what sharing is all about.

KPIs are created within a browser window that is part of the web portal user interface. No additional tool to download for this one. Well, you will need Report Builder to create shared datasets, but we already have that in place

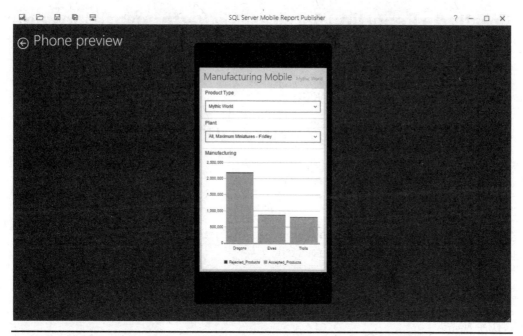

Figure 17-23 *The Phone preview of the Manufacturing Mobile report*

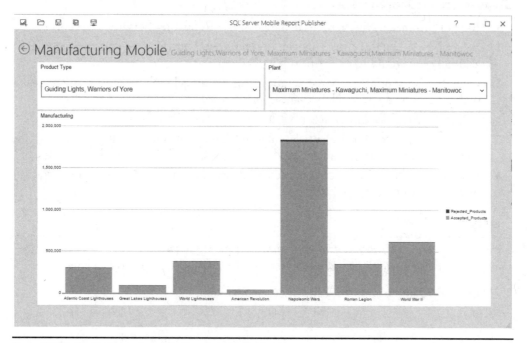

Figure 17-24 *The Master preview of the Manufacturing Mobile report*

Creating a Reporting Services Key Performance Indicator

In this Learn By Doing exercise, we will create a KPI in the Reporting Services web portal. This exercise will give you an introduction to the KPI creation process. Even though KPIs are pretty straightforward, this is not a comprehensive look at the features of Reporting Services web portal KPIs.

Learn By Doing: Creating a Web Portal KPI

Feature Highlighted

▶ Creating a web portal KPI

Business Need The Maximum Miniatures production manager would like to see a KPI based on percent of product rejected.

NOTE

Report Builder and a Reporting Services native mode web portal instance are required to complete this Learn By Doing exercise.

Steps to Create Shared Datasets

1. In your browser, navigate to an instance of the Reporting Services web portal.
2. Select New | Dataset from the web portal menu. You will receive a message asking if you would like to run Report Builder.
3. Click the appropriate response to allow this action. The New Report or Dataset dialog box appears with New Dataset preselected.
4. Select the MaxMinManufacturing data source and click Create.
5. If you are prompted for credentials, enter the appropriate credentials to connect to the MaxMinManufacturing Tabular model and click OK. The query dialog box appears.
6. Expand KPIs and the Percent Rejected KPI, and then drag the Value onto the query area. The query executes.

NOTE

We do not have to use a KPI from the data model when creating a web portal KPI. However, we may as well use it after taking the time to create it. We will take advantage of the fact the KPI has a goal already assigned to it.

7. Drag Goal and Status onto the query area as well.

8. In the filter area, click "<Select dimension>" and click the drop-down arrow that appears.

9. Select Time from the drop-down list.

10. Click under the Hierarchy heading in the same row and click the drop-down arrow that appears.

11. Select Date Hierarchy.

12. Click under Operator in the same row and the Equal entry appears.

13. Click under Filter Expression in the same row, and click the drop-down arrow that appears.

14. Expand the All entry.

15. Expand the 2015 entry.

16. Expand the 2015-Q4 entry.

17. Check 2015-12 to select December 2015.

18. Click OK. The query now shows the percent rejected in December 2015, as shown in Figure 17-25.

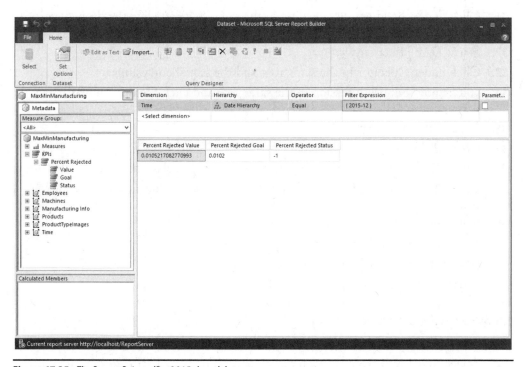

Figure 17-25 *The PercentRejectedDec2015 shared dataset*

19. Click Save in the upper-left corner of the window. The Save As Dataset dialog box appears.

20. Enter **PercentRejectedDec2015** for Name.

21. Navigate to the Max Min Reports/Datasets folder.

22. Click OK to exit the Save As Dataset dialog box.

23. Click the File tab of the ribbon and select New from the popup menu. The New Report or Dataset dialog box appears.

24. Select New Dataset.

25. Select the MaxMinManufacturing data source.

26. Click Create. The query dialog box appears.

27. Expand KPIs and the Percent Rejected KPI, and then drag the Value onto the query area. The query executes.

28. Expand the Time table and the Date Hierarchy, and then drag the Month attribute onto the query area.

29. In the filter area, click "<Select dimension>" and click the drop-down arrow that appears.

30. Select Time from the drop-down list.

31. Click under the Hierarchy heading in the same row and click the drop-down arrow that appears.

32. Select Date Hierarchy.

33. Click under Operator in the same row, and the Equal entry appears.

34. Click under Filter Expression in the same row and click the drop-down arrow that appears.

35. Expand the All entry.

36. Check 2015.

37. Click OK. The query shows the percent rejected for each of the months of 2015.

38. Click Save in the upper-left corner of the window. The Save As Dataset dialog box appears.

39. Enter **PercentRejected2015** for Name.

40. Navigate to the Max Min Reports/Datasets folder.

41. Click OK to exit the Save As Dataset dialog box.

42. Close the Report Builder query dialog box.

Steps to Create a Web Portal KPI

1. Navigate to the Max Min Reports folder in the web portal.

2. Select New | KPI from the web portal menu. The New KPI page appears.

3. Enter **Percent Rejected** for KPI Name.

4. Select Percent with decimals from the Value format drop-down list.

5. Select Dataset field from the Value drop-down list.

6. Click the ellipsis (...) button for Pick dataset field next to Value. The Choose a Dataset dialog box appears.

7. Navigate to the Max Min Reports/Datasets folder.

8. Select PercentRejectedDec2015. The Choose a Field from PercentRejectedDec2015 dialog box appears.

9. Select the Percent_Rejected_Value option.

10. Click OK to exit the Choose a Field from PercentRejectedDec2015 dialog box.

11. Select Dataset field from the Goal drop-down list.

12. Click the ellipsis (...) button for Pick dataset field next to Goal. The Choose a dataset dialog box appears.

13. Navigate to the Max Min Reports/Datasets folder.

14. Select PercentRejectedDec2015. The Choose a Field from PercentRejectedDec2015 dialog box appears.

15. Select the Percent_Rejected_Goal option.

16. Click OK to exit the Choose a Field from PercentRejectedDec2015 dialog box.

17. Select Dataset field from the Status drop-down list.

18. Click the ellipsis (...) button for Pick dataset field next to Status. The Choose a Dataset dialog box appears.

19. Navigate to the Max Min Reports/Datasets folder.

20. Select PercentRejectedDec2015. The Choose a Field from PercentRejectedDec2015 dialog box appears.

21. Select the Percent_Rejected_Status_ option.

22. Click OK to exit the Choose a Field from PercentRejectedDec2015 dialog box.

23. Select Dataset trend from the Trend set drop-down list.

24. Click the ellipsis (...) button for Pick dataset trend next to Trend set. The Choose a Dataset dialog box appears.

25. Navigate to the Max Min Reports/Datasets folder.

26. Select PercentRejected2015. The Choose a trend from PercentRejected2015 dialog box appears.

27. Select the Percent_Rejected_Value option.

28. Click OK to exit the Choose a trend from PercentRejected2015 dialog box. The New KPI page appears, as shown in Figure 17-26. Our trend bar is flat because the differences in our rejection percents are very small.

29. Click Create to create the KPI. The KPI appears in the Max Min Reports folder, as shown in Figure 17-27.

30. Close the browser you are using to access the Reporting Services web portal.

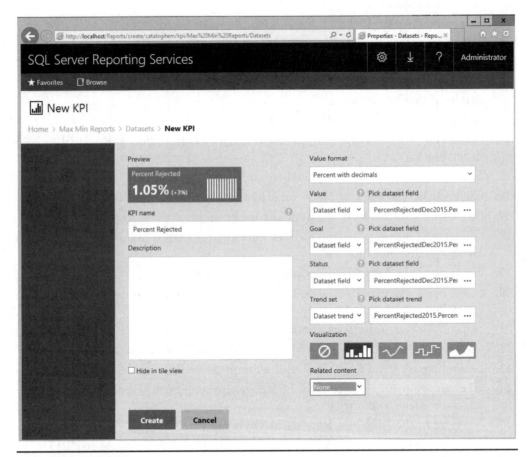

Figure 17-26   *The New KPI page*

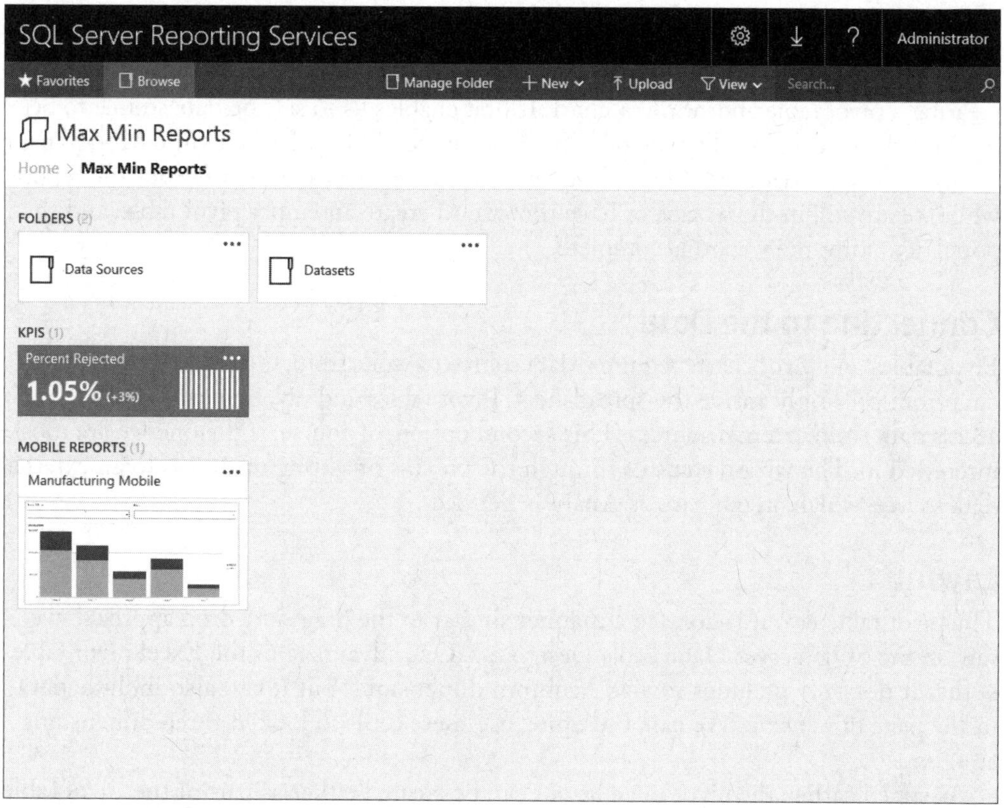

Figure 17-27 *The Percent Rejected KPI*

Excel

Most business decision makers are comfortable with the applications that make up Microsoft Office. Spreadsheets were some of the first tools for doing what we now call ad hoc analysis and reporting. In almost every organization, decision makers depend heavily on spreadsheets as data repositories and tools for analysis. Wouldn't it make sense to allow our business intelligence information to be incorporated and manipulated in this comfortable and ubiquitous environment as well? Microsoft provides us the means to do this in Excel with the PivotTable and PivotChart Wizard.

Creating Pivot Tables and Pivot Charts

The PivotTable and PivotChart Wizard takes us step by step through the process of creating a pivot table and/or pivot chart. It first enables us to set the data source to be used for the pivot items. Fortunately, the data source can be a BI Semantic Model in an Analysis Services database. Once the data source is set, we can either lay out the report while we are still in the wizard or have the wizard create an empty pivot table, and then populate it after the wizard is complete.

Connecting to the Data

Pivot tables and pivot charts require a data source to work from. One option is to use data from cells right inside the spreadsheet. Pivot tables and pivot charts can also access data from external sources. This second option, of course, is the one we are most interested in. The wizard steps us through the process of setting up access to an external data source, which, in our case, is Analysis Services.

Layout

The pivot table layout is done in a manner similar to the drag-and-drop approach we saw on the SQL Server Data Tools Design tab. One advantage of the Excel pivot table is that it not only includes row and column dimensions, but it can also include data in the page dimension. We can, therefore, use these tools to look at three dimensions at a time.

As stated earlier, the pivot table layout can be created either as part of the PivotTable and PivotChart Wizard or after the wizard completes. In most cases, the layout is created after exiting the wizard. Waiting until after the wizard is complete provides a cleaner and more capable report creation environment. The one time we may want to create the layout in the wizard is in a situation where the underlying data has gotten large and unwieldy. By creating the layout in the wizard, we can specify a field to serve as the page grouping. Once this is done, data is retrieved one page at a time, eliminating the need to retrieve the entire data set before displaying results.

Learn By Doing: Creating an Excel Pivot Table

Feature Highlighted

► Creating a pivot table in Microsoft Excel

Business Need The vice president (VP) of production for Maximum Miniatures, Incorporated would like to do some of his own analysis of the information in the Max

Min Manufacturing DM cube. He is a big Excel user and is comfortable with this program. To fulfill the VP's needs, we show him how to create a pivot table in Excel, pulling data from the MaxMinManufacturingDM cube.

> **NOTE**
>
> *Pivot tables can be created in Excel 2003 and later. Excel 2016 was used for the Learn By Doing exercises in this chapter.*

Steps to Create the Connection to a Cube on Analysis Services

1. Open Microsoft Excel. If asked, create a new blank workbook.
2. Select the Insert ribbon and click the PivotTable icon, as shown in Figure 17-28. The Create PivotTable dialog box appears.
3. Select the Use an external data source option to use data from outside the workbook, as shown in Figure 17-29.
4. Click Choose Connection. The Existing Connections dialog box appears.
5. Click Browse for More. The Select Data Source dialog box appears.
6. Click New Source. The Data Connection Wizard dialog box appears.
7. Select Microsoft SQL Server Analysis Services from the list of data source types, as shown in Figure 17-30.
8. Click Next. The Connect to Database Server page of the Data Connection Wizard appears.
9. Enter the name of the Analysis Services server hosting the MaxMinManufacturingDM database.
10. Enter the appropriate credentials for accessing this server. The Connect to Database Server page of the wizard appears, as shown in Figure 17-31.
11. Click Next. The Select Database and Table page of the Data Connection Wizard appears.

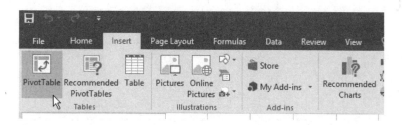

Figure 17-28 *Creating a pivot table in Excel*

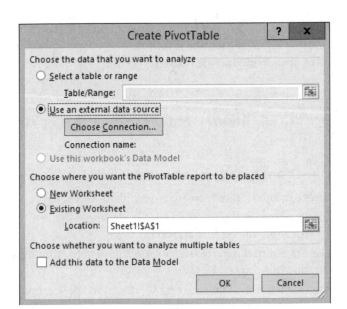

Figure 17-29   *The Create PivotTable dialog box*

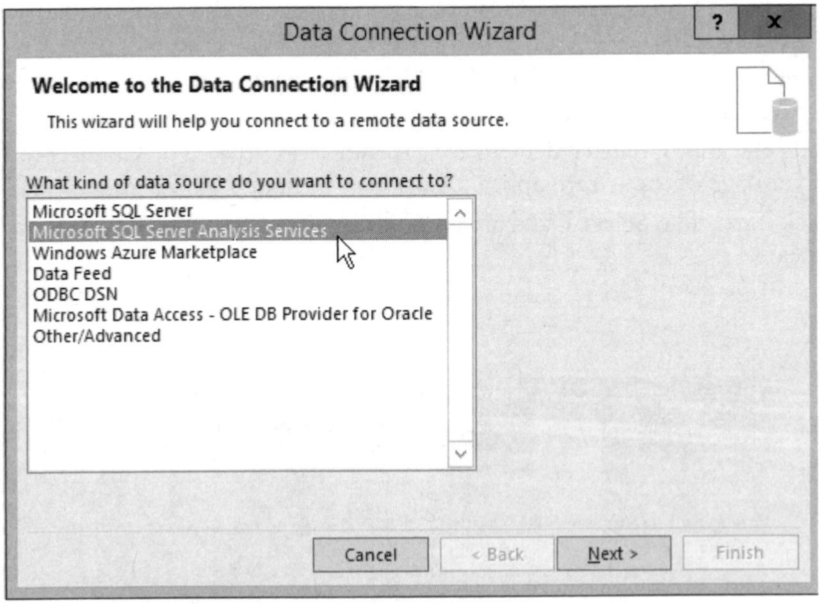

Figure 17-30   *The Data Connection Wizard dialog box*

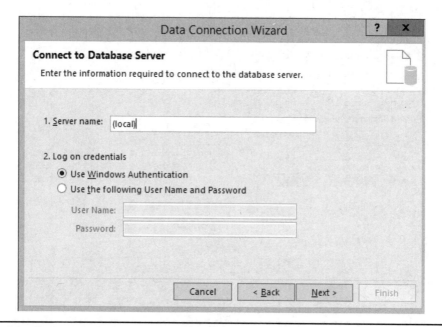

Figure 17-31   *The Connect to Database Server page of the Data Connection Wizard*

12. Select MaxMinManufacturingDM from the database drop-down list, if it is not selected by default.

13. Select the Max Min Manufacturing DM cube from the list of cubes and perspectives. The Select Database and Table page of the wizard appears, as shown in Figure 17-32.

14. Click Next. The Save Data Connection File and Finish page of the Data Connection Wizard appears, as shown in Figure 17-33.

15. Enter a description of the data source and click Finish. We return to the Create PivotTable dialog box.

16. Click OK to exit the Create PivotTable dialog box. An empty pivot table is created, as shown in Figure 17-34.

NOTE

In this example, we queried data from one of our Multidimensional BI Semantic Models. We can use a similar approach to connect to a Tabular instance of SQL Server Analysis Services and query data from our Tabular BI Semantic Model for use in a PivotTable or PivotChart.

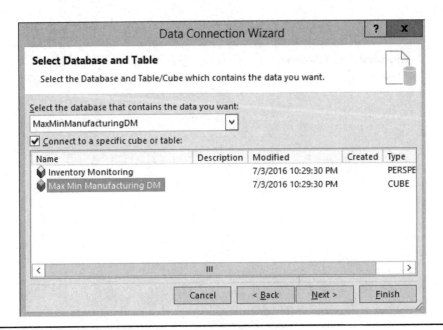

Figure 17-32 *The Select Database and Table page of the Data Connection Wizard*

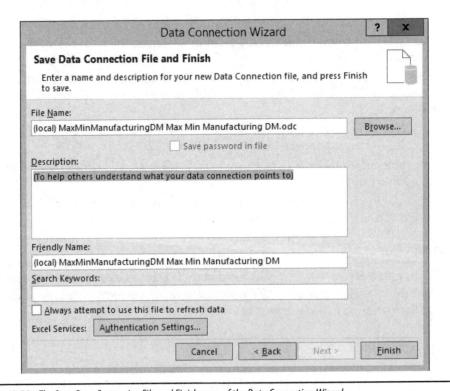

Figure 17-33 *The Save Data Connection File and Finish page of the Data Connection Wizard*

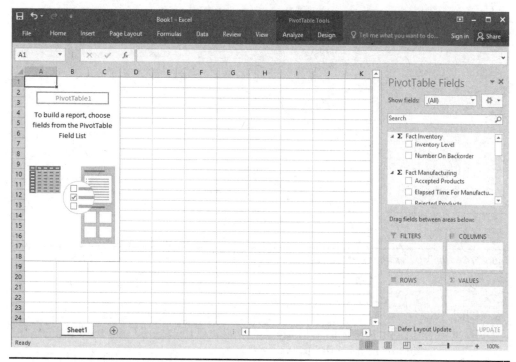

Figure 17-34 *The empty pivot table layout in the Excel spreadsheet*

Steps to Create the PivotTable Layout

1. In the PivotTable Fields List, locate the Date Hierarchy. Drag the Date Hierarchy and drop it on the Filters area. This creates a report filter in the upper-left corner of the spreadsheet, as shown in Figure 17-35.

2. Click the filter (funnel) icon next to 2015 in the upper-left corner of the spreadsheet.

3. Check the Select Multiple Items check box. We can now select multiple dimension members.

4. Expand the 2015 item in the list.

5. Uncheck the 2015Q3 and 2015Q4 items in the list. The Date Hierarchy drop-down window appears, as shown in Figure 17-36.

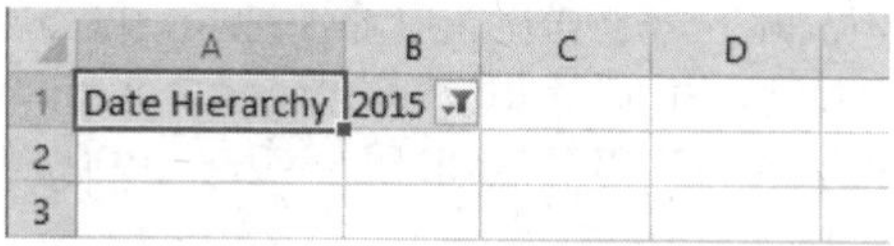

	A	B	C	D
1	Date Hierarchy	2015 ⊤		
2				
3				

Figure 17-35 *A filter added to the pivot table layout*

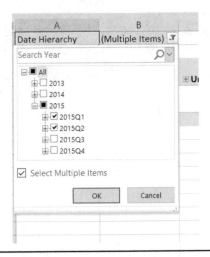

Figure 17-36 *The Date Hierarchy report filter*

6. Click OK.

7. In the PivotTable Fields List, locate the Product Hierarchy. Drag the Product Hierarchy and drop it on the Rows area.

8. Rows are created in the pivot table for the highest level in the hierarchy, the Product Type. Click the drop-down arrow next to Row Labels. The Row Labels drop-down menu appears.

9. Uncheck the Warriors of Yore and Woodland Creatures items. The Row Labels drop-down window is shown in Figure 17-37.

10. Click OK.

11. In the PivotTable Fields List, locate the Plant Hierarchy. Drag the Plant Hierarchy and drop it on the Columns area. Columns are created for the highest level of the Plant Hierarchy, which is the Country level.

12. In the PivotTable Fields List, locate the Accepted Products measure. Drag the Accepted Products measure and drop it on the Values area. The Accepted Products measure is added to the pivot table, as shown in Figure 17-38. When a pivot table includes a single measure, the label for that measure appears in the upper-left corner of the pivot table.

13. Drag the Rejected Products measure and drop it in the area where you dropped the Accepted Products measure. Both measures are included in the layout. The labels for the measures are now at the top of each column, as shown in Figure 17-39.

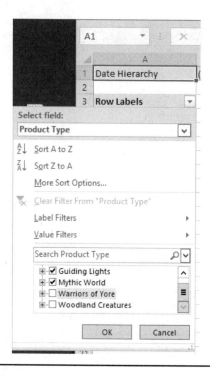

Figure 17-37 *The Row Labels drop-down window*

14. Now that we are done placing items on the layout, we can close the PivotTable Fields List window. We can close the window or click the Field List button under the Show drop-down in the Analyze ribbon, as shown in Figure 17-40. We can bring back the PivotTable Field List window by clicking this ribbon button a second time.

15. Select one of the cells containing the Accepted Products measure label. Change the text to # **Accepted**. When we exit the modified cell, all occurrences of the measure label are changed.

16. Change the Rejected Products measure label to # **Rejected**. The completed pivot table appears, as shown in Figure 17-41.

17. Save the workbook in an appropriate location.

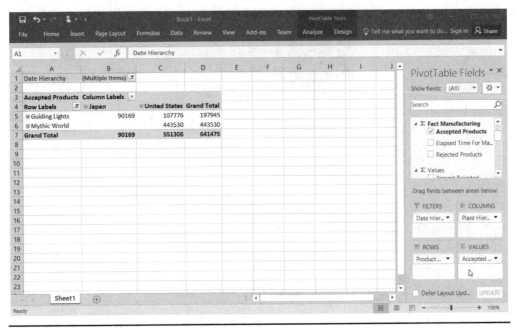

Figure 17-38   *A pivot table with a single measure*

Pivot Chart

Now that we have seen how to work with pivot tables, let's try a pivot chart.

Learn By Doing: Creating a Pivot Chart

Feature Highlighted

▶   Creating a pivot chart in Microsoft Excel

Business Need   Our intrepid VP of production is extremely happy with the information he has been able to discover using the pivot table in Excel. Now, he would like to create a chart from this information to use at an upcoming presentation. We can show him how to create a pivot chart in Excel.

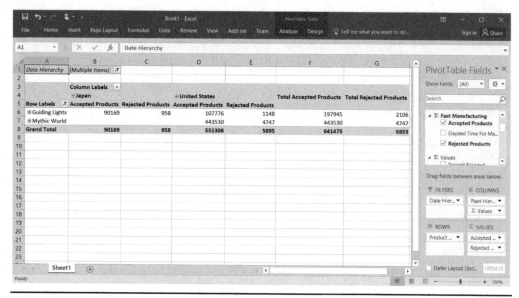

Figure 17-39 *A pivot table with multiple measures*

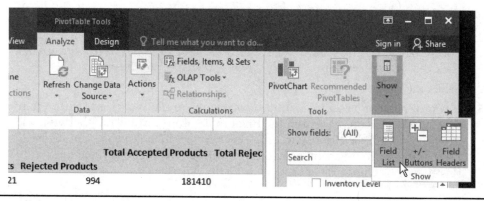

Figure 17-40 *The Field List button in the Options ribbon*

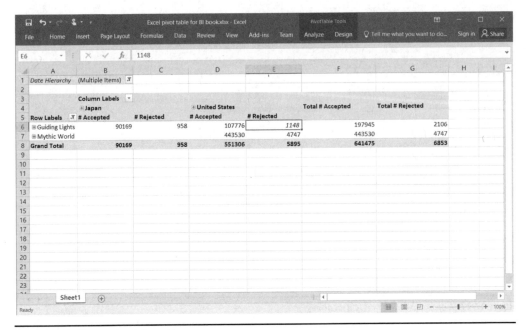

Figure 17-41 *The completed pivot table*

Steps to Create a Pivot Chart Layout

1. If the Excel workbook file used in the previous Learn By Doing exercise has a Sheet2 tab, select the Sheet2 tab. If that workbook does not have a Sheet2 tab, click the New Sheet button to add a new spreadsheet to the workbook.

2. Select the Insert ribbon.

3. If your version of Excel has a drop-down arrow on the PivotTable button in the ribbon, select PivotChart from the PivotTable drop-down list. Otherwise, select PivotChart from the PivotChart drop-down in the ribbon, as shown in Figure 17-42. Depending on your version of Excel, you will see a dialog box titled Create PivotChart or Create PivotTable with PivotChart.

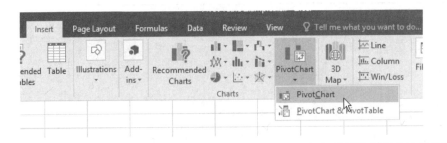

Figure 17-42 *Creating a pivot chart*

4. Select the Use an external data source option to use data from outside the workbook and click Choose Connection. The Existing Connections dialog box appears.

5. Select the connection to the Analysis Services MaxMinManufacturingDM database you created in the previous Learn By Doing exercise.

6. Click Open to return to the previous dialog box.

7. Click OK to exit the dialog box. An empty pivot chart is created, as shown in Figure 17-43. If the field list is not visible on the right, select Field List in the Analyze tab of the ribbon.

NOTE

In older versions of Excel, a pivot table will be visible along with the pivot chart.

8. In the Pivot Chart Fields List, locate the Plant Hierarchy. Drag the Plant Hierarchy and drop it on the Filters area.

9. Expand the Plant Hierarchy drop-down window in the upper-left corner of the spreadsheet or chart—wherever it appears in your version of Excel.

10. Expand the All entry, and then expand the United States entry.

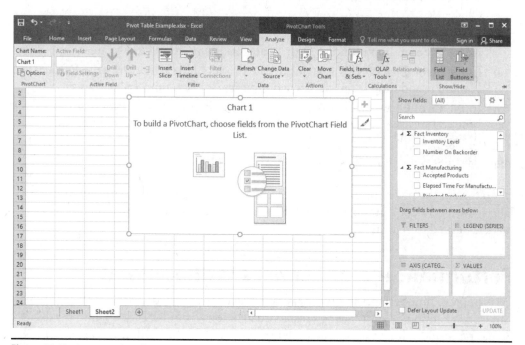

Figure 17-43 *An empty pivot chart*

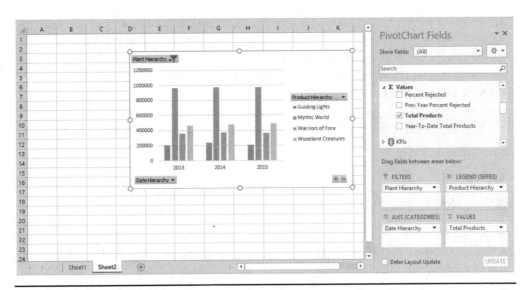

Figure 17-44 *A pivot chart*

11. Select the Maximum Miniatures—Fridley entry.

12. Click OK.

13. In the Pivot Chart Fields List, locate the Date Hierarchy. Drag the Date Hierarchy and drop it on the "Axis (Categories)" or "Row Labels" area.

14. In the Pivot Chart Fields List, locate the Product Hierarchy. Drag the Product Hierarchy and drop it on the "Legend (Series)" or "Column Labels" area.

15. In the Pivot Chart Fields List, locate the Total Products measure. Drag the Total Products measure and drop it on the Values area. The chart should appear, similar to Figure 17-44.

16. Save the workbook and close Excel.

To format the pivot chart, select a section of the chart you want to format: the axis labels, the legend, or a graph area itself. Right-click and use the context menu to carry out the desired formatting.

PerformancePoint Services in SharePoint

PerformancePoint Services is a business intelligence tool provided as part of SharePoint Enterprise Edition. It allows us to create visualizations from KPIs defined in our BI Semantic Models. It also allows us to define new KPIs to be used in visualizations. The KPI visualizations can then be incorporated into scorecards and dashboards.

The features of PerformancePoint Services are accessed through a site collection created using the Business Intelligence Center template. A Business Intelligence Center SharePoint site provides access to the Dashboard Designer. Using the Dashboard Designer, we can create scorecards and dashboards to display our KPIs. Look for additional information about PerformancePoint Services in books covering SharePoint.

NOTE

Microsoft appears to be putting its resources into developing and enhancing other platforms for creating dashboard content. PerformancePoint has not had any significant enhancements in a number of years. Something to keep in mind when making a tool selection. The processes in this section of the book were completed with SharePoint 2010.

Creating a Site Collection Using the Business Intelligence Center Template

For our work with PerformancePoint in this chapter, we use a SharePoint site with a site collection created from the Business Intelligence Center template. You can follow the directions in the next Learn By Doing exercise to create this site collection. You will need access to SharePoint Central Administration and rights to create a site collection on the SharePoint server. As always, do not complete these exercises on a production server.

Learn By Doing: Preparing SharePoint to Allow the Use of PerformancePoint Services

Features Highlighted

▶ Creating a site collection using the Business Intelligence Center template

▶ Configuring PerformancePoint Services

Business Need   Maximum Miniatures would like to create dashboards using PerformancePoint Services. We need to perform the appropriate installations and customization to get PerformancePoint Services up and running.

Steps to Create the Site Collection Using the Business Intelligence Center Template

1. Open SharePoint Central Administration.
2. Click Application Management on the left side of the page. The Application Management page appears.

3. Under the Site Collections heading, click the Create site collections link. The Create Site Collection page appears.

4. Enter an appropriate title and description for the site collection.

5. Complete the URL for the site collection. Make note of this URL so you can navigate to the site collection later.

6. In the Select a template area, select the Enterprise tab, and then select the Business Intelligence Center template, as shown in Figure 17-45.

7. Enter the user name of the Primary Site Collection Administrator.

8. Click OK to create the site collection.

Steps to Configure PerformancePoint Services

1. Click OK.

2. Click the Central Administration heading on the left side of the page.

3. Under the Application Management heading, click the Manage service applications link. The Service Applications page appears.

4. Click Application Management on the left side of the page. The Application Management page appears.

5. Click New in the ribbon. A drop-down menu appears.

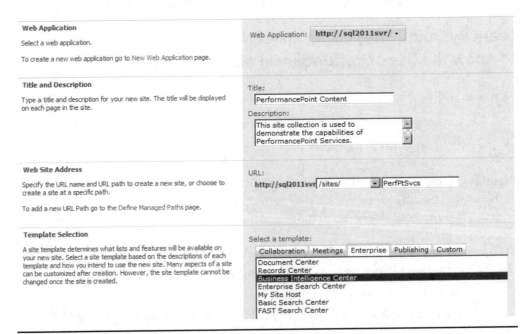

Figure 17-45 *Creating a site collection using the Business Intelligence Center template*

6. Select PerformancePoint Service Application from the drop-down menu. The New PerformancePoint Service Application page appears.

7. Enter **PPS Service App BI Book** for Name.

8. Check the "Add this service application's proxy to the farm's default proxy list" check box.

9. Scroll down to the Application Pool section.

10. Select the Create new application pool radio button, if it is not already selected.

11. Enter **PPSServiceAppPool** for Application pool name.

12. The Configurable radio button should be selected under "Select a security account for this application pool."

13. Select an appropriate domain account from the Configurable drop-down list or use the "Register new managed account" to specify another domain account to be used by this application pool.

14. Click Create to create the PerformancePoint Services service application.

15. Click OK after the service application is successfully completed. You will be taken to a list of service applications.

16. Scroll down and click the entry for the "PPS Service App BI Book" service application we just created. The Manage PerformancePoint Services: PPS Service App BI Book page appears.

17. Select PerformancePoint Service Application Settings. The PerformancePoint Service Application Settings page appears.

18. Enter a domain user name and password for the Unattended Service Account, as shown in Figure 17-46. These credentials are used to authenticate to PerformancePoint data sources. Therefore, this domain account must be granted access rights to those data sources.

19. Click OK to save your changes to the PerformancePoint Services configuration.

20. Click the System Settings link on the left side of the page. The Systems Settings page appears.

21. Under the Servers heading, click the Manage services on server link. The Services on Server page appears.

22. Scroll down and make sure both the PerformancePoint Service and the Secure Store Service are started. If either is not started, click the link to start that service.

Creating a Dashboard Using PerformancePoint Services

Now that we have PerformancePoint Services activated and configured on our SharePoint 2010 Enterprise site, we can give it a try. We create a new KPI based on the number of items on backorder. Then we combine this with a chart to create a simple dashboard.

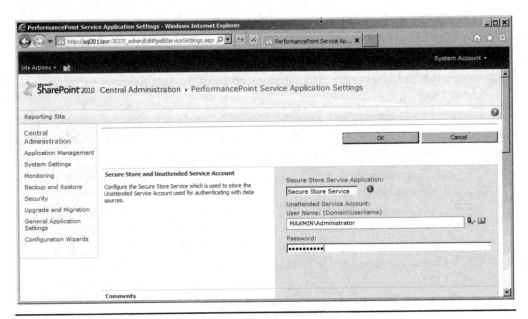

Figure 17-46 *Configuring PerformancePoint Services*

Learn By Doing: Creating KPIs and a Dashboard Using PerformancePoint Services

Features Highlighted

- ▶ Creating a KPI using PerformancePoint Services
- ▶ Creating a dashboard using PerformancePoint Services

Business Need The operations manager at Maximum Miniatures would like a dashboard with a KPI showing items on backorder along with a chart showing the number of products accepted by product type for the past three years. The KPI and the chart need to be created using PerformancePoint Services.

Steps to Defining a Data Connection

1. Navigate to the site you created from the Business Intelligence Center template. The main page of this site should appear, as shown in Figure 17-47.
2. Click the PerformancePoint Content link on the left side of the page. The PerformancePoint Content library appears.

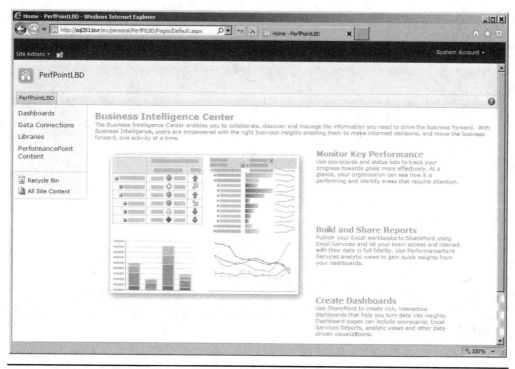

Figure 17-47 *The main page of the Business Intelligence Center SharePoint site*

3. Click the Add new item link. The first time you do this, the Dashboard Designer application will download and install. If prompted to run the Dashboard Designer application, click Run. The Dashboard Designer will appear, as shown in Figure 17-48.

4. In the Workspace Browser, select the Data Connections item.

5. Select the Create tab of the ribbon and click Data Source. The Select a Data Source Template dialog box appears, as shown in Figure 17-49.

6. Select the Analysis Services template, if it is not already selected, and click OK.

7. A new data source appears in the Workspace Browser area. The center of the screen allows you to fill in the details for this new data source. Replace "New Data Source" with **MaxMinManufacturingDM** for the name of the data source.

8. For Server, enter the name of the server where the Max Min Manufacturing DM cube was deployed.

9. Select MaxMinManufacturingDM from the Database drop-down list.

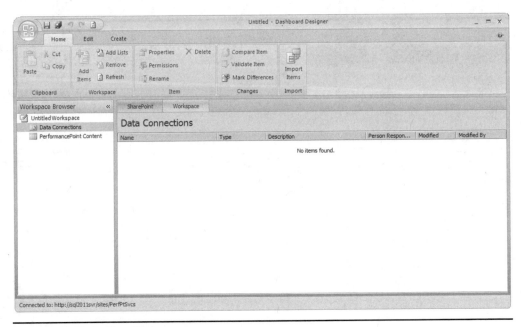

Figure 17-48 *The Dashboard Designer*

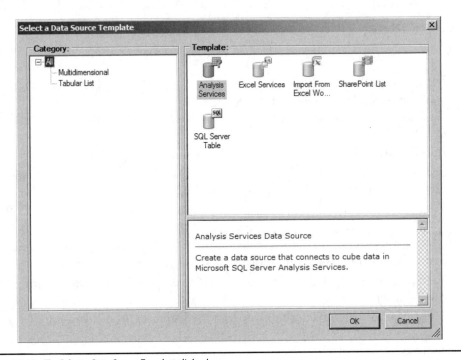

Figure 17-49 *The Select a Data Source Template dialog box*

10. Select Max Min Manufacturing DM from the Cube drop-down list. The Dashboard Designer should appear similar to Figure 17-50.

11. Click the Save button in the upper-left corner of the Dashboard Designer.

Steps to Create a KPI

1. In the Workspace Browser, select the PerformancePoint Content item.

2. Click KPI on the Create tab of the ribbon. The Select a KPI Template dialog box appears, as shown in Figure 17-51.

3. Select Blank KPI, if it is not already selected, and click OK.

4. A new KPI appears in the Workspace Browser area. The center of the screen allows you to fill in the details for this new KPI. Replace "New KPI" with **Backorder KPI**.

5. Click the link in the first row under the Data Mappings column. This is the Actual row. The Fixed Values Data Source Mapping dialog box appears.

6. Click Change Source. The Select a Data Source dialog box appears.

7. Select the MaxMinManufacturingDM Analysis Services data source, as shown in Figure 17-52.

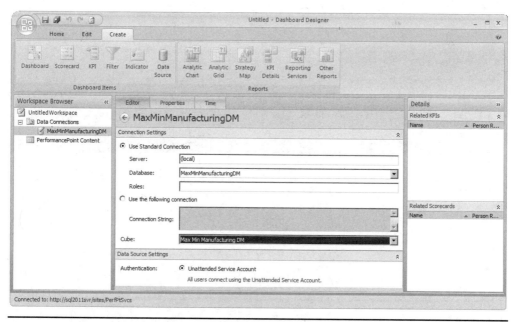

Figure 17-50 *The Dashboard Designer with a new data connection*

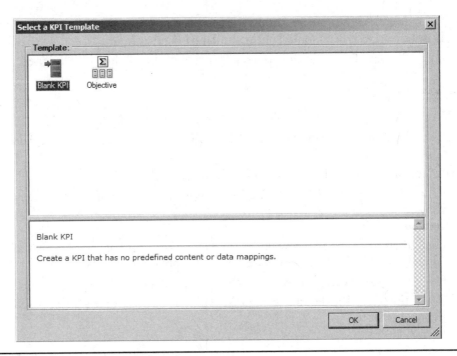

Figure 17-51   *The Select a KPI Template dialog box*

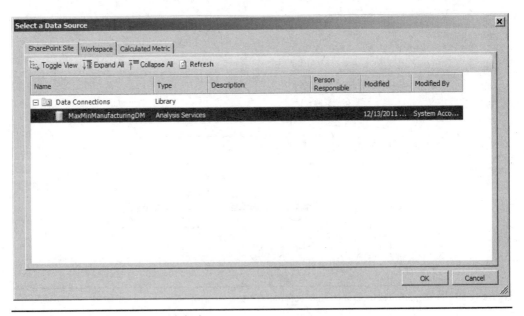

Figure 17-52   *The Select a Data Source dialog box*

8. Click OK. The Fixed Values Data Source Mapping dialog box has changed to the Dimensional Data Source Mapping dialog box.

9. Check the Use MDX tuple formula check box.

10. Enter the following in the formula area:

```
ABS(ROUND([Number On Backorder] /
    COUNT(DESCENDANTS([Product Hierarchy].CurrentMember,
                [Product Hierarchy].[Product])), 0))
```

This MDX expression takes the number on backorder for a given product type, product subtype, or product and divides it by the number of products in that grouping. This gives the average amount on backorder for the grouping. The expression rounds the result to a whole number because you can't really have half of a product on backorder. It also takes the absolute value of the backorder amount to allow us to deal with positive numbers in the KPI. The Dimensional Data Source Mapping dialog box should appear, as shown in Figure 17-53.

11. Click OK.

12. Click the link in the second row under the Data Mappings column. This is the Target row. The Fixed Values Data Source Mapping dialog box appears.

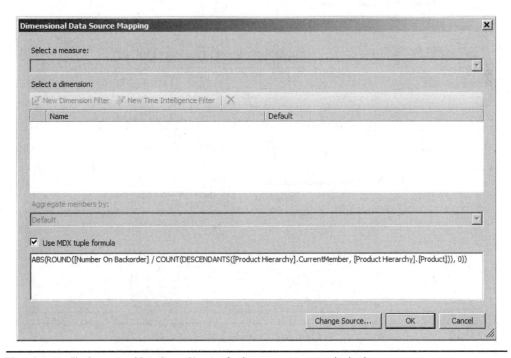

Figure 17-53   *The Dimensional Data Source Mapping for the average amount on backorder*

13. Replace 1 with **600**.

14. Click OK.

15. In the Thresholds area, click the Set Scoring Pattern and Indicator button. The Select the Scoring Pattern page of the Edit Banding Settings dialog box appears. (If the Thresholds area is not visible, click anywhere in the Target row.)

16. Select Decreasing is Better from the Scoring pattern drop-down list. The dialog box should appear, as shown in Figure 17-54.

17. Click Next. The Select an Indicator page of the Edit Banding Settings dialog box appears.

18. Leave the default settings and click Next. The Specify the worst value page of the Edit Banding Settings dialog box appears.

19. Leave the default setting and click Finish. The Dashboard Designer should appear similar to Figure 17-55.

20. Click Save.

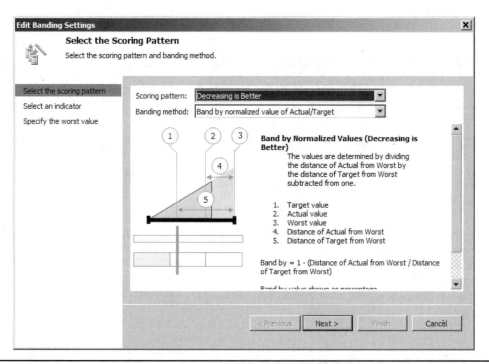

Figure 17-54 *The Select the Scoring Pattern page of the Edit Banding Settings dialog box*

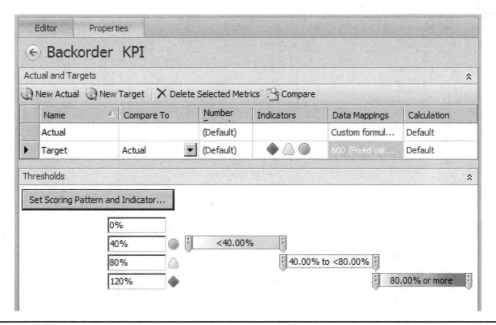

Figure 17-55 *The Dashboard Designer with a new KPI*

Steps to Create a Scorecard Using a PerformancePoint KPI   A PerformancePoint Scorecard combines a KPI with dimensions and filters to produce meaningful information.

1. In the Workspace Browser, select the PerformancePoint Content item.
2. Click Scorecard on the Create tab of the ribbon. The Select a Scorecard Template dialog box appears. Click All in the Category pane to see the various types of scorecards that can be created, as shown in Figure 17-56.
3. Make sure Analysis Services is selected in the Template pane and click OK. The Select a data source page of the Create an Analysis Services Scorecard dialog box appears.
4. Select the MaxMinManufacturingDM Analysis Services data source.
5. Click Next. The Select a KPI Source page of the Create an Analysis Services Scorecard dialog box appears.
6. Make sure the Create KPIs from SQL Server Analysis Services measures radio button is selected and click Next. The Select KPIs to Import page of the Create an Analysis Services Scorecard dialog box appears.
7. Click Select KPI. The Select a KPI dialog box appears with our brand-new Backorder KPI, as shown in Figure 17-57.

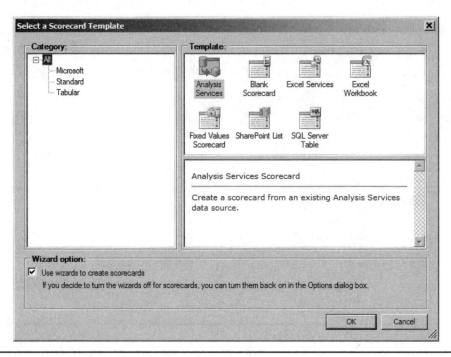

Figure 17-56   *The Select a Scorecard Template dialog box*

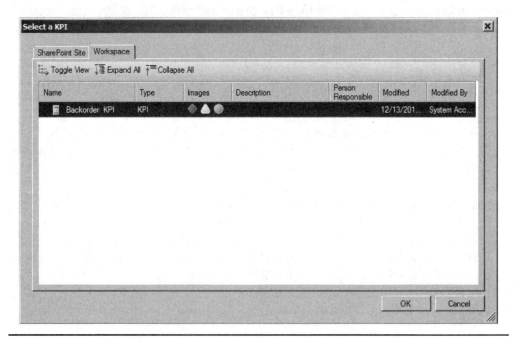

Figure 17-57   *The Select a KPI dialog box*

8. With the Backorder KPI selected, click OK. The Backorder KPI is added to the list on the Select KPIs to Import page.

9. Click Next. The Add Measure Filters page of the Create an Analysis Services Scorecard dialog box appears. This page allows us to apply filter conditions to the KPI.

10. Click Next. The Add Member Columns page of the Create an Analysis Services Scorecard dialog box appears.

11. Check the Add column members check box.

12. Click Select Dimension. The Select Dimension dialog box appears.

13. Select Dim Product.Product Hierarchy.

14. Click OK.

15. Click Select Members. The Select Members dialog box appears.

16. Check Guiding Lights, Mythic World, Warriors of Yore, and Woodland Creatures, as shown in Figure 17-58.

17. Click OK.

18. Click Finish.

19. Replace "New Scorecard" with **Backorder Scorecard**. The scorecard appears, as shown in Figure 17-59. Try drilling into the Product Subtype and Product levels.

20. Click Save.

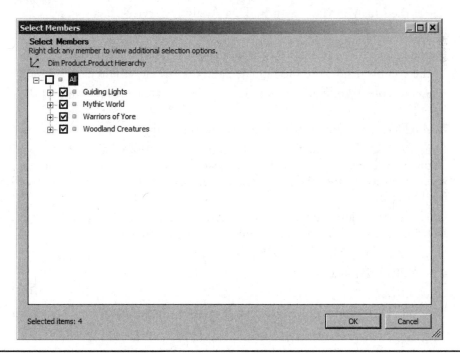

Figure 17-58 *The Select Members dialog box*

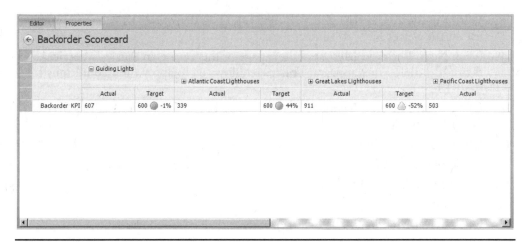

Figure 17-59 *The Backorder Scorecard*

Steps to Create an Analytic Chart

1. In the Workspace Browser, select the PerformancePoint Content item.
2. Click Analytic Chart on the Create tab of the ribbon. The Select a Data Source page of the Create an Analytic Chart Report dialog box appears.
3. Select the MaxMinManufacturingDM Analysis Services data source.
4. Click Finish.
5. Replace "New Report" with **Accepted Products Chart**.
6. In the Details window to the right, expand the Measures entry.
7. Drag Accepted Products and drop it in the Series area at the bottom of the chart layout.
8. In the Details window, expand the Dimensions entry.
9. Drag the Dim Time hierarchy and drop it in the Bottom Axis area at the bottom of the chart layout. A column chart is created with one column showing the accepted products for 2015 (the default member of the Time dimension, as you might recall).
10. Click the drop-down arrow next to the Dim Time Date Hierarchy entry in the Bottom Axis area. The Select Members dialog box appears.
11. Uncheck Default Member (2015).
12. Check 2013, 2014, and 2015.
13. Click OK.
14. Drag the Dim Product hierarchy and drop it in the Series area below Accepted Products.

15. Click the drop-down arrow next to the Dim Product Product Hierarchy entry in the Series area. The Select Members dialog box appears.

16. Uncheck Default Member (All).

17. Check Guiding Lights, Mythic World, Warriors of Yore, and Woodland Creatures.

18. Click OK. We have a bar chart showing the number of products accepted by product type by year, as shown in Figure 17-60.

19. Click Save.

Steps to Create a Dashboard

1. In the Workspace Browser, select the PerformancePoint Content item.

2. Click Dashboard on the Create tab of the ribbon. The Select a Dashboard Page Template dialog box appears, as shown in Figure 17-61.

3. Select "2 Rows," as shown in Figure 17-61.

4. Click OK.

5. Replace "New Dashboard" with **Manufacturing Dashboard**.

6. In the Details window, expand the Scorecards item.

7. Expand the PerformancePoint Content item under Scorecards.

8. Drag the Backorder Scorecard item from the Details window and drop it in the Top Row zone of the new dashboard.

9. In the Details window, expand the Reports item.

10. Expand the PerformancePoint Content item under Reports.

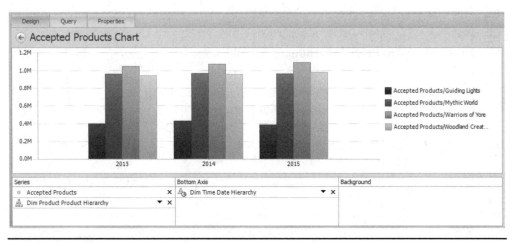

Figure 17-60 *Analytic chart of products accepted by product type by year*

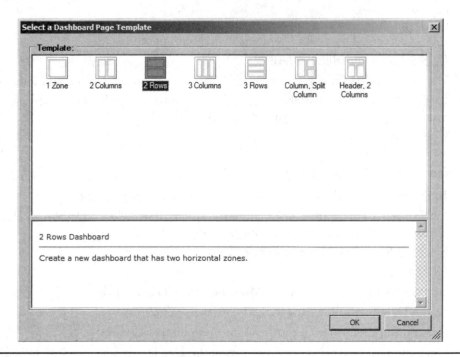

Figure 17-61 *The Select a Dashboard Page Template dialog box*

11. Drag the Accepted Products Chart from the Details window and drop it in the Bottom Row zone. The dashboard layout appears, as shown in Figure 17-62.

12. Click Save All. The Save As dialog box appears.

13. Navigate to an appropriate folder to save the Dashboard Designer workspace.

14. Enter **Max Min PerfPt Dashboard** for File name.

15. Click Save.

16. In the Workspace Browser window, right-click the Manufacturing Dashboard entry and select Deploy to SharePoint from the context menu. The Deploy To dialog box appears with the Dashboards folder selected.

17. Click OK. The Manufacturing Dashboard will be deployed and will display in a new browser tab, as shown in Figure 17-63.

18. Hover your mouse over a bar in the chart. A ToolTip will tell you which product type is being represented.

19. We have already explored drilldown in our scorecard. Let's try it in the chart. Right-click any of the green bars showing Warriors of Yore information in the chart.

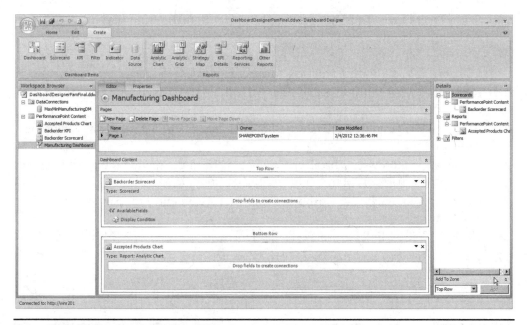

Figure 17-62 *The Manufacturing Dashboard layout*

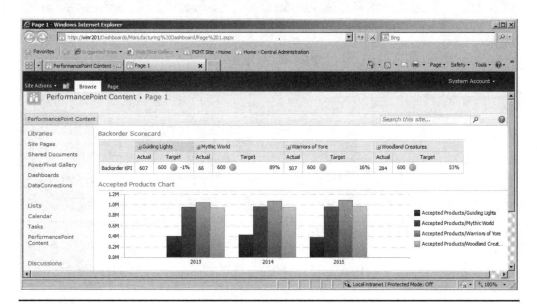

Figure 17-63 *The Manufacturing Dashboard after deployment*

20. Select Drill Down To | Dim Product | Product Subtype from the context menu, as shown in Figure 17-64.

21. The chart will drill down to show information for the product subtypes in the Warriors of Yore product type, as shown in Figure 17-65.

22. Right-click a bar in the chart and select Drill Up from the context menu to return the chart to its original form.

23. After you have explored the new dashboard, close the browser tab displaying the dashboard.

24. In the original browser tab, select Dashboards from the menu on the left. You see the entry we just created by deploying the dashboard.

25. Click the Manufacturing Dashboard link. You see an entry for page 1 of the dashboard.

26. Click the Page 1 link to display the dashboard.

27. Close the browser and the Dashboard Designer.

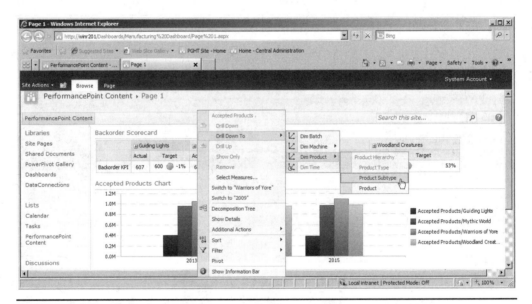

Figure 17-64 *Drilling down in the chart*

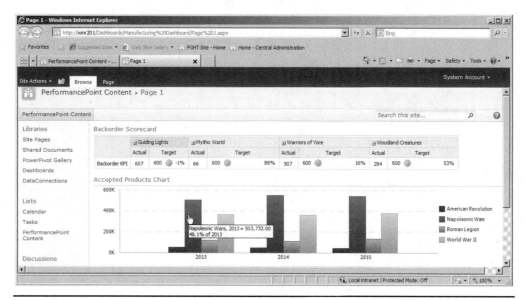

Figure 17-65 *The Manufacturing Dashboard with drilldown*

Putting It All Together

Business intelligence that simply sits on a relational or OLAP server without ever getting to the users does no good for anyone. To make a difference, this information must reach its target audience. In many cases, the target audience is too busy with other commitments to seek out the information. It is up to us to put business intelligence at their fingertips.

In this chapter, we saw several tools that can be part of the solution for getting information to the decision makers. In the next chapter, we look at ways developers can integrate business intelligence right into their applications.

Chapter 18

Let's Get Together: Integrating Business Intelligence with Your Applications

In This Chapter

► **ADOMD.NET**
► **Integrating a Reporting Services Report with an Application**
► **Great Capabilities, Great Opportunities**

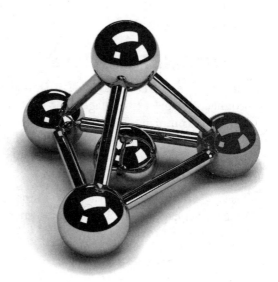

If you want to make beautiful music, you must play the black and the white notes together.

—Richard Milhous Nixon

I n the previous chapter, we looked at several tools that make our BI Semantic Models available to business decision makers. In some situations, however, our users don't want a separate tool. At times, our business intelligence must integrate tightly with other programs and solutions.

Once again, SQL Server 2016 provides us with the tools to fulfill this need. The ADOMD.NET data provider enables us to execute queries against BI Semantic Models on Analysis Services servers. Analysis Management Objects (AMO) provides a programming interface for the management of an Analysis Services server and the objects residing on that server. Reporting Services also offers a number of methods for integrating reports with applications.

With these features, we can provide our users with the complete package, the integrated solution, the all-in-one application, the tightly coupled, well-oiled . . . well, you get the picture.

ADOMD.NET

ADOMD.NET, the multidimensional counterpart to ADO.NET, is our means to programmatically access the wealth of business intelligence we have been creating on the Analysis Services server. With ADOMD.NET, our client applications can query databases on an Analysis Services server. ADOMD.NET also allows these applications to programmatically view and manipulate the structures residing in Analysis Services databases. ADOMD.NET uses XML for Analysis (XML/A) to interact with the Analysis Services server.

ADOMD.NET Structure

The structure of ADOMD.NET is similar to the structure of ADO.NET. Both use a connection object to manage the connection string and set up access to the server. Both use a command object to execute queries against a database. And both provide structures for connected and disconnected access to data.

AdomdConnection

The *AdomdConnection* manages the connection between the client application and the Analysis Services server. A connection string similar to the following is used to initiate the connection to a server:

```
Data Source={ServerName};Catalog={AnalSvcsDB};Provider=msolap;
```

The connection to the server is made using either Transmission Control Protocol/Internet Protocol (TCP/IP) or Hypertext Transfer Protocol (HTTP). This enables connections to be made with a minimum of firewall and network interference.

Once the connection is open, an AdomdCommand object can be used to interact with the Analysis Services database. When the session has concluded, the connection must be explicitly closed with the Close method. An AdomdCommand object does not automatically close the connection when it goes out of scope in your code. (This is done to facilitate connection sharing.)

AdomdCommand

The *AdomdCommand* manages the execution of queries against a multidimensional server. The query is set using either the CommandText property or CommandStream property. The query itself must be an MDX command or an XML/A-compliant command that is valid on the target server.

AdomdCommand offers the following methods for executing the query:

▶ **Execute** The Execute method returns the result of the command either as a CellSet or as an AdomdDataReader, depending on the format of the results themselves.

▶ **ExecuteCellSet** The ExecuteCellSet method returns the result of the command as a CellSet.

▶ **ExecuteNonQuery** The ExecuteNonQuery method executes a command that does not return a result.

▶ **ExecuteReader** The ExecuteReader method returns the result of the command as an AdomdDataReader.

▶ **ExecuteXMLReader** The ExecuteXMLReader method returns the result of the command in the native XML/A format using an XMLReader.

AdomdDataReader

The *AdomdDataReader* provides a means for reading a forward-only result set from a query. While this result set is being read, the connection to the data source remains busy. This is a connected result set. Connected access requires more server overhead to maintain the active connection.

CellSet

Unlike the AdomdDataReader, the *CellSet* facilitates a disconnected result set. The CellSet contains the entire structure of the multidimensional result set. Therefore, an application can interact with this result set without having to maintain a connection to the server.

A portion of the CellSet structure is shown in Figure 18-1. The CellSet contains one or more axis objects. These represent the query dimensions: Column, Row, Page, and so on. Review Chapter 14 if you need a refresher on query dimensions in an MDX query. Each axis contains a set of tuples. A set can have zero, one, or many tuples. As we discussed in Chapter 13, tuples are made up of dimension and hierarchy members.

In addition to the items shown in Figure 18-1, the CellSet contains a collection of cells called Cells. These *cells* contain the measures that are included in the MDX query. The cell collection contains one index for each dimension in the MDX query. For example, if the MDX query contains Column, Row, and Page dimensions, the cell collection will have three indexes, and an individual cell would be addressed as shown:

```
CellSet.Cells(x, y, z)
```

The measure calculated for an individual cell is accessed through the Value property, as shown:

```
CellSet.Cells(x, y, z).Value
```

ADOMD.NET Example

Let's look at an example using ADOMD.NET to incorporate an MDX query result into an application. A Maximum Miniatures developer has created a Windows program

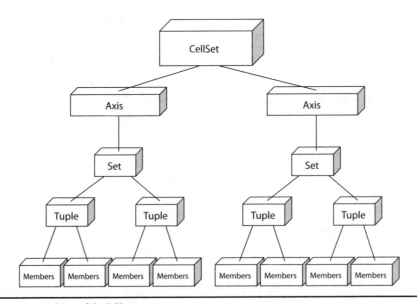

Figure 18-1   *A partial view of the CellSet structure*

for analyzing prospective customers called *Prospect Analyzer*. The method of analysis being used by this program is to take a prospective customer's city of residence and display the buying habits of other residents of that city for the past three years. Many of Max Min's products have regional appeal, so this type of analysis can be helpful when planning a sales approach to a prospective customer.

The program displays the number of product sales by store by year. Because we have three dimensions in the result set, a bit of creativity was required. Two of the three dimensions are represented by the rows and columns of a data grid. Multiple data grids are placed on a set of tab pages to represent the third dimension. The user interface for the Prospect Analyzer is shown in Figure 18-2.

Recall the MDX Query window in SQL Server Management Studio only allows two dimensions in query results. Here, we have an MDX query result viewer that allows three. Your homework is to design your own MDX query result viewer that will display four dimensions.

> **NOTE**
>
> *The Prospect Analyzer sample application is included in the Zip file available for download from the publisher's website for this book.*

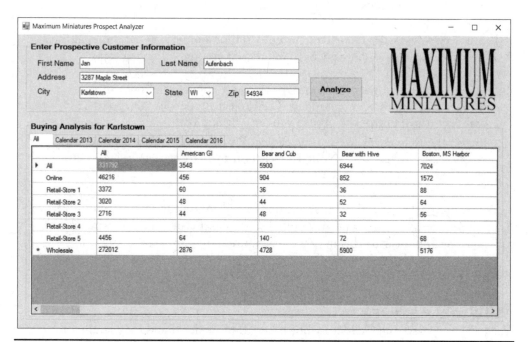

Figure 18-2   *The Prospect Analyzer sample application with a three-dimensional MDX query result viewer*

Setting a Reference

We can use ADOMD.NET in a number of different .NET project types. But before we can use ADOMD.NET in the project, we must first set a reference to the assembly that implements it. That reference is set within your Visual Studio project by doing the following:

1. Right-click the project entry in the Solution Explorer window and select Add | Reference from the context menu. The Add Reference dialog box appears.
2. Select the Assemblies | Framework page.
3. Click the Name heading to sort the list by name.
4. Scroll down in the .NET tab, and select the entry for Microsoft.AnalysisServices .AdomdClient. If this entry is not present, click the Browse button and navigate to the following folder if you are using a 32-bit version of Windows:

   ```
   C:\Program Files\Microsoft.NET\ADOMD.NET\130
   ```

   or to the following folder if you are using a 64-bit version of Windows:

   ```
   C:\Program Files (x86)\Microsoft.NET\ADOMD.NET\130
   ```

   and then select Microsoft.AnalysisServices.AdomdClient.dll.
5. Click OK to exit the Add Reference dialog box and add a reference to this assembly in your project.

If you need to view the references currently set for a project to determine if the ADOMD.NET client has already been referenced, use the following steps:

1. Right-click the project entry in the Solution Explorer window and select Properties from the context menu. The Project Properties tab appears. (This tab will have the name of the project you are working with.)
2. Select the References page of the Project Properties tab. This page appears as shown in Figure 18-3. Notice the entry for Microsoft.AnalysisServices. AdomdClient at the top of the list of references.

We will import AdomdClient so we don't need to use the prefix "Microsoft. AnalysisServices.AdomdClient" in front of every object type. The following line of code must be at or near the beginning of each program:

```
Imports Microsoft.AnalysisServices.AdomdClient
```

Retrieving a CellSet

The code to retrieve the CellSet is shown here. This code should look familiar to anyone who has used ADO.NET because it has the same format. We connect to the

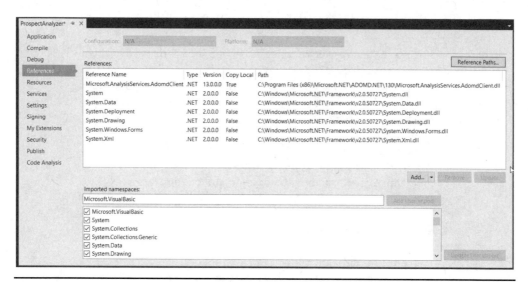

Figure 18-3   *The References page of the Project Properties tab*

database server, we create and execute the query on this server, and then we pick up the query result and pass it back:

```
Imports Microsoft.AnalysisServices.AdomdClient

Public Class ADOMDWrapper

    Public Function BuyingByProductByStoreByYearMDX( _
                    ByRef CityName As String) As CellSet
        Dim conn As AdomdConnection
        Dim cmd As AdomdCommand
        Dim cst As CellSet
        Dim strServer As String = "local"
        Dim strDatabase As String = "MaxMinSalesDM"
        Dim strMDXQuery As String

        strMDXQuery = "SELECT [Date].[Year].members ON PAGES, " & _
                      "[Store].[Store].members ON ROWS, " & _
                      "[Product].[Product].members ON COLUMNS " & _
                      "FROM [MaxMinSales] " & _
                       "WHERE ([Measures].[Sales in Units], " & _
                          " [Customer].[City].[" & CityName & "])"
```

```vbnet
    ' Open the connection to the Analysis Services server
    Try
        ' Create a new AdomdConnection object, providing the
        ' connection string.
        conn = New AdomdConnection("Data Source=" & strServer & _
        ";Catalog=" & strDatabase & ";Provider=msolap;")
        ' Open the connection.
        conn.Open ()
    Catch ex As Exception
        Throw New ApplicationException( _
            "An error occurred while connecting.")
    End Try

    ' Execute the MDX Query
    Try
        ' Create a new AdomdCommand object,
        ' providing the MDX query string.
        cmd = New AdomdCommand(strMDXQuery, conn)
        ' Run the command and return a CellSet object.
        cst = cmd.ExecuteCellSet()

        ' Return the CellSet object
        Return cst

    Catch ex As Exception
        Throw New ApplicationException( _
            "An error occurred while opening the cellset.")
    End Try

    ' Release resources.
    Try
        conn.Close ()
    Catch ex As Exception
        ' Ignore errors
    Finally
        cst = Nothing
        cmd = Nothing
        conn = Nothing
    End Try

    End Function
End Class
```

The next code listing shows how to parse the information into our fancy three-dimensional viewer. First, we loop through the content of Axes(2), the Pages dimension, to create a tab page for each one. Each tab page has a DataGridView control for displaying columns and rows on that tab. Second, we loop through the content of Axes(0), the Column dimension, to create columns in the DataGridView. Third, we loop through the content of Axes(1), the Row dimension, to create row labels in the DataGridView. Finally, we loop through the cells in the CellSet to populate the content of the DataGridView on each tab page:

```
Imports Microsoft.AnalysisServices.AdomdClient

Public Class ProspectAnalyzer

    Private Sub cmdAnalyze_Click(ByVal sender As System.Object, _
            ByVal e As System.EventArgs) Handles cmdAnalyze.Click
        Dim ADOMDBWpr As New ADOMDWrapper
        Dim CSet As CellSet
        Dim i, j, k As Integer
        Dim DataGridView As System.Windows.Forms.DataGridView
        Dim DataGridViewColumn As _
            System.Windows.Forms.DataGridViewTextBoxColumn

        ' Don't do any analysis if there is no city selected
        If String.IsNullOrEmpty(cboCity.Text) Then
            Return
        End If

        ' Set the label on the buying analysis group box
        gbxBuyingAnalysis.Text = "Buying Analysis for " & cboCity.Text

        ' Call the function to get a CellSet
        ' with the results for the specified city
        CSet = ADOMDBWpr.BuyingByProductByStoreByYearMDX(cboCity.Text)

        ' Create a tab for each Page in the resulting CellSet
        TabForPages.TabPages.Clear()

        For i = 0 To CSet.Axes(2).Set.Tuples.Count - 1
            ' Label the tab using the caption for
            ' each Page in the CellSet
```

```
TabForPages.TabPages.Add( _
    CSet.Axes(2).Set.Tuples(i).Members(0).Caption)

' Place a DataGridView on the new tab
DataGridView = New System.Windows.Forms.DataGridView
DataGridView.ReadOnly = True
DataGridView.Width = TabForPages.TabPages(i).Width
DataGridView.Height = TabForPages.TabPages(i).Height
DataGridView.RowHeadersVisible = True
DataGridView.RowHeadersWidth = 123

' Create a column in the DataGridView for
' each Column in the CellSet
For j = 0 To CSet.Axes(0).Set.Tuples.Count - 1
    DataGridViewColumn = New _
        System.Windows.Forms.DataGridViewTextBoxColumn

    ' The headers for the column is the caption
    ' for each Column in the CellSet
    DataGridViewColumn.HeaderText = _
      CSet.Axes(0).Set.Tuples(j).Members(0).Caption

    DataGridViewColumn.Width = 150

    DataGridView.Columns.Add(DataGridViewColumn)
Next

' Create an empty row in the DataGridView
' for each Row in the CellSet
DataGridView.RowCount = CSet.Axes(1).Set.Tuples.Count

' The headers for each row is the caption
' for each Row in the CellSet
For k = 0 To CSet.Axes(1).Set.Tuples.Count - 1
    DataGridView.Rows(k).HeaderCell.Value = _
        CSet.Axes(1).Set.Tuples(k).Members(0).Caption
Next

' Place the values from the CellSet in the DataGridView
' cells
For j = 0 To CSet.Axes(0).Set.Tuples.Count - 1
    For k = 0 To CSet.Axes(1).Set.Tuples.Count - 1
        DataGridView(j, k).Value = CSet.Cells(j, k, i).Value
```

```
            Next
        Next

        ' Place the DataGridView on the tab page
        TabForPages.TabPages(i).Controls.Add(DataGridView)
    Next

    ' Set the Buying Analysis group box visible
    gbxBuyingAnalysis.Visible = True

    End Sub
End Class
```

Integrating a Reporting Services Report with an Application

In addition to writing our own code to query a BI Semantic Model and display the result, we can integrate a Reporting Services report with an application. There are several ways to accomplish this, such as using URL links or using the Report Viewer control. In the Learn By Doing exercises in this chapter, we will accomplish this integration using a call to the report server web service.

In order to give this a try, we need to deploy our Reporting Services reports to a report server. First, a little information about the report server. As was discussed in Chapter 17, Reporting Services can operate in either native mode or SharePoint Integrated mode. The discussion and Learn By Doing exercises here pertain to Reporting Services operating in native mode.

Report Server

The report server is the piece of the puzzle that makes Reporting Services the product it is. This is the software environment that enables us to share our reports with the masses—at least those masses who have rights to the report server. The report server holds a copy of each report that is deployed to it. It then allows users to locate and run those reports in a secure environment.

When a report is deployed to a report server, a copy of the report's RDL definition is put in that server's Report Catalog. The *Report Catalog* is a set of databases used to store the definitions for all the reports available on a particular report server. It also stores the configuration, security, and other information necessary for the operation of that report server.

Folders

Before we deploy reports to the report server, we need to have an understanding of the way the report server organizes reports in the Report Catalog. In the *Report Catalog*, reports are arranged into a system of folders similar to the Windows file system. Folders can contain reports, supporting files (such as external images and shared data sources), and even other folders. The easiest way to create, view, and maintain these folders is through the web portal.

Although the Report Catalog folders look and act like Windows file system folders, they are not actual file system folders. You cannot find them anywhere in the file system on the computer running the report server. *Report Catalog folders* are on-screen representations of records in the databases that hold the Report Catalog.

The Web Portal

The *web portal* application provides a straightforward method for creating and navigating folders in the Report Catalog. We used the web portal in Chapter 17 when we worked with mobile reports and the web portal KPI. As you saw, the web portal gives us an easy-to-use interface for interacting with the report server.

By default, the web portal is installed in the default website on the server. It is located in a virtual directory called Reports. As we discussed in Chapter 17, the default URL for the web portal is as follows, where *ComputerName* is the name of the computer hosting Reporting Services:

```
http://ComputerName/reports
```

No matter how we get there, the web portal appears similar to Figure 18-4.

NOTE

Figure 18-4 shows the web portal as it appears for a user with content manager privileges. If you do not see some of the menu options, you do not have content manager privileges and will be unable to complete the exercises in this section of the chapter. If possible, log out and then log in with a Windows login that has local administration privileges on the computer running the report server.

The web portal will work with any modern browser.

Deploying Reports Using SQL Server Data Tools

In the following Learn By Doing exercise, we are going to deploy the report we created in Chapter 17 to a report server. We will deploy the report from the SQL Server Data Tools environment where we originally created it.

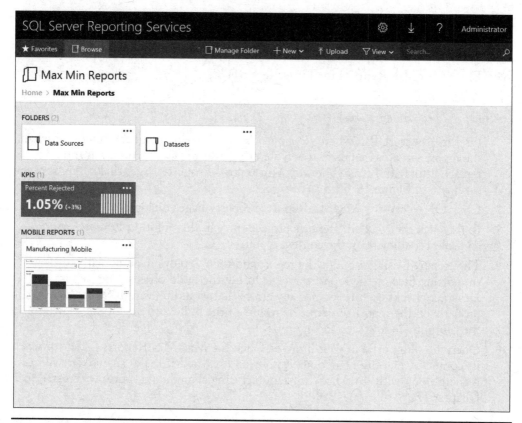

Figure 18-4   *The web portal*

Learn By Doing: Deploying a Report

Feature Highlighted

▶ Deploying a report from SQL Server Data Tools

Business Need   The Maximum Miniatures Marketing Department would like the Wholesale Sales By Month Report integrated with a custom application. The first step toward making that happen is to deploy the report to a report server.

Steps to Create a Report Server Project

1. Open SQL Server Data Tools.
2. Open the MaxMinReports project.

3. Select Project | MaxMinReports Properties from the main menu. The MaxMinReports Property Pages dialog box appears.

4. Enter **Max Min Reports/Data Sources** for TargetDataSourceFolder.

5. Enter **Max Min Reports** for TargetReportFolder.

6. Type

    ```
    http://{ComputerName}/ReportServer
    ```

    for TargetServerURL, where *{ComputerName}* is the name of the computer where the report server is installed. If you are using a secure connection, you should replace http: with https:. The MaxMinReports Property Pages dialog box appears as shown in Figure 18-5.

7. Click OK to exit the MaxMinReports Property Pages dialog box.

8. Right-click the MaxMinReports project entry in the Solution Explorer window and select Deploy from the context menu.

9. The Report Designer builds the report and then deploys it, along with any supporting files, to the report server. (During the build process, the Report Designer checks each report for any errors that would prevent it from executing properly on the report server.) The results of the build and deploy are shown in the Output window seen in Figure 18-6.

10. Open the web portal in your browser. Click the Max Min Reports folder to view its content. Click the Data Sources folder. Our MaxMinSales shared data source is there along with the MaxMinManufacturing shared data source we created in Chapter 17.

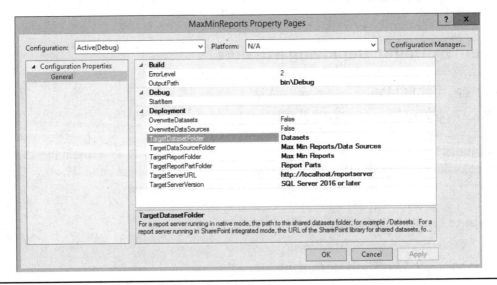

Figure 18-5   *The MaxMinReports Property Pages dialog box*

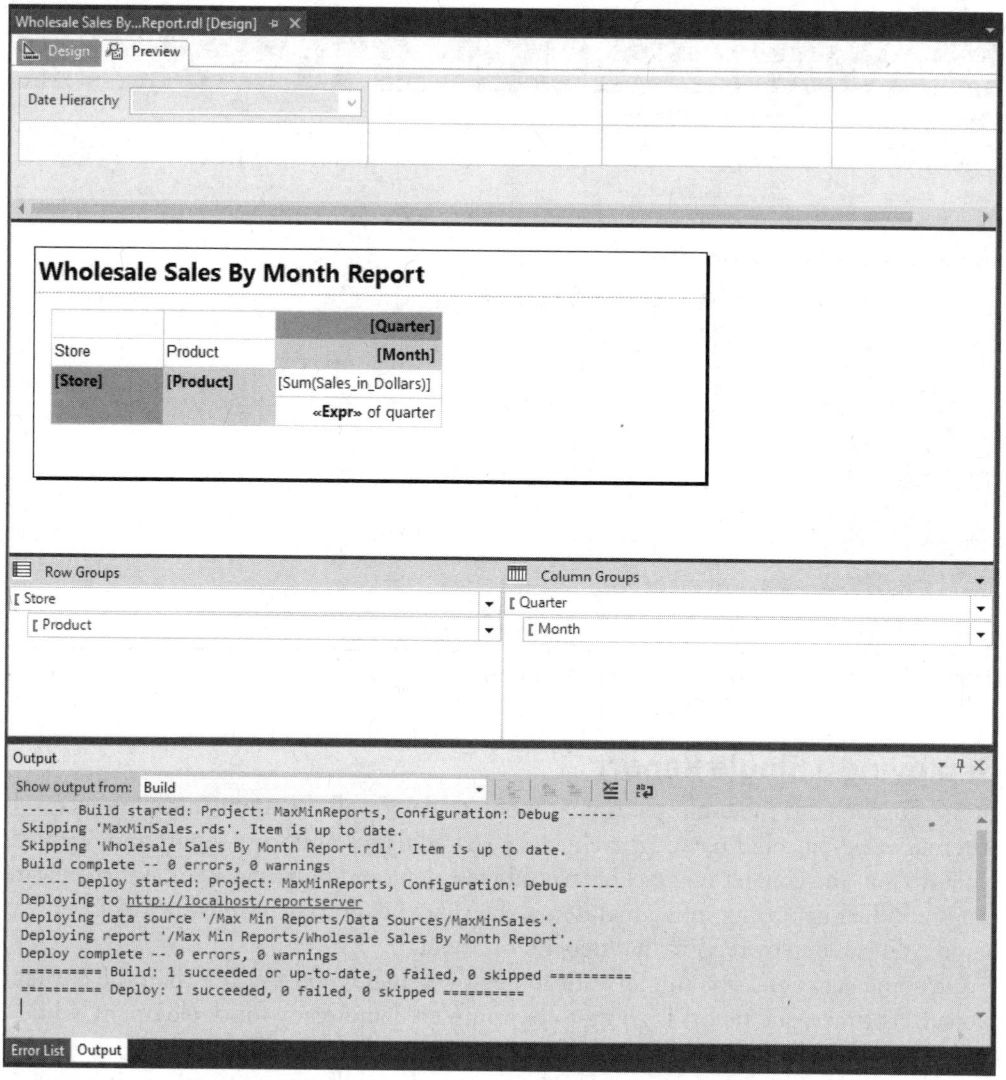

Figure 18-6 *Deploying a report project*

11. Use the breadcrumbs at the top of the page to navigate back to the Max Min Reports folder.

12. Click the entry for the Wholesale Sales By Month Report. The report displays as shown in Figure 18-7.

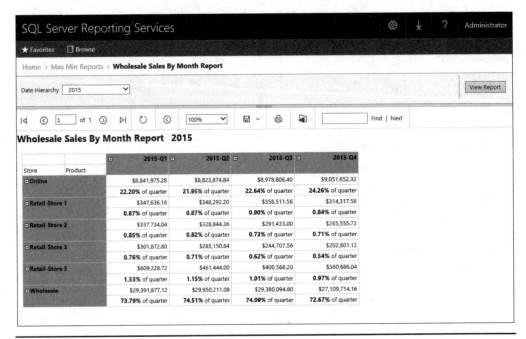

Figure 18-7   *The Wholesale Sales By Month Report in the web portal*

Deploying a Single Report

In Step 8, you used the project's context menu to deploy all the items in the project. Alternatively, you could have right-clicked a shared data source or a report and selected Deploy from the context menu. This would have deployed only that item, not the entire project. When deploying individual items, the shared data sources must be deployed before you can deploy reports that depend on them.

On some occasions, you might want to deploy a single report rather than the entire project. At times, one report is going to be completed and ready for deployment, while the other reports in the project are still under construction. At other times, one report is revised after the entire project has already been deployed. In these situations, it is only necessary to redeploy the single revised report.

Web Service Access

The web portal provides a nice interface for finding and executing reports, but sometimes, the web portal is not the best way to deliver a report to your users. Perhaps the user is browsing your website and needs to view a report. In these situations, we want to provide an integrated approach with reporting available within the application. We want to deliver the report to the user right where they are.

It is possible to access reports programmatically using the Reporting Services web service interface. This is the same interface used by the web portal to interact with Reporting Services. This means anything you can do in the web portal, you can also do through the web service interface.

The *web service interface* enables you to specify a set of credentials to use when executing a report. This allows your custom application to use a set of hard-coded credentials to access reports through the web service interface. This can be a big benefit in situations where you want Reporting Services reports to be exposed on an Internet or extranet site where each user does not have a domain account.

Learn By Doing: Displaying a Report in an Application

Feature Highlighted

▶ Using the Reporting Services web service

Business Need With our report deployed to the report server, let's build an application that accesses the report.

Steps to Create a Project and a Web Reference

1. Start Visual Studio.
2. Create a new project.
3. Select Visual Basic | Web in the Installed Templates area.
4. Select ASP.NET Web Application from the list in the center of the dialog box.
5. Enter **MaxMinRptFrontEnd** for Name.
6. Enter an appropriate path for Location.
7. Click OK. If you are prompted for a template, select Web Forms and click OK.
8. When the new project has been created, right-click the MaxMinRptFrontEnd project entry in the Solution Explorer and select Add | Service Reference from the context menu. The Add Service Reference dialog box appears.
9. Click Advanced. The Service Reference Settings dialog box appears.
10. Click Add Web Reference. The Add Web Reference dialog box appears.
11. Enter the following address for URL:

```
http://localhost/ReportServer/ReportExecution2005.asmx
```

NOTE

If Reporting Services is not on your computer, replace "localhost" with the name of the computer where Reporting Services is installed.

12. Click Go.
13. When the "ReportExecutionService" Description appears, enter **RptExec** for Web reference name. The completed dialog box is shown in Figure 18-8.
14. Click Add Reference.

To use a web service, you need to create code that knows how to send data to and retrieve data from that web service. Fortunately, this code is generated for you by Visual Studio through the process of creating a web reference. Once the web reference is in place, you can call the methods of the web service the same way you call the methods of a local .NET assembly.

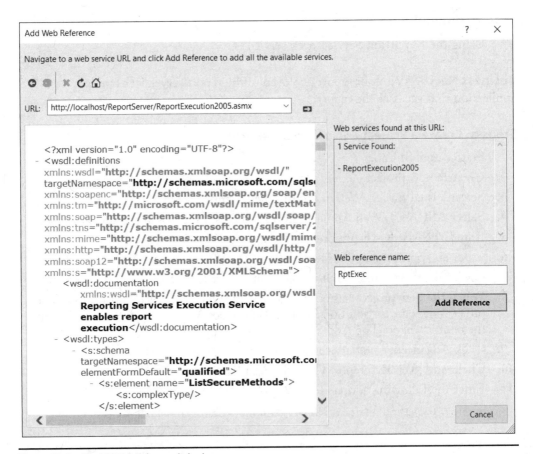

Figure 18-8   *The Add Web Reference dialog box*

Steps to Create a Web Form for the User Interface

1. Right-click the MaxMinRptFrontEnd project entry in the Solution Explorer and select Add | Web Form. The Specify Name for Item dialog box appears.
2. Enter **ReportFrontEnd.aspx** for Item name and click OK.
3. Click Design near the bottom of the screen to switch to the Design tab.
4. Place two labels, one drop-down list, and a button on the web form, as shown in Figure 18-9.
5. Change the ID property of the drop-down list to **lstYear**.
6. Populate the Items collection as follows:

Text	Value
2013	[Time].[Date Hierarchy].[Year].&[2013]
2014	[Time].[Date Hierarchy].[Year].&[2014]
2015	[Time].[Date Hierarchy].[Year].&[2015]

7. Change the ID property of the button to cmdExecute.
8. Change the Text property of the button to Display Report.
9. Double-click the cmdExecute button to open the code window.

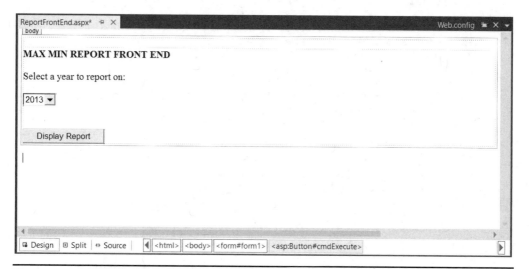

Figure 18-9   *The Report Front End form*

10. Enter the following code for cmdExecute_Click:

```
Private Sub cmdExecute_Click(sender As System.Object,_
                            e As System.EventArgs) _
                        Handles cmdExecute.Click
    Dim report As Byte () = Nothing

    ' Create an instance of the Reporting Services
    ' Web Reference.
    Dim rs As RptExec.ReportExecutionService _
                    = New RptExec.ReportExecutionService

    ' Create the credentials that will be used when accessing
    ' Reporting Services. This must be a logon that has rights
    ' to the Manufacturing By Machine report.
    ' *** Replace "LoginName", "Password", and "Domain" with
    ' the appropriate values. ***
    rs.Credentials = New _
            System.Net.NetworkCredential("LoginName", _
            "Password", "Domain")
    rs.PreAuthenticate = True

    ' The Reporting Services virtual path to the report.
    Dim reportPath As String = _
    "/Max Min Reports/Wholesale Sales By Month Report"

    ' The rendering format for the report.
    Dim format As String = "PDF"

    ' The devInfo string tells the report viewer
    ' how to display with the report.
    Dim devInfo As String = _
        "<DeviceInfo>" + _
    "<Toolbar>False</Toolbar>" + _
    "<Parameters>False</Parameters>" + _
    "<DocMap>True</DocMap>" + _
    "<Zoom>100</Zoom>" + _
    "</DeviceInfo>"

    ' Create an array of the values for the report parameters
    Dim parameters (0) As RptExec.ParameterValue
    Dim paramValue As RptExec.ParameterValue _
                            = New RptExec.ParameterValue
    paramValue.Name = "TimeDateHierarchy"
    paramValue.Value = lstYear.SelectedValue
    parameters (0) = paramValue

    ' Create variables for the remainder of the parameters
    Dim historyID As String = Nothing
    Dim credentials () As _
                RptExec.DataSourceCredentials = Nothing
```

```vb
        Dim showHideToggle As String = Nothing
        Dim encoding As String
        Dim mimeType As String
        Dim warnings () As RptExec.Warning = Nothing
        Dim reportHistoryParameters () As _
                     RptExec.ParameterValue = Nothing
        Dim streamIDs () As String = Nothing

        ' Prepare for report execution.
        Dim execInfo As New RptExec.ExecutionInfo
        Dim execHeader As New RptExec.ExecutionHeader
        rs.ExecutionHeaderValue = execHeader
        execInfo = rs.LoadReport(reportPath, historyID)
        rs.SetExecutionParameters(parameters, "en-us")

        Try
            ' Execute the report.
            report = rs.Render(format, devInfo, "", mimeType, _
                                      "", warnings, streamIDs)

            ' Flush any pending response.
            Response.Clear ()

            ' Set the HTTP headers for a PDF response.
            HttpContext.Current.Response.ClearHeaders ()
            HttpContext.Current.Response.ClearContent ()
            HttpContext.Current.Response.ContentType = "application/pdf"
            ' filename is the default filename displayed
            ' if the user does a save as.
            HttpContext.Current.Response.AppendHeader ( _
                "Content-Disposition", _
                "filename=""WholesaleSalesByMonthReport.pdf""")

            ' Send the byte array containing the report
            ' as a binary response.
            HttpContext.Current.Response.BinaryWrite(report)
            HttpContext.Current.Response.End ()
        Catch ex As Exception
            If ex.Message <> "Thread was being aborted." Then
                HttpContext.Current.Response.ClearHeaders ()
                HttpContext.Current.Response.ClearContent ()
                HttpContext.Current.Response.ContentType = _
                        "text/html"
                HttpContext.Current.Response.Write ( _
                    "<HTML><BODY><H1>Error</H1><br><br>" & _
                                    ex.Message & "</BODY></HTML>")
                HttpContext.Current.Response.End ()
            End If
        End Try
    End Sub
```

11. Replace LoginName, Password, and Domain in the NetworkCredentials() method call with credentials that have rights to execute the Wholesale Sales By Month Reports on the report server.

12. Click Save All on the toolbar.

13. Select Debug | Start Debugging from the main menu. This executes your program.

14. When the browser window appears with the web application front-end page, select a year and click Display Report. The report appears as a PDF document using the year selected on the front-end page.

15. Switch back to Visual Studio and select Debug | Stop Debugging from the main menu.

You can refer to the comments in the code sample for information on the purpose of each section of code.

Managing Reporting Services Through Web Services

In addition to executing reports through the web service interface, you can manage Reporting Services using the web services. If you choose, you can write an application that completely replaces the web portal application for controlling Reporting Services.

NOTE

You can also integrate reports with .NET applications using the Report Viewer control. The Report Viewer control can be used to display reports rendered by a report server, or it can provide the rendering engine for reports running local to the application.

Great Capabilities, Great Opportunities

The business intelligence tools in SQL Server 2016 offer us tremendous capabilities. We can create powerful analysis tools to provide business intelligence to decision makers at every level of our organization. We can define, construct, deploy, and analyze with greater speed and efficiency than ever before.

The complexity that made data warehousing, enterprise-wide reporting, and the integration of those items with line-of-business applications a lengthy, expensive, and risky venture has been reduced, if not eliminated.

The reputation of business intelligence projects as not worth the time, money, and headaches involved is widespread and deeply ingrained. Too many times, business intelligence projects delivered less than expected, in a less effective manner than anticipated, over a longer timeline than allowed for, while requiring more money than budgeted. Most small and mid-size organizations would never dream of creating a data mart or using Tabular or Multidimensional data models. Yet, these are the same organizations that stand to benefit the most from what SQL Server 2016 has to offer. A number of large organizations have been down the business intelligence road with huge, all-encompassing projects that ended up failing miserably. With SQL Server 2016, these large organizations can implement business intelligence with an incremental approach that leads to a much higher success rate.

Those of us working with business intelligence in SQL Server 2016 have a job ahead of us. We need to let organizations of all sizes know that the tools, the architecture, and, indeed, the rules of business intelligence have changed. SQL Server 2016 allows for more of an iterative style and less of the all-or-nothing approach to business intelligence projects of the past. With SQL Server 2016, it is possible to get *more* than you expected in a *more* effective manner than anticipated with a *shorter* timeline than allowed, requiring *less* money than budgeted.

Those organizations that hear this message can reap the rewards offered by the business intelligence tools in SQL Server 2016 and the strategic advantages that go along with them. They can efficiently create tools to achieve effective decision making!

Index